THE WORLD'S GREATEST TREASURY OF
WOMEN'S HEALTH SECRETS

From the
Editors of
Bottom Line
REVISED AND
UPDATED

BottomLineBooks

BottomLineInc.com

Bottom Line Books® publishes the advice of expert authorities in many fields. These opinions
may at times conflict as there are often different approaches to solving problems.
The use of this material is no substitute for health, legal, accounting or other professional
services. Consult competent professionals for answers to your specific questions.

Telephone numbers, addresses, prices, offers and websites listed in this book are
accurate at the time of publication, but they are subject to frequent change.

Bottom Line Books® is a registered trademark of Bottom Line Inc.,
3 Landmark Square, Suite 201, Stamford, CT 06901

BottomLineInc.com

Bottom Line Books® is an imprint of Bottom Line Inc., publisher of print periodicals,
e-letters and books. We are dedicated to bringing you the best information from the most
knowledgeable sources in the world. Our goal is to help you gain greater wealth,
better health, more wisdom, extra time and increased happiness.

Printed in the United States of America

Contents

6 • YOUR FAMILY'S HEALTH

7 • EMBARRASSING CONDITIONS

9 • NUTRITION FOR A SLIMMER, TRIMMER YOU

10 • FIT FOR LIFE

11 • HEALTHY BEAUTY SECRETS

Preface

We are proud to bring you *The World's Greatest Treasury of Women's Health Secrets*. We trust that you'll find the latest discoveries, best treatments and money-saving solutions to your health concerns.

Whether it's breast cancer prevention, new heart therapies, breakthrough osteoporosis treatments or cutting-edge nutritional advice, our editors talk to the people—from top women's health doctors to consumer health advocates—who are creating the true innovations in health care.

How do we find all these top-notch medical professionals? Over the past two decades, we have built a network of literally thousands of leading physicians in both alternative and conventional medicine. They are affiliated with the premier medical institutions and the best universities throughout the world. We read the important medical journals and follow the latest research that is reported at medical conferences. And we regularly talk to our advisors in major teaching hospitals, private practices and government health agencies.

The World's Greatest Treasury of Women's Health Secrets is a result of our ongoing research and contact with these experts, and is a distillation of their latest findings and advice. We trust that you will enjoy the presentation and glean new, helpful and affordable information about the health topics that concern you and your family.

As a reader of a Bottom Line book, please be assured that you are receiving reliable and well-researched information from a trusted source.

But, please use prudence in health matters. Always speak to your physician before taking vitamins, supplements or over-the-counter medication…changing your diet…or beginning an exercise program. If you experience side effects from any regimen, contact your doctor immediately.

The Editors, Bottom Line Books, Stamford, CT.

1

Health Myths That Harm Women

Diseases Your Doctor May Miss

She died of a heart attack in the parking lot outside the emergency room—after the ER physician sent her away with a prescription for tranquilizers and a referral for gastrointestinal tests. The doctor had seen that she was sweaty and short of breath, and she had told him she felt tired, weak, achy and nauseous, so he considered it an obvious case of nerves. None of her complaints had sounded like classic heart attack symptoms—a feeling of crushing pressure on the chest and/or pain radiating down the left arm.

Fact: Fatigue, nausea, upper-body aches, perspiring and shortness of breath are indeed symptoms of a heart attack—in about 20% of women who have heart attacks. The "classic" signs are typical primarily among men. I hear about case after case like the one above.

The medical community still struggles, if not with actual gender bias, at least with persistent ignorance about women's unique health concerns.

Here are specific diseases that doctors most often overlook in women...the warning signs to watch for...and the steps you can take to protect yourself.

HEART DISEASE

Heart disease is the number-one killer of women in the US. The incidence of the disease is on the rise even among women in their 20s and 30s, though this increase may be due to our improved diagnostic abilities. Still, test results are too often misinterpreted.

Recent finding: A common test for heart disease is coronary angiography, in which a doctor injects dye into the arteries and then

Marianne J. Legato, MD, FACP, professor of clinical medicine at Columbia University College of Physicians and Surgeons, and founder and director of the Partnership for Gender-Specific Medicine at Columbia University, New York City. She is author of *The Female Heart: The Truth About Women and Heart Disease* (Perennial Currents).

takes an angiogram (X-ray) that reveals blockages of fatty plaque inside blood vessels. A recent study shows that for many women, this test is not accurate—because instead of forming identifiable blockages (as plaque does in men), in women the plaque is spread more evenly throughout the artery walls.

Consequence: As many as 3 million American women who are at high risk for heart attack may be incorrectly told that they're at low risk—so they go untreated.

Self-defense: Other warning signs of heart attack include insomnia, irregular heartbeat, jaw pain, or pain in the upper abdomen or back during physical activity or intense emotion. If you experience any such symptoms—especially if you smoke, have diabetes or have a family history of heart attack before age 55—it is vital to be tested for heart disease.

Initial tests may include an electro-cardiogram (a recording of the heart's electrical activity) …echocardiogram (ultrasound of the heart)… exercise (treadmill) stress test…and/or non-invasive nuclear scan (in which an injection of radioactive liquid produces three-dimensional images of the heart).

Important: Memorize the warning signs of heart attack in women mentioned above —and if you experience symptoms, call 911 immediately. (For more information on protecting yourself against heart disease, see page 463.)

OVARIAN CANCER

Ovarian cancer strikes about 22,000 women in the US yearly, most of them over age 50. It is the second most common gynecologic cancer —and the deadliest. If the cancer is caught before it spreads beyond the ovary, a woman has a 90% chance of living at least five years. Unfortunately, only 20% of ovarian cancers are discovered at this early stage because the disease exhibits only vague symptoms.

Recent study: Up to a year before being diagnosed, women with ovarian cancer were more likely than cancer-free women to experience abdominal pain and swelling, pelvic pain, gas, constipation or diarrhea and/or frequent urination.

Self-defense: If any of the above symptoms persist for more than a month, see a gastro-enterologist. If no digestive problem is found, ask your gynecologist about ovarian cancer screening tests—ultrasound, magnetic resonance imaging (MRI), computed tomography (CT) and a blood test for CA-125, a protein produced by ovarian cancer cells.

THYROIDITIS

One of the most commonly missed auto-immune diseases is Hashimoto's thyroiditis. This disease impairs the thyroid gland's ability to produce proper amounts of the thyroid hormones T3 and T4, which affect the body's metabolic rate (speed at which calories are burned) and other biological processes.

Symptoms of Hashimoto's thyroiditis may include fast heart rate, anxiety, swollen neck, brittle nails, thinning hair, heavy or frequent periods, muscle cramps or weakness, weight gain, constipation, chills, fatigue and/or depression. Some people have no symptoms. Untreated, Hashimoto's can lead to high cholesterol, heart disease, birth defects and other health problems.

Self-defense: If you have several of the symptoms above, ask your doctor about blood tests that measure levels of hormones and antibodies associated with the disease. Low levels of T3 and T4 and/or high levels of thyroid stimulating hormone (which the pituitary gland produces more of when the thyroid gland is underactive) indicate Hashimoto's.

Treatment: Thyroid hormone therapy— generally, for life.

SLEEP APNEA

Many doctors describe a typical sleep apnea patient as "a fat man who snores and gasps in his sleep." Yet this sleep disorder—in which a sleeping person repeatedly stops breathing because the tongue blocks the airway or the brain fails to signal muscles that control respiration— is just as common in postmenopausal women not on hormone replacement therapy as it is in men. Symptoms include morning headaches, weight gain, lethargy and memory loss. Without treatment, sleep apnea can contribute to high blood pressure, heart disease and accidents brought on by sleep deprivation.

Self-defense: Before bed, set a tape recorder to "voice activation." If the playback is a cacophony of snorts and gasps, ask your doctor for a referral to a sleep disorder center. Sleep apnea may be relieved by weight loss…an oral appliance that positions the jaw and tongue… or a continuous positive airway pressure (CPAP) machine, which gently blows air through a face mask to keep your airway open.

More from Dr. Marianne Legato…

Get the Care You Deserve

To make sure your doctor takes your health concerns to heart…

• **Be assertive.** Arrive at appointments with a written list of questions, and don't leave until you've gotten clear, complete answers.

• **Keep track of all medical tests performed,** and phone the doctor if you are not notified about results within the expected time frame.

• **Go elsewhere for your health care** if your physician rushes through exams or brushes off your questions.

Women Underestimate Their Heart Disease Risk

Women ages 30 to 50 who have a family history of heart disorders are less likely to take preventive measures—including exercising and not smoking—than men with the same family history.

Theory: Health-care providers may be less apt to educate women about cardiovascular risk factors…and women may not realize that a family history of heart disease can affect their health risk and that they should be screened for risk factors. Heart disease is the number-one killer of women in the US.

Amit Khera, MD, MSc, associate professor of internal medicine, University of Texas Southwestern Medical Center, Dallas, and leader of a study of 2,404 people, published in *American Heart Journal*.

Beware of Heart Attack Treatment Delays

Women with heart attack symptoms are not treated as promptly as men. Response time for ambulances is the same for women and men, but when the patient is a woman, there are more delays after ambulances arrive.

Among the reasons: Women don't always have classic heart attack symptoms and often minimize symptoms that they do have.

Self-defense: Know the warning signs of a heart attack, such as chest pain. Women often experience symptoms as indigestion, shortness of breath, extreme fatigue and/or a feeling of throat tightness. Tell emergency workers if you have a family history of heart attacks. Explain symptoms in detail. Do not self-diagnose, and do not minimize your pain.

Nieca Goldberg, MD, a cardiologist and nationally recognized pioneer in women's heart health. Her New York City practice, Total Heart Care, focuses primarily on caring for women. Dr. Goldberg is clinical associate professor of the New York University Women's Heart Program. She is author of *The Women's Healthy Heart Program* (Ballantine).

Smoking Risk Worse For Women

Among smokers with less than 30 pack-years (packs smoked daily multiplied by years of exposure), women were almost twice as likely as men to develop significant precancerous colorectal growths.

Best: Ask your doctor how to quit and whether to have more frequent colonoscopies.

Joseph C. Anderson, MD, associate professor of medicine, University of Connecticut Health Center, Farmington, and head of a study of 2,707 colonoscopy patients, reported at a meeting of the American College of Gastroenterology.

The 7 Big Cancer Myths

Gregory Pennock, MD, medical oncologist who specializes in lung cancer, sarcoma (cancer of the soft tissue) and melanoma (skin cancer). He is medical director of clinical trials at UF Health Center at Orlando Health, Orlando, Florida. *www.orlandohealth.com*

Despite all the medical information in the media, many people are misinformed about the realities of cancer. These misconceptions can prevent people from getting appropriate treatment. *Here, the truth behind common myths about cancer...*

Myth: **Cancer usually is fatal.**

In a recent American Cancer Society (ACS) survey, 68% of respondents said that they believe the risk of dying of cancer is increasing. Not true. Though the number of Americans diagnosed with cancer has increased (because the US population is increasing and getting older), the risk of dying of cancer has decreased due to early detection and improved treatment. More than half of people diagnosed with cancer survive the disease—and for some cancers, such as lymphoma and leukemia, the cure rate is between 70% and 80%.

Cancer isn't a single disease. It includes many types of tumors, all of which behave differently. Some tumors, such as those in the breast, are very responsive to chemotherapy and other treatments. Lung tumors are more resistant to treatment. The likelihood of a cure depends not only on the type of tumor but how far advanced it is at the time of diagnosis.

Myth: **Cancer runs in families.**

Only about 8% of cancers are genetically linked. These usually are cancers that occur in younger patients, such as sarcoma or early-onset colon cancer. The vast majority of cancers occur without a known cause or are related to lifestyle.

A family history does increase risk for certain cancers. For example, if a woman has a first-degree relative (such as a mother or sister) who developed the BRCA1 form of breast cancer at an early age, her risk for getting that cancer is increased.

However, only about 10% to 20% of women diagnosed with breast cancer have a family history of the disease. That's why it's important for every woman to undergo regular mammograms and do breast self-exams on a regular basis.

Myth: **Stress causes cancer.**

There's a long-standing belief that people who experience a lot of stress or lack a positive attitude are more prone to cancer. A survey of long-term breast cancer survivors in Canada found that 42% attributed cancer to stress. This causes many people with cancer to blame themselves or feel that they always have to be upbeat to prevent a recurrence.

There's no evidence that stress or a negative attitude causes cancer. In a study reported in the journal *Cancer,* 8,500 people were scored on factors such as fatigue, irritability, etc. After following the participants for almost nine years on average, researchers found no link between emotional distress and cancer risk.

However, positive thinking may play a role in recovery. Patients with a positive attitude are more likely to do things that improve outcomes, such as following medical instructions and maintaining a healthy lifestyle.

Myth: **Surgery causes cancer to spread.**

In the ACS survey, 41% of respondents said they believe that cancer spreads through the body during surgery. In reality, the risk of cancer spreading during surgery is close to zero. This myth probably started in the days before early detection of cancer. It was common for doctors to find advanced cancers during surgery—even in patients who may have had only mild symptoms. Patients and their families concluded that the surgery itself made the disease worse.

Some cancers in the abdomen or ovaries produce large amounts of malignant fluid. In those cases, it's theoretically possible for cancer cells to spread if the fluid leaks into the abdomen during surgery, but there is no actual evidence of that happening.

Myth: **Injuries cause cancer.**

More than one-third of respondents in the ACS survey thought that injuries such as a bruised breast or a hard fall could cause cancer later in life.

These types of injuries don't cause cancer. What may happen is that people hurt a part of the body, see a doctor about the injury and then learn that they have a tumor—but the tumor was already there. The injury just triggered the discovery.

That said, a few cancers are caused by certain types of injuries. A serious sunburn during childhood, for example, increases the risk of skin cancer later in life. Chronic reflux disease (heartburn) can burn the esophagus and increase the risk of esophageal cancer.

Myth: **It's okay to keep smoking after a lung cancer diagnosis.**

Some people believe that because the damage is done, they don't have to quit smoking —but those who continue to smoke after a lung cancer diagnosis have significantly poorer outcomes than those who quit. People with lung cancer who quit smoking respond better to the treatments.

Important: Lung cancer is the leading cause of cancer deaths in men and women. Lung tissue gradually returns to normal when people quit smoking. Ten years after quitting, lung cancer risk is reduced to one-third of what it was.

Myth: **Cell phones cause brain cancer.**

Large population studies have shown no evidence that cell phones cause any kind of cancer, including brain cancer.

Cell-phone use today is vastly higher than it was a decade ago. If there were any truth to the cancer/cell-phone link, we would be seeing an increased incidence of brain cancers by now, but that hasn't happened.

Why Are So Many Women Getting "Old Man's" Lung Disease?

Meilan Han, MD, assistant professor of internal medicine and medical director of the Women's Respiratory Health Program at the University of Michigan Medical Center in Ann Arbor.

M any people think of chronic obstructive pulmonary disease (COPD) as an old man's disease—but that is no longer true.

Facts: COPD is on the rise among women …its severity and symptoms tend to be worse for females…women with COPD seem to experience more anxiety and depression and a lower quality of life than men with the disease do…and more American women than men now die of COPD each year.

Some women who develop COPD may not even have known risk factors for it. What's going on, and how can women protect themselves?

WHAT IS COPD?

COPD is a progressive lung disease that can cause serious, long-term disability. In severe cases, sufferers may become short of breath so easily that they cannot walk half a block. *Patients with COPD have one or both of the following…*

• **Chronic bronchitis,** which involves inflammation of the lining of the bronchial tubes (the two large tubes that carry air from the windpipe into the lungs). The inflammation narrows the airways, making it hard to breathe. Over time, the bronchial tubes become scarred and produce too much mucus, further blocking airflow.

Symptoms: Labored breathing, wheezing and a mucus-producing chronic cough.

• **Emphysema,** which involves damage to the lung's tiny air sacs (alveoli). As these sacs lose elasticity, it is increasingly difficult to draw in air and expel it from the lungs.

Symptoms: Shortness of breath, chronic cough, wheezing and a tendency to exhale through pursed lips to force out trapped air.

COPD is the fourth-leading cause of death in the US and is expected to be third by 2020. More than 12 million Americans have been diagnosed with COPD, and another 12 million may have it but not know it. Symptoms usually appear after age 40. More than one-third of COPD patients are under age 65.

The most common cause of COPD is smoking. Since the disease may take decades to develop, some of the increased incidence in women today is attributed to the rise of smoking among women starting in the 1950s. About 20% of smokers get COPD.

Even after a person quits smoking, his/her lungs may have some permanent damage—so a former smoker also is at increased risk for COPD.

Long-term exposure to secondhand smoke also can contribute to COPD.

Troubling: From 5% to 12% of COPD patients are not smokers or ex-smokers—and the majority of these patients are women.

THE GENDER BIAS

Theories on why COPD is hitting women harder…

•**Since COPD is still thought of as a man's disease,** women may not be correctly diagnosed in a timely fashion. COPD is commonly mistaken for asthma and treated with the wrong drugs. In general, primary care doctors refer a smaller percentage of female patients to the specialists most likely to order diagnostic tests.

•**Some evidence suggests that women smokers may be more likely to develop COPD than men smokers**—perhaps women's lungs are more sensitive to toxins.

•**Once addicted to cigarettes, women have a harder time quitting than men.** Among my patients, women tend to feel more keenly the stigma of using an oxygen tank in public. Embarrassment contributes to the anxiety and depression that often accompany COPD.

HOW TO PROTECT YOURSELF

COPD tends to develop gradually, so you may not notice it for years—yet the longer treatment is delayed, the worse the condition gets. COPD cannot be cured but often can be controlled. The sooner you are diagnosed and treated, the better your outcome is likely to be.

What every woman should do…

•**If you have any symptoms of COPD,** see your doctor or a pulmonologist for a physical, chest X-ray and a spirometry test—a noninvasive breathing test that measures how much and how fast you can blow air out of your lungs.

Referrals: American College of Chest Physicians, 800-343-2227, *www.chestnet.org*.

•**If you smoke, stop now.** Giving up cigarettes leads to even greater improvement in lung function for women than for men. Call 800-QUIT-NOW (784-8669), a free government service that provides trained "quit coaches"…or visit *www.smokefree.gov* for a how-to guide.

If you're diagnosed with COPD…

•**Investigate your health-care options.** These may include medication…supplemental oxygen therapy…surgery to remove damaged lung tissue…and in very severe cases, a lung transplant. The American Lung Association offers a personalized online guide to the latest research. Go to *www.lung.org/lung-disease/copd*.

•**Use drugs properly.** Broncho-dilators relax airway muscles, and corticosteroids suppress inflammation. However, one-third of COPD sufferers do not correctly use a hand-held device, called a dry powder inhaler, to administer medication. If your doctor prescribes an inhaler, get instructions on proper use and follow them precisely.

•**Get vaccinated against flu and pneumonia.** These illnesses can be fatal for COPD patients.

•**Ask your physician about pulmonary rehabilitation.** It combines training in the use of breathing techniques, aerobic and strengthening exercises and nutrition counseling.

•**Call your doctor without delay if you develop a fever…**mucus that is green, yellow or tinged with blood…worsening of your cough… or increased difficulty breathing. These may be signs of an infection, pneumonia or other problem that should be treated immediately.

•**Make sure your doctor monitors your overall health.** COPD patients are at increased risk for cardiovascular disease, muscle problems, brittle bones (a side effect of steroid medication) and depression.

•**Join a COPD support group.** Contact the American Lung Association (800-586-4872, *www.lung.org*). Support groups provide information, plus the emotional benefits of sharing with others who know what you are dealing with.

Women Still Need to Work Harder!

Women must work harder than men in the workplace.

Recent study: Statistical analyses show that the gender discrepancy is not due to differences in job levels, qualifications or family responsibilities.

The results imply that women must work harder and produce superior performance to obtain the same evaluations as men who do the same jobs.

Elizabeth Gorman, PhD, associate professor of sociology, University of Virginia, Charlottesville, and co-author of a study analyzing five surveys, published in Gender and Society.

Can We Talk?

Did you know women don't talk more than men? The belief that women talk much more than men has no basis in science. Studies show no significant difference between the sexes.

Psychology Today, 115 E. 23 St., New York City 10010.

Clinical Trials: What You Can Do to Help

JoAnn E. Manson, MD, DrPH, professor of medicine and women's health at Harvard Medical School and chief of the division of preventive medicine at Brigham and Women's Hospital, both in Boston. A lead investigator for two important studies on women's health, Dr. Manson is coauthor of Hot Flashes, Hormones & Your Health *(McGraw-Hill).*

Until about 20 years ago, researchers generally excluded women from clinical trials of drugs and other therapies, fearing possible harm to women of childbearing age—and assuming that what worked for men also would work for women.

What we now know: Women often respond differently than men do to tests and treatments.

Example: Earlier studies showed that daily low-dose aspirin significantly reduced the risk for a first heart attack among men—but later research found this benefit to be much more modest in women.

It also is important that women participate in trials for conditions that affect us more than men, such as osteoporosis and arthritis—yet few women do.

Survey: 93% of women said their doctors had never mentioned the possibility of joining a medical research study.

To find a clinical trial: For a list of recruiting studies funded by the National Institutes of Health, visit *www.clinicaltrials.gov.* For cancer trials, see *www.cancer.gov/clinical trials.* For links to disease-specific trials, see *www.rarediseases.org.* For more information on women and research, visit the Society for Women's Health Research at *www.swhr.org* or phone 202-223-8224.

Find out before signing on...

• **Purpose of the trial.** Studies typically test new drugs for safety and effectiveness...older drugs for long-term effects or usefulness for additional conditions...natural treatments, such as diet and exercise...or prevention methods.

• **Type of study.** Observational studies track behavior and health outcomes without intervening in participants' lives. In randomized clinical trials, participants are assigned at random to receive treatment or a placebo.

• **Benefits.** If you're healthy, volunteering for a study may provide information that helps you and others stay healthy. If you are at risk for a disease, you may learn ways to lessen your risk. If you have a disease, participating may help expand treatment options for you and others—and though you may be assigned to the placebo group, you could instead receive a breakthrough therapy.

• **Potential risks**—such as harm or side effects from the drug or test procedures. Be sure

7

you understand the potential risks and have read the informed consent form carefully. If you have a disease, make sure you will at least get the generally accepted level of treatment for that condition.

EFFECT ON YOUR LIFE AND FINANCES

Consider whether you can handle time and travel commitments. Ask if expenses are reimbursed and/or stipends paid.

Who funds the study—government, industry or another source. A potential conflict of interest does not necessarily mean the study should be avoided, but you do want assurance that the investigators work independently from a commercial sponsor and that the sponsor cannot suppress the trial's findings.

What's Really Making Us Add on the Pounds

JoAnn E. Manson, MD, DrPH, professor of medicine and women's health at Harvard Medical School and chief of the division of preventive medicine at Brigham and Women's Hospital, both in Boston. A lead investigator for two important studies on women's health, Dr. Manson is coauthor of *Hot Flashes, Hormones & Your Health* (McGraw-Hill).

The statistics are scary—62% of American women are now overweight, and more than half of these women are obese. *Everyone knows that too much food and too little exercise lead to weight gain—but to reach and maintain a healthy weight, it's important to recognize lesser-known culprits...*

• **Stress.** When we're stressed, our adrenal glands release the hormone *cortisol,* which boosts activity of the enzyme lipoprotein lipase, causing the body to store extra fat.

Smart: Make exercise a priority—it triggers the release of soothing brain chemicals called endorphins. Talk to your doctor if you suffer from depression or an anxiety disorder, as these also are linked to elevated levels of cortisol.

• **Sleep deprivation.** The average American sleeps fewer than seven hours per weeknight —and many of us log six hours or less. In surveys, overweight people generally report sleeping less than slim people do.

Theories: Sleep deprivation may slow carbohydrate metabolism...increase cortisol levels ...reduce the hunger-suppressing hormone leptin...and increase the appetite-stimulating hormone *ghrelin.*

Solutions: Avoid late-evening meals and caffeine...turn off telephones (including cell phones) at night...get the computer and TV out of the bedroom...and maintain a consistent bedtime that allows for eight hours of rest.

• **Stillness.** Obese people tend to sit still (literally), spending, on average, 2.5 fewer hours per day pacing and fidgeting than lean people do.

Surprising: These seemingly insignificant movements burn about 350 calories per day—preventing a gain of about 36 pounds per year. A tendency toward stillness may be genetically determined, but long hours at a desk or in a car exacerbate the situation.

Good habit: Don't sit when you can stand or ride when you can walk.

• **Fat friends and family.** Our chances of becoming obese may rise by 57% if a close friend becomes obese...40% if a sibling becomes obese...and 37% if a spouse becomes obese.

One reason: When judgments are based on comparison with others, a loved one's obesity may shift our perception of an acceptable weight.

Best: Ask loved ones to start a weight-loss program with you, and avoid picking up their bad habits.

• **Diet composition.** High-glycemic foods rapidly increase blood sugar levels, triggering a surge of the hormone insulin. These foods may be more likely to cause weight gain, independent of their calorie content, because insulin increases fat storage and prevents fat breakdown in the body.

Slenderizing: Limit high-glycemic foods, such as white bread, pasta, sugary cereals, baked goods and soda. Eat more low-glycemic foods—fruits, vegetables, legumes and whole grains—which stabilize blood sugar.

Daily Chocolate May Harm Bones

In a recent study, older women who ate chocolate daily had an average bone density 3.1% lower than women who ate chocolate less than weekly.

Possible reason: Chocolate contains *oxalate,* a salt that can hinder calcium absorption…and sugar, which can increase calcium excretion.

Jonathan M. Hodgson, PhD, senior research fellow, Western Australian Institute for Medical Research, Perth, and lead author of a study of 1,001 women, reported in *The American Journal of Clinical Nutrition.*

Get the Best Treatment— No Matter What Your Age

Charles B. Inlander, consumer advocate and health-care consultant based in Fogelsville, Pennsylvania. He was founding president of the People's Medical Society, a consumer health advocacy group active in the 1980s and 1990s. He is author of more than 20 books, including *Take This Book to the Hospital with You* (St. Martin's).

Not long ago, a new study confirmed why older adults need to be especially careful when seeking medical care. The study, published in the *Journal of the American Medical Association*, found that women over age 70 who had been diagnosed with breast cancer were not being offered effective—often lifesaving—chemotherapy by their doctors as often as younger women with the same diagnosis. When treated with chemotherapy, women over age 70 who were otherwise healthy had the same success rate as those under age 70, the researchers found.

This study is only the latest in a stack of research suggesting that age should not be the deciding factor in withholding aggressive treatment for most conditions. What is more important, according to researchers, is the overall health of the patient. For example, a man with diabetes, prostate cancer and a chronic respiratory ailment may not be a good candidate for coronary bypass surgery—regardless of his age—due to the increased risk for complications associated with those conditions. For such a patient, medication may be a safer option.

Until a few years ago, little research was conducted on the effectiveness of aggressive treatment in older adults. As a result, doctors did not recommend all available medical options for these patients, fearing that the treatment would do more harm than good. Surveys show that many doctors still adhere to this philosophy. If you are over age 70, how do you know that you're getting the most effective treatment? *My advice…*

• **Ask your doctor,** "What treatment would you recommend for a person who is 20 years younger?" If the treatment (for any medical condition) is different from that recommended for a younger person, ask the doctor why. There may be very good reasons. For example, some people with kidney ailments cannot tolerate chemotherapy because of its toxic effects on the kidneys. By asking the question, you will get the information you need to make an informed decision.

• **Consult a geriatrician.** These physicians specialize in the care of older adults. Tens of thousands of Americans use geriatricians as their primary care doctors. Or you can consult a geriatrician for a second opinion on a suggested course of treatment. To find a geriatrician in your area, check the Yellow Pages under "Physicians—Geriatric" or contact the American Geriatrics Society referral service at 212-308-1414 or *www.healthinaging.org* and click on "Find a Geriatrics Healthcare Professional."

• **Know thyself!** For many older adults, enough is enough. When my mother was 91, she had the option of receiving surgery for her heart ailment. She decided that it wasn't worth the risk or the likelihood of a long recovery period. At her age, she didn't want to go through an additional hospitalization and operation that would probably add little to the length and quality of her life. This is a decision that only you can make. It's okay to say "no," but you should be given all the realistic options. In the end, the choice should be yours.

Get the Care You Need In an Emergency

Kathleen Clem, MD, associate professor of pediatrics and chair of the department of emergency medicine at Loma Linda University Medical Center, Loma Linda, California. She also is a spokesperson for the American College of Emergency Physicians and a winner of its "Heroes of Emergency Medicine" award.

Overcrowding in the emergency room (ER) keeps getting worse. A recent study from Harvard Medical School reported that, between 1997 and 2004, the number of ER patients in the US increased by 18%...the number of hospitals with 24-hour ERs fell by 12%...patients' average waiting time to see an ER doctor increased by 36%, to 30 minutes...and the average wait for heart attack patients increased by 150%, to 20 minutes.

Concern: Women wait, on average, 5.6% longer than men. This may not sound like much—but often a minute makes the difference between life and death.

One reason for the gender discrepancy is that doctors—and patients—do not always recognize how symptoms can differ between the sexes.

Example: Women with heart attacks are less likely than men to experience "classic" crushing chest pain and more likely to feel nauseous, dizzy and/or breathless—vague symptoms easily dismissed as indigestion or anxiety.

Another factor is that women, brought up to give care rather than receive it, often are reluctant to demand attention.

Here's how to get the care you need...

LONG BEFORE YOU NEED THE ER...

• **Ask your primary care doctor which hospital he/she prefers,** so that you are not forced to make this decision during a crisis. You may be advised to go to the closest ER if your situation is potentially life-threatening... or to the hospital with which the doctor is affiliated if your condition is not as serious.

• **Create a written, portable personal health record** to keep on hand for emergencies.

Include: Your doctors' names, specialties and phone numbers...your current and past medical conditions and surgeries...names and dosages of all prescription and nonprescription medications that you take (including supplements)... and family history of serious health problems. Always carry this record with you.

• **Carry your medical insurance card.** ERs provide care regardless of patients' ability to pay, but having insurance information handy speeds the administrative process.

• **Talk to your doctor about your personal risk factors,** such as high cholesterol or blood sugar problems. Discuss warning signs that merit immediate care—for instance, decreased urination in a patient with chronic kidney disease.

THE INSTANT AN EMERGENCY ARISES...

• **Decide if you need an ambulance.** *Call 911 if you experience...*

• Sudden onset of severe headache or dizziness...severe abdominal pain...extreme shortness of breath not caused by exertion... numbness in a limb or trouble walking...or altered vision or speech.

• More than a few minutes of squeezing or burning pain in the neck or torso.

• Any occurrence of uncontrolled bleeding ...copious blood in vomit or stool...a broken bone penetrating the skin...or fainting not caused by emotional stress.

• **If you do not need an ambulance**—for instance, a cut requires stitches but is not bleeding profusely or you have twisted your ankle and may need X-rays to determine if a bone is broken—ask a relative or friend to drive you to the ER, or call a taxi. Do not drive yourself if you are in a lot of pain or feel woozy.

• **Drive yourself only if the problem is minor**—a condition that normally would be handled in your doctor's office (had it not occurred after hours or when you were out of town) but that should not go untended for many hours.

Example: A skin rash or other sign of a systemic allergic reaction that does not affect breathing.

BEFORE HEADING FOR THE ER...

• **Call your own doctor if you are able or,** if your condition is too severe, ask someone to call for you. Your doctor may want to alert the ER to prepare for your arrival.

• **If you haven't made a list of your medications,** put all your drug bottles in a bag (or ask another person to) and take them with you. The ER staff needs to see what you take.

• **If you ingested someone else's medication** or a toxic household product, bring the container.

• **If a loved one is not accompanying you to the ER,** *try to arrange for someone to meet you there.* A companion can help you remember what the doctor says, provide emotional support and notify family.

• **Bring a pen and paper to write down the doctors' instructions.**

WHEN YOU ARRIVE AT THE ER...

• **A nurse will assess you to determine how critical your condition is.** Don't downplay your symptoms!

• **Show the nurse the personal health record you created previously.** Share any suspicions—for instance, "My mother had blood clots. I'm worried that this lump in my leg might be a clot, too."

• **If you are or may be pregnant,** tell everyone who assesses or treats you.

• **If pain is severe,** ask a nurse if you can have pain medication.

WHILE YOU WAIT TO BE EXAMINED...

• **If your symptoms change or worsen,** tell the nurse immediately.

• **In the waiting room, if someone near to you is coughing or vomiting,** change your seat and/or ask a nurse for a face mask.

• **Exercise patience.** Unless your situation is dire, other patients may be in more critical condition. The ER staff tries to attend to patients in order of patients' needs—not first-come, first-served.

WHEN YOU SEE THE DOCTOR...

• **Again, describe your symptoms and share your personal health record.** Don't assume that the doctor already knows everything you told the nurse who first assessed you.

• **Listen carefully,** ask questions and take notes if you can.

• **Discuss the risks and benefits of tests and treatments** that the doctor is considering.

• **If the ER physician suggests that you be admitted to the hospital** for additional testing and/or overnight observation, agree. Many patients refuse because they would rather see their own doctors the next day—but staying at the hospital allows tests to be done quickly and gives you instant access to care if your condition worsens.

BEFORE LEAVING THE ER...

• **Make sure that you understand your diagnosis and instructions for care after discharge.**

• **Review with the doctor or nurse any warning signs that merit an immediate return to the ER.**

• **Request that test results be sent to your primary care doctor.** (This is not necessary if your doctor is affiliated with the hospital.)

• **If you are told to see a specialist for follow-up, get a name.**

WHEN YOU GET HOME...

• **Follow discharge instructions.**

• **Call the ER if concerns arise.**

• **Contact your own doctor during normal office hours** to see if a follow-up exam is recommended.

Prevent "Change of Life" Weight Gain

Mark A. Stengler, NMD, licensed naturopathic medical doctor in private practice, Encinitas, California... adjunct associate clinical professor at the National College of Natural Medicine, Portland, Oregon...author of *The Natural Physician's Healing Therapies* and co-author of *Prescription for Natural Cures* (both from Bottom Line Books).

W omen often assume the change of life means a change in dress size. Even though research has proven that postmenopausal weight gain is not at all inevitable, the myth is so common many women don't question the pounds that pile up with the years. So it was with "Myrna," a 74-year-old woman who had gone through her menopause 25 years earlier. In the ensuing years she had gained only a moderate amount of weight, gradually—but when she turned 70, she started to gain rapidly and inexplicably, even though she walked almost every day and watched her diet. Within four years, 20 pounds had piled on, mostly around her waist. Her confusion and dismay about this unhappy circumstance brought her to naturopathic physician Mark Stengler, ND, for a consultation.

WHAT'S THE CULPRIT?

When Dr. Stengler reviewed Myrna's health history with her, she told him she was taking several routine medications, including one for blood pressure, another for cholesterol and a daily one-milligram tablet of Estrace, an oral form of estrogen known as estradiol. This is a high estrogen dosage for a 74-year-old, but Myrna told Dr. Stengler that her doctor had prescribed it as hormone replacement therapy (HRT) when she was 50 to treat menopause symptoms. She had been taking the same dosage ever since. (Because she had had a hysterectomy, she did not take the combination therapy of estrogen/progesterone prescribed for women with an intact uterus to keep the endometrial lining from building up, a possible cancer risk.) The furor caused by the 2002 Women's Health Study demonstrating HRT's negative implications for health had worried her, but Myrna's doctor had advised that she continue the estrogen regimen. Given this information and his patient's symptoms, including the rapid weight gain, Dr. Stengler ordered a saliva test to determine Myrna's current estrogen level. The results showed that it had soared, and was in fact, 10 times higher than it should have been.

According to Dr. Stengler, Myrna had developed a condition known as "estrogen dominance." The body uses estrogen to promote growth of certain types of tissue but ordinarily natural levels of progesterone serve to prevent excessive estrogen growth effects. With age, however, the liver's elimination function begins to slow, making the body less efficient at metabolizing estrogen. Other reasons estrogen dominance can develop include obesity (the adipose tissue makes estrogen) and a low-fiber diet that results in improper elimination, along with a few other more obscure causes. In Myrna's case, the problem had caused water retention and fat deposition, especially in the abdomen. The excess estrogen can also suppress thyroid function (as it did in Myrna's case). A poorly functioning thyroid can result in yet more weight gain, not to mention fatigue.

WEANING OFF HRT

To resolve her problem, Dr. Stengler reduced Myrna's estrogen levels. It's important to note that getting off HRT is not something anyone should do cold turkey, he says. But Myrna had such high levels of estrogen he took the unusual step of stopping estrogen right away, while starting her on a natural progesterone cream both to more efficiently offset the high estrogen levels and ease any withdrawal symptoms, including hot flashes and depression. Following Dr. Stengler's advice, Myrna continued eating carefully and exercising each day as she had been doing previously, and in three weeks she lost five pounds. Her bloating subsided, as did her abdominal protrusion.

Hormones are powerful chemicals, critical to many aspects of the body's proper function throughout life. Any kind of hormone treatment should therefore be evaluated and monitored with great care, says Dr. Stengler. *Before starting on hormones, discuss the following questions with your physician…*

•**Are your symptoms serious enough that you really need to take hormones?**

•**Are the hormones you will be taking the best form of them, i.e., bioidentical hormones in the case of HRT?**

•**Are you taking the right dosage for you?**

The only safe way to take hormones is with careful supervision by a health-care professional thoroughly trained in, and experienced with, their use. HRT can be valuable for some situations, but incorrect use of them can harm rather than enhance health, as Myrna's case demonstrates.

Myth Buster: Thin Women Actually Have Fewer Hot Flashes

Because body fat can convert male hormones into estrogen, many people have long assumed that heavy women have an estrogen reserve that helps prevent menopausal hot flashes.

But: Recent research contradicts that notion. According to a study of 1,776 women ages 47 to 59, those who had a higher percentage of body fat were more likely to experience hot flashes and night sweats than those with less body fat.

Bottom line: If you are carrying extra pounds, try losing some weight. Not only will it improve your health, it just might help your hot flashes.

Rebecca C. Thurston, PhD, is an assistant professor in the departments of psychiatry, epidemiology and psychology at the University of Pittsburgh, and leader of a study on weight and menopausal hot flashes.

Recent Discoveries Put Vitamin K Back on the Map

The late Shari Lieberman, PhD, CNS, author and co-author of several books including *The Real Vitamin and Mineral Book* (Avery) and *Easy-to-Use Glycemic Index Food Guide* (Square One). Dr. Lieberman was the founding dean, New York Chiropractic College's MS Degree program in Applied Clinical Nutrition.

Some conventional doctors urge patients to avoid vitamin K-containing foods and supplements. Why? Because vitamin K is essential for clotting…and it can interfere with the anti-clotting effects of Coumadin.

But reports have been emerging recently about vitamin K's amazing powers. It plays a role in bone building. Some research shows that it may be involved in the prevention of atherosclerosis. Some forms of vitamin K are being used in current cancer research. Could there be more to the vitamin K story?

BONE HEALTH

As it turns out, yes. When it comes to bones, we talk about calcium and magnesium and vitamin D, which of course are all very important, but the lesser-acclaimed vitamin K is critically important for building strong bones as well. "Vitamin K actually activates a compound called *osteocalcin* that acts like studs inside the walls of a house. It's a structural framework that anchors calcium molecules inside the bone," explained the late Shari Lieberman, PhD, coauthor of *The Real Vitamin and Mineral Book* (Avery). So you can take all the calcium you want, but if it's not getting into the bones, it's not going to do you very much good and it actually can do you some harm by calcifying in other places in the body. "Vitamin K makes sure that you get that calcium into the bone where it belongs," she said.

HEART DISEASE AND OSTEOPOROSIS

Vitamin K helps protect against heart attacks and osteoporosis. Dr. Lieberman explained that the very actions of vitamin K that protect the bones also help protect against calcification in the blood vessels, a prime risk factor for a type of heart disease called atherosclerosis. "Vitamin K produces opposite effects in bone and blood vessels. Proteins in bone increase mineralization when they're activated by vitamin K…but similar proteins in blood vessels decrease calcification in blood vessels." The end result? Vitamin K both helps build bones and protect against calcification in the blood vessels. In a well-known study based on data from the Rotterdam Study (which tracked the effects of vitamin K-2 on 4,800 seniors), subjects with higher intake of one form of vitamin K had reduced mortality from coronary heart disease. (Researchers also noted that higher vitamin K intake was associated with reduced aortic calcification.) They also had a lower death rate in general. The authors suggested that adequate intake of vitamin K-2 could be important in coronary heart disease prevention.

And, in the Nurses' Health Study of more than 72,000 women, those who got the most vitamin K were about one-third less likely to get a hip fracture.

13

VITAMIN K AND CLOTTING

Vitamin K got its name from the German "koagulation" when it was discovered that the vitamin was necessary in order to make the blood clot. It's for this reason that some conventional doctors warn patients against vitamin K-containing foods when they're on blood-thinning medications like Coumadin. But this information could be woefully out of date, said Dr. Lieberman.

"The latest research shows that people on Coumadin can safely take 100 mcg of vitamin K a day," continued Dr. Lieberman, "but they should certainly check with their doctors to monitor their clotting levels."

HOW TO GET VITAMIN K

Researchers now think that vitamin K is needed in larger quantities than what was once thought, particularly in aging adults. "According to the NIH, the optimal daily intake (DV or daily value) for vitamin K is only 80 micrograms (mcg)," said Dr. Lieberman. "In my book I have a higher recommendation. Most multivitamins don't contain any vitamin K or have very little, and most don't contain enough for optimal health." Considering the importance of this vitamin, it's reasonable to ask yourself if you're getting enough. Fortunately, it can be found in assorted vegetables such as broccoli, turnip greens, green cabbage, spinach and tomatoes.

Vitamin K actually has three forms—K1 is found primarily in foods and as phylloquinone or phytonadione...K2 is made in the body by intestinal bacteria and is found in some foods...and K3 is a synthetic form not available generally for humans. "Vitamin K2 appears to be the most active and biological form," said Dr. Lieberman. However, as usual, it is best to get your vitamins from food, especially since taking too much vitamin K can be problematic. As much as 45 mg per day is being used for osteoporosis, cancer and heart disease—but under a doctor's supervision, said Dr. Lieberman. Recent research suggests that eating foods rich in vitamin K does not appear to interfere with anticoagulants (but don't make any drastic changes in your diet without consulting with your doctor). If you are taking additional vitamin K for health reasons and you are on an anticoagulant, check with your physician before taking additional vitamin K.

"Vitamin K is one of the most exciting vitamins of the decade," said Dr. Lieberman. "By keeping calcium in bone where it belongs, vitamin K may help prevent heart disease, stroke, osteoporosis, Alzheimer's disease and more. Researchers are just now focusing on its potential roles in the prevention and treatment of cancer. And, high-dose vitamin K has been approved in Japan for the treatment of osteoporosis since 1995." Yet another great reason to eat your greens.

Older Women Have Less Access to Kidney Transplants

Despite comparable risks and survival rates, women over age 55 are 15% less likely to be referred to a waiting list for a kidney transplant than men of the same age...the disparity rises to 59% in women over 75.

Best: If you are approaching kidney failure, insist that your doctor refer you for a transplant.

Dorry Segev, MD, PhD, director of clinical research, transplant surgery, Johns Hopkins Medicine, Baltimore, and lead author of a study of 563,197 patients, published in *Journal of the American Society of Nephrology.*

A Gender Bias on Knee Pain?

Knee replacement is considered for patients with moderate osteoarthritis if other therapies (a brace, injections of cortisone) fail to ease pain. Two arthritis patients—one man, one woman—with the same level of pain visited 67 doctors. In total, 67% of the physicians recommended knee replacement for the man, but only 33% recommended it for the woman.

Possible reason: Unconscious gender bias.

Best: Ask your doctor about knee replacement if knee pain limits daily activities.

Cornelia Borkhoff, PhD, assistant professor, clinical epidemiology program, University of Toronto Faculty of Medicine, Canada, and lead author of a study published in *Canadian Medical Association Journal*.

Surgery Danger For Women

Patients often receive unfractionated heparin to prevent postsurgical blood clots. Sometimes this leads to heparin-induced thrombocytopenia (HIT), a decrease in platelet count that paradoxically increases clotting risk.

Recent finding: HIT is more common in women than in men.

Self-defense: Studies show that HIT risk is lower with low-molecular-weight heparin or the anticoagulant *fondaparinux* (Arixtra)— ask your doctor before surgery.

Theodore Warkentin, MD, professor of pathology and molecular medicine, McMaster University, Hamilton, Ontario, and leader of a study of 290 people, published in *Blood*.

6 Common Symptoms That Can Be Very Dangerous

Marie Savard, MD, medical contributor for ABC News, former director of the Center for Women's Health at the Medical College of Pennsylvania (now part of Drexel University), Philadelphia. A board-certified internist, she is author of three books, including *How to Save Your Own Life* (Warner). *www.drsavard.com*

Conditioned to be care-givers rather than care-getters, women frequently downplay their own seemingly insignificant symptoms, such as bloating and headaches. Many doctors trivialize women's complaints, too.

Example: Among patients with chest pain, men are more likely than women to be given a screening test for heart disease, while women are more likely than men to be offered tranquilizers—even though heart disease is the number-one killer of Americans of both sexes.

Self-defense: Familiarize yourself with the conditions that a new or persistent symptom could signal, then see your doctor as soon as possible and insist on being given the appropriate diagnostic tests—the first step toward successful treatment. When a worrisome symptom suggests multiple possible causes, a thorough physical examination should help your doctor prioritize the tests.

1. Swelling could be due to fluid retention from your period, varicose veins, eating too much salt or sitting too long. *But watch out for…*

• **Chronic kidney disease**—especially if swelling is severe enough to leave indentations when the skin is pressed. This common condition, which often goes undiagnosed, increases the risk for heart attack, stroke and kidney failure.

Action: Diagnosis requires a urine test for the protein albumin…a blood test for the waste product urea nitrogen…and a glomerular filtration rate calculation based on blood and urine levels of the waste product creatinine and other factors.

• **Heart failure,** in which the heart's pumping action is insufficient to meet all of the body's needs. Other telltale symptoms include shortness of breath and rapid pulse.

Action: Get blood tests and imaging tests— most importantly, an echocardiogram (heart ultrasound).

• **Blood clot**—if swelling appears in only one leg and the area is tender. A clot that breaks off and travels to the lungs can be fatal.

Action: Go to the emergency room. You need an ultrasound or computed tomography (CT) scan.

2. Change in bowel habits may signal the onset of lactose intolerance (dairy food sensitivity) or irritable bowel syndrome (bouts of constipation and/or diarrhea that are uncomfortable but not dangerous). *But watch out for…*

• **Celiac disease,** a genetic disorder in which gluten—a protein in wheat, rye, barley and certain other grains—damages the small intestine. Celiac disease is more common in women than men, can develop at any time, may lead to malnutrition and loss of bone density and increases the risk for digestive tract cancers.

Action: Diagnosis is made with a tissue transglutaminase (tTG) and/or an endomysial antibody (EMA) blood test.

• **Inflammatory bowel disease (IBD),** which involves chronic inflammation of, and ulcers in, the digestive tract. IBD increases colorectal cancer risk.

Action: You should have X-rays of the gastrointestinal tract. If X-rays suggest IBD, blood tests for certain types of antibodies can help determine your specific type of IBD. Also get a colonoscopy (visual examination of the colon using a flexible lighted tube) to check for precancerous polyps and cancerous growths. Abnormal tissue must be biopsied.

• **Colorectal cancer,** the number-two cause of cancer deaths in the US after lung cancer. Other signs include blood in the stool, abdominal pain and unexplained weight loss.

Action: You must have a colonoscopy, including removal of suspicious polyps and biopsy of tissues.

3. Abnormal vaginal bleeding (heavy bleeding or bleeding between periods) prior to menopause suggests fibroids (benign uterine growths)...irregular ovulation...or menstrual changes typical of perimenopause. *But watch out for...*

• **Gynecologic cancer,** such as cancer of the endometrium (uterine lining) or cervix. Even light vaginal bleeding can signal cancer or precancer if it occurs between cycles...and after menopause, any vaginal bleeding at all is cause for concern.

Action: Call your gynecologist right away. If a pelvic exam and transvaginal ultrasound detect suspicious tissue, a biopsy is needed.

4. Breast changes, such as lumps and tenderness, often are signs of benign breast cysts (fluid-filled sacs). *But watch out for...*

• **Breast cancer**—particularly if you also have nipple discharge, puckered or pitted skin, redness or a change in breast contours. Don't dismiss symptoms just because your last mammogram was negative—mammograms miss up to 20% of breast cancers. An aggres-

sive type called inflammatory breast cancer is especially hard to detect with mammography because it forms no lumps, but instead causes tenderness, swelling, itching and/or redness.

Action: If you notice something abnormal or different, a biopsy is almost certainly warranted. Your doctor also may order magnetic resonance imaging (MRI). When a woman's symptoms or high-risk status indicate a medical need for a breast MRI, insurance generally pays.

5. Headaches may occur because you are prone to tension headaches or migraines, which are more common in women. *But watch out for...*

• **Brain tumor**—if you recently started having headaches, especially in the mornings, or have experienced a change in headache patterns.

Action: Call your doctor immediately. An MRI or CT scan can rule out a brain tumor.

• **Meningitis**—if the headache is accompanied by a fever and stiff neck. This deadly infection causes inflammation of the membranes around the brain and spinal cord.

Action: Go to the ER immediately. You need a lumbar puncture (spinal tap) to check for white blood cells and bacteria in the cerebrospinal fluid.

• **Bleeding in the brain**—particularly if head pain is sudden and extremely severe. Possible causes include a cerebral aneurysm (a bulging, weakened area in a brain artery)... subarachnoid hemorrhage (bleeding beneath the tissues covering the brain)...or hemorrhagic stroke.

Action: Call 911. You need magnetic resonance angiography (MRA), which produces detailed images of blood vessels...and a lumbar puncture to check for red blood cells in the cerebrospinal fluid.

6. Chest pain frequently can be a symptom of heartburn. *But watch out for...*

• **Heart disease.** Although chest pain is more typical in men with heart disease, it also is a common sign of heart trouble in women. Be especially vigilant if you have high blood pressure, high cholesterol, a history of smoking or a family history of heart problems.

Action: If you are at risk for heart disease, ask for an ultrafast heart CT scan, a noninvasive test that measures calcium buildup in coronary arteries. Chest pain with fatigue, shortness of breath, dizziness or back pain could signal a heart attack—so call 911.

Diabetes Deaths a Concern for Women

Death rates for women with diabetes have not fallen in the past 29 years, even though they have fallen steeply for men.

Possible reason: Women often get less aggressive care for health problems associated with diabetes.

If you have diabetes: Make sure your doctor checks your blood sugar, cholesterol and blood pressure every three months. Maintain a healthy weight, and take medications as directed.

Edward W. Gregg, PhD, epidemiologist, Centers for Disease Control and Prevention, Atlanta, and lead author of a study of 26,057 people, published in *Annals of Internal Medicine*.

Women Less Likely To Control Cholesterol

In an analysis of 194 health-care plans, researchers found that women were significantly less likely than men to maintain their LDL "bad" cholesterol at the recommended levels (below 100 mg/dL for healthy women and below 70 mg/dL for women with heart disease or risk factors).

Theory: Women and their health-care providers underestimate risk for high cholesterol, yet heart disease is the number-one killer of women.

Ask your doctor to check your cholesterol. If it's high, ask how you can lower LDL levels through diet, exercise and/or medication.

Ileana Piña, MD, professor of medicine, Case Western Reserve University, Cleveland.

Medical Studies: Media Hype May Not Be Right

JoAnn E. Manson, MD, DrPH, professor of medicine and women's health at Harvard Medical School and chief of the division of preventive medicine at Brigham and Women's Hospital, both in Boston. A lead investigator for two important studies on women's health, Dr. Manson is coauthor of *Hot Flashes, Hormones & Your Health* (McGraw-Hill).

When the media reports on medical news, complex research gets reduced to sound bites—which may be misleading. *Find a full account of the study (try www.medlineplus.gov) and ask…*

•**Are this study's results consistent with other evidence?** Accuracy usually involves consistent results from different researchers… using different types of studies…and involving different people.

•**Is it an observational study or a randomized clinical trial?** An observational study tracks behavior and health outcomes without intervening in participants' lives. This can uncover "associations" but cannot prove a cause-and-effect link.

Example: The apparent health benefits of vitamin supplements seen in observational studies simply may reflect that people who choose to use such supplements tend to have healthier habits overall.

In a randomized clinical trial, researchers actively intervene by assigning participants at random to receive treatment or a placebo—making this the "gold standard" of research.

•**Is it an animal study?** Animal studies allow far greater control than human studies—but results from other species may not apply directly to people.

•**How many participants were there?** The larger the study, the less likely its findings are due to chance.

•**How long did the study last?** A long-term study may detect risks or benefits that go unnoticed in shorter studies.

Example: Hormone therapy using estrogen plus progestin increases risk for breast cancer—but only after four to five years.

A two-year study would not uncover this relationship.

- **Did the study look at actual disease outcomes?** Because it takes years for certain diseases to develop, many studies examine "markers" of disease.

    Example: Lower cholesterol levels suggest a reduced risk for heart disease—though cholesterol reductions do not always lead to actual decreases in heart disease risk. Research looking at concrete outcomes, such as the occurrence of heart attacks, is more reliable.

- **Who were the participants?** A study is less valid if participants are not typical of the people who use the therapy.

    Example: The first clinical trial of estrogen therapy to reduce heart disease was done on men, not women!

- **What does increased risk really mean?** It is scary to hear that a risk factor (such as exposure to a toxin) increases risk for a certain disease by, say, 50%. But suppose that two cases of disease normally occur per 10,000 women who haven't been exposed to the toxin. In that case, a 50% increase would mean that toxic exposure leads to three cases per 10,000 women—which isn't so scary.

Cholesterol Drugs Do Not Strengthen Bones

Some preliminary research suggested that cholesterol-lowering statin drugs, such as *atorvastatin* (Lipitor), had beneficial effects on the skeleton.

But: A recent clinical study of postmenopausal women found that Lipitor had no effect, either positive or negative, on bone mineral density.

Michael R. McClung, MD, director, Oregon Osteoporosis Center, Portland, and coauthor of a study of 626 women, published in *Journal of Clinical Endocrinology and Metabolism.*

To Drink or Not to Drink

JoAnn E. Manson, MD, DrPH, professor of medicine and women's health at Harvard Medical School and chief of the division of preventive medicine at Brigham and Women's Hospital, both in Boston. A lead investigator for two important studies on women's health, Dr. Manson is coauthor of *Hot Flashes, Hormones & Your Health* (McGraw-Hill).

Alcohol is a double-edged sword for women. It reduces the risk for certain diseases but raises the risk for others.

Upside: Moderate drinking can lower a woman's risk for heart disease by 20% to 40% and for ischemic (clot-caused) stroke by 20% to 30%. The ethyl alcohol in all types of wine, beer and liquor increases the liver's production of HDL "good" cholesterol, which removes fat from arteries and prevents plaque buildup...and decreases the liver's synthesis of clotting factors, lowering blood clot risk. Moderate drinking cuts diabetes risk by improving insulin sensitivity (cells' ability to use the hormone insulin) and may slow mental decline, possibly by boosting the brain's neurotransmitters (chemical messengers).

Downside: Even moderate drinking increases risk for breast cancer, probably by raising estrogen levels...and for colorectal, esophageal, oral and liver cancers, perhaps by damaging cell DNA. By decreasing clotting, alcohol raises hemorrhagic (bleeding) stroke risk. Excessive drinking contributes to obesity and perhaps endometrial cancer, and can lead to accidents, addiction, liver disease, heart failure and death.

To make your decision, consider...

- **Age.** In your 30s and 40s, breast cancer is a bigger risk than heart disease, so drinking may do more harm than good. Alcohol's benefits may outweigh its hazards in your 50s, 60s and beyond, when risks for heart disease and cognitive decline overtake breast cancer risk.

- **Hormones.** Estrogen is linked to breast cancer. If you use estrogen therapy to ease menopause symptoms, it's best to drink only occasionally.

- **Current health.** Do not drink if you have liver disease, ulcers or bleeding problems...

take narcotics, tranquilizers, sleeping pills or blood thinners…use *acetaminophen* (Tylenol) regularly…are pregnant or plan to get pregnant soon…are breastfeeding…or find it hard to stop drinking once you start.

• **Family history.** If you have a family history of alcoholism or a type of cancer linked to alcohol (as mentioned previously), drink only lightly, if at all.

• **Current abstinence.** If you don't drink now, do not feel compelled to start. You can protect your health by exercising, watching your weight, limiting saturated fats and not smoking. If you do decide to drink, start slowly—with one ounce of wine once or twice a week—until your tolerance builds.

Women metabolize alcohol differently than men, so we can drink only half as much before becoming intoxicated. For women, moderate drinking means no more than one drink per day (five ounces of wine, 12 ounces of beer or 1.5 ounces of liquor). I think the best balance between risks and benefits comes from having one-half drink daily…or one drink three or four times per week.

Does Red Wine Protect the Heart?

Mark A. Stengler, NMD, licensed naturopathic medical doctor in private practice, Encinitas, California…adjunct associate clinical professor at the National College of Natural Medicine, Portland, Oregon…author of *The Natural Physician's Healing Therapies* and co-author of *Prescription for Natural Cures* (both from Bottom Line Books).

You might have read the headlines in recent years—moderate consumption of alcohol, especially red wine, decreases the risk of cardiovascular disease. Before you assume that's reason enough to consume alcohol on a regular basis, let's look at this issue more closely.

It is true that alcohol consumption provides some cardiovascular protection. For example, when researchers combined data from 51 epidemiological studies, they found that the risk of heart disease decreased by about 20% when one to two alcoholic drinks were consumed per day. (One drink of alcohol is equivalent to 1.5 ounces of liquor, 5 ounces of wine or 12 ounces of beer.) The people who seemed to benefit most from light drinking (about 1.2 drinks a day) to moderate drinking (2.2 drinks daily) were middle-aged men and women.

Red wine has additional benefits over other alcoholic beverages, studies suggest. That's because several chemicals in red wine may protect the heart, including resveratrol, a polyphenol (plant pigment) with antioxidant effects. (White wine has smaller amounts of resveratrol.)

The natural compounds in red wine seem to prevent buildup of plaque in the arteries by reducing inflammation and promoting good tone in blood vessel walls. The compounds also play a role in preventing blood clots, which can obstruct blood flow and cause a heart attack or stroke. Alcoholic beverages of any type increase HDL "good" cholesterol, which removes LDL "bad" cholesterol from circulation, thereby minimizing plaque formation.

Despite these positive effects, I don't recommend that people rely on wine or any alcoholic beverages for heart disease prevention. If you do not drink alcohol on a regular basis, don't start. One of the obvious risks of regular alcohol consumption is alcoholism, a very serious and common disease in our country. *Other reasons not to drink alcohol…*

• **Cancer risk.** According to the American Cancer Society, men who have two alcoholic drinks a day and women who have one alcoholic drink a day increase their risk of certain cancers—of the esophagus, pharynx, mouth, liver, breast and colon. If you enjoy drinking each day, limit consumption to half a drink for women and one drink for men so as not to increase cancer risk.

• **Heart risk.** Paradoxically, the same amount of alcohol that has been shown to have a heart-protective effect—two drinks daily for men and one for women—also has been shown to raise triglyceride levels. High levels of these fats increase heart disease risk. Excessive drinking also raises the risk of high blood pressure, heart failure and stroke.

•**Obesity risk.** Alcohol contains simple carbohydrates. Consuming large amounts of simple carbs increases the risk of obesity and diabetes.

•**Fetal risk.** Mothers who drink alcohol during pregnancy predispose their babies to birth defects.

You can dramatically reduce your risk of heart disease without negative effects by not smoking, avoiding secondhand smoke, exercising regularly and consuming a Mediterranean-style diet. This diet is rich in fruits and vegetables, whole grains, nuts, seeds, legumes and olive oil—and has low to moderate amounts of dairy, fish and poultry, and little red meat. You also might take fish oil with a combined EPA and DHA total of 500 mg daily to get heart-healthy essential fatty acids.

Also drink purple grape juice. It makes arteries more flexible and reduces the susceptibility of LDL cholesterol to cause damage in patients with coronary artery disease. Purple grape juice has potent antioxidant activity and, like red wine, contains resveratrol. It is high in simple sugars, so drink only six ounces daily—with a meal to slow sugar absorption. If you have diabetes, have no more than four ounces daily with a meal.

Drugs for Men Not the Same for Women

Marianne Legato, MD, FACP, physician and professor of clinical medicine at Columbia University, New York City, and founder and director of Columbia's Partnership for Gender-Specific Medicine. She is author of several books, including *Why Men Never Remember and Women Never Forget* (Rodale).

Medical researchers have long known that men and women differ in their susceptibility to common diseases, such as diabetes, heart disease and cancer.

Now: Researchers are discovering that men and women often respond differently to the same medication.

Example: The allergy drug *terfenadine* (Seldane) was removed from the market when it was discovered that women taking it had a higher risk for potentially deadly heartbeat irregularities (arrhythmias). Men taking the drug didn't experience the same risk.

THE GENDER FACTOR

Until recently, the pharmaceutical industry mainly tested new drugs on men. Women were not included in drug trials to protect them and any children they might conceive if pregnancy occurred during testing. Also, the hormone fluctuations experienced by women were thought to make them less desirable than men as study subjects.

In 1993, after researchers had discovered that men and women respond differently to drugs, the FDA began requiring that women be included in drug trials for medications that would be taken by them.

Among the most popular theories to explain gender-related differences in drugs…

•**Hormones.** The enzymes that metabolize drugs are affected by hormones, which differ greatly in men and women. For example, the "female" hormone progesterone, which increases just prior to menstruation, accelerates the breakdown of the steroid *prednisone* in the body. This means that a woman with asthma might require a higher dose of the drug just before her menstrual period to avoid an attack.

•**Fatty tissue.** Some drugs are stored in fatty tissue. Because women typically have a higher percentage of body fat than men, women might require a lower drug dose in some cases because the drug is stored in the fatty tissue and is available for a longer time after dosing.

Common drugs with sex-specific differences…

ANALGESICS

Women may be biologically more sensitive to pain than men—and they are known to experience more inflammation from infection and injury. Therefore, women may require higher doses of analgesics that have an anti-inflammatory component.

Women often do better with *ibuprofen* (Advil) or another nonsteroidal anti-inflammatory drug (NSAID), such as *naproxen* (Aleve), than with pain relievers, such as *acetaminophen* (Tylenol), that do not treat inflammation.

Best advice: For severe pain—following surgery, for example—women should ask their doctors for a "kappa opioid," such as *butorphanol tartrate*, a morphine-like painkiller. This class of drugs is much more effective for women than other analgesics. In men, kappa opioids aren't as effective as other drugs.

ANESTHESIA

Women tend to wake up quicker than men following anesthesia—an average of six minutes faster—even when they're given the same dose relative to their body weight. Women experience more side effects from anesthesia than men do and are more likely than men to report some consciousness during surgical procedures.

Despite this, women tend to be given less pain-relieving medication in the recovery room following surgery.

Reason: A man's blood pressure rises when he's in pain. Doctors rely on this to indicate when to use drugs and how much to give. Women in pain frequently have a drop in blood pressure—and a more rapid heart rate as a result, which is a better indicator of how much distress they are feeling.

Best advice: Before an operation, women should request that their heart rate be monitored as a pain indicator along with blood pressure. If the heart rate increases, their doctors should consider giving more pain medication.

ANTI-ARRHYTHMICS

This class of drugs is used to treat heart arrhythmias. One popular anti-arrhythmic, *sotalol* (Betapace), is more dangerous for women than for men. Due to differences in the characteristics of the cardiac cell membranes in men and women, sotalol, which acts on these cell membranes, can increase a woman's risk for ventricular tachycardia, a potentially life-threatening arrhythmia.

Best advice: A woman who needs an anti-arrhythmic drug can sometimes be treated with another drug in the same class. If she requires sotalol, she should be advised to stay in a hospital or other facility that can provide continuous heart monitoring—and cardiac resuscitation, if necessary.

ASPIRIN

Millions of healthy Americans take aspirin daily or every other day to "thin" the blood and reduce the risk for clots, which can contribute to heart attack and/or stroke. However, doctors must weigh the potential benefits of aspirin therapy against the potential risks. In both sexes, regular use of aspirin has been shown to increase the risk for gastrointestinal bleeding.

Recent finding: In men, daily aspirin can lower heart attack risk by 32%, according to a recent analysis of aspirin therapy conducted by researchers at Duke University Medical Center in Durham, North Carolina. Aspirin does not have this effect in all women. However, women who take a daily or every-other-day aspirin were found to have a 17% reduction in the risk for stroke.

Best advice: For men who are at risk for heart attack (due to smoking, high blood pressure or family history), aspirin therapy is often a good choice.

Women under age 65 who are concerned about heart protection alone may want to forgo aspirin therapy and focus on other protective strategies, including weight control, not smoking, regular exercise, etc.

In women over age 65, the heart benefits of aspirin therapy may outweigh the risks for stomach problems.

Because women suffer strokes about as often as men—and their risk of dying from stroke is even higher—they should consider aspirin therapy if they have stroke risk factors, such as smoking, high blood pressure, etc.

Important: Consult your doctor before starting or discontinuing aspirin therapy.

2

Money-Saving Secrets

Natural Remedies a Pharmacist Has in Her Own Medicine Cabinet

As a pharmacist for more than two decades, Suzy Cohen knows the importance of medication—but she also has learned to "think outside the pill" and recommend natural options that often are just as good or better at promoting health without the risk of dangerous side effects.

Here are the remedies she recommends most often. All are free of significant side effects unless otherwise noted, but always talk with your doctor before using any supplements.

TEA TREE OIL FOR WOUNDS

This oil kills germs, reduces pain and helps wounds heal more quickly. You can use it in place of antibiotic ointment for minor cuts, scratches and burns...to treat toenail fungus

...and, when diluted, as a gargle to kill the germs that cause sore throat.

How it works: It's a strong antiseptic that kills bacteria as well as fungi.

How to use: Moisten a cotton ball or swab with one or two drops of the oil, and apply it to the area two to three times daily until it heals.

For a gargle for sore throat: Mix a few drops in a cup of water, gargle and spit it out.

Caution: Do not swallow it.

GINGER FOR NAUSEA

Studies have shown that ginger can relieve nausea—due to pregnancy, seasickness, etc.—as well as or better than over-the-counter drugs.

How it works: Ginger increases the pH of stomach acid, reducing its acidity. In one study,

Suzy Cohen, RPh, registered practicing pharmacist and author of *The 24-Hour Pharmacist* (Rodale). She has a syndicated newspaper column, "Dear Pharmacist." She is a member of the Association of Natural Medicine Pharmacists and the American Holistic Health Association. *www.suzycohen.com*

published in *The Lancet*, volunteers were given either ginger or Dramamine (a nausea-preventing drug), then were seated in a chair designed to trigger motion sickness. Those given ginger were able to withstand the motion 57% longer than those given the drug.

How to use: Put one teaspoon of peeled, grated fresh gingerroot in a cup of boiling water. Let it steep for 10 minutes, then drink (you can filter out the ginger if you want). Or chew and swallow a piece of crystallized ginger, sold in health-food stores.

Caution: Ginger can increase the risk of bleeding when taken with blood-thinning drugs, such as *warfarin* (Coumadin).

RHODIOLA ROSEA FOR STRESS

This herb acts like a natural form of Valium by reducing physical and emotional stress. The supplement is made from the root of the Siberian plant.

How it works: Herbalists classify Rhodiola as an adaptogen, a class of herbs that "sense" chemicals in the body and either raise or lower them. It normalizes levels of brain chemicals that affect mood, such as monoamines and beta-endorphins, which help counter the effects of stress. Rhodiola also may increase serotonin, which enhances feelings of well-being.

How to use: During times of stress, take 100 milligrams (mg) of rhodiola rosea in capsule form, two to three times daily. It's best taken on a cyclical basis—two months on, two weeks off.

CALCIUM PLUS MAGNESIUM FOR CRAMPS

Many people who experience frequent and/or painful menstrual or muscle cramps often have a deficiency of calcium and magnesium.

How it works: Calcium and magnesium regulate the contraction and relaxation of muscles.

How to use: Before going to bed, take 500 mg to 600 mg of calcium, along with 150 mg to 200 mg of magnesium (using the chelate or glycinate forms—check the label). Combination formulas are easy to find and fine to use.

For menstrual problems, start 10 days before you expect your period to begin each month and continue until your period is complete.

GABA FOR INSOMNIA

Gamma-aminobutyric acid (GABA) is a neurotransmitter (mood-related brain chemical) that is naturally present in the body. It's taken in supplement form to reduce insomnia, as well as anxiety and depression.

How it works: GABA is an inhibitory neurotransmitter that slows activity in the brain and makes it easier to fall asleep.

How to use: Take 500 mg to 1,000 mg one hour before bedtime if you have trouble getting to sleep. If your problem is that you wake in the middle of the night and can't get back to sleep, take it then. Don't exceed recommended doses on the package. Do this for two weeks. If it doesn't help, talk to your doctor.

Caution: Combining GABA with prescription or over-the-counter sleep aids can cause excessive sedation.

CAPSAICIN CREAM FOR PAIN

Capsaicin is the chemical compound that puts the "hot" in chili peppers. It is effective for easing muscle aches, back and joint pain and nerve pain caused by the herpes virus (post-herpetic neuralgia).

How it works: When applied as a cream, it causes nerve cells to empty their reservoirs of substance P, a pain-causing chemical. This results in less pain from the underlying disorder.

How to use: Start with a 0.025% concentration. Apply it two to three times daily—the initial burning sensation diminishes with continued use. If needed, you can always buy the stronger 0.075% concentration—but it's best to work your way up to this strength.

Caution: Wear latex gloves when applying capsaicin—and wash your hands thoroughly after using to prevent residual cream from getting into the eyes, nose, etc.

PROBIOTICS FOR DIGESTIVE DISCOMFORT

A healthy digestive tract contains trillions of bacteria, many of which have beneficial effects. These so-called "good" (probiotic) organisms promote digestive health, improve immunity and aid in the synthesis of B vitamins, among many other functions.

How they work: Probiotic supplements replenish beneficial bacteria and crowd out harmful organisms that can cause gas, bloating, diarrhea and other digestive problems.

How to use: Take a daily supplement of at least 10 billion organisms that contains a variety of living organisms, such as *L. bulgaricus*, *L. bifida* and *B. longum*. Some yogurts contain these live active cultures, but avoid those that contain sugar or artificial sweeteners.

BIOTIN FOR CRACKED NAILS

The B vitamin biotin is the only nutrient that has been shown to improve nail health in generally healthy adults. People with a deficiency of biotin often have fragile nails that crack easily.

How it works: Biotin is absorbed by the nail matrix, the part under the fingernail where nail cells are generated.

How to use: Take 2,000 micrograms (mcg) to 4,000 mcg of biotin daily, as well as a B-complex supplement. Most people will notice an improvement in nail strength and thickness in one to two months.

Migraine Relief

Eliminate migraine pain with pepper. Capsaicin, an ingredient in cayenne pepper, cuts off neurotransmitters in the brain that cause headache pain.

Best: Dissolve one-quarter teaspoon of cayenne powder in four ounces of warm water. Dip a cotton swab into the solution, and apply the liquid inside your nostrils. It will burn—and by the time the burning stops, the headache pain will be reduced and sometimes gone altogether.

Eric Yarnell, ND, assistant professor, department of botanical medicine, Bastyr University, Kenmore, Washington.

Simple, All-Natural Personal-Care Products To Make at Home

Dorie Byers, RN, author of *Natural Beauty Basics: Create Your Own Cosmetics and Body Care Products* (Vital Health). She is a registered nurse and herbalist in Bargersville, Indiana.

Why buy high-priced toiletries and over-the-counter medications filled with chemicals and preservatives?

Better: Make your own body-care products and healing remedies, often for pennies. Grow herbs yourself or buy them, along with other ingredients, at health-food stores.

BAD BREATH

What you need...

- **1 cup distilled water**
- **2 tablespoons vodka**
- **2 drops peppermint essential oil**
- **2 drops myrrh essential oil**

Preparation: In a small bowl, mix vodka and oils. Stir in distilled water (which is free of minerals and impurities). With 1 tablespoon of mixture, rinse mouth, then spit out. Repeat daily.

Good to know: Place remaining mixture in a covered, airtight container. Store away from light (to preserve the oils' potency) for up to 6 weeks.

Caution: Do not swallow. These essential oils can be toxic in high amounts if ingested.

DULL HAIR COLOR

What you need...

- **2 cups distilled water**

For dark hair...

- **¼ cup fresh rosemary leaves**

For blonde hair...

- **¼ cup chamomile flower petals**

Preparation: Boil water. Then add rosemary or chamomile, cover and simmer 30 minutes. Strain, discarding leaves. Lean head forward and pour infusion over hair, catching run-off in a basin. Repeat twice. Do not rinse off your hair.

Good to know: The herbs help restore natural highlights. For best effect, use after every shampoo.

FOOT ODOR

What you need…

• **1 cup apple cider vinegar**

• **½ cup dried sage leaves**

Preparation: Boil vinegar. Add sage, cover and simmer 15 minutes. Strain, discarding leaves. Fill a basin with 1 gallon of warm water, add infusion and soak feet for 15 minutes. Repeat daily.

Good to know: If you prefer a different fragrance, substitute dried thyme or fresh rosemary leaves for the sage.

ITCHY, FLAKY OR DRY SKIN

What you need…

• **1 cup coarsely ground sea salt**

• **¼ cup olive oil**

Preparation: Stir oil into salt. Standing in the shower, massage 2 tablespoons of mixture into skin (reserving remainder for later). Rinse. Repeat weekly.

Good to know: For a pleasing scent, add 6 drops of lavender essential oil to the mixture before using. Store remainder in a glass jar in a cool, dark place.

PIMPLES

What you need…

• **1 cup distilled water**

• **1 tablespoon dried thyme leaves**

• **1 tablespoon dried calendula blossoms**

Preparation: Boil all ingredients, covered, for 10 minutes. Strain, discarding leaves and blossoms. Cool infusion. Apply 2 tablespoons to clean skin. Air dry. Repeat twice daily.

Good to know: Also use this preparation to improve an oily, shiny complexion. Store remainder in a glass bottle in a cool, dry place.

PUFFY, TIRED OR IRRITATED EYES

What you need…

• **2 chamomile tea bags**

• **1 cup distilled water**

Preparation: Boil distilled water. Add tea bags and steep until water is lukewarm. Remove bags and squeeze out most of the water. Place bags over closed eyes for 15 minutes.

Good to know: If you have ragweed allergies, do not use this preparation.

SUNBURN

What you need…

• **1 cup distilled water**

• **¼ cup dried *or***

• **½ cup fresh peppermint leaves**

Preparation: Boil water. Add peppermint, cover and simmer 15 minutes. Strain, discarding leaves. Fill bathtub with tepid water and add infusion. Soak 20 minutes. Repeat as needed.

Good to know: Substitute lemon mint, lavender mint or other types of mint leaves for the peppermint to vary the aroma.

Unique Honey Helps Heal Wounds

Manuka, or *Leptospermum,* honey is made by bees from the flowers of the New Zealand wild tea tree. Applied over a superficial wound, this honey slowly releases the antiseptic hydrogen peroxide, which kills bacteria without damaging tissues. Manuka honey can be purchased online or in health-food stores for $20 to $30 a jar.

How to use: Apply to the wound side of a waterproof sterile dressing. Use adhesive tape or bandages to hold the dressing over the wound. Change dressing three times daily.

Mark A. Stengler, NMD, licensed naturopathic medical doctor in private practice, Encinitas, California…adjunct associate clinical professor at the National College of Natural Medicine, Portland, Oregon…author of *The Natural Physician's Healing Therapies* and co-author of *Prescription for Natural Cures* (both from Bottom Line Books).

A Very Frugal New Englander's Favorite Money Savers

Richard Gray, author of *The Frugal Senior: Hundreds of Creative Ways to Stretch a Dollar!* (Linden) and creator of *FrugalWorld.com*, an online warehouse of information on saving money. He lives in Wells River, Vermont.

Being frugal isn't just about scrimping and saving money. It can help you reduce stress over your finances, as well as get more enjoyment out of life.

Here are author Richard Gray's favorite money-saving tricks…

HOME PRODUCTS

• **Use low-cost alternatives to store-bought health and beauty products and household cleaners.** Most specialty cleaning and beauty solutions weren't developed until the past few decades. Many of them are expensive and include harsh chemical ingredients. *Until a few generations ago, everyone used more basic mixtures—with excellent results…*

• **Burn ointment.** An aloe plant. Grow one on your kitchen windowsill. Aloe contains dozens of vitamins, amino acids and enzymes that relieve pain and help burned skin heal. Simply tear off a leaf, and squeeze the liquid onto the burn.

• **Ice/frozen gel packs.** Mix one part rubbing alcohol with two parts water in a plastic freezer bag placed inside a second freezer bag. Put it in the freezer. The alcohol prevents the pack from freezing completely, so you can mold it to any part of your body.

• **Skin exfoliants.** Plain yogurt—the lactic acid sloughs off dead skin cells. Rinse your face with warm water. Massage in one tablespoon of plain yogurt. Let sit for a few minutes, then rinse with warm water. Olive oil and sugar—wet your face, and massage olive oil into your skin to moisturize. Then scrub your face with a teaspoon of sugar to remove dead skin cells. Rinse with warm water. Wipe off any excess with a warm, wet towel to complete the facial.

PETS

• **Substitute homemade remedies.**

Instead of store-bought flea treatments: Mix a little sage into your cat's or dog's food.

Instead of ear-cleaning treatments: Make your own ear rinse by mixing a solution of one-third rubbing alcohol, one-third white vinegar and one-third water. Squirt a few drops of the liquid into your pet's problem ear…let set a minute…then wipe out the ear with a tissue.

ONLINE FREEBEES

• **My favorite sites for free stuff.**
  • *www.bestdealsontheweb.net*
  • *www.coolfreebielinks.com*
  • *www.fabfree.com*
  • *freebies.about.com.*

Six Ways to Ease Anxiety

Michael McKee, PhD, cognitive-behavioral therapist in private practice in Scarsdale, New York, and research scientist at the Anxiety Disorders Clinic, New York State Psychiatric Institute, New York City.

Here are six simple ways to ease anxiety on your own—without help from a therapist.

• **Exercise.** Research shows that all kinds of exercise will make you feel more confident and at ease. Aerobic exercise stimulates the release of *endorphins,* neurotransmitters that are the body's natural "feel good" drug. Yoga can calm nerves.

• **Deep breathing.** Slow breathing from deep in the diaphragm (belly breathing) slows racing thoughts and restores a sense of control.

• **Progressive muscle relaxation.** To remove tension from your muscles, clench them tightly for a full five seconds, then slowly release. Do this for individual body parts starting with your toes and working all the way up to your face.

• **Cut back on coffee.** The caffeine in coffee is a stimulant, so if you are nervous, it will make you more so. Switch to green tea—it has much less caffeine. Green tea also contains amino acids that researchers believe have a calming effect on the brain.

- **Limit alcohol consumption.** It stimulates stress hormones, so have no more than one alcoholic beverage a day.

- **Keep a "joy journal."** Write down on a piece of paper a list of all the good things in your life. Take notes during the day of any funny, entertaining or rewarding things that occur. By consciously thinking about them, they will become more meaningful than stressful parts of your life.

Licorice for Sore Throats

A licorice gargle before surgery can reduce sore throat afterward. Patients who gargled with a licorice solution five minutes before an operation also had less postsurgical coughing. Sore throats and coughs are common after surgery involving general anesthesia with intubation. The licorice gargle is easy to make.

How to do it: Boil about one teaspoon of licorice powder in one-and-a-half cups of water, then filter. Gargle should stay at room temperature and be used within 24 hours. Licorice contains compounds with anti-inflammatory and anti-irritant effects. Ask your doctor for details.

Anil Agarwal, MD, department of anaesthesiology, Sanjay Gandhi Post Graduate Institute of Medical Sciences, Lucknow, India, and leader of a study published in *Anesthesia & Analgesia*.

Meditate for a Bigger Brain

Compared with nonmeditators, people who had meditated between 10 and 90 minutes a day for five to 46 years had significantly greater brain volume in some regions linked to emotion.

Theory: Meditation may promote better nerve connections or larger cells in certain brain regions—which may explain many meditators' emotional stability and mental focus.

Eileen Luders, PhD, assistant professor, Laboratory of Neuro Imaging, University of California, Los Angeles School of Medicine, as well as lead author of a study of 44 people.

DHEA Supplements May Build Bones

Older women (not men) who supplemented daily with the hormone *dehydroepiandrosterone* (DHEA) plus calcium and vitamin D had a 4% average increase in spinal bone density after two years—enough to reduce spinal fracture risk by up to 50%. Women who took only calcium and vitamin D had no bone density increase. Ask your doctor about taking 50 mg of DHEA daily. Avoid DHEA if you have a history of breast or endometrial cancer.

Edward Weiss, PhD, RD, professor of nutrition and dietetics, D'Youville College, Buffalo, New York, and leader of a study of 136 seniors.

Ginger Relieves Arthritis Pain

Ginger supplements soothe osteoarthritic joints by inhibiting production of pain-causing prostaglandins.

Best: Take a 100-mg supplement, such as Gingerforce, one to three times a day.

Sung Woo Kim, PhD, professor of nutrition and digestive physiology, department of animal and food sciences, Texas Tech University, Lubbock, and leader of a study published in *Journal of Medicinal Food*.

10 Natural Medicines For Every Home

Jamison Starbuck, ND, naturopathic physician in Missoula, Montana. She is past president of the American Association of Naturopathic Physicians and a contributing editor to *The Alternative Advisor: The Complete Guide to Natural Therapies and Alternative Treatments* (Time-Life).

Most Americans make a mad dash to the nearest drugstore if an acute illness, such as sore throat or diarrhea, or a minor injury, such as muscle strain, needs attention. But that's not always necessary. It's easy to keep a few well-chosen natural medicines on hand to treat most minor ailments. At my home, we keep rubbing alcohol, 3% hydrogen peroxide, adhesive bandages, gauze and medical tape for basic first aid. Here are the natural medicines (available at health-food stores) that I keep at home (unless I've indicated otherwise, follow manufacturers' recommendations for dosing)...

1. Traumeel. *Use for:* Sprain, muscle strain or pain after surgery or dental procedures. This homeopathic anti-inflammatory/analgesic (topical or oral) contains a variety of plant medicines, including arnica.

2. Rescue Remedy. *Use for:* Emotional stress, anxiety and worry. This Bach flower remedy contains essences of five plants, including impatiens and clematis. Use four drops on the tongue as needed—up to five times daily.

3. Calendula spray. *Use for:* Skin injuries— cuts, abrasions, insect bites and burns. Used topically, tincture of calendula flowers acts as a mild antiseptic and anti-inflammatory.

4. Echinacea tincture. *Use for:* Cold, flu or sore throat. At the onset of illness, take 60 drops in one to two ounces of water every four waking hours—continue for two to five days.

5. Cough formula. *Use for:* Dry cough and sore throat. Use a tincture formula that contains the herbs elecampane, marshmallow, osha, cherry bark, fennel and licorice mixed in a honey base. This remedy moistens the throat and reduces the frequency of coughs.

6. Charcoal. *Use for:* Acute diarrhea. Take two tablets every two to three waking hours. *Caution:* Charcoal should not be taken with any medication—it can block the drug's absorption.

7. Aloe plant. *Use for:* Burns. Immediately after a burn, cut off a small piece from the tip of an aloe leaf (I keep an aloe plant in my kitchen), slice it open and place the moist inner gel directly on your burn to reduce pain. (If you prefer to buy aloe gel, be sure to refrigerate it.)

8. Peppermint leaf. *Use for:* Fever, nausea, gas and sore throat. To make peppermint tea, steep loose-leaf peppermint tea or tea bags covered for at least five minutes in boiled water. Drink one to four cups daily.

9. Epsom salts. *Use for:* Sore muscles or tension headaches. Rich in magnesium, which helps relax muscles, Epsom salts (two cups) can be used in a bath.

10. Homeopathic flu remedies. *Use for:* Flu. Take at the first signs. *My favorite homeopathic flu remedies:* Muco Coccinum by UnDA and Oscillococcinum by Boiron.

For safety and optimal effectiveness, keep all medicines, including natural ones, in a cool, dry place that is out of the reach of children...and check the expiration dates of your products.

Popular Herbs with Unexpected Health Benefits

Holly Phaneuf, PhD, expert in medicinal chemistry and author of *Herbs Demystified* (Avalon). She is a member of the American Chemical Society.

You may know that the tiny, fiber-rich seeds of the flax plant can be used as a laxative and that ginger helps ease nausea. But can you name any of the other health benefits provided by these plant-derived remedies?

Few people can. However, credible scientific evidence shows that many herbs that are well-known for treating a particular ailment have other very important—but little-known—uses.* *For example…*

ARTICHOKE LEAF

Artichoke leaf extract is used by some people with mildly elevated cholesterol levels as an alternative to prescription statin drugs. Exactly how the herb works is unknown, but animal studies suggest that it inhibits *HMG CoA-reductase,* an enzyme that plays a key role in the liver's production of cholesterol.

In a placebo-controlled, randomized study conducted at the University of Reading in England, adults who took 1,280 mg of artichoke leaf extract daily for three months reduced their cholesterol levels by 4.2%, on average, while levels increased by 1.9%, on average, in those taking a placebo.

What else artichoke leaf can do: Calm indigestion. In a placebo-controlled, randomized study, patients rated their chronic indigestion as significantly improved after taking artichoke leaf extract twice daily for six weeks. Tests on rats suggest that the herb stimulates the gallbladder's production of bile, which helps facilitate the digestion of dietary fat.

Typical dose: About 320 mg daily of artichoke leaf soothes digestive complaints. This dosage can be taken until the indigestion is no longer a problem.

Caution: Avoid artichoke if you are allergic to plants in the daisy family or if you have gallstones (artichoke appears to make the gallbladder contract).

FLAX

Often used as a gentle laxative, the seed of the flax plant (flaxseed) contains fiber and phytonutrients known as lignans—a combination that helps draw water into the gut to speed digestion. For laxative effects, eat one tablespoon of whole or ground seeds (sprinkled on

*If you use prescription drugs and/or have a chronic medical condition, such as diabetes, cancer or heart disease, speak to your doctor before trying herbal remedies. In some cases, herbs may interfere with medication or cause an undesired effect on a chronic medical problem. Women who are pregnant or breast-feeding also should consult a doctor before taking herbs.

cereal, for example) daily. Be sure to drink at least eight ounces of water when eating flaxseeds to prevent them from forming a temporary blockage in the intestines.

What else flaxseed can do: Help prevent breast and prostate cancers. Lignans form estrogen-like compounds that inhibit the body's production of the hormone in women and men. This effect is believed to reduce risk for estrogen-dependent malignancies, including some breast and prostate cancers.

Typical initial dose: One to two tablespoons of ground flaxseed daily, which can be increased gradually to as many as five tablespoons daily.

Grinding flaxseed (in a coffee grinder, for example) rather than eating it whole releases more of its cancer-fighting compounds. Also, ground flaxseed is better than flaxseed oil, which lacks the plant's beneficial lignans unless they are replaced during the manufacturing process.

Helpful: Be sure to refrigerate flaxseed to prolong freshness and preserve potency.

Caution: Do not consume flaxseed within two hours of taking an oral medication—flaxseed may interfere with absorption of the drug.

GARLIC

With its powerful blood-thinning effects, garlic is widely used to help prevent artery-blocking blood clots that can lead to a heart attack or stroke. The typical recommendation for this purpose is one clove of fresh garlic or one-half to three-quarters of a teaspoon of garlic powder daily.

What else garlic can do: It can help prevent stomach and colorectal cancers. The National Cancer Institute funded an analysis of 23 clinical studies that linked garlic consumption (raw, cooked or from garlic supplements) to a 10% to 50% decrease in risk for these types of cancers. This cancer-fighting effect is believed to result from the antioxidant activity of garlic's sulfur-containing molecules. Garlic also is a popular remedy to stave off the common cold, but research on its virus-fighting properties has shown mixed results.

Recommended: A fresh crushed garlic clove four to seven times a week.

GINGER

Ginger is widely used to treat nausea, including that due to motion sickness (one-quarter to one-half teaspoon of ginger powder)…and chemotherapy (one to two teaspoons daily of ginger powder).

Ginger is believed to quell queasiness by stopping intense stomach motions that can interfere with digestion.

What else ginger can do: Relieve arthritis pain. With its aspirin-like effects, ginger inhibits both COX-1 and COX-2 enzymes, two substances that are involved in the production of inflammatory hormones known as prostaglandins.

Typical dose: One-quarter to one-half teaspoon daily of ginger powder.

TURMERIC

In India, turmeric is a popular remedy for indigestion. It contains curcumin, an oily, yellow pigment that appears to prevent gut muscles from contracting and cramping.

What else turmeric can do: Relieve arthritis, morning stiffness and minor sprains. Turmeric reduces levels of an inflammatory, hormone-like substance known as PGE2.

In lab studies, researchers also are finding that turmeric helps prevent colorectal and skin cancers, but its cancer-fighting mechanism has not yet been identified.

In addition, turmeric is being studied for its possible role in decreasing risk for Alzheimer's disease. Test tube and animal studies suggest that turmeric interferes with the formation of amyloid plaque, a hallmark of this neurodegenerative disease.

Recommended: Consume turmeric powder regularly by adding it to food, such as Asian dishes.

Caution: Because turmeric can cause gallbladder contractions, people with gallbladder problems should avoid the herb.

Hooray! Home Remedies For Headaches

Joan Wilen and Lydia Wilen, folk-remedy experts based in New York City. They are coauthors of many books, including *Bottom Line's Treasury of Home Remedies & Natural Cures* and *Bottom Line's Household Magic* (both from Bottom Line Books, 866-444-2086, *www.bottomlinestore.com*).

Next time your head starts to ache, instead of popping a pain pill, try a natural remedy. Science cannot explain why these alternative approaches work—but they have stood the test of time, have no side effects and often work faster than drugs.

Caution: If headaches recur regularly or are severe, seek professional medical help.

Most of the categories below include several options. Try one or more remedies to see which work best for you. Products are sold in health-food stores.

•**Acupressure.** Clip a clothespin to the earlobe that is closest to your headache and leave on for one minute.

•Stick out your tongue about one-half inch, and bite down as hard as you comfortably can… continue for five minutes.

•Ask your partner or a friend to slowly move one thumb down the right side of your back, heading from your shoulder blade toward your waist and stopping to exert steady pressure for one minute on any tender spots.

•**Aromatherapy.** Rub a dab of essential oil of rosemary or peppermint on your forehead, temples and behind the ears…and inhale the fumes from the open bottle four times.

•Crumple a fresh, clean mint leaf, roll it up and gently insert it into one nostril (leaving a bit sticking out for easy removal)…remove after two to three minutes.

•Boil one cup of water mixed with one cup of apple cider vinegar…remove from heat… drape a towel over your head to trap steam and bend over the pot…breathe deeply through your nose for five minutes.

•**Compress.** Dip a white cotton scarf in distilled white vinegar and wring it out…tie it around your forehead as tightly as possible without causing discomfort…leave in place for 15 to 30 minutes.

• **Food.** Eat an apple, a cup of strawberries, a handful of raw almonds (chew thoroughly), one teaspoon of gomasio (Japanese sesame salt), or one teaspoon of honey mixed with one-half teaspoon of garlic juice.

• Drink a cup of chamomile tea.

• **Water.** Fill a sink with water that is as hot as you can tolerate and dunk your hands for one minute.

• Fill a bathtub ankle-high with very cold water…dress warmly but leave feet bare…walk around in the tub until feet start to feel warm (from one to a maximum of three minutes)…then get out, dry your feet, slip under the bed-covers and relax.

Fight Sinusitis

Effective, low-cost ways to fight sinusitis: Use nasal irrigation or a saline nasal spray twice a day. Steam the sinuses by draping a towel over your head while breathing in the steam from a bowl of hot (not boiling) water three times per day for 10 minutes. Take hot showers. Apply warm compresses around the nose, eyes and cheeks for 20 to 30 minutes, two to four times a day. Drink plenty of fluids to dilute mucus and aid drainage. Avoid alcohol, which can worsen swelling of the nose and sinuses. Do not smoke, and avoid secondhand smoke.

Mayo Clinic Women's HealthSource, (now Mayo Clinic Health Letter, *healthletter.mayoclinic.com*).

Healing Spices: Surprising New Discoveries

David Winston, RH, a Broadway, New Jersey–based registered herbalist and professional member of the American Herbalist Guild. He is author of several books, including *Adaptogens: Herbs for Strength, Stamina and Stress Relief* (Healing Arts). *www.herbalstudies.net*

Researchers have now identified new health benefits for several of the popular spices. You may recognize the names of these spices, but the latest studies suggest uses that are not widely known. *Intriguing research…*

CAYENNE PEPPER

• **Cholesterol.** Artery-clogging fatty build-ups are created or worsened when cholesterol oxidizes, a biochemical process similar to metal rusting. Cayenne pepper (also known as chili pepper) contains a plaque-fighting antioxidant (capsaicin), which is also available in supplement form.

Recent research: When researchers asked 27 people to eat a diet that included cayenne-spiced chili or same diet with no chili for one month, the spicy-chili group had much lower harmful cholesterol than those who did not eat chili. In addition to protecting cholesterol from oxidation, cayenne pepper also stimulates digestion and improves circulation—an important benefit for people with chronically cold hands and feet.

My recommendation: Use a cayenne-based hot sauce, to taste. I add it to a variety of foods, including chicken dishes and sandwiches.

Caution: In some people, cayenne causes digestive problems. If you experience stomach upset or anal irritation, use a milder hot sauce, cut back the amount or stop using it.

SAGE

• **Alzheimer's disease.** Herbalists and many doctors report that sage may help patients with mild to moderate Alzheimer's disease.

Recent research: Neurons of lab animals exposed to amyloid beta (the main constituent of harmful plaques in Alzheimer's) and sage leaves or rosmarinic acid (an active ingredient in sage) were less damaged than when the cells were exposed to amyloid beta alone. However, you cannot achieve this potential health benefit from the amount of sage used in cooking.

My recommendation: Drink sage tea.

What to do: Pour eight ounces of boiling water over a tea strainer or tea ball that contains one-half teaspoon of ground sage. Let sit for 15 to 20 minutes. Drink four ounces twice a day. (Refrigerate any unused portion and gently reheat before drinking.)

Alternative: Use sage tea bags. Or add 20 to 30 drops of sage tincture to one ounce of water—drink this amount three times daily.

ROSEMARY

• **Cancer.** Laboratory studies of human cells show that rosemary may help prevent certain types of cancer.

Recent research: The rate at which human leukemia and breast cancer cells multiplied in a laboratory study was reduced when researchers exposed the cells to rosemary extract. More research is needed to confirm these benefits in human study subjects, but rosemary extract is safe to use in the meantime. Cooking with rosemary does not provide this potential health benefit.

My recommendation: Drink rosemary tea.

What to do: Pour 12 ounces of boiling water over a tea strainer or tea ball that contains one-half teaspoon of rosemary. Let sit for 15 to 20 minutes. Drink four ounces, three times a day. (Refrigerate unused tea.)

Alternative: Use rosemary tea bags. Or add 40 to 60 drops of rosemary tincture to one ounce of water—drink this amount three times daily.

HOW TO USE SPICES

The active ingredients in spices can eventually deteriorate after processing. For example, the levels of antioxidants, known as carotenoids, in paprika drop by 75% after three months of storage.

My recommendation: Buy no more than a one-year supply of any spice you plan to use—and replace it annually. Keep your spices away from light, moisture and heat—for example, not near the oven. Consider buying whole rather than powdered spices, and grind them right before using, with a mortar and pestle or spice grinder. To tell whether a spice is rich in health-promoting compounds, smell and/or taste it—the richer the odor and flavor, the better the spice.

Natural Ways to Ease Menopause Symptoms

Ann Louise Gittleman, PhD, nutritionist based in Post Falls, Idaho, and author of 30 books, including *Hot Times: How to Eat Well, Live Healthy, and Feel Sexy During the Change* (Avery).

For decades, women relied on hormone replacement therapy (HRT) to relieve symptoms of menopause—hot flashes, sleep disturbance, anxiety and mood swings. But several large studies have linked long-term HRT with increased risk of breast cancer, dementia, heart attack and stroke.

Fortunately, there are safer, natural alternatives to HRT.

MORE THAN JUST ESTROGEN

People typically attribute menopausal symptoms to declining production of the female hormones estrogen and progesterone. But poor eating and lifestyle habits also play a role, by overtaxing the adrenal glands. For women who are going through menopause, the adrenal glands are nature's backup system. When the ovaries decrease their production of estrogen and progesterone, the adrenals have the ability to produce hormones to compensate. Poor diet and lifestyle choices put stress on the adrenals, creating an imbalance in body chemistry and contributing to the uncomfortable symptoms that we associate with menopause.

If you are a woman with menopausal symptoms, adopting healthier habits can help to even out these imbalances.

If you are a man and the woman you love is going through menopause, you can help by understanding that she is experiencing a profound physiological change. Your kindness and patience can ease her transition through a time that is confusing—for her as well as for you.

Common symptoms and natural solutions...

HOT FLASHES

As many as 80% of women experience hot flashes during menopause. One theory is that the hypothalamus, which controls body temperature, is triggered in some way by hormonal fluctuations.

●**Avoid spicy foods.** Foods containing cayenne or other peppers have a thermogenic effect, meaning that they raise your body temperature.

●**Cook with garlic, onion, thyme, oregano and sage.** These seasonings contain very small amounts of phytoestrogens (plant-based estrogens such as lignans and isoflavones that occur naturally in certain foods) and can help restore hormone balance.

●**Cut down on caffeine.** Caffeine stimulates the adrenal glands, leading to a spike in blood sugar levels followed by a plunge in blood sugar to even lower levels than before. This stresses the body and aggravates menopause woes.

If you don't want to give up coffee completely, have one cup a day with food. Don't use coffee as a stimulant between meals. Instead, eat frequent small meals for energy.

Better than coffee: Green, white and black teas have less caffeine and are high in disease-fighting antioxidants. Try substituting tea for coffee. Then transition to herbal tea or hot water with lemon.

●**Add flaxseed.** Ground flaxseed contains lignans, which seem to modulate fluctuating estrogen and progesterone levels. Aim for two tablespoons a day. Ground flaxseed has a pleasant nutty flavor—sprinkle it on cereal, yogurt and salads.

Bonus: Flaxseed reduces cholesterol, helps prevent certain cancers and relieves constipation (be sure to drink plenty of water).

●**Eat soy foods in moderation.** Some countries with diets high in soy report low rates of menopausal symptoms and breast cancer. But I'm cautious about soy. Preliminary research suggests that while isoflavones in soy appear to protect against some breast cancers, they may stimulate growth of other types of breast cancer.

I'm especially concerned about isolated soy protein, which often is added to protein powder, energy bars and supplements. This puts far more soy isoflavones into the diet than

other cultures typically consume—and these high amounts may not be healthful.

If you enjoy soy foods, limit your consumption to two servings a week, and eat them in their whole-food form—as tofu, tempeh, miso and edamame.

●**Be wary of herbal remedies.** I'm cautious about black cohosh, red clover and other plant remedies with estrogenlike properties. Research has not demonstrated clearly that they help, and some can have harmful side effects if not properly monitored. However, some women do report good results from these remedies. Check with your doctor first. If you don't notice a clear change in symptoms after two to three weeks of trying a new remedy, ask your doctor about trying something else.

What men can do: Buy a dual-control electric blanket so that you both will be comfortable. Make her a cup of herbal tea. Join her in eating flaxseed—it is good for your colon and prostate.

INSOMNIA

During menopause, elevated levels of the stress hormone cortisol make it difficult to fall asleep and can trigger intermittent awakening throughout the night. *Natural sleep aids…*

●**Wild yam cream.** This topical cream extracted from yams grown in Mexico is a source of natural progesterone. It's available at most health-food stores and some pharmacies. Applying small amounts of wild yam cream daily may help to balance cortisol levels and enhance sleep. (The cream also helps reduce anxiety and hot flashes.)

Apply one-quarter teaspoon once in the morning and once at night. Gently rub the cream into areas where you see capillaries, such as the wrist, back of the knee and neck—these are the places where skin is thinnest and the cream is easily absorbed. Alternate where you apply the cream on a daily basis.

●**Magnesium.** Levels of magnesium, a natural sleep aid, are depleted when you consume too much coffee, cola, alcohol, sugar or salt. Foods high in magnesium include halibut…whole-wheat bread…leafy green vegetables such as spinach…nuts…and dried beans (soaked and cooked). If your diet is low in magnesium, take 200 milligrams (mg) to 400 mg in supplement form at bedtime.

• **Zinc.** This mineral can help quiet an overactive mind. Foods rich in zinc include poultry, red meat and nuts, but it is hard to get enough zinc from food. Take 25 mg to 45 mg in supplement form before bed.

• **Exercise.** One study found that women over age 50 who walked, biked or did stretching exercises every morning fell asleep more easily. Try to get a half-hour of exercise most mornings. Avoid working out in the evening—you may have trouble winding down. And don't go to extremes. Overexercising (more than two hours of strenuous, nonstop activity every day) can lead to hormonal imbalance.

What men can do: Exercise with her in the morning. Make sure there is a bottle of magnesium tablets by the bedside at home and when traveling.

MOOD SWINGS

Drinking less coffee and eating frequent small meals will go a long way toward balancing your moods by reducing spikes in blood sugar and stress on adrenals. *In addition…*

• **Eat a balanced diet.** The emotional and mental stress of menopause can lead to a vicious cycle in which stress depletes important mineral stores, further taxing the adrenals.

Among the minerals depleted by stress are copper, calcium, magnesium, potassium, sodium and zinc. To restore these minerals, eat an adrenal-supportive diet rich in bright-colored fruits and vegetables, legumes, lean meats and whole grains. Avoid sugar and other refined carbohydrates.

Recommended: Sea vegetables, such as nori, arame, wakame and hijiki. These are especially high in key minerals. Health-food stores sell them in dried form. They can be crumbled into soup and over fish, salad and vegetables.

• **Get the right kind of fat.** Though you should avoid saturated fats (found in pork, beef and high-fat dairy products) and hydrogenated fats (in margarine, shortening and many packaged baked goods), certain fats are necessary for hormonal regulation and proper functioning of the nervous system. Known as essential fatty acids (EFAs), these healthy fats help to stabilize blood sugar.

Strive to consume two tablespoons a day of healthy oil (use it in cooking, salad dressings, etc.). Olive, sesame, almond, macadamia and flaxseed oils are especially high in EFAs. (Flaxseed oil does not cook well.)

• **Take B-complex vitamins.** B vitamins are known as the antistress vitamins because they nourish the adrenals. Good sources of B vitamins include whole grains and dried beans (soaked and cooked). Most diets are too low in these vitamins, so supplements usually are needed to make up the deficit. Take 50 mg to 100 mg of a vitamin-B complex daily.

What men can do: Make it easy for her to avoid sugar and caffeine by cutting back on them yourself—your health will benefit, too. If she seems distant or on edge, don't take it personally. Remind yourself that it is not you—it is her biochemistry that is acting up.

WEIGHT GAIN

One of the reasons so many women gain weight during menopause is that the ovulation process burns calories—as many as 300 per day during the first 10 days of the menstrual cycle. When ovulation stops, fewer calories are burned and metabolism slows. *Foods to counter the slowdown…*

• **Protein.** Increasing protein intake can raise the body's metabolic rate by as much as 25%. Aim for three to four ounces of lean protein from fish, poultry, beef or lamb twice a day. Eggs and beans also are good sources.

• **Healthy carbohydrates.** Whole grains, vegetables and fruits metabolize slowly and give you energy throughout the day. Try to consume daily at least two servings of fruits, three servings of vegetables and three servings of whole grains.

What men can do: Don't nag her about her weight. Support her by not buying high-calorie foods, such as potato chips and rich desserts.

Drug-Free Ways to Fight Colds

Effie Poy Yew Chow, PhD, RN, founder and president of East West Academy of Healing Arts in San Francisco, *www.eastwestqi.com*. A licensed acupuncturist, qigong grandmaster and registered psychiatric and public health nurse. Dr. Chow is coauthor of *Miracle Healing from China: Qigong* (Medipress).

When a cold makes you miserable, you want relief fast. But drugs designed to ease cold symptoms can have side effects—increased blood pressure and heart rate, gastric upset, blurred vision, trouble concentrating, insomnia.

Instead, I recommend the practices of traditional Chinese medicine, which have been used for thousands of years. These practices may ease inflammation...fight infection...boost the immune system...and promote the healthful flow of qi (energy) through the body.

YIN OR YANG?

According to traditional Chinese medicine, two seemingly opposing yet interdependent natural forces called yin and yang must be in balance for a person to maintain good health. When one force predominates, illness results.

Colds can be characterized as either yin or yang. With a yin cold, you have chills...feel exhausted...and want to crawl into bed. With a yang cold, you have a fever...perspire...and feel agitated. *To reestablish the body's natural balance...*

• **Feed a yin cold—primarily with yang foods.** Yang foods are warming. Generally, they include meat, chicken and fish...and vegetables that grow in the earth, such as carrots, beets, jicama, turnips and yams. Eat as much as you comfortably can. Drink three six-ounce cups of ginger tea daily—ginger has anti-inflammatory and antiseptic effects.

Also soothing: Submerge yourself up to your earlobes in a bathtub of comfortably hot water mixed with Epsom salts.

• **For a yang cold, eat lightly.** Avoid yang foods, and instead focus on cooling yin foods —especially green vegetables, sprouts, fruits and other foods that grow in the open air. Drink eight to 10 cups of water daily. Also

drink two or three cups of garlic tea daily —garlic is an antibacterial, antiviral and anti-inflammatory agent.

To make garlic tea: Boil a cup of water... add a clove of garlic cut in half...steep five to 10 minutes...remove garlic...add honey and lemon juice to taste.

Also helpful: Use garlic liberally when cooking.

TIME-HONORED REMEDIES

Many traditional treatments may be helpful no matter what type of cold you have. Products mentioned below are sold at health-food stores, Asian markets and/or online. Check with your health-care provider before taking supplements, especially if you have a chronic health condition or take any medication. *Consider...*

• **Loquat syrup.** Made from the yellow pear-shaped loquat fruit, this syrup quiets coughs and soothes sore throats. Try a brand called Nin Jiom Pei Pa Koa cough syrup or a natural loquat extract. See product labels for specific dosage guidelines.

• **White Flower Analgesic Balm.** This brand-name product combines essential oils of wintergreen, menthol, camphor, eucalyptus, peppermint and lavender.

To relieve nasal congestion: Put a drop of White Flower on your palm, rub palms together, then bring your hands up to your nose (avoiding the eyes) and inhale for four to eight breaths. Repeat up to four times daily as needed.

To ease headache or body aches: Massage a few drops into achy areas up to four times daily.

• **Acupressure.** This practice stimulates certain points along the body's meridians (energy channels) to eliminate qi blockages. To open sinuses, squeeze the acupressure point on the fleshy area between your thumb and index finger, near the thumb joint. The more blocked your qi is, the more tender this spot may feel. Apply enough pressure to cause mild discomfort. Hold for several minutes, then switch sides. Repeat as needed.

• **Diaphragmatic breath work.** This technique uses the diaphragm as a piston to improve oxygen flow and blood circulation and relieve congestion. Sit or stand up straight to allow lungs to fill…gently draw in air through your nose (if you're not too congested), letting your abdomen expand outward…then pull your abdomen in so that it pushes the air out through your mouth. Continue for one minute. Consciously repeat several times daily, aiming for this to become the way you automatically breathe throughout the day.

More from Dr. Effie Poy Yew Chow, PhD, RN…

How to Not Catch a Cold

The best defense against colds is to avoid getting them in the first place. That requires a strong immune system—and certain nutrients can help.

Advised: In addition to a daily multivitamin, take any or all of the following supplements. For maximum effect, use year-round.

•**Coenzyme Q10 (CoQ10).** This vitamin-like substance boosts cellular energy.

Recommended dosage: 100 mg to 200 mg twice daily.

•**Fish oil.** This is rich in the omega-3 fatty acids *eicosapentaenoic acid* (EPA) and *docosahexaenoic acid* (DHA), which reduce disease-promoting inflammation. Take fish oil liquid or capsules at a dosage that provides 3,000 mg daily of combined EPA and DHA.

•**Vitamin D.** This is a fat-soluble vitamin that benefits the body in many ways, including by strengthening the immune system. I recommend taking 2,000 international units (IU) daily of vitamin D3 (*cholecalciferol*).

Alternative: Take one teaspoon of cod-liver oil daily for each 50 pounds of body weight.

Kick the Salt Habit

Cut back on salt by changing cooking habits and reading food labels.

•**Go light on soy sauce in a stir-fry**—two tablespoons include almost one day's recommended sodium intake. Instead, drizzle a small amount of toasted sesame oil for flavor without the sodium.

•**Use fresh or frozen vegetables**—not canned ones, which have high salt content.

•**Make plain pasta or rice,** and add herbs and spices instead of buying prepackaged mixes.

•**Cook meat without salt,** then sprinkle a little on it to enhance the flavor.

•**Read labels** of ketchup, mustard and other condiments—many have high salt levels.

•**Eat foods rich in potassium,** which helps counteract the effects of salt. Good potassium sources include sweet and white potatoes, white and lima beans, plain yogurt, bananas and spinach.

Marisa Moore, RD, spokesperson, American Dietetic Association, Atlanta.

Simple Ways to Help You Save on Health Care

Charles B. Inlander, consumer advocate and health-care consultant based in Fogelsville, Pennsylvania. He was founding president of People's Medical Society, a consumer health advocacy group active in the 1980s and 1990s. He is author of more than 20 books, including *Take This Book to the Hospital with You* (St. Martin's).

Sadly, many people continue to cut back on their medications to save money. Doing this may save dollars in the short run—but over time, it is likely to cost people much more as their medical troubles return or worsen. Fortunately, there are plenty of ways to save a lot of money on your health-care expenses without jeopardizing your health. *How you can start saving today…*

•**Call rather than visit your doctor.** I recently saved $300 in office-visit and consultation fees by calling a specialist who had been treating me and talking about a problem on the phone rather than going to his office. This doctor was able and willing to review the status of my condition by talking to me, and he called in a prescription. In a nonemergency situation, such as following up on an office visit or asking about a symptom, this approach may save you money.

Important: Some doctors are starting to charge nominal fees for telephone consultations, which are not covered by insurance.

•**Get free supplies.** Doctors' offices are a great place to get free medical supplies. My wife recently got several free boxes of contact lens solution from her optometrist. She saved $60! Endocrinologists and family doctors often have diabetes supplies…urologists often have large supplies of catheter bags…and your other specialists may have supplies you use. When it comes to samples of prescription drugs, be careful. Patients often receive free samples of new, costly medications. While such drugs may be appropriate, it's best to ask your doctor if there is a less expensive medication that is just as effective for your condition.

•**Borrow equipment.** Check with friends or relatives if you need a walker, crutches, wheelchair or even a hospital bed. A friend of mine has saved thousands of dollars this way. Just be sure to disinfect the equipment.

•**Use store-brand products.** We all know that the generic versions of prescription medications are much less expensive than brand-name drugs. But the savings don't stop there. Store-brand over-the-counter medications, such as aspirin, cold remedies and cough syrups, are often half the price of the big-name brands. Store-brand incontinence products, foot-care supplies and other health products are also cheaper.

•**Review your insurance.** If you are covered by Medicare, compare "Medigap" plans (Medicare supplemental insurance) each year to see if you are getting maximum coverage for the price. Go to the Medicare Web site, *www.medicare.gov*, click on "Supplements & Other Insurance," then "How to compare Medigap policies." At the same Web site, you can compare Medicare Part D prescription drug benefit plans as well. If you are not eligible for Medicare, but need health insurance, check Web sites such as AARP's, *www.aarp. org*, or local health plans in your area. Most insurance companies now offer many individual and family plans. If you have been insured until very recently, you can buy plans that cover

even pre-existing conditions at affordable prices. So don't wait. Start saving today.

Low-Cost Doctor and Eye Care

Jim Miller, an advocate for senior citizens, writes *Savvy Senior,* a weekly information column syndicated in more than 400 newspapers. Based in Norman, Oklahoma, he is a contributor to the NBC *Today* show. *www. savvysenior.org*

There are a variety of programs and services that provide free or low-cost medical care…

•**Health centers.** Federally funded by the Health Resources and Services Administration (HRSA), these health centers provide low-cost health and dental care. You pay what you can afford based on your income. 888-275-4772, *http://findahealthcenter.hrsa.gov*.

•**Hill-Burton facilities.** There are about 200 Hill-Burton health-care facilities around the country that offer free or reduced-cost health care. Eligibility standards vary by facility, but most require your income to be at or below two times the US poverty guideline (see *http://aspe. hhs.gov/poverty*). 800-638-0742 (800-492-0359 for Maryland residents), *www.hrsa.gov/get-health-care/affordable/hill-burton/index.html*.

•**Free clinics.** Nationwide, there are about 1,000 privately funded, non-profit, community-based clinics that provide care to those in need at little or no cost. To locate a clinic in your area, call your local hospital or go to *www.free medicalcamps.com*.

•**Indian Health Service (IHS).** An agency within the Department of Health and Human Services, IHS provides free medical care to approximately 1.5 million American Indians and Alaska Natives. *www.ihs.gov*.

•**Remote Area Medical.** A nonprofit, all-volunteer, charitable organization that provides free health, dental and eye care to uninsured or underinsured people in remote areas of Kentucky, Tennessee, and Virginia. *www.ramusa.org*.

EYE CARE

• **EyeCare America.** This program, coordinated by the American Academy of Ophthalmology, provides a medical eye exam and up to one year of treatment at no out-of-pocket expense for seniors and diabetics. 877-887-6327, *www.eyecareamerica.org.*

• **Mission Cataract USA** provides free cataract surgery to people of all ages who don't have Medicare, Medicaid or private insurance and have no other means to pay. 559-797-1629, *www.missioncataractusa.org.*

• **Vision USA.** Coordinated by the American Optometric Association (AOA), Vision USA provides free eye-care services to uninsured and low-income workers and their families who have no other means of obtaining care. 800-766-4466, *www.aoafoundation.org.*

• **New Eyes for the Needy.** A not-for-profit eyeglass program that accepts donations of used prescription eyeglasses and distributes them to people in need. 973-376-4903, *www.neweyesfortheneedy.org.*

• **Lions Club.** Your local Lions Club can help you find free or discounted eye-care and eyeglasses programs, including the OneSight program (*www.onesight.org*), along with other local services. Go to *www.lionsclubs.org* to get the number of your state Lions Club office, which can refer you to your community representative.

Smart Ways to Save on Prescription Drugs

Edward Jardini, MD, a family physician at Twin Cities Community Hospital, Templeton, California, where he has served as chair of the pharmacy and therapeutics committee. He is author of *How to Save on Prescription Drugs: 20 Cost-Saving Methods* (Celestial Arts).

The high cost of prescription medication creates a heavy financial burden for many Americans. According to a study in *American Journal of Medicine*, more than one in five Americans over the age of 50 with a chronic health problem has been forced to cut back on essentials—including food—to pay for prescription drugs. Nearly one in five has had to skip doses of prescribed medications to save money.

High deductibles and high copayments mean that these problems can affect even people who have prescription drug coverage through health insurance.

But there are ways to reduce out-of-pocket prescription drug costs...

• **Decline free samples.** Receiving things for free sounds like a wonderful money-saver—but accepting free samples to start a new long-term treatment could cost you a bundle. Pharmaceutical companies typically supply doctors with free samples of expensive new drugs with which they are trying to win market share from lower-cost, better proven alternatives. These free sample drugs often require long-term use, so receiving the first dose for free will mean much less to your bottom line than the hefty price you will pay for subsequent doses.

• **Unless your doctor has reason to believe that this drug is better for you than the alternatives, say, "No, thank you, Doctor.** Keep the samples. Just give me a prescription for a trusted medication that's within my budget."

Exception: Free samples will save you money if your doctor is willing to give you enough samples for a complete course of treatment. Though uncommon, this might be possible with, say, an antihistamine for a case of hives or an antibiotic for an infection.

• **Split tablets.** You may know that splitting tablets can save you money. But most people, including doctors, don't realize just how much you can save. Most prescription drugs are sold in a range of dosages. There might be a 20-milligram (mg) pill, a 40-mg pill and an 80-mg pill.

The higher-dose pills usually are a relative bargain, per milligram of medication, compared with lower-dose pills. In other words, an 80-mg pill will almost always cost substantially less than twice the price of a 40-mg pill and less than four times the price of a 20-mg pill. In some cases, pills of different dosages are priced exactly the same.

Example: The 20-mg, 40-mg and 80-mg versions of the cholesterol medication Lipitor cost the same per pill.

Whenever you are prescribed an expensive medication, ask your doctor if it would be possible for him/her to prescribe half-tablet doses of pills twice as strong as you need—half an 80-mg tablet rather than one 40-mg tablet, for example. Most doctors aren't very familiar with medication prices, so you might have to explain that this could save you a lot of money. Pill-splitting devices, sold at pharmacies, can help you divide pills accurately.

Caution: Certain types of pills, including capsules, gelcaps and extended-release tablets, cannot be split safely. Discuss any plans you have to split pills with your doctor and pharmacist.

•**Apply to pharmaceutical company patient-assistance programs.** Most major pharmaceutical companies will supply their drugs for free to patients who are unable to afford them. These underpublicized, underutilized assistance programs are not necessarily restricted to people who are very poor. Families making as much as $80,000 per year can qualify for the most liberal programs. Other pharmaceutical company programs cap income at $40,000 or less, but exceptions may be made or applicants may be allowed to deduct the cost of medical expenses when determining their annual income. Income, not assets, is used to determine need, so retirees often qualify even if they have considerable savings.

There is no downside to applying. Look for details and an application on the pharmaceutical company's Web site or call its 800 number.

Attention veterans: Anyone who has been honorably discharged from the military following active service can obtain many prescription drugs for $8 per month per prescription through the US Department of Veterans Affairs' Health Care System. Contact the VA for more information on health-care eligibility (877-222-8387, *www.va.gov*).

Ask your doctor to prescribe a cheaper alternative to a name-brand drug. Most people know that generic versions of expensive prescription pharmaceuticals are just as effective at a fraction of the cost.

Examples: The generic equivalents of the popular drugs Ambien, Prozac, Soma, Xanax and Zantac cost less than 10% as much as the name brands.

However, you may not realize that there are less expensive medications within the same class of drugs that might be equally effective for you.

Example: Beta-blockers are a class of drugs used to treat high blood pressure. Though all beta-blockers are very similar, 100 tablets of Zebeta costs about $375...90 tablets of Inderal is closer to $410. Even generic versions of these drugs differ substantially in price—about $100 for 100 tablets of the generic version of Zebeta...and $125 for 100 tablets of generic Inderal.

Sometimes it is possible to switch to a different, cheaper class of drugs without any health consequences. New classes of drugs are heavily marketed, but that does not mean they are any better than older, cheaper drugs that treat the same problems. Ask your doctor whether there is evidence that the expensive new class of drug he/she wants to prescribe will be any more effective for you than a drug from an older, less expensive class.

Example: Januvia, a newer class of drug used to treat type 2 diabetes, costs more than $600 for a 90-day supply. Studies suggest that for many people it is often less effective than far cheaper diabetes drugs previously on the market.

•**Don't ask your doctor for advertised drugs.** Pharmaceutical companies now market prescription medications directly to consumers. Asking your doctor about an advertised drug could be bad for both your financial and physical health. Not only are heavily advertised prescription drugs usually very expensive, research suggests that mentioning advertised drugs to your doctor could lead to prescriptions that you do not need.

Example: In a study published in *The Journal of the American Medical Association*, medical researchers had actors pose as patients suffering from depression-related symptoms. The symptoms that the actors described did not indicate the need for prescription antidepressants, and only 10% of the actors were given prescriptions. But when the actors presented the same set of symptoms and asked the doctor, "Do you think Paxil will help me?" they were prescribed Paxil or a similar antidepressant more than 50% of the time.

•**Don't use insurance for very low-cost drugs.** Patients who have prescription drug coverage typically use this insurance every time they purchase medication. When these prescriptions are for low-cost generic drugs, however, their copayments can exceed the cost of purchasing the drugs out-of-pocket. Ask your pharmacist the cash cost of a generic drug before producing your insurance card.

Example: I prescribed one-half tablet per day of *hydrochlorothiazide,* a high blood pressure medication, to a patient. This patient used his prescription drug plan to buy the medication, paying a $10 copayment each month, for a total cost of $120 per year. These pills would have cost him only around a nickel apiece had he paid cash—approximately $10 per year.

Also, check Walmart and Target for their $4 prescription drug plans.

More from Dr. Edward Jardini...

Get Your Drugs at 50% Off—Or Even Free

Anyone who regularly takes prescription medication knows how pricey drugs can be. Fortunately, there are places where you can buy your drugs for less—or even get them for free. The key is knowing where to look.

Important: Although most low-cost drug programs have income eligibility requirements, do not assume that you won't be accepted into a program just because your income is officially too high. Many programs will consider applications on a case-by-case basis.

Best resources for finding low-cost or free medications...

DRUG DISCOUNT NETWORKS

Some groups connect patients to public and private assistance programs that provide discounted or free drugs to eligible patients. *These include...*

•**Partnership for Prescription Assistance** (888-477-2669, *www.pparx.org*). This collaborative network of professional medical organizations, including the American Academy of Family Physicians, and private groups links patients with more than 475 public and private patient assistance programs that offer more than 2,500 drugs at reduced cost or no charge. Income qualifications vary by state.

PHARMACEUTICAL PATIENT-ASSISTANCE PROGRAMS

Major pharmaceutical companies have their own patient-assistance programs that offer many—though not all—drugs at a discount, or even for free, to people who cannot afford them. Eligibility requirements vary—even families earning up to $80,000 a year can qualify. Some companies evaluate applications on a case-by-case basis.

To obtain a free copy of Directory of Prescription Drug Patient Assistance Programs, call the Partnership for Prescription Assistance at 800-762-4636. To determine the manufacturer of a particular drug, ask your pharmacist. *Among the pharmaceutical companies with programs...*

•**AstraZeneca's AZ & Me Prescription Savings Program** (800-292-6363, *www.astrazeneca-us.com*, click on "Affordability").

•**GlaxoSmithKline** (888-825-5249, *www.gskforyou.com*).

•**Lilly TruAssist Patient Assistance Programs** (Lilly USA, 800-545-6962, *www.lillytruassist.com*).

•**Merck Patient Assistance Program** (800-727-5400, *www.merckhelps.com*).

•**Novartis Patient Assistance Now** (800-245-5356, *www.patientassistancenow.com*).

•**Pfizer RxPathways** (844-989-7284, *www.pfizerRxPathways.com*).

•**Genentech Access to Care Foundation** (866-422-2377, *www.genentech-access.com*).

Some pharmaceutical companies also offer coupons that can be printed from their Web sites, as well as discount-card programs offering savings on some products. Check the drug manufacturer's Web site for details.

Also from Dr. Edward Jardini…

More Ways to Save on Drugs

There are a number of ways to dramatically reduce your medication costs. Unfortunately, most drug-discount programs don't advertise their services, so few people are aware of all the available options. Some programs even waive income eligibility requirements.

Among the best resources…

PHARMACY BENEFIT MANAGERS

Because of their size, large companies that act as third-party managers of prescription drug programs can provide discounted medications. *Ones to consider…*

• **Caremark: RxSavingsPlus** (877-673-3688, *www.rxsavingsplus.com*). This program offers a card that is accepted at more than 65,000 US pharmacies and provides an average savings of 22%. You can use the card as long as you're not receiving insurance reimbursement, including Medicare. For up to a 50% discount, order a 90-day supply by mail.

• **Rx Outreach** (888-796-1234 *www.rxout reach.com*). For low-income patients, this nonprofit charitable organization sets annual income limits of less than $36,810 for most individuals or less than $48,720 a year for couples. Most drugs can be purchased for $90 or 180-day supply.

GOVERNMENT PROGRAMS

Federal, state and local governments also offer eligible patients access to low-cost drugs…

• **US Department of Veterans Affairs** (877-222-8387, *www.va.gov*). For people who were honorably discharged from active duty in a branch of the military, the VA will provide prescription drugs at a cost of $8 a month. The prescription must be written by a doctor in a VA clinic. To qualify, you must fill out application form 10-10EZ (available at local VA

offices and medical centers or online at *www. va.gov*, search 10-10EZ and provide a copy of your discharge document.

The VA also offers a separate health-care program, called CHAMPVA, for family members of a veteran who has a permanent disability or who died in the line of duty or due to a service-connected disability—as long as they're not eligible for TRICARE.

• **TRICARE** (*www.tricare.mil*). TRICARE is a healthcare benefit for active-duty service members, reserve members, retired uniformed armed services members, their families and survivors. Widows and widowers of active-duty members also may qualify unless they remarry. The plan includes prescription coverage.

If the medication is obtained at a military treatment facility, it is free. Generic drugs by mail are also free. Medications obtained at retail network pharmacies cost significantly less for a 90-day supply.

• **National Conference of State Legislatures**, *www.ncsl.org/research/health/state-pharmaceu tical-assistance-programs.aspx*). In recent years, several states had established some type of program to provide prescription drug coverage or subsidies to low-income older adults or disabled persons who do not qualify for Medicaid. The programs vary widely—and the information is available through state departments of health or social services.

PATIENT ADVOCACY GROUPS

Some groups charge a set fee to help patients find free or low-cost medications. This works well for people who don't want to deal with the application process required for most drug-assistance programs.

MASS-MARKET RETAILERS

Some large retail stores, such as Walmart, Target, Costco and Kmart, offer low-price prescriptions on generic and some brand-name medications. Target, for instance, offers a program that covers mostly generic drugs at a cost of $4 for a 30-day supply and $10 for a 90-day supply. For information, go to store Web sites or ask at your local store's pharmacy.

Save Money on Medications

Marjory Abrams, chief content editor, *Bottom Line* newsletters, Bottom Line, Inc., 3 Landmark Square, Stamford, Connecticut.

My eyebrows went up when I read recently about a North Carolina insurance program that saved $6.6 million over a three-year period through prescription drug "cost-control interventions." Individuals covered by the plan saved, too. Their average monthly drug expenditures dropped by about 11%, from $11.52 to $10.23 per prescription.

The study, published in *The American Journal of Managed Care*, was led by David P. Miller, Jr., MD, assistant professor at Wake Forest University School of Medicine in Winston-Salem, North Carolina. The study focused on the university medical center's own health insurance plan, which covers more than 22,000 people.

The bulk of the savings came from prescribing generic instead of branded drugs—an option that is becoming more widely available. Popular medications that have become available in generic versions include the antihistamine *fexofenadine* (Allegra)...the sleep aid *zolpidem* (Ambien)...the heart drug *carvedilol* (Coreg)...the herpes/shingles drug *famciclovir* (Famvir)...*terbinafine* (Lamisil), which treats nail fungus...the cholesterol-lowering drug *simvastatin* (Zocor)...and the antidepressant *sertraline* (Zoloft).

Pharmacists are your best source of information about new generics. They also can tell you which ones are not yet available legally. Some Internet suppliers sell what are purportedly generic forms of drugs that are still under patent protection.

Examples: *atorvastatin* (Lipitor), a cholesterol-lowering drug which came off patent in November 2011.

People with prescription drug coverage save with generic drugs because co-payments are lower (typically $10 versus $25 or more). Savings can be much more substantial for people who lack such coverage and for Medicare recipients whose annual drug expenses are approaching the infamous "doughnut hole," when no drug costs are covered.

Good for everyone: Some large chain stores, such as Target and Walmart, now charge only $4 for a 30-day supply of any of hundreds of generic drugs.

More ways to save...

• **Buy OTC.** In the study, medications were moved out of the insurance formulary (the list of drugs that an insurance plan covers) if there were comparable over-the-counter (OTC) drugs available. Dr. Miller says that consumers, especially those without prescription drug coverage, may indeed save in two particular categories—the nonsedating antihistamines, such as *loratadine* (Claritin), and the acid-reducing proton pump inhibitors, such as *omeprazole* (Prilosec). In some cases, even if a person has insurance, the cost of the OTC drug still may be lower than the co-payment. Ask your physician which medications may help you the most, and then compare costs.

• **Split pills.** Because many medications are priced about the same regardless of dose, buying a double-dose pill and halving it gives you two pills for the price of one. Check with your pharmacist to make sure that a pill can be split safely. Pill-splitting devices can be purchased in drugstores and online for less than $10.

• **Avoid drugs altogether.** In this study, the plan limited the quantity of sleep aids supplied to members. Members were provided with only enough tablets for every-other-day use, instead of the usual 30-day supply. Because sleep medications can have serious side effects, including daytime drowsiness and slower reaction time, Dr. Miller urges people with insomnia to try to restore a healthy sleep pattern without medication, whenever possible.

Bottom line: If you eat right, exercise regularly and guard your health in other ways, you are likely to need fewer drugs altogether.

Free or Low-Cost Flu Shots

Norman H. Edelman, MD, chief medical officer, American Lung Association, and professor of medicine, State University of New York at Stony Brook.

Free or low-cost flu shots are available at an increasing number of locations, including county health departments and pharmacies. At most of these locations, however, the shots are offered for a very limited time. The American Lung Association's online Flu Vaccine Finder (*www.lung.org,* search Find a Flu Shot) can search for upcoming flu shot clinics in your area so you don't miss your chance.

Virtually everyone should get an annual flu shot, particularly people over age 50... between ages two and 18...suffering from a chronic lung or heart problem...or in regular contact with someone who falls into any of these increased-risk categories. The shot usually becomes available in late September. Flu and flu complications kill about 36,000 Americans each year.

Brand-Name vs. Generic Drugs

Brand-name heart drugs are no better than generics. In a recent review, 53% of medical journal editorials and commentaries favored the use of brand-name cardiovascular drugs.

Additional recent finding: When researchers analyzed 47 studies comparing the use of generic or brand-name cardiovascular drugs, they found no evidence that brand-name drugs led to better results for patients.

If you take heart medicine: Ask your doctor about taking a less-expensive generic version...and start saving money today.

Aaron Kesselheim, MD, instructor of medicine, Harvard Medical School, Boston.

Negotiate the Cost of Health Care

Ask hospitals and doctors for a price break. When choosing a facility, consider cost—an urgent-care center may charge $150 for services that could cost $1,000 at a hospital emergency room. Use generic drugs whenever possible—and when one is not available, ask your doctor if you can try a less expensive medicine designed to treat the same condition.

Also: Find out about benefits through your insurance company. Some offer discounts on gym memberships, stop-smoking and weight-loss programs, and other services.

The Washington Post.

Now Is the Time to Go Medical Bargain-Hunting

Charles B. Inlander, health-care consultant and founding president of the Peoples Medical Society, a consumer advocacy organization active in the 1980s and 1990s. He is the author of 20 books, including *Take This Book to the Hospital with You: A Consumer Guide to Surviving Your Hospital Stay* (St. Martins).

With health insurance policy still up in the air, this may be the best time we've had in years to get some deep discounts on medical services and equipment. For example, an optometrist I recently spoke with told me that his business is off significantly from one year ago, so now he is discounting all the eyeglasses he sells by at least 30%. A psychologist told me that she has begun offering up to three sessions of counseling at 50%.

In general, recent reports show that doctor visits are down by as much as 7%. Add to that a decline in elective surgeries, including knee replacements, cataract removal and cosmetic surgery, and what we have is a unique opportunity for consumers to do some medical bargain-hunting.

Here are the best ways to find good deals on high-quality services in your community...

• **Ask the right question.** Many times, getting a discount is as easy as asking for it. Don't be afraid to ask a surgeon (if you are contemplating surgery) or any type of health provider if he can do better after discussing the cost of a medical procedure or service. This is especially helpful if a big out-of-pocket cash outlay is involved because you have no insurance or your insurance does not cover a particular service, such as dental care or cosmetic surgery.

Insider secret: Don't worry about getting lower-quality care if you pay a discounted price. Research shows that price does not affect quality when it comes to medical care.

• **Get the ammunition you need to negotiate.** When my wife recently needed a dental implant, our dentist and the surgeon he recommended quoted her a price of more than $3,000. But we shopped around and found two other highly recommended surgeons and dentists who were offering the same procedure at a price of $2,000. When we told that to our dentist, he and the surgeon matched the price.

Insider secret: When negotiating for a discount, you'll have the best luck if you comparison shop and are able to quote a lower price from a competitor.

• **Don't forget about discounts on equipment.** You've probably seen those TV commercials for motorized scooters and wheelchairs. If youre insured, the deal may look good. But if you are not covered, you may be able to match the price or do even better at a local medical equipment shop that's looking for customers. And even if you are insured, many local stores will throw in a maintenance contract at no additional charge just to get your business. Hearing aids also are being sold at the steepest discounts in years. With a few phone calls, you often can find deals at 20% to 50% off retail price.

Don't put off what you thought you couldn't afford. Like all other businesses these days, medical and health providers badly need your patronage and very often will reduce their prices to get it.

How to Shrink Your Medical Bills By 25% Or More

Sue Goldstein, founder of Underground Shopper, a 40-year-old company focused on bargain-shopping tips. Goldstein has written more than 70 books on shopping and hosts a morning radio show on KVCE-AM in Dallas/Fort Worth.

The cost of medical care continues to climb. And even if you do have insurance, it rarely covers everything. *But you can cut costs...*

NEGOTIATE A BETTER DEAL

More patients are negotiating with their doctors for reduced fees. If you would like to try, call your doctor before scheduling an appointment. Ask what you can do to lower your bill. Would there be a discount if you paid with cash...or scheduled your appointment for an off-peak time? What if you agreed to come in on short notice when the doctor had a cancellation? You could get 25% off your bill—possibly more.

You might even be able to barter for medical care if you have a skill or service that the medical professional needs. Are you a Web designer, landscaper, architect or accountant? Ask the physician if he/she is interested in trading services.

If a procedure is medically necessary but you have no insurance and money is tight, tell your doctor. Most physicians are willing to bend on price under these circumstances.

COSMETIC SURGERY SAVINGS

Cosmetic surgery is rarely covered by health insurance, so cosmetic surgeons are often open to negotiation. Some board-certified surgeons may offer significant discounts to patients who are flexible about scheduling.

About 13% of all scheduled cosmetic surgeries are postponed for one reason or another. This can leave doctors with open operating-room time. If you're ready to jump in when one of these gaps occurs, the doctor might cut his usual rate by as much as 15%.

Important: Ask the surgeon to show you his portfolio of patients' before-and-after pictures. Get at least three references. Also call your state's medical society—listed in the *Yellow Pages* under "Medical Associations"—to learn about disciplinary actions, license suspensions or other complaints.

GO TO A TEACHING HOSPITAL

Local teaching hospitals, dental schools and chiropractic schools often offer inexpensive medical care. Students lack the experience of older doctors, but they typically are well supervised. If they can't handle something, more experienced doctors are on hand to help. Contact local teaching hospitals or schools for details.

Resource: The Association of American Medical Colleges, 202-828-0400…or visit *www. aamc.org.*

FREE MEDICATIONS

Major pharmaceutical companies may provide drugs to certain people at no cost or at steep discounts. More than 1,500 drugs are available through more than 100 pharmaceutical company programs. Go to *www.rxassist. org* for a directory.

To be eligible for these discounts, your insurance must not cover the prescription. You also must make enough money that you don't qualify for government health-care programs —but not so much that the pharmaceutical company thinks you can afford to pay.

Income requirements vary from company to company, but people making less than $25,000 a year are generally eligible for most programs. Anyone with big drug bills—$300 a month or more—making less than $50,000 annually may also qualify.

The programs are based on income, not assets. Even if you own a nice home, you still could qualify if you are retired or temporarily unemployed.

To find out if you are eligible and if the drug you need is covered, you can call the drug manufacturer.

FREE COUPONS

Many pharmaceutical companies run free, week- to month-long trial-offer programs for certain drugs. All consumers need to do is clip a coupon from a magazine or download one from a Web site and have a doctor write a prescription. Rules vary, but in many cases, you can use the coupon even if it is not your first prescription for the medication.

Don't assume that these coupons always are good deals. The drugmaker might be offering the free trial because a competing drug— perhaps even a cheaper generic version of the drug—will come to market. The drug company is banking that you won't later go to the bother of switching medications. Always ask your doctor if there are cheaper or more effective alternatives.

To find out if a coupon is available for a particular drug, check the company's Web site.

DISCOUNTS ON ADJUSTABLE BEDS AND NONALLERGENIC MATTRESSES

For people with certain heart conditions or back problems, adjustable beds are medical necessities. For allergy sufferers, nonallergenic mattresses can be a must.

•**City Mattress Factory** (800-834-2473, *www. citymattress.com*) sells all types of mattresses and adjustable bed frames, typically for half the retail price of brand-name mattresses even after factoring in shipping.

Example: An adjustable double bed at City Mattress can cost about $800, rather than the $2,000 you would pay for one advertised on television.

IF MONEY IS EXTREMELY TIGHT

If you have no insurance and require medical treatment, one option is to participate in a clinical trial. You receive free complete medical exams, free treatment and may even get paid for your trouble.

Downside: The treatment you receive might not yet be proven effective—it could even be dangerous, although this is rare. Also, if you participate in a "blind" study, you might be given a placebo instead of the experimental drug.

If you are interested in participating in a clinical trial, contact Research Across America (*www.researchacrossamerica.com*), Radiant Research (480-535-8111, *www.radiantresearch. com*) or *www.clinicaltrials.gov*.

Free Online Answers to Your Health Questions

Trisha Torrey, a patient advocate, health columnist and radio talk-show host based in Syracuse, New York. Torrey is the founder of the Web sites *www.everypa tientsadvocate.com* and *www.diagknowsis.org*, and an expert in patient empowerment for About.com (*www. patients.about.com*).

With a few computer keystrokes, people who have Internet access can find literally thousands of health-related Web sites. But much of this information is misleading or simply incorrect.

Reliable health information that's free of charge online…

1. Information on medications and supplements. Your doctor and pharmacist are good resources, but there are several Web sites that also can help.

Best sites: The Physicians' Desk Reference (PDR) Web site (*www.pdrhealth.com*) explains the conditions for which a prescription or over-the-counter drug, or dietary supplement or herbal remedy, may be prescribed…how best to take it…and whether it may interact with foods or other medications.

If you can't find a particular medication listed at the PDR Web site or if you're taking an expensive brand-name drug and want to see whether it's available in a less expensive generic equivalent, check the FDA's Electronic Orange book (*www.fda.gov/cder/ob*).

For a list of other Web sites that provide information on medications and supplements, consult the resource library on the health information Web site *www.diagknowsis.org*,

which gives advice on how to research medical diagnoses and treatments, along with links to credible health Web sites.

2. Doctors' credentials. Your neighbor may have had a good experience with his orthopedist, but is this doctor the best one to perform your hip surgery? It's important to check the credentials of any doctor you may consider using.

At a minimum, a doctor should be licensed, the basic credential issued by each state. The Federation of State Medical Boards Web site (*www.fsmb.org/directory_smb.html*) provides a directory of state boards that allows you to confirm that a particular doctor is licensed to practice.

To check whether a doctor is board-certified in his/her medical specialty, which ensures that the physician has met minimum competency and continuing education requirements, go to the American Board of Medical Specialties Web site (*www.abms.org*) or call 866-275-2267. To inquire about a doctor of osteopathy, consult the American Osteopathic Association (*www.osteopathic.org*) or call 800-621-1773.

3. Secrets to living with medical conditions. Let's say you're wondering how to get through a long movie when you have arthritis, what to say to a friend with cancer or how to tell your boss about your diabetes. These kinds of questions are ideal to ask at online health forums, where you can get input on problems that you might want to discuss with a friend—if only you had one who had been in a similar situation.

How online health forums work: People with access to the Internet can share their experiences and advice on a "message board" where others who log on to the same Web site are able to read the messages and respond to them, if they so desire. Keep in mind that the people who post comments on these message boards are not medical professionals. They are patients and caregivers who are speaking from their own experience.

Good sites: HealthBoards (*www.health boards.com*) offers more than 150 message boards on a variety of health topics…Daily Strength (*www.dailystrength.org*) provides access to more than 500 online support groups dedicated to physical and mental health issues. Some Web sites sponsored by organizations that focus on specific diseases, such as the American Cancer Society (*www.cancer.org*) or the Leukemia & Lymphoma Society (*www.lls.org*), also offer online message boards.

Important: Communications posted on an online health forum's message board are anonymous, so any information or advice that involves specific treatment recommendations or medical products should always be verified with a medical professional. When participating in these forums, do not provide identifying details, such as your last name, phone number or address. It's okay to provide your first name and city or state.

HONCODE

Look for the "HONcode" accreditation from the Health on the Net Foundation in Switzerland, which guides lay users and medical professionals to reliable sources of health-care information online. This accreditation ensures that the Web site has been deemed a reliable source of health information and meets standards, including those related to the qualification of the authorities cited on the site, privacy of personal data submitted by a visitor to the site and financial disclosures of funding sources.

Get Dental Care for Less Money

Jordan Braverman, MPH, former director of legislative and health policy analysis at Georgetown University's Health Policy Center, Washington, DC. He is author of several books on health-care policy and financing, including *Your Money & Your Health* (Prometheus).

Dental care is rarely covered by Medicare …few retirees have dental insurance… and those who have dental insurance often find that their coverage is very limited.

Dental bills average around $677 per year for the typical senior, and a major procedure, such as a root canal or a dental implant, can push that tab into four or even five figures.

Exception: Medicare usually will pay dental bills if they are related to a medical incident that requires a hospital stay, such as jaw reconstruction following a car accident.

Some resources that could help you dramatically reduce your dental bills or even provide dental care for free…

HEALTH INSURANCE

Insurance can help pay dental bills. *Options to consider…*

• **Dental insurance.** If you have access to subsidized group dental insurance through an employer or former employer, it likely is worth having. If not, the case for dental insurance is less compelling.

Dental insurance typically features copayments as high as 50%…annual benefit caps in the low four figures…often long waiting periods before expensive procedures are covered …and usually only 80% coverage if your dentist is out of network. Dental insurance premiums for seniors are about $430 per year for individual plans. That's a steep price for such limited coverage, but not necessarily an awful deal if you have reason to believe that you will require significant dental work within a few years, perhaps because your dentist has warned you that a major procedure cannot be put off too much longer.

If you do decide to sign up for dental insurance, consider the policies offered through AARP. Rates on AARP dental policies often are a bit lower than what comparable individual dental coverage would cost elsewhere.

More information: Visit *www3.deltadentalins.com/aarp/.*

If you do have dental insurance, confirm that your dentist will accept it before agreeing to any procedure. Work with him/her to get the most out of the insurance if he does.

Example: If the dental work you require is not an emergency and significantly exceeds your coverage's annual benefits cap, ask your dentist if the work—and the bill—could be spread out over two or more plan years.

• **Private health insurance.** If you do not have dental insurance but have private health insurance in addition to Medicare, this health insurance could include some basic dental benefits. Read the plan literature or call the insurance company's customer service department to find out.

• **Medical flexible spending accounts (FSAs).** FSAs can substantially trim the effective cost of dental care by allowing patients to pay for health-care bills—including dental bills—with pretax dollars. Unfortunately for retirees, FSAs are available only to employees whose employers offer FSAs as part of their benefits packages.

HAGGLING

Dentists' bills often are negotiable—but only if you discuss costs before having the dental work done. Ask if you can get a senior discount or a cash discount if you pay in cash. Either of these appeals could net you savings of 5% to 10%.

Call other dentists' offices to ask their prices for the procedure. If you find a better rate, tell your dentist that you are on a tight budget and ask if he can match the lower price.

Get a second opinion before agreeing to any major procedure. There's a chance that your dentist could be recommending an expensive procedure that is not necessary. Have your dental files, including the most recent test results and X-rays, forwarded to the dentist who will provide this second opinion so that you do not have to pay to have these repeated. You will have to pay for the second opinion, but the cost of a simple office visit is so much lower than the cost of an elaborate dental procedure that it can be a smart investment if there is any chance that the original dentist was wrong.

IF YOU HAVE A LIMITED INCOME

You probably can get dental care even if your financial resources are very limited…

• **Medicaid.** Medicaid is available only to those with low incomes and limited assets. Eligibility rules and program benefits vary by state. In most states, Medicaid provides at least basic dental care for those living near or below the poverty line.

To find out if you qualify, contact your state's Medicaid Office. (Visit *www.benefits.gov*, se-

lect "By State" from the Benefits menu, then choose your home state. Or call 800-333-4636 for a contact phone number for your state's Medicaid office.)

Helpful: Nursing homes are legally required to arrange for dental care for residents who use Medicaid to pay for their stays. That typically means that they must either bring a dentist to the nursing home or transport the resident to a dentist's office to receive care.

• **Local and state dental associations.** Many have programs that provide dental services for free or reduced rates to those in financial need. Services are provided by dentists who volunteer their time. Eligibility requirements vary.

State and local dental associations can be found on the Web site of the American Dental Association (ADA)—at *www.ada.org*, select "About ADA," then "National, State & Local Organizations," then check both the "State (Constituent) Organizations" and the "Local Component Organizations" to find relevant associations. Or call the ADA at 312-440-2500 and ask for your state dental association's phone number.

Example: The Connecticut Dental Association sponsors an annual "Mission of Mercy" program that provides free cleanings, extractions and fillings on a first-come, first-served basis. Unlike most programs of this sort, Connecticut's Mission of Mercy does not require proof of limited income. See the Connecticut State Dental Association's Web site for more information (*www.csda.com/ctmom/ctmom4.html*).

• **Public or nonprofit dental clinics.** Available in many regions, these typically charge very low rates, perhaps linked to the patients' ability to pay. In some cases, treatment is free.

Your area Agency on Aging should be able to direct you to any dental clinics in your region and might know of other local low-cost dental options for seniors. (Call the US Administration on Aging's Eldercare Locator, 800-677-1116, or use the Locator on the Web at *www.eldercare.gov* to find your local Agency on Aging if you cannot locate it in your phone book.) Your local or state dental association also might know of area clinics.

MONEY-SAVING OPTIONS

If you are too well off to qualify for low-income dental programs, consider these options…

• **Local dental colleges.** Performed for perhaps half the usual cost, the work is done by dental students under the supervision of qualified instructors. The quality of the dental care tends to be good…however, a dental school might not provide a full range of dental services.

The American Dental Education Association Web site can help you find dental schools in your region. (At *www.adea.org*, click "About ADEA" then "Who We Are," and "Predoctoral Dental Education Programs.") Typing "dental schools" and the name of your state into Google.com also can help you find any schools in your region.

• **Retail dental centers.** Usually located in shopping malls, they typically charge 10% to 20% less than traditional dentists' offices.

Dangers of Medical Identity Theft

James C. Pyles, Esq., principal, Powers, Pyles, Sutter & Verville PC, a law firm specializing in health care, education and government relations, Washington, DC.

A thief uses your Social Security number or insurance data to get free medical treatment—or to collect insurance money for services that were never performed.

Problem: This can cause incorrect or fictitious information about you to appear in medical databases—leading to incorrect treatment or future refusal of insurance benefits.

Thieves change the address to which claims and statements are sent, so you may not know of their actions for years. In addition, patient privacy laws can make it harder to find out about phony information—and make doctors reluctant to change errors, for fear of liability.

Self-defense: Every year, get a copy of your medical records from all of your health-care providers and a list of benefits paid in your name by your insurer.

Question any charges or payments that you do not recognize—and contact police if you suspect fraud.

The Simple 25¢ Remedy For Back, Hip, Leg and Foot Pain

Burton S. Schuler, DPM, podiatrist and director of the Ambulatory Foot Clinic at the Podiatric Pain Management Center in Panama City, Florida. He is author of *Why You Really Hurt: It All Starts in the Foot* (La Luz). *www.footcare4u.com*

Millions of Americans live with chronic pain in their backs, hips, legs and feet. Many self-medicate with ibuprofen or other analgesics…or they undergo expensive tests to identify the underlying problem.

Do this first: Take off your socks and look at your toes. If the second toe is even slightly longer than the big toe, you might have *Morton's toe*, a condition that disrupts normal alignment and can cause pain throughout the body, particularly in the back, legs and feet.

The condition is named after Dudley J. Morton, MD, of Yale Medical School, who first wrote about it causing foot problems. Janet Travell, MD—White House physician to Presidents Kennedy and Johnson—took the concept further by explaining that Morton's toe could cause pain all over the body.

It's estimated that up to 15% of Americans have Morton's toe. Among those with chronic musculoskeletal pain, the prevalence might be as high as 80%. People are born with Morton's toe, but it usually takes decades of accumulated stress and the age-related loss of tissue elasticity to start producing symptoms.

WHY IT HURTS

When we walk and our feet push off from the ground, the big toe typically touches before the other toes. For a fraction of a second, it absorbs virtually all of the body's weight. Then as the foot rolls forward, some of the pressure is shifted to the adjoining, weaker toes.

In patients with Morton's toe, the first metatarsal bone (in the big toe) is abnormally short and the longer second metatarsal bone typically touches the ground first and absorbs most of the body's weight. The second metatarsal bone isn't strong enough for this much pressure. To compensate, the foot overpronates—it rolls in the direction of the big toe to support the excess weight.

Overpronation makes the foot unstable. It also prevents the big toe from pushing your weight upward. This means that other muscles and joints have to compensate.

The result: Decades of abnormal stress that can disrupt your posture and potentially damage joints throughout the body, causing pain.

THE 25¢ FIX

The simple, inexpensive remedy for Morton's toe is a toe pad. It will act like a shim under the first metatarsal bone and cause the big toe to meet the ground a fraction of a second sooner. This will prevent overpronation and help keep the foot stable. It often relieves symptoms within a few weeks—and sometimes right away.

Exception: Because a toe pad changes the body's alignment, some people experience a temporary increase in pain. This usually diminishes within a few days.

Once the pain goes away, you still will need to wear a toe pad every day, just as someone with sight problems needs to wear glasses or contact lenses every day. *To make a toe pad…*

• **Buy a package of inexpensive foam shoe inserts.** I have found that Dr. Scholl's Molefoam is a good product for making a toe pad (one pack provides six to eight toe pads). Just about any product will work—even no-name brands available at most pharmacies and discount stores, usually for less than $2.

• **Cut out a rectangle about one-inch wide and two-and-a-half inches long.** That's about the size of a stick of chewing gum or a Band-Aid. Put it over the first *metatarsal head,* the bulge on the bottom of the foot that is below the point where the big toe joins the foot. Position the pad so that the longer dimension runs lengthwise with the foot. If the insole doesn't have an adhesive backing, tape it to the foot with duct tape, electrical tape or even Scotch tape. It does not have to look pretty.

You can take the toe pad off at night and put it back on the foot in the morning. One toe pad usually lasts two to four days.

Helpful: If you don't have a foam insert, a quarter can work. Anything that adds thickness to the first metatarsal head will help restore proper alignment.

APPLY HEAT

If a toe pad doesn't eliminate the pain right away, you might want to apply heat. Rest your feet on a heating pad or soak them in warm water for about 15 minutes, once or twice a day.

If after two to three weeks you still have pain, see your physician.

Health Web Sites You Can Trust

Suzy Cohen, RPh, registered practicing pharmacist for 22 years and author of *The 24-Hour Pharmacist* (Rodale). She has a syndicated newspaper column, "Dear Pharmacist." She is a member of the Association of Natural Medicine Pharmacists and the American Holistic Health Association. *www.suzycohen.com*

It can be tricky to search the Internet for answers to health questions—because mixed in with a bounty of valid information are countless unsubstantiated claims and even some downright dangerous advice.

Best: Put your faith in the following reliable Web sites. *For information on…*

DIAGNOSIS AND TREATMENT
www.mayoclinic.com

Features: Reports on symptoms, causes, complications, tests, treatments and coping strategies for thousands of illnesses.

• **Multimedia presentations.**
• **Links to disease-specific organizations.**
Click-worthy: "Healthy Living Program."

DRUGS AND SUPPLEMENTS
www.drugs.com

Features: Consumer-friendly information on uses, dosages, side effects and contraindications for prescription as well as nonprescription drugs, herbs and dietary supplements.

• **Interactions checker**—to see if the effect of a particular drug is altered when it is taken with another drug, supplement or food.

• **New drug approvals and alerts from the FDA.**

Click-worthy: "Pill Identifier" (including photos) that searches by color, shape and/or imprint.

INTEGRATIVE MEDICINE
www.naturalstandard.com

Features: Free e-newsletter.

• **Blogs and newsfeed.**

• **In-depth databases on thousands of herbs as well as supplements** (requires a paid subscription).

Click-worthy: Webinars focused on alternative medicine.

LIFESTYLE AND SPIRITUAL WELL-BEING
www.lifescript.com

Features: Blogs from doctors, psychologists, nutritionists, fitness experts and alternative health-care providers.

• **Calculators for body mass index, calorie burn and more.**

• **"Ask the Doctor."**

Click-worthy: Quizzes that test your knowledge (for instance, on acupuncture or hygiene) or assess your risk (such as for cancer, depression or thyroid disease).

NATURAL HEALTH AND HEALING
www.naturalnews.com

Features: Breaking news reports.

• **Cartoons and satire.**

• **"Citizen journalism" program that invites articles from independent writers.**

Click-worthy: Podcasts from author Mike Adams (aka the "Health Ranger") interviewing preeminent experts on alternative medicine.

SCIENTIFIC STUDIES
www.pubmed.gov

Features: More than 27 million citations for biomedical articles dating back to 1948.

• **Interactive tutorials on very newsworthy topics,** such as flu outbreaks.

Click-worthy: ClinicalTrials.gov, a locator for studies recruiting participants.

3

The Childbearing Years

Before Conceiving, Take Folic Acid for One Full Year

When taken for at least a year before conception, supplements of folic acid can help reduce the chance of a premature birth by at least 50%, University of Texas researchers say.

Their study, published in *PLoS Medicine*, found no link to a reduction in the odds of giving birth before 37 weeks of pregnancy if the supplements were taken for less than a year before conception. The researchers also found no ties between adding folic acid, also known as vitamin B-9, to a woman's diet and any pregnancy complications.

BACKGROUND

About 12% of US babies are born before 37 weeks' gestation, according to a Public Library of Science news release. Premature babies can have breathing issues, learning or developmental disabilities, and are less likely to survive than those born closer to 40 weeks' gestation. Other research has linked low levels of folate (folic acid) in the mother with a shorter length of pregnancy, the release noted.

STUDY FINDINGS

The recent study, which looked at the pregnancies and childbirth experiences of nearly 35,000 women, found that compared to those who did not take folate supplements, those who took folate supplements for at least one year before conception were 70% less likely to spontaneously give birth between 20 and 28 weeks of gestation. These same women were also 50% less likely to give birth between weeks 28 and 32.

LEARN MORE

For more on preventing a premature birth, visit the March of Dimes' Web site, *www.march ofdimes.org*. Under "Health Topics" choose "Preterm Labor and Premature Birth."

Public Library of Science, news release.

Iron Increases a Woman's Chance of Becoming Pregnant

Women who take daily iron supplements have, on average, 40% lower risk for infertility caused by ovulation problems than those who don't take iron supplements. The higher the iron dosage, the lower the risk for infertility. Women who take the highest doses—41 mg a day—reduced their risk for infertility by 62%.

Caution: Take iron supplements only under a doctor's supervision. Iron overload can cause damage to internal organs.

Jorge E. Chavarro, MD, research fellow, department of nutrition, Harvard School of Public Health, Boston, and lead author of an eight-year study of women ages 24 to 42, published in *Obstetrics & Gynecology*.

Freezing Ovaries Preserves Fertility, Scientists Report

Sherman J. Silber, MD, director, Infertility Center of St. Louis at St. Luke's Hospital, Saint Louis, Missouri.

Richard J. Paulson, MD, professor of obstetrics and gynecology, chief, Division of Reproductive Endocrinology and Infertility, University of Southern California Keck School of Medicine, Los Angeles.

American Society for Reproductive Medicine annual meeting, San Francisco.

Scientists are reporting the ability to freeze and transplant ovaries, a development that could help preserve fertility in women facing cancer therapy.

"We can transplant ovaries without any loss of ovarian tissue or eggs, and it functions perfectly normally whether it's fresh or frozen," said coresearcher Sherman Silber, MD, director of the Infertility Center of St. Louis at St. Luke's Hospital.

Dr. Silber said women who want to delay having children could also use the technique. He reported the findings at the American Society for Reproductive Medicine annual meeting, in San Francisco.

EGG FREEZING vs. OVARY FREEZING

Currently, women can have their eggs frozen and put back after cancer treatment is complete, Dr. Silber noted. "But there are disadvantages," he said. "If you put all those eggs in one basket, and she goes through *in vitro fertilization* (IVF), she can't have any better chance of pregnancy than 50%. If she is not pregnant from that, then she's finished."

With ovary transplantation, however, "She's got a normally functioning ovary just like she would have if she were younger. Freezing the ovary and putting it back is much more sure for the patient than egg freezing," he said.

OVARY TRANSPLANTATION TO TWIN

In one paper, Dr. Silber reported that he and his colleagues had transplanted an ovary from one identical twin to her twin sister, allowing the twin with premature ovarian failure to conceive a child. One year after the transplant, the twin with the transplanted ovary became pregnant.

OVARY FROZEN AND RESTORED

Dr. Silber and his colleagues also reported at the meeting on one woman who had her ovary removed, frozen and then restored. They said they've done the procedure nine times. "It's very repeatable," Dr. Silber said. "It's not just a fluke."

Dr. Silber said the ability to remove an ovary, freeze it and put it back into the same woman represents the real breakthrough. "We can freeze the ovaries of young women who are going to lose their fertility over time and transplant them back later, and they [the ovaries] won't have aged," he explained.

The technique can benefit cancer patients about to undergo radiation, chemotherapy or bone marrow transplant, which would leave them sterile, Dr. Silber said. "But if we take the ovary out, freeze it, save it and transplant it back later, they will be fertile again," he said.

RECOMMENDATION

Dr. Silber said that if a woman receives a cancer diagnosis, "ask about freezing your ovary. In addition, young women who are going to put off childbearing should also think about having one of their ovaries frozen," he added.

EXPERT COMMENTARY

Richard J. Paulson, MD, chief of the Division of Reproductive Endocrinology and Infertility at the University of Southern California Keck School of Medicine, in Los Angeles, thinks the new reports are encouraging but preliminary.

"This is very exciting," Dr. Paulson said. "Fertility preservation is our next major frontier, because what we have found is that women with cancer are increasingly surviving their chemotherapy but are infertile. It would be very helpful if we could have a method to preserve their fertility."

Although women are having their eggs frozen, many women can't go through the procedure to harvest the eggs, Dr. Paulson said. "It would be very appealing to take the ovary out and freeze it for the future," he said.

However, Dr. Paulson noted that, so far, no woman had become pregnant after her ovary had been removed, frozen and put back.

LEARN MORE

For more, visit the US Department of Health and Human Services' Office on Women's Health Web site, *http://womenshealth.gov,* and search "infertility."

This diet also promotes good weight control. A healthy body weight—neither too heavy nor too slim—can dramatically improve ovulation and fertility.

Wise: Taking a multivitamin with iron.

Acupuncture May Boost Fertility

Advocates say acupuncture improves hormone levels and increases blood flow to the uterus.

Cost: $100 or more per session, which is sometimes covered by insurance. Ask a fertility specialist for a referral to a licensed acupuncturist, or contact National Certification Commission for Acupuncture and Oriental Medicine (904-598-1005, *www.nccaom.org*) or American Academy of Medical Acupuncture (310-379-8261, *www.medicalacupuncture.org*).

Gary Kaplan, DO, clinical associate professor, Georgetown University School of Medicine, Washington, DC, and medical director, the Kaplan Center for Integrated Medicine, McLean, Virginia.

What to Eat to Increase Fertility

Jorge E. Chavarro, MD, ScD, instructor of medicine, Harvard Medical School, Boston, and coauthor of *The Fertility Diet* (McGraw-Hill).

Women whose infertility is due to ovulation disorders, such as polycystic ovary syndrome, should favor monounsaturated fats over trans fats...vegetable protein over animal protein...and complex carbohydrates, such as whole grains.

Also helpful: One to two servings daily of high-fat dairy, such as whole milk. These dietary practices improve the cells' response to the blood sugar–regulating hormone insulin, which in turn influences blood levels of testosterone and other hormones, increasing fertility.

Placebo Acupuncture Tied to Higher IVF Pregnancies

European Society for Human Reproduction and Embryology, news release.

Compared to real acupuncture, placebo acupuncture was associated with significantly higher overall pregnancy rates among women undergoing *in vitro fertilization* (IVF), says a University of Hong Kong study.

REAL vs. PLACEBO ACUPUNCTURE

In real acupuncture, fine needles are inserted into particular points on the body. In placebo acupuncture, blunt needles that look identical to real acupuncture needles retract into the handle of the needle when pressed on the skin, but still give the sensation and appearance of entering the skin.

THE STUDY

The researchers gave real or placebo acupuncture to 370 women on the day of embryo transfer and found that 55.1% of those who received placebo acupuncture became pregnant, compared to 43.8% of those who received real acupuncture. The findings were published in *Human Reproduction*.

"We found a significantly higher overall pregnancy rate following placebo acupuncture when compared with that of real acupuncture," said study author Ernest Hung Yu Ng, MD, an associate professor in the department of obstetrics and gynecology at the University of Hong Kong.

IMPLICATION

The results suggest that placebo acupuncture may not act as an inert control for real acupuncture and may be having a real effect. That theory is supported by the fact that the researchers noted significant changes in measurements for uterus receptivity and patient stress levels after the women received both the real and placebo acupuncture.

POSSIBLE EXPLANATIONS

There are two possible explanations for the study results.

"Placebo acupuncture is similar to acupressure and therefore is good enough to improve the pregnancy rate," said Dr. Ng, who added it's also possible that real acupuncture may, in some way, reduce the pregnancy rate. Acupressure utilizes the same pressure points as acupuncture, but uses gentle to firm finger pressure instead of needles.

"So far, there is no evidence that real acupuncture would adversely affect IVF outcomes because, in a previous meta-analysis of several acupuncture studies, the pregnancy rate was higher in the acupuncture group than in the control group. However, we cannot draw a firm conclusion about this from our current study, as we did not compare the two groups with a third control group of patients who received neither form of acupuncture. Further studies should be conducted to compare

placebo or noninvasive acupuncture and controls without acupuncture," Dr. Ng said.

LEARN MORE

For more information on acupuncture, visit the Web site of the National Center for Complementary and Alternative Medicine, *http://nccam.nih.gov/health/acupuncture/*.

Hormone Might Help Restore Female Fertility

Society for Endocrinology, news release.

A hormone called *kisspeptin* may offer treatment for infertility, according to British researchers who found that the hormone can activate the release of sex hormones that control the menstrual cycle.

According to the researchers, kisspeptin is an important regulator of reproductive function. Animals that lack kisspeptin function don't go through puberty and remain sexually immature.

THE STUDY

The study included 10 women who were not menstruating and were infertile due to a hormone imbalance. The researchers injected the participants with either kisspeptin or saline and then measured levels of two sex hormones—*luteinizing hormone* (LH) and *follicle stimulating hormone* (FSH)—essential for ovulation and fertility.

The women who received kisspeptin had a 48-fold increase in LH and a 16-fold increase in FSH, compared to those who received the saline. The study is the first to show that kisspeptin can stimulate production of sex hormones in infertile women, according to the study's authors.

The findings were presented at a meeting of the Society for Endocrinology in the United Kingdom.

IMPLICATIONS

"This research shows that kisspeptin offers huge promise as a treatment for infertility," said study author Waljit Dhillo, PhD, of Imperial College London.

"From our previous results, we know that kisspeptin can stimulate release of reproductive hormones in healthy women. We have now extended this research to show that kisspeptin treatment has the same effect in women with infertility. In fact, our current data show that kisspeptin causes a greater increase in luteinizing hormone production in non-menstruating women than in fertile women in the previous study," Dr. Dhillo said.

"This is a very exciting result and suggests that kisspeptin treatment could restore reproductive function in women with low sex hormone levels. Our future research will focus on determining the best protocol for repeated kisspeptin administration with the hope of developing a new therapy for infertility," he added.

Can This Patient Be Cured? Infertility

Mark A. Stengler, NMD, licensed naturopathic medical doctor in private practice, Encinitas, California… adjunct associate clinical professor at the National College of Natural Medicine, Portland, Oregon…author of *The Natural Physician's Healing Therapies* and co-author of *Prescription for Natural Cures* (both from Bottom Line Books).

For three years, Sarah, a 36-year-old medical doctor, and her husband, Ray, had been trying to start a family—but each month brought disappointment. Conventional medical testing found no reason why she or her husband would be infertile (defined medically as being unable to achieve pregnancy after a year of unprotected intercourse). After in vitro fertilization failed, they consulted me.

First, we reviewed how to time sexual relations to maximize the chances of conception.

Optimal: One day before or on the day of ovulation, when an egg is released from the ovary. Sarah had been using an at-home urine test (sold in drugstores) that detects a surge in luteinizing hormone, indicating that ovulation is imminent. I recommended that she also pay attention to her cervical mucus, because fertility rises when there is an increase in its amount, slipperiness and stretchiness.

Some studies suggest that caffeine decreases female fertility, for unknown reasons. Also, regular and decaf coffee, as well as black and green tea, contain tannic acid, which may decrease sperm production. I advised Sarah and Ray to avoid coffee, cola, chocolate and tea (except herbal).

Wisely, Sarah had eliminated alcohol from her diet. Alcohol can sporadically halt ovulation (and contribute to birth defects). I suggested that Ray also avoid alcohol, because it can reduce sperm count and quality. I was pleased that Sarah's weight was normal. Being overweight raises levels of the hormone estrogen and may lead to irregular ovulation. Being underweight inhibits production of the hormones required to stimulate ovulation. I also was glad that neither partner smoked, because toxins in tobacco can damage eggs and sperm.

Sarah was unaware that nutritional and herbal therapies can help a woman get pregnant. I told her to take a daily multivitamin to guard against nutritional deficiencies that impair fertility. In addition, I suggested supplementing with the herb *Vitex* (chasteberry), which stimulates the pituitary gland to release luteinizing hormone…in turn increasing the ovaries' release of progesterone, a hormone that prepares the uterine lining for implantation of a fertilized egg.

A longstanding naturopathic treatment for female infertility is to enhance the level of thyroid hormone, because even a minor deficiency can prevent ovulation and increase the risk for miscarriage. Blood testing revealed that Sarah had a very low level of the most potent thyroid hormone, T3. I prescribed Armour Thyroid, a natural brand that contains T3 and other thyroid hormones found in the human body. Synthetic brands usually contain T4, the less potent form of the hormone.

Two months after her first visit, Sarah phoned and exclaimed, "I'm pregnant!" After congratulating her, I recommended that Sarah stop taking chasteberry, which was no longer needed…continue her thyroid medication… and switch to a prenatal multivitamin that provided more folic acid, vitamin B-12 and iron.

A few weeks later, Sarah came to my clinic again—this time, for morning sickness.

Obesity Lowers Fertility

Men who weigh too much are likely to have poor sperm quality. Overweight women have trouble conceiving naturally—and are less likely to become pregnant even when embryos are fertilized in the lab and implanted.

David Ryley, MD, clinical fellow, reproductive endocrinology and infertility, Beth Israel Deaconess Medical Center, Boston, and leader of a study of more than 5,800 attempts at in vitro fertilization, published in *Fertility and Sterility*.

Fruits and Veggies May Improve Sperm Quality

Plataforma SINC, news release.

Eating a diet rich in fruits and vegetables plays an important role in semen quality, according to recent research from Spain.

THE STUDY

The study included 61 men—30 with reproductive problems and 31 who did not have such issues. It appeared online in the journal *Fertility and Sterility*.

The study found that "men with good semen quality ate more vegetables and fruit (more vitamins, folic acid and fiber and less protein and fats) than those men with low seminal quality," said the lead author, Jaime Mendiola, PhD, a researcher at the University of Murcia.

EXPLANATION

Antioxidants, found mainly in fruits and vegetables, lower the level of oxidative stress that can affect semen quality, the researchers explained, and also improve sperm concentration and mobility.

MEAT AND DAIRY LOWER SEMEN QUALITY

An earlier study by the same team "showed that men who eat large amounts of meat and full-fat dairy products have lower seminal quality than those who eat more fruit, vegetables and reduced-fat dairy products," Dr. Mendiola said.

But the study "found that people who consume more fruits and vegetables are ingesting more antioxidants, and this is the important point," Dr. Mendiola said. "A healthy diet is not only a good way of avoiding illness but could also have an impact on improving seminal quality."

FOOD VERSUS SUPPLEMENTS

"What we still do not understand is the difference between taking these vitamins naturally and in the form of supplements," the researcher added. "In the studies we are going to carry out in the United States (where the consumption of vitamins in tablet form is very common), we will be looking at the role of supplements."

LEARN MORE

The Web site of the US National Institute of Child Health and Human Development has more about reproductive health at *www.nichd.nih.gov/*. Under "Health & Research," select "A to Z Topics," then choose "M" and click on "Men's Reproductive Health."

Simple Procedure Improves Male Fertility

Sebastian Flacke, MD, PhD, associate professor, radiology, Tufts University School of Medicine, Boston.
Hossein Sadeghi-Nejad, MD, associate professor, urology, UMDNJ New Jersey Medical School, Hackensack University Medical Center.
Radiology.

A simple, minimally invasive procedure can treat a common cause of male infertility and improve a couple's chances of having a baby, a recent study finds.

BACKGROUND

The condition, called varicocele, is a network of tangled blood vessels in the scrotum, which prevents the normal circulation of blood through the veins in the testicles. A minimally invasive radiological procedure called embolization can, in most cases, correct the problem.

In embolization, a small catheter is inserted into the groin and, using X-ray guidance, is placed in the varicocele. Once the catheter is placed, a tiny platinum coil and a few milliliters of an agent to ensure the closure of the gonadic vein are also inserted.

The minimally invasive procedure has a short recovery time; most patients go home the next day.

Varicoceles are very common, said lead researcher Sebastian Flacke, MD, PhD, an associate professor of radiology at Tufts University School of Medicine in Boston. In fact, about 20% of all men have them. Not all of these cause infertility or need to be treated, he said. The problem is usually treated if it causes pain, shrinkage or fertility problems.

THE STUDY

For the study, Dr. Flacke's team collected data on 223 infertile men with at least one varicose vein. All the men had healthy partners with whom they wanted to have a baby.

Dr. Flacke's group used embolization to successfully relieve 226 of the 228 varicose veins among the men. Three months after the procedure, the researchers analyzed the sperm of 173 patients. The analysis showed, on average, that sperm motility and sperm count had significantly improved.

After six months, 45 couples (26%) reported a pregnancy. "That's a very large number for a simple procedure," Dr. Flacke said.

The report was published in an issue of the journal *Radiology*.

ADVICE

"If you're dealing with infertility and have varicoceles, this should be treated," Dr. Flacke said. By improving sperm count, the treatment could also be valuable in situations where the woman is having problems conceiving, he added.

"Most of the time, infertility is on both the male and female side," Dr. Flacke said. "Most of the time females get treated first if there is an issue, and men are neglected. I think you could boost the performance of the sperm if a varicocele is present and treated."

Dr. Flacke noted that the success rate of the treatment is very high. More than 95% of the time the procedure corrects the problem.

EXPERT COMMENTARY

Infertility expert Hossein Sadeghi-Nejad, MD, an associate professor of urology at UMDNJ New Jersey Medical School and Hackensack University Medical Center, noted that, as a rule, infertility treatment begins with a woman. "The fact is that a male factor is responsible for infertility in about half of the cases," he said. "Varicoceles are one example of the male factor that can affect fertility."

If you do treat varicoceles properly, you do get improvement in sperm counts and pregnancy rates, Dr. Sadeghi-Nejad said.

However, there are drawbacks to embolization, Dr. Sadeghi-Nejad added. These include a steep learning curve to get used to doing the procedure and the danger of prolonged or misdirected radiation, especially if there are varicoceles on both sides of the scrotum.

LEARN MORE

For more on male infertility, visit the Web site of the US National Library of Medicine, *www.medlineplus.gov*. Under "Health Topics," click on "Male Reproductive System," then "Male Infertility."

Antidepressants May Reduce Male Fertility

F ragmented sperm increased from 13.8% to 30.3% in healthy men within four weeks after they started taking the antidepressant *paroxetine* (Paxil) daily. Further studies are being done to determine the effect that antidepressants have on sperm.

Peter Schlegel, MD, chairman, department of urology, Weill Cornell Medical College, New York City, and leader of a study of 35 men, published in *New Scientist*.

Is the Pill Still Right For You?

Richard P. Dickey, MD, PhD, clinical professor and chief of reproductive endocrinology and infertility in the department of obstetrics and gynecology at Louisiana State University Medical School in New Orleans. He also is founder of the Fertility Institute, which has three clinics in Louisiana, and author of *Managing Contraceptive Pill/Drug Patients* (EMIS). *www.fertility institute.com*

Recent research provides surprising revelations about the benefits and risks of oral contraceptives. So if you are not taking "the Pill" now, you might want to reconsider. If you are on it, you need to make sure that it is still safe, given your lifestyle and medical history…and also make sure that the type you are taking has minimal side effects for you.

Have you heard? To minimize the risk for an unintended pregnancy, you should continue to use birth control until one full year has passed without a menstrual period. And despite what many women think, oral contraceptives do *not* delay the onset of menopause.

Heres what you need to know now about oral contraceptives…

A recent study in *BMJ* (British Medical Journal), which involved more than 46,000 women who were observed for up to 39 years, found a significantly lower rate of death from any cause among women who had ever used the Pill, compared with women who had never used it. Also, a study published in *Contraception* found that oral contraceptives strongly protected against death from uterine cancer and ovarian cancer. Surprisingly, many of these protective effects persisted for years after users stopped taking the Pill—which means that oral contraception often is a particularly good choice for women with a family history of uterine or ovarian cancer.

Good news for the perimenopausal: Oral contraceptives (particularly the low-dose type) often lighten perimenopausal menstrual symptoms and periods or make them stop altogether.

All birth control pills are not created equal —different brands have different ratios of estrogen to progestin—so if one brand causes side effects for you, talk to your doctor about other options.

Some studies indicate that being overweight interferes with the contraceptive effects of the Pill. To reduce pregnancy risk, overweight women may be advised against using a low-dose formulation and also should be careful to take their pills exactly as prescribed.

Important: Many drugs and supplements (including acetaminophen, antibiotics and St. John's wort) can interact with progestin, reducing the Pill's effectiveness. Be sure to tell your doctor about any medications or supplements you take.

Who should not use the Pill: There is a clear link between Pill users who smoke and an increased risk for breast cancer, cardiovascular disease and potentially life-threatening blood clots. Oral contraceptives containing estrogen are also not appropriate for women with a history of heart disease, uncontrolled hypertension, blood clots or estrogen-dependent cancer.

Acupuncture May Relieve Heartburn in Pregnancy

Joao Bosco Guerreiro daSilva, MD, PhD, department of internal medicine, Rio Preto Medical College, Sao Jose do Rio Preto, Brazil.

Richard Frieder, MD, obstetrician-gynecologist, Santa Monica-UCLA Medical Center, and clinical instructor, obstetrics and gynecology, David Geffen School of Medicine, University of California, Los Angeles.

Marshall H. Sager, DO, past president, American Society of Medical Acupuncture, acupuncturist, Bala Cynwyd, Pennsylvania.

Acupuncture in Medicine.

Acupuncture relieves the indigestion and heartburn that bother many women as their pregnancy progresses, a new Brazilian study shows.

"Although small, this study suggests that acupuncture can relieve symptoms of indigestion that are pretty common in pregnancy and may provoke loss of quality of life in the final days, disturbing not only eating but also sleeping," said lead researcher Dr. Joao Bosco Guerreiro da Silva, MD, PhD, from the department of internal medicine at Rio Preto Medical College.

BACKGROUND

Indigestion is common during pregnancy, with up to 80% of moms-to-be suffering heartburn, stomach pain or discomfort, reflux, belching and bloating. Symptoms tend to worsen as the pregnancy progresses, and women who avoid taking medicine for fear of harming the developing fetus might welcome an alternative treatment.

THE STUDY

For the study, the researchers randomly assigned 42 pregnant women with indigestion to dietary counseling plus antacids, or to dietary counseling and antacids plus acupuncture, once or twice a week. The researchers assessed the women's symptoms at the beginning of the study and every two weeks after that for eight weeks.

Heartburn, the main symptom, was reduced by half in 75% of the women treated with acupuncture. Women receiving acupuncture also ate and slept better, he said.

The 20 women who underwent acupuncture and completed the study reported having milder symptoms and took less medication than the 16 women getting conventional therapy, the researchers found.

Fewer than half the women receiving traditional treatment said their heartburn was halved.

Among the 14 women who took antacids, seven in each group, those receiving acupuncture took 6.3 fewer doses, while those receiving conventional treatment upped the amount of medication they took by 4.4 doses, the researchers found.

In addition, 15 women in the acupuncture group said that their eating habits improved by 50%, compared with fewer than one in three in the other group. Fourteen women receiving acupuncture said their sleep had improved by 50%, compared with just one in four women treated conventionally.

The report was published in *Acupuncture in Medicine*.

IMPLICATION

"Dyspepsia [indigestion] in pregnancy is a very common problem," Guerreiro da Silva said. "Medication is always a concern. Acupuncture can be effective. It is safe and simple to apply and every pregnant woman can be treated."

EXPERT COMMENTARY

Richard Frieder, MD, an obstetrician-gynecologist at Santa Monica-UCLA Medical Center and clinical instructor of obstetrics and gynecology at the David Geffen School of Medicine, University of California, Los Angeles, doesn't think that acupuncture works any better than conventional treatment.

"This is an interesting idea but far from proves any benefit, as the control group did not have any type of placebo treatment, such as fake acupuncture to make the control and test group comparable," Dr. Frieder said.

Indigestion and heartburn are common in pregnancy and usually successfully treated with diet, sleep positioning and medication with no known harmful effects, Dr. Frieder noted.

"Acupuncture might be a nice alternative for women who are inclined to this option, but it is doubtfully more effective than standard treatment if the study had been done in an apples-to-apples comparison," he said.

AN ACUPUNCTURIST WEIGHS IN

Another expert thinks that acupuncture does relieve indigestion, but he won't perform it on pregnant women because of litigation concerns.

"It is a well-done study and it is expected that there would be positive results," said Marshall H. Sager, DO, past president of the American Society of Medical Acupuncture and an acupuncturist in Bala Cynwyd, Pennsylvania.

However, he worries that he would be sued if something went wrong with the pregnancy. "I wouldn't touch a pregnant lady with acupuncture because of the malpractice situation. Not that it's not effective, but that's my problem with the medical/legal aspects of it," he said.

Eating Nuts During Pregnancy Increases Baby's Asthma Risk

Saskia Willers, MSc, doctoral candidate, Utrecht University, the Netherlands.

Jennifer Appleyard, MD, chief, allergy and immunology, St. John Hospital and Medical Center, Detroit.

American Journal of Respiratory and Critical Care Medicine.

I f you've got a strong family history of food allergies or allergic asthma, you might want to think twice before munching a handful of nuts when you're pregnant.

That's because recent research has found that daily consumption of nut products during pregnancy raises the odds of having a child with asthma symptoms by nearly 50%.

The study, published in the *American Journal of Respiratory and Critical Care Medicine,* found "consistent positive associations between maternal nut product consumption, such as peanut butter, during pregnancy and wheeze, dyspnea (shortness of breath), steroid use, doctor-diagnosed asthma and persistent wheeze in children from 1 to 8 years of age," said study author Saskia Willers, a doctoral candidate at Utrecht University in the Netherlands.

BACKGROUND

As many as 4% of American children have food allergies, according to the American Academy of Allergy, Asthma & Immunology. Slightly more than 1% of people in the United States—or about 3 million—are allergic to peanuts or tree nuts.

Most allergies develop as a result of repeated "sensitization" to an allergen in susceptible individuals, and each time the body is exposed to the allergen, the reactions tend to increase. It's already recommended that children under age 3 not be given nuts or nut products, because their immune systems are still developing and may be more susceptible to allergens, explained Jennifer Appleyard, MD, chief of allergy and immunology at St. John Hospital and Medical Center in Detroit.

"If you say avoid nuts in children, and for nursing mothers because peanut protein can be transferred through milk, do we need to take it a step further and limit nuts during pregnancy?" said Dr. Appleyard.

THE STUDY

To try to answer that question, Willers and her colleagues reviewed information gathered from interviews of more than 4,000 pregnant women—1,327 with a history of allergy or asthma and 2,819 with no such history. The women were asked about their diets, and their children were followed from birth to 8 years of age to assess whether or not diet impacted the risk of developing asthma.

They found no association between maternal consumption of vegetables, fish, eggs, milk or milk products and the development of asthma, according to the study.

However, daily consumption of nut products increased the odds that a child would have wheezing by 42%, shortness of breath by 58% and steroid use to ease asthma symptoms by 62%, compared to children born to mothers who rarely consumed nuts. Overall, the odds of developing asthma symptoms for a child whose mother ate nuts daily were 47% higher, according to the study.

WHAT TO DO

But, Willers said, it's too soon to recommend a complete nut ban during pregnancy. "The associations we found are pretty strong, only we are the first to find these effects, so they need to be confirmed by other studies before recommending the avoidance of peanuts and nuts during pregnancy," she said.

Dr. Appleyard agreed. "This subject definitely needs further investigation. And, if you can pass on the antibodies that cause nut allergy from mother to fetus, why not other allergies as well?" she asked.

However, she did suggest that women with a strong family history of food allergy might want to limit the amount of nut products they consume during pregnancy.

LEARN MORE

For more information about peanut allergy, visit the Food Allergy Research & Education's Web site, *www.foodallergy.org.* Under "Common Allergens," click on "Peanut."

Smoking May Harm The Egg, Embryo

American Society for Reproductive Medicine, news release.

In research that might have implications for human reproduction, US and Chinese scientists have found that cigarette smoke damages mouse eggs and embryos.

STUDY DESIGN

The study was designed to examine whether cigarette smoke causes oxidative stress, cell death and dysfunction, and the shortening of telomeres (DNA at the ends of chromosomes that protect them from degradation).

Two groups of female mice were exposed to cigarette smoke or cigarette smoke condensate for four weeks and compared to a control group of mice. Cigarette smoke condensate, chemicals created when tobacco is burned, is often used in scientific research to test the effects of smoke in animals.

STUDY FINDINGS

The mice exposed to cigarette smoke or the condensate were more likely than the unexposed mice to show increased fragmentation and delayed fertilization, resulting in impaired embryo development, the study found.

The fragmented eggs also showed oxidative stress, and embryos from mice exposed to cigarette smoke or condensate for four weeks before fertilization were more likely to contain dead cells and altered expression of the protein Oct4, which plays an important role in the formation of viable blastocysts (a stage of embryonic development).

The association between cigarette smoke or condensate and embryo development was dependent on the length of exposure, the team noted. But even embryos exposed to smoke for as little as four days showed reduced telomere length in cells and decreased blastocyst development, suggesting that embryos may be more sensitive to smoke-induced oxidative stress than eggs, the researchers said.

The study was published in the journal *Fertility and Sterility*.

EXPERT ADVICE

"Here is even more evidence demonstrating the dreadful effects smoking has on reproductive tissues and function. While there are some data implying that the effects may not be permanent, every woman planning to become pregnant would be wise to quit smoking or, better yet, never start," said William Gibbons, MD, past president of the American Society for Reproductive Medicine.

Smoking During Pregnancy May Turn Unborn Children Into Smokers

Children whose mothers smoked while they were pregnant were three times more likely to begin smoking by age 14—and twice as likely to start after age 14—as children of women who did not smoke during pregnancy. Children of women who either never smoked or who quit during pregnancy but returned to smoking afterward were less likely to begin smoking.

Abdullah Al Mamun, PhD, senior lecturer, division of epidemiology and social medicine, University of Queensland, Herston, Australia, and leader of a study of 3,000 mothers and their children, published in *Tobacco Control*.

Zinc May Counter Effects of Alcohol in Early Pregnancy

Alcoholism: Clinical & Experimental Research, news release.

Zinc supplements may help mothers-to-be reduce the risk for birth defects linked to alcohol use early in pregnancy, Australian researchers report.

The animal study was published in the journal *Alcoholism: Clinical & Experimental Research*.

BACKGROUND

"Alcohol's damage to the fetus depends not only on the amount and duration of alcohol exposure, but also on the timing of the exposure relative to the development of the cells and tissues involved," said study coauthor Peter Coyle, PhD, an associate professor at the Hanson Institute in Adelaide.

"Earlier work had shown that prenatal alcohol, as well as other toxins, can result in fetal zinc deficiency and (developmental malformations) by inducing the zinc-binding protein, *metallothionein*, in the mother's liver. Since then, our group has confirmed the importance of metallothionein in alcohol-mediated birth defects," he said.

RECENT STUDY

In this study, Dr. Coyle and colleagues injected either saline or a 25% solution of alcohol into pregnant mice on their eighth day of gestation. In mice, the eighth day of gestation is equivalent to weeks three to eight during a human pregnancy. The mice were fed either a regular or zinc-supplemented diet from conception to day 18 of gestation, when some fetuses were assessed for birth defects. The growth of the surviving offspring was monitored for 60 days after birth.

"There were three key findings," Dr. Coyle said. "One, fetal abnormalities caused by acute alcohol exposure in early pregnancy can be prevented by dietary zinc supplementation. Two, dietary zinc supplementation throughout pregnancy can protect against post-natal death caused by acute alcohol exposure in early pregnancy. Three, dietary zinc supplementation increases the mother's blood zinc to overwhelm the transient drop in zinc caused by alcohol, which we believe prevents the fetal zinc deficiency and subsequent fetal damage."

IMPLICATIONS

These findings don't mean that taking zinc makes it safe for women to drink during pregnancy, however.

"We have not determined whether zinc protects against all of the possible negative outcomes from alcohol exposure in pregnancy," Dr. Coyle said. "Nor would we recommend that makers of alcoholic beverages include zinc in their product so that women can drink while pregnant. Indeed, we take the conservative stand of a 'no alcohol policy' during pregnancy."

What the studies do indicate is that dietary zinc supplementation could be as important as folic acid in helping to prevent damage to the fetus during pregnancy, according to Dr. Coyle.

LEARN MORE

The US National Institute on Alcohol Abuse and Alcoholism has downloadable fact sheets about drinking during pregnancy at *http://www.niaaa.nih.gov*. Under "Publications & Multimedia," click on "Brochures and Fact Sheets."

Morning Sickness Drug Gets Green Light in Study

Amalia Levy, PhD, senior lecturer, Department of Epidemiology and Health Service Evaluation, Ben-Gurion University of the Negev, Israel.

Eva K. Pressman, MD, director, maternal fetal medicine, University of Rochester Medical Center, Rochester, New York.

New England Journal of Medicine.

A new study suggests that women who experience morning sickness early in pregnancy can safely take the medication *metoclopramide* (Reglan), a drug developed to treat gastrointestinal (GI) problems, to relieve their symptoms.

The study, which included nearly 3,500 pregnant women who took metoclopramide, found no significant increases in the risk of birth defects, premature delivery, low birth weight or fetal death.

Results of the study appear in the *New England Journal of Medicine*.

BACKGROUND

In Europe and in Israel, metoclopramide is often prescribed early in pregnancy to help quell that queasy feeling so common in the first trimester, according to the study's authors. Yet, like many drugs used in pregnancy, the effects of the drug on the growing fetus have not been well studied. In the United States, the medication is usually reserved for women with severe morning sickness because the Food and Drug Administration (FDA) has not approved it for use in pregnancy, the authors report.

And despite the study's findings, the use of metoclopramide is not without controversy. The FDA added what's known as a "black box" warning to metoclopramide to alert people that long-term use of the medication (more than 12 weeks) or its use at high dosages has been associated with serious side effects. After long-term use, some people develop uncontrollable movements of the limb, face and tongue that don't go away even after they stop taking the drug.

But the current study focused only on short-term use during pregnancy, and use of metoclopramide in pregnancy is "usually for short terms and as needed," said the study's senior author, Amalia Levy, PhD, a senior lecturer in epidemiology at Ben-Gurion University of the Negev in Israel.

STUDY DETAILS

For the study, the researchers reviewed 81,703 births between 1998 and 2007, all to mothers registered with a particular Israeli health system that has a computerized database of medical information. From that group, 3,458 women—4.2%—were given metoclopramide during the first trimester of their pregnancies.

The study found no significantly increased health risks for babies of women exposed to the drug compared with the offspring of women who hadn't taken it. The risk of birth defects, for instance, was 5.3% in the metoclopramide group and 4.9% in the group not exposed to the drug. The researchers also found no significantly increased risk of low birth weight, premature delivery or fetal death.

IMPLICATION

"It appears that metoclopramide is safe for short-term use to control GI problems in pregnant women when used as prescribed," said Dr. Levy. "Physicians are reassured about the safety of metoclopramide use in pregnancy in recommended doses."

EXPERT COMMENTARY

"We worry about women with extensive nausea and vomiting during pregnancy," said Eva Pressman, MD, director of maternal fetal medicine at the University of Rochester Medical Center in New York. "There's concern about dehydration and losing weight. The largeness of this study is clearly better than anything we've had to date on the safety of metoclopramide, and it shows that there are safe medications that you can use in pregnancy."

Pregnant women who are having morning sickness shouldn't just suffer through it, Dr. Pressman said. Instead, she said, talk to a doctor about ways to lessen the stomach upset.

Preeclampsia in Pregnancy Boosts Future Health Risks

Yale University, news release.

Women who experience preeclampsia during pregnancy are at increased risk for future health problems, such as hypertension, diabetes and blood clots, American and Danish researchers report.

Preeclampsia is a condition marked by high blood pressure that if left untreated can lead to serious complications for the mother and baby.

THE STUDY

The researchers analyzed data on more than 11 million women who gave birth in Denmark from 1978 to 2007. Among women with preeclampsia, the risks for developing hypertension in the future were compounded with each pregnancy.

The findings were presented at the Society for Maternal-Fetal Medicine's annual meeting in San Diego.

IMPLICATION

"The only reliable treatment for preeclampsia is delivery of the baby. But while delivery may 'cure' preeclampsia in the moment, these mothers are at high risk of chronic hypertension, type 2 diabetes and blood clots for the rest of their lives," said senior author Michael J. Paidas, MD, director of the Program for Thrombosis and Hemostasis in Women's Health in the department of obstetrics, gynecology & reproductive science at Yale.

This research contributes to the growing data on the link between hypertension during pregnancy and subsequent heart disease and death among women, Dr. Paidas said. He and his colleagues are conducting ongoing research into the genetic links between pregnancy complications, cardiovascular disease and diabetes.

LEARN MORE

For more information about high blood pressure during pregnancy, visit the Web site of the Preeclampsia Foundation, *www.pree clampsia.org.*

Dietary Fiber Cuts Risk of Pregnancy Complication

Jennifer Wu, MD, obstetrician/gynecologist, Lenox Hill Hospital, New York City.
American Journal of Hypertension online edition.

Eating more fiber during the first trimester of pregnancy seems to reduce the risk of developing preeclampsia, a potentially fatal condition characterized by elevated blood pressure.

The finding appears to be another good reason for pregnant women to maintain good fiber intake, one expert said.

BACKGROUND

According to the Preeclampsia Foundation, some 5% to 8% of women experience the dangerous condition during pregnancy. The only way to end preeclampsia is to deliver the baby—obviously a more reasonable strategy the further along a pregnancy is.

Risk factors for the condition include obesity, a family history of type 2 diabetes and/or hypertension, depression, anxiety, diets low in fruits and vegetables, and low levels of physical activity.

The findings, published in an online edition of the *American Journal of Hypertension*, seem to corroborate previous findings on the subject from somewhat smaller studies.

RECENT STUDY

For this study, more than 1,500 pregnant women in Washington State filled out a 121-item questionnaire listing the types of food they ate, both before they conceived and during the early weeks of their pregnancy.

Women who consumed 21.2 grams a day or more of fiber were 72% less likely to develop preeclampsia compared with women who ate less than 11.9 grams a day, the researchers found triglyceride levels were lower and levels of HDL or "good" cholesterol higher in women consuming more fiber, the study noted.

The authors, from the Swedish Medical Center and the University of Washington School of Public Health and Community Medicine in Seattle, noted that adding an extra 5 grams of fiber a day was associated with a 14% reduction in the risk of developing preeclampsia. Consuming two slices of whole-grain bread daily would be the equivalent to adding 5 grams of fiber a day, they said.

EXPERT ADVICE

"There's not really a downside to taking more fiber," noted Jennifer Wu, MD, an obstetrician/gynecologist at Lenox Hill Hospital in New York City. "Many women suffer from constipation in pregnancy, and it can only help that. If you can increase your fiber anyway for constipation, it may also decrease preeclampsia."

Unnecessary C-Sections Can Be Deadly for Infants

Babies born via C-sections to women who did not require Cesarean section have twice the risk of death within the first month as those born vaginally.

Self-defense: Only have a C-section if your doctor feels it is medically necessary.

Marian F. MacDorman, PhD, statistician and senior social scientist, division of vital statistics, National Center for Health Statistics, Centers for Disease Control and Prevention, Atlanta.

What Your C-Section Scar Can Tell You About Your Next Delivery

Emmanuel Bujold, MD, associate professor, obstetrics and gynecology, Laval University, Quebec City, Canada.
Shoshana Haberman, MD, director, perinatal testing services, Maimonides Medical Center, Brooklyn, New York.
Alessandro Ghidini, MD, maternal-fetal medicine specialist, Alexandria, Virgina.
Society of Maternal-Fetal Medicine, news release.

Measuring the thickness of the uterine scar from a Cesarean delivery can help physicians predict which women would be at low risk for uterine rupture and may safely try to have a vaginal delivery, according to a new study by Canadian researchers.

"The thicker the scar is, the stronger the scar is, and the smaller the chance of rupture," said Emmanuel Bujold, MD, associate professor of obstetrics and gynecology at Laval University in Quebec City, Canada. Dr. Bujold is the lead author of the study, which was presented at the Society for Maternal-Fetal Medicine's annual meeting in San Diego.

BACKGROUND

The issue of repeat Cesarean deliveries is of concern, because delivery of a baby by C-section has been linked to higher rates of complications for both mother and infant, Dr. Bujold said.

C-section rates have been climbing in the United States and elsewhere. In 2011, about a third of births were by Cesarean, with 1.3 million Cesarean births and 2.7 million vaginal deliveries, according to the US National Center for Health Statistics.

In deciding which women can safely try a vaginal birth after a C-section, doctors must decide if a vaginal delivery would be safe or if risks—such as uterine rupture—would make it unwise.

STUDY DETAILS

Dr. Bujold's study involved 236 pregnant women who had delivered previously by C-section but who planned a vaginal delivery. The researchers used ultrasound to measure the lower part of the uterus, which correlates with scar thickness from the previous C-section, and then followed the women through their deliveries.

During labor and delivery, three of the women had a complete uterine rupture. In six, the scar reopened. Women who had uterine rupture had a very thin scar, Dr. Bujold said.

"We found the cutoff is probably 2.3 millimeters" in terms of scar thickness, he said. The average risk of rupture is about 1%, Dr. Bujold said, but in the study, "if you had a scar smaller than 2 mm, your risk of rupture [was] about 10%."

THE PRACTICE OF MEASURING THE UTERINE SCAR

Measuring the uterine scar is very common in France and in Quebec, Dr. Bujold said, and is becoming more common in the United States.

The study confirms results published in 1996 that also found that uterine rupture and uterine scar opening during labor could be predicted by ultrasound measurements of the previous scar.

Dr. Bujold suggested that measuring the scar could predict who would be and would not be at risk for uterine rupture and could help physicians decide which women would be candidates for a vaginal delivery.

EXPERT COMMENTARY

Shoshana Haberman, MD, director of perinatal testing services at Maimonides Medical Center in Brooklyn, New York, said she has been doing this measurement on women with previous C-sections for a few years. And while the new study results are interesting, she said, the prediction method is not yet definitive.

"We need more data—that's the bottom line," Dr. Haberman said. "We need more data to decide the cutoff."

The ultrasound measure is also operator-specific, she added, so it could vary from person to person.

EARLIER RESEARCH CONFIRMED

Another expert welcomed the study, saying it confirms the previous research.

"Not all women with previous C-sections are created equal," said Alessandro Ghidini, MD, a maternal-fetal medicine specialist in Alexandria, Virginia, and president of the scientific committee for the meeting at which the study was being presented.

Taking into account the measurement, plus other factors—including the reason for the previous C-section—will help a woman and her doctor decide the best course for the current pregnancy, he said.

Though the test is not done as often in the United States as elsewhere, he said, women who've had a Cesarean delivery could ask their doctors about having the test.

Early Deliveries May Be a Sign of Heart Disease

Women who had delivered before 37 weeks of pregnancy were more than twice as likely to have heart disease decades later as women who had delivered at full term (after 37 weeks).

Theory: Inflammation and blood fats may affect both pregnancy and heart health.

Best: Women with a history of preterm delivery may benefit from early cardiac interventions, such as exercise and weight control.

Janet M. Catov, PhD, assistant professor of obstetrics, gynecology and reproductive sciences, University of Pittsburgh, and leader of a study of 446 women, published in *American Journal of Epidemiology*.

Should You Diet When Pregnant?

Yvonne S. Thornton, MD, MPH, clinical professor, obstetrics and gynecology, New York Medical College, Valhalla, New York.
Robin Kalish, MD, director, clinical maternal-fetal medicine, NewYork-Presbyterian Hospital/Weill Cornell Medical Center, New York City.
Journal of the National Medical Association.

In a study that reinforces recent changes in pregnancy weight gain recommendations, obese women who gained little or no weight while pregnant had better outcomes than obese women who gained more.

BACKGROUND

About 35% of US women are obese, according to the US Centers for Disease Control and Prevention.

Though doctors know that obesity during pregnancy raises the risk for hypertension, gestational diabetes and other complications, no one is certain what the optimal weight gain for pregnant women should be.

THE STUDY

In the new study, published in the *Journal of the National Medical Association*, researchers divided 232 obese women, all with a body mass index (BMI) greater than 30 (a BMI of 30 and over is considered obese), into two groups. One group was given the standard advice to "eat to appetite." The other group was given nutritional counseling, told to keep a food diary and placed on a diet that limited calories to between 2,000 and 3,500 a day, depending on their pre-pregnancy weight.

By the end of the pregnancy, the average weight gain in the group of women who stuck to their normal diets was 31 pounds. The average weight gain for women in the calorie-restriction group was 11 pounds. Twenty-three extremely obese women actually lost weight during their pregnancy.

CALORIE RESTRICTION BENEFITS SEEN

The results seem to support less, not more, weight gain during pregnancy. Women in the calorie-restricted group had fewer C-sections and lower rates of gestational diabetes and hypertension and had retained less weight six weeks after delivery.

Fewer women in the calorie-restricted group delivered newborns weighing more than 10 pounds, which can make deliveries risky for both mother and child. There were no growth-restricted babies in either group.

HEALTHY EATING DURING PREGNANCY

"Women who are obese when beginning a pregnancy are, by definition, unhealthy," noted Yvonne Thornton, MD, MPH, a clinical professor of obstetrics and gynecology at New York Medical College and the study's lead author. "To say that they should gain even more weight is counterintuitive, and our study bears that out."

Still, Dr. Thornton does not favor establishing a one-size-fits-all weight gain number for obese women.

Instead, "we need to focus on making these women healthier by getting them to eat a well-balanced diet, similar to the types of moderate calorie-restricted diets that women with gestational diabetes are put on with no ill effects," she said.

"Over the past decade, obstetricians have become more aware that the idea of 'eating for two' is really not a good thing, especially for patients who start out obese," said Robin Kalish, MD, director of clinical maternal-fetal medicine at NewYork-Presbyterian Hospital/Weill Cornell Medical Center.

STUDY AUTHOR'S WEIGHT STRUGGLE

The idea for the study came from Dr. Thornton's own lifelong struggle with weight. During her first pregnancy in the late 1970s, she gained 67 pounds and hit a peak weight of 225 pounds.

After the pregnancy, she signed up for Weight Watchers and lost 20 pounds, only to become pregnant again.

But with her second child, she continued the focus on nutrition and gained less than a half-pound.

"I was the first test case," Dr. Thornton said.

NEW WEIGHT-GAIN GUIDELINES

Experts at the US Institute of Medicine and the National Research Council recently updated their gestational weight gain guidelines to urge that obese women gain only 11 to 20 pounds during pregnancy—down from a minimum weight gain of 15 pounds that had been recommended in 1990.

Guidelines for Pregnancy Weight Gain

Physicians are less strict than they used to be about weight gain in pregnancy. Although most doctors like to see a gain of about 25 to 35 pounds, 40 pounds should be okay if the due date is near or if you were underweight before the pregnancy. If your physician considers the weight gain excessive, he/she will check for excess fluid retention (a sign of the potentially dangerous condition called preeclampsia) and for gestational diabetes...and may recommend nutritional counseling.

Jonathan Scher, MD, assistant clinical professor of obstetrics, gynecology and reproductive science, Mount Sinai Medical Center, New York City, and author of *Preventing Miscarriage* (Harper & Row).

Do Cereal Eaters Have More Boys?

Women who ate high-calorie diets with a wide range of nutrients around the time of conception were more likely to deliver boys. Women who ate breakfast cereal daily had more boys...those who seldom ate cereal had more girls.

Caution: Even if you hope for a girl, do not restrict calories—your baby needs nutrients. Do not avoid cereal—it often has folic acid, which combats birth defects.

Fiona Mathews, PhD, lecturer, University of Exeter, England, and head of a study of 740 women, published in *Proceedings of the Royal Society B: Biological Sciences.*

Pregnant Mom's Flu Shot Protects Baby

New England Journal of Medicine.

A flu shot provided to a woman during her pregnancy can help shield her newborn against the potentially deadly infection, researchers report.

The study, which was conducted in Bangladesh, bolsters longstanding US recommendations that pregnant women get vaccinated against influenza—especially since it is also recommended that infants under 6 months of age not receive the shot.

"Our data show that one dose of maternal influenza vaccine provides a considerable two-for-one benefit to both mothers and their young infants," wrote a team led by Mark C. Steinhoff, MD, of Johns Hopkins University's Bloomberg School of Public Health, in Baltimore.

The study was published in the *New England Journal of Medicine.* Dr. Steinhoff also presented the findings at a Washington, D.C., meeting focused on the flu shot, sponsored by the US National Vaccine Advisory Committee.

INFLUENZA RISKS FOR MOTHER AND CHILD

In the study, Dr. Steinhoff's group pointed out that maternal influenza infection during pregnancy carries health risks for the mother and her offspring, including fetal malformation and even infant death. In fact, "childhood deaths associated with influenza are most frequent in infants under the age of 6 months," the authors noted.

FLU VACCINE GUIDELINES

For more than a decade, experts at the US Centers for Disease Control and Prevention (CDC) have recommended that pregnant women get a flu shot. The vaccine is also recommended for infants between 6 and 24 months of age. It is not recommended for younger babies.

However, the researchers knew that newborns could pick up some immunity to the flu virus from maternal antibodies circulating in the fetal environment.

So, would antibodies stimulated by a flu vaccine given to the mother protect her baby?

RECENT STUDY

To find out, Dr. Steinhoff's team tracked the health of a group of 340 Bangladeshi mother-infant pairs during 2004–2005. Some of the women received a flu shot during their pregnancy, while others did not. The researchers then tracked levels of respiratory illness among both moms and babies for the first 24 weeks after delivery. Infants were not vaccinated against the flu during this time.

The researchers found that babies born to vaccinated mothers had a 63% lower risk of laboratory-confirmed influenza compared to babies whose mothers who had not received the flu shot. The incidence of any type of respiratory illness with fever also declined, from 153 cases among infants born to unvaccinated mothers to 110 cases among babies whose mothers had gotten the flu shot.

"In other words, five pregnant women would need to be vaccinated to prevent a single case of respiratory illness with fever in a mother or infant," the team concluded. One case of laboratory-confirmed influenza among infants would be prevented for every 16 shots given to pregnant women, they found.

CONCLUSION

The researchers noted that, despite the current CDC recommendations, few expectant mothers in the United States currently receive the flu shot—even though "the general safety of this strategy has been shown." This trial—the first randomized, prospective study on the topic yet conducted—offers what they call "unique evidence supporting the strategy of maternal immunization to prevent influenza infection in young infants and their mothers."

Hooray! Big Hips Mean Brainier Babies

Researchers analyzed data from the National Center for Health Statistics. On average, children born to mothers with relatively more fat in the hip area and narrower waists performed better on tests of cognitive function than other children did.

Theory: Women with hourglass figures store more fat on their thighs and buttocks... and this fat contains polyunsaturated fatty acids that aid fetal brain development.

William D. Lassek, MD, adjunct assistant professor of epidemiology, University of Pittsburgh, and coauthor of a study of 16,325 women, published in *Evolution and Human Behavior.*

Magnesium Sulfate Reduces Threat of Cerebral Palsy

Dwight J. Rouse, MD, MSPH, professor of obstetrics and gynecology, University of Alabama at Birmingham.

William Zinser, MD, pediatric neurologist, Children's Medical Center, Dallas, and associate professor of pediatric neurology, University of Texas Southwestern Medical Center at Dallas.

New England Journal of Medicine.

M agnesium sulfate, given to mothers at risk of preterm delivery, cut the rate of cerebral palsy in their babies by nearly half, a new study found. The findings were published in the *New England Journal of Medicine.*

BACKGROUND

Cerebral palsy, marked by abnormal movement control and postures that cause limited activity, is caused by damage or dysfunction to the developing fetal or infant brain. Preterm birth is itself a risk factor for the condition. About one third of cerebral palsy cases are associated with preterm birth.

In past studies, magnesium sulfate hasn't borne out as an effective treatment for delay of early labor. But it has proven effective for treatment of maternal high blood pressure associated with pregnancy, said study lead author Dwight J. Rouse, MD, a professor of obstetrics and gynecology at the University of Alabama at Birmingham.

And some previous research had found magnesium sulfate effective for reducing the risk of cerebral palsy, but other studies had been inconclusive. So, Dr. Rouse and his colleagues embarked on this large, more comprehensive study.

RECENT STUDY

In the study, the largest of its kind, Dr. Rouse and his colleagues randomly assigned 2,241 women at risk of delivering early—between 24 and 31 weeks—to receive either magnesium sulfate or a placebo. (Babies born after 37 to 42 weeks of pregnancy are considered full term, according to the March of Dimes.) The magnesium sulfate was given intravenously as the women entered labor as a 6-gram dose followed by a constant infusion of 2 grams per hour until 12 hours had passed, labor had subsided, or they had given birth.

The researchers then compared infants born to each group of mothers to see if there were differences in the rates of death or the occurrence of cerebral palsy.

They found no significant differences in the proportion of deaths between the magnesium sulfate group and the placebo group. But they did find that moderate or severe cerebral palsy was diagnosed in just 1.9% of the group treated with magnesium sulfate, compared to 3.5% in the placebo group.

POSSIBLE EXPLANATION

Dr. Rouse said it's not known for certain how the compound may work. But, he said, it may "stabilize the vessels in the vulnerable preterm brain," protect against damage from lack of oxygen, and guard against injury caused by swelling and inflammation.

"Our findings are applicable only to early preterm birth," he added. "We define high risk as threatening delivery prior to 32 weeks."

ADVICE

"If deemed to be at high or immediate risk of delivery prior to 32 weeks, women and their doctors should consider using magnesium sulfate to prevent their child from having cerebral palsy," Dr. Rouse said.

EXPERT REACTION

William Zinser, MD, is a pediatric neurologist at Children's Medical Center, and an associate professor of pediatric neurology at the University of Texas Southwestern Medical

Center, both in Dallas. He said, "It's too early to know if magnesium sulfate has an overall effect on the incidence rate of cerebral palsy."

Dr. Zinser reviewed the study but was not involved with it. "More research needs to be done, certainly," he said.

Study Links Pesticides To Birth Defects

Indiana University School of Medicine, news release.

Pesticides may increase the risk for birth defects, say researchers from Indiana University School of Medicine. They found that the highest rates of birth defects in US babies occur among those conceived in the spring and summer, the same time that there are increased levels of pesticides in surface water.

THE STUDY

Researchers analyzed all 30.1 million births in the United States between 1996 and 2002. They found a strong association between higher rates of birth defects among women whose last menstrual period was in April, May, June or July and elevated levels of nitrates, *atrazine* and other pesticides in surface water during those same months.

The data showed a statistically significant correlation between the last menstrual period and higher rates of birth defects for half of 22 categories of birth defects, including spina bifida, cleft lip, clubfoot and Down syndrome.

"Elevated concentrations of pesticides and other agrochemicals in surface water during April through July coincided with significantly higher risk of birth defects in live births conceived by women whose last menstrual period began in the same months," said study first author Paul Winchester, MD, professor of clinical pediatrics at the Indiana University (IU) School of Medicine. "While our study didn't prove a cause and effect link, the fact that birth defects and pesticides in surface water peak during the same four months makes us suspect that the two are related," he said.

FIRST STUDY TO MAKE CONNECTION

It's long been believed that these chemicals pose a threat to developing embryos, but this is the first study to make the connection between birth defects and elevated levels of pesticides at the time of conception, the authors said. The study was published in the journal *Acta Paediatrica*.

"Birth defects, which affect about three out of 100 newborns in the US, are one of the leading causes of infant death. What we are most excited about is that if our suspicions are right, and pesticides are contributing to birth defect risk, we can reverse or modify the factors that are causing these lifelong and often very serious medical problems," Dr. Winchester said.

Known risk factors for birth defects include alcohol use, smoking, diabetes, and advanced age among pregnant women. But even mothers who didn't have these risk factors had higher overall birth defect rates for babies conceived from April to July, the study found.

EXPERT REACTION

"These observations by Dr. Winchester are extremely important, as they raise the question for the first time regarding the potential adverse effect of these commonly used chemicals on pregnancy outcome—the health and well-being of our children," said James Lemons, MD, a professor of pediatrics at the IU School of Medicine.

The Low Birth Weight–Autism Link

Autism risk is more than double among infants who are born prematurely or at low birth weight. Risk is higher for premature and low-birth-weight girls than for similar boys, even though autism itself is more common in boys. About one in 150 children in the US is autistic.

Diana Schendel, PhD, lead health scientist, National Center on Birth Defects and Developmental Disabilities, Centers for Disease Control and Prevention, Atlanta, and researcher on a study of 565 children, published in *Pediatrics*.

Prenatal Nutrition, Postnatal Allergy Protection

Jennifer Appleyard, MD, chief, allergy and immunology, St. John Hospital and Medical Center, Detroit.

Devang Doshi, MD, director, pediatric allergy and immunology, Beaumont Hospital, Royal Oak, Michigan. *Thorax.*

An apple a day while you're pregnant may indeed keep the doctor away. But the real beneficiary could be your unborn child.

Recent research suggests that when women eat apples during pregnancy, their offspring have lower rates of asthma.

And, mothers who consume fish during pregnancy may lower their child's risk of developing eczema, an allergic skin condition.

"There are influences that occur in utero that can have lasting impact," said Jennifer Appleyard, MD, chief of allergy and immunology at St. John Hospital and Medical Center in Detroit. "More and more, we're finding influences for later health develop earlier than we anticipated."

BACKGROUND

More than 20 million Americans have asthma, according to the US Centers for Disease Control and Prevention, and about 6.2 million of those are children.

Eczema is an allergic condition that makes the skin dry and itchy. It's most common in babies and children and is sometimes called atopic dermatitis.

THE STUDY

Dutch researchers recently followed 1,253 children from before birth to age 5. Their mothers completed food questionnaires during their pregnancies, and their children's health was assessed with a symptom questionnaire. The children's diets were also assessed.

The study was published in the medical journal *Thorax.*

APPLES vs. ASTHMA

Women who consumed the most apples during pregnancy—more than four a week—had children who were 37% less likely to have ever wheezed than children of mothers who had the lowest consumption of apples during pregnancy. Additionally, youngsters born to apple-loving moms were 46% less likely to have asthma symptoms and 53% less likely to have doctor-confirmed asthma than those whose mothers shunned the fruit.

The mechanism behind apples' apparent protective effect needs further study, but may have something to do with the flavonoids and other antioxidants contained in apples, said Devang Doshi, MD, director of pediatric allergy and immunology at Beaumont Hospital in Royal Oak, Michigan.

FISH vs. ECZEMA

The study also found that mothers who ate fish more than once a week had children who were 43% less likely to have eczema than children of women who never ate fish.

"This was a good study, but we need a lot more evidence still," said Dr. Doshi, who pointed out that the children in the study generally had well-balanced, nutritious diets, and that may have played a role as well.

EXPERT ADVICE FOR PREGNANT WOMEN

So, what's a pregnant woman to do? "The general consensus is that women should consume a good, well-balanced diet with lots of fruits and vegetables, and not to overindulge in any one food," Dr. Doshi said.

Dr. Appleyard recommends avoiding nuts, peanuts and shellfish while you're pregnant to reduce the risk of your child developing a food allergy. While this advice applies to everyone, it may be even more important for those with a family history of allergies.

Dr. Appleyard also suggested that pregnant women might want to "pick your foods wisely, because what you're eating today may not only nourish your body, but may have an impact on your baby's future health."

She added that for preventing asthma, avoiding cigarette smoke both before and after birth is crucial.

LEARN MORE

For more information on eating right during pregnancy, visit the KidsHealth Web site of the

Nemours Foundation, *http://kidshealth,* under "Nutrition & Fitness," click on "Special Dietary Needs," then "Eating During Pregenancy."

Mom and Baby Both Benefit from Exercise

Raul Artal, MD, chairman of obstetrics, gynecology and women's health, Saint Louis University School of Medicine, St. Louis.

Thomas Wang, MD, Kaiser Permanente, San Diego.

American Congress of Obstetricians and Gynecologists (*www.acog.org*).

American Pregnancy Association (*www.american pregnancy.org*).

It's natural that a woman might be worried about exercising while she's pregnant. So many changes are occurring in her body, it makes sense to have second thoughts about whether exercise might harm her or her unborn child.

But it turns out that a thoughtful exercise program is good for both mother and child, according to medical experts.

"We know that women who exercise during pregnancy have less chance of developing certain conditions like gestational diabetes," said Raul Artal, MD, chairman of obstetrics, gynecology and women's health for the Saint Louis University School of Medicine. "Not only that, exercise maintains musculoskeletal fitness. Women can cope with the anatomical and physiological changes of pregnancy better when they're in good shape. They also tolerate labor better and recover more quickly from delivery."

The baby also benefits. One study found that when an expectant mother works out, her fetus reaps cardiac benefits in the form of a lower fetal heart rate.

CHOOSING APPROPRIATE EXERCISE

When choosing what sort of exercise to pursue, a woman should take into account the shape she was in before becoming pregnant, said Thomas Wang, MD, a family practitioner for Kaiser Permanente in San Diego.

"A lot of things depend on the level of fitness they had before," Dr. Wang said. A mom-to-be should pursue activities that will provide a good level of exertion without testing the limits of her body's current conditioning. If she's just starting a fitness program to improve her health during pregnancy, she should start out slowly and be careful not to overexert herself.

The American Congress of Obstetricians and Gynecologists recommends that pregnant women do at least 30 minutes of moderate exercise a day most days of the week. First, though, all women should consult a doctor to make sure it's okay.

ACTIVITIES TO AVOID

But there are certain activities that should at least be undertaken with caution, if not avoided altogether. Pregnant women, for instance, should not go scuba diving, as that activity exposes the fetus to a risk of developing decompression sickness, also known as the bends.

Women also should think twice before engaging in activities where the risk of falling is high, such as gymnastics, horseback riding, downhill skiing and high-intensity racquet sports. And they should avoid contact sports, such as ice hockey, soccer and basketball.

"Anything that involves impact or the chance of abdominal trauma, they should try to avoid," Dr. Wang explained.

SAFE EXERCISE

Exercise that's perfectly safe for expectant mothers includes Kegel exercises (which strengthen the pelvic floor muscles), swimming, walking, light dancing and yoga. Riding a stationary bicycle or working out on aerobic gym equipment—elliptical or stair-climbing machines, for instance—is also fairly safe, as long as care is taken to prevent a fall.

Most pregnant women also can take part in jogging, running and aerobics, especially if those were exercises they regularly performed before pregnancy.

WEIGHT TRAINING

Pregnant women who weight train should emphasize improving their muscle tone, particularly in the upper body and abdominal area, according to the American Pregnancy Association. They should avoid lifting weights above their heads and performing exercises that strain the lower back muscles.

"There have been some studies that show heavy lifting causes a temporary drop in the baby's heart rate," Dr. Wang said. "It usually corrects pretty quickly, but they might want to be careful."

EXERCISE PRECAUTIONS

Other things to keep in mind if exercising while pregnant...

• **Avoid exercising to the point of exhaustion or breathlessness,** as that could affect the oxygen supply to the fetus.

• **Avoid overheating,** which can affect the baby's development. Don't exercise in hot weather.

• **During the second and third trimesters,** avoid exercise that involves lying flat on your back as this decreases blood flow to the womb.

Though that might seem like a lot of precautions for something that's supposed to be safe, doctors insist that women can and should engage in a well-thought-out fitness program during their pregnancy.

"By and large, if there are no medical complications of pregnancy, women can continue engaging in the same type of activities," Dr. Artal said. "Women should be encouraged to continue living an active lifestyle."

For an Easygoing Baby, Quit Smoking

Researchers rated nine-month-old babies on mood, receptivity to new things, and eating and sleeping regularity. Compared with babies whose mothers smoked throughout pregnancy, babies whose mothers gave up cigarettes while pregnant were significantly more easygoing.

Upshot: Here's yet another reason to quit smoking.

Kate E. Pickett, Phd, department of health sciences, University of York, England, and leader of a study of about 18,000 babies, published in *Journal of Epidemiology and Community Health.*

Eating Fish, Breast-Feeding Boost Infant Development

Harvard Medical School, news release.

Greater maternal consumption of fish and longer periods of breast-feeding are tied to better physical and cognitive development in infants, according to a recent study.

The report, which looked at mothers and infants from Denmark, provides further evidence that the omega-3 fatty acids found in fish and compounds in breast milk aid infant development.

"These results, together with findings from other studies of women in the US and the United Kingdom, provide additional evidence that moderate maternal fish intake during pregnancy does not harm child development and may on balance be beneficial," said study lead author Emily Oken, MD, MPH, an assistant professor at Harvard Medical School.

Researchers from the Maternal Nutrition Group at the Department of Epidemiology at Statens Serum Institut in Copenhagen, Denmark, also collaborated on the study, which was published in the *American Journal of Clinical Nutrition.*

THE STUDY

The research, which looked at 25,446 children born to mothers participating in a Danish study between 1997 and 2002, found that children whose mothers ate the most fish during pregnancy (about two ounces a day on average) were more likely to have better motor and cognitive skills. Meanwhile, those whose mothers ate the least fish had the lowest developmental scores at 18 months of age.

Children who were breast-fed for longer periods of time also scored better, especially at 18 months. Breast milk also contains omega-3 fatty acids. The benefit of fish consumption was similar among infants breast-fed for shorter or longer durations.

RECOMMENDATIONS FOR FISH CONSUMPTION

US women are advised to limit their fish intake to two servings a week because some fish contain high traces of mercury, a known toxin. Most women in the study, however, consumed cod, plaice, salmon, herring and mackerel—fish that tend to have low mercury levels.

"In previous work in a population of US women, we similarly found that higher prenatal fish consumption was associated with an overall benefit for child cognitive development, but that higher mercury levels attenuated this benefit," Dr. Oken said. "Therefore, women should continue to eat fish—especially during pregnancy—but should choose fish types likely to be lower in mercury."

LEARN MORE

For a table listing the amount of mercury in different species of fish, visit the Web site of the US Food and Drug Administration, *www.fda.gov/*, and search "Mercury levels in fish."

Breast-Feeding Lowers Stress for Life

Liz Maseth, RN, outpatient lactation services, department of maternal-fetal medicine, Akron Children's Hospital, Ohio.
Judy Hopkinson, PhD, assistant professor of pediatrics, Baylor College of Medicine, Houston.
Archives of Diseases in Childhood, online.

Breast-feeding offers a host of benefits to both mother and baby, including a stronger immune system for the baby and faster weight loss for mom. There are even some known psychological benefits from breast-feeding, such as a stronger parent–child bond.

And now British researchers have recently discovered another mental bonus—children who are breast-fed seem to cope with stress and anxiety more effectively when they reach school age.

STUDY FINDINGS

In a group of nearly 9,000 children between the ages of five and 10, those who weren't breast-fed and whose parents were getting divorced or separated were 9.4 times more likely to be highly anxious when compared to other children. Children who were breast-fed as infants, however, whose parents were getting divorced were only 2.2 times more likely to be highly anxious, the study found.

"Breast-feeding is associated with resilience against the psychosocial stress linked with parental divorce/separation," concluded the authors of the study published in the *Archives of Diseases in Childhood.*

POSSIBLE EXPLANATIONS

The authors theorized that the physical contact between mother and child in the first few days of life could help form certain neural and hormonal pathways that affect a person's ability to cope with stress later in life.

Breast-feeding experts have long been aware of the mother–baby bond that occurs during breast-feeding. "There's a lot less verbal communication, but lots of tactile communication and eye contact that promotes positive physiological responses," said Liz Maseth, RN, an outpatient lactation consultant at Akron Children's Hospital in Ohio.

"Breast-feeding does seem to suppress stress responses in babies, and it does seem that there's a protective effect," she said.

"In terms of the biological possibility, breast milk is pretty amazing stuff, and the tactile interaction that goes along with breast-feeding does have an influence on the development of neurons," explained Judy Hopkinson, PhD, an assistant professor of pediatrics in the section of nutrition at Baylor College of Medicine in Houston.

Dr. Hopkinson added that babies who aren't breast-fed might be able to reap similar benefits with lots of holding and touching.

The study authors also suggested that the bond created during breast-feeding might affect the way the child and the mother interact, and that effect might be long lasting.

Hopkinson pointed out that mothers who are successful at breast-feeding often have a

75

supportive social network, which could also help lessen a child's stress in times of crisis.

Whatever the reason for the association, it was clear that children who had been breast-fed were less stressed.

HELPFUL RECOMMENDATIONS

Both Maseth and Dr. Hopkinson said it's very important to try to begin breast-feeding as soon as possible after birth—no more than one hour. Maseth said this is because the breasts contain glands that release the same scent as amniotic fluid, a scent that babies will recognize.

"For most mothers, breast-feeding doesn't come naturally. If the baby doesn't latch on, it can lead to feelings of failure and concern about whether or not the baby is getting enough milk. Women need lots of encouragement and education," Maseth said.

"Don't give up, though; seek help," she advised, adding that your baby's pediatrician will likely have information on what local breast-feeding resources are available.

"Breast-feeding is something for mothers and babies to enjoy. A time for them to cherish and nurture each other," said Dr. Hopkinson. For women who can't breast-feed, she said, that skin-to-skin contact between mother and baby can also help build a similar bond.

Breast-Feeding Scores Great Grades

Joseph Sabia, PhD, assistant professor, public policy, American University, Washington, D.C.

Daniel Rees, PhD, professor, economics, University of Colorado Denver.

David L. Katz, MD, director, Prevention Research Center, Yale University School of Medicine, New Haven, Connecticut.

Journal of Human Capital.

C hildren who were breast-fed do better in high school and are more likely to go to college than their bottle-fed siblings, researchers report.

While the health benefits of breast-feeding to both infants and mothers is well known, this study suggests the practice may have educational benefits as well. This is the first study using data on siblings to examine the effect of breast-feeding on high school completion and college attendance, the researchers noted.

"We compare sibling pairs—one of whom was breast-fed and one of whom was not, or siblings who were breast-fed for different durations—and find consistent evidence that breast-fed children have higher high school grade point averages and a higher probability of attending college," said study coauthor Joseph Sabia, PhD, an assistant professor of public policy at American University in Washington, D.C.

The researchers ruled out factors, such as socioeconomic status, in the connection between breast-feeding and educational achievement, Dr. Sabia said.

The report was published in the *Journal of Human Capital.*

STUDY DETAILS

For the report, Dr. Sabia and his colleague Daniel Rees, PhD, a professor of economics at the University of Colorado Denver, used data from the National Longitudinal Study of Adolescent Health. They looked at the breast-feeding histories and high school grades of 126 siblings from 59 families; high school graduation and college attendance data was obtained for 191 siblings from 90 families.

"If you're breast-fed, your high school GPA goes up substantially, and the likelihood that you go on to college goes up," Dr. Rees said.

For every month you are breast-fed, your high school GPA goes up about 1% and your probability of going to college goes up about 2%, Dr. Rees added.

"We found that more than one-half of the estimated effect of being breast-fed on high school grades can be linked to improvements in cognitive ability and health," Dr. Sabia said. "Thus, we conclude that improvements in cognitive ability and adolescent health may be important pathways through which breast-feeding affects long-term academic achievement," he said.

About one-fifth of the increased likelihood of going to college appears to be due to breast-feeding, Dr. Rees added.

"This is another benefit of breast-feeding," Dr. Rees said. "We know that breast-feeding leads to better health, higher IQ, but the next step is what are the implications, and this is an important implication," he said.

EXPERT REACTION

David L. Katz, MD, director of the Prevention Research Center at Yale University School of Medicine, said this study may not prove a connection between school performance and breast-feeding, but it could be another reason to breast-feed your baby.

"An array of health benefits is convincingly associated with breast-feeding, including a reduced risk of both infections and obesity in the breast-fed child," Dr. Katz said. "Less certain, but long suggested, is enhanced cognitive development in breast-fed children as well."

It could be that factors that determine whether or not a baby is breast-fed are an important piece of the puzzle, Dr. Katz noted. "Why a baby is fed one way or another may matter as much as which way a baby is fed," he said. "A study of association such as this cannot fully resolve that issue."

Blood Test May Predict Postpartum Depression

Ilona S. Yim, PhD, associate professor, psychology, University of California, Irvine.
Jeanelle Sheeder, MSPH, clinical sciences senior instructor, obstetrics and gynecology and pediatrics, University of Colorado Medical Center, Denver.
Archives of General Psychiatry.

Measuring the levels of a hormone produced by the placenta during pregnancy might predict whether a woman is likely to develop postpartum depression, a recent study suggests.

"If we know early on that a woman is at high risk to develop postpartum depression, then we can implement interventions before symptoms actually occur," said lead researcher Ilona S. Yim, PhD, an associate professor of psychology at the University of California, Irvine.

"By means of a simple blood draw, we could correctly identify 75% of women who would later develop postpartum depression," she said. The report was published in the *Archives of General Psychiatry*.

BACKGROUND

Approximately 13% of women will experience postpartum depression, a condition that holds significant consequences not only for women but for their infants and families as well, experts say. Once a woman has had postpartum depression, she is more likely to have future bouts of depression, and that puts infants and children at risk for cognitive, behavioral and social problems.

Postpartum depression generally begins within four to six weeks after delivery. Risk factors include a history of depression, stressful life events, a lack of social support, low self-esteem and depression, anxiety or stress during pregnancy.

THE STUDY

For the study, Dr. Yim's group looked for a link between *placental corticotropin-releasing hormone* (pCRH) and postpartum depression. The researchers took blood samples from 100 pregnant women at various stages during their pregnancy and tested for levels of pCRH.

They also assessed the women for signs of depression during pregnancy and about eight weeks, on average, after delivery.

In all, 16 women developed postpartum depression. In each case, the women had had high levels of pCRH at 25 weeks into their pregnancies, the study found.

The blood test could identify about 75% of women who would develop postpartum depression, Dr. Yim's team found. The test misclassified about 25% of the women.

When the blood test was combined with assessing symptoms of depression during pregnancy, Dr. Yim noted, it was even more predictive of postpartum depression.

IMPLICATIONS

If the findings can be replicated, then testing the level of this hormone might become standard care, Dr. Yim said.

"Postpartum depression affects so many women that it would be great to have something that would help to identify being at risk early on, and perhaps develop strategies to prevent it," she said.

Women who know they are at risk for postpartum depression can take steps to reduce stress that might ward off the condition, Dr. Yim said. "They could take yoga classes and avoid severe stressors," she said.

EXPERT REACTION

Postpartum depression expert Jeanelle Sheeder, MSPH, a clinical sciences senior instructor of obstetrics and gynecology and pediatrics at the University of Colorado Medical Center in Denver, said she was not sure that the blood test would add more than what can be gleaned from screening women for signs of depression before and during their pregnancies.

"It is encouraging to have a prenatal biologic measure that predicts postpartum depression," Sheeder said. "However, I am not sure about the practicality of using pCRH as a screening tool. It has been shown that prenatal depression is predictive of postpartum depression, and it is easier and cheaper to do that type of screening than pCRH in most clinical settings."

Fans Lower Sudden Infant Death Syndrome Risk 72%

SIDS (Sudden Infant Death Syndrome) may occur when babies' access to fresh air is blocked.

Study: Infants who slept in a room with a fan were 72% less likely to die of SIDS…those who slept in a room with an open window were 36% less likely.

Theory: Airflow reduces the chance of rebreathing trapped carbon dioxide.

De-Kun Li, MD, PhD, MPH, senior research scientist, Kaiser Permanente, Oakland, California, and head of a study of 497 babies, published in *Archives of Pediatric & Adolescent Medicine.*

Don't Use Crib Bumper Pads

All 22 bumper pads examined in a recent study were found to carry a risk of causing suffocation or strangulation.

Reasons: An infant's head can get wedged between the pad and mattress…and some pads have ties longer than the industry standard of nine inches.

Bradley T. Thach, MD, professor of pediatrics, Washington University in St. Louis School of Medicine and staff physician, St. Louis Children's Hospital, and head of a study of crib bumper deaths, published in *The Journal of Pediatrics.*

4

Very Personal Problems

How to Choose the Best Gynecologist for You

You're in the gynecologist's office, feeling vulnerable as can be—naked except for that flimsy gown... feet up in the stirrups... exposing yourself to the world. Your physician is going about her exam, and when you muster up the nerve to mention some weird cramps you had, she sighs and looks at her watch.

If this sounds all too familiar, it's time to ask yourself, *Does my gynecologist see me as a whole person or just a pelvis?* For optimal wellness, you need to have at least one doctor who answers all of your questions and treats you with respect, acknowledging you as a collaborative member of your own health-care team. After all, you know your body better than anyone else.

When you feel pressured, the levels of certain brain chemicals are altered, making it likely that you will forget some of the questions

you had planned to ask the doctor. This could be dangerous.

Example: Suppose that along with those weird abdominal cramps, you've had a few embarrassing incidents with incontinence. If you're too flustered to mention these or if your doctor brushes you off with, "Every woman has those problems occasionally," you've missed the opportunity to investigate these early warning signs of ovarian cancer.

SHOULD YOU SAY "SO LONG"?

Ideally, a gynecologist will invite you to share information about your whole self—your home environment, workplace, emotional concerns, social support systems, family history, overall health and energy, and personal approach to health care. This makes accurate diagnoses much more likely. For instance, after taking appropriate steps to rule out potentially serious

Joel M. Evans, MD, obstetrician/gynecologist and founder/director of the Center for Women's Health, an integrative health-care facility in Stamford, Connecticut. He is founding diplomate of the American Board of Integrative Holistic Medicine.

health problems, the doctor can reassure you that your cramps are related to the stress of your new job, or that your occasional incontinence is caused by a pot-a-day coffee habit—but only if she knows about those aspects of your life.

I'm not saying that you should immediately leave your current gynecologist if she takes the hurry-up, waist-down approach. If you have an involved, caring internist or family physician as your primary care provider, you can stick with a gynecologist who focuses only on your reproductive organs if that feels right for you.

It's quite a different story if you lack confidence in the care you are receiving or feel objectified by a gynecologist who never looks beyond the speculum—especially if you use your gynecologist as your primary care physician, as many women do. In that case, try talking with the doctor about your needs. If that doesn't help, it is time to find a physician who is a better fit. Don't feel disloyal. You have a right to be cared for in a way that reflects who you are as a human being.

SHOPPING FOR A DOCTOR

The first step in finding a new gynecologist is to formulate a personal definition of the ideal doctor. To do this, make a list of what bothers you about your current doctor, as well as what you appreciate.

Examples: "He 'joked' that I was a hypochondriac"…"She gives only one-word answers to my questions"…"She's punctual." This clarifies that you want a doctor who takes your concerns seriously, answers questions completely and knows your time is valuable.

Next, get referrals from other doctors you respect—or from any nurses you know (they often have inside information about physicians). Ask friends to provide the names of their doctors.

Request a 30-minute consultation with any gynecologist you are considering switching to. For such a nonemergency visit, she should be able to accommodate you within a month or two. *During your initial consultation, ask the doctor…*

• **Where she was trained and how long she has been in practice.**

• **What certifications she holds.** She should be board-certified in gynecology, ideally with a subspecialty certificate in an area important to you, such as maternal/fetal medicine or gynecologic oncology.

• **What her philosophy on patient care is.** Beware of any response like, "I expect patients to trust in my expertise and comply with my instructions," which suggests a dogmatic approach that does not acknowledge patients' individual personalities and preferences.

• **How she would handle any specific concern you might have, such as whether to get genetic testing for breast cancer.** If you don't understand her response, ask for clarification. Discussing your particular health issues allows you to judge whether the doctor is right for you (and also increases the chances that insurance will pay for the visit).

If the doctor seems offended, recalcitrant, dismissive of your questions or eager for the consultation to be over, simply thank her for her time and leave.

THE INTEGRATIVE OPTION

In your deliberations, consider interviewing an integrative gynecologist—one who combines traditional gynecology with complementary and alternative medicine. The general philosophy of such physicians is that real health springs from prevention and involves an integration of the emotional, spiritual and physical. In other words, no one symptom is treated as a single event, but rather as a part of a larger picture.

For treatment, integrative gynecologists use numerous therapies, such as stress-reduction techniques, nutritional and herbal supplements, and diet and lifestyle changes to promote optimal health. The very nature of this approach to wellness—in which the patient is encouraged to be an active participant in her self-care—guarantees that an integrative gynecologist views a patient as a whole person, rather than a body part with a problem.

Integrative gynecologists graduate from a regular medical school and are board-certified in gynecology. In addition, they are certified through the Academy of Integrative Health & Medicine (858-240-9033, *www.aihm.org*), which requires specific additional training.

At present, in the US, there are only about 200 integrative physicians specializing in women's health, but this number is growing. *To find out if there is one in your area, contact…*

• **The Academy of Integrative Health & Medicine** (858-240-9033, *www.aihm.org*).

• **The Center for Mind-Body Medicine** (202-966-7338, *www.cmbm.org*).

• **The Institute for Functional Medicine** (800-228-0622, *www.functionalmedicine.org*).

Keep looking until you find a gynecologist who can provide the care and respect you deserve.

Nature's Rx for Women's Problems

Jamison Starbuck, ND, a naturopathic physician in family practice in Missoula, Montana. She is past president of the American Association of Naturopathic Physicians and a contributing editor to *The Alternative Advisor* (Time-Life).

Women often resort to quick drugstore fixes when they experience "female complaints." I advise women to consider their alternatives. Many women's health problems respond to gentle, natural medicines …and to lifestyle changes that help to improve your overall health. *My recommendations…*

• **Bacterial vaginosis (BV)** causes a gray-white discharge, mild burning and vaginal itching. Gynecologists often prescribe antibiotics to treat this condition.

But antibiotics can create problems. Like the digestive tract, the vagina is filled with bacteria that keep mucous membranes in good health. Antibiotics disrupt the vaginal "ecosystem" by eliminating not only the offending bacteria, but also the beneficial ones, like *lactobacillus.*

This can bring on another type of vaginal infection—*Candida vaginitis.* Also known as yeast infection, this causes vaginal itching and burning and a thick, white discharge.

For this condition, doctors typically prescribe antifungals—again upsetting the vaginal ecosystem and increasing the likelihood of BV. Many women get stuck in this cycle. *I tell my patients with these conditions to…*

• Avoid refined foods, sweets and alcohol. Each can weaken the immune system. Stick to these restrictions for at least one month after the infection clears up.

• Use capsules to encourage growth of beneficial bacteria. During the acute infection, insert one capsule of Oregon grape root (*Berberisaquifolium*) powder into the vagina each evening. Each morning, insert one lactobacillus acidophilus capsule. The capsules are available at most health food stores.

• Abstain from sex during treatment. It can irritate vaginal tissue.

An infection that's acute should clear up in one week. For stubborn cases, repeat the capsule protocol on alternating weeks for a total of four treatments.

• **Urinary tract infections (UTIs)** often occur when bacteria migrate from the vagina through the urethra into the bladder. Sexual intercourse, vaginal infection and chronic vaginal dryness increase your risk.

If you suffer from recurrent UTIs, see your family doctor for antibiotic treatment for the acute infection. *Then follow these steps to prevent relapse…*

• Drink about 64 ounces of water daily to rid your bladder of pesky bacteria.

• Take an acidophilus/bifidis supplement that contains three billion of these live organisms every night at bedtime.

• Drink 12 ounces of unsweetened cranberry juice each day. It acidifies your urine, preventing bacteria from adhering to the bladder wall. If you don't like cranberry juice—or don't want the extra calories—take a daily capsule containing 900 milligrams (mg) of cranberry extract.

• **Fibrocystic breasts and premenstrual syndrome (PMS)** can both be caused by poor dietary habits. If you have fibrocystic breasts, avoid caffeine and sugar…and cut back on fat and refined food. Eat more whole grains, beans, peas, fruits and veggies.

In addition, take 50 mg of vitamin B-6, 200 international units (IU) of vitamin E and 3,000 mg of flaxseed oil or 1,500 mg of evening primrose oil daily to curb inflammation.

Low progesterone levels may contribute to PMS. For this condition, follow the fibrocystic breast protocol and try chasteberry (*Vitex agnus-castus*) to boost production of the hormone progesterone. Two weeks before your menstrual period starts, take 60 drops of Vitex tincture daily. Discontinue for two weeks following menstruation, then repeat.

Note: Women who are pregnant or breast-feeding should check with their doctors before taking any herb.

Better Breast Health

Know how your breasts feel. Breast tissue might normally feel like butter…bubble wrap…gravel…even rocks. If you notice any difference between or change in the texture of your breasts, call your doctor—you may need to be screened for cancer.

M. Ellen Mahoney, MD, breast surgeon, Stanford University, and cofounder of the Community Breast Health Project, both in Palo Alto, California.

PMS Improves Memory

Perhaps due to fluctuating hormone levels, women with premenstrual syndrome (PMS) have heightened sensitivity to their surroundings—which helps memories form more permanently.

Bert S. Moore, PhD, dean of the School of Behavioral & Brain Sciences, University of Texas, Dallas.

Heavy Periods May Be Due to a Clotting Disorder

Duke University Medical Center, news release.

Bleeding disorders often go undiagnosed in women, say experts who've developed a new list of signs that might indicate a problem. The guidelines, published in the *American Journal of Obstetrics & Gynecology*, aren't meant only for doctors.

Women with heavy menstrual cycles should watch for these signs as well because about 25% of women with heavy menstruation have an undiagnosed bleeding disorder, said Andra James, MD, an obstetrician at Duke University Medical Center and the study's lead author. "Heavy bleeding should not be ignored," Dr. James said. "When a woman's blood can't clot normally, the most obvious sign is a heavy period."

But in many such cases, doctors don't suspect a blood-clotting problem. "Sometimes they think hormones are the cause, or fibroids," Dr. James said. "In some cases they recommend removal of the uterus or offer another gynecologic explanation when the real contributing factor is a blood-clotting disorder."

The researchers recommended that doctors and women be on the lookout for…

- **A personal history of heavy periods.**
- **Blood disorders among family members.**
- **Bruises when no injury has occurred.**
- **Bleeding for more than five minutes with minor wounds.**
- **Excessive or prolonged bleeding after dental extractions.**
- **Surgical bleeding that is greater than expected.**
- **Hemorrhaging that requires blood transfusions.**
- **Postpartum hemorrhaging that occurs in the days after delivery.**

"Too often, women think heavy bleeding is OK because the women in their family—who may also have an undiagnosed bleeding disorder—have heavy periods as well," Dr. James said. "We want women who continually experience abnormal, reproductive-tract bleeding, specifically heavy menstrual bleeding, to be alert to these other signs and approach their physicians about being evaluated."

For more information about bleeding disorders, visit the Web site of the U.S. Department of Health and Human Services Office on Women's Health (OWH), *www.womens health.gov.*

Chasteberry for Women

Mark A. Stengler, NMD, licensed naturopathic medical doctor in private practice, Encinitas, California... adjunct associate clinical professor at the National College of Natural Medicine, Portland, Oregon...author of *The Natural Physician's Healing Therapies* and co-author of *Prescription for Natural Cures* (both from Bottom Line Books).

If you were to examine some of the many "women's hormone-balancing" products in health-food stores and pharmacies, you would most likely see chasteberry (also known as *Vitex agnus-castus*) listed as an ingredient. It has been recommended for female conditions, including hormone-related acne, fibrocystic breast syndrome, endometriosis, infertility, lactation difficulties, menopausal hot flashes, menstrual disorders, ovarian cysts and uterine fibroids. In other words, it is touted as helping almost all major female conditions.

The herb comes from the berries of the chasteberry tree, actually a shrub found in subtropical climates. The ancient Greeks used chasteberry as a symbol of chastity in young women, hence the name "chaste berry" or "chaste tree."

HOW IT WORKS

Chasteberry does not contain hormones. It acts on the pituitary gland in the brain to increase the production of *luteinizing hormone* (LH). LH stimulates the ovaries to release eggs, as occurs with ovulation. Ovulation triggers a surge in levels of the hormone *progesterone*. This release of progesterone is important in maintaining a balance with the other major female hormone, *estrogen*. Research has shown that some premenopausal women do not ovulate regularly. This sets the stage for what is known as "estrogen dominance"—too much estrogen relative to progesterone. By helping to normalize progesterone levels, chasteberry promotes hormone balance. This is why it is effective for so many female conditions, including premenstrual syndrome and fibrocystic breast disease as well as uterine fibroids in women of all ages, which are in large part caused by estrogen dominance.

Chasteberry also has been shown to lower levels of the hormone *prolactin*. When elevated, this hormone, which is secreted by the pituitary gland, is associated with premenstrual syndrome, irregular menstrual cycles and infertility.

DOSAGE

For all of these conditions, I commonly recommend 160 mg to 240 mg daily of a 0.6% *aucubin* or 0.5% *agnuside* extract (important active ingredients) in capsule form—available directly from Enzymatic Therapy (800-783-2286, *www.enzy.com*) and Natural Factors (sold by Vitacost, 800-381-0759, *www.vitacost.com*). Or I suggest 40 drops of the tincture in four ounces of water, taken once daily.

For best results, chasteberry should be used until the problem is alleviated and then for an additional three months. Women may notice improvements within two menstrual cycles.

Chasteberry often needs to be taken for four to six months or longer for long-standing cases of hormone imbalance that have resulted in infertility, amenorrhea (no menstrual cycles), irregular menstrual cycles or endometriosis.

Mild digestive upset, nausea, headaches and skin rash are infrequent side effects of chasteberry. Stop taking it if they occur.

Chasteberrry should not be used by women taking birth control pills or injections. It also should be avoided by those taking drugs that block dopamine receptors, such as the antipsychotic medication *haloperidol* (Haldol).

As with most herbs, chasteberry should be avoided during pregnancy, although it is helpful for lactation in nursing mothers.

Lastly, some women experience an "adjustment phase" during the first few months of taking chasteberry. It is not uncommon for the menstrual cycle to shorten or lengthen, and flow can become lighter or heavier than what it was previously. This adjustment phase almost always normalizes after two to three months of use.

Natural Treatment For Endometriosis

Pycnogenol, an antioxidant plant extract from the bark of the French maritime pine tree, can reduce by one-third symptoms of endometriosis, such as severe menstrual pain, lower abdominal pain, painful intercourse and infertility. It has fewer side effects than the conventional treatment for endometriosis—contraceptive hormone therapy, such as birth control pills.

Dosage: 30 milligrams, twice a day. Pycnogenol is available in most health-food stores. It is generally safe, but do check with your doctor before starting any new treatment.

Takafumi Kohama, MD, chief, department of obstetrics and gynecology, Keiju Medical Center, Kanazawa University School of Medicine, Ishokawa, Japan, and leader of a study of 58 women, published in *The Journal of Reproductive Medicine.*

Do You *Really* Need A Hysterectomy?

Togas Tulandi, MD, professor of obstetrics and gynecology and Milton Leong Chair in reproductive medicine at McGill University and chief of the department of obstetrics and gynecology at the Sir Mortimer B. Davis Jewish General Hospital, both in Montreal.

I magine this scenario—a woman has uterine fibroids (benign growths on the uterine wall) that cause heavy menstrual bleeding and pelvic pain. Her doctor says that she needs a *hysterectomy* (surgical removal of the uterus). She complies—then experiences several days of severe postoperative pain, misses several weeks of work and feels an unexpected sense of loss. Eventually she switches to a different physician—and is shocked to learn that her hysterectomy may not have been necessary at all.

This is an all-too-common occurrence. Many women are told that hysterectomy is the only appropriate treatment for their conditions —even when medical advances may provide nonsurgical treatments or less invasive surgical options.

Self-defense: If your physician insists that a hysterectomy is the only way to go, seek a second or even a third opinion.

SURGERY WORRIES

Second only to cesarean section, hysterectomy is the most common surgical procedure performed on women in the US. By age 60, one in three women has had a hysterectomy.

Gynecologic problems often can be treated without resorting to hysterectomy—yet as many as two-thirds of women who undergo hysterectomy do so without a compelling medical necessity. *Concerns...*

• **Like any major surgery, hysterectomy involves risks**—the possibility of blood clots, excessive bleeding, infection and adverse reactions to anesthesia. In rare cases, the urinary tract and/or rectum are damaged during surgery.

• **In premenopausal women, hysterectomy brings an abrupt end to menstruation.** If ovaries also are removed, it can trigger severe or persistent menopausal symptoms, such as hot flashes, lowered libido and depression.

• **Some women undergo hysterectomy only to find that the surgery does not completely relieve their symptoms.** This often occurs with chronic pelvic pain (which may be caused by an undiagnosed intestinal or urinary tract problem, rather than a uterine problem)...and with *endometriosis*, a condition in which tissue from the uterine lining (which should stay inside the uterus) attaches itself to organs outside the uterus.

Note: Hysterectomy generally is warranted for the following conditions...

• Uncontrolled uterine bleeding, due to complications of childbirth, or extreme fibroid-related bleeding.

• Cancer of the uterus, cervix or ovary.

• Severe uterine prolapse (in which the uterus protrudes outside the vaginal opening).

WHAT YOU NEED TO KNOW

If your physician suggests hysterectomy, be sure to ask...

• **What could happen if I don't have the hysterectomy?** If the risks are modest, you may prefer to continue as you are. If potential consequences are serious, such as severe hemorrhaging or debilitating pain, ask how commonly they occur.

•**How urgent is my situation?** Unless it's an emergency, you may be able to take several months to decide about surgery.

•**Will my condition improve on its own after menopause?** For example, once menstruation ends, hormones that prompt endometriosis and fibroids generally no longer cause problems—so consider whether you are close enough to menopause (which typically occurs between ages 48 and 52) to wait it out. On the other hand, uterine prolapse tends to worsen with age—so waiting won't help.

•**Are there less invasive surgical alternatives or nonsurgical therapies?** Discuss the risks and benefits of your treatment options (as described below), including how each affects fertility, if this is relevant for you.

•**How effective are these alternatives?** To put an end to symptoms permanently, hysterectomy could be the best choice. If you would be satisfied with partial or temporary improvement, try other options first.

ALTERNATIVES TO HYSTERECTOMY

Here are common gynecologic problems and treatments that may allow you to avoid hysterectomy...

•**Abnormal vaginal bleeding,** due to menstrual problems, endometriosis or endometrial hyperplasia (overgrowth of the uterine lining).

•Intrauterine device (IUD) with progesterone is a small hormone-coated contraceptive device that can be left in the uterus for up to five years.

•Endometrial ablation, an outpatient procedure, uses a surgical device to destroy the inner layer of the lining of the uterus, stopping or severely reducing menstrual flow.

•**Endometriosis,** which can cause pain, heavy bleeding and infertility.

•Oral contraceptives taken continuously —without the usual week off each month— relieve mild-to-moderate symptoms.

•GnRH agonists (medications that block estrogen production) temporarily halt menstruation and shrink endometrial tissue, buying you time if you are close to menopause.

•Laparoscopic excision involves inserting a lighted fiber-optic tube (laparoscope) and surgical instruments through small abdominal incisions, then removing the errant endometrial tissue.

•**Uterine fibroids,** growths that can vary in size from a speck to a melon and may number from one to hundreds. With the procedures below, fibroids may not recur.

•GnRH agonist medications temporarily shrink fibroids.

•High-intensity focused ultrasound combines ultrasound waves and magnetic resonance imaging to destroy fibroid cells.

•Myomectomy removes individual fibroids with a laser, electrical current or scalpel.

•Uterine fibroid embolization shrinks fibroids by blocking their blood supply with tiny plastic beads injected into small blood vessels.

•**Uterine prolapse** that is mild to moderate (the uterus drops into the vagina but does not yet bulge out of the vaginal opening).

•Oral estrogen therapy helps thicken supporting pelvic tissues.

•A pessary is a plastic cap worn in the vagina to reposition the uterus.

IF YOU OPT FOR HYSTERECTOMY

Once the decision has been made to have a hysterectomy, discuss the following with your doctor...

•**What will surgery remove?**

•Supracervical hysterectomy removes the uterus but not the cervix. It should not be used if your Pap test reveals potentially precancerous cervical cells.

•Hysterectomy with bilateral salpingo-oophorectomy removes the uterus, fallopian tubes and ovaries. I typically recommend this procedure to patients who are close to or past menopause.

•Total hysterectomy removes the uterus and cervix, leaving ovaries intact. This often is used for women with severe uterine bleeding.

•Radical hysterectomy removes the uterus, cervix, top of the vagina and most tissue surrounding the cervix. It generally is used to treat cancer.

•**How will the surgery be done?**

•Abdominal hysterectomy requires an abdominal incision of about six inches. I use the procedure when a woman has a very large uterus

85

or scarring from previous abdominal surgeries. *Recovery:* About six weeks.

• Laparoscopic hysterectomy is done through several small abdominal incisions. It often is used for endometriosis or persistent pelvic pain. *Recovery:* About two weeks.

• Vaginal hysterectomy involves a small incision in the vagina through which the uterus is cut and removed. Often used for uterine prolapse, it leaves no visible scars. *Recovery:* About two weeks.

Better Alternatives To Hysterectomy

Esther Eisenberg, MD, MPH, professor of obstetrics and gynecology, and director, division of reproductive endocrinology, Vanderbilt University School of Medicine, Nashville. She is coauthor of *Hysterectomy: Exploring Your Options* (Johns Hopkins).

During the past 25 years, advances in gynecologic surgery have caused a steady decline in the number of hysterectomies (removal of the entire uterus) performed in the US.

Now: Recent surgical techniques are giving women even more options for treating abnormal uterine bleeding as well as fibroid tumors.

ABNORMAL UTERINE BLEEDING

This condition typically occurs in women older than age 45. It results from a high level of estrogen that is not balanced by progesterone. Ovulation does not occur, but the *endometrium* (lining of the uterus) thickens and is then shed incompletely and irregularly, causing bleeding.

In the past, abnormal uterine bleeding was treated by a complete hysterectomy.

Alternatives to hysterectomy…

• **Endometrial ablation.** This approach, requires no incision and is performed on an outpatient basis. It stops uterine bleeding in up to 80% of women.

How it works: A *hysteroscope* (a thin, lighted fiber-optic tube) is inserted through the vagina and cervix into the uterus. An electric current or laser is then used to heat and destroy the endometrium. Scar tissue may develop, which is likely to impair a woman's ability to become pregnant. Other potential risks include perforation of the uterine wall and injury to adjacent structures, such as burns to the bowel.

• **Thermal balloon ablation.** This newer technique appears to be as effective as endometrial ablation, and typically, has fewer risks. However, not all hospitals have the equipment that is needed to perform thermal balloon ablation.

How it works: A balloon that is filled with fluid is placed in the uterus and heated until it destroys the endometrium without damaging surrounding tissue.

UTERINE FIBROIDS

Up to 40% of hysterectomies are performed to remove uterine fibroids. Although the cause of these tumors is unknown, recent research has linked them to a genetic mutation. Fibroids are almost always benign and often produce no symptoms.

However, fibroids can cause extremely heavy or frequent menstrual flow (sometimes leading to anemia)…chronic pain…bloating…pressure on the bladder and other internal organs… infertility…and/or abdominal swelling. In these cases, surgery is often the best solution.

Procedures to consider…

• **Myomectomy.** Currently the preferred treatment for women who want to keep their reproductive options open, this procedure removes fibroids but retains the woman's uterus to allow for pregnancy.

How it works: A surgeon makes an abdominal incision, cuts the fibroid out and repairs the wall of the uterus using sutures.

• **Laparoscopic myomectomy.** This procedure is less invasive than the standard myomectomy, but it may not be advisable if the fibroid is too large.

How it works: A *laparoscope* (a thin, lighted viewing tube) and other instruments are introduced through a small (less than 1 inch) abdominal incision. The fibroids are cut into fragments small enough to be removed through the abdominal incision or another small incision made through the vaginal wall. Most women can sustain a pregnancy after they have undergone laparoscopic myomectomy.

However, there is increased risk of uterine rupture at delivery because the laparoscopic closure of the uterine muscle may not be as effective as in a standard myomectomy.

In one out of three women who receive standard or laparoscopic myomectomy, fibroid tumors eventually recur.

• **Hysteroscopy.** An even less invasive technique than laparoscopic myomectomy, hysteroscopy is now being used for some submucus fibroids, which protrude inside the uterine cavity. (Many fibroids are embedded in the uterine muscle.)

How it works: After the cervix is dilated, a hysteroscope is passed through the cervix into the uterus, which is inflated with gas or fluid to provide a better view. Because dilation is painful, a local or regional anesthetic is usually administered.

In a hysteroscopy, fibroids are removed using an electrosurgical tool that burns the tissue so that the fibroids can be removed in pieces. The procedure, which requires no incision, is performed on an outpatient basis, and recovery takes two to three days.

• **High-intensity focused ultrasound.** This is a promising experimental procedure.

How it works: While the patient lies in a *magnetic resonance imaging* (MRI) scanner, a doctor uses the image to aim heat-producing, high-intensity focused ultrasound beams at the tumor to destroy it.

The patient is awake throughout the high-intensity focused ultrasound, and no incisions are required. Currently available at such institutions as the Johns Hopkins Hospital in Baltimore, Brigham and Women's Hospital in Boston and the Mayo Clinic in Rochester, Minnesota, this procedure has been found to be safe and effective in preliminary studies.

MORE RECENT HYSTERECTOMY OPTIONS

Despite the availability of newer treatments, up to 600,000 women each year still choose to have a hysterectomy.

Reason: A hysterectomy provides a permanent cure for abnormal uterine bleeding and fibroid tumors and also eliminates the risk of uterine cancer.

Newer, less invasive types of hysterectomy have sharply reduced hospitalization—to just two to three days for many patients—and hastened recovery to as little as a week.

• **Supracervical hysterectomy.** The uterus, but not the cervix, is removed through an abdominal incision. This surgery has fewer complications than total hysterectomy, but it still leaves a woman at risk for cervical cancer.

• **Laparoscopic hysterectomy.** The uterus is removed using a laparoscope inserted through a small abdominal incision.

• **Vaginal hysterectomy.** The uterus is removed through an incision inside the vagina. This procedure includes removal of both the cervix and the uterus. It can only be performed on fibroids that are small enough to pass through the vagina. Vaginal hysterectomy can also be performed with laparoscopic assistance.

Noninvasive Treatment For Fibroids

Phyllis J. Gee, MD, obstetrician-gynecologist and medical director, North Texas Uterine Fibroid Institute, Plano, Texas.

InSightec, the privately held company that developed ExAblate 2000, *www.insightec.com.*

US Food and Drug Administration, *www.fda.gov.*

Fibroid tumors can cause very troubling symptoms in some women, including heavy or prolonged menstrual periods, pelvic pain and pressure on the bladder or bowel, to name just a few.

The problem is that most treatment options—especially life-altering hysterectomy—are really not "good." Hence, fibroid sufferers were fated to "pick their poison" with regard to the least unpleasant treatment option. The good news is that there's a noninvasive alternative that uses ultrasound…and it's been approved by the US Food and Drug Administration (FDA).

AN INTERACTIVE COMBINATION— MRI AND ULTRASOUND

Magnetic resonance guided focused ultrasound (MRgFUS) has been available to women in the US since it was approved by the FDA in

2004, but treatment centers are limited. Phyllis J. Gee, MD, an obstetrician-gynecologist and medical director of the North Texas Uterine Fibroid Institute in Plano, Texas, explains more about this innovative approach.

According to Dr. Gee, ExAblate combines *magnetic resonance imaging* (MRI) with focused ultrasound to seek out and destroy cells. For many women, this procedure represents a safe and effective alternative to invasive surgery such as hysterectomy (surgical removal of the uterus) and myomectomy (surgical removal of fibroids while leaving the uterus intact).

The treatment, developed by the Israel–based firm InSightec, is available in many states (visit *www.insightec.com* for more details about locations).

HOW IT WORKS

ExAblate is performed on an outpatient basis, and usually takes three to four hours. During the procedure, a woman lies inside an MRI scanner, which generates three-dimensional images of the fibroid and surrounding tissue. The role of MRI is to guide and monitor ultrasound treatment, allowing for precise targeting of highly focused waves to the fibroid. The high-intensity ultrasound energy waves raise fibroid tissue temperature sufficiently to coagulate it, in a process known as thermal ablation. Over time, the tumor continues to shrink and the body eventually reabsorbs it. Among the benefits of ExAblate is that it is not as "messy" as other fibroid procedures, which can be more risky and invasive.

Throughout ExAblate, the patient is mildly sedated, so she is conscious but not fully alert. It is normal to experience a feeling of warmth in the abdomen. The treatment is generally well tolerated and the incidence of side effects is relatively low. So far, side effects do not appear to be severe or lasting. Possible risks of the procedure include skin burns, back or leg pain, abdominal cramping, nausea, vaginal discharge and urinary tract infection.

However, Dr. Gee points out that as more procedures are done, there are fewer complications. For example, to prevent burns, practitioners have learned to make adjustments such as making sure the patient is well shaved, and the skin has been thoroughly cleansed with alcohol so that no oils or talc interfere with the passage of waves.

WEIGHING THE PROS AND CONS

ExAblate is not for everyone, including women who plan future pregnancies (since it may alter the composition and strength of uterine tissue)…women who have a large number of fibroids…and cases in which fibroids are close to vital organs such as the bowel or bladder. Like any medical procedure, ExAblate has both advantages and disadvantages.

Advantages…

• **Focused ultrasound is noninvasive,** so does not carry the risks of surgical procedures and general anesthesia.

• **No hospital stay is required.** (Traditional invasive surgeries require one to several days of hospitalization.)

• **Most women can resume normal activities** within one to three days of treatment.

Disadvantages…

• **There is always the risk of the aforementioned side effects**.

• **New fibroids can develop,** and more than two out of 10 women are likely to require additional treatment within a year either to treat new fibroids or to complete the destruction of the original one. Tumors that were treated will not regrow.

However, problems can develop with new or untreated fibroids. This can occur with all fibroid treatments except, of course, hysterectomy.

• **Because focused ultrasound is relatively new, it does not have a significant track record for safety,** and insurance may not cover it. The average cost is several thousand dollars.

We asked Dr. Gee how claustrophobic women tolerated ExAblate and she told us that in her experience, this has not been a problem. Women are positioned stomach down, feet first in the MRI machine, so their heads are not actually in the tunnel. They're also medicated, and most women simply sleep through the procedure, says Dr. Gee.

LOOKING TOWARD THE FUTURE

Recent studies of this treatment have been promising, such as research from Germany that showed focused ultrasound to be technically successful for 93.5% of the women studied. Current trials to study ExAblate are ongoing.

Only time will tell whether ExAblate is a long-term, safe and effective answer to treating fibroids. In the meantime, if you suffer from fibroids and are considering invasive surgery, it's a worthwhile option to explore with your physician. For a list of treatment sites, go to *www.fusfoundation.org/diseases-and-conditions/womens-health/uterine-fibroids*. (For another nonsurgical option, see page 90.)

Exercise May Help Prevent Fibroids

These benign uterine tumors, which may cause infertility, bleeding and pain, are the leading cause of hysterectomies in the US.

Recent finding: Women who do recreational exercise or walk seven or more hours a week are less likely to develop fibroids than sedentary women.

Donna Day Baird, PhD, epidemiologist, division of intramural research, National Institute of Environmental Health Sciences, Research Triangle Park, North Carolina, and lead author of a study of 1,189 women, published in *American Journal of Epidemiology*.

Breakthrough Surgery

Ralph V. Clayman, MD, professor and dean of the University of California, Irvine School of Medicine. The founder and coeditor of the *Journal of Endourology*, he is also on the editorial board of the *Journal of Robotic Surgery* and has published many peer-reviewed articles and book chapters.

If you've ever had an operation, chances are your surgeon did not explain in detail the trauma that commonly occurs to a patient's body—some surgeries require incisions up to 12 inches long, and tissues and organs routinely get pushed aside to improve the surgeon's visibility.

Recent development: With sophisticated new technology, patients can now undergo robotic-assisted surgery performed by surgeons who sit at a console several feet from the operating table, moving joysticks (similar to those used for video games) and other controls to manipulate lights, cameras and instruments inside the patient's body.

The FDA has approved the use of a robotic system for several procedures, such as gallbladder removal, hysterectomy (removal of the uterus), certain procedures performed in the chest (including repair of heart valves and surgeries involving the lungs) as well as radical prostatectomy (removal of the prostate gland).

A NEW FRONTIER

Robotic-assisted surgery is the latest development in endoscopic surgery, which aims to reduce pain and trauma by using minimally invasive devices, such as tiny, flexible viewing tubes (endoscopes) through which surgical instruments can be introduced.

Increased training among surgeons and greater accessibility to costly robotic-assisted systems (a complete system can easily exceed $1.2 million) has only recently made this type of surgery widely available.

About 500 to 600 robotic units are now in use in the US—mostly at large, university-based medical centers.

WHAT THE TECHNOLOGY DOES

Robotic-assisted devices are designed to do things that are difficult for humans to do on their own. *Important benefits...*

•**No hand tremor.** With delicate procedures, the slightest amount of hand tremor can compromise the results. Robotic arms have no tremor.

•**Better visibility.** The imaging devices used in robotic-assisted surgery can magnify up to 15 times, compared with the two- to four-times magnification that's possible using a surgical loupe (a small magnifying lens) with conventional surgery.

•**Greater access.** The mechanical arms of robotic-assisted systems have a greater degree of movement—including flexing and rotation—than human wrists and hands. In addition, many of the instruments are much smaller than human fingers, allowing surgeons to more easily reach out-of-the-way places.

• **Less surgeon fatigue.** Rather than spending four to seven hours standing over the patient, the surgeon can sit down…and have an easier time staying mentally focused.

POTENTIAL LIMITATIONS

If problems occur during robotic-assisted surgery—an inability to repair a heart valve, for example—surgeons have the equipment and resources on hand to complete the procedure with conventional surgery. But the new technology does present unique challenges.

Important considerations…

• **Lack of sensation.** With conventional surgery, surgeons depend on their sense of touch to tell if they're cutting at the right pressure, when they're making stitches tight enough, etc. Because robotic devices don't provide such "force feedback," surgeons must learn to use visual feedback to achieve the same results— such as adequately tight stitches—that are possible with conventional surgery.

• **Lengthier operations.** At the University of Michigan Medical Center, surgeons reported that robotic-assisted radical prostatectomies took an average of 3.5 hours, compared with 2.6 hours for open procedures. Lengthier procedures can potentially increase a patient's risks for blood loss during the procedure as well as slow recovery.

Important: The length of robotic-assisted operations will probably decline as surgeons gain expertise with the new technology—and the potentially improved results may outweigh the slight risks resulting from increased operating times.

IS IT RIGHT FOR YOU?

Robotic-assisted surgery is best suited to reconstructive procedures that involve extensive suturing and rejoining of tissues, such as uterine prolapse repair and heart valve replacement. Conventional open or laparoscopic surgery (which entails use of an endoscope) is best for such procedures as removal of a large cancerous tumor. The preparation steps and anesthesia for robotic and conventional surgery are the same, but robotic-assisted surgery has a lower risk for infection because of the smaller incisions typically used.

Insurance covers the cost of robotic surgery for many procedures. When considering whether robotic-assisted surgery is right for you, ask your surgeon about his/her overall experience in the planned procedure, as well as his experience in performing the procedure as robotic-assisted surgery.

Nonsurgical Fibroid Removal Can Improve Sex Life

Painful uterine fibroids can be removed without surgery—and the procedure also can improve a woman's sex life. The nonsurgical option uterine fibroid embolization eliminates fibroids by blocking their blood supply. The 90-minute treatment is very safe and has been shown to improve sexual desire, arousal and satisfaction by eliminating excessive menstrual bleeding as well as the pain and pressure of fibroids. The procedure is not used as often as it could be because not enough physicians are familiar with it. The risks are infection (less than 1%) and possibly pushing a woman into menopause (1% to 5% depending on age).

Robert Vogelzang, MD, Albert Nemcek Education Professor of Radiology, Northwestern University Feinberg School of Medicine, Chicago.

Ovaries Should Stay…

Most women undergoing hysterectomy should not have their ovaries removed. A hysterectomy is the surgical removal of all or part of the uterus. Women past child-bearing age often have their ovaries removed at the same time to protect against ovarian cancer.

Recent finding: Ovary removal increases risk of dying from heart disease and hip fracture. Prophylactic ovary removal still should be considered for women whose family history puts them at high risk for developing ovarian cancer.

William H. Parker, MD, clinical professor, David Geffen School of Medicine, University of California, Los Angeles, and coauthor of *A Gynecologist's Second Opinion* (Plume). His analysis of ovary removal was published in *Obstetrics & Gynecology*.

Ovarian Torsion

Ovarian torsion is a twisting of the ovary around the vessels that supply it with blood. The twisting interferes with blood flow, causing extreme abdominal pain, nausea, vomiting, diarrhea or constipation. Torsion is usually caused by a large cyst or benign tumor inside the ovary. If this condition is not treated promptly, the ovary can die. Ovarian torsion is treated with laparoscopic surgery to remove the cyst and/or reposition the ovary. The condition is not hereditary.

Jonathan Scher, MD, assistant clinical professor of obstetrics, gynecology and reproductive science, Mount Sinai Medical Center, New York City.

Surgery Reduces Cancer Risk

More evidence that breast and ovary removal reduces cancer risk for women at high risk for breast and ovarian cancer. For women with the BRCA-1 or BRCA-2 mutations, which increase risk for both types of cancer, surgery is more effective than rigorous screening.

Recent study: Four years after preventive double mastectomy, none of the high-risk women developed breast cancer…but 7% who had intensive screening without surgery did. Only 1% of women at high risk for ovarian cancer who had at least one ovary and fallopian tube removed developed the disease, versus 6% of women who did not have the surgery.

Claudine Isaacs, MD, medical director of cancer assessment and risk evaluation program, Georgetown Lombardi Comprehensive Cancer Center, Washington, DC.

Is PCOS Hurting Your Health?

Richard S. Legro, MD, professor of obstetrics and gynecology specializing in reproductive endocrinology at Pennsylvania State University College of Medicine in Hershey. He is coauthor of *Polycystic Ovary Syndrome: A Guide to Clinical Management* (Informa Healthcare).

A little-known syndrome may be putting older women at increased risk for heart disease, diabetes, even cancer.

For years, many doctors believed that *polycystic ovary syndrome* (PCOS)—which is caused by excessive production of male hormones (androgens), such as *testosterone*—was a disorder affecting mostly younger women. Today, more health-care providers are aware that PCOS not only continues beyond the childbearing years, but it can put women in midlife and beyond at risk for serious health problems.

Worrisome: Many older women who have PCOS have never been accurately diagnosed, and so they are not getting the treatment they need.

RECOGNIZING THE SYMPTOMS

PCOS can cause many different symptoms. Some are similar to symptoms we associate with both menopause and aging. Also, not all women with PCOS share the same symptoms. For these reasons, PCOS often goes unrecognized—even though the condition may affect 5% to 10% of all women. *Symptoms can include…*

• **Infrequent or irregular menstrual periods or periods** that stop altogether before the typical age of menopause (ages 48 to 55).

• **Excess hair growth on the face and body.**

• **Thinning hair on the scalp.**

• **Sleep apnea** (repeated halts in breathing during sleep).

- **Acne.**
- **Obesity.**
- **High blood sugar or diabetes.**
- **High cholesterol.**
- **High blood pressure.**
- **Multiple ovarian cysts** (though not all women with PCOS have cystic ovaries, and not all women with ovarian cysts have PCOS).

DIAGNOSING PCOS LATER IN LIFE

A diagnosis of PCOS during perimenopause (the years leading up to menopause) or after menopause is complicated because physicians can't use the pattern of a woman's periods to guide them. Still, if I see a patient who has many of the symptoms associated with PCOS, I ask what her periods were like before. If they were infrequent or irregular, PCOS is likely.

Because PCOS is defined by a cluster of symptoms, there is no single simple test for the disease. A typical workup for PCOS includes blood tests for glucose (sugar) levels and for elevated levels of male hormones. However, the key to diagnosis is the overall pattern—a history of absent or irregular periods, obesity, high blood sugar levels and the presence of other symptoms associated with PCOS.

DANGERS OF PCOS

Our biggest concern for patients with PCOS is that they are at increased risk for serious—even life-threatening—diseases, such as...

- **Cardiovascular disease.** Data from the ongoing Nurses' Health Study, the 11-state study of women's health, found a connection between highly irregular periods and the later development of heart disease, possibly due to undiagnosed PCOS.
- **Diabetes.** With PCOS, the body's ability to metabolize sugars is impaired, which can lead to high blood sugar levels and diabetes. Complications of diabetes can include heart problems, kidney disease, nerve damage to the feet and eye problems that can lead to blindness.
- **Endometrial (uterine) cancer.** Irregularities of the menstrual cycle increase the supply of estrogen to the uterus, raising the risk for abnormal bleeding and cancer.

One positive aspect: The male hormones that cause PCOS symptoms also may increase bone density, giving postmenopausal PCOS patients some degree of protection from osteoporosis and fractures.

PREVENTION AND TREATMENT

Until we learn more about why some women get PCOS, much of our focus is on treating individual symptoms and encouraging women to make healthy lifestyle changes.

- **Keep weight at an appropriate level.** This is the number-one thing you can do to lower your risk for heart disease and diabetes. Studies show that dietary changes and exercise are helpful weight-management tools for women with PCOS. If you are overweight, consider working with a nutritionist to devise a suitable weight-loss plan. I advise everyone to exercise at least three times per week, for a total of at least two-and-a-half hours weekly.
- **See your doctor regularly.** Cholesterol and blood pressure checks, a discussion of any family history of heart disease (especially cardiac disease at an early age), weight-management encouragement and glucose tolerance testing all should be performed as a matter of routine health care by either your regular physician or an endocrinologist.

Important: If you are postmenopausal, immediately report any vaginal bleeding to your doctor—it needs to be investigated.

- **Consider medication,** such as the oral diabetes medication *metformin* (Glucophage) and/or cholesterol-lowering statin drugs. Work with your physician to find medications that are appropriate for you.

If You Have an Ovarian Cyst...

Arnold P. Advincula, MD, professor of obstetrics and gynecology, University of Central Florida School of Medicine and co-director of minimally invasive surgery at Florida Hospital Celebration Health, in Celebration. He is a pioneer of robotic gynecologic surgery.

Ovarian cysts are fluid-filled sacs that develop in a woman's ovaries. They occur in about 15% of postmenopausal women and a greater percentage of premenopausal women. Although most ovarian cysts produce no symptoms, some cause abdominal aches or pressure...discomfort during intercourse...heavy or irregular periods...bloating, indigestion and frequent urination ...and/or facial and body hair growth (due to hormonal imbalances).

Dangers: A cyst can rupture, hemorrhage or lead to ovarian torsion (twisting), causing extreme abdominal pain that requires emergency care. While most cysts are benign, some can be cancerous.

•**Cyst formation.** Each month during a woman's reproductive years, one of her ovaries develops a saclike follicle that releases an egg. Usually, the empty follicle eventually dissolves —but sometimes it persists and fills with fluid, forming what is called a *corpus luteum cyst.* Similarly, if a follicle does not release its egg, it can continue to grow and form a *functional cyst.* These are common in women who have polycystic ovary syndrome (PCOS) or who take fertility drugs, such as *clomiphene* (Clomid). They are rare after menopause.

Other types of benign cysts include *cystadenomas,* which form from cells on the ovary's outer surface...*dermoids,* which contain many types of cells...and *endometriomas,* which can form on the ovaries of women who have endometriosis (a condition in which tissue of the uterine lining grows outside the uterus).

•**Detection.** Symptomless cysts usually are detected during a pelvic exam and confirmed with ultrasound. Occasionally, they are found when an imaging test has been done for some other reason. A blood test known as the CA-125 *protein* may be ordered if there are concerns about potential malignancy. If a cyst is small, causes no symptoms and is not suspected of being malignant, the doctor may opt to observe it closely through a series of follow-up exams. For premenopausal women, birth control pills can help prevent more cysts from forming but do not necessarily treat existing ones.

•**The right doctor.** Your regular gynecologist can diagnose and treat an ovarian cyst that appears to be benign. If screening tests suggest a malignancy, see a gynecologic oncologist.

Referrals: Society of Gynecologic Oncology, 312-235-4060, *www.sgo.org.*

•**Treatment.** *Options for cysts that are symptomatic...*

•Surgical removal of the cyst (cystectomy). This usually is an outpatient laparoscopic procedure performed through tiny incisions in the abdomen. It typically is used when a cyst becomes large or painful, or on an emergency basis in cases of rupture, hemorrhage or torsion. Because ovaries remain intact, this procedure preserves fertility and normal hormone production for premenopausal women.

•Surgical removal of one or both ovaries (oophorectomy). In cases where a cystectomy is not appropriate, the entire ovary can be removed. This often is done as an outpatient laparoscopic procedure, though sometimes more invasive surgery is needed.

PAP After Hysterectomy?

Lauren F. Streicher, MD, assistant clinical professor, department of obstetrics and gynecology, Northwestern University Feinberg School of Medicine, Chicago, and author of *The Essential Guide to Hysterectomy* (M. Evans).

Often hysterectomy does not include removal of the cervix. If you have a cervix or had a total hysterectomy to treat either invasive cervical cancer or a precancerous condition, you still need to get annual Pap smears and, if your doctor recommends it, a test for human papillomavirus (HPV).

But that's not the end of the story. Your gynecologist is the only one of your physicians who routinely checks for vaginal cancer. Although rare, vaginal cancer often goes undetected until it has progressed because it causes no symptoms in the initial stages. To get an early diagnosis—which increases survival rates —your doctor must visually check your vagina and also do a vaginal smear to screen for abnormal cells.

Your gynecologist also needs to check your outer genitalia for cancer of the vulva, the fourth-most-common gynecologic malignancy. In addition, the doctor should do a bimanual exam—one hand on your belly and two fingers inside your vagina—to check for ovarian cancer and colon cancer.

Check for This Little-Known Skin Cancer

The sexually transmitted *human papillomavirus* (HPV), linked to cervical cancer, can cause genital skin cancer. This cancer—squamous cell carcinoma—is more common in the genitalia of women than men. If treated early, there is a high cure rate. Women are three times more likely to die from this type of skin cancer than men.

Self-defense: Examine genitals monthly using a mirror, and contact your gynecologist if you find anything unusual.

Martin A. Weinstock, MD, professor of dermatology and community health, Brown University, Providence, and senior author of a study of 75,000 skin cancer deaths, published in *Journal of Investigative Dermatology*.

Cervical Cancer Vaccine Not Just for Teens

The Lancet, news release.

The human papillomavirus (HPV) vaccine works for women ages 24 to 45 who aren't already infected by HPV, the virus that has been linked to cervical cancer and other cervical diseases.

That's the finding from Nubia Munoz, MD, of the National Institute of Cancer in Bogota, Columbia, who noted that women's rising age at first marriage and increasing divorce rates have led to more widespread premarital intercourse and pairing with new sexual partners around middle age.

THE STUDY

Their study included more than 3,200 women, ages 24 to 45, with no history of cervical

disease or cancer or genital warts caused by HPV types 6, 11, 16 and 18. The women received either the quadrivalent HPV vaccine, which protects against the four HPV types, or a placebo at day one and months two and six of the study.

The women were followed for about 2.2 years and the researchers identified four cases of infection or disease in the vaccinated group, compared to 41 cases in the placebo group. That means the vaccine was 91% effective against all four virus strains.

When they looked at only the two most common HPV strains, 16 and 18, the researchers found four cases in the vaccine group and 23 in the placebo group, making the vaccine 83% effective against those two HPV types.

For women infected with at least one of the HPV types or an HPV-associated disease, the vaccine was only 30% effective. "[This result] suggests that the public health effect of vaccinating women aged 25 to 45 years will be smaller than that recorded after vaccinating susceptible adolescents. This notion will be assessed in future cost-benefit analyses," the study authors wrote.

The findings were published in *The Lancet*. For more information on HPV, visit the Web site of the US National Cancer Institute (NCI), *www.cancer.gov/about-cancer*.

The Cervical Cancer Vaccine Can Save Lives

The vaccine gardasil protects against two high-risk strains of the sexually transmitted human papillomavirus (HPV) which are responsible for about 70% of cervical cancer cases. It also shields those vaccinated from two more types of HPV that cause 90% of genital warts cases. Gardasil, which is given in three doses over a six-month period, is currently recommended for girls and young women ages 12 through 26.

Important: Vaccinated individuals should still have regular Pap tests to check for cervical cell changes caused by HPV.

William Schaffner, MD, chair of preventive medicine, Vanderbilt University School of Medicine, Nashville, and board member of the National Foundation for Infectious Diseases, Bethesda, Maryland. *www.nfid.org*

Guideline Urges HIV Tests for All Patients 13 and Older

American College of Physicians, news release.

Physicians should routinely screen all patients 13 years and older for HIV, says a practice guideline recently released by the American College of Physicians (ACP). HIV is the virus that causes AIDS.

BACKGROUND

In the United States, HIV affects more than one million people, and about 20,000 new infections are caused each year by people who don't know they have HIV. Screening can help identify undiagnosed cases of HIV infection and prevent further transmission of the virus.

NEW SCREENING GUIDELINE

"The purpose of the guideline is to present the available evidence to physicians as a way to help guide their decisions around screening for HIV in their practice," said guideline lead author Amir Qaseem, MD, PhD, senior medical associate in ACP's Clinical Programs and Quality of Care Department. "ACP recommends that physicians adopt a routine screening policy for HIV and encourage their patients to get tested, regardless of their risk factors."

The new guideline says doctors should offer initial screening to all patients and should determine the need for repeat screening intervals on a case-by-case basis. Patients at higher risk for HIV infection should be retested more frequently than patients at average risk.

High-risk patients include those who have shared injection needles, had a blood transfusion between 1978 and 1985, have had unprotected sex with multiple partners, have a sexually transmitted disease, or have had unprotected sex with anyone in any of these risk categories.

Patients should talk to their doctors about their individual risk, says the guideline.

"The intent of this guideline is to help prevent the unwitting spread of HIV infection," said Vincenza Snow, MD, director of clinical programs and quality of care at ACP. "I would tell my patients that it's important to know your HIV status, so that you do not risk infecting anyone else. Besides, an AIDS test is very simple and quick, and can be performed during a routine exam."

The U.S. Centers for Disease Control and Prevention has more information about HIV testing at *gettested.cdc.gov*.

Cream Might Prevent Herpes Transmission

Harvard Medical School, news release.

A topical treatment that disables genes that play a key role in the transmission of the herpes virus has been developed by US researchers.

HERPES VIRUS

According to the World Health Organization, about 536 million people worldwide are infected with herpes simplex virus type 2 (HSV-2), the most common strain of this sexually transmitted disease.

Women are much more likely than men to be infected with HSV-2, and the virus can easily pass from mother to child during birth. Infants with untreated HSV-2 infection can suffer brain damage and death.

In adults, HSV-2 infection isn't life threatening, but does increase vulnerability to other viruses, such as HIV.

HOW IT WORKS

The treatment fights the virus in two ways: by disabling its ability to replicate and by blocking the host cell's ability to take up the virus. In mice, the treatment is effective when used from one week before to a few hours after exposure to the herpes virus.

"As far as we could tell, the treatment caused no adverse effects, such as inflammation or any kind of autoimmune response," said Judy Lieberman, MD, PhD, a professor of pediatrics at Harvard Medical School and a senior investigator at the Immune Disease Institute. In addition, there was no indication that the treatment interfered with normal cellular function.

BENEFITS OF NEW CREAM

"People have been trying to make a topical agent that can prevent transmission, a microbicide, for many years," Dr. Lieberman said. "But one of the main obstacles for this is compliance. One of the attractive features of the compound we developed is that it creates in the tissue a state that's resistant to infection, even if applied up to a week before sexual exposure. This aspect has a real practicality to it."

If the findings can be reproduced in people, she said, this cream could have a powerful impact on preventing transmission of the herpes virus.

The research was published in the journal, *Cell Host & Microbe*. The American Sexual Health Association has more information about herpes. Visit their Web site at *www.ashasexual health.org*.

When It Hurts To Make Love

Barbara Bartlik, MD, a psychiatrist in private practice in Manhattan and assistant professor of psychiatry and sex therapist at NewYork–Presbyterian Hospital/ Weill Cornell Medical College in New York City.

When it comes to sex, sometimes the spirit is willing but the flesh says, "Ow!" If lovemaking has become painful, see your gynecologist.

Possible causes…

• **Dryness.** Insufficient vaginal lubrication can be caused by dehydration…side effects of birth control pills or antidepressants…and

decreased levels of the hormone estrogen after menopause.

What helps: Drink 64 ounces of water daily. Try an over-the-counter (OTC) lubricant, such as Replens, available at drugstores. Extend foreplay to give your body time to create lubrication.

Prescription topical estrogen also can help. It is less likely than oral estrogen to increase risk for cardiovascular problems and breast cancer. Options include a vaginal estrogen cream or an estrogen-containing ring inserted into the vagina.

Recent research: A low-dose vaginal estrogen suppository or ring (about 10 to 25 micrograms) is as effective as a higher-dose product for relieving dryness yet is less likely to cause side effects, such as headache and breast pain.

• **Endometriosis.** When tissue from the endometrium (uterine lining)—which should stay inside the uterus—instead attaches itself to organs outside the uterus, it causes pelvic pain and inflammation for women in their reproductive years.

Options: Take an OTC nonsteroidal anti-inflammatory drug (NSAID), such as *ibuprofen* (Advil) or *naproxen* (Aleve), starting the day before your period is due and continuing until bleeding stops. To halt disease progression, your doctor may prescribe oral contraceptives. In severe cases, surgery to remove endometrial tissue and adhesions can relieve pain while preserving fertility—though symptoms may recur. If pain is extreme and you are done having children, you may want to consider a hysterectomy.

• **Pelvic inflammatory disease (PID).** A bacterial infection of the reproductive organs, PID results from a sexually transmitted disease (such as chlamydia or gonorrhea) or other vaginal infection. Repeated douching and using an IUD (intrauterine device for birth control) can increase risk. PID symptoms include painful intercourse, vaginal discharge and abdominal or back pain.

Caution: PID can cause scarring that leads to infertility and chronic pain. Antibiotics cure the infection but cannot reverse damage.

Your partner: He must see his doctor, even if he has no symptoms of infection (such as pain or discharge from the penis)—without treatment, he could reinfect you.

• **Trichomoniasis.** This parasitic infection usually is transmitted sexually but in rare cases can occur if genitals come in contact with an object that harbors the parasite, such as a wet towel. It causes vaginal odor, yellow-green discharge, sores on vaginal walls, genital itching and pain during sex.

Cure: One large dose of an antibiotic, such as *metronidazole* (Flagyl), can work as well as a seven-day lower-dose course of treatment —but it increases risk for side effects, such as nausea and vomiting. Your partner also must be tested.

• **Uterine prolapse.** This occurs when weakened muscles and ligaments of the pelvic floor allow the uterus to drop into the vagina, creating pressure in the vagina or a lump at the vaginal opening. Contributing factors include pregnancy, childbirth, obesity, chronic constipation and decreased estrogen.

Self-help: Kegel exercises strengthen the pelvic floor. Contract vaginal muscles as if to stop the flow of urine…hold five seconds…relax…repeat. Aim for 30 repetitions daily.

Treatment: Your doctor may fit you with a pessary—a flexible plastic device worn in the vagina to reposition the uterus. Some pessaries can be worn during sex. If a bulge protrudes from the vagina, your doctor may recommend surgery to repair the pelvic floor…or a hysterectomy.

• **Vaginismus.** Involuntary spasms of the pubococcygeus (PC) muscles surrounding the vagina make intercourse extremely painful. Possible causes include pelvic or vaginal infection or injury…lingering pain (or fear of pain) …hormonal changes…or psychological issues.

Relief: Treat any underlying physical cause —with medication to cure an infection or with hormone therapy for low estrogen. Kegel exercises, physical therapy and biofeedback help relax the PC muscles.

In the privacy of your home: Your doctor may recommend vaginal dilators, phallic-shaped rods of various sizes. Starting with the smallest (tampon-size), you gently insert the dilator into your vagina, working up to larger dilators over time until you can comfortably accommodate penetration by your partner.

• **Vulvodynia.** This chronic condition is characterized by stinging or stabbing pain in the vagina or vulva. The cause may be related to genetics…infection…or injury to vulvar nerves, such as during childbirth, especially if you had an incision or tear at the vaginal opening. There is no known cure.

What helps: Medication options include an anticonvulsant or tricyclic antidepressant to block pain signals…and injections of the anesthetic lidocaine. Physical therapy and biofeedback help relax pelvic muscles.

Avoid: Hot tubs, tight underwear, scented toilet paper and perfumed soaps.

For more comfortable sex: Apply a topical anesthetic, such as lidocaine cream, 30 minutes before intercourse. This will diminish sensations of pain (and also, unfortunately, of pleasure). Use a vaginal lubricant…and apply cold compresses after lovemaking.

More from Dr. Bartlik…

When to Consult a Sex Therapist

See a trained sex therapist (a psychiatrist, psychologist or social worker) if medical treatment does not ease pain…your doctor finds no medical cause for your discomfort …or you suspect an emotional cause for painful lovemaking. A sex therapist can suggest sexual techniques and positions that minimize discomfort…allow you to examine fears or relationship problems in a supportive setting…and help you change behaviors that interfere with pleasure. *Referrals…*

• **American Association of Sexuality Educators, Counselors and Therapists (AASECT),** 202-449-1099, *www.aasect.org.*

• **Society for Sex Therapy and Research,** 847-647-8832, *www.sstarnet.org.*

Dietary Links To Pelvic Pain

Spicy food can cause pelvic pain in women who have a type of chronic bladder condition called interstitial cystitis. Citrus, caffeine, tomatoes and alcohol can also cause pain and an urgent need to urinate frequently. The foods cause gastrointenstinal irritation that, in turn, leads pelvic pain to flare up due to perceived bladder pain. The pain may be treatable with a suppository or gel containing anesthetic or an anesthetic patch applied to the skin—but further research is needed. Ask your doctor for details.

David Klumpp, PhD, assistant professor of urology, Feinberg School of Medicine, Northwestern University, Chicago.

What Is Pelvic Floor Disorder?

When researchers recently surveyed 4,000 women (ages 25 to 84), they found that one-third suffered from one or more pelvic floor disorders, such as overactive bladder, stress urinary incontinence or pelvic organ prolapse (sagging of the vaginal walls). Women who had given birth vaginally were twice as likely to have these disorders as women who had never given birth or had delivered only by cesarean section.

If you suffer from pelvic floor disorder symptoms: Consult a urogynecologist (an obstetrician/gynecologist who specializes in pelvic floor disorders). To find a urogynecologist in your area, contact the American Urogynecologic Society (*www.augs.org*). Treatment options include losing weight, physical therapy to strengthen pelvic floor muscles and Kegel exercises (contraction and release of pelvic floor muscles).

Emily S. Lukacz, MD, associate professor, clinical reproductive medicine, University of California, San Diego Medical Center, La Jolla, California.

Testosterone Injections Offer Hope for Male Contraceptive

The Endocrine Society, news release.

Injectable testosterone may be an effective form of male contraception, recent research suggests.

THE STUDY

Chinese researchers injected 1,045 healthy, fertile Chinese men, ages 20 to 45, with a 500-milligram formulation of testosterone once a month for 30 months.

All of the study participants had a normal medical history and had fathered at least one child within two years of beginning the study. The study participants' female partners, ages 18 to 38, also had normal reproductive function.

THE RESULTS

After 24 months, there was a contraceptive failure rate of 1.1 per 100 men, resulting in pregnancy.

The researchers noted that no serious adverse events were reported in any of the men and, in all but two men, reproductive function returned to normal after the study period.

IMPLICATIONS

"For couples who cannot, or prefer not to use only female-oriented contraception, options have been limited to vasectomy, condom and withdrawal," said Yi-Qun Gu, PhD, of the National Research Institute for Family Planning in Beijing, China. "Our study shows a male hormonal contraceptive regimen may be a potential, novel and workable alternative."

This is the largest multi-center, male hormonal contraceptive efficacy clinical trial of an androgen preparation, Dr. Gu said.

MORE RESEARCH ON SAFETY NEEDED

"Despite the present encouraging results, the long-term safety of this hormonal male contraceptive regimen requires more extensive testing with a focus on cardiovascular, prostate and behavioral safety," Dr. Gu said.

The study was published in the *Journal of Clinical Endocrinology & Metabolism*. For more information on male hormonal contraception, visit the Male Contraception Initiative's Web site, *www.malecontraceptive.org*.

The Pill May Limit Muscle Gains in Women

Chang Woock Lee, doctoral student, Department of Health and Kinesiology, Texas A&M University, College Station.

Jennifer Wu, MD, obstetrician/gynecologist, Lenox Hill Hospital, New York City.

Amanda Weiss-Kelly, MD, director, pediatric sports medicine, Rainbow Babies & Children's Hospital, University Hospitals Case Medical Center, Cleveland.

American Physiological Society annual meeting, New Orleans.

Lower hormone levels in women who exercise regularly and take birth-control pills may result in less muscle mass increases, a recent study suggests. But the muscle-mass differences between women taking the Pill and those not taking the Pill did not affect performance.

BACKGROUND

There is some existing research into the effect of oral contraceptives on body composition, according to Amanda Weiss-Kelly, MD, director of pediatric sports medicine at Rainbow Babies & Children's Hospital, part of University Hospitals Case Medical Center in Cleveland. But most studies have been small, and results have been conflicting, she said.

The authors of the recent research studied two groups of 18-to-31-year-old active and healthy women. Of the 73 total women, 34 were on the Pill and 39 were not on the Pill. All of the women participated three times a week in a 10-week resistance-exercising training program and also underwent analysis of their body composition both before and after the program.

FINDINGS

Those women who were not taking oral contraceptives were observed to have gained more than 60% more muscle mass than those on the Pill. There were other changes noted in participants on the Pill, including reduced concentrations of the hormone DHEA, which is a hormone that builds muscle.

The study findings were presented at the annual meeting of the American Physiological Society in New Orleans.

IMPLICATIONS

At this point there is no reason to stop taking oral contraceptives, experts said. "It is premature to say anything conclusively at this point," said study lead author Chang Woock Lee, a doctoral candidate in the department of health and kinesiology at Texas A&M University, College Station. "Vigorous future studies with more stringent control and clever design will be definitely needed to confirm the results and/or elucidate the underlying mechanism conclusively."

EXPERT REACTION

Others agreed. "It's just one small group of women. If you think of how many women actually are on the Pill, how significant is the difference in terms of patients noticing anything or even an actual health effect?" asked Jennifer Wu, MD, an obstetrician/gynecologist at Lenox Hill Hospital in New York City. "This might make a difference for a high-performance athlete in a competition, but, for your normal patients who have a healthy exercise routine, this might not make a difference."

"I don't disagree with the statistical significance, but the clinical significance is very questionable," added Dr. Weiss-Kelly. "The difference didn't translate into improvement in performance," she added.

For more information on birth control pills, visit the Web site of the United States National Women's Health Resource Center (NWHRC), *www.healthywomen.org*.

If You Take (or Ever Took) Birth Control Pills

JoAnn E. Manson, MD, DrPH, professor of medicine and women's health at Harvard Medical School and chief of the division of preventive medicine at Brigham and Women's Hospital, both in Boston. Dr. Manson is coauthor of *Hot Flashes, Hormones & Your Health* (McGraw-Hill).

Women in their 40s often ask, "Will it hurt my health if I keep taking birth control pills?"—while women past menopause ask, "Am I at risk because I *used* to take the Pill?" Here's what you need to know...and what not to worry about.

• **Pregnancy.** Women in their 40s may assume that they're too old to get pregnant—yet the unintended pregnancy rate in this age group rivals that of teens.

Current users: For many midlife women, low-dose birth control pills provide safe contraception, make periods lighter and more regular, and minimize mood swings.

Caution: The Pill is not appropriate if you are at high risk for cardiovascular problems (see below)...have a history of breast cancer ...or are a smoker over age 35.

• **Cardiovascular problems.** For most women, the Pill raises the risk for heart attack, stroke and blood clots only slightly—but significantly increases risk in women already at elevated risk due to smoking, high blood pressure or diabetes.

Recent finding: The Pill may raise stroke risk in migraine patients.

Current users: If you have cardiovascular risk factors, ask your doctor about pills that contain only *progestin* (synthetic progesterone hormone). These are less likely than combined estrogen-progestin pills to boost risk.

Past users: Don't worry. Cardiovascular risk drops within weeks after you stop taking the Pill.

• **Benign tumors.** Oral contraceptives are linked to liver *adenomas*, noncancerous growths that carry a small risk for bleeding or becoming malignant.

Current users: If you develop pain or a lump in the upper abdomen, alert your doctor —you may need to stop using the Pill. Rarely, surgery is required.

Past users: Adenomas usually shrink soon after you go off the Pill.

• **Breast cancer.** Studies are contradictory. Some suggest that long-term Pill use raises risk slightly.

Current users: Pregnancy diminishes breast cells' sensitivity to hormonal effects. If you've never been pregnant and have taken the Pill for close to a decade or longer, ask your doctor about using nonhormonal contraception.

Past users: Be extra conscientious about mammograms and breast exams if you took the Pill in the 1960s or 1970s (when doses were higher) or before your first pregnancy...were never pregnant...or stopped taking the Pill less than a decade ago.

• **Ovarian cancer.** Ovulation itself contributes to ovarian cancer risk. The Pill halts ovulation, reducing risk.

Current users: For every five years on the Pill, risk falls by 20%.

Past users: Protective effects persist for many years after you go off the Pill. Your long-term risk for uterine cancer and possibly colon cancer also is lower, perhaps because progestin decreases cell growth in these organs.

Birth Control After 40

Anita L. Nelson, MD, professor of obstetrics and gynecology, David Geffen School of Medicine, University of California, Los Angeles, and coauthor of *Contraceptive Technology* (Thomson Reuters).

During perimenopause—from your early 40s until menopause—the birth control methods you used in the past may not be appropriate.

Examples: If you have high blood pressure or a history of breast cancer, smoke or are obese, your doctor may recommend against hormone-based contraception...and natural family planning is less reliable now that menstruation is irregular. Ask your doctor about the risks and benefits of the following options (all prices are approximate). *If you're looking for...*

•**Convenience**—try an intrauterine device (IUD), a small T-shaped plastic device. A doctor inserts it into the uterus...then you simply feel for a string indicating that the IUD is still in place. The Mirena IUD contains a *progestin* hormone, can be left in for five years and often makes periods lighter. A nonhormonal IUD with copper, called ParaGard, lasts 10 years but may make periods heavier.

Cost: $750 to $900.*

Alternative: Implanon is a matchstick-size plastic rod with a progestin that a doctor inserts under the skin of your arm. It works for three years. Periods often become irregular.

Cost: $400 to $800.*

•**No monthly periods**—try a continuous-use estrogen/progestin oral contraceptive, such as Seasonique.

Bonus: No menstrual migraines or cramps.

Cost: Seasonique, about $200 for a three-month supply.*

•**PMS relief**—try Yaz. Combining a very low dose of estrogen with the progestin *drospirenone*, this pill may ease irritability.

Bonus: Lighter periods.

Cost: $60–$80 a month.*

•**More comfortable sex**—try Nuvaring, a low-dose estrogen/progestin vaginal ring that increases vaginal lubrication (and often decreases menstrual flow). You insert it yourself every four weeks.

Cost: $40 to $70 a month.*

*Prices subject to change.

Understanding Perimenopause

Marcie Richardson, MD, a member of the North American Menopause Society. She is a consultant at Harvard Vanguard Medical Associates and a clinical instructor in obstetrics, gynecology and reproductive biology at Harvard Medical School, both in Boston.

Perimenopause is the time of transition from the reproductive years to menopause. It can last for several years and is often hard to track. The transition is rooted in hormonal changes—and hormone production is very erratic during this time. What's a woman to do?

There is no reliable diagnostic test, hormonal or otherwise, that accurately determines whether a woman is perimenopausal.

Clinicians usually make the diagnosis on the basis of signs and symptoms.

Changes that women typically experience during perimenopause...

•**Periods that first come closer together and then become less and less frequent.**

•**Irregularity in the timing and extent of flow during periods.**

•**Hot flashes that tend to occur just before a period.**

The benchmark that menopause has occurred is when you have gone 12 months without a menstrual period.

Some menopause symptoms—such as hot flashes and vaginal dryness—may continue for some years after a final period.

5

Sex & Relationship Secrets

An Expert Answers Your Most Intimate Questions

ver time, lovemaking can fall into a too-familiar routine, turning sex into a bore or a chore…and as we age, hormonal changes can make intercourse uncomfortable for women and erections unreliable for men. Yet it can be embarrassing to discuss such matters for men. And it can be embarrassing to discuss such matters even with a doctor. *Here are explicit answers to the questions women secretly wish they could ask…*

•**Is there any such thing as being "too old for sex"?** Absolutely not. Basically, sexual activities are the same whether a person is 25 or 85. Older bodies may not be as fit, firm and responsive as younger ones—but with age comes the advantage of experience.

•**My husband was never big on foreplay. In the past, I didn't mind—but now it takes me longer to get aroused. How can I get him to change his technique?** Tell him, "I've always loved making love with you, but my body has changed and my nerves need different sensations now." Then show and tell him exactly what you want—for instance, "It feels great when you stroke my breasts like this for a few minutes before we move on." If you're not sure what your body needs now, read *Sex Over Fifty* by Joel D. Block, PhD (Perigee), or *Better Than I Ever Expected: Straight Talk About Sex After Sixty* by Joan Price (Seal).

•**Without his medication for erectile dysfunction, my husband can't get an erection —but he hates taking a pill to have sex. Are there alternatives?** For older men, a firm erection often requires direct stimulation—so

Lou Paget, certified sex educator, American Association of Sex Educators, Counselors and Therapists, CEO of Frankly Speaking, Inc., a sex education firm in Beverly Hills, and author of five books, including *The Great Lover Playbook* (Gotham).

102

during foreplay, maintain constant contact with his genitals. Using your hand, emphasize the upstroke to help bring blood into the penis. For added sensation, use a silicone-based lubricant, such as Astroglide X ($11.25 for 2.5 ounces at drugstores)—it won't dry out the way a water-based lubricant may.

Also, be aware that reactions to medications vary among individuals—so if your husband's objection is to the way a particular drug makes him feel, he should ask his doctor about other brands. Many men swear by *sildenafil* (Viagra)…some say that *vardenafil* (Levitra) works faster…others prefer long-lasting *tadalafil* (Cialis).

Another option is a vacuum erection device. This cylindrical device uses suction to increase blood flow to the penis ($90 to $250 online, in adult stores or through doctors who treat erectile dysfunction, such as urologists). Or his doctor can teach him (or you) to inject the drug *alprostadil* (Caverject) into his penis, which produces an erection within 20 minutes and lasts up to one hour.

If your husband is unwilling to try any of these alternatives, suggest to him that you see a marriage counselor together to explore his reasons.

•**Sometimes my husband balks at giving me oral sex because he says that I have an unpleasant taste. How can I avoid this problem?** Your diet can affect your genital aroma and taste for several hours. On days when you anticipate making love, eat lots of fruits, especially pineapple and grapes, which may impart a lighter scent and taste. Before sex, avoid eating asparagus, broccoli, cauliflower, garlic or onions, which often produce overly strong body odors and tastes.

Certain drugs and supplements can alter body chemistry, so use trial-and-error to determine which ones are problematic, then ask your doctor about alternatives. Do not use a douche or feminine hygiene spray—these often have an unpleasant taste. Ask your partner if he likes or dislikes the scent of a cologne or fragranced lotion on your inner thighs. Also, to be at your freshest, bathe on "date nights."

•**What can I do to relieve vaginal dryness?** Drink more water in order to prevent dehydration. Also try an over-the-counter vaginal lubricant, such as Very Private Intimate Moisture ($15 for two ounces at drugstores or online). Antihistamines and antidepressants often contribute to vaginal dryness, so ask your doctor about alternatives.

If these measures do not help, consider using hormone therapy to improve vaginal lubrication. Ask your doctor about the risks and benefits of prescription topical estrogen cream…an estrogen ring inserted into the vagina and left in place for three months…or oral hormone replacement therapy.

•**It takes longer for me to climax, and my orgasms are less powerful than they were before menopause. What will rev things up again?** A mental turn-on sets the stage for stronger orgasms.

Possible solutions: Alone or with your partner, watch adult films designed for couples (try ordering DVDs from Femme Productions, *www.amazon.com*).

You also may benefit from more intense physical stimulation, so experiment with vibrators or other sex toys.

Discreet source: Natural Contours (800-865-9165, *www.natural-contours.com*).

•**I would like to be able to perform oral sex for my husband, but I find it physically uncomfortable. What will help?** The key is for you to control the depth of penetration. Encircle his penis with your hand, then position your mouth so that the side of your thumb and index finger remain connected to the edge of your mouth. If you prefer for him not to ejaculate in your mouth, when you sense that he is about to climax, remove your mouth and finish with your hand. Then use a damp warm washcloth to gently wash his genitals for him.

•**Why does my husband fall asleep right after sex—and how can I get him to stay awake and cuddle?** Typically, couples have sex at the end of a stress-filled day, following a soothing dinner, and while lying in bed in a dark room. After an orgasm, stress leaves the mind and body—so it's natural to fall asleep.

To keep your husband awake for snuggling or love talk after sex, try making love in the morning or early evening...or with the bedroom lights on...or somewhere other than the bed, such as on the living room couch...or with him in a kneeling or standing position, so he can't just roll over and conk out afterward.

Sex Headaches

S ex-related headaches usually are caused by changes in blood pressure and by tension in head and neck muscles before and during orgasm. One hour before sex, take a nonprescription anti-inflammatory, such as aspirin or *ibuprofen* (Advil). If that doesn't help, ask your doctor about the prescription anti-inflammatory *indomethacin* (Indocin) or blood pressure drug *propranolol* (Inderal). Also take 100 mg twice daily of magnesium, which helps many types of headache.

Barbara Bartlik, MD, sex therapist and assistant professor of psychiatry at NewYork–Presbyterian Hospital/Weill Cornell Medical College in New York City. She is the medical advisor for the book *Extraordinary Togetherness: A Woman's Guide to Love, Sex and Intimacy* (Rodale).

Why Women Kiss

M ost women would never engage in sex without kissing—although many men would. Women kiss to assess a partner's level of commitment based on unconscious mechanisms that respond to touch and chemical and postural cues—and on that basis, they may be prompted to end a potential relationship after a single kiss. Men are more likely to kiss as a means to a shorter-term goal, such as sexual intimacy or reconciling after a fight.

Gordon G. Gallup, Jr., PhD, evolutionary psychologist, University of Albany, New York, and coauthor of a study of 1,041 people, published in *Evolutionary Psychology*.

Reasons Sex Drive Drops

Barbara Bartlik, MD, sex therapist and assistant professor of psychiatry at NewYork–Presbyterian Hospital/Weill Cornell Medical College in New York City. She is the medical advisor for the book *Extraordinary Togetherness: A Woman's Guide to Love, Sex and Intimacy* (Rodale).

W e all know that a woman's libido can take a nosedive when she's stressed, depressed or menopausal. But other, less-known health issues also can cause difficulties with sex drive and/or arousal. If you're having problems in bed, consider the conditions below and discuss your situation with your doctor.

BLAME IT ON BLOOD FLOW

A flagging libido, limited arousal and trouble reaching orgasm often have the same root cause—reduced blood flow to the genitals. Any health problem that interferes with blood flow throughout the body can impede genital blood flow. *Culprits...*

•**High cholesterol.** Cholesterol is a fatlike substance that contributes to plaque formation in the arteries. As arteries become clogged and narrowed, blood flow is restricted. Total cholesterol above 200 milligrams per deciliter (mg/dL) can contribute to arousal problems.

Medication concern: There are no studies that have shown that cholesterol-lowering statin drugs cause sexual dysfunction in women, but we do know that statins can lower men's levels of testosterone, a hormone that strongly influences sex drive. Statins may have a similar effect in women (who also produce testosterone, though at lower levels than men do).

What helps: Regular exercise and a low-fat diet that includes cholesterol-lowering foods, such as ground flaxseeds, walnuts, and most fruits and vegetables. Also, talk to your doctor about cholesterol-lowering supplements, such as niacin, red yeast rice extract and/or fish oil.

•**Diabetes.** The hormone insulin allows blood sugar (glucose) to move from the blood into the muscles and other cells for use as fuel. Type 1 diabetes occurs when the body does not produce enough insulin. Type 2 diabetes develops when cells cannot use insulin properly—often due to excess weight, a high-sugar diet and/or lack of exercise. One consequence of either type of diabetes is reduced blood flow, because blood vessels narrow and harden. Also, a condition called diabetic neuropathy, in which there is damage to nerves, can contribute to sexual dysfunction.

Note: A prediabetes condition called insulin resistance also can interfere with blood flow.

What helps: Catch the problem early, and sexual responsiveness will return—but if the condition progresses very far, sexual dysfunction may be irreversible. From age 45 onward, have your doctor give you an oral glucose-tolerance test every three years to screen for diabetes. To reduce your risk for diabetes or to keep it from worsening, stabilize blood glucose levels by adopting a low-sugar diet, losing excess weight and exercising regularly.

• **Hypertension.** Blood pressure is the force of the blood pushing against the walls of the arteries whenever the heart beats (the systolic pressure, or top number) and between beats (the diastolic pressure, or bottom number). Hypertension, or high blood pressure, means that the heart has to work harder, the arteries harden and blood flow is impaired. Blood pressure above 120/80 is cause for concern.

Medication concern: Hypertension drugs themselves can contribute to an inability to reach orgasm because they reduce blood pressure overall, including blood supply to the genitals. Beta-blockers and diuretics are more likely to cause sexual dysfunction than other drugs. If you need medication, work with your doctor to find one with a minimum of side effects.

What helps: For some people, a low-salt diet can lower blood pressure, so keep sodium intake below 1,500 mg per day. When possible, avoid over-the-counter *nonsteroidal anti-inflammatory drugs* (NSAIDs), such as *ibuprofen* (Advil), which can increase blood pressure. Talk to your doctor about natural supplements that can lower blood pressure, such as magnesium and *coenzyme Q10* (CoQ10). Supplementing with the amino acid

L-arginine can help, but it is not advisable for anyone with a history of heart attack.

• **Smoking.** Obviously, smoking cigarettes is not a disease (although it can lead to a plethora of health problems)—but it is a primary cause of sexual dysfunction in both women and men. Smoking delivers a double whammy to blood flow—the toxins damage the smooth inner lining of blood vessels…and nicotine triggers the release of fats into the blood, which then stick to artery walls.

What helps: Easier said than done—stop smoking!

New approach: Women typically have a harder time giving up cigarettes than men do. However, a study from the University of Chicago found that smoking-cessation rates among women rose by almost 50% when nicotine patches or nasal sprays and behavioral therapy were used in combination with the oral medication *naltrexone* (Vivitrol), which blocks nicotine's pleasurable chemical signals to the brain.

More from Dr. Barbara Bartlik…

In the Privacy of Your Home

A device called Eros is useful for arousal problems associated with health conditions that reduce genital blood flow.

What it is: A clitoral therapy device, available by prescription, that consists of a small suction cup (to be placed over the clitoris) combined with a small, battery-operated vacuum pump.

How it helps: The gentle suction action increases blood flow to the clitoris, which enhances arousal, sensation and lubrication, and allows the buildup of sexual tension that precedes orgasm. Eros can be used before sex to get you in the mood or during foreplay with your partner.

Nonprescription alternative: A vibrator, which also can increase genital blood flow.

Whether or not you opt for "high-tech" arousal aids, it is easier to overcome arousal problems if you communicate openly with your partner about the specific type of genital stimulation you find most pleasurable.

Check Your Meds

Your sex drive can be affected by different medications.

Talk to your prescribing doctor about changing medications. Some antidepressants, such as *bupropion* (Wellbutrin) and *duloxetine* (Cymbalta), may cause fewer sexual side effects than others.

If switching is not recommended, your doctor may prescribe a second drug that counteracts your antidepressant's sexual side effects, such as the antianxiety medication *buspirone*.

Oral contraceptives sometimes cause sexual dysfunction—so if you are taking both an antidepressant and the Pill, your risk for low libido is further increased. In this case, consider a different form of birth control.

Anita H. Clayton, MD, professor of psychiatry and neurobehavioral sciences, University of Virginia Health System, Charlottesville, and author of *Satisfaction: Women, Sex and the Quest for Intimacy* (Ballantine).

Libido Boost

In order to wake up your libido, try combining and drinking equal parts of the tincture form of the herbs *damiana* and *Panax ginseng* to stimulate arousal and increase levels of the hormone testosterone. This formula works for women and for men.

Consult a health-care professional knowledgeable in herbal medicine to determine if the formula is right for you and what dosage you should use.

If that doesn't work: Ask your doctor to check you for a deficiency in *dehydroepiandrosterone* (DHEA). The steroid hormone is available at health-food stores and is a precursor to such hormones as estrogen and androgen. Ask your doctor if this is right for you.

Jane Guiltinan, ND, dean of naturopathic medicine, Bastyr University and a clinical supervisor at Bastyr Center for Natural Health, both in Seattle.

Don't Let Your Sexual Desire Fade

Marianne Brandon, PhD, clinical psychologist and director of Wellminds Wellbodies, Annapolis, Maryland. She is coauthor, with Andrew Goldstein, MD, of *Reclaiming Desire: 4 Keys to Finding Your Lost Libido* (Rodale). *www.wellminds.com*

Even though we live in a culture that sometimes seems to be obsessed with sex, we're not always very knowledgeable about sexuality. And one of the worst myths in our society is the idea that sexual desire—or libido—always fades with age.

Our sexuality does change as we grow older, but the reality is that we can stay as tuned in to our senses and remain as sensual as we want to be. For both men and women, sexuality and libido can stay an important and enjoyable part of life.

UNDERSTANDING LIBIDO

Sexual desire differs between men and women. That seems obvious, but it's actually a major source of misunderstanding in our culture. For a woman, a healthy libido tends to be experienced as being receptive. She responds to her partner, but her libido is less assertive. Over time in long-term relationships, women tend to become less spontaneous in their desire and less interested in initiating sexual activity.

Men, on the other hand, generally remain more eager to initiate sex throughout a long-term relationship. That's a very basic difference between men and women, and it's important to understand—because a woman might misinterpret her response and think that she has low libido, when in fact she's perfectly normal and is responding as a healthy woman would.

Similarly, as a man ages, his ability to have sex (though not his desire) changes. The quality of his erections may diminish, and he may not be able to have an erection as frequently as when he was younger. These changes are normal, but they can cause a lot of distress.

Important: There's a big difference between low desire and genuine dysfunction. Psychologists do recognize a disorder called *hypoactive* sexual desire disorder. In both men and women, it's characterized by a lack of interest in sex and a lack of sexual fantasy. The disorder must cause marked distress to be considered diagnosable. And even then, it's a controversial diagnosis. Some professionals feel it's motivated by drug companies that want to have a disorder that can be diagnosed and treated with prescription drugs, such as supplemental testosterone. Many feel that there haven't yet been enough high-quality scientific studies to confirm that the disorder affects as many people as some researchers claim.

THE PHYSICAL PIECE OF THE PUZZLE

The physiological aspects of sex and desire are just a small piece of what makes up our experience of our sexuality. Our society is very focused on the physical aspects of sex, but if you're in a loving relationship and you want to expand intimacy, having a high libido isn't the primary requirement.

When two individuals share intimacy—their hearts and bodies—they create something beautiful. That intimacy doesn't have to rely on intercourse and orgasm. When the sexual patterns that used to work for you start to change, as they naturally do as we age, it's time to look into other aspects of how to give and receive love well with your body.

But if your body isn't healthy, it's hard to enjoy any kind of sex life. *Many things can interfere with your libido…*

• **Sleep deprivation.** Someone who is tired from lack of sleep, too much travel, chronic illness or some other reason, is far less likely to be interested in sex.

• **Poor diet.** Not eating right can cause fatigue, digestive upsets and other problems that interfere with your sex drive. Being obese can also cause sexual difficulties.

• **Medications.** Some common prescription medications, including antidepressants and blood pressure drugs, can interfere with sexual pleasure by altering blood flow to the genital area. Antidepressant drugs, such as *fluoxetine* (Prozac), *citalopram* (Celexa) and *sertraline* (Zoloft), can also lower libido. Sometimes reducing the dose or changing to a different medication helps. Don't hesitate to have a frank discussion with your doctor if you think that a drug you take is impacting your sex life.

• **Chronic conditions,** such as diabetes, arthritis and high blood pressure, can affect your libido by interfering with blood flow or making sex uncomfortable. There are ways to work around these medical challenges.

Unfortunately, many doctors don't know much about this. Also, you and your doctor may be too embarrassed to discuss the topic. But don't give up on sex! Consider consulting a trained sex therapist instead.

• **Menopause.** The hormonal changes of menopause can make intercourse physically uncomfortable for women. This problem can easily be solved with lubricants, such as K-Y jelly and Vagisil, and, when appropriate, the use of hormones to relieve vaginal dryness. Discuss the issue with your doctor.

EMOTIONAL ASPECTS

When a man or woman is feeling depressed, anxious or stressed, he/she is unlikely to be interested in sex or feel a desire to be close. In fact, low libido is one diagnostic indicator of depression.

When serious depression is ruled out, however, we can still have anxiety and negative feelings about our bodies. Our culture tells us that to be "sexy," bodies should look a certain way, but very few of us actually ever looked like that, and we certainly don't look that way when we get older.

Being comfortable with our bodies and avoiding unrealistic expectations helps avoid a lot of emotional anguish.

Understanding what arouses your desire—and what doesn't—is an important part of improving your libido. This means exploring your own sexuality and sharing that knowledge frankly with your partner.

By learning what you enjoy most and communicating it in an emotionally open way, you increase your own enjoyment of sex. And when you start to enjoy something more, you become more interested in participating in it and initiating it.

Our culture tells us that as people age, they lose their sensuality and sexuality, but that's simply not true. We don't lose the need for intimate contact, we don't lose the need for touch and we don't have to lose our sexual desire. Research shows us that people can be sexually active for as long as they want to be.

As we get older and our bodies change, making love can be a fabulous way to feel pleasure in our bodies and have a sense of growing and expanding.

SPIRITUAL FULFILLMENT

Spiritual contentment is what turns sex into making love. I'm referring to the experience of a deeper and more profound sense of life and also of a deeper and more profound connection to yourself and your partner. That's achieved through an open heart—by living more fully in a loving way.

Spiritual contentment in a relationship can be nurtured in part simply by slowing down and taking more time for each other. Spending quality time together outside of sex, for instance, will help partners share life goals and get to know each other at a deeper level.

Older adults often have more time to experiment with this way of thinking because they're at a point in life where they're less focused on schedules and the rat race. They can relax more into the experience of being loving outside of sex as well as during sex, and they can more fully experience giving and receiving.

"Sweaty" New Finding

Male sweat boosts women's sexual arousal in a matter of minutes.

Recent finding: Within 15 minutes of sniffing *androstadienone*, a compound in male perspiration, women's levels of the stress hormone cortisol rose...their moods improved... and blood pressure, heart rate and breathing increased—all indicating heightened arousal.

Study by researchers at University of California, Berkeley, Kaiser Permanente Hospital, Oakland, California, and Weizmann Institute of Science, Rehovot, Israel, published in *The Journal of Neuroscience*.

A Spray that Boosts Satisfaction

A daily spritz of hormones may boost sexual satisfaction in some women.

Recent finding: Among premenopausal women who lacked interest in sex, a daily dose of a testosterone spray to the abdomen led to significant improvement in their sexual satisfaction.

Susan Davis, PhD, professor of medicine, Monash University, Victoria, Australia, and leader of a study of 261 women ages 35 to 46, published in *Annals of Internal Medicine*.

You're OK!

One in 100 adults reports never having felt sexual attraction to anyone at all. Campaigns are under way to promote awareness and acceptance of asexuality.

Anthony Bogaert, PhD, psychologist and human sexuality expert, Brock University, St. Catharines, Ontario, Canada.

Orgasm Concern

Diminished orgasms can stem from several causes. Medications can affect brain chemicals involved with sexual satisfaction.

Examples: Beta-blocker heart drugs, such as *carvedilol* (Coreg) and *atenolol* (Tenormin) ...SSRI antidepressants, such as *fluoxetine* (Prozac) and *sertraline* (Zoloft). Low testosterone levels, which commonly occur soon after age 50 or from medications, such as those used to treat prostate cancer. Nerve damage—from long-term bicycle riding or other perineal injuries—may lessen sensation. Also, diabetics and alcoholics may experience less sensation. Stress, anxiety and depression can interfere with satisfaction.

Best course of action: Consult a physician specializing in sexual medicine. Your primary care provider or local hospital may be able to recommend a sexual medicine clinic in your area. Treatment may include sex therapy, medications to increase hormone levels or the antidepressant *bupropion* (Wellbutrin).

Irwin Goldstein, MD, editor in chief, *The Journal of Sexual Medicine*, Boston.

Enhance Your Sex Drive

Sex drive may be enhanced with a nasal spray. PT-141, also called *bremelanotide*, is a hormone that stimulates regions of the brain responsible for arousal.

Michael A. Perelman, PhD, codirector, human sexuality program, NewYork–Presbyterian Hospital, and clinical associate professor of psychiatry, reproductive medicine and urology, Weill Cornell Medical College, both in New York City.

Sex...an Antidote to Fear

Having sex releases endorphins and other brain chemicals that are calming.

Another sex–fear connection: Moderate levels of fear can stimulate sexual arousal by causing the release of the hormone *adrenaline*. Controlled situations that can promote this response include scary movies or amusement park rides...walking in the dark...crossing a narrow or swinging bridge.

Caution: Too much fear makes people draw inward, lessening intimacy.

Judy Kuriansky, PhD, clinical psychologist and sex therapist on the adjunct faculty of Columbia University Teachers College in New York City. She is author of five books, including *The Complete Idiot's Guide to a Healthy Relationship* (Alpha). *www.sexualtherapy.com/therapists/jkuriansky.htm*

What Is Your Reason?

The top reason for having sex for both men and women is "attraction to the person." This refutes the gender stereotype that men want sex only for the physical pleasure and women want love. Overall, the top 10 reasons for both genders are similar and include "It feels good"..."I wanted to experience physical pleasure"..."It's fun"...and "I wanted to show my affection to the person."

Some notable differences: Men are more likely than women to be open to having sex when presented with the opportunity...and women are more likely to have sex because they feel the need to please their partners.

Cindy M. Meston, PhD, clinical psychology professor, University of Texas at Austin, and coauthor of a study of 1,549 people, published in *Archives of Sexual Behavior*.

Natural Aphrodisiacs

Chris D. Meletis, ND, executive director, the Institute for Healthy Aging. He is author of several books, including *Better Sex Naturally* (Harper Resource), *Complete Guide to Safe Herbs* (DK Publishing) and *Instant Guide to Drug-Herb Interactions* (DK Publishing). *www.drmeletis.com*

A woman who suffers from low libido may think that testosterone cream is the most effective way to boost her flagging desire. Men who are troubled by erectile dysfunction (impotence) often assume that drugs—such as *sildenafil* (Viagra), *tadalafil* (Cialis) and *vardenafil* (Levitra)—are the answer.

While both of these approaches may offer a temporary solution, they will not remedy the underlying causes of these problems. Discovering and curing the cause of a sexual problem can be the key to long-term enjoyment of sex.

To identify the cause, a detailed medical history and diagnostic tests, including a prostate-specific antigen (PSA) test for men and a Pap test for women are performed.

In addition to low levels of testosterone, the hormone that fuels sex drive in both men and women, there are a number of possible scenarios. These include circulation problems that inhibit blood flow to the genitals...psychological stress, which diminishes interest in sex...and insomnia, which steals the vitality necessary to pursue sexual activity.

There are safe, natural medications, such as herbs* to trigger the healing process.

ERECTILE DYSFUNCTION

More than half of men over age 40 have some degree of erectile failure, according to one recent study. The condition can be caused by a variety of health problems, such as poor circulation or nerve damage. For this reason, it's important to see your primary-care physician for a diagnosis. *The most effective herbal treatment for optimal erectile function...*

•**Ginkgo biloba.** An erection depends on healthy blood flow to the penis. Clogged arteries reduce circulation, which compromises a man's ability to achieve an erection. The herb ginkgo biloba dilates blood vessels, improving circulation and helping restore erections.

In a recent study, 78% of men with erectile dysfunction who took the herb regained their ability to have erections.

Good news for women: Women who use ginkgo biloba may experience longer, more intense orgasms.

People most likely to benefit from ginkgo biloba have circulatory symptoms, such as dizziness, varicose veins, cold hands or feet and/or high blood pressure.

Typical use: 40 milligrams (mg), three times daily. Look for a formula containing 24% *flavonglycosides,* the active ingredient.

Warning: Ginkgo should not be taken by anyone who uses blood-thinning medication, such as aspirin, antidepressants known as MAO inhibitors or anyone who has had a stroke or has a tendency to bleed or bruise easily.

*The US Food and Drug Administration does not regulate herbal supplements. Check with your physician before taking any of these products. Some may interact with prescription medications.

INHIBITED SEXUAL DESIRE

A flagging libido can plague both men and women. *Fortunately, both sexes can benefit from the following...*

•**Panax Ginseng.** This herb energizes the body, helping it respond better to almost any health problem. It also boosts the production of sex hormones, such as testosterone in men and women, to enhance sexual response.

People likely to get the most benefit from ginseng have anxiety, blood sugar problems, fatigue, high levels of stress, menopausal symptoms or frequent infections like colds.

Typical use: Look for a product that contains *ginsenoside Rg1,* the active ingredient. Take 10 mg, twice daily.

Warning: Ginseng is a stimulant, and it is not recommended for people with high blood pressure or anyone taking medication for diabetes, bipolar disorder or heart disease. Common side effects are nausea, diarrhea and insomnia.

DANGEROUS NATURAL REMEDIES

Stay away from...

•**Damiana.** Derived from the leaves of a shrub found in the Southwest US and Mexico, this herb has many possible side effects, including diarrhea, vomiting, heart palpitations and anxiety. Use it only under the supervision of a doctor or naturopathic physician.

•**Spanish Fly.** This beetle is pulverized and eaten. It contains the chemical *cantharidin,* which can damage your heart, kidneys, stomach and intestines—or even kill you.

Viagra for Women?

Viagra may help women who experience sexual dysfunction caused by the antidepressants they take.

Recent finding: Seventy-two percent of women who took Viagra because of antidepressant-related sexual dysfunction experienced improvement, compared with 27% of women who took a placebo. There were no serious side effects among women using Viagra. Note that Viagra has not been approved by the Food and Drug Administration for women and sexual dysfunction.

Even more recent: In August 2015, the FDA approved Addyi (flibanserin), "the little pink pill," to enhance sexual drive in women.

H. George Nurnberg, MD, executive vice chair, department of psychiatry, University of New Mexico School of Medicine, Albuquerque, and leader of a study published in *The Journal of the American Medical Association.*

The Secret to Great Sex At Any Age

Judy Kuriansky, PhD, clinical psychologist and sex therapist on the adjunct faculty of Columbia University Teachers College in New York City. She is author of five books, including *The Complete Idiot's Guide to a Healthy Relationship* (Alpha). *www.sexualtherapy.com/therapists/ jkuriansky.htm*

What you used to look forward to twice a week (or even twice a night!) can drop off, as the years pass, to twice a month…or once in a blue moon. As a woman gets older, sex—which used to provide unparalleled pleasure and promote emotional intimacy—can start to feel like a chore or a bore or a bother.

But it doesn't have to be this way. One effective and enjoyable way to keep your sex drive stimulated—no matter what your age or stage of life—is for you and your partner to explore the mysteries of the highly erotic and deeply sensitive *G-spot.* Just say to him, "Let's explore something new tonight, as we would on a vacation in Italy or the Islands." Chances are good that he'll happily race you to the bedroom.

SPOT CHECK

Popularized by the book *The G-Spot: and Other Discoveries About Human Sexuality* by Alice Khan Ladas, Beverly Whipple and John D. Perry, first published in 1982, and named after German gynecologist Ernst Grafenberg, who described it in the mid-twentieth century, the Grafenberg spot, or G-spot (more accurately an area or space), can be a locus of strong sexual arousal and powerful orgasms in women. Yet controversy surrounds this erogenous zone, with some people saying it's a must for satisfying sex while experts insist on not increasing expectations. Some experts even contest its existence in every woman despite evidence to the contrary.

As a psychologist and a sex therapist, I assure you that this area does indeed exist—and that every woman has one. The G-spot can be an added source of pleasure, though I warn against considering it the "holy grail" of female sexuality, because preset expectations can raise performance anxiety and put a damper on sex.

Despite its reputation, once you know where it is and what it feels like, the G-spot is not hard to find. It is located on the front wall of the vaginal "barrel," about one-third of the way up. Compared with the smoothness of the rest of the vaginal wall, the G-spot feels slightly rippled, with grooves—and its texture increases as the spot is stimulated. When a woman is aroused, blood and fluid rush to the area and the G-spot swells, sometimes doubling in size.

In some women, G-spot stimulation triggers an emission of fluid (like an ejaculation), helping to lubricate the external area—a special plus for older women, for whom uncomfortable dryness is often a deterrent to sex. Of course, if dryness is a problem, don't hesitate to also use a lubricating product, such as K-Y Jelly, Astroglide, Zestra or Eros.

TO TRY TONIGHT

There are a number of simple, straightforward ways to stimulate the G-spot. During foreplay, the man can insert his index or middle finger into the vagina, crook the finger upward and then gently, repeatedly and rhythmically make a "come hither" gesture.

The G-spot also can be stimulated during intercourse, using positions that are angled to allow the best access. *Positions to try…*

• **The woman on her back** with a pillow under her bottom to raise the pelvis and hips, and the man on his knees before her.

• **The doggie position,** with the man angling his thrusts downward.

• **The woman on top,** guiding the man's thrusts to make contact with the G-spot.

What to avoid: It's essential for your partner to take his time and be very delicate in his attentions toward the G-spot, especially at the outset. For successful arousal, he must not push too hard, rub too vigorously or force the stimulation in any way. The unfamiliar pressure and sensations may feel uncomfortable and confusing to you at first—so don't give up too quickly. Also, due to the G-spot's proximity to the urethra, stimulation may at first produce an urge to urinate. To prevent this distracting sensation, it's a good idea to empty your bladder before sexual activity.

Practice makes perfect: As with all aspects of lovemaking, every woman is different, and it may require some patience and experimentation until you find what works best for you. Once you do, awareness of the G-spot can become a very satisfying addition to your lovemaking. You may decide that, when it comes to your sex life today, the "G" stands for great.

Herbal Aphrodisiacs

Laurie Steelsmith, ND, author of *Natural Choices for Women's Health* (Three Rivers). Her private practice in naturopathic and Chinese medicine is in Honolulu. *www.naturalchoicesforwomen.com*

I f your libido is lagging, rekindle the spark with herbs used by practitioners of traditional Chinese medicine (TCM). Try them one at a time, in the order presented (*epimedium* and *rehmannia* can be taken together). If you don't see results with one herb after two months, discontinue it and try the next. Typically an herb corrects the underlying problem within six months and is then discontinued. These herbs are sold in health-food stores. Do not use while pregnant or breastfeeding. If you have any health problems, talk to your doctor before beginning herbal therapy.

Cordyceps (a mushroom) improves kidney health, according to TCM, by supporting *kidney qi* (vital energy)—and abundant qi is necessary for a strong libido. Take 500 mg in tablet form two to three times daily. Do not use if you have a fever because it could worsen symptoms.

Ginseng contains compounds called *ginsenosides,* which may boost enzymes that help to break down or otherwise dispatch stress hormones, such as cortisol. Stress dampens libido, so decreasing stress helps to increase desire. Ginseng "modulates" the nervous system, boosting sexual energy if you are lethargic and helping you relax if you are tense. Using an extract labeled "standardized to 4% ginsenosides," take 100 mg in pill form or 50 drops in tincture form, two or three times daily. Do not use if you have hot flashes, insomnia, dry mouth or dry skin—ginseng could exacerbate symptoms.

Epimedium (horny goat weed) stimulates the nervous system, especially nerves in the genitalia, by increasing the flow of qi to the pelvis. It usually is sold in a combination herbal formula. Choose a brand that provides 800 mg of epimedium per day. Do not use if you have a fever, hot flashes or insomnia.

Rehmannia is an herb that draws energy into the reproductive organs through the body's meridians (energy pathways). Usually it is sold in combination with other herbs. Select a brand that has 300 mg of rehmannia per tablet, and take three times per day. Do not use if you have diarrhea, because it can loosen stool.

Bonus: Rehmannia eases anxiety and hot flashes—making it even easier to get into the mood for love.

Chemical Attraction

A woman is attracted to a man's scent based on one gene. The OR7D4 gene reacts strongly with the chemical *androstenone,* formed when a man's body breaks down the hormone testosterone. Depending on a woman's variation of OR7D4, a man's androstenone may smell like vanilla, urine or nothing.

Bottom line: Some aspects of attraction really are chemical.

Leslie B. Vosshall, PhD, professor, laboratory of neurogenetics and behavior, Rockefeller University, New York City, and coauthor of a study of 400 people, published online in *Nature*.

Sex Can Ease Migraine Pain

Women who have sex when they feel a migraine coming on experience less head and neck pain, fatigue and moodiness. Nearly one-third of women who had sex at the start of a migraine reported reduced symptoms...and for 12%, sex stopped the migraine completely.

Possible reason: Sex and orgasm boost levels of the pleasure hormone serotonin—which is known to be low in migraine sufferers.

James R. Couch, MD, PhD, professor and former chair of neurology, University of Oklahoma Health Sciences Center, Oklahoma City, and leader of a study of 82 women with migraines, published in *Headache: The Journal of Head and Face Pain.*

Persistent Arousal

Irwin Goldstein, MD, director of San Diego Sexual Medicine at Alvarado Hospital, San Diego. He is clinical professor of surgery, University of California at San Diego and editor in chief of *The Journal of Sexual Medicine.*

Often, without physical or psychological stimulation, some people feel intense and uncomfortable arousal in their genitals. Persistent sexual arousal syndrome (PSAS)—also known as persistent genital arousal disorder (PGAD)—is uncommon, but it can cause enormous distress. Women with PSAS have a dysfunctional neurotransmitter system that allows messages to travel too freely from the brain to the genitals. Reasons for the dysfunction are not well-understood—but sometimes women develop PSAS when they stop taking *fluoxetine* (Prozac) or other antidepressants, especially if the medication is halted abruptly.

Women who think they may have PSAS should consult a physician familiar with female sexual problems. Treatments, including biologic and psychologic therapies, need to be tailored to the individual.

For more information and referrals: Call San Diego Sexual Medicine, 619-265-8865—or contact the International Society for the Study of Women's Sexual Health, *www.isswsh.org.*

Sex Studies

Most Americans had sex before getting married. This is true going back decades. Even among women born in the 1940s, nearly nine in 10 had sex before marriage.

Lawrence B. Finer, PhD, director of domestic research, The Guttmacher Institute, New York City, and author of "Trends in Premarital Sex in the United States, 1954–2003," published in *Public Health Reports.*

Have Much Better Sex As You Age

Dagmar O'Connor, PhD, sex therapist in private practice in New York City. She is the creator of a self-help sex therapy video and book packet: *How to Make Love to the Same Person for the Rest of Your Life—and Still Love It* (Dagmedia).

Most older Americans grew up not talking about sex. Through others' silence, they were taught to believe that sex was shameful and taboo. Any mention of sex between "old folks," in particular, made people shudder.

Sexual activity is a natural and healthy part of life. In fact, you can get better at sex and enjoy it more—at any age. I treat couples in their 80s and 90s who wouldn't dare tell their children or grandchildren that they're seeing a sex therapist. Typically, whatever the state of their sex life, therapy improves it.

With retirement's gift of time, you can learn how the aging body works differently from its younger self, what pleases you individually and how to please each other in new ways.

PRACTICAL MATTERS

Yes, bodies change with age. Many women start to feel old and asexual at menopause.

113

Men may develop erectile problems. But most difficulties can be overcome.

Physical change: Chronic conditions, such as diabetes, thyroid disease, cancer, Parkinson's disease and depression, can affect sexual function. With heart disease, sex can cause chest pain, and with asthma, breathlessness.

Remember, intercourse is the equivalent of walking two city blocks. Check with your doctor first.

Physical change: Joint pain and stiffness from arthritis makes sex difficult.

Solution: Relax in a Jacuzzi or bath before sex...vacation together in a warm climate... find new positions that won't stress your sore spots.

Physical change: Many drugs—antidepressant, hypertension, heart disease and some cancer medications, as well as alcohol —can affect sexual function.

Solution: If your sex drive is down or you're having other sexual problems, ask your doctor whether your medications could be the cause and if switching might help.

Physical change: After menopause, vaginal tissue becomes less elastic, the vaginal opening becomes smaller and lubrication decreases.

Result: Discomfort during intercourse.

Solution: Don't avoid sex—increase it. The more tissue is exercised, the more it stretches and the more you relax your muscles. Using your finger or a dildo, gently widen the vaginal opening every day. If the problem persists for more than two months, see a gynecologist or sex therapist.

Meanwhile, smooth the way with a nonprescription water-based lubricant, such as Astroglide or K-Y Jelly.

Not as good: Oil-based lubricants or petroleum products such as Vaseline. They may linger in the vagina and irritate it.

Bonus: Applying lubricant may get you in the mood for sex. Or let your partner apply it as part of lovemaking. Good foreplay makes lubrication flow naturally.

Physical change: With age, men require more manual stimulation for erections, take longer to ejaculate and have a longer refractory period—the amount of time between an orgasm and the next erection.

Solution: Patience. These changes are an invitation to discover the slow, loving sex that many women, in particular, have always wanted but haven't received.

Erectile problems can be treated medically, too. Discuss the situation with your doctor. You may be referred to a urologist for medication or other treatment.

BEYOND INTERCOURSE

Couples in their 60s and 70s and older often ask me what to do about erectile problems and other issues that interfere with intercourse. I tell them to slow down—expand their sexual horizons, develop new sexual habits and start all over again. The goal is simply to feel more.

Our society fears low-level arousal— pleasurable excitement that doesn't lead to penetration or orgasm. But those who have always resisted "just touching" become gluttons for such physical connection once they realize how great it is.

Exercise: During the day or with a light on at night, one partner lies back and is touched by the other—but not on the breasts or genitals —for 15 minutes to an hour. The person being touched stipulates what's wanted in a non-verbal way. If you would like your partner to touch more slowly, put your hand over your partner's and slow it down. When the "touchee" is finished, switch places.

Simple interludes set a loving, sensual tone and encourage you both to overcome shyness about requesting what pleases you. Prolonged sensual touching without genital contact removes sexual anxieties...helps you become relaxed, sensitized and responsive...revives a sense of trust and well-being that you may not have experienced since you were stroked as a child.

You'll emerge from the interlude feeling wonderful about each other. Resentments and recriminations will evaporate. Making sensual, uninhibited love often follows naturally. If not, there's always next time.

LOVE YOUR BODY AS IT IS

Our society presumes that only the young and skinny are (or should be) sexually active.

As a result, many older people avoid sex out of embarrassment about spotted skin, a protruding stomach, wrinkles and flab. (Do remember that while you are ashamed of your wrinkles and protruding belly, your partner's eyesight has probably also diminished!) A mastectomy or other surgery can interfere with self-esteem, too, especially with a new partner.

Your body is miraculous. Learn to love it the way it really looks. One woman attending my sexual self-esteem workshop said, "I did not learn to love my body until I lost it." But your body at any age is a gift. Value it for itself …not as it compares with anyone else's or to how you looked when younger.

Exercise: Stand together before a full-length mirror. Say what you like about your own body out loud. Do this exercise alone first, before sharing it with your partner. Then try the exercise with your partner, taking turns. Listen, but don't respond.

To learn to appreciate your body, admire it often. Come away from this event loving five things about your body.

If you look better, you'll feel better. I recommend exercise—walking, swimming, Pilates —to couples of all ages. Getting stronger makes both women and men look better and feel more powerful…more sexual.

EDUCATE YOUR PARTNER

The young body works without thought. As you grow older, you can—and may need to— benefit from learning more about your body and your lover's. The key to intimacy is to express your needs—once you have learned what they are—and to insist on knowing the needs of your partner so that you can try to fulfill them.

Special note to women: If you rarely initiated sex but would like to, take baby steps. Try asking for different ways of being touched, or take his hand and show him how you like to be touched.

Exercise: Turn up the thermostat, and hang out nude together. Sleep nude in the same bed even if you haven't done so for years.

Sex and Sleep

People with sleep disturbances, such as sleep walking or apnea, also may exhibit sexual behavior ("sexsomnia") during sleep— fondling another person, masturbation, etc.

How to Talk to Your Partner About Sex

When is the best time to give a man feedback on his lovemaking—before, during or after sex?

All of the above.

Before: When his self-confidence is high— after a great golf game, for instance—say, "You know what I'd love to do in bed?" Then tell him.

During: Gently guide him toward what pleases you. When he gets it right, say, "That's fantastic!"

After: Express appreciation for whatever you enjoyed. He'll want to give an encore.

Judy Kuriansky, PhD, clinical psychologist and sex therapist on the adjunct faculty of Columbia University Teachers College in New York City. She is author of five books, including *The Complete Idiot's Guide to a Healthy Relationship* (Alpha). *www.sexualtherapy.com/therapists/ jkuriansky.htm*

Shocking Research: People Pick Chocolate Over Sex

Baby boomers prefer chocolate to sex. Seniors feel the same way. Both age groups said that the hardest thing to give up permanently would be reading…the second most difficult thing would be chocolate. Sex came in third for both groups.

50 Plus Research, which conducts research for companies serving the baby boomer and senior markets, San Francisco. The firm conducted a survey of more than 500 people designed to provide a broad overview of boomer and senior attitudes and beliefs.

Postmenopausal Women And Infections

Postmenopausal women are more prone to vaginal infections, irritation and pain during intercourse. That's because the labia—the folds of tissue that surround and protect the vagina—loses plumpness when estrogen levels drop after menopause.

Self-defense: Ask your doctor about local estrogen therapy—creams, suppositories, rings or tablets inserted into the vagina—that can deliver small amounts of estrogen to help keep tissues plump.

Irwin Goldstein, MD, director of San Diego Sexual Medicine at Alvarado Hospital, San Diego. He is clinical professor of surgery, University of California at San Diego and editor-in-chief of *The Journal of Sexual Medicine.*

Ladies—Even Your Testosterone Can Be Too Low

Culley C. Carson, MD, Rhodes distinguished professor and chief of urology, University of North Carolina Medical Center, Chapel Hill.

Approximately 30 million American women are thought to have low levels of the androgens (so-called male hormones) they need, including testosterone and DHEA.

Common causes of these low levels include diminished ovarian function, estrogen supplementation (either by birth control pills or by hormone-replacement therapy) and impaired adrenal function.

Symptoms include: Osteoporosis, reduced sex drive (which could be due to diminished libido or lack of interest due to pain or dryness), loss of muscle tone, low energy, lack of mental clarity and decreased enjoyment of life.

Diagnosis: To check for androgen deficiency in women, it's best to measure levels of testosterone and DHEA-sulfate (DHEA-S), another androgen. Total testosterone less than 30 nanograms per deciliter (ng/dL) and/or DHEA-S levels less than 100 micrograms per deciliter (mcg/dL) may be reason to consider supplementation.

Treatment: Among women who have sexual dysfunction due to low androgens, treatment using low-dose testosterone or low-dose DHEA significantly increases sex drive—approximately 70% of the time. Although the US Food and Drug Administration (FDA) has not yet approved testosterone supplements for use in women, many doctors are prescribing them anyway.

Warning: Unnecessary supplementation can lead to excessive androgen levels, resulting in heavier pubic hair growth, clitoral enlargement, acne, increased facial hair growth, lowered voice, and reduced levels of HDL ("good") cholesterol. Close monitoring of testosterone levels is advised.

The Romance Gene

Differences in sexual desire and performance may be determined by normal genetic variations rather than by learned behavior or emotional problems. Researchers report that some variations in the D4 receptor gene depress sexual desire and function, while other variations have the opposite effect.

Hebrew University of Jerusalem.

Dating for Adults

Judy Kuriansky, PhD, clinical psychologist and sex therapist on the adjunct faculty of Columbia University Teachers College in New York City. She is author of five books, including *The Complete Idiot's Guide to a Healthy Relationship* (Alpha). *www.sexualtherapy.com/therapists/ jkuriansky.htm*

Looking for love in midlife or beyond may feel silly, scary or self-delusional—but you're never too old for a new romance. *To find companionship...*

•**Replace insecure thoughts with confident ones.** Instead of worrying, "I'm too old-fashioned for this new age," tell your-self, "I'll just be me and that's enough."

•**Let go of the past.** If you're a widow, imagine your beloved giving you permission to date. If you're divorced, set aside old resentments.

•**Be realistic, not pessimistic.** Older women do outnumber older men—but you're an individual, not a statistic. Many men value maturity and shared interests more than youthful beauty.

•**Expand your image of a good man.** Look twice at men who are shorter or older or even younger than you, or who come from a different background. Labels don't matter—people matter.

•**Circulate.** Ask friends to introduce you… get active in community groups…take a class.

•**Stay safe on dates.** Meet blind dates in public places. Take your own car and money. Give out your cell-phone number, not your home phone number or address.

•**Prepare your adult children.** Tell them that you're dating, but don't share intimate details—you're the parent, not a pal. Introduce a beau only when the relationship gets serious.

Today's Rules of Online Romance

Judsen Culbreth, journalist and author of *The Boomers' Guide to Online Dating* (Rodale).

More and more of us are communicating by e-mail. Even romances develop through exchanges of e-mails, not phone calls or face-to-face encounters.

Here's how to compose e-mails that will win your correspondent's heart…

STRIKING THE RIGHT TONE

When we converse via e-mail, we can't count on tone of voice to convey our mood or meaning, so it's vital that our words strike the right note. *To do so, keep in mind that…*

•**Happy is better than heavy.** Don't burden a potential partner with your problems during the early months of the relationship. Don't bring up past relationships either. Rehashing old romances may prevent the two of you from focusing on each other. It could even make it appear that you haven't gotten over your past partner. If asked about a previous relationship, keep your answer brief and neutral.

Example: "My ex and I are on good terms now."

Also avoid focusing on where you would like the relationship to lead. Mentioning marriage or children early on could scare away a potential partner.

•**Flirtatious is better than sexually permissive.** Sexual advances and innuendo can seem overly forward in e-mail. Write your messages as if you were looking for friendship first and foremost.

Example: Write about your favorite activities, and ask your correspondent to tell you about the things that he/she enjoys.

That doesn't mean you can't be flirtatious. One effective way to subtly flirt via e-mail is simply to use the person's name.

Example: "Sam, what do you like about Martha's Vineyard?"

•**Warmth is better than sarcasm.** Sarcasm can come off as mean-spirited in print. If you want to be funny, aim for jolly or self-deprecating.

Also, reread your correspondent's notes before responding. Did he mention that he had an upcoming dentist's appointment? Ask how it went. Did he say that he loves a particular old movie? Let him know the next time it's showing on cable. Remembering what was said shows that you care.

•**Colorful is better than bland.** Descriptive language makes your writing fun and interesting.

Example: "I'm long and leggy" is better than "I'm tall."

MINDING THE DETAILS

The body of the text isn't the only way you present yourself in an e-mail relationship. *Pay attention to the…*

- **Subject line.** If you build up a long string of replies with the same subject line, you risk making the relationship feel stale. Instead, vary the line by being funny, friendly or even enigmatic.

    Examples: "Loved your note!" "Sigh…" or "Are you ready for this?"

- **Greeting.** "Dear Pat," works as a greeting in a traditional letter, but it seems formal in an e-mail. Consider opening with "Hello Pat," then shifting to "Hi Pat" as the relationship progresses.

- **Ending.** "Sincerely," "Regards" and "Best Wishes" are too stiff for e-mail. One great way to end an e-mail is to say what you're about to do. This makes you seem like a happy, active person who is fun to be with.

    Examples: "I'm off to the gym," "Got to go meet my friends," or "Time to pack for my trip."

- **Timing.** Wait a day before responding to messages you receive, particularly early in the relationship. Immediate answers make you appear too eager.

- **Spelling.** Always use the spell-check tool and heed the rules of grammar. A poorly written e-mail can make you seem unintelligent or sloppy.

Co-Worker Smarts

Alan L. Sklover, partner, Sklover & Associates LLC, which specializes in employment law for executives, New York City, and author of *Fired, Downsized or Laid Off: A Guide to Negotiating Severance Packages* (Henry Holt).

B e extra cautious about dating a coworker. The resignation of Harry Stonecipher, Boeing's CEO in 2005, for an office affair is a cautionary tale of the dangers of dating coworkers. No law expressly forbids consensual relationships between coworkers, but more companies are making their own policies to discourage such liaisons.

Bosses: Don't go into a room with a member of the opposite sex and close the door—a closed-door meeting might be considered

unnecessarily confining or suggest intimacy. Don't give frequent gifts to a subordinate or coworker. If you choose to date someone from the office, take along other people the first few times so they can witness that the dates are consensual.

Employees: Dress in a businesslike fashion. When telling stories or jokes, pretend that your grandmother is in the room so that you'll tone down any off-color expressions that could give the wrong impression.

Close Relationships= A Healthy Immune System

L ack of close relationships may weaken immunity.

Recent finding: Women who say they have difficulty forming attachments to others have decreased activity of their natural killer cells, key defenders against illness.

Possible reason: An inability to form close relationships may increase stress, which causes the body to produce the stress hormone cortisol. Cortisol inhibits the function of natural killer cells.

Angelo Picardi, MD, senior researcher, Center of Epidemiology and Health Surveillance and Health Promotion, Italian National Institute of Health, Rome, and lead author of a study of 61 women, published in *Psychosomatic Medicine*.

Little Words You Should Never Use

Judy Kuriansky, PhD, clinical psychologist and sex therapist on the adjunct faculty of Columbia University Teachers College in New York City. She is author of five books, including *The Complete Idiot's Guide to a Healthy Relationship* (Alpha). *www.sexualtherapy.com/therapists/jkuriansky.htm*

R emarks made with the best of intentions may unwittingly cause hurt feelings. *Here are common words to avoid…*

• **Don't.** This word backfires, reinforcing undesirable behavior by conjuring up a mental image of it. That's why telling your husband in bed, "Don't touch me so hard," actually may make it more likely that he'll unintentionally continue to be heavy-handed.

Better: "Do." Helping him to visualize the desirable behavior ("Please do touch me lightly here, because it feels great") increases the odds that he'll remember—which will be gratifying to you both.

• **But.** This word voids a compliment. "That's a chic haircut, but you must spend all day fussing with it," actually is an insult.

Better: "And." This reminds you to keep comments positive, as in, "…and the bangs accent your pretty eyes."

Smart Women Don't Marry

Smart women are less likely to marry. Check your IQ score to be sure.

Recent finding: For every 15-point increase in IQ score above the average of 100, a woman's likelihood of marrying falls by almost 60%.

The Atlantic Monthly, The Watergate, 600 New Hampshire Ave., NW, Washington, DC 20037.

Marital Stress Causes Cardiac Changes

Among people in unhappy marriages, those who spend less time with a spouse have lower blood pressure than those with a lot of contact. In good marriages, those who spend a lot of time with a spouse have lower blood pressure than those who don't.

Unknown: Whether it is better for your health to try to improve a troubled marriage or get a divorce.

Harvey B. Simon, MD, associate professor of medicine, Harvard Medical School, Boston, and editor, *Harvard Men's Health Watch.*

The Power of the Pill

Women's choice of mates is affected by birth control pills. Women typically are attracted to the scent of men whose MHC genes—which affect the immune and reproductive systems—are unlike their own.

But: The Pill alters preferences for male scents, so users tend to choose men with MHC genes similar to their own. Couples with similar MHC genes have more fertility problems… and because scent influences sexual attraction, relationships may suffer when women go off the Pill.

S. Craig Roberts, PhD, lecturer, evolutionary psychology, University of Liverpool, England, and leader of a study of 110 women and 97 men, published in *Proceedings of the Royal Society.*

What's Your Love Personality?

Helen Fisher, PhD, research professor of anthropology at Rutgers University, New Brunswick, New Jersey, and chief scientific adviser to the online dating site Chemistry.com, a division of Match.com. She is author of four books including, most recently, *Why We Love: The Nature and Chemistry of Romantic Love* (Holt). *www.helenfisher.com*

When your spouse does things that mystify you or drive you crazy, you probably wish he/she would behave more reasonably. Yet your partner may not be "programmed" to behave any other way.

My research suggests that each of us has a "love personality"—how we are naturally inclined to behave with a romantic partner—that may depend on the particular chemicals dominant in one's brain. This research comes from my analysis of existing genetic and pharmaceutical studies, as well as from my work as chief scientific adviser to the Internet dating site Chemistry.com. I devised a series of questions to establish to what degree we express specific chemicals in the brain and collected data on 28,000 men and women. I determined that love personalities can be divided into four main types, based on which brain chemicals—serotonin, dopamine, estrogen and testosterone—are predominant. Some people show characteristics of one type...others are a combination. *The four types...*

BUILDERS

Serotonin promotes orderly, cautious behavior and respect for authority. More than the other three types, Builders enjoy planning far ahead. They are literal and predictable, fastidious about their possessions, conscientious and dutiful. They tolerate routine well.

What the Builder brings to a relationship: Builders are good at forming strong networks and run businesses and households with great efficiency. A Builder will never keep you waiting, forget to fill the gas tank or write down the wrong flight departure time.

Sources of stress: Builders are stubborn—if you helpfully suggest to a Builder a better way to mop the floor, you may find yourself in an argument. Builders can be moralistic and overly rule-bound. They are suspicious of new experiences and ideas—in fact, they will be quick to point out all the reasons why an idea might not work.

Sex and fidelity: Builders are most likely to be attracted to other Builders. They are serious when they court. Sex may become routine, but Builders like routines, and two Builders will rarely fight about their life in the bedroom. Highly loyal, Builders are unlikely even to consider divorce.

Living with a Builder: Let the Builder do things his way, even if you're convinced there is a better way. If you crave more adventure than the Builder, map out a new experience beforehand so that it doesn't look like a risk ...or let the Builder plan the details.

EXPLORERS

High dopamine activity is associated with curiosity, spontaneity, risk-taking, novelty-seeking, irreverence, mental flexibility and optimism.

What the Explorer brings to a relationship: Explorers are enthusiastic and full of energy. Charming and creative, Explorers don't like to be told what to do—they chafe at rules, plans and schedules. They can be extravagant gift givers.

Sources of stress: The Explorer's impulsiveness can grate on someone who would like to know what time to be ready for dinner or who prefers to buy theater tickets in advance. An Explorer doesn't like repetitive tasks, so you shouldn't depend on an Explorer to take out the garbage every night.

Sex and fidelity: Explorers tend to be attracted to other Explorers, and they make exciting sex partners. Instead of discussing the deep meaning of a relationship, an Explorer would rather make love or go out together for a good time. Big fights may be followed by passionate lovemaking. It is important to have adventures with an Explorer, lest he decide to find someone else to share his experiences with.

Living with an Explorer: Don't try to keep an Explorer from doing what interests him. Instead of imposing rules, find parameters that the Explorer can live with.

Example: A Builder husband and Explorer wife had repeated showdowns over the Explorer's chronic lateness. They finally agreed that the Explorer would call her husband when she was running late...and that the Builder would go ahead with plans instead of waiting for his wife, who would join him later.

NEGOTIATORS

Men, as well as women, can have high estrogen activity in the brain, promoting connection-seeking.

What the Negotiator brings to a relationship: Negotiators are highly verbal, agreeable and good at reading people. They are skilled at coming up with the right thing to say to make others feel valued. Negotiators have rich imaginations and think holistically—they see creative and unusual connections between disparate pieces of information. They are flexible and willing to change their minds.

Sources of stress: The ability to see many sides of an issue can make it difficult for Negotiators to reach decisions. They are so imaginative about possibilities that they may create constant anxiety for themselves. Because Negotiators want everyone to be happy, they don't always say clearly what they need or mean, leading to confusion and misunderstanding.

Sex and fidelity: Negotiators tend to be most attracted to Directors. The Negotiator needs the Director's logic, forthrightness and decisiveness to get things done.

Negotiators seek deep intimacy with their partners—they want a soul mate—so they will be patient, forgiving and compassionate. But if a Negotiator feels that he won't ever "reach" you to share an intimate life together, he may eventually turn elsewhere for the romance he craves.

Living with a Negotiator: Recognize that what sounds to you like endless processing is a way for the Negotiator to address the needs of everyone involved. Don't rush the Negotiator's decision. Trust that once he has examined all the angles, the solution will make a lot of people happy, including you.

DIRECTORS

Both women and men can have high testosterone activity in the brain, leading them to be competitive, straight-forward, logical and pragmatic.

What the Director brings to a relationship: You don't have to second-guess Directors—they say what they mean without nuance. Because of their ambition and competitiveness, they are dedicated to their work and typically well-paid. Directors like to focus very deeply on a few subjects and learn everything about them.

Sources of stress: Directors can alienate people with their bluntness, coming across as dictatorial and aloof. They get impatient when others are not as focused as they are or don't immediately grasp their ideas. They have a hard time leaving work behind—at the beach, the Director is the one checking E-mail.

Sex and fidelity: Directors are most likely to be attracted to Negotiators. The Director relies on the Negotiator's people skills. Sex is a genuine form of intimacy for them. They tend to be loyal, but if they cannot get the physical connectedness they need, they will seek it elsewhere.

Living with a Director: Don't give a Director hints or make gentle requests—the message will not get through. Instead of "Would you have time to…" say, "I need you to do this by Friday." During disagreements, appeal to logic ("This would be more efficient") rather than emotion ("This makes me frustrated").

To get Directors to relax outside work hours, encourage activities that are absorbing, challenging or competitive enough to distract them, such as joining a tennis league or a book club.

More from Dr. Helen Fisher…

Our Love Quiz Can Improve Your Marriage

Chemistry is more than just a metaphor for romantic compatibility. Brain chemicals really do play a role in determining whom we are attracted to and the strengths and tensions in our relationships.

My research has identified four main "love types"—Explorer, Builder, Director and Negotiator—based on whether the chemical dopamine, serotonin, testosterone or estrogen is dominant in a person's brain. In "What's Your Love Personality?" I reported on some of my research. *Here, more on how to make your relationships stronger by knowing your love type…*

WHICH TYPE ARE YOU?

Each of us is a combination of all four types and may express any of the four styles depending on the situation. However, we tend to act according to one type most often. *For clues to your love type, answer "yes" or "no" to the following questions…*

1. I do things spur of the moment.

2. I have a wide range of interests.

3. I am more creative than most.

4. My friends and family would say that I have traditional values.

5. I think consistent routines keep life orderly and relaxing.

6. People should behave according to standards of proper conduct.

7. I am able to solve problems without letting emotion get in the way.

8. Debating is a good way to match my wits with others.

9. I am more analytical and logical than most people.

10. I like to get to know my friends' deepest needs and feelings.

11. After an emotional film, I often still feel moved by it hours later.

12. When I wake from a vivid dream, I need a few seconds to return to reality.

SCORING

If you answered "yes" to questions 1, 2 and 3, you probably are an Explorer. (Dopamine is dominant.)

Explorers love novelty, spontaneity, freedom and risk. They are curious, creative, offbeat, magnetic, flexible, optimistic and full of energy.

If you answered "yes" to questions 4, 5 and 6, you probably are a Builder. (Serotonin is dominant.)

Builders are guardians of tradition and respecters of authority. Cautious but not fearful, they prefer rules and routines and are comfortable with statistics and concrete details. They are calm, orderly, persistent, patient and frugal. Builders also are highly social—community-oriented, cooperative and loyal.

If you answered "yes" to questions 7, 8 and 9, you probably are a Director. (Testosterone is dominant.) Although testosterone is popularly thought of as a male hormone, Directors can be male or female.

Directors are decisive, exacting, competitive, ambitious and self-contained. They say what they mean. Logical and analytical, they excel in technical fields, such as engineering, computer sciences and mechanical repairs. Their focus tends to be narrow, but they go deep in areas that interest them.

If you answered "yes" to questions 10, 11 and 12, you probably are a Negotiator. (Estrogen is dominant, but Negotiators can be female or male.)

Negotiators are big-picture thinkers—imaginative, open to possibility and comfortable with ambiguity. They are empathetic, intuitive, emotionally expressive and sensitive to others' needs, as well as introspective and aware of their own internal processes. Negotiators are adept with words and have good people skills—they are agreeable and read tone and gesture well.

If you answered "yes" to questions in more than one category, choose the category in which you had the most "yes" answers. If there is a tie, you exhibit traits from those categories.

NATURAL PAIRINGS

Some love types are natural fits...

• **Explorer-Explorer.** Explorers make ideal playmates for each other. They delight in spur-of-the-moment adventures and lusty sex. They don't bicker over details or get on each other's nerves.

Advice for Explorer-Explorer pairs: Be willing to set limits together—unrestrained Explorers can burn each other out. Because novelty is so appealing to Explorers, adultery is a danger—both partners need the resolve to say a strong "no" to temptation.

• **Builder-Builder.** Builders enjoy sharing family traditions and social networks. They make joint plans, stick to schedules and appreciate frugality.

Advice for Builder-Builder pairs: Because Builders believe that there is one right way to do things, stubbornness can be a problem—disagreements over trivial matters can lead to a stalemate. Builders need to work on letting go of the little things and focusing on their shared values.

• **Director-Negotiator.** The see-all-sides Negotiator benefits from the Director's decisiveness, while the demanding, analytical Director appreciates the Negotiator's social skills. They have lively discussions—the Director's depth of knowledge is complemented by the Negotiator's contextual perspective.

Advice for Director-Negotiator pairs: When this couple argues, the Director is likely to fly off the handle and then quickly forget about the incident, while the Negotiator may nurse hurt feelings for years. A Director and Negotiator should agree on how they will deal with flare-ups—perhaps by going to separate rooms until tempers cool.

The Director needs to risk revealing deeper feelings to the Negotiator. And when the Negotiator needs something, he/she needs to say so.

CHALLENGING PAIRINGS

These pairings are more challenging, but any pairing can work if partners make allowances for their differences...

•**Explorer-Builder.** An Explorer can add stimulation to a Builder's quiet life, while the Builder provides security. But over time, the Explorer may feel constrained and the Builder neglected.

Advice for Explorer-Builder pairs: Look for ways to combine adventure and stability.

Example: A trip with friends to a mountain lodge, where the Builder can socialize by the lake while the Explorer goes rock climbing.

•**Builder-Director.** Both types are emotionally contained and value persistence, calm and order. However, both like to be in control, leading to potential conflict. Also, the Director's boldness and self-reliance may clash with the Builder's cautious nature.

Advice for Builder-Director pairs: Focus on mutual goals. The Director's ambition, combined with the Builder's planning skills and social network, can make for a comfortable home and stature in the community.

•**Explorer-Negotiator.** Both are curious, imaginative and open-minded. Tensions stem from different expectations of intimacy. For the Explorer, intimacy means doing things together ...talking helps the Negotiator feel close.

Advice for Explorer-Negotiator pairs: The Negotiator needs to recognize that fun can be bonding. The Explorer should practice looking the Negotiator in the face during conversations and make an effort to speak the language of emotions.

Example: The Explorer might tell stories about past adventures that include some speculation about how the experience changed him/her.

•**Director-Explorer.** Both types are unconventional, inventive, irreverent and highly sexual—all areas of strong compatibility. But the Director spends long hours at work, while the Explorer is more interested in having a good time. The Director's deep knowledge about a subject may seem obsessive to the Explorer. The Explorer's broad interests and hedonism may strike the Director as superficial.

Advice for Director-Explorer pairs: Since neither is possessive, each can pursue his/her interests independently without worrying that the other will feel left out. But schedule shared activities to avoid drifting apart.

•**Builder-Negotiator.** Both value strong, stable relationships. However, the Builder may be befuddled by the Negotiator's emotionalism and the Negotiator disappointed by the Builder's lack of introspection and imagination.

Advice for Builder-Negotiator pairs: Make the most of commonalities—nurturing, nest-building, community ties.

•**Director-Director.** Directors tend to appreciate each other's straightforward style, competence and drive. Directors don't like to fail, which makes them willing to ride out difficulties.

Advice for Director-Director pairs: Beware of workaholism. Directors often don't make time for each other, so put shared activities on the schedule and commit to them.

•**Negotiator-Negotiator.** These couples are highly sensitive to each other's feelings, have inspired conversations and go to great lengths to please each other. Yet they easily can become mired in analysis of the relationship and paralyzed by minor decisions.

Advice for Negotiator-Negotiator pairs: Set time limits on discussions of relationship dynamics.

What's in a Name?

More newly married women are changing their names. Those taking their husbands' last names went from 77% in 1990 to 83% by the year 2000.

Claudia Goldin, PhD, Henry Lee Professor of Economics, Harvard University, Cambridge, Massachusetts, and leader of a study of female college graduates and name changes, published in *Journal of Economic Perspectives.*

Good Marriages Help Women Destress

After a busier-than-usual day at work, women who come home to a loving spouse have a bigger drop in the stress hormone cortisol than women whose marriages are less happy. Men's cortisol levels drop when they come home regardless of the state of their marriages.

Darby E. Saxbe, CPhil, researcher, University of California, Los Angeles, and leader of a study of 30 married couples, published in *Health Psychology*.

Little Tricks to Make Your Marriage Much, Much Happier

Harville Hendrix, PhD, therapist and chancellor of the Institute for Imago Relationship Therapy, New York City. *www.harvilleandhelen.com*. He is author of several books and coauthor, with his wife, Helen LaKelly Hunt, PhD, of *Receiving Love: Transform Your Relationship by Letting Yourself Be Loved* (Atria).

It doesn't take a major change to improve a marriage. The path to a more loving relationship is tread with small steps—with an unexpected compliment…the touch of a hand…or a call just to say "hello." You can spend thousands of dollars on a big anniversary bash for your spouse, but the celebration won't mean much if you haven't said "I love you" on the other days of the year.

Some little things that can make your marriage better…

• **Honor "otherness."** The longer we're married, the more we tend to forget that we're married to another person. We begin to think of our spouses as extensions of ourselves—then we get frustrated when they act in ways that we wouldn't. We say things like, "Why would you do something like that?" or "How can you think that?" These reactions overlook the fact of difference, that our partners are not a part of us and that they have their own reality.

"Otherness" is part of being married—no two people are completely compatible. Be curious about these differences, not critical. Ask your spouse why he holds an opinion or took a certain action. Don't make him feel that he is wrong. Validate the opinion or action with a response such as, "I can see the sense of that."

• **Eliminate negativity.** If there's something about your relationship or your partner's behavior that you don't like, it rarely helps to complain about it. Instead, it is better to ask for what you want.

Examples: Rather than say, "You never take me out to eat," try, "I'd like it if we went out to eat more." Instead of "We don't have sex anymore," say, "I'd like us to have sex more often." Then turn your statement into a dialogue by adding, "What do you think?"

This approach makes it less likely that your partner will feel attacked and more likely that you'll get what you want. Strive to eliminate negativity—it injures your partner and ruptures your connection. Requests change behavior more often than complaints.

• **Make the bedroom a problem-free zone.** Everyone needs a place where he can feel safe and happy. If you and your spouse agree to ban arguments and serious discussions from the bedroom, you will end each day together in a place of serenity. Select another place in your home for serious discussions, such as the living room—and set a time limit on those discussions.

• **Acknowledge some of the little things your partner does for you.** Perhaps your spouse makes you breakfast every morning or changes the oil in your car. You might consider such chores to be his responsibilities, but that doesn't free you from your responsibility to express thanks. It's wonderful to have someone in your life who does things for you. The fact that your partner helps you out on a regular basis makes his efforts even more worthy of praise, not something to be ignored.

Helpful: When you express gratitude for your spouse's contributions, say it like you mean it and be specific about what you appreciate. A heartfelt statement such as, "I love that you look at me when I am talking. Thank you," means more than an offhand "Thanks."

•**Take the initiative.** We forget that feelings of tenderness between partners don't just happen—we must take the initiative to remind our spouses that we still love them.

What you do to accomplish this isn't terribly important, so long as you do something daily that shows your spouse you're thinking of him. Call her from work on your lunch hour just to say "hello"...bring him a cup of coffee in the morning...or touch her shoulder and say, "I love you," as you walk by.

Touch your partner the way he likes to be touched. Sharing a touch makes us feel closer to each other—yet few couples take the time to enjoy each other's touch in nonsexual ways. Some people like back rubs...others prefer foot rubs or just a touch on the face. If you're not sure what your partner likes, ask him. Make touch an everyday routine until it becomes second nature.

•**Laugh together.** Share a funny anecdote or cartoon. Do whatever it takes to laugh with your spouse on a regular basis, even if it's simply watching a humorous movie or television show together.

Emotional memories stay with us on a much deeper level than other memories. If you laugh often with your spouse, the whole emotional center of your lives together will improve.

•**Receive compliments well.** Many people don't know how to handle a compliment. If you say that you like his shirt, he might say, "Oh, it's old."

People brush off compliments because they have inner doubts about their abilities or they're trying to be modest. If you regularly dismiss compliments from your spouse, you'll hurt his feelings, strain your relationship and bring the compliments to an end. Instead say, "Thank you. I like hearing that and appreciate your noticing." Let your spouse's compliment in and accept the warmth being sent your way.

Love the Spouse You Have

Mark O'Connell, PhD, clinical instructor of psychology at Harvard Medical School in Boston. He also is a marriage therapist in private practice in Chestnut Hill, Massachusetts, and author of *The Marriage Benefit: The Surprising Rewards of Staying Together* (Springboard). *www.markoconnellphd.com.*

When a marriage becomes contentious, cold or boring, too many couples point fingers or pack bags, lamenting lost dreams of marital bliss. Yet the disappointments behind today's dismal divorce rate often result not from truly unacceptable situations (serial affairs, spousal abuse)—but instead stem from couples' seriously unrealistic expectations of what a marriage can and should be.

The fix: By recognizing that relationships evolve over time and adapting to those inevitable changes, we can come to understand ourselves better...love our spouses better... and experience a deeply satisfying partnership that will last the rest of our lives.

MONEY MATTERS

One way we measure happiness is by comparing ourselves with people around us—and in that regard, the most tangible factor is wealth. When your neighbor's house is nicer or your brother's paycheck is bigger, whom are you likely to resent? Your spouse.

Be realistic: More money is not the key to permanent peace, because there always will be people who are richer. *Instead, resolve the underlying conflict by figuring out what money means to each of you...*

•**Is money a sign of self-worth**—because you were ashamed of growing up poor or for another reason? If so, remind yourself of nonmaterial achievements—the way you raised wonderful children together or serve as community leaders.

•**Is money a safeguard against insecurity**—because you were horrified when a cousin lost her home or you experienced some other financial trauma? Work with a financial planner to set up a long-term budget.

• **Is money an expression of love**—because your father lavished your mother with jewelry? Appreciate the way your husband shows his love by bringing you breakfast in bed.

Helpful: Make a list of your top five financial goals, and have your husband do the same. Together, compare the lists…agree on several goals you both share…and brainstorm ways to achieve them. When you know what truly matters, money becomes merely a means to an end, not the end goal itself.

BEDROOM BATTLES

He wants more sex…you want more cuddling. You crave variety…he's happy on top. Toss in the influence of Hollywood—gorgeous couples who are eternally lusty and lip-locked —and unrealistic expectations about sex can run wild.

Be realistic: Take a compassionate look at the underlying reasons why lovemaking has become disappointing. Maybe she avoids sex because she thinks her body is not as beautiful as it once was. Maybe he sticks with one position not because he's indifferent to your preferences, but because he's worried about losing his erection. The key is to talk specifically about what you need or want—and encourage your spouse to do the same. When you both share honestly and listen with open minds, you can reach a satisfying compromise and find joy in your continuing mutual attraction.

Try this: Agree to share a kiss (a real kiss, not a peck) at least once a day—not necessarily with the goal of having it lead to intercourse, but simply to enhance the bond between you. Research shows that kissing sparks sexual desire and reduces levels of the stress hormone cortisol. Less stress is always a good thing—in or out of the bedroom.

AGE PREJUDICE

Have you ever caught sight of yourself in a mirror and thought, "Who is that old person?" Looking at your husband can be like looking in that mirror. In his paunch and wrinkles, you

see evidence of your own advancing age—and wish you didn't have to be reminded.

Be realistic: Growing old actually can improve a marriage—once you give up the fantasy that starting over with someone else will automatically make you feel young again.

The trick: Face up to whatever bothers you about aging. Perhaps you're disappointed that your bad shoulder has put an end to your tennis games together…or you're afraid that your husband's couch potato habits will lead to a heart attack. If so, try new activities together that can accommodate your not-as-young body, such as bicycling…or gently urge him to go for walks with you, not because he's a "lazy old bum," but because you want him to be with you for years to come.

IDEALIZATION OF LOVE

If only we could bottle that passion of the first year of a relationship, when romance made life dreamy. But it's biologically impossible to sustain that intensity of feeling day in and day out for years on end.

Reason: The early stages of romance are associated with big physiological changes—in fact, the brain pathways that govern falling in love appear to be the same as those involved in addiction. However, studies using magnetic resonance imaging (MRI) suggest that about 18 months into a relationship, brain chemistry again begins to alter—this time in ways that promote a change in focus from romance and lust to long-term attachment and contentment.

Be realistic: If love stayed at a fevered pitch, we would never get anything else done…and we would never move past the starry-eyed stage and *really* get to know each other. Love between two people is not stagnant or defined solely by romance—it is a combination of fascination, friendship, passion, shared purpose, trust, continuity and companionship.

What to do: Make a list of everything your spouse does that pleases you. Does he listen to your mother's endless complaints with a kind ear? Is he a thoughtful planner—for fun activities as well as important life issues? Does he keep his word? Look for the qualities you value in any long-term friendship. Maybe he's not composing adoring poems for you anymore, but he shares your commitment to family and supports you in times of crisis—and that kind of partnership provides a path to lifelong marital happiness.

Revive Your Romance

Judy Kuriansky, PhD, clinical psychologist and sex therapist on the adjunct faculty of Columbia University Teachers College in New York City. She is author of five books, including *The Complete Idiot's Guide to a Healthy Relationship* (Alpha). *www.sexualtherapy.com/therapists/jkuriansky.htm*

Everyday life can quash the romance in even the best of relationships. *To restore the magic…*

• **Relive the past.** Reminisce with your partner about the dawn of your romance—how you first flirted at a party…that time you filled his briefcase with love letters…how he wrapped you in his coat one chilly night and promised to keep you warm forever.

Write down details as if scripting a movie, then read scenes aloud or even revisit locales to recapture the heady emotions of falling in love.

• **Add spark to the present.** Agree on an activity—a painting class, a book club—you both would enjoy doing together. Hold hands for 10 minutes daily while expressing appreciation ("Thanks for driving Mom to the doctor") or admiration ("I adore your eyes").

Do something overtly romantic each day—dance in the kitchen, kiss in the moonlight—and end each evening by saying, "I love you."

• **Make promises for the future.** Create surprises that give anticipatory pleasure. Leave a message on his phone saying, "I have a treat for you waiting at home," and be ready with his favorite DVD or some sexy lingerie.

Write an IOU for a backrub or homemade cookies. Establish a weekly "date night" and take turns planning—and dropping hints about—romantic events to come.

Simple Secrets to a Stronger Marriage

Barton Goldsmith, PhD, psychotherapist based in Westlake Village, California. He writes "Emotional Fitness," a syndicated newspaper column, and is author of *Emotional Fitness for Couples* (New Harbinger). *www.bartongoldsmith.com*

Do you feel that your marriage isn't as strong as it could be? A few simple strategies can make the difference between a happy couple and an unhappy couple. *Ways to strengthen your marriage…*

• **Don't start a serious discussion unless you have your partner's full attention.** One person may pick a time to talk that is good for him/her but not good for his partner—then get angry when the partner is distracted.

• **If your partner springs a serious discussion on you when you're busy, explain that you very much want to talk with him, but now isn't a good time**—then suggest a time that is good.

That said, stopping what you're doing to have a conversation with your partner can be a winning move.

Example: Few things score a man as many points with his wife as turning off a sporting event on TV, looking her in the eye and saying, "Okay, let's talk."

• **Give in on the little things.** Remind yourself that "it isn't worth fighting over" when tensions rise on a minor matter.

Helpful: If neither spouse will back down on a particular point, each should rate the importance of the issue on a scale of one to 10. The spouse who rates it higher wins, and the other yields. Of course, you have to play fair—not everything can be a 10.

• **Hold a weekly relationship meeting.** This way, problems won't fester and escalate, and serious discussions are less likely to take place at inopportune moments. Limit meetings to one hour. Select a place where you both feel comfortable. Schedule a fun date afterward so this isn't something you dread.

• **Find alternate ways to say "I love you."** Many people are self-conscious about saying

"I love you," particularly in public. Use a code to say the same thing, and the message will be private and meaningful.

Examples: A professional couple pages each other with "111" to mean "I love you," and "112" to mean "I love you, too." A man squeezes his wife's hand three times before releasing it, as a silent message of "I love you."

• **Do nice things.** It's easy for a spouse to feel taken for granted after years of marriage. In successful relationships, both partners find small ways to make loving gestures on a regular basis.

Example: I know one husband who will take his wife's car to be washed and gassed up every Saturday. His wife brings him coffee every morning.

Don't be confrontational or accusatory.

Example: If the sound of your spouse cracking his knuckles drives you up the wall, say, "Could you warn me before you do that? The noise gets to me for some reason," instead of "Cut that out. I hate it."

• **Give 100% under every circumstance.** Some couples think that the spouse who created a problem is entirely responsible for solving it.

That's a recipe for relationship failure. Both partners must give everything they have whenever there's a problem, no matter who is to blame.

• **Fight fair.** Never call your partner names. Always leave the past in the past, and don't bring up old mistakes to win a new argument. Don't threaten to walk out unless you mean it—emotional blackmail only makes things worse.

• **Act romantic, and you'll feel romantic.** Couples often put off sex for weeks or months because one partner "doesn't feel like it" or doesn't feel "turned on" by the other. Instead of waiting for the mood to strike you, decide to do it and see what happens. Chances are that you will start to feel turned on.

Ten Habits of Happy Couples

Mark Goulston, MD, Los Angeles–based psychologist and consultant, *www.markgoulston.com*. He is coauthor of *The 6 Secrets of a Lasting Relationship* (Perigee).

Happy couples know that the real relationship begins when the honeymoon is over. *Here are the habits of highly happy couples…*

1. Go to bed at the same time. Remember the beginning of your relationship, when you couldn't wait to go to bed with each other to make love? Happy couples resist the temptation to go to bed at different times even if one partner wakes up later to do things while his/her partner sleeps.

2. Cultivate common interests. Don't minimize the importance of activities you can do together that you both enjoy. If you don't have common interests, develop them. At the same time, be sure to cultivate interests of your own. This will make you more interesting to your mate and prevent you from appearing too dependent.

3. Make trust and forgiveness your default mode. When happy couples have a disagreement or an argument that they can't resolve, they default to trusting and forgiving rather than distrusting and begrudging.

4. Focus on accentuating the positive. If you look for things that your partner does wrong, you always can find something. If you look for what he/she does right, you always can find something, too.

5. Hug each other as soon as you see each other after being apart for the day. Couples who say hello with a hug reaffirm their love for each other.

6. Say "I love you" and "Have a good day" every morning. This is a great way to buy some patience and tolerance as each partner sets out each day to battle traffic jams, long lines and other annoyances.

7. Say "good night" every night, regardless of how you feel. This tells your partner that regardless of how upset you are with him, you still want to be in the relationship. It says that what you and your partner have is bigger than any single upsetting incident.

8. Do a "weather" check during the day. Call your partner at home or at work to see how his day is going. This is a great way to adjust expectations so that you're more in sync later in the day. For instance, if your partner is having an awful day, it might be unreasonable to expect him to be enthusiastic about something good that happened to you.

9. Walk hand in hand. Happy couples are pleased to be seen together and often are in some kind of affectionate contact—hand in hand or hand on shoulder, for example. They are saying that they belong with each other.

10. Stick with it. Even if these actions don't come naturally, happy couples stick with them until they do become a part of their relationship. It takes 30 days for a change in behavior to become a habit and a minimum of six months for a habit to become a way of life—and love.

Married Women Sleep Well

Women who are happily married are more likely to fall asleep quickly and stay asleep than those with unhappy marriages. Both men and women who are divorced tend to sleep more poorly than married people.

University of Pittsburgh.

"New Ways" to Have a Happier Marriage

Do new things together as a couple to keep a marriage happy. Just going out on a date is not enough if you only go to places with which you are already familiar and only do things you have done before. Trying a new restaurant—or going for a whole new experience, such as taking an art class together or visiting an amusement park—can bring new sparks to a relationship. The brain's reward system—the same system that responds when you first fall in love—appears to respond positively to new, exciting experiences.

Arthur Aron, PhD, professor of social psychology, State University of New York at Stony Brook.

Happy Marriage by The Numbers

Pamela C. Regan, PhD, professor of psychology at California State University, Los Angeles. Her work with thousands of couples over the years led her to write the book *The Mating Game* (Sage).

When 4,000 couples in the UK who had been married for more than 16 years, on average, were polled on the keys to a long-lasting relationship, some interesting facts were discovered. On average, these married couples wanted four cuddles a day…romantic gestures from their partners every 10 days…unsolicited helpful gestures three times a month…and seven cozy nights in and two dinner dates out a month.

We can make our own marriages happier by incorporating these "happy marriage behaviors" into our lives. Striving to give your spouse, say, four cuddles a day might start out feeling artificial but eventually will become a rich part of the fabric of your relationship. Because kindness reaps kindness in relationships, you will encourage your spouse to reciprocate.

ROMANTIC GESTURES EVERY DAY

In a long-term relationship, we tend to think romantic gestures are no longer necessary. But surprising your spouse with flowers or a romantic dinner reminds your partner that you still are in love with him/her. If you decide to run a bath for your wife because she had a bad day, it shows that you are thinking specifically about what would please her, and that thoughtfulness is far more important than even the action itself. To be truly romantic, don't ask your partner what he might want. Instead

129

come up with your own idea—something that shows great attention to your partner's unique likes and dislikes.

CUDDLES A DAY

Make sure to hug or affectionately touch your partner at least four times a day. The happiest couples touch a lot. Try a slight squeeze on the shoulder at breakfast or a hug before you run off to work.

HELPFUL ACTIONS A MONTH

Thoughtful actions that lighten a partner's load are perceived as tender and caring—especially when done without anyone asking. Taking the initiative to do the dishes or make your spouse coffee in the morning shows that you are paying attention and makes your partner realize how central he/she is in your thoughts. You even can come right out and tell your partner, "I'm doing this because I love you and I want to make sure you know that."

COZY NIGHTS IN AND DINNER DATES OUT A MONTH

Your "cozy nights in" should be different from your everyday routine—make sure you aren't parked in front of the television. Instead, have dinner together, talk about your week, make plans, check in about upcoming activities.

Also, reserve special nights two times a month. Making the effort to dress up and go outside the family home together reinforces your "coupleness" and adds vitality and fun to a relationship.

Wedded Bliss Fights Depression

People who are depressed show greater psychological benefits after getting married than those who aren't depressed—possibly because they have more to gain from intimacy and emotional closeness.

Ohio State University.

Peaceful Relationships

An easy way to more peaceful relationships is to stop assuming that you know what someone else is thinking. Whatever you think another person is thinking, you are wrong. Assuming and acting on what you think another person is thinking leads to misunderstandings and upset. If we remember and accept that we're all different and we see the world in our own ways, relationships improve and we are happier.

Andy Feld, entrepreneur based in Morrison, Colorado, and author of *Simple Happy: Finally Learning to Listen to Yourself* (iUniverse).

How to Avoid Five Common Marriage Mistakes

Robert Stephan Cohen, Esq., founding partner of the law firm of Cohen Lans LLP in New York City. He is author of *Reconcilable Differences: 7 Keys to Remaining Together from a Top Matrimonial Lawyer* (Atria).

In my 30 years as a matrimonial lawyer, I have listened to countless men and women tell me why their marriages have failed. Disagreements over money and lifestyle, and, of course, infidelity lead all kinds of couples to divorce court. Divorce is so common nowadays —expected, even—that couples start thinking about it at the first sign of trouble.

I have seen enough divorce battles up close to have a good handle on the marital mistakes couples make. Many issues can be worked out—if there's a real desire on both sides. *Here are the most common problems that endanger marriages and strategies to deal with them…*

• **Parallel lives.** A couple might live in the same house and share the same bed, but their communication may be perfunctory. They could go for days without really talking.

Both spouses are so busy with their "own" lives that they more or less forget they're married. Whether because of busy careers, child-rearing or even time-consuming hobbies, they never make time for each other.

Strategy: Carve out time for each other by picking one night a week to go on a "date." That means time together—no phone calls or kids. Also, don't let a day go by without having a conversation, even if it is by phone.

I recall one professional couple who had little free time for each other. They decided to share part of every day by walking their dog together. This simple change helped get their marriage back on track.

• **Infidelity.** Cheating spouses who want to save their marriages need to stop cheating and—assuming that they haven't been discovered—keep their mouths shut.

Strategy: That's right—don't tell. Telling a spouse about a one-night stand or an affair that has ended may make you feel less burdened and more virtuous, but you'll have created an enormous obstacle that the marriage may never overcome. Marriages fail not because of an affair, but because of the aftermath.

Warning: If the cat is out of the bag, don't try to fix things alone. Couples who successfully get past a known affair almost always do so with the help of a neutral party, such as a member of the clergy or a therapist.

• **Sexual incompatibility.** Most people who have been married for a while have sex less frequently than they once did. Some people are fine with that. For others, a lack of sex colors their view of the entire marriage.

How powerful is the sexual aspect of a marriage? In three decades, I have never had anyone come into my office wanting a divorce even though sex at home was great.

Strategy: Couples must discuss their sexual needs and wants. The increasing popularity of sexual topics in mainstream media may make it easier to broach the subject. One spouse could refer the other to a relevant article, for example, or they could go to a therapist together.

• **Problem children.** I have seen a number of marriages collapse over differences in how to deal with troublesome children. In the cases that I have dealt with, the children were heavy drug users or had serious mental illness, but even minor problems with children can damage a marital relationship.

If spouses already are leading parallel lives, they begin to line up in separate camps with their children. For instance, one spouse might hide a child's misconduct from the other. Then when the misconduct becomes impossible to ignore, the parents take opposite positions. In my experience, mothers frequently think that love and affection will alter their children's behavior, while fathers are more apt to take a tough stance. The fierce arguments that follow can destroy a marriage.

Stepparents have a particularly tough time. The children often try to undermine the new marriage because they see it as a threat to their own relationships with their parents and they still hope that their parents will get back together.

Strategy: Enlist the help of a neutral authoritative third party. When doctors or therapists take over much of the decision-making in terms of the child's treatment, the husband and wife can address marital issues and comfort each other, which often brings them closer together.

• **Money matters.** Financial disagreements can cause serious trouble for any couple, no matter how well-off they are. Historically, wives often have been in the dark about a couple's finances—and this is true even today.

Whether the husband insists on handling the money alone or the wife is willfully ignorant, the result often is heated arguments about finances that spiral into personal attacks on each other's values, common sense and honesty. It undermines a marriage when, for instance, one spouse simply tells the other that the couple can't afford a trip this year.

Strategy: For the best chance of marital success, both spouses should be familiar with the household's finances and have a say in spending and investing. Then the couple's expectations will be similar and, in many cases, more realistic.

Some people think a prenuptial agreement is unromantic, but I'm a big fan of them—and the lessons I've learned through using prenups can be applied at any time during a marriage.

I recommend that engaged, newlywed or even long-married couples talk to an accountant, financial planner or even a divorce lawyer to get a sense of how the economics of the marriage can work. Then they should keep talking about money so that things stay out in the open at home.

Six Ways Men Can Make Their Marriages Much Happier...and What Wives Can Do, Too

Scott Haltzman, MD, a Distinguished Fellow of the American Pychiatric Association. He is a psychiatrist in private practice in Woonsocket, Rhode Island, and author of *The Secrets of Happily Married Men: Eight Ways to Win Your Wife's Heart Forever* (Jossey-Bass). *www.drscott.com*

Men often are told that to improve their marriages, they must share their hopes and fears with their wives and become more emotionally connected—in short, that they must behave in ways that are totally unnatural for the average man.

Good news: There are steps men can take that will make their marriages happier but still let them be themselves...

1. Treat your wife like a business client. Many men say they don't know what's expected of them in romantic relationships—yet the same men know what to do in business relationships. The two aren't as different as you might think.

If a client made you unhappy, you wouldn't fight with him/her. Instead, you would try to smooth things out. If this client made a crucial error, you would not criticize him—you would try to help him recover. Overall, you would try to understand who your client is, what his goals are and how you can help him succeed.

Treat your wife like this, and you won't go too far wrong. Of course, don't tell her you're treating her like a client. Just do it!

2. Forget the golden rule. "Do to others as you would have them do to you" isn't the best

advice for married men. When we treat our wives as we would like to be treated, we ignore the fact that our wives are quite different from us.

Forget whatever you think you know about what makes people happy, and observe your wife for a while. What does she really appreciate? What are her deepest interests and goals? Have your past gifts and gestures of love been on target? You might not have to work much harder to make your wife happier—you might just have to stop doing things that you would appreciate if someone did them for you and start doing things she will appreciate.

Example: Buy her a greeting card when there's no special occasion, and inside write how much you love her and need her. Leave the card someplace she will stumble on it unexpectedly. Such a gesture would mean little to the average husband but lots to the average wife.

3. Do more than say "I'm sorry." A single "I'm sorry" won't balance the scales when you say something critical of your wife...dismiss her ideas or her feelings...or make her feel ignored. It will most likely take five positive interactions for every negative one before you're back to par.

According to research by the Gottman Institute, a Seattle–based couples therapy organization, marriages tend to be happy when spouses—wives as well as husbands—interact with each other in a positive manner at least five times as often as they interact in a negative manner. Positive interactions might include paying her compliments, saying, "Thank you" or "I love you," offering to do something for her, holding her hand or paying attention to her.

4. Master the makeup. The happiness of your marriage is not determined by whether you fight—all couples do. It's determined by how well you patch things up afterward. Wait until you cool down—that typically takes about 20 minutes—then make a peace offering. Bring her a cup of tea...say you're sorry you argued...or tell her that you love her. Such gestures generally help couples get past the fight fast and back to the happy marriage.

Helpful: Makeups are easier if you avoid the four mistakes that turn arguments into lingering problems—criticizing, showing contempt, acting defensive and stonewalling (shutting down when your partner reaches out to you).

5. Seek your wife's opinion. Wives often feel that they don't have an equal voice in the decision-making. As far as most husbands are concerned, the issue isn't who is making the decisions, but whether the correct decisions are being made. Still, you can make your married life happier if you seek your wife's approval on your ideas, even when you believe you're right. Who knows? Maybe she is right. Don't dismiss her opinion out of hand—even when it isn't feasible. Instead, say something positive about the idea, then later express disappointment if together you "discover" that it won't work.

Example: She wants to fly across the country to visit your daughter next month. You know the trip won't fit into your budget. Rather than tell her no and invite her anger, establish that you're on her side. Say something like, "I always love to see our daughter. Let's see if we can afford it." Together, review the family's finances, and let her make the decision that you can't afford to go—or perhaps she'll think of a clever way so that you can afford it.

6. Do some cleaning. Most wives think their husbands should help more with housework. Many husbands think they do so much work around the yard and with the car that housework isn't their responsibility. Who's right? Studies by University of Michigan Institute for Social Research show that husbands are. When work hours both inside and outside the home are added up, even husbands who don't help with the cleaning often put in about as many hours of effort as their wives.

Unfortunately, if you try to argue this point, you're sure to lose. You can either spend your life bickering about whether you get enough credit for your contributions—working long hours at the office, tending the lawn and handling the car repairs—or you can do some housework and have a happier marriage. To make your wife really happy, figure out which household task is her least favorite and do it without being asked.

More from Dr. Scott Haltzman…

What Wives Can Do

Here's how wives can make their husbands happier and their marriages stronger…

• **Show a sense of humor.** Men are happier in their marriages when their wives don't take things too seriously. (Oddly, this doesn't work in reverse. Women usually prefer their husbands to take problems seriously—even when they initially were attracted to men who made them laugh.)

• **Don't overload him with problems.** Most men like to deal with one topic at a time. The rule of thumb is one problem per discussion.

• **Give him credit.** Even if your husband doesn't help with the housework, he probably does plenty. Let him know you appreciate his efforts.

• **Accept a physical gesture as a sign of love.** Men aren't always great at verbalizing their emotions, but holding your hand might mean the same thing as saying "I love you." If you press him for more words, you may only make him feel uncomfortable.

• **Make him feel like a hero.** Silly as it might seem, men want to be heroes to their wives. Compliment him for carrying something heavy or for making you feel safe when you walk down the street together at night.

• **Give him some space when he first gets home from work.** Many men have trouble transitioning from the workplace to home life. Give him 10 or 15 minutes of quiet time.

A Couple's Guide to Boosting Desire

Michele Weiner-Davis, MSW, social worker and relationship expert who is founder and director of the Divorce Busting Center in Boulder, Colorado, *www.divorcebusting.com*. She is author of seven books, including, *The Sex-Starved Wife: What to Do When He's Lost Desire* (Simon & Schuster).

One out of five marriages is virtually sexless—these couples have sex 10 or fewer times a year. In about one in three marriages, one spouse has a considerably larger sexual appetite than the other. If you see yourself in these statistics, don't despair—there's a great deal that can be done to boost your marriage's libido.

WHO'S SEX-STARVED?

A sex-starved marriage occurs when one spouse is desperately longing for more physical affection. Sex-starved marriages can't be defined by the number of times per week or month that a couple has sex, because there are no daily or weekly minimum requirements to ensure a healthy sex life. What works for one couple is grounds for divorce for another.

Most people believe that it is principally women who struggle with low sexual desire. While it's true that more men than women complain about the frequency of sex, the difference between genders isn't great. In fact, low desire in men is one of America's best-kept secrets. Too many men are simply unwilling to discuss their low desire with doctors, therapists or even their wives.

In a sex-starved marriage, the less interested spouse, whether male or female, typically thinks, *Why are you making such a big deal out of this? It's just sex.* But to the spouse wanting more physical closeness, sex is extremely important because it's not just a physical act. It's about feeling wanted, attractive, appreciated and emotionally connected. When the low-desire spouse doesn't understand sex's significance and continues to reject sexual advances, intimacy on many different levels tends to fall off. The couple stops cuddling on the couch, laughing at each other's jokes, going on dates together. In short, they stop being friends. This places their marriage in jeopardy.

CATCH-22

Frequently, the lower-desire spouse needs to feel close and connected on an emotional level before he/she is interested in being sexual. This usually entails spending quality time together and talking about intimate issues.

The catch-22 is that typically the higher-desire spouse needs to feel connected physically in order to open up with conversation or feel that spending time together is a priority.

One spouse waits for time together and heart-to-heart talks before investing in the physical relationship, while the other spouse waits to be touched before initiating time together or intimate conversation.

Each waits for the other to change.

THE NOs HAVE VETO POWER

The spouse with the lower sexual drive usually controls the frequency of sex—if he doesn't want it, it generally doesn't happen. This is not due to maliciousness or a desire for power—it just seems unimaginable to be sexual if one partner is not in the mood.

Furthermore, there is an unspoken and often unconscious expectation that the higher-desire spouse must accept the no-sex verdict, not complain about it—and, of course, remain monogamous. After decades of working with couples, I can attest that this is an unfair and unworkable arrangement. This is not to say that infidelity is a solution, but as with all relationship conflicts, being willing to find middle ground is the best way to ensure love's longevity.

If you're in a sex-starved marriage, you and your spouse need to make some changes. Don't worry about who takes the lead. Relationships are such that if one person changes, the relationship changes.

ADVICE FOR HIGH-DESIRE SPOUSES

Tune in to your spouse's needs outside the bedroom. High-desire people usually try to boost their spouses' desire by doing things that would turn themselves on, such as buying sexy lingerie and renting X-rated videos. However, these actions often don't work for their spouses, who are more likely to be responsive to loving behaviors outside the bedroom, such as helping more with housework and offering more compliments and fewer criticisms.

•**Talk from the heart.** Some people talk to their spouses about their sexual unhappiness, but instead of speaking from their hearts—which might prompt their spouses' empathy—harsh words are exchanged and tempers flare. Although it's understandable that unending rejection might lead to anger and resentment, these emotions are not aphrodisiacs. Instead of complaining, say, "I miss being close to you physically. We seem to get along so much better after we make love. I'm hoping that we can be more affectionate this week."

ADVICE FOR LOW-DESIRE SPOUSES

• **Don't ignore the problem.** If you and your spouse have been arguing about sex, don't stick your head in the sand. Your differences won't disappear—the only thing that will disappear is your intimate connection and friendship. There are many excellent resources to help you feel more sexual. Good books include *Hot Monogamy* by Patricia Love, MD, and Jo Robinson...*Rekindling Desire: A Step-by-Step Program to Help Low-Sex and No-Sex Marriages* by Barry and Emily McCarthy...and my book, *The Sex-Starved Marriage*. Also, licensed sex therapists can be found through the American Association of Sexuality Educators, Counselors and Therapists (*www.aasect.org*).

• **Just do it.** Perhaps you've had the experience of not being in the mood when your spouse approached you, but you gave it a try, and once you got into it, you enjoyed it. You're not alone. There are millions of people who simply don't experience out-of-the-blue sexy thoughts—unlike their more highly sexed spouses who may have lusty thoughts many times every day.

Try this: For the next two weeks, initiate sex twice each week. Also, flirt, call your spouse pet names, dress more provocatively and be more physically affectionate. Do this whether you feel like it or not. Then carefully watch your spouse for any changes in his behavior. An irritable, withdrawn, uncooperative spouse most likely will become much more fun and exciting to be around.

Why Women "Look for Love"

Two new small studies show that women experience heightened lust during ovulation, when they are most likely to conceive.

Women who don't find their regular partners sexy are especially likely to look outside their relationships during ovulation.

Martie G. Haselton, PhD, associate professor of communication studies, department of psychology, UCLA Center for Behavior, Evolution, and Culture, and leader of a study of campus volunteers, reported in *Evolution and Human Behavior*.

Affair-Proof Your Marriage

Steven D. Solomon, PhD, licensed clinical psychologist based in La Jolla, California. *www.therelationshipinstitute.org*. He is past president of the San Diego Psychological Association and coauthor of *Intimacy After Infidelity: How to Rebuild & Affair-Proof Your Marriage* (New Harbinger).

It seems that every week we learn about another politician, sports star or celebrity caught having an extramarital affair. But public figures are hardly the only ones guilty of infidelity. Surveys show that between 40% and 60% of husbands and between 30% and 50% of wives will be unfaithful at some point during their marriages.

Loneliness is the most common cause of infidelity. Almost everyone who enters into marriage does so intending to remain faithful to his/her partner, but long-term relationships are difficult. Partners often drift apart. The romance and the excitement of the initial period eventually ends. Many people do not know how to recover the closeness of a relationship once it fades, so they look outside the marriage for the fulfillment that they no longer receive at home.

The secret to a fulfilling and faithful long-term marriage is maintaining "emotional intimacy"—openness, trust, communication and caring between partners. When spouses feel this intimate closeness, they are unlikely to cheat.

Emotional intimacy is not just one skill—it is a combination of several different abilities...

SELF-INTIMACY

In order to have an emotionally intimate relationship with someone else, you first must understand your own emotions. Men in particular tend to pay insufficient attention to their emotions.

What to do: Take one to two minutes a few times a day to ask yourself three questions—What emotion(s) am I feeling right now? What specific situation is causing me to feel these emotions? What, if anything, do I need to do about this situation to take care of myself?

Example: I'm feeling anger...I'm feeling it because that guy cut me off on the highway ...The best thing I can do to take care of myself is let the anger go.

Run through these questions two or three times each day for 60 days and you will become much more aware of, and in charge of, your own emotions.

CONFLICT INTIMACY

All couples fight, but couples with emotionally intimate marriages fight productively. They don't just try to win arguments—they listen to their partners and come to understand their points of view, even if they do not agree.

What to do: When you are at odds with your spouse, you can try an established technique called Initiator to Inquirer or I to I. One spouse serves as "initiator." This spouse raises a troubling issue and shares his feelings and opinions on the matter. The initiator presents these thoughts as his perspective on the situation, not as the only way to look at it.

Example: The wife, as the initiator, says, "I felt hurt because it seemed to me as if you intentionally were trying to hurt my feelings," rather than "You intentionally hurt my feelings."

The other spouse's role is "inquirer." He is to repeat back the substance of what the initiator has said to show that he has heard and understood. The inquirer then asks questions that aid in understanding.

The inquirer is not allowed to question the validity of the initiator's feelings. When the desire to do so arises (and it will), the inquirer should silently remind himself that "this is not about me—it is only about my partner's perspective on the situation, and it is important for me to understand this perspective." When the initiator has had her say, the partners can switch roles. Avoid distractions during I to I time, and do not try this when one or both of you are exhausted.

This will not be a comfortable process at first, particularly if lots of negative feelings exist between you and your spouse. If you practice it two or three times each week for about 20 minutes at a time, it can become a very useful process for working through the marital conflicts that could lead to unhappiness. You and your partner will get good at fighting productively, which will end up bringing you closer.

AFFECTION INTIMACY

Being in love with your partner is not enough to prevent infidelity. You also must show your love and affection in the ways that your partner needs. Even a well-meaning spouse can run into trouble here if he fails to realize that the type of affection he is providing is not the type that his partner desires. *Types of marital affection include...*

• **Verbal.** How often do you tell your partner that you love him? How often do you express your gratitude for all of the things your partner does for you?

• **Actions.** How often do you do things just because your partner enjoys having them done? This might include buying a gift or doing some favor or chore for the partner that goes beyond your normal responsibilities.

• **Physical (nonsexual).** How often do you hold hands, hug or kiss your partner? How often do you provide foot massages or back rubs?

• **Sexual.** How often do you have sex with your partner?

What to do: Do not assume that your partner desires the same types of affection that you do or that you know what your partner needs because you have been together for years. Come right out and ask your partner what types of affection he/she would like you to provide more often. Get specifics. Then communicate your own needs. Do not take it personally if your partner says you have not shown enough affection. This reflects the partner's personal affection needs, not your own shortcomings.

Example: A man thinks he shows his wife plenty of affection by buying gifts, holding hands and helping out around the house. His wife feels he is never affectionate, because she wants verbal affection and he never says, "I love you."

If you fail to provide the types and amounts of affection that your partner considers appropriate, your spouse may stray. Provide the desired affection, and your spouse is less likely to seek it from others.

More from Dr. Steven Solomon...

To Tell or Not to Tell

My patients who have had or are having extramarital affairs often ask me if they should tell their spouses about the affair. I tell them that if the affair is ongoing and you have no intention of ending it, then you must. Infidelity is a major violation of marital trust, and the very least you owe your partner is the opportunity to deal with the violation as he sees fit, whether that means divorce, separation, couples therapy or something else.

If your infidelity has ended and you have no intention of repeating it, it might be better to leave the past in the past. Do not confess to unfaithfulness simply because it will feel good to get it off your chest. Telling your spouse could cause more pain and problems than it solves.

Is Your Parents' Marriage in Trouble? How to Help

Joseph Ilardo, PhD, and Carole Rothman, PhD, mental-health professionals specializing in elder care and family communication issues, Somers, New York. They are professional speakers and coauthors of the expanded and reissued *Are Your Parents Driving You Crazy?* (VanderWyk & Burnham).

Your parents have been arguing for decades—but now their marriage seems worse than ever. Or maybe they have always seemed happy together, but the marriage suddenly is on the rocks. A marriage can hit rough spots even late in the journey. When that happens, the couple's adult children typically wish to help their parents save the relationship, but what can they do to help?

STRATEGIES

When a marriage falters after decades, the best question to ask yourself is "What's changed?" *Certain changes are particularly likely to create problems for older married couples, including...*

• **Increased togetherness.** Your mother and father probably spent many hours apart each week for most of their married lives. Retired couples often are together 24 hours a day, which can be a difficult adjustment.

What to do: Help your parents find individual hobbies. Suggest they return to activities enjoyed long ago...join clubs on their own... or spend more time with their own same-sex friends.

• **Different plans.** Perhaps one of your parents wants to travel, but the other just wants to be near the grandkids.

What to do: Help them reach a compromise by suggesting, for example, that they travel for a few months each year but spend the rest of the time at home.

• **Depression.** If one of your parents isn't happy—perhaps because of a health problem, adjusting to retirement or a child moving away—that unhappiness can taint the whole marriage.

What to do: Help this parent see that his/her marriage isn't to blame for the unhappiness. Suggest that he seek help—a therapist or support group, perhaps.

• **Financial difficulties.** Your parents' retirement savings might not have lasted as long as they had expected. Money problems can strain even the strongest relationship.

What to do: Remind your parents that they're not unhappy with each other—they're just tense about money. Help them find ways to trim expenses...offer financial support if you're able...

137

and point out that living separately is even pricier than living together.

- **Medication side effects.** Has either of your parents changed medications recently? Drugs sometimes cause changes in behavior or personality, potentially resulting in marital conflicts.

What to do: Consult a doctor about possible behavioral side effects of your parent's medications and alternative drug options.

- **Chronic illness or dementia.** The onset of dementia, perhaps as yet undiagnosed, can alter a person in ways that might frustrate his spouse. Illness or dementia can alter your parents' roles in ways that strain a marriage, forcing one spouse to become the caregiver and the other the dependent.

What to do: Help your parents locate appropriate support groups. If acceptable to your parents and financially feasible, consider hiring someone to ease the caregiver's burden.

- **Loss of friends.** Parents may be dealing with friends dying or retiring to different parts of the country. This can alter their social circles and outlook on life.

What to do: Encourage your parents to continue to expand their social circle by joining clubs or other groups.

- **Declining driving ability.** The loss of the ability to drive safely is a common source of arguments in older couples.

What to do: Ask a family doctor to decide if a parent can still drive safely, or let a driver's test decide so that it isn't just one parent telling the other he's not capable. Look into senior transport programs in your area, or arrange for family, friends or volunteer drivers to provide rides on a regular basis so that your parent isn't stranded.

YOUR PROPER ROLE

If your parents don't want your help with their marital problems, don't force the issue. Some parents aren't comfortable sharing their problems with their kids. When that's the case, you'll only make things worse by interfering. If you're not confident that your input will be welcomed, ask, "Is this something you would like my help with?" If the answer is no, let your parents know that you love them both…that you're there for them if they change their minds…and that you can help them find a third party to help, such as a professional marriage counselor, if they would prefer.

You won't help your parents' marriage by taking sides in their arguments. As soon as you side with one parent, the other will feel ganged up on and become wary of your continued involvement. Even if you're certain one parent is completely to blame, remember that you might not know the whole story.

Exception: If one parent is suffering from dementia or serious depression, you may need to take a more active role in helping both parents find appropriate medical and psychological help.

If your parents burden you with their problems but won't listen to your advice, tell them they must let you help or leave you out of it. Make it clear that you'll cut visits short if they can't be civil to each other. Keep in mind that you're not responsible for their marriage. If you have offered assistance and a sympathetic ear, you have done all you can do.

The Surprising Reason Couples Fight

Yukio Ishizuka, MD, psychiatrist in private practice in Rye, New York. He is author of the eBooks *Breakthrough Intimacy* and *Sad to Happy Through Closeness.*

When we argue with our partners, we typically attribute the fight to a recent incident. A couple might fight over who forgot to pay the utility bills or why they got lost during a drive.

What couples do not realize is that the event that seems to trigger a marital fight usually is just an excuse to argue, not the true root cause. The actual cause of fights between partners in close relationships may be closeness itself.

My research with hundreds of married couples has shown that fights are most likely when relationships reach new levels of closeness and intimacy.

This increased closeness makes the partners feel more dependent on each other and, therefore, more vulnerable and threatened.

Example: A couple argues seemingly because a mother-in-law is coming for yet another visit.

They do not realize that the real reason they are fighting is that they just had a romantic weekend and felt particularly close to each other, an unfamiliar feeling that left at least one of them feeling more vulnerable.

The good news is that arguments brought on by increasing closeness offer an opportunity for the couple to get even closer.

GETTING PAST FIGHTS

Four key steps to getting closer…

1. Recognition. The first step is recognizing warning signals, catching yourself in a familiar emotional confrontation with the very person that you care for the most.

Recognize negative emotions, such as anxiety, anger and depression, as warning signals that you are facing a challenge.

2. Perspective. Consider why you are facing this challenge, what your options are for solving it and what the consequences are for each of those options.

Recognize that closeness is the top priority over all other considerations, such as being right or wrong…or winning or losing an argument.

3. Decision. Should you apologize? Agree to forget the whole thing? The best decision is to take whatever action is necessary to overcome the crisis.

4. Action. Implement your decision to the best of your ability. Think, feel and act in ways that increase closeness.

Sometimes all it takes is to say, "Sorry, I didn't mean any of those nasty things I said. I love you." Or simply reach out affectionately as if nothing had happened.

Fight Right: New Rules For Couples

Marjory Abrams, chief content editor, *Bottom Line* newsletters, Botton Line Inc., 3 Landmark Square., Stamford, Connecticut 06901.

Cain versus Abel. Captain Ahab versus Moby Dick. Hamlet versus Claudius and Polonius. The best stories have conflict and so do the best marriages, according to Bonnie Eaker Weil, PhD. Bonnie is a relationship therapist in New York City, and she has an amazingly high success rate with clients. Ninety-eight percent of the couples she counsels end up staying together.

Bonnie notes that adultery is most common in relationships in which the partners are "too polite" to fight. Without conflict, there is no passion, but people need to know how to fight right. Bonnie has an unusual approach to handling disputes, quite contrary to how most people handle them.

Here are her time-tested guidelines…

•**Make an appointment to talk with your spouse about a given issue.** Early evening is best. Don't make it for just before bedtime, during a meal, while drinking alcoholic beverages or while out on a date.

•**One person should talk and the other just listen during your appointment.** The listener must suppress his/her own responses and wear an emotional bulletproof vest so that he takes in the information without taking things personally. (He will get a turn to talk later on, so be patient!)

•**Talk for no more than 10 minutes.** Honor the other person's feelings, motivations and accomplishments while expressing your needs in emphatic, loving language.

Example: If the issue is that your husband seems to work too much, tell him that you respect what he is doing and his role as a provider and that you love him for it.

•**Avoid words that wound.** Criticism, sarcasm and contempt are out-of-bounds.

•**Suggest several options for solving the problem**—say, a regular Saturday night date or a time when both of you can be together, away from cell phones and other forms of interruptions.

• **Have the listening spouse repeat what he has heard.** Bonnie says that the spouse should mirror not only the request for change but also any praise.

After at least 24 hours have passed—and yes, you really should wait the 24 hours—the listening spouse then validates your feelings ("I understand how you feel") and either chooses a course of action or asks for his own turn to speak. Several rounds may be required to resolve a particularly thorny issue, such as how to spend your money. (In her book, *Financial Infidelity*, Bonnie calls money the number-one relationship wrecker.)

• **Link the end of the quarrel to a positive experience.** Reconnect physically with a long hug or kiss, cuddling, etc. The action serves as a bridge to reconciliation and stimulates the same brain chemicals as falling in love. Bonnie's routine is to dance around the room with her husband, which helps them focus on shared fun instead of the disagreement.

Important: Give up the idea of winning. If one person wins and the other loses, both of you lose.

Though the process may seem cumbersome at first, it provides comfort and safety in stormy times. Bonnie says that often people feel bad after an argument because nothing has been resolved. Using her method, couples resolve their disagreements without hurting one another and then move on.

Arguments conducted à la Bonnie manage to avoid that trap by preventing power struggles and helping both partners feel safe, taken cared of and loved.

Ouch! Fighting Slows Down Healing

E ven low-level stress from a minor disagreement with a spouse can delay wound healing after surgery by a day. A major disagreement can delay healing by two days.

Reason: Hostility hinders the regulation of *cytokine,* an important chemical messenger in the immune system. When cytokine stays in the blood too long, it causes an increase in inflammation, which can slow healing.

Janice Kiecolt-Glaser, PhD, director, division of health psychology, department of psychiatry, and member of the Institute for Behavioral Medicine Research, the Ohio State University, Columbus, and lead author of a study of 42 married couples, published in *Archives of General Psychiatry.*

Why Fighting Is Bad For Your Heart

I n a new study, 150 healthy married couples discussed a contentious topic for six minutes while being videotaped. Two days later, each spouse had a computed tomography (CT) scan of the chest.

Result: Wives who were hostile and husbands who were controlling had a greater degree of hardening of the arteries than spouses who did not display these behaviors.

Theory: Hostility and dominance can release chemicals that may increase heart disease risk.

Cynthia Berg, PhD, professor of psychology, University of Utah, Salt Lake City.

When a Relationship Ends

B reaking up is easier to do than most people realize—even though it is painful.

Recent finding: Relationship breakups typically cause less distress than most people expect—and the unhappiness lasts for less time than predicted. Most people in a recent study were back to their prebreakup level of happiness within two months, even though they anticipated that it would take longer.

Paul Eastwick, PhD, and Eli Finkel, PhD, psychology researchers, Northwestern University, Evanston, and coauthors of a study published online in *Journal of Experimental Social Psychology.*

"All You Need Is Love..." And Other Lies About Marriage

John W. Jacobs, MD, psychiatrist and couples therapist in private practice in New York City. He is an associate clinical professor at New York University School of Medicine and author of *All You Need Is Love, And Other Lies About Marriage* (HarperCollins).

Marriage is more fragile today than ever before, as evidenced by the shockingly high 48% divorce rate among American couples. With so many marriages breaking up, it is clear that some of our basic assumptions about the modern institution are misguided—and even outright wrong. *Understanding the realities of marriage today can help make your relationship more satisfying...*

Myth: All you need is love.

Reality: Love is not enough to keep you together. Marital love is conditional and based on how you behave toward one another day after day.

What to do: First, be clear to your spouse about what you need from the relationship—what you can live with and what you cannot live with.

Ask your partner to think about that, too. Then share your views and negotiate how you each can fulfill each other's wishes.

Example: You may feel the need to go out with friends regularly without your partner, but your partner may feel hurt by this. You might negotiate to go out one night with friends in exchange for one night out with your partner.

Myth: Talking things out always resolves problems.

Reality: Communication has been oversold as the key to a good marriage, but many couples actually make things worse by talking things out. Brutal honesty often backfires, causing a spouse to dig in his/her heels instead of making changes in behavior.

What to do: Learn how to communicate skillfully by focusing on problems rather than fault. Use "I language," not "you language." With "I language," you take responsibility for your emotional experience rather than blaming it on your partner.

Example: "I feel anxious when we don't have things planned in advance, and it would be a big help to me if we could make dates with friends as far in advance as possible." That's better than making accusatory statements such as, "You always wait until the last minute to make plans, and then our friends are too busy to see us."

Myth: People don't change.

Reality: Change is always possible, and small changes often can produce big results. But most people go about trying to change their relationships in unproductive ways—by trying to get their spouses to change. Marital problems are rarely the fault of just one partner, and the biggest impediment to change is the belief that you aren't the one who needs to change.

What to do: Change your own behavior—this often is the best way to prompt shifts in your partner's behavior.

Example: If your spouse always seems to criticize you, try praising his actions on a regular basis. Eventually, he may reciprocate by praising you.

Myth: Our culture's shift in gender roles has made marriage easier.

Reality: The modern marital arrangement—in which both husband and wife work outside the home, and family responsibilities and decisions are handled by both partners—may be "fairer," but it has created its own problems. Confusion about roles, as well as mutual feelings of being taken for granted, can lead to resentment and conflict.

What to do: When discussing your expectations of your relationship, be on the alert for gender stereotypes, such as the idea that women cook and men take out the garbage. Apportion your duties and responsibilities fairly.

Example: You cook two days a week, and your spouse cooks two days a week. Order takeout on the other days.

Myth: Children solidify a marriage.

Reality: The stress of having children is a serious threat to a couple's harmony. Even when you feel that you are prepared for their impact on your relationship, your natural devotion to them will leave little time and energy for your marriage.

What to do: If you want to preserve your marriage, your children cannot always come first. Commit to regular alone time as a couple with weekly or biweekly date nights and occasional trips away from the kids.

Myth: The sexual revolution has made great sex easier.

Reality: Movies, television shows and advertisements have raised our expectations about sex, making it seem like everyone is having great sex on a regular basis and you're abnormal if you're not. But many married couples have sexual problems—they just don't talk openly about them.

What to do: Expect ebbs and flows in your sex life, and don't buy into the Hollywood image of what your sex life should be. Consider seeking help from a couples counselor or sex therapist if you can't resolve sexual problems on your own.

To locate a qualified practitioner, contact...

• **American Association of Sexuality Educators, Counselors, and Therapists,** 202-449-1099, *www.aasect.org.*

• **American Association for Marriage and Family Therapy,** 703-838-9808 or visit *www. aamft.org.*

When Communication Hurts a Marriage

Joel D. Block, PhD, senior psychologist at North Shore–Long Island Jewish Health System, Glen Oaks, New York, and assistant clinical professor of psychiatry at Albert Einstein College of Medicine, Bronx, New York. He is author of *Naked Intimacy: How to Increase True Openness in Your Relationship* (McGraw-Hill). *www.drblock.com*

T he happiest, most passionate couples are those who are emotionally open and unafraid to reveal themselves to each other. Yet the potential for deception always is present.

The "big" lies, such as having an affair, tend to have the worst repercussions (often divorce). Yet a lifetime of small lies also can erode a relationship.

Examples of little lies: Maybe you bought something that you didn't really need—and lied to your partner about the cost. Or your partner noticed your lingering glance at another person—then you swore up and down that you really didn't find that person attractive.

We tell ourselves that these small lies are harmless—or even beneficial because they protect our partners' feelings. But little lies can be just as detrimental to a relationship as telling a whopper. They just take more time to tear couples apart—and are not always easy to detect.

People who tell lies really are protecting themselves by hiding their own true feelings. When the truth is discovered (it almost always is eventually), the other person naturally feels betrayed. *Here, the many kinds of lies...*

INDIRECT COMMUNICATION

Rather than stating clearly what they do or don't want, people tend to talk around subjects that they find uncomfortable. The more afraid you are of rejection or potential criticism, the more likely you are to communicate indirectly. The "lie" is not owning up to what is wanted.

Example: I once counseled a couple who had been married for 12 years. The husband, who was in the restaurant business, had once been arrested for selling drugs. His wife noticed that he recently had a lot more money. She also noticed a spike in their cell-phone bills and a spate of hang-up calls.

She secretly wondered whether her husband was back in the drug world—but rather than confronting him about her fears, she tried to gather information indirectly. She suggested, for example, that she might start spending more time at the restaurant. He said he didn't need extra help, but she kept pressing and their disagreements escalated. Finally, she blurted, "You're hiding something. I know it!"

If a couple is going to argue, they should at least have a disagreement based on an accurate understanding of each other's position. With indirect communication, no one is even sure what the argument is about. In this case, the real issue was the wife's (unfounded) suspicions.

Solution: Openly request information. Had the wife stated directly what she was worried about or had the husband asked why coming to the restaurant was so important, they could have had a real conversation instead of an argument. If you're uncomfortable making a request, say so—"I feel uncomfortable asking you, but…" That's the truth. To circle around it is to avoid the truth.

BROKEN CONTRACTS

How often have you made a promise and failed to keep it? Not keeping your word is a kind of lying that can seriously harm a relationship by undermining trust. Even when the promises are trivial—maybe you agree to start projects but fail to follow through—breaking your word can make everything you say seem unreliable.

There is a concept in psychology called "secondary gains." It means that someone gets positive reinforcement from negative patterns. We're all guilty of occasional broken promises. Someone who consistently "forgets" may be unconsciously creating emotional distance— forgetting puts the other person off—so that the "forgetter" feels less vulnerable.

Solution: If you're a forgetter, try to understand the secondary gains that arise from disappointing your partner. Merely understanding this concept can be a powerful step.

Also helpful: A quid pro quo, which roughly means "a favor for a favor." If someone is persistently forgetful, his/her partner can insist on having something done before giving something in return. While this is a bit adversarial, it's sometimes warranted.

Example: The forgetter asks you to mail a package at the post office. You respond, "Absolutely—as soon as you clean out the backseat of the car as you promised to do two weeks ago."

WITHHOLDING INFORMATION

We all have a right to privacy, but some people take this to extremes and withhold important information. This is a form of concealment

that borders on lying—and is the opposite of true intimacy.

Example: A husband might avoid certain issues—for example, his feelings about a mutual friend—because he feels that his wife is critical of his opinions. If he gets in the habit of not saying what he thinks, she might criticize his persistent silence—at which point, he'll conclude that his wife is too critical.

Solution: This is a very slippery slope and should be addressed by sharing everything. It is the premise of a good partnership. Sharing private personal thoughts with each other creates intimacy. If sharing is met with harsh judgment, don't withdraw. Talk this out with your partner to clear the way for future non-judgmental discussion.

BLAMING

When something goes wrong, the aggrieved party knows precisely whom to blame. It's the other person's fault. When a person blames someone else, he/she is omitting his part in the issue—that's the lie.

In all of my years as a therapist, I've rarely encountered a conflict that truly was just one person's fault—and blame never, ever makes things better.

The person who is blamed feels defensive. He/she will probably respond with counter-blame and anger.

Solution: Instead of pointing fingers, the partners should avoid the language of blame. Substitute sentences that start with "I" for those that start with "you."

Example: Rather than saying, "You never help in the kitchen," say something like, "I feel resentful when you don't help out."

Unlike "you" statements, which can typically lead to adversarial reactions, "I" sentences are more honest and less confrontational. They can lead to understanding rather than a continuation of the disagreement.

SEXUAL SECRETS

Sexual desires are among the most sensitive secrets. A partner might reveal something about his/her sexual desires (or sexual history) and then be judged harshly. It's natural for that person, under these circumstances, to be reluctant to reveal himself again.

At the same time, sharing sexual desires with one's partner can build intimacy.

Solution: When you take responsibility for what pleases you, you increase the probability of being pleased. For a couple to have a satisfying sex life, both partners need to be aware of their preferences. If you find it hard to initiate this kind of conversation, perhaps an opportunity will arise while watching a sexy scene in a movie. "Would that kind of thing be exciting to you?" could be a way to start the conversation.

After Infidelity

Joy Browne, PhD, clinical psychologist in New York City. Her internationally syndicated call-in radio show, "The Dr. Joy Browne Show," is the longest-running of its kind (*www.drjoy.com*). She is author of many books, including *Getting Unstuck: 8 Simple Steps to Solving Any Problem* (Hay House).

N o woman in her right mind would suggest that adultery strengthens a marriage. *But a relationship can survive and even thrive afterward if the wounded partner finds the courage to demand answers to three questions…*

•**Why did this happen?** Saying, "I was drunk" or "It just happened" doesn't cut it. If it "just happened" once, it could just happen again—so there's no basis for resurrecting trust. The unfaithful partner must figure out the real reason—"I felt old and was trying to feel young again" or "I miss the way we used to make love." Once the problem is acknowledged, it can be worked on.

•**How can you promise it won't happen again?** A fidelity plan identifies the lesson learned ("No fling is worth endangering our marriage")…puts constraints in place ("I'll be home by 6 pm every night")…and offers options ("I'll go with you for counseling or do whatever you want to show how sorry I am").

•**What's in it for me if you cheat again?** This idea came about when a caller to my radio show said her cheating husband wanted another chance. He loved his boat—so I said, "If he'll sign a document saying that if he cheats, you get the boat, then you've got a shot. Before he's unfaithful again, he'll think, 'Bimbo? Or boat?' If he won't sign, he's not willing to put his heart into fidelity."

More from Dr. Joy Browne…

The Art of the Apology

T he three most difficult words in the English language, contrary to popular opinion, are not "I love you," but rather "I am sorry." Perhaps it's because these words make us feel vulnerable or less than perfect or afraid of being sent to our rooms. Yet fear of 'fessing up makes human interaction unnecessarily tense. *To right a wrong…*

•**Avoid the unsorry apology.** A self-righteous "I'm sorry you feel that way," or an equivocating "I'm sorry if I hurt you," or a resentful "I'm always wrong, you're always right," will not repair a relationship.

•**Figure out where you erred.** If you're mystified by a friend's cold shoulder, a clueless "What did I do?" only makes her angrier. Think about recent events, paying attention to your "belly barometer"—the memory that makes your stomach churn probably is key to the problem. Even if your apology misses the mark, you open a dialogue that can clear the air.

•**Explain, don't excuse.** The injured party doesn't want rationalization ("I missed your speech because traffic was terrible")—she wants the real reason ("I left the house too late, and I'm terribly sorry").

•**Make amends.** If you spill water on a friend's sweater, simply say "Pardon me!" But if you spill red wine, you must offer to pay for a new sweater. You're not just buying a garment —you're investing in a relationship.

Familiarity Breeds... Irritation?

Couples find each other more irritating over the course of their marriages. Over time, nitpicking and frequent demands make spouses more negative about each other. Increasing irritation seems to be a normal part of close, long-lasting marital relationships that include a lot of daily contact.

Self-defense: Couples should use constructive strategies to deal with conflict and irritations—for example, calmly discussing problems rather than ignoring them.

Kira Birditt, PhD, research fellow, University of Michigan's Institute for Social Research, Ann Arbor, and coauthor of an analysis of survey responses by more than 800 adults, presented at a meeting of the Gerontological Society of America.

Good Marriages Bring a Lifetime of Happiness

Widowed men and women who had good marriages are less likely to be depressed following their spouses' deaths than those whose marriages were bad.

Recent study: Good marriages seem to have a protective impact on surviving spouses, while those who were unhappily married often remain unhappy even years after the loss of their spouses.

Toni Antonucci, PhD, professor of psychology, senior research scientist, and Nina Rhees, Hartford fellow, both at Institute for Social Research Life Course Development Program, University of Michigan, Ann Arbor, and coauthors of a study of 1,532 widowed adults, presented at a meeting of the Gerontological Society of America.

Important Information On Suicide and Marriage

A spouse's suicide significantly raises the suicide risk of the surviving partner.

A woman whose partner kills himself is 15 times more likely to commit suicide. A man is 46 times more likely—possibly because men are less likely to seek support after a partner's death.

Important: Spouses whose partners suffer from a severe psychiatric disorder also are at increased risk for suicide themselves. If you, your spouse or a loved one is experiencing thoughts of suicide, consult your doctor or a mental health professional immediately.

Esben Agerbo, MS, associate professor, National Centre for Register-Based Research, University of Aarhus, Denmark, and leader of a study of 475,000 Danes, including 9,000 who committed suicide, published in *Journal of Epidemiology and Community Health.*

Long-Distance Love

Long-distance relationships require a different kind of intimacy.

To keep the flame alive: Consider handwritten letters—studies have shown that couples who stay together send each other twice as many letters as those couples who eventually break up.

Greg Guldner, MD, founder, Center for the Study of Long Distance Relationships, Corona, California, and author of *Long Distance Relationships: The Complete Guide* (Milne).

No More Stress

Nonsexual, caring touch between couples alleviates stress and controls blood pressure. Hand-holding, hugs and sitting or lying cuddled up produces higher levels of *oxytocin,* also known as the "love hormone."

Included in the study: A 30-minute massage (neck, shoulder or forehead) three times a week.

For men: Warm partner touch may be especially good for the heart.

Julianne Holt-Lunstad, PhD, assistant professor of psychology, Brigham Young University, Provo, Utah.

Why Men Never Remember And Women Never Forget

Marianne Legato, MD, FACP, physician and professor of clinical medicine at Columbia University, New York City, and founder of Columbia's Partnership for Gender-Specific Medicine. She is author of several books, including *Why Men Never Remember and Women Never Forget* (Rodale).

Neither men nor women can claim that their brains are "better." While men's brains are 10% larger on average, women's brains have more elaborate connections that make them more efficient. Male and female brains unquestionably are different, in terms of both structure and chemistry, and that can cause problems when we try to communicate with one another.

Most of us speak to our spouses just as we would speak to members of our own sex—then wonder why they don't seem to understand.

Here's how to communicate more effectively with the opposite sex…

NONVERBAL CUES

The female brain is good at decoding nonverbal signals, including facial expressions and tone of voice, perhaps because mothers must understand the needs of children too young to speak. When women send nonverbal signals to men, women are often dismayed to find that these signals are ignored.

Women don't realize that the typical male brain is not skilled at interpreting nonverbal communications. Men are particularly bad at identifying signs of sadness in women—though men are pretty good at spotting signs of anger and aggression.

Women: Tell him verbally when something is bothering you. A sad expression or the silent treatment won't get you anywhere. It's not that he is ignoring your feelings—he is just unaware of them.

If a man asks you what he can do to make you feel better, tell him. If you say "nothing," he'll assume that you mean nothing and he'll do nothing. He isn't trying to hurt you—men's brains just work in a more linear, literal manner. Because men often like to be left alone when they're upset, he might conclude that he is doing you a favor by giving you some space.

Men: Search for clues beyond her words when she seems unusually quiet or terse. She might be sending signals that you're not picking up. If you can't figure out the signals and she won't tell you what she needs, remind her that you really want to help, but it's hard for you to pick up her nonverbal cues.

LISTENING

The female brain seems to be better at listening than the male brain—women have more nerve cells in the areas known to process language and put a larger percentage of their brains to work when they hear someone speak.

The more elaborate wiring of the female brain also makes women better multitaskers than men. Evolution likely made women this way so that mothers could keep an eye on the children and still get other things done. Evolution shaped the male brain to focus on one very difficult task at a time. Tiger hunts were more successful when the hunters could focus all their attention on the tiger.

Add men's inferior listening ability to their superior focus, and the result is a phenomenon most wives know well. Tell a man something important while he's watching a ball game, and he might not remember a word of it. He isn't purposely ignoring you—his brain simply isn't wired to hear what you said.

Women: Put him on alert that what you're about to say is important. If it's particularly vital information, begin with a gentle "I need you to look me in the eyes." If there are too many distractions in your present location, ask him to go with you for a walk or out to a quiet restaurant.

Men: Don't be insulted if she doesn't stop what she is doing when you want to talk. Chances are that she can pay attention to you even if she's occupied. If you want her undivided attention, ask for it.

PROBLEM SOLVING

The structure of the male brain makes men straight-ahead thinkers—when they see a problem, their instinct is to try to solve it.

Women are more likely to ruminate over decisions. They'll verbalize a problem and talk through all the implications and issues before they proceed. When women try to talk through their problems with men, they're often dismayed and insulted that the men try to tell them what to do. This confuses the men, who thought they were being asked for a solution.

Women: Tell a man the specific type of response you want before you share a problem. Are you asking the man for a solution, or do you just want to talk through the issue so it's clear in your mind? If you don't specifically tell him that it's the latter, he'll assume it's the former. If he tries to solve your problem anyway, understand that this is just how his brain responds.

As for how to respond to a man's problems, this rarely comes up. Men tend not to share their problems with anyone.

Men: Understand that women like to verbalize their thinking and don't always want you to solve their problems.

Instead, wait for a question before providing an answer. Ask what you can do to help rather than assume you know. And if your wife starts crying, holding her quietly works better than telling her she's being too emotional.

DIFFERENT INTERESTS

Women tend to expect their male partners to be interested in every subject they wish to discuss. That isn't fair. A woman wouldn't expect her female friends to chat about a subject that she knows bores them.

Women: Tailor your conversation to your partner's interests. (Men should do this, too, but because men talk less, it isn't as often an issue.) Find other conversation partners for topics that don't interest him.

Men: Encourage your partner to spend time with female friends so there's another outlet for the conversations that don't interest you. Don't get upset if she's busy with friends when you want to see her.

BETTER ARGUMENTS

During an argument, women are more likely to bring up past events. Estrogen increases the amount of cortisol, a memory-boosting hormone, released by the adrenal glands during stressful moments. Because the female brain has more estrogen, memories of old fights remain fresher in a woman's mind. The male brain finds it easier to forget emotional situations and move on. Maybe forgetting a close call on a tiger hunt made it easier for men of the past to continue to hunt.

Women: Use simple, declarative sentences, and state what you want in outline form when imparting important information to men. Leave out anecdotes and unnecessary adjectives. Take advantage of your ability to read his emotions to spot the signs of boredom. When you see them, sum up your argument with a closing statement and end the conversation. Try not to rehash old arguments.

Men: Try to keep women focused on the point under discussion. If during an argument she brings up a fight you had five years ago, tell her, "We've discussed that already and it isn't going to help to go over it again. Let's focus on the current problem."

Questions About Sleep And Sex You Were Afraid to Ask

Billy Goldberg, MD, emergency room physician at Bellevue Hospital and New York University Medical Center, both in New York City. He is coauthor, with Mark Leyner, of *Why Do Men Fall Asleep After Sex? More Questions You'd Only Ask a Doctor After Your Third Whiskey Sour* (Three Rivers).

The human body is so complex that we can't come close to understanding everything that goes on inside of us. Emergency room physician Billy Goldberg, MD, answers some of the medical questions many people wonder about but often are embarrassed to ask. *Here are his answers to some of your questions...*

• **Why are men more likely to snore than women?** Women's airways are wider and less prone to collapse than men's airways—which allows for freer breathing. Also, men are more likely than women to gain fat around the neck, where it can squeeze the airway closed, causing snoring. And men are more likely to smoke or drink to excess, either of which can contribute to snoring.

Women are considerably more prone to snoring when they're pregnant. Blood flow to the nasal area can increase during pregnancy, causing the lining of the nose and throat to swell.

To reduce snoring: Adhesive nasal strips, marketed to athletes as a way to increase oxygen intake, have been shown to reduce snoring for some people by opening nasal passages and making breathing easier. The Breathe Right brand is available at most drugstores. Also, consider losing weight and cutting down on smoking or drinking if these issues apply to you.

•**Why do men fall asleep after sex?** Endorphins, *gamma-aminobutyric acid* and the hormones *oxytocin* and *prolactin* are released into a man's body after he has an orgasm. All of these hormones and chemicals have been found to contribute to sleepiness. Interestingly, these same chemicals are also released into women's bodies after orgasm. The difference might be that women are less likely to have orgasms when they have sex.

Why We Love...the Science Of Sexual Attraction

Helen Fisher, PhD, research professor of anthropology at Rutgers University, New Brunswick, New Jersey, and former research associate at American Museum of Natural History in New York City. She is author of several books on human sexual and social behavior, including *Why We Love* (Holt). *www.helenfisher.com*

I f you've ever been a "fool for love," blame it on evolution. The phenomena of love, lust and the desire for attachment aren't just emotions. They are drives as powerful as hunger and crucial to our survival as a species.

Helen Fisher, PhD, one of the country's leading experts on love administered a series of experiments to look into the brains of people who are deeply in love and those who were recently rejected. *What she discovered...*

Does the brain actually change when we fall in love?

There's a complex interplay of chemicals. My colleagues and I performed brain scans (functional magnetic resonance imaging) on 20 men and women in love. The people in our study had increased activity in the *caudate nucleus*, part of the brain's reward system that produces the focus and motivation to meet your goals. The subjects also showed activity in the *ventral tegmental* area, which is responsible for the intense energy and concentration that people in love experience. Increased blood flow in these areas explains the all-night talk sessions and endless letters and e-mails between lovers, as well as the outpouring of love-related poetry and art.

How does lust differ from love?

Humans have three basic mating drives—lust, romantic love and attachment. They occur in different regions of the brain and involve different hormones and neurochemicals—but they work together to ensure reproduction and survival of the species.

•**Lust** is associated primarily with *testosterone,* the hormone that motivates men and women to have sex. People with higher levels of testosterone tend to have sex more often than those with lower levels.

•**Romantic love** is linked to *dopamine* and also most likely to *serotonin* and *norepinephrine,* brain chemicals that can produce feelings of ecstasy. In specific combinations, these chemicals motivate a person to focus his/her attention on a preferred individual and think obsessively about that person.

•**Attachment,** the desire of couples to stay together, is linked to elevated activities of *vasopressin* and *oxytocin,* neurohormones that promote the urge to bond and cuddle as well as to care for offspring.

Romantic love is metabolically expensive because people lavish so much energy and attention on their beloved. It pays off in evolutionary terms because it leads to attachment and the desire to nurture and raise a family.

Can lust lead to love?

Love is far more likely to lead to lust than lust is to love. We find our new partners sexually attractive in part because increases in dopamine enhance the activity of testosterone.

Is "love at first sight" possible?

I think that love at first sight comes out of nature. With animals, brain circuitry must be triggered rapidly because they don't have much time to mate. We inherited this ability to prefer certain partners almost instantly.

Do men and women experience love differently?

Both exhibit similar elation and obsessive behavior—but men show more activity in a brain region associated with the integration of visual stimuli. Women have more activity in brain areas associated with memory recall.

Why this difference? Men are more visual than women, probably because for millions of years they sized up women by looking for signs of youth and fertility, such as clear skin, bright eyes, a big smile, etc. These and other visual cues caused men to become aroused and initiate the mating process.

On the other hand, a woman can't tell just from looking at a man if he would protect and provide for her and her future offspring. As we evolved, women probably depended more on memory—remembering if a man kept promises, was truthful, etc.

Why is rejection so difficult?

There are two stages, each associated with different chemical changes…

• **The protest stage** is very painful. You love even more deeply after you've been dumped. This is the time when you call constantly, write pleading e-mails, show up unannounced and generally make a fool of yourself.

Dopamine activity most likely spikes during the protest stage because the brain's reward system keeps churning it out in an attempt to recapture the beloved.

The behavior of jilted lovers often alienates the ones they love. This seems counterproductive from an evolutionary point of view, but it might be a way of conserving energy in the long run. The rejected one behaves in ways that sever the ties and allow both partners to move on and find new mates.

• **The resignation stage** is accompanied by a drop in dopamine. People experience lethargy, depression and a lack of motivation. This stage may allow the body to rest and recover. It also sends signals to others in the community that you need support, which can attract potential mates.

How can we diminish the pain?

It can take several months, even years, to recover from rejection. Treat it as you would an addiction. Remove cards, letters and photos of the beloved. Don't call or write. Stay busy and get more exercise—physical activity increases dopamine activity. Sunlight also improves mood.

People who are seriously depressed may benefit from psychotherapy and/or antidepressants.

Is falling in love just a matter of brain chemistry?

Chemical factors clearly are involved, but many environmental elements also are at work. For example, you must be interested in meeting someone in the first place. If the timing isn't right, you won't trigger the brain chemistry for romantic love.

How can long-married couples keep their love alive?

Novelty drives up the activity of dopamine. Couples who are spontaneous and try new things are aroused mentally as well as physically. Just going on vacation can spark your sex life and rejuvenate a relationship.

Sexy Stride

Experts can accurately estimate a woman's history of vaginal orgasms just by watching her walk.

Telltale sign: The sum of stride length and pelvic and vertebral rotation is higher in women who experience vaginal orgasms.

The Journal of Sexual Medicine.

How to Handle Your Teen's Breakup

To help your teenager get through a romantic breakup, be available as a willing ear and shoulder to cry on—not as a source of advice or commentary. Do not minimize a teenage romance by calling it "puppy love" or saying anything else that a teen would perceive as demeaning. Don't tell your child that he/she is overreacting and will get over the breakup in time. Do not give your own opinions of the former boyfriend or girlfriend, and don't try to reassure a teen that he will look back on the breakup with a better perspective in the future. All these well-meaning comments will push a teen away and possibly trigger depression.

Best: Simply be there for your child, let him initiate any conversation, and be sympathetic and nonjudgmental.

Deborah P. Welsh, PhD, associate professor of psychology, University of Tennessee, Knoxville.

Solving Relationship Problems

Relationship problems are solved by different ways including...

• **Focusing on one issue at a time,** not on global statements about the relationship.

• **Describing a problem** as *a difficulty we have,* not as something your partner does *to* you.

• **If you cannot discuss problems without arguing,** write your partner a letter, or make an audio- or videotape in which you tell your side of the story calmly—and suggest he/she do the same.

• **Doing something nice for your partner,** even if the argument is not yet resolved. A smile or cup of coffee, offered without strings attached, often defuses conflict.

Andrew Christensen, PhD, professor of psychology, University of California, Los Angeles, and coauthor of *Reconcilable Differences* (Guilford).

6

Your Family's Health

How to Protect Against Killer Food Allergies

Many people with food allergies have mild symptoms, such as a rash, runny nose or itchy eyes, when they eat small amounts of a problem food. But they may still be at risk for a potentially deadly reaction.

In the US, food allergies cause up to 30,000 emergency room visits and 200 deaths annually due to *anaphylaxis*, an acute reaction that can cause respiratory distress and/or a heart arrhythmia (irregular heartbeat).

Helpful: The Food Allergen Labeling and Consumer Protection Act, which went into effect in January 2006, requires food manufacturers to list eight major allergens on food labels to help people with food allergies identify and avoid problem foods.

IS IT REALLY AN ALLERGY?

Not all reactions to food are due to allergies. Tens of millions of Americans suffer from food intolerance. A food intolerance, such as a sensitivity to the lactose in milk, can begin in childhood. The most common symptom of *lactose intolerance* is gastrointestinal discomfort, including diarrhea, cramping and flatulence.

Food allergies affect about 11 million to 12 million Americans. With a food allergy, the immune system mistakenly identifies as harmful the various proteins—or even a single kind of protein—within one or more foods. This triggers a cascade of events that causes immune cells to respond to the "threat" by releasing large amounts of histamine and other chemicals that produce the allergic symptoms.

The most common food allergen is shellfish. Up to 2% of Americans are allergic to

Steve L. Taylor, PhD, professor of food science and director of the Food Allergy Research and Resource Program at the University of Nebraska, Lincoln. He is a specialist in food allergies and serves on the editorial board of the *Journal of Food Protection*.

shrimp and/or other shellfish, such as lobster, crab and crayfish. This type of allergy often is ignored—primarily because most people tend to eat shellfish far less often than other allergenic foods, such as eggs, peanuts and fish.

TESTING FOR ALLERGIES

A food allergy usually can be diagnosed with a thorough medical history taken by an allergist.

The doctor will want to know...

•**When do symptoms occur?** Food allergies typically cause symptoms within a few minutes to several hours after exposure. Symptoms include stomach cramping, hives, lip swelling, runny nose, congestion and asthma. With a food intolerance, symptoms may not occur until the next day.

•**How much did you eat?** With food allergies, *any* exposure can trigger symptoms. For some patients, 1 mg—an amount that's almost impossible to see—will provoke an allergic response. A reaction can even be triggered by kissing—or sharing utensils with—someone who has eaten a substance to which you are allergic. A skin reaction can occur from touching the substance.

With a food intolerance, symptoms usually are linked to the amount consumed. Someone who's sensitive to milk, for example, can often drink a small amount without a reaction.

Two tests can identify most food allergies. *They are...*

•**Skin prick.** Extracts of suspected foods are introduced into the skin with a needle. The appearance of a rash within a few hours—or even a few minutes—indicates an allergy.

Caution: The skin-prick test isn't advisable for patients with severe allergies. The tiny amounts of food used in the test could trigger a life-threatening reaction.

•**Radioallergosorbent test (RAST).** This blood test detects antibodies to specific food proteins. The test occasionally produces false positives—indicating an allergy where none is present. It's often combined with the skin-prick test for more accurate results.

TREATMENT

People with a history of serious food reactions *must* carry an EpiPen. Available by prescription, it's a self-injector that delivers a dose of *epinephrine*. Epinephrine stimulates the heart and respiration and helps counteract deadly anaphylaxis.

Important: Use the EpiPen immediately if you experience difficulty breathing or throat constriction. Even if you take the shot promptly, get to an emergency room as soon as possible for follow-up treatments.

Also helpful: Take an antihistamine, such as Benadryl, according to label instructions. It can lessen the severity of symptoms while you get to an emergency room.

New development: Omalizumab (Xolair), a medication currently used for asthma, appears to significantly blunt reactions in food–allergy patients who receive a monthly injection of the drug. In an early study, patients who reacted to trace amounts of peanuts were able to eat eight to 10 nuts without experiencing problems. Further studies must be completed to determine whether the FDA deems it an effective—and safe—therapy for food allergies.

AVOIDING PROBLEM FOODS

Because there isn't a cure for food allergies—and even trace amounts of a protein can trigger reactions—strict avoidance is the best defense...

•**Always read food labels**—even if you've safely eaten that product in the past. Manufacturers frequently change or add ingredients.

•**Ask about "hidden" ingredients in medications.** Some prescription and over-the-counter (OTC) drugs, as well as vitamins and supplements, contain milk proteins or other common food allergens. This information should be on the label, but check with your doctor or pharmacist before taking any medication or supplement.

•**Talk to the chef or restaurant manager when eating out.** The waiter or waitress doesn't always have accurate information about food ingredients and preparation. Ask to speak to the chef or manager instead and tell him/her what you're allergic to. Explain that any contact with the offending food can be life-threatening.

- **If you're allergic to shellfish,** for example, tell the chef or manager you can't eat a hamburger that was cooked on the same grill used to cook shrimp.

Other hidden sources of food allergens: Cooking oils that are used to cook different foods...knives and cutting boards that aren't washed clean between uses.

- **Wear a medical alert bracelet/necklace.** Anaphylaxis can cause a loss of consciousness within minutes. A medical alert bracelet/ necklace lets medical personnel know that you require urgent treatment for your allergy.

Simple Ways to Avoid a Cold

Joyce Frye, DO, a clinical assistant professor of family and community medicine at the University of Maryland School of Medicine and an integrative family physician at the school's Center for Integrative Medicine in Baltimore. Trained in a variety of complementary modalities, Dr. Frye is certified by the American Board of Holistic Medicine and has served as president of the National Center for Homeopathy and the American Institute of Homeopathy.

If you would like to be one of those people who doesn't get sick even if you do come in contact with a cold virus, be sure to follow these prevention steps during the cold season...

- **Adopt smart lifestyle strategies.** To keep your immune system functioning optimally, eat at least five different-colored vegetables and fruits per day (the different colors ensure that you're ingesting different types of immune-boosting phytonutrients)...and avoid high-sugar foods, including all fruit juice— sugar depresses immune function.

Also: Get plenty of sleep...and keep stress and emotional conflicts to a minimum. If you have some stress that cannot be avoided, take regular "stress breaks"—for example, set aside time to meditate and/or enjoy a social or recreational activity each day.

- **Take a cold-prevention vitamin regimen.** To ensure that youre getting adequate amounts of immune-boosting nutrients, I recommend taking a vitamin D supplement— 2,000 international units (IU) daily. Vitamin D plays a key role in the body's immune system, and most people in the US don't get enough of the vitamin from their diets and sun exposure—particularly in the winter months.

Also: Take a daily multivitamin or other supplement containing the recommended daily allowance of vitamin C—75 mg to 90 mg...and vitamin A—4,000 IU for women and 5,000 IU for men. Both of these vitamins help the body resist microbial infection.

- **Nasal irrigation.** Dry or irritated mucous membranes are much more vulnerable to infection from a cold virus. That's why I'm a big fan of doing preventive nasal irrigation daily to flush out toxins from the membranes and keep them moist.

My favorite approach: Using a Neti pot, a centuries-old technique that originated in India as a part of Ayurvedic medicine.

How it's commonly used: Pour a solution containing about one pint of warm tap or filtered water and one teaspoon of noniodized salt into the ceramic Neti pot.

My advice: To prevent the salt from possibly stinging, add one-half teaspoon of baking soda to the mixture.

Then tilt your head over a sink and pour the mixture into one nostril, allowing it to drain out the opposite nostril. Use the Neti pot daily or less frequently depending on your preference.

Neti pots are available for about $15 at drugstores and health-food stores. Sanitize the pot between uses in the dishwasher or with soap and hot water.

Also: Prepackaged saline solutions and irrigation devices, such as plastic bottles or rubber squeeze bulbs, are widely available at drugstores.

Best Care for Your Toothbrush

Paula Shannon Jones, DDS, past president, Academy of General Dentistry, Chicago, and a founding contributor to the Academy's free dental health forum for the public, *www.agd.org*.

Y ou rely on it to promote oral health— but a toothbrush that is not properly maintained may house bacteria and viruses that transmit colds, flu, cold sores and other ailments.

What to do for your toothbrush…

• **Give it a good home.** When several toothbrushes are jumbled together, germs can migrate from brush to brush—so use a holder that keeps toothbrushes upright and separate. Place the holder at least six feet from the toilet —water particles can travel several feet with each flush. (Better yet, close the toilet lid before flushing.)

• **Keep it clean.** Rinse the toothbrush well with running water after each use. Swish the bristles once daily in an antiseptic mouthwash that contains alcohol—and once a week, soak the toothbrush in the mouthwash for five minutes.

Caution: Do not put toothbrushes in the microwave or dishwasher to clean them—high heat damages bristles.

• **Dry it off.** Wet bristles are a breeding ground for bacteria. Dry your brush completely between uses, using a clean towel or blow-dryer on low heat or by leaving it exposed to air in a well-ventilated place. If you store your toothbrush in a medicine cabinet or in a toothbrush case or cover (even one labeled "antibacterial"), first dry it thoroughly.

• **Replace it regularly.** Invest in a new toothbrush whenever bristles begin to look frayed or splayed—or at least every three months. If you get sick, replace your toothbrush when you are well again so you don't reinfect yourself.

Your Nagging Cough Could Be the Sign of A Serious Illness

Peter V. Dicpinigaitis, MD, professor of clinical medicine at Albert Einstein College of Medicine and founder and director of the Montefiore Cough Center at Montefiore Medical Center, both in the Bronx, New York.

C oughing is so prevalent—especially during the winter months—that most people dismiss it as a minor ailment that will go away on its own.

Coughing is a vital reflex that helps clear mucus, airborne chemicals and other substances from the airways, which extend from the throat to the lungs. Foreign substances trigger coughing by irritating receptors (nerve endings that line the airways).

Recent development: A highly contagious type of cough that often is accompanied by classic cold symptoms, such as sneezing and a runny nose, is on the rise among American adults. Reported cases of *pertussis*, commonly known as whooping cough, recently reached a 40-year high in the US—and the disease now strikes up to 600,000 Americans each year.

SHOULD YOU SEE A DOCTOR?

A cough that accompanies a cold usually goes away within a matter of days. But sometimes a cough can linger for weeks or months. If a cough lasts more than two months, it is considered chronic and should be evaluated by a physician. Regardless of how long it has lasted, any cough that seriously disturbs your sleep, work or family or social life should be treated by a doctor. If violent enough, a cough can cause sore muscles—and even break ribs or precipitate bouts of fainting or vomiting.

Important: A cough that occurs with certain other symptoms may signal a potentially serious illness. For example, if you have a high fever and/or cough up dark-colored phlegm or blood, it may indicate pneumonia…chest pain and shortness of breath could mean a collapsed lung…and blood-streaked sputum and wheezing could indicate lung cancer. These conditions require immediate medical care.

To treat a nagging cough that occurs without the additional symptoms described above, the underlying cause must be identified.

MAIN CULPRITS

If you exclude smoking and medication side effects—blood pressure–lowering drugs known as angiotensin-converting enzyme (ACE) inhibitors, such as *enalapril* (Vasotec), often trigger coughing—more than 90% of all chronic coughs are caused by three conditions (in order of prevalence)…

•**Upper-airway cough syndrome** is a new term for what used to be called *postnasal drip*. The syndrome includes coughing due not only to postnasal drip (mucus accumulation in the back of the nose or throat), but also resulting from other effects of nose, sinus or throat irritation or inflammation.

Best treatment options: Older antihistamines, such as *chlorpheniramine* (Chlor-Trimeton), and decongestants, such as *pseudoephedrine* (the active ingredient in Sudafed), are the only medications shown in studies to provide much relief—especially when taken in combination. (Pseudoephedrine is available "behind-the-counter" at drugstores.) Newer antihistamines, such as *loratadine* (Claritin) and *fexofenadine* (Allegra), are easier to take because they don't make you as drowsy but don't seem to work as well against cough.

There's little evidence that expectorant or suppressive cough syrups do much—they don't get at the cause of the cough. But a potent cough suppressant, such as one with *codeine* or *hydrocodone*, can offer temporary relief when a severe cough prevents sleep. For allergic rhinitis (due to such conditions as hay fever or an allergy to animal dander), inhaled steroids are the best choice, while antibiotics treat chronic sinusitis.

•**Asthma** is the next most common cause of cough. If accompanied by wheezing and shortness of breath, asthma is easy to diagnose. But much of the time, cough is the only symptom. This condition is known as *cough-variant asthma*.

Best treatment options: Cough-variant asthma usually responds to the same treatments as traditional asthma—inhaled steroids, plus other drugs, such as bronchodilators, if needed. Some of the newest asthma medications—*leukotriene receptor antagonists*, such as *montelukast* (Singulair)—are particularly effective for asthmatic cough.

Important: Once cough-variant asthma goes away, it's tempting to stop treatment. But experts now agree that this type of asthma may affect the lungs much the way traditional asthma does, causing chronic inflammation and thickening of the airway wall that could lead to irreversible obstruction. For this reason, it's safest to continue treatment as instructed by your physician.

New development: Nonasthmatic eosinophilic bronchitis (NAEB) recently has been recognized as a cause of chronic cough. The prevalence of this condition in the US is unknown, but European studies have found that 13% of people with chronic cough have NAEB. Like asthmatic cough, NAEB responds well to inhaled steroids.

•**Gastroesophageal reflux disease (GERD)** is one of the most common causes of chronic cough in the US. GERD is associated with heartburn but also can cause a cough—with or without heartburn. Coughing results when stomach contents back up into the esophagus, stimulating cough receptors. If acid reaches the voice box (larynx), coughing may occur with other upper respiratory symptoms, such as hoarseness.

Best treatment options: Cough caused by GERD generally improves with standard lifestyle changes (such as avoiding alcohol, caffeine and chocolate…and not eating within two hours of bedtime) and acid-suppressing medication prescribed for ordinary reflux. In some cases, two drugs—a proton pump inhibitor, such as *omeprazole* (Prilosec), and an H2 blocker, such as *ranitidine* (Zantac)—may be needed to eliminate cough-causing GERD.

In some people, bile and other nonacidic contents of the stomach are to blame, and drugs, such as *metoclopramide* (Reglan), are needed to strengthen the sphincter valve at the base of the esophagus and hasten stomach emptying.

A type of laparoscopic surgery (which involves wrapping part of the upper stomach around the sphincter to strengthen it) is helpful if drugs don't work, but may only reduce—not cure—the cough.

• **Pertussis,** which was first identified in the early 1900s, causes a nagging cough that often lingers for weeks or even months. The disease was largely eradicated in the US with widespread use of a childhood vaccine, but pertussis is now re-emerging as immunity from the illness has begun to weaken in some people during adulthood.

The Centers for Disease Control and Prevention now recommends a booster pertussis vaccine, which has been approved for adults ages 19 to 64. Because the vaccine is *acellular* (made from bacterial fragments, rather than the whole organism), it is unlikely to cause arm soreness, fever or other adverse reactions.

If treated during the two weeks of acute infection, pertussis responds well to antibiotics, such as *erythromycin.* But because early symptoms resemble those of the common cold—and there's often nothing distinctive about the cough (adults are unlikely to display the loud and forceful "whoop" from which the disease gets its name)—pertussis often remains undiagnosed until the cough has become severe. At this point, antibiotics are less effective, because the infection is too advanced. The infection resolves with time.

Caution: Pertussis is *extremely* contagious —one person can infect most or all of the people in his/her household. If a member of your household has pertussis, you should be seen by a physician as a precaution.

WHY WE COUGH

Coughing is a vital reflex that helps clear mucus, airborne chemicals and other substances from the airways, which extend from the throat to the lungs. Foreign substances trigger coughing by irritating receptors (nerve endings that line the airways). Coughing usually results from respiratory infections, allergies or smoking, but lesser-known causes (described in this article) also may be to blame.

Natural Ways to Prevent Pneumonia

Jamison Starbuck, ND, a naturopathic physician in family practice in Missoula, Montana. She is past president of the American Association of Naturopathic Physicians and a contributing editor to *The Alternative Advisor* (Time-Life).

Even though many people think of pneumonia as a wintertime illness, it can strike during any season of the year. It can be caused by one of many different types of bacteria, viruses, fungi—or even an injury, such as exposure to chemical fumes (from a chlorine spill, for example). People who are at greatest risk for pneumonia are older adults and newborns, smokers, heavy drinkers, people with pre-existing lung disease or compromised immune systems, or anyone who is bedridden or has limited mobility (which increases risk for buildup of mucus in the lungs). Fortunately, you can take steps to protect yourself. *My secrets to avoiding pneumonia...*

• **Consider getting a pneumonia vaccination.** Discuss the vaccine with your doctor if you are age 65 or older—or at any age if you have congestive heart failure, a compromised immune system, liver or lung disease or diabetes, or if you are a smoker or heavy drinker. The vaccine can help prevent a common type of pneumonia caused by the Streptococcus pneumoniae bacterium.

• **Take vitamin A daily.** Vitamin A deficiency can cause drying of the respiratory-tract lining and a reduction in cilia, the hairlike tissues that move mucus and debris out of the lungs. Both changes make the lungs vulnerable to infection and inflammation. A total daily dose of 10,000 international units (IU) of vitamin A can help keep your lungs healthy.

Caution: Vitamin A is toxic when consumed in high doses over long periods of time. Consult your doctor before taking more than 10,000 IU of vitamin A daily. If you have liver disease or are pregnant, do not take supplemental vitamin A. In addition, some research suggests that smokers should not take vitamin A supplements.

•**Get more vitamin C daily.** The results of studies on the immune-enhancing effects of vitamin C have been mixed. However, I'm convinced—based on my clinical experience —that a daily dose of vitamin C does, in fact, help the immune system resist disease and is essential to combating the immune-draining effects of stress, a chief cause of illness.

I recommend a daily total of 1,000 mg of vitamin C.

•**Treat upper respiratory infections (URIs) promptly and effectively.** Quite often, pneumonia develops from the spread of inflammation caused by a viral infection, such as bronchitis.

My advice: Rest (forgo your usual activities, including going to work)...and hydrate (drink 68 ounces of water daily). For a cold or bronchitis, I recommend drinking a tincture made from extracts of the powerful antiviral botanical medicines elder, echinacea, eyebright and licorice—15 drops of each in one ounce of water, 15 minutes before or after meals, every four waking hours for several days.

Caution: Omit licorice if you have high blood pressure or heart disease—the herb may affect blood pressure or cause heart problems.

•**Don't delay a doctor visit if you suspect pneumonia.** Typical symptoms include a cough, fever, shortness of breath and fatigue. An early diagnosis increases your chance of a good outcome.

Antibiotics for Ear Infections?

Mark A. Stengler, NMD, licensed naturopathic medical doctor in private practice, Encinitas, California... adjunct associate clinical professor at the National College of Natural Medicine, Portland, Oregon...author of *The Natural Physician's Healing Therapies* and co-author of *Prescription for Natural Cures* (both from Bottom Line Books).

When a patient has an earache, he/she (or the parent, if the patient is a child) often asks for an antibiotic, thinking that the drug will alleviate the pain and cure the infection. But the American Academy of Pediatrics advises against prescribing antibiotics for mild-to-moderate ear infections in patients age two and older.

Reasons: Overuse of the drugs contributes to the rise in antibiotic-resistant bacteria... antibiotics reduce beneficial intestinal flora, interfering with digestion and immunity...and ear infections are caused mostly by viruses or occasionally by fungi, neither of which respond to antibiotics.

Natural treatments are more effective than antibiotics for reducing pain and hastening recovery.

Evidence: In a German study of 131 children with ear infections, one group of children received conventional antibiotics, decongestants and fever-reducing medicines, while the rest were treated with homeopathic remedies. On average, children treated with homeopathy experienced two days of pain after treatment began and required four days of treatment... and 71% were free from recurrent infection in the year that followed. Children treated with conventional drugs had three days of ear pain and required 10 days of treatment (the standard length of antibiotic treatment)...and only 57% remained free from recurrence.

Antibiotics do not prevent complications, either. A study in the *British Medical Journal* analyzed data from 3.36 million episodes of respiratory tract infections, from which ear infections commonly develop.

Results: Serious complications from ear infections were rare...and antibiotics prevented complications for only one person out of every 4,000 who took the drugs.

I consider antibiotics when a patient has pus in the middle ear (seen during an exam)...has a fever of 104°F or higher for more than 24 hours or any fever for more than 48 hours...has rapidly worsening symptoms...or does not respond to natural treatments within two days.

The natural treatments below work well for most bacterial and viral ear infections. For mild pain, try eardrops alone. If pain is moderate to severe or does not ease after one or two applications of eardrops, use all three remedies. Therapies generally are safe for adults and children of all ages. Products are sold in health-food stores.

• **Garlic/mullein/St. John's wort eardrops** relieve pain and have antibacterial and antiviral effects. Hold the capped bottle under hot water until warm…then place three drops in the affected ear three to four times daily. Do not use if the eardrum is ruptured (indicated by pus in the ear).

Try: Eclectic Institute Ear Drops (800-332-4372, *www.eclecticherb.com*).

• **Homeopathic chamomilla** (from the chamomile plant) reduces pain and fever.

Dosage: Two 30C potency pellets to be taken four times daily.

• **Echinacea/goldenseal herbal formula** strengthens the immune response. Use as directed, typically four times daily. For children, choose an alcohol-free product.

Pain relief: Run one facecloth under hot water and another under cold water to make compresses. Hold the hot compress over the ear for two minutes, then switch to the cold compress for 30 seconds. Repeat twice. Do in the morning, midday and evening for two days to reduce congestion and draw healing immune cells to the area.

Nosebleed Know-How

D on't tilt your head back during a nosebleed. It can let blood run into the esophagus, which can cause choking, or run into the stomach, which can lead to irritation and vomiting.

Instead: Sit down, lean forward and keep your head above your heart. Use your thumb and index finger to squeeze the soft tissue below the bridge of your nose for five to 20 minutes. Also, a small wad of cotton or gauze sprayed with a topical decongestant can be placed in the bleeding nostril for 10 to 15 minutes.

American Academy of Family Physicians, Leawood, Kansas, *www.aafp.org*.

Medical Symptoms You Should Never Ignore

Maurice A. Ramirez, DO, PhD, former emergency room doctor in Dade City, Florida. He is a specialist in emergency and disaster medicine and founding chair of the American Board of Disaster Medicine.

M illions of people ignore symptoms that they should pay attention to right away. They think a high fever will go down or stomach pain will go away—but symptoms such as these can be signs of dangerous, even life-threatening, conditions. *Here, symptoms that should never be ignored…*

ABDOMINAL PAIN

Severe abdominal pain often is a symptom of a medical crisis.

Possibly happening…

• **Appendicitis.**

• **Gallbladder problems.**

• **Diverticulitis** (an infection of the wall of the intestines).

• **Aortic aneurysm** (weakened or bulging area in the aorta, the major vessel that feeds blood to the body).

• **Tumor.**

Urgent: If the pain doesn't go away within five minutes, call 911 or have someone drive you to the emergency room (ER).

If you wait too long: While most of these conditions can be resolved quickly with immediate surgery, waiting can make the problem worse.

Example: Appendicitis can become a ruptured appendix—and instead of going home the day after your surgery, you may end up in the intensive care unit.

SHORTNESS OF BREATH

You start to have trouble breathing.

Possibly happening…

• **Chronic Obstructive Pulmonary Disease (COPD),** such as emphysema.

• **Congestive heart failure,** in which the heart doesn't pump strongly enough to keep blood from backing up into the lungs.

- **Heart attack.**
- **Asthma attack or anaphylaxis** (throat constriction caused by a severe allergic reaction).
- **Pneumonia.**

Urgent: If you are slightly short of breath—you can still speak a sentence without having to stop and take another breath—you can drive yourself or ask someone to drive you to the ER unless you also have chest pain.

If you are huffing and puffing, turning blue and/or cannot finish a sentence without taking another breath—what ER doctors call "one-sentence dyspnea"—you are in severe trouble. And "four-word dyspnea"—you cannot speak four words without taking a breath—is extremely dangerous, and you should be on a ventilator. In either case, call 911.

If you wait too long: Depending on the condition, there could be damage to the heart and possible death from lack of oxygen.

HIGH FEVER

A fever is cause for concern if it is higher than 103°F and is accompanied by a stiff neck, severe headache and/or a rash.

Possibly happening…

- **Meningitis.**
- **Rocky Mountain spotted fever.**
- **Pneumonia.**

Urgent: Go to the ER fast.

If you wait too long: Serious infection can lead to shock (when the body's circulatory system fails to maintain adequate blood flow).

If you have pneumonia and wait more than four hours to have the high fever treated, you are more likely to die of pneumonia.

HIVES ALL OVER

You suddenly have itchy, red bumps over much of your body. This may be accompanied by difficulty breathing…pale, cool and clammy skin…or a weak or rapid pulse.

Possibly happening: You're having an allergic reaction to an insect bite or sting, a food or other type of allergen.

Urgent: Go to the ER, and don't leave without a prescription for *epinephrine* (EpiPen). Cases of "hives all over" often will spontaneously recur over the next month—even if you aren't exposed to the allergen again—getting worse each time. The epinephrine can short-circuit a severe allergic reaction.

Caution: Once you use your EpiPen, don't assume that the problem is gone. Go to the ER immediately.

If you wait too long: Anaphylactic shock, a life-threatening drop in blood pressure that also can result in difficulty breathing, dizziness and/or loss of consciousness.

SUDDEN VISION OR HEARING LOSS

You're suddenly blind in one or both eyes and/or deaf in one or both ears.

Possibly happening: This is almost always a stroke.

Urgent: Call 911.

If you wait too long: Loss of vision and/or hearing, as well as other stroke damage, possibly leading to death.

DIFFICULTY MOVING OR SPEAKING

You can't move part of your body, and/or you start slurring words.

Possibly happening…

- **Stroke,** caused by a clot blocking an artery to the brain.
- **Cerebral aneurysm** (ruptured blood vessel in the brain).
- **Brain tumor.**
- **Tumor or bone chip** in the spinal canal, pressing on a nerve.

Urgent: Call 911, even if the paralysis or slurred speech goes away. A temporary disconnection between your brain and the rest of your body is always cause for concern.

If you wait too long: If you don't receive treatment for a stroke or ruptured blood vessel within six hours, your odds of future disability are 50%. If you are treated within three hours, there is a 70% chance of full recovery.

An undiagnosed tumor can damage the brain. An undiagnosed impediment in the spinal canal can destroy the nerve, causing permanent loss of function, even paralysis.

CHEST PAIN

Most people know that chest pain is a dangerous sign—and yet people with chest pain typically wait six hours before going to the ER. Then it's often too late to receive treatments that can stop or reverse damage to the heart, brain and other vital organs.

Possibly happening…

• **Heart attack.**

• **Pulmonary embolism** (blood clot in a lung artery).

• **Aortic aneurysm** (a tear in the body's largest artery).

Urgent: If you have chest pain for more than five minutes, call 911. Do not drive to the ER or ask someone to drive you. You need emergency care in an ambulance.

If you wait too long: Heart muscle can die, causing permanent heart damage or death…a partial aortic tear can develop into a full tear, causing a stroke.

Get the Ultimate Medical Checkup

Leo Galland, MD, director, Foundation for Integrated Medicine, New York City. He is author of *The Fat Resistance Diet* (Three Rivers, *www.drgalland.com*). Dr. Galland is a recipient of the Linus Pauling award.

The managed-care revolution has drastically reduced the amount of time doctors spend with their patients. During the typical office visit, your doctor barely has enough time to investigate troublesome symptoms and check your weight…pulse…heartbeat…blood pressure, etc. That simply does not go far enough.

A thorough exam should also address your overall physical and emotional well-being…diet…lifestyle…and any "silent" symptoms that could potentially increase your risk for developing health problems.

Most doctors take a medical history, listing current health problems…prescribed medications…allergies, etc. This information is critical.

Helpful: When writing down your concerns, give your doctor additional information that he/she may fail to include in the medical history. *For example…*

• **How's your diet?**

• **Are you taking any herbal or dietary supplements?**

• **Do you get enough sleep?**

• **Are you physically active?**

• **Are you experiencing sexual problems?**

Also mention if you smoke, how much alcohol you drink and whether you're having difficulty in your personal relationships. Try to keep the list to one page.

THE PHYSICAL

To save time, doctors often take shortcuts during the physical. This can affect not only your current diagnosis and treatment—but also your future health. *Here are the steps most commonly omitted…*

• **Blood pressure.** This vital sign is typically checked in one arm while the patient is sitting. For a more accurate reading, blood pressure should be tested in both arms, preferably while you're lying down.

If blood pressure differs by 15% or more between arms, there may be blockages in the large blood vessels.

Important: If you're taking blood pressure medication—or if you get dizzy when you change positions—your doctor should check your blood pressure immediately after you stand up. If blood pressure drops by more than 10%, a change in dosage of blood pressure medication may be needed.

• **Eyes.** Most people visit an ophthalmologist or optometrist. But if you don't see an eye specialist regularly and you're age 40 or older, your internist or family practitioner should measure the pressure on your eyeballs to test for glaucoma and look for lack of lens clarity—an early sign of cataracts.

• **Lymph nodes.** The lymph nodes in your neck are typically checked, but doctors should also check those in the groin and under arms. Swollen lymph nodes may signal infection. Lumps could indicate cancer.

• **Pulse points.** Your doctor probably checks your pulse in your neck and/or groin—but may skip your feet. If pulse strength differs in these three areas, it can be a sign of peripheral arterial disease.

• **Skin.** Many doctors ignore the skin altogether, assuming that it should be examined by a dermatologist. Not true. The skin should also be checked during a general medical checkup.

To thoroughly examine your skin, your doctor should ask you to disrobe so he can look for moles on every part of your body, even your scalp and the bottoms of your feet.

If you have moles larger than one-half inch —or if your moles have gotten larger, darkened or changed their shape—you should get a referral to a dermatologist for a melanoma screening.

• **Thyroid.** This butterfly-shaped gland at the base of the neck is often missed during the lymph node exam. By palpating the thyroid, your doctor can screen for thyroid cancer.

FOR WOMEN ONLY

• **Breast and reproductive organs.** Most doctors check the breasts for suspicious lumps, but few doctors show women how to perform monthly exams at home.

Helpful: When performing a self-exam, move all eight fingers, minus the thumbs, up and down instead of in a circle. That way, you will be covering the entire breast.

If you don't see your gynecologist regularly, your primary physician should also perform rectal and vaginal exams. These exams should be performed simultaneously—it makes it easier to identify suspicious masses.

LABORATORY TESTS

Routine blood tests include cholesterol levels …liver and kidney function…blood glucose levels…and a white blood cell count. But we now know that other blood tests can be important if a patient shows signs of certain conditions. *These tests include…*

• **C-reactive protein.** An elevated level of this inflammation marker can indicate heart disease risk.

• **Homocysteine.** Elevated levels of this amino acid are associated with heart disease and stroke risk.

Helpful: The B vitamin folate, when taken at 200 to 400 micrograms (mcg) daily, reduces homocysteine levels.

• **Iron.** Elevated levels of this mineral contribute to iron overload (hemochromatosis).

• **Lipoprotein (a).** Elevated levels of this blood protein increase the risk for blood clots.

• **Magnesium.** Low levels of this mineral can bring about fatigue, generalized pain and/or muscle spasms.

• **Zinc.** If you're deficient in this immune-strengthening mineral, you may be prone to frequent infection.

More from Dr. Leo Galland…

Important Medical Tests Doctors Don't Tell You About

Special screening tests—for detecting heart disease, aneurysms, lung cancer and ovarian cancer—could save your life. But there's a good chance that your doctor won't order them because insurance companies rarely pay for them.

Reason: Insurance companies typically pay for tests only when you have been diagnosed with a particular condition or when there is a high likelihood that you might have it. With some exceptions, such as mammograms, insurance rarely pays for screening tests aimed at early detection.

Ask your doctor if you should have any of the following tests, even if you have to pay for them yourself. They are available at most diagnostic and medical centers around the country. Ask your doctor for a referral.

These tests aren't appropriate for everyone, but early research suggests that they could be lifesavers for those with key risk factors…

CHOLESTEROL TEST

Traditional cholesterol tests only measure HDL ("good") cholesterol and triglycerides. The formula used to calculate levels of harmful LDL cholesterol isn't always accurate. This partly explains why half of people who have heart attacks have cholesterol levels that appear normal.

Better: Expanded cholesterol tests measure LDL specifically, giving more accurate readings. About 40 million American adults have hidden heart disease. Expanded cholesterol tests could identify 95% of these patients before a heart attack occurs.

The tests also look at individual HDL and LDL particles and determine how helpful—or harmful—they are likely to be.

Example: HDL protects against heart disease, so high levels are desirable. But some people who appear to have high levels actually have a subtype of HDL that isn't very helpful. Also, though all LDL particles are bad, the smaller ones are more dangerous than the bigger ones. These kinds of differences aren't detectable with conventional tests—but they can be detected with the expanded tests.

Who should consider them: Patients with mildly elevated cholesterol levels (200 mg/dL to 230 mg/dL) who smoke or have cardiovascular risk factors, such as heart problems, high blood pressure or a family history of heart disease.

Cost: $75 to $175.

ANEURYSM TEST

Aneurysms are bulges in artery walls. They can be deadly when they rupture, killing 80% to 90% of people who have ruptured aneurysms. About 30,000 Americans die from this annually.

Better: An aneurysm scan uses an ultrasound wand to detect aneurysms in the abdominal aortic arteries. It's the only noninvasive test that allows doctors to identify aneurysms before they rupture. Surgery to repair aneurysms can increase survival rates to 99%.

Who should consider it: Anyone over age 60 who has cardiovascular risk factors, such as high blood pressure, or who smokes…anyone over age 50 who has a family history of heart disease.

Cost: $60 to $200, depending on the extent of the scan.

HEART DISEASE TEST

Current methods for detecting heart disease risk, such as checking blood pressure, miss up to 75% of patients who later develop heart problems.

Better: The electron-beam tomography (EBT) heart scan is the first direct, noninvasive way of identifying atherosclerosis, the main risk factor for heart disease. The patient lies in a doughnut-shaped machine while electron beams map calcium deposits in the arteries. Calcium buildups indicate the presence of plaque—fatty deposits that hamper blood flow to the heart and increase the risk of clots. Patients who are found to have early signs of heart disease can take the appropriate steps—such as lowering cholesterol, controlling blood pressure, stopping smoking, etc.—to prevent problems from progressing.

Drawback: Calcium deposits don't always indicate an elevated risk of heart attack. The deposits may be harmless. On the other hand, a person who has a clear scan could actually have dangerous levels of plaque.

Patients with high calcium levels also may have to take a follow-up stress test. If this test is positive, the patient may have to undergo an angiogram—an invasive procedure. If the angiogram shows no heart disease, the patient has undergone these extra tests unnecessarily. Still the EBT is considered useful because traditional tests don't catch most heart problems.

Who should consider it: All men over age 45 and women over age 55. If you have heart disease risk factors—smoking, a family history of heart disease, etc.—consider having an EBT 10 years sooner.

Cost: About $500.

LUNG CANCER TEST

Lung cancer rarely causes symptoms until it reaches an advanced stage. The five-year survival rate is about 15%. Conventional X-rays may fail to detect early-stage tumors.

Better: The spiral CT scan can detect cancerous tumors as small as a grain of rice. Eighty percent of lung cancers spotted in scanning studies were caught at a potentially treatable stage.

Drawbacks: The test can result in false-positives—findings that indicate cancer when none is present. This could lead to unnecessary and risky lung biopsies. The false-positive rate improves when patients have follow-up scans.

Who should consider it: Smokers and former smokers age 50 and over who have smoked at least one pack daily for 10 years or two packs daily for five years.

Cost: $200 to $450.

OVARIAN CANCER

More than 14,000 American women die from ovarian cancer annually. It's the deadliest female cancer. Like lung cancer, it often has no symptoms until it reaches an advanced stage.

Better: An ultrasound device inserted into the vagina allows doctors to inspect the ovaries for malignant changes. University of Kentucky researchers used the test on 23,000 women. Twenty-nine had cancerous ovarian tumors, 76% of which were detected at an early, more treatable stage. Typically, only 25% of ovarian cancers are caught early.

Drawback: The test isn't able to differentiate between malignant and benign growths—so positive test results could result in unnecessary procedures.

Who should consider it: Women age 45 and older with risk factors, such as a family history of ovarian, breast or colon cancer…or a history of fertility or hormone-replacement treatment…or who never have been pregnant.

Cost: About $250.

Best Home Medical Tests

Steven I. Gutman, MD, former director of the Food and Drug Administration's Division of Clinical Laboratory Devices in Rockville, Maryland. *www.fda.gov*

Home medical testing kits and devices sold at pharmacies and on the Internet allow anyone to conveniently test for illnesses and other medical conditions in the privacy of his/her own home.

Home-test manufacturers must prove to the Food and Drug Administration (FDA) that their products are as accurate as the laboratory tests used by medical offices.

None of the tests requires a doctor's prescription, but they aren't substitutes for doctor visits. These tests are not covered by insurance.

Important: Carefully read the instructions that come with any test. Doing a test improperly —taking urine at the wrong time of day, for example—can invalidate the results.

Editor's note: Home medical tests are available from retail and online pharmacies and the Web companies *www.homehealthtesting.com* and *www.homeaccess.com*.

Some of the best home tests…

CHOLESTEROL

High cholesterol is a leading risk factor for stroke, heart disease and other cardiovascular conditions.

How the test works: Place some blood from a finger prick on a chemically treated strip. Cholesterol readings will appear on a thermometer-like scale in about 10 minutes. Some tests provide separate breakdowns for LDL (bad) and HDL (good) cholesterol. For this, you must send the blood sample to the manufacturer and wait several weeks for the results.

Average cost: $13 to $40 for a package of two tests.

COLON CANCER

Fecal Occult Blood Tests (FOBTs) detect small, often invisible amounts of blood in the stool—an early sign of colon cancer.

How the test works: Traditional FOBTs require you to take stool samples at home, then bring them to a lab for analysis. A newer FOBT doesn't require stool samples. You drop a chemically treated tissue into the toilet after you've had a bowel movement. A color change indicates blood is present. If so, you need additional tests, such as a colonoscopy, to check for cancerous or precancerous growths.

To ensure accuracy: You must repeat the test for three consecutive bowel movements. Don't take aspirin, ibuprofen or other nonsteroidal anti-inflammatory drugs for one week prior to testing. They may cause bleeding that can skew the results.

For three days prior to the test, avoid eating red meat and don't take vitamin C supplements in excess of 250 mg daily. Don't use this test if you have bleeding hemorrhoids or anal fissures.

Average cost: $10 for five-pad test kit.

DRUG USE

Parents who suspect their children of drug use may want to do a home test. Some tests check for a specific drug, such as marijuana. Broader tests detect multiple drugs—including cocaine and amphetamines.

How the test works: Some urine is dropped in a test cassette. Markings or color changes show if drugs are present. Marijuana generally can be detected within two to 30 days after use.

Important: About 5% of all urine drug tests result in false positives—they indicate that drugs are present when they're not. A positive home test should be confirmed with a laboratory drug test, such as a gas chromatography.

Average cost: $10 for three urine-test strips.

Drugs can also be detected in hair clippings, which are sent to a laboratory for analysis.

Cost: About $70.

HIV

Privacy concerns prevent many people from getting tested for HIV, the virus that causes AIDS. Home-test manufacturers that analyze the results follow strict confidentiality guidelines.

How the test works: Prick your finger, and apply the blood to special paper. Call a toll-free number to activate your personal code. Mail the blood sample and an anonymous personal identification number to a laboratory. To get the test results, you call a toll-free number and give your personal code.

Average cost: $60 for one test.

MENOPAUSE

Women in their 40s and 50s commonly experience hot flashes, mood swings or other menopause-like symptoms. They can confirm that they are entering menopause with a home test.

How the test works: Place a few drops of urine on a test strip. Premenopausal levels of follicle-stimulating hormone are lower than 25 IU/L. Readings that are above 25 indicate a woman has entered menopause.

Home-test manufacturers advise women to repeat the test every six to 12 months when the symptoms of menopause occur.

Average cost: About $23 for two tests.

OVULATION

Home test kits have taken much of the guesswork out of when women may be able to get pregnant.

How the test works: Wet a test strip with urine to measure luteinizing hormone. Levels peak 24 to 36 hours prior to ovulation, which is the optimal time to try to conceive.

Average cost: $10 for five-test strip.

URINARY TRACT INFECTIONS (UTIs)

With a home test, you can confirm that you have an infection. Then your doctor may prescribe antibiotics for you over the phone.

How the test works: Wet a plastic strip with urine. Part of the strip will change color if a UTI is present.

These tests are recommended only for people who get recurrent UTIs and are familiar with the symptoms, including frequent and/or painful urination.

If you have not experienced a UTI before, you should see your doctor to rule out any other possible conditions, such as chlamydia or kidney stones.

Important: The test fails to detect infections about 30% of the time. See your doctor if the test is negative but you have symptoms.

Average cost: $10 for six test strips and collection cups.

Shingles Linked to Family History

When researchers analyzed data for 504 people who had been treated for shingles and 523 people who had been treated for other skin conditions, about 39% of the shingles patients reported having a family member (parent, child or sibling) with a history of the condition, compared with 10.5% of those in the other group.

Theory: Genetic factors may raise risk for shingles.

If one or more of your family members has had shingles: Ask your doctor whether you should get the shingles vaccine.

Stephen Tyring, MD, PhD, clinical professor, department of dermatology, University of Texas Health Science Center, Houston.

Aluminum: This Toxic Metal Is Everywhere

Mark A. Stengler, NMD, licensed naturopathic medical doctor in private practice, Encinitas, California…adjunct associate clinical professor at the National College of Natural Medicine, Portland, Oregon…author of *The Natural Physician's Healing Therapies* and co-author of *Prescription for Natural Cures* (both from Bottom Line Books).

You may think of aluminum mostly as a handy foil for wrapping leftovers, but in fact, aluminum is just about everywhere…in our air, water, soil and food. It also is in many drugs…as well as in household and personal products, such as kitchen pans and antiperspirants.

I am concerned about the aluminum humans have added to our surroundings. Although conventional medicine has long maintained that aluminum is not a problem for most people, the holistic view is that any metal is unsafe when present in excess.

Unfortunately, there is limited research on the risks of aluminum buildup in the body. *What we know for certain…*

• **Aluminum can accumulate in the bones, liver, kidneys and brain.**

• **It is toxic to the nervous system.**

• **It can cause brain cells to degenerate.**

Symptoms of aluminum toxicity include headache…fatigue…bone pain…anemia (low red blood cell count)…and dementia. Because these symptoms can mimic those of other medical conditions, doctors often do not recognize aluminum as the root cause of the problem.

That is why, whenever I see such symptoms in my patients, I order a urine test to check aluminum levels.

RISKY VACCINES?

I am especially concerned about aluminum in vaccines, for children in particular. Shots that are supposed to help keep us healthy may, in this way, do us harm.

A decade ago, the biggest concern around childhood vaccines had to do with *thimerosal*, a preservative that contains mercury. As clear evidence of mercury's toxicity mounted, demands were made that thimerosal be removed from vaccines. Manufacturers finally complied, eliminating or reducing it to trace levels in all vaccines. This was possible because thimerosal was not crucial to the effectiveness of the vaccine.

But aluminum is a different story. It is an *adjuvant*, which means that it makes vaccines work better. It allows the body's immune system to more easily recognize the vaccine and get busy creating antibodies against the disease being targeted. Eliminating the aluminum would necessitate a complete reformulation of current vaccines—plus many years of clinical trials to determine whether new alternatives were effective.

In healthy adults, the current guideline for a safe amount of aluminum delivered via a vaccine is considered to be up to 850 micrograms (mcg). Many of the vaccines typically given to adults—for tetanus, diptheria, pertussis (whooping cough), HPV and Hepatitis A and B—contain aluminum. I would argue that *no* amount of aluminum is healthy.

However, adults have, on average, five liters of blood, and they generally do not receive multiple vaccinations at the same time. These factors make the consequences of receiving an aluminum-laced vaccine less worrisome for them than it is for children. In newborns, as pediatrician Robert W. Sears, MD, points out in *The Vaccine Book* (Little, Brown), an acceptable aluminum dose ranges from just 10 mcg to 20 mcg. Yet this number is far exceeded by some of the new vaccines.

Example: The Hepatitis B shot with 250 mcg, which was added by the American Academy of Pediatrics to the childhood vaccination schedule in the early 1990s. Furthermore, throughout the first year of life, several vaccines are administered at each checkup. Add up the amount of aluminum in all the vaccines recommended in a single round—given at two months of age, four months and six months—and you will see that babies are getting as much as 1,225 mcg in a single vaccination day. For a one-year old, the known safe amount is only about 50 mcg daily.

Much of what is known about aluminum's effects in human infants comes from research in premature babies. Years ago, it was discovered that preemies who received more than 10 mcg to 20 mcg of aluminum in their intravenous feeding solutions each day suffered aluminum toxicity in their bones and brain tissue, resulting in impaired neurologic and mental development. Aluminum is now filtered out of such solutions. Yet preemies are still allowed to receive a Hep B vaccine with 250 mcg of aluminum!

SAFER STEPS YOU CAN TAKE...

•**Ask your doctor for aluminum-free vaccines for yourself and your loved ones.** Certain vaccine brands contain little or no aluminum.

Examples: Fluzone and FluMist for influenza...Pneumovax for pneumonia...RotaTeq for rotavirus. The Centers for Disease Control and Prevention has a complete list on its Web site, *www.cdc.gov/vaccines.*

•**Do not receive more than one vaccine per month.** Ideally, adults and children should space out getting any shots that have aluminum by three or more months. *The Vaccine Book* offers a safer vaccination schedule for children.

SNEAKY SOURCES

Each person in the US ingests, on average, about 30 mg to 50 mg of aluminum daily, according to the National Library of Medicine.

Reason: Aluminum can be present in a number of common substances, including...

•**Air**—via dust from mining and agricultural processes.

•**Baking aids,** such as cake mixes, self-rising flour and baking powder. Try aluminum-free varieties, available from Bob's Red Mill

(800-349-2173, *www.bobsredmill.com,* and in natural food stores).

•**Beverages**—from the cans that hold juice, soda, beer, infant formula.

•**Cheeses (processed).**

•**Cookware, utensils (some brands) and aluminum foil**—it is especially important to avoid using these items when preparing acidic substances, such as tomato sauce, which make them more likely to leach aluminum.

•**Health and beauty products,** including some antiperspirants, shampoos and sunscreens.

•**Jet fuel.**

•**Medications,** including some antacids and anti-diarrheals, and buffered aspirin.

•**Nondairy creamers.**

•**Tap water,** especially fluoridated.

Watch for "alum-" on labels. Once you are aware of these sneaky sources, you can take care to avoid them as much as possible. More research is needed to understand how aluminum affects our health and to formulate guidelines about its use. When it comes to aluminum—or any toxic metal—it's better to be safe than sorry.

TESTING & TREATMENT

While we all should watch our exposure to aluminum, certain people are at especially high risk for aluminum toxicity. *I recommend all adults be tested at some point, but it is especially important for...*

•**People with severe memory problems and/or dementia,** including Alzheimer's disease

•**People with neurological problems,** such as tremors and neuropathy (nerve pain)

•**Children with learning or developmental disorders** (autism, ADHD)

•**Anyone with impaired kidney function**

•**Those with known aluminum exposure,** such as workers in factories where it is used.

Your doctor can perform the test. If your aluminum levels appear to be elevated, see a holistic doctor for urine or stool testing to confirm that excess aluminum is present.

If so, your doctor should prescribe a chelating agent—a drug that binds to metal, pulling it out of the body's tissues and sending it into the blood. It can then be filtered through the liver and kidneys and excreted via urine and stool. After three months or more, your doctor will want to retest you to see if your aluminum level has dropped. I have had great success using this therapy and detoxifying supplements for my patients.

More from Dr. Mark Stengler...

Get the Lead Out

The recent discovery that toddlers' toys were causing lead toxicity called attention to a problem many people thought was behind us.

Reality: In the US, lead toxicity continues to be a serious health threat—and not just in children. I regularly see adult patients whose bodies harbor dangerous levels of lead.

Reason: Lead that entered the body decades earlier can linger indefinitely. Not too long ago, lead was part of everyday life, appearing in paints, gasoline, household pipes, tin can soldering, crystal goblets and glazed ceramic dishware.

Current laws have improved the situation, but lead is still associated with numerous industries and hobbies (see page 168). Lead is found in some lipsticks...herbs from China and Japan...and soil contaminated by car exhaust and other pollutants. In up to 90% of currently occupied homes in the US built before 1940, residents are exposed to lead that leaches into tap water from plumbing. Paint manufactured before 1978 may produce dust or flakes that contain lead. Researchers suggest that the consequences of lead exposure for people born in the latter half of the 20th century will persist through the first half of the 21st century.

HOW LEAD AFFECTS US

Lead inhibits enzymes that affect brain chemicals and oxygen-carrying red blood cells, causing malfunctions in nerve signal transmission, muscle contraction and heartbeat. It depletes the liver's stores of glutathione, an amino acid vital to detoxification and liver cell regeneration. Lead may contribute to autoimmune disorders (in which the immune system attacks the body's own tissues), such as rheumatoid arthritis and multiple sclerosis.

Children are particularly at risk because they absorb lead more readily...and because their developing organs and nervous systems are more vulnerable to lead's damaging effects.

Symptoms of lead toxicity include...

• **Gastrointestinal problems**—abdominal pain, diarrhea, constipation.

• **Muscular weakness and fatigue.**

• **Impaired kidney and liver function.**

• **Neurological effects**—headache, dizziness, tremors, poor memory and possibly dementia.

• **Central nervous system problems**—mood disorders, sleep disorders, seizures, decreased libido.

• **Cardiovascular effects**—high blood pressure, hardening of the arteries.

• **Reproductive problems**—decreased sperm count, menstrual irregularities, increased risk of miscarriage and stillbirth.

• **Developmental and behavioral problems in children.**

TESTING TROUBLES

Blood tests can detect lead only if exposure was recent or extreme. Most adults do not meet these criteria. In adults, lead generally has been present for many years, so the body has had time to remove it from the blood and lock it away in the fat, nerves, kidneys and bones. Only 2% of the total lead in an adult body typically remains in the blood, making blood testing unreliable.

Urine-testing accuracy depends on how it is done. I spoke with Mary James, ND, a medical education specialist with Genova Diagnostics, a major testing lab for toxic metals. Dr. James explained that the best tests (which I use with my own patients) involve a chelating agent—a substance that binds to metal, pulling it out of the body's tissues and sending it into the blood, from which it can then be filtered through the liver and kidneys and eliminated via urine and stool. When an oral chelating agent is used, urine tests reveal higher-than-normal lead levels in about 75% of people tested, said

Dr. James—compared with a 25% positive rate when a chelating agent is not used.

Who should be tested: Request testing if you have been exposed to lead or exhibit any symptoms of toxicity. Parents who suspect lead exposure should have their children tested.

PREVENTION AND TREATMENT

Calcium competes with lead for absorption in the digestive tract and for storage sites in the bones. With adequate calcium, you retain less lead. As a general preventive measure, I recommend that all teens and adults take 500 mg to 600 mg of calcium twice daily...and that children ages three to 12 take 500 mg once daily.

If lead toxicity is diagnosed, do not delay treatment. The longer lead remains in the body, the more difficult it is to get out. Still, even if the metal has been inside the body for decades, treatment can improve symptoms considerably, especially for young to middle-aged adults. Sadly, some damage may be irreversible in older adults and in children whose cognitive function has been impaired.

Chelation treatment is needed to pull lead from tissues so that it can be excreted. The form used depends on the severity of toxicity. Options (from least to most aggressive) include oral medication taken five to seven days per week...rectal suppositories used every other night before bedtime...or intravenous (IV) therapy for one to three hours weekly.

Patients must have kidney and liver function tests done before starting chelation to ensure that treatment will not overtax the organs responsible for detoxification. Naturopathic physicians and holistic medical doctors administer all types of chelation...chiropractors provide oral chelation. Most people experience little or no discomfort, though side effects may include skin rash, digestive upset, fatigue, cloudy thinking and/or moodiness. Treatment typically takes from two to eight months, depending on symptom severity. Follow-up testing indicates when treatment is complete. Unfortunately, insurance rarely covers chelation.

To guard against mineral loss during treatment, supplement daily with a high-potency multivitamin/mineral plus an additional 1,200 mg of calcium and 600 mg of magnesium. I also recommend Heavy Metal Support from

Thorne Research (800-228-1966, *www.thorne.com*), available online...or OptiCleanse GHI or OptiCleanse Plus by Xymogen (800-647-6100, *www.xymogen.com*), available through health-care professionals.

If you have lead toxicity, ask your doctor for a blood test to measure iron levels. Iron-deficient people absorb two to three times more lead than those with adequate iron. If necessary, your doctor can prescribe iron supplements.

Caution: Do not take iron unless diagnosed with a deficiency—excess iron damages the liver.

Smart: If you suspect that any portion of your home was last painted before 1978—when paint containing lead was banned—paint over it to minimize flakes or dust that might pose a threat. If your home was built before 1940, install a charcoal filter on each water tap.

JOBS AND HOBBIES LINKED TO LEAD EXPOSURE

Lead exposure continues to be a potential problem in more than 900 vocations and avocations. If you are involved in any of the following, ask your doctor to test you for lead toxicity.

- **Battery manufacturing**
- **Ceramics**
- **Chemical industries**
- **Construction or demolition**
- **Firing ranges**
- **Foundries**
- **Gasoline additives production**
- **Jewelry-making**
- **Lead mining, smelting, soldering or refining**
- **Pigment manufacturing**
- **Pipe-fitting**
- **Plastics industries**
- **Sewage treatment**
- **Stained glass-making**
- **Welding.**

Dangerous Toxins May Be Lurking in Your Home

The late Mitchell Gaynor, MD, former assistant clinical professor of medicine at Weill Medical College of Cornell University, and founder of Gaynor Integrative Oncology, both in New York City. He is author of *Nurture Nature/Nurture Health* (Nurture Nature Press).

As long as you breathe, eat and drink, you can't entirely escape environmental toxins. Research on the risks associated with these toxins is ongoing, but many scientists believe that existing evidence suggests that toxic buildup in our bodies contributes to the development of Parkinson's disease and may increase risk for some types of cancer and other serious conditions. A Centers for Disease Control and Prevention study that tested 10,000 men and women for the presence of 116 chemicals, including phthalates and dioxin, found that most Americans carried some combination of these toxins in small amounts in their blood.

TOXICITY IN THE HOME

Household sources of toxins that are under investigation...

• **Home furnishings.** *Polybrominated diphenyl ethers* (PBDEs), common ingredients in flame retardants that are used to treat upholstered chairs and sofas, foam mattresses and cushions, may be carcinogenic. PBDEs also may disrupt thyroid function and brain development.

What to do: When buying foam mattresses, upholstered furniture, etc., ask whether PBDEs were used during manufacturing.

• **Pressed wood and fiberboard,** which often are used in furniture and shelving, are common sources of *formaldehyde*, a gaseous compound that is used as a disinfectant. Formaldehyde has been found to be a probable carcinogen.

What to do: Look for solid wood products or those carrying the seal of the American National Standards Institute (ANSI), which certifies that the item is low in formaldehyde emissions.

• **Cleaning products.** Most people use a wide variety of cleaning products, many of which contain toxic chemicals. Chlorine bleach is potentially carcinogenic and can damage the respiratory system. Among its by-products are *chlorinated hydrocarbons, chloroform* and *trihalomethanes,* all of which act like weak estrogens and cause breast cells to divide more rapidly. These by-products have been shown to cause breast tumors in animals.

What to do: Use commercial cleansers that are free of chlorine and most chemicals. Seventh Generation and Sun & Earth are two brands that are widely available at health food stores.

Or use natural cleaning alternatives—baking soda to scrub sinks, tubs and toilets...white distilled vinegar in a pump-spray bottle to clean mirrors and windows. If you must use chlorine-containing cleaners, make sure the room is well-ventilated.

• **Pesticides.** Research has shown that pesticides increase risk for Parkinson's disease—and may be a cause of some cancers.

What to do: Use baits and traps instead of sprays. Try organic alternatives to toxic bug killers, including oil sprays, such as Sharpshooter, an all-natural insect killer containing plant oils...Burnout II, a natural herbicide that contains vinegar, clove and lemon...and corn gluten meal, a natural weed killer. All of these products are available at most garden centers that carry organic products.

For more information on pesticides and other toxic household products, visit the Web site of Earth Share (a nationwide network of environmental organizations) at *www.earthshare.org.*

• **Cosmetics.** *Paraphenylenediamine,* a chemical found in some dark hair dyes, increases risk for bladder cancer in humans, according to a study in the journal *Carcinogenesis. Other toxic ingredients used in cosmetics...*

• *Phthalates,* typically used as a solvent and plastic softener, have been linked to cancer and to birth defects of the male reproductive system. They are found in many shampoos and other hair products, cosmetics, deodorants and nail polish. To learn more about phthalates and get a list of products that contain them, go to

169

www.safecosmetics.org, a Web site of several consumer environmental groups.

• *Talc*, in talcum powder, has been linked to a 60% increase in the risk for ovarian cancer in women who use it in the genital area.

• *Propylene glycol*, an ingredient found in some moisturizing products and skin creams, is absorbed through the skin, and high levels may damage the kidneys and liver.

What to do: Read labels carefully. By law, cosmetic ingredients must be listed on the label, starting with those in largest amounts. Choose all-natural alternatives, such as products made with olive oil, safflower oil or oatmeal, whenever possible. To find companies that produce hair products, lotions, deodorants and other products that are free of toxic ingredients, go to *www.safecosmetics.org* and click on "What's in Your Products" then on "Safer Cosmetics Companies."

SELF-DEFENSE

Antioxidants such as vitamins C and E are known to promote health by scavenging free radicals (harmful by-products of metabolism), which damage our cells and contribute to cancer and other diseases.

But antioxidants have another role that is possibly even more important in protecting against environmental toxins. Antioxidants stimulate an area of the DNA called the *antioxidant responsive element* (ARE), which activates a gene that produces detoxifying enzymes. This is the body's way of breaking down carcinogens and other toxins.

In addition to commonly known antioxidant sources, such as brightly colored produce (carrots, beets, kale and tomatoes), be sure your diet contains...

• **Cruciferous vegetables,** such as cauliflower and brussels sprouts, which contain *sulforaphane*, a potent enzyme inducer.

• **Green tea,** an antioxidant source that is 20 times more potent than vitamin E, according to the American Chemical Society. Drink two to five cups daily.

• **Rosemary,** a source of *carnosol*, which has antioxidant and anticarcinogenic properties. Use rosemary in cooking, or drink one cup of rosemary tea daily.

• **Curry,** a spice mixture with turmeric, a potent cancer-fighting herb that contains curcumin. Cook with curry three times a week.

Check on Produce Pesticide Levels

Apples, cherries, grapes, celery, lettuce and winter squash retain high levels of pesticide residue. Bananas, blueberries, mangoes, watermelon, broccoli, cauliflower and eggplant are likely to have little residue.

Self-defense: Buy organic produce, which has less residue...wash all produce thoroughly before you serve it.

Caroline Smith DeWaal, JD, food safety director, Center for Science in the Public Interest, Washington, DC, and author of *Is Our Food Safe?* (Three Rivers).

Hyperactive Children Should Avoid Food Dye

Some FDA-approved additives—including allura red, known as Red No. 40...and tartrazine, known as Yellow No. 5—can cause significant increases in hyperactivity in some children under age 10. These colors are added to many foods, including yogurt, so check labels carefully.

William Sears, MD, pediatrician, Sears Family Pediatrics, Capistrano Beach, California, and coauthor of *The Healthiest Kid in the Neighborhood* (Little, Brown).

Limit Cell Phone Use

Children of women who use cell phones two to three times a day while pregnant may be more likely to develop behavioral problems.

Recent study: Children born to women who frequently used cell phones were 54% more

likely than other children to be hyperactive and have difficulties with conduct, emotions and relationships.

Reason: Unknown. These results should be viewed with caution. More research is needed.

Leeka Kheifets, PhD, professor of epidemiology at UCLA and one of the leaders of a study of 13,159 children, published in *Epidemiology*.

Honesty Is the Best Policy on Drug Use

How do you warn kids about drugs if you used them yourself? Be honest, and tailor your message to your child, who may want lots of information or only a little. Say immediately that you do not want him/her using drugs, and explain why. Explain your own drug use directly—for instance, you might say that you tried them because other kids did…or that you made a mistake and ended up doing things you are not proud of. Listen as much as you talk—ask what your child thinks and what his friends think.

Recommendations from the Partnership for a Drug-Free America. *www.drugfree.org*

Another Reason Why Mom Should Not Smoke

Roni Grad, MD, associate professor, clinical pediatrics, University of Arizona College of Medicine, Tucson, Arizona.

Danny McGoldrick, vice president, research, Campaign for Tobacco-Free Kids, Washington, DC.

Norman H. Edelman, MD, scientific consultant, American Lung Association.

Gina Lovasi, PhD, a Health and Society Scholar, Columbia University, New York City.

American Thoracic Society's 105th International Conference, San Diego.

Smoking while pregnant "biologically primes" the unborn child to become a regular smoker as a teen and young adult, according to a theory put forth by University of Arizona researchers.

"Somehow smoke is changing the brain chemistry," said the lead researcher, Roni Grad, MD, an associate professor of clinical pediatrics at the university. "If you are exposed to smoking prenatally or in the early years of life, you are much more likely to be a chronic smoker at the age of 22," Dr. Grad said.

In fact, these children are four times more likely to become regular smokers, according to the research, which was presented at an American Thoracic Society's international conference in San Diego.

THE STUDY

For the study, Dr. Grad's team used data from the Tucson Children's Respiratory Study to see whether a mother's smoking during pregnancy and during her child's early years affected whether the child smoked later on. The researchers assessed maternal smoking during pregnancy and when infants were 1.5 months and 1.5 years old and again when the children were 6, 9 and 11 years old. They then looked at the children's smoking behavior when they were ages 16 and 22.

THE FINDINGS

They found that women who smoked during pregnancy and during their children's early years were more likely to have kids who smoked at age 22. This proved true whether the mother smoked or did not smoke during the child's school years. In addition, the children of mothers who smoked during pregnancy and their early years were less likely to quit smoking than were the offspring of mothers who never smoked or who started smoking when their children were school-age. The impact of early maternal smoking was not affected by whether the children's fathers smoked or by peer pressure during adolescence, the study found.

"Nobody should smoke," Dr. Grad said. "I would definitely discourage any mother from smoking around her child. If children have been exposed in early life to smoke, I would really go the extra mile to try to keep them from experimenting, because they may be at higher risk of becoming nicotine dependent very quickly."

EXPERT COMMENTARY

Norman H. Edelman, MD, a scientific consultant to the American Lung Association, said that the research provides another reason for women to stop smoking before becoming pregnant. "We know that smoking during pregnancy confers many health risks upon the fetus, including premature birth and increased risk for asthma," Dr. Edelman said. "Now we see a new risk—increased rates of smoking during subsequent early adulthood."

Dr. Edelman said that the researchers seem to favor a biologic explanation, such as an alteration of brain neurochemistry during pregnancy. "However, the study does not include enough information to rule out social factors, such as increased smoking of others in the household even though the mother stops after childbirth. When you decide to become pregnant, there are certain steps to take to optimize the health of the hoped-for child, such as taking folic acid and weight reduction for the very overweight," Dr. Edelman said. "Now, even more forcefully, we add stop smoking—and get others in the household to do so as well."

Danny McGoldrick, vice president for research at the Campaign for Tobacco-Free Kids, agreed that the study highlights the importance of not smoking during pregnancy. "We already know how bad smoking during pregnancy is for the fetus and the health of the child," he said. "This new research shows that smoking during pregnancy also makes the child more likely to become a smoker as an adult—even if the mother quits smoking when the child is young. Aside from protecting their own health, this is one more reason that female smokers who are pregnant or considering becoming pregnant should try to quit," McGoldrick said.

STUDY ON EXPOSURE TO SMOKE AND EMPHYSEMA

Another study on the effects of smoking, also presented at the conference, found that children exposed to smoke may be more likely to develop emphysema later in life. The researchers explained that smoke can damage young children's lungs, creating what's known as "emphysematous holes" in the lung. The holes begin as small areas of damage or impaired development but can lead to breathing problems later in life, even among nonsmokers, they said.

"The take-home message from our analysis is that exposure to tobacco smoke during childhood may be associated with detectable differences in lung structure, and perhaps early emphysema, later in life among people who do not themselves smoke," said Gina Lovasi, PhD, a Health and Society Scholar at Columbia University.

For information on helping kids not to smoke, visit the Web site of the U.S. Centers for Disease Control and Prevention, *www.cdc.gov/tobacco*.

Better Asthma Treatment

Up to half of all adults with severe asthma are allergic to airborne fungi, which can worsen asthma.

Recent research: In a study of 58 patients with severe asthma and a fungal allergy (determined by skin and blood testing), one group took the oral antifungal drug *itraconazole* (Sporanox)—200 mg twice daily—and the rest took a placebo for 32 weeks.

Result: Within the drug group, 62% reported significant improvement in lung function, while the placebo group reported a worsening of lung function.

If you have both severe asthma and a fungal allergy: Ask your doctor if itraconazole is right for you.

David Denning, MD, professor of medicine and medical mycology, University of Manchester, UK.

Herbs to Fight Hay Fever

Ara DerMarderosian, PhD, professor of pharmacognosy and Roth Chair of Natural Products at the University of the Sciences in Philadelphia. He also is the scientific director of the university's Complementary and Alternative Medicines Institute.

Over-the-counter and prescription antihistamines and decongestants are heavily advertised and are a mainstay of treatment for most of the approximately 30 million Americans who suffer from hay fever. The fact that herbal therapy also can be effective as a treatment for hay fever is less well known.

Stinging nettle (Urtica dioica) is a flowering plant found in most temperate regions of the world.

In a clinical double-blind trial of 69 hay fever sufferers, 58% taking freeze-dried stinging nettle leaf daily for one week experienced a reduction of symptoms, such as sneezing and itchy eyes, compared with 37% of those receiving a placebo. The mechanism for stinging nettles' beneficial effect is unknown.

Typical dose: 450 mg in freeze-dried stinging nettle leaf capsules two to three times daily …or 2 ml to 4 ml of tincture three times daily. Take at the onset of symptoms and continue as needed.

Side effects are rare, but some people taking oral stinging nettle formulations experience mild gastrointestinal upset.

Stinging nettle should be avoided by people taking blood-thinning medication, such as *warfarin* (Coumadin). Stinging nettle has a diuretic (water-excreting) effect, so it should not be used by people with kidney disease.

Because herbs can interact with medication, consult an allergist or herbalist before trying stinging nettle.

Allergic to Contact Lenses?

Strictly speaking, it is unlikely that anyone is allergic to contact lenses. Instead, some suffer from an inflammatory condition called papillary conjunctivitis. The condition sometimes develops suddenly in near-sighted people who have used soft contact lenses for years, and it is not preventable. Symptoms include itching, tearing and/or small bumps on the underside of the eyelid.

Once the inflammation develops, it is unlikely that switching brands of lenses or simply not wearing them for a few months will help.

Better: Switch permanently to eyeglasses… or to rigid, gas-permeable contact lenses…or consider corrective LASIK surgery.

Robert Abel, Jr., MD, ophthalmologist, Delaware Ophthalmology Consultants, Wilmington, Delaware, and co-founder of the alternative medicine curriculum, Thomas Jefferson University, Philadelphia. He is author of *The Eye Care Revolution* (Kensington).

How Contagious Is Pinkeye?

Robert Maiolo, OD, an optometrist in private practice in Stamford, Connecticut, and former guest lecturer, Yale University School of Medicine, New Haven, Connecticut.

Most forms are very contagious. Pinkeye is often used as a general term to describe any type of eye inflammation, but the condition is most often due to *conjunctivitis,* which is typically caused by a viral or bacterial infection or by an allergy. Both viral and bacterial conjunctivitis can spread via hand-to-hand contact or by touching an object, such as a metal door handle, that has been contaminated with the virus or bacterium and then touching one's eyes. Allergic conjunctivitis is not contagious.

Primary symptoms: Pink discoloration of the eye accompanied by a light watery discharge (often due to a viral infection) or a thicker discharge that can create a sticky build-up on the eyelashes (often due to a bacterial infection). Red in the white of the eye or inner eyelid may accompany itchy eyes (often due to an allergy).

Main treatment: Over-the-counter drops are rarely helpful, but antibiotic eyedrops (available by prescription) can effectively treat pinkeye caused by a bacterial infection. If the condition is caused by an allergy, prescription eyedrops, including antihistamines, can relieve symptoms. Viral conjunctivitis requires individual treatment. See your optometrist.

Hot Help for Allergies

Washing clothes in 140°F water kills all dust mites versus just 6.5% of those in clothes washed at 104°F. Hot water is also more effective at removing pet dander and pollen.

American Thoracic Society (ATS), New York City, *www.thoracic.org*.

Pets That Don't Make You Sneeze

Marty Becker, DVM, resident veterinarian on ABC-TV's *Good Morning America* and author of *The Healing Power of Pets* (Hyperion).

Most people who are allergic to dogs or cats react to the animal's dander—the dried, flaky material that typically comes off when a dog or cat sheds. There are no allergen-free cats or dogs, but some breeds produce less dander than others, and, in general, female pets cause fewer allergic reactions than male ones.

Best dog breeds: Small basenji...soft-coated Wheaten terrier...bichon frise...poodle...Portuguese water dog...Chinese crested...or mixed breeds, such as the labradoodle or other poodle mixes.

Cat breeds: Cornish Rex...Devon Rex...Siberian...or Sphynx (a mostly hairless breed). Dark cats cause allergic reactions more frequently than lighter-coated cats. To lessen your chance of allergy, bathe your pet once a week with a quality pet shampoo and feed your pet a premium diet, as recommended by a veterinarian.

Lock Out Allergies

Leave shoes at the door to keep allergens out of the house. Pollen, moss, mold, etc. stick to shoes as you walk outdoors. Walking indoors then spreads them through your home. Protect allergy sufferers in your home by having everyone take off their shoes at the door.

Kathleen Sheerin, MD, Atlanta Allergy & Asthma Clinic, *www.atlantaallergy.com*.

7

Embarrassing Conditions

Always Looking for a Bathroom?

USA Today founder Allen H. Neuharth made headlines when he publicly announced a few years ago that he wears adult diapers. This disclosure was news because few people are willing to admit—even to their doctors—that they suffer from urinary incontinence.

With age, bladder size typically decreases and pelvic floor muscles, which help control urination, weaken. But urinary incontinence (UI)—the involuntary or unwanted loss of urine—is not normal. Even so, about 38% of women age 60 or older and 17% of men in that age group suffer from the condition.

DO YOU HAVE UI?

To determine whether you may have one of the four common varieties of UI, ask yourself if any of the following applies to you…

• **Stress incontinence** refers to urine leakage during any physical exertion, such as exercise, or sneezing, coughing or laughing. Stress incontinence also can occur in men after prostate treatments and in women after pregnancy.

• **Urge incontinence** (which is also called over-active bladder) is an increase in urgency and frequency, typically accompanied by urine leakage on the way to the bathroom.

• **Mixed incontinence** is stress and urge incontinence combined.

• **Overflow incontinence** occurs when the bladder does not empty completely because of a blockage in the urethra or diseases of the brain or spinal cord.

Diane Kaschak Newman, RN, codirector of the Penn Center for Continence and Pelvic Health and director of clinical trials, division of urology, both at the University of Pennsylvania Medical Center in Philadelphia. She is author of *The Urinary Incontinence Sourcebook* (McGraw-Hill).

UNDERSTANDING THE BLADDER

When full, an adult's bladder expands to about the size of a softball and holds 12 to 16 ounces of urine. If you're under age 65, it's normal to urinate every four to five waking hours…and every three to four waking hours if you're age 65 or older.

As you age, it can be normal to get up once or twice a night to empty your bladder. This is partly due to a shift in the circadian rhythm of water excretion, causing the greatest proportion of urine production to occur when the body is at rest.

In addition, certain medical conditions, such as diabetes, can predispose a person to UI. For example, excess blood sugar (glucose) causes people with diabetes to urinate more often and suffer frequent urinary tract infections (UTIs) —both of which raise the risk for UI.

Certain medications also can cause UI. For example, diuretics (often used to treat blood pressure) lead to urinary frequency and urgency for up to six hours after the drug is taken…and calcium channel blockers (typically used for heart conditions) can result in urinary retention.

SIMPLE STEPS THAT WORK

For about eight out of 10 people, lifestyle interventions reduce or eliminate most types of UI.

My advice…

•**Do not cut back on fluids.** If you suffer from UI, you may be tempted to reduce your fluid intake to help minimize trips to the bathroom and urine leakage. This is a mistake. If you don't drink enough fluids, your urine may become highly concentrated (dark yellow and strong-smelling). This puts you at risk for bladder infections, which can worsen UI. Aim for about 64 ounces of fluids daily.

Good beverage choices: Water as well as apple, cherry and grape juices.

Surprising fact: Citrus juices—along with alcohol and carbonated beverages—may cause bladder overactivity, for unknown reasons, in many people. Even cranberry juice, which contains an enzyme that can help prevent UTIs, can irritate the bladder. For this reason, two 500-mg cranberry supplements daily may be a better choice.

•**Limit caffeine—in all forms.** Caffeine acts as a diuretic, causing the bladder to fill more quickly, so you have to urinate more urgently and frequently. If you have urinary problems, limit your caffeine intake to 200 mg daily. An eight-ounce cup of brewed coffee contains 95 mg, while the same amount of decaf contains 2 mg to 4 mg. Five ounces of black or green tea contains about 40 mg of caffeine.

"Hidden" sources of caffeine: Hot chocolate (2 mg to 15 mg per five ounces)…chocolate ice cream (5 mg per two-thirds cup)…and some over-the-counter medications, such as Excedrin (65 mg per tablet).

•**Watch out for little-known bladder irritants.** Highly acidic foods, such as tomato-based products, and spicy foods, such as Mexican food, can irritate the bladder.

Surprising fact: For unknown reasons, foods that contain milk and/or artificial sweeteners also can reduce bladder control.

•**Perform pelvic floor muscle exercises correctly.** Tightening and relaxing the pelvic floor—the hammock-like muscle that supports all the pelvic organs, including the bladder —can improve symptoms of UI in women and men.

Don't make this mistake: When attempting to locate the muscles to tighten, many people tense the muscles of the legs, buttocks or abdomen.

Proper form: Imagine that you are trying to control the urge to pass gas. The rectal muscles you use to hold in the gas are the pelvic floor muscles. This technique is preferable to the widely used method of stopping the flow of urine to isolate the muscles. It is not a good practice to interrupt the voiding process.

Once you find these muscles, tighten them for three seconds, then release them for three seconds. This constitutes one set. Practice while sitting, standing and lying down so that you strengthen these muscles while in the positions that you will be in over the course of a day. Aim for 20 sets of squeezing and relaxing the muscles a day in each position, and gradually increase the hold to 10 seconds. When

performed diligently, pelvic floor muscle exercises should reduce urine leakage within eight weeks.

• **"Retrain" your bladder.** If you have strong, frequent urges to urinate (more than eight times in a 24-hour period), ask your doctor about bladder retraining. This technique involves emptying your bladder on a predetermined schedule (roughly every two hours).*

Little-known strategy: You can use deep breathing and meditation while you are waiting out the urge to urinate. Bladder retraining minimizes strong, frequent urges to urinate. It may take four to six weeks before you see improvement.

• **Prevent constipation.** Being constipated (having fewer than three bowel movements per week) can worsen UI because the hard stool can press against the bladder. Eating more fiber-rich foods usually improves constipation.

Examples: Prunes and figs…and whole grains (such as All-Bran and Bran Flakes cereals).

Natural constipation fighter: Blend one-half cup of prune juice…one cup of applesauce …and one cup of unprocessed wheat bran flakes. Eat two tablespoons of this mixture with breakfast daily when you experience constipation.

WHEN NOTHING ELSE WORKS

If the strategies described earlier don't improve urge incontinence, you may need a medication—such as *darifenacin* (Enablex), *fesoterodine* (Toviaz), *oxybutynin gel* (Gelnique), *tolterodine* (Detrol), *trospium* or *solifenacin* (Vesicare). Side effects may include dry mouth and constipation.

For stress UI that is not improved with pelvic floor muscle exercises, a procedure known as sling surgery, which involves the insertion of synthetic tape to support the urethra, may be needed. Overflow UI can be improved through removal of an obstruction or through catheterization to empty the bladder.

*To find a nurse incontinence specialist to help with pelvic floor muscle exercises or bladder retraining, contact the Wound Ostomy and Continence Nurses Society (*www.wocn.org*).

More from Diane Kaschak Newman, RN…

How to Stay Dry

Many products can help protect people who suffer from urinary incontinence avoid "accidents." Women who have light-to-moderate urine leakage can wear absorbent panty liners and pads. Men can use products, such as socklike, drip-collecting pouches and guards that are worn inside briefs. Options for moderate-to-heavy urine loss include disposable protective underwear…and pads-and-pants systems that combine cloth underpants and disposable pads. All are available at most drugstores.

Why Soda Makes You Go…

Soda doesn't actually cause incontinence—but if you already have incontinence, it can make symptoms worse than other beverages might because carbonation can irritate the bladder. Caffeinated soda delivers a double whammy because caffeine acts as a diuretic and an irritant.

Because soda has no nutritional value, limit your intake to no more than 12 ounces daily. If you don't like plain water, try noncaffeinated tea or flavored water.

Linda Brubaker, MD, director of the division of female pelvic medicine and reconstructive surgery at Loyola University Medical Center in Maywood, Illinois.

Incontinence Updates…

Tomas L. Griebling, MD, MPH, the John P. Wolf 33° Masonic Distinguished Professor of Urology at The University of Kansas (KU) School of Medicine, Kansas City. He is also professor and vice-chair in the department of urology and faculty associate in The Landon Center on Aging.

There are more recent options for overactive bladder that may cause fewer side effects than drugs and/or be more convenient to use.

New development I: The FDA recently approved for women with OAB an over-the-counter version of Oxytrol in a patch that is placed on the skin every four days. The patch's possible side effects, including dry mouth and constipation, are believed to be milder than those that can occur with the pills, since the dose is lower. The patch may cause minor skin irritation where it is placed.

New development II: The FDA recently approved Botox injections for patients with OAB who do not respond to medication. Small amounts of botulinum toxin are injected at various sites in the bladder.

Other OAB treatments now covered by some insurance companies (check with your insurer)…

• **Peripheral tibial nerve stimulation** involves inserting a small needle electrode near the ankle to stimulate the tibial nerve, which helps control urination. The electrode is then charged with electrical current (it is not painful). Thirty-minute sessions are typically scheduled once weekly for 12 weeks. Thereafter, maintenance sessions are usually required every two to three weeks.

• **Sacral neuromodulation (SNM).** This treatment, also known as sacral nerve stimulation (SNS), and sometimes referred to as a "pacemaker for the bladder," involves implanting a device near the tailbone where it can send electrical signals to the sacral nerve, which helps control the bladder and muscles that are related to urination.

What to Do About Urine Leakage

Rebecca Rogers, MD, chief of the division of urogynecology at the University of New Mexico Health Sciences Center in Albuquerque and coauthor of *Regaining Bladder Control* (Prometheus).

If you have a urine leakage problem, the key to fixing that problem is to strengthen your pelvic floor muscles.

Hardest part: Identifying the right muscles to exercise.

To find them: Squeeze your rectum as if trying not to pass gas (this works the muscles under the bladder).

Next, place a finger inside your vagina and try to squeeze it with your vaginal muscles.

Once you've isolated these two sets of muscles, practice contracting them by doing three sets of 10 repetitions daily.

For each repetition, squeeze for three seconds, then relax for three seconds…gradually working up until you can hold each squeeze for 10 seconds.

You should see improvement within three to six weeks.

Then, whenever you feel a sneeze coming, purposely contract these muscles to prevent leaks.

Fixes for Urinary Tract Infections

Larrian Gillespie, MD, freelance writer and retired urogynecologist in Beverly Hills, California, and author of numerous books, including *You Don't Have to Live with Cystitis* (William Morrow). *www.larriangillespie.com*

Urinary tract infections (UTIs) have undoubtedly been around for as long as we've had urinary tracts—and, unfortunately, haven't gotten any more comfortable over the eons. When an infection includes not only the urethra (the tube that carries urine away from the bladder) but also invades and causes inflammation of the bladder, it is called *cystitis.*

What you may not know: Your stream of urine normally flushes out any bacteria that could cause a UTI. If the bladder cannot empty completely, some urine and bacteria are left inside. Sometimes there is a temporary reason, such as when an overly large tampon compresses the urethra, partially blocking urine flow. In other cases, it's a chronic problem. If your pelvis and spine are perpetually pushed out of alignment—by habitually wearing high

heels or using improper form while exercising, for instance—you could develop *lordosis* (swayback). This strains the nerves between the low back and bladder, weakening bladder contractions and making it hard to drain your bladder entirely.

A UTI also may develop when the chemistry within the vagina is altered, allowing bacteria to flourish there and to easily migrate to the urinary tract. Common culprits include too-tight pants, nonbreathable underwear, douching, an ill-fitting diaphragm and increased sexual activity.

Common mistake: Urinating immediately after intercourse. A little dribble of urine won't wash away bacteria. Instead, wait until you feel the need and can produce a forceful stream.

Easier treatment: While it's common for a doctor treating a UTI to prescribe a three- to seven-day course of antibiotics, I usually recommend a one-day treatment—generally three antibiotic pills taken all at once. This short course is safe, effective and eliminates the risks for diarrhea and yeast infections that commonly occur with longer courses of antibiotics.

Drinking cranberry juice can help prevent UTIs, but it takes a lot of juice—and if an infection develops, the juice's acidity worsens pain. Cranberry extracts or capsules also help to prevent but not to treat UTIs. If you do get a UTI, see your doctor—and relieve discomfort by using over-the-counter Cystex, which contains *methenamine*, an antibacterial that prevents bacteria from sticking to urinary tract walls.

Acupuncture Helps Overactive Bladders

Women with overactive bladders received either acupuncture using acupuncture points targeted for bladder control or general, nontargeted acupuncture once weekly for four weeks.

Result: Women who received bladder-specific acupuncture had improved bladder capacity, while the other group showed no change in symptoms.

Theory: Targeted acupuncture decreases the excess nerve stimulation that causes the bladder to feel full even when it is not.

Sandra L. Emmons, MD, associate professor of obstetrics and gynecology, Oregon Health and Sciences University, Portland.

Natural Ways to Prevent Urinary Tract Infections

Mark A. Stengler, NMD, licensed naturopathic medical doctor in private practice, Stengler Center for Integrative Medicine, Encinitas, California...adjunct associate clinical professor at the National College of Natural Medicine, Portland, Oregon...author of many books, including *The Natural Physician's Healing Therapies* and coauthor of *Prescription for Natural Cures*

Women tend to be more susceptible than men to urinary tract infections (UTIs). That's because they have a shorter urethra than men, and hormonal changes that occur in women during pregnancy and after menopause can contribute to susceptibility. *Here's what I recommend for my female patients who suffer from UTIs...*

• **First, be sure that your urologist has ruled out any structural cause of your infections,** such as a bladder or kidney abnormality. Then, remove all the immune-suppressing foods from your diet, including refined grains, candies, soda pop and fruit juice, with the exception of unsweetened cranberry juice—cranberry prevents bacteria from adhering to the urinary tract. Drink at least 10 ounces a day of unsweetened cranberry juice (available at health food stores), or take a 400-mg to 500-mg cranberry supplement twice daily. If the juice is too tart, dilute it with an equal amount of water.

• **Consume a lot of vegetables and one cup per day of blueberries,** which contain constituents similar to cranberries that may prevent bacteria from adhering to the bladder wall, as well as fish and lean poultry. Also consume onions and garlic—both have strong antimicrobial properties and improve immunity. Drink 50 to 60 ounces of water daily to keep flushing the bacteria out of your urinary tract.

• **Since you may have been taking repeated courses of antibiotics,** you may have a buildup in the urinary tract and gastrointestinal tract of *Candida albicans* or some other fungal species that can suppress immunity. As a result, you'll need to repopulate your gastrointestinal tract with friendly flora, which keep the immune-suppressing species from taking over. Yogurt with live cultures, kefir (a cultured product similar to yogurt that contains good bacteria), miso and sauerkraut are natural food sources of friendly flora. Try to consume at least one serving of one of these foods each day.

I also recommend a probiotic supplement containing up to 20 billion organisms of *Lactobacillus acidophilus* and *Bifidobacterium bifidum* daily—there are many brands available, such as Nutrition Essentials and Dr. Tobias, both available at *Amazon.com*.

Urinary Incontinence Treatments That Work

Jonathan M. Vapnek, MD, urologist, assistant professor of urology and a consultant for the Autonomic Disorders Research Program at Mount Sinai Medical Center, New York City. He is a member of the American Urological Association.

A s the bladder fills with urine, it eventually sends signals to the brain that tell the person "it's time to go." Before that happens, the bladder walls relax to permit urine to accumulate. This gradual process is what allows most people to wait hours before going to the bathroom. Urinary control also is achieved by a ring of muscles called the urinary sphincter. It contracts to keep urine in, then relaxes to let it out.

Incontinence occurs when there's a problem with either muscular or nervous system control—or a combination of both. Women are about twice as likely as men to have incontinence, although men who have prostate enlargement or have had prostate surgery have an increased risk of incontinence.

The main types...

• **Stress incontinence is most common,** affecting at least 50% of the women who have urinary incontinence. It occurs when the urinary sphincter isn't strong enough to hold in urine, particularly during activities that cause an increase in abdominal pressure, including laughing, coughing, sneezing and exercise.

Stress incontinence frequently occurs during pregnancy and can persist in women who have had several vaginal births. The drop in estrogen that occurs after menopause can weaken the urethra, inhibiting its ability to hold back the flow of urine.

• **Urge incontinence often is caused by inflammation or irritation of the bladder or urethra**—due to infection, urinary stones or, in men, irritation of the prostate gland. This causes frequent (and sudden) urges to urinate. This type of incontinence also may be caused by bowel problems and neurological problems, such as stroke or Parkinson's disease.

• **Overflow incontinence.** Patients with nerve damage (from diabetes, for example) or damage to the bladder may constantly dribble urine because they're unable to empty the bladder completely when they urinate.

Other potential causes of incontinence are an enlarged prostate gland, a tumor in the urinary tract or bladder cancer. The majority of patients have either stress or urge incontinence —or a combination of both, known as mixed incontinence.

DIAGNOSIS

Most cases and types of incontinence can be diagnosed with a medical history alone. Keep a bladder diary for a week or two before you see your doctor. Write down how often you urinate...when you leak...and if you have trouble emptying your bladder. Also, note fluid consumption as well. The answers to these questions usually are sufficient to allow a definitive diagnosis.

Tests may be required to provide additional information. *Most common...*

• **Stress test.** The doctor examines the urethra while the patient coughs or bears down. A leakage of urine indicates that the patient has stress incontinence.

• **Urodynamic testing.** There are a variety of tests that measure pressure in the bladder and how much fluid it can hold.

Example: The doctor might insert a catheter into the bladder, inject small amounts of fluid and measure changes in bladder pressure. Sudden increases in bladder pressure and/or spasms could indicate urge incontinence.

• **Patients may require an ultrasound to check how well the bladder empties.** Your doctor also should perform urinalysis to check for blood or signs of infection in the urine.

TREATMENT

Some forms of incontinence are transitory and will go away when the underlying problem (an infection or inflammation, for example) improves. Most incontinence requires one or more of the following treatments, which can bring about significant improvement for most patients.

• **Behavioral techniques.** These techniques are used to help patients achieve better bladder control and are considered the mainstay of treatment. *Examples...*

• Bladder training requires patients to avoid going to the bathroom for longer and longer periods. A person might try to wait an extra 10 minutes when he/she has the urge to urinate. The goal is to lengthen the waiting time over a period of days or weeks. With practice, most patients are able to wait several hours. This is for patients with bladder overactivity and frequent urination.

• Timed urination means going to the bathroom at specific intervals—say, once every hour, even if you don't feel as though you have to go. This might be used for frail, elderly people who tend to wet themselves because they can't hold it once the urge hits. The idea is to void before the bladder hits that point of no return.

• **Kegel exercises.** Patients are advised to tightly squeeze the same muscles that they would use to stop the flow of urine. Contract the muscles for three to five seconds, relax, then repeat again. Do the cycle several times daily, working up to more repetitions each time. Kegels are helpful for men and women and for both stress and urge incontinence cases.

• **Medications.** Antispasmodic drugs reduce bladder contractions that contribute to urge incontinence. These drugs often cause dry mouth as a side effect. They're usually used in combination with behavioral treatments.

• **Surgery.** If behavioral changes and medications don't adequately control incontinence, patients may require surgery. *Main approaches...*

• Tension-free vaginal tape (TVT) procedure. This is standard for women with stress incontinence. A mesh-like tape is slung under the urethra like a hammock. It compresses the urethra to prevent leaks.

• Bulking injections. Collagen or synthetic bulking agents are injected into tissue surrounding the urethra or urinary sphincter. The extra bulk causes surrounding tissue to tighten the seal of the sphincter. The procedure usually needs to be repeated every six to 18 months because collagen is absorbed by the body over time.

• Sphincter replacement. An artificial, doughnut-shaped device is implanted around the urethra. When patients are ready to urinate, they press a valve that causes the device to deflate and let out urine. This procedure is mainly used for men who have had prostate surgery.

Don't Lose Sleep Over Nighttime Urination

Jamison Starbuck, ND, naturopathic physician in Missoula, Montana. She is a past president of the American Association of Naturopathic Physicians and a contributing editor to *The Alternative Advisor: The Complete Guide to Natural Therapies and Alternative Treatments* (Time-Life).

Doctor, I'm here because I get up eight times a night to use the bathroom. I'm exhausted and frustrated." These were the words of my 38-year-old patient Jan. She already had seen her family physician and two urologists. Extensive testing, including an X-ray, did not find a cause for her condition.

Frequent nighttime urination, known as *nocturia,* is a common but often-overlooked medical problem. To most people, a mild case —waking a few times a night—is bothersome, but not a reason to see a doctor.

In my view, ignoring even mild nocturia is a mistake. Our kidneys and bladder are designed to retain urine during an eight-hour sleep. Waking to urinate more than twice a night is a medical problem. People need good sleep to lead healthy, productive lives, and we cannot sleep well if we are getting up. *If you wake to urinate more than twice a night, consider these suggestions...*

• **See a doctor.** Hypertension, diabetes, prostate problems, stroke, kidney disease and, in some cases, a tumor in the bladder can cause nocturia. Get a thorough physical, including a urinalysis, to check for a bladder infection.

• **Cut back on beverages.** Certain beverages have a diuretic effect that can lead to nighttime urination—coffee, black or green tea, alcohol, caffeinated soda and herbal teas containing dandelion, burdock, linden, nettle or parsley. Abstain from these beverages after 6 pm, and limit your total fluid intake after dinner to 12 ounces of water or a nondiuretic, non-caffeinated tea, such as chamomile or peppermint.

• **Review your prescriptions.** Many commonly prescribed drugs, including diuretics used to treat hypertension, increase urinary frequency. If you have nocturia, ask your pharmacist whether any of the drugs you take may be causing the problem. If so, ask your doctor for a substitute or whether you can take the medication before 6 pm.

• **Get quercetin.** In people with allergies or certain medical conditions, including benign prostatic hyperplasia and interstitial cystitis, inflammation is the cause of nocturia. Quercetin, a strong antioxidant, decreases inflammation and inhibits cell damage in the kidneys. Cranberries and other dark red or purple berries, such as blueberries and raspberries, contain quercetin. Eat one cup of fresh berries daily, or take a 500-mg quercetin supplement twice daily with meals.

• **Test for food allergies.** Food allergens act as irritants, so your body tries to eliminate them quickly through a variety of mechanisms, including urination. In Jan's case, we found that she was allergic to eggs, dairy and corn. When she avoided these foods, she woke to urinate only twice each night. To test for food allergies, consult a naturopathic physician or

a nutritionally minded allergist or internist for a blood test.

Can IBS Be Treated Without Drugs?

For many people, a change in diet reduces irritable bowel syndrome (IBS) symptoms such as abdominal pain, cramping, constipation and/or diarrhea. IBS often is a result of sensitivity to gluten, a protein in wheat, rye and barley. Many IBS patients also are sensitive to dairy foods. As a first step, eliminate gluten from your diet (gluten-containing foods include many breads, cereals, crackers, cookies, cakes, pies, gravies and sauces) for two to three weeks to see if symptoms improve. In addition, keep a daily journal noting the foods that seem to cause a flare-up of IBS. If your symptoms don't improve, try eliminating dairy products for two to three weeks. If these elimination diets don't help, consult your doctor or a certified nutrition specialist, who can recommend dietary changes that are appropriate for you.

The late Shari Lieberman, PhD, CNS, FACN, nutrition scientist and author of *The Gluten Connection* (Rodale).

Better Irritable Bowel Treatment

Researchers analyzed 38 studies on treatments for irritable bowel syndrome (IBS), a disorder that causes such symptoms as abdominal pain, constipation and/or diarrhea.

Result: Soluble fiber treatments, including *psyllium* (such as Metamucil)...peppermint oil capsules (about 200 mg, two to three times daily)...and some antispasmodic drugs—especially *scopolamine* (Transderm Scop)—significantly reduced IBS symptoms.

If you suffer from IBS: Ask your doctor if one or more of these treatments—which often have been overlooked since the introduction of IBS drugs—would be appropriate for you.

Alexander C. Ford, MD, clinical fellow, gastroenterology division, McMaster University Health Sciences Center, Ontario, Canada.

Relief from Anal Fissures

Andreas M. Kaiser, MD, FACS, associate professor of clinical surgery, University of Southern California, Los Angeles, and author of the manual *Colorectal Surgery* (McGraw-Hill).

An anal fissure is a tear in the skin of the anus, typically the result of chronic constipation with large, hard stools or of prolonged diarrhea. It can cause bleeding and severe pain during and after bowel movements. A fissure may become a chronic problem if the internal anal sphincter muscle develops increased tone (the level of muscle contraction when the muscle is at rest). This causes painful spasms and interferes with healing by reducing blood flow to the area.

Treatment includes medication and/or dietary changes to prevent constipation or diarrhea. Also, prescription ointment applied to the anus can relax the sphincter...or the muscle relaxant Botox can be injected into the sphincter.

If nonsurgical methods fail, a colorectal surgeon can do an outpatient procedure to cut part of the internal sphincter muscle, weakening it enough to restore normal sphincter tone. The fissure usually then heals within a few weeks.

Inactivity = Constipation

Being inactive for several hours and/or becoming dehydrated (which can occur during a plane flight) can slow the movement of stool through the colon, leading to constipation. To stay well-hydrated, drink plenty of water and other liquids, such as fruit and vegetable juices and clear soups. In addition, take an over-the-counter fiber supplement, such as Citrucel, to help prevent constipation. Take two capsules twice a day or one heaping tablespoon of the powdered form in eight ounces of liquid three times daily for three days before your trip. When taking a plane trip, bring some high-fiber food, such as prunes, to eat during the flight.

Charles D. Gerson, MD, codirector, Mind-Body Digestive Center, and clinical professor of medicine, Mount Sinai School of Medicine, both in New York City.

Foods That Explode In Your Bowel

Elizabeth Lipski, PhD, CCN, has been working in the field of holistic and complementary medicine for more than 25 years. She is director of doctoral studies at Hawthorn University in Whitethorn, California. She is author of *Digestive Wellness* (McGraw-Hill). *www.lizlipski.com*

Your abdomen bloats and cramps. You pass so much gas that you think you might be contributing to global warming. You have diarrhea or constipation or an alternating assault of both.

Your problem: Irritable bowel syndrome (IBS), the most common gastrointestinal complaint, accounting for 10% of doctor's visits and about 50% of referrals to gastroenterologists. But the fact that doctors see a lot of IBS doesn't mean that they understand the condition or treat it effectively.

IBS is a well-recognized but unexplained set of symptoms—medical science knows what is happening but not exactly why. A diagnosis isn't made by detecting telltale biochemical or structural changes unique to IBS—it's made after other digestive disorders, such as colorectal cancer and inflammatory bowel disease, have been ruled out.

At that point, the typical doctor offers a predictable prescription—eat more fiber, drink more water, get more exercise, reduce stress.

While that regimen may work for some people, it fails many people because it overlooks a common but often ignored trigger of IBS—food hypersensitivity.

TRIGGER FOODS

To understand food hypersensitivity, you first need to understand what it is not—a food allergy. Food allergies are relatively rare, affecting 1% to 2% of the adult population. The ingested food attracts the immune system's immunoglobulin E (IgE) antibodies, which identify the food as "foreign" and attack it, sparking the release of histamine and cytokines, inflammatory chemicals that cause tissue to swell, eyes to tear, skin to itch and other allergic symptoms. Eggs, milk, nuts, shellfish, soy and wheat are common allergy-causing foods.

Food hypersensitivity involves other antibodies, such as IgA, IgG and IgM. Their attack isn't immediate—it can occur hours or days after eating an offending food and cause bloating, cramping, constipation and/or diarrhea.

What to do: For one week, eat an "elimination diet" consisting solely of foods that almost never cause hypersensitivity—fruits (except citrus), vegetables (except tomatoes, eggplant, white potatoes and peppers), white rice, fish and chicken. You can use olive and safflower oils. *If after seven days you are symptom-free, food hypersensitivity is triggering your IBS. Follow these steps…*

Step 1. Reintroduce one category of food every two to three days. Start with one of the foods that together account for 80% of food hypersensitivity—beef, citrus, dairy products, eggs, pork and wheat. For two days, stay on the elimination diet and eat as much of the reintroduced food as you like.

If IBS symptoms return, you have detected a hypersensitivity. Stop eating the offending food, and wait until symptoms disappear to reintroduce another food.

If you don't get symptoms, try the next food after the two days of eating the previous one. Repeat this process, reintroducing foods one by one.

Step 2. For the next six months, avoid all foods that caused IBS during the elimination testing. This will help your bowel heal.

Step 3. After the six months, you can try a "rotation diet"—reintroduce the offending foods (as long as they don't cause symptoms), but eat any offending food no more than once every four days. Now that your digestive tract is healed, you may be able to handle small amounts of the offending foods.

Also helpful: Digestive enzyme supplements can help reduce gas and bloating. Effective products include Transformation Enzymes DigestZyme and TPP Digest…Enzymedica Digest and Digest Gold…and Enzymatic Therapy Mega-Zyme. These products are available at most health-food stores and many drugstores.

INFECTIONS

It is my opinion that food hypersensitivity may trigger 50% to 75% of all cases of IBS. Another 25% or so is caused by infections.

Research: Israeli doctors studied 564 travelers. While traveling, people are more likely to be exposed to new microbes that can cause diarrhea. Those who developed traveler's diarrhea were five times more likely to later develop IBS. In reviewing eight studies, American scientists found a seven times higher risk of IBS among those who had infections in the gastrointestinal tract.

What to do: See your doctor—he/she can perform tests to detect abnormal bacteria, fungi and parasites, and prescribe the appropriate treatment.

NATURAL REMEDIES

Supplements that help to relieve IBS symptoms…

• **For diarrhea.** Probiotic supplements provide friendly intestinal bacteria that can help restore normal bowel function. *Saccharomyces boulardii* is an unusual probiotic—it's yeast, not bacteria—but doctors have used it for decades to control diarrhea effectively.

Look for a product called Florastor or other probiotic brands containing the yeast. Take 250 milligrams (mg), three times a day. If that works, try twice a day and then once a day, finding the lowest dosage that works for you.

• **For constipation.** You've probably tried fiber supplements—and found that they didn't work. Instead, take a magnesium supplement, which naturally loosens bowels.

Use magnesium glycinate, starting with 300 mg a day. If that dosage doesn't work, increase the dose by 100 mg per day, until you develop diarrhea. Then cut back by 100 mg—to produce regular bowel movements.

Probiotic supplements can help as well.

THE PROBLEM WITH MEDICATIONS

Doctors have tried a range of drugs for IBS—bulking agents for constipation, antidepressants to affect brain chemicals that play a role in digestion, spasmolytics to decrease cramping. A review by Dutch doctors of 40 studies on medications for IBS concluded, "The evidence of efficacy of drug therapies for IBS is weak."

The drugs also can be dangerous. In March 2007, the FDA pulled the IBS drug *tegaserod maleate* (Zelnorm) from the market when studies showed that it increased the risk for heart attack and stroke 10-fold.

supplement, antidepressant or blood pressure drug.

When you are constipated, try the remedies below, one at a time, in the order listed. If one does not help within a week, switch to the next. All are sold in health-food stores (see labels for dosages).

• **Flaxseed oil,** which lubricates stool.

• **Triphala tablets,** an herbal formula that stimulates digestive contractions.

• **Dandelion root capsules** to promote the flow of bile.

• **Probiotics (beneficial bacteria)**—supplements that restore the digestive tract's normal balance of flora.

Constipation can signal an underlying medical problem, such as a thyroid disorder, uterine prolapse (uterus dropping into the vagina) or colon cancer. If natural remedies don't help, see your doctor.

Natural Cures for Constipation

Mark A. Stengler, NMD, licensed naturopathic medical doctor in private practice, Encinitas, California. He is author of *The Natural Physician's Healing Therapies* and coauthor of *Prescription for Natural Cures* (both from Bottom Line Books).

Twice as many women as men suffer from constipation and its side effects—abdominal pain, bloating, hard stool and hemorrhoids. Long-term laxative use worsens the problem by halting digestive contractions. *Prevention...*

• **First thing every morning,** drink eight ounces of warm water with two teaspoons of lemon juice to improve flow of bile, a laxative digestive fluid.

• **Sit on the toilet for two minutes at the same time each morning,** even if you can't move your bowels, to help train your nervous system to go on schedule.

• **Avoid cow's milk,** bananas and fried foods...eat high-fiber whole grains, fruits and vegetables.

• **Ask your doctor about nonconstipating alternatives if you use an antacid,** iron

Common Causes of Flatulence

Anil Minocha, MD, FACP, professor of medicine and director of division of digestive diseases, University of Mississippi Medical Center, Jackson.

Diseases such as irritable bowel syndrome, Crohn's disease, ulcerative colitis and cancer can lead to excess gas and bloating. Certain medications, including calcium channel blockers, tricyclic antidepressants and narcotic-based painkillers, slow digestion and lead to excess gas. Diet changes, such as adding fiber to ease constipation, can create gas. Lactose intolerance leads to flatulence because lactose-laden foods are improperly digested. Loss of muscle tone around the anal sphincter and loss of elasticity of the valve itself can weaken control.

Self-defense: Limit intake of milk products, except for yogurt with active cultures. Avoid carbonated beverages and foods that are heavy in carbohydrates, such as beans, brussels sprouts, broccoli and cauliflower. Also avoid foods that contain sugars such as fructose (including onions, artichokes, pears and wheat) and sorbitol (apples, peaches and prunes). Eat slowly and chew food thoroughly.

Got Gas?

To get rid of uncomfortable (and embarrassing) gas, go somewhere private, and let it out. Don't be embarrassed—the average person passes gas 14 times a day. Holding it in can be painful. Gassiness may increase after ingesting carbohydrates—such as lactose (in milk), fructose (in fruit), raffinose (in vegetables and grains) and sorbitol (in sugar-free gum). If you're bloated, nonprescription *simethicone* (Gas-X) or activated charcoal tablets (CharcoCaps) may help you release gas. To ease discomfort, try peppermint tea—it contains menthol, which may ease cramping.

Samuel Meyers, MD, clinical professor of medicine at Mount Sinai School of Medicine, New York City.

Ahhh...Safe, Quick Relief from Hemorrhoid Pain— You Don't Need Surgery!

Mark A. Stengler, NMD, licensed naturopathic medical doctor in private practice, Encinitas, California. He is author of *The Natural Physician's Healing Therapies* and coauthor of *Prescription for Natural Cures* (both from Bottom Line Books).

My hemorrhoids are driving me crazy," said Doris, a 55-year-old woman who recently visited me for a consultation. "The bleeding and itching have been really bad this year, so my doctor is recommending surgery. What do you think?"

I could tell that Doris was desperate for relief, but I felt obligated to share my concerns about the procedure.

"Have you ever spoken with someone who has had hemorrhoid surgery?" I asked.

"Well, no," Doris replied.

"Believe me, it's the last thing you want to consider," I said. "The pain can be excruciating for several days, or even weeks, afterward, and the hemorrhoids can return."

I presented Doris with an alternative to surgery—she could change her diet, take nutritional supplements and get more exercise (physical activity improves circulation and promotes bowel regularity). Doris agreed to try the plan, and after two months, her pain and bleeding were completely eliminated. She thanked me for saving her from the ordeal of surgery.

COMMON CAUSES OF HEMORRHOIDS

According to the National Institutes of Health, an estimated 50% of American adults develop hemorrhoids by age 50. However, when you speak with proctologists (medical doctors who specialize in diseases of the rectum, anus and colon), they will tell you that everyone has at least some hemorrhoidal tissue, even though many people don't experience symptoms. Problematic hemorrhoids are found equally in men and women, and the prevalence of this condition peaks between ages 45 and 65.

Hemorrhoids, also known as piles, occur when veins and soft tissue around the anus or lower rectum become swollen and inflamed as a result of pressure from straining or carrying extra body weight and/or irritation due to diet. The most common culprits are constipation (especially when a person strains to pass stools)... obesity (extra body weight bears down on veins in the lower rectum, causing pressure)...and pregnancy/childbirth (the fetus increases pressure on the pelvic and rectal tissues), and hormonal changes (make blood vessels more lax). Diarrhea associated with inflammatory bowel diseases, such as Crohn's disease and ulcerative colitis, can cause irritation that predisposes sufferers to hemorrhoids.

Hemorrhoids are often the cause of bleeding from the anus. This is due to the rich network of veins in tissues of the rectum and anal canal. Besides pain, other common hemorrhoidal symptoms include itching and burning in the anal area.

Caution: If you experience excessive or re-current rectal bleeding, discuss it with your doctor.

Although hemorrhoids are a common cause of such bleeding, other conditions, such as colon cancer, may trigger it. To determine the cause of rectal bleeding, your doctor may perform a rectal exam and/or order tests, such as flexible sigmoidoscopy or colonoscopy. For both tests, a tube with a fiber-optic light and lens are inserted through the rectum. Flexible sigmoidoscopy examines one-third of the colon. Colonoscopy examines the entire colon.

Internal hemorrhoids are located at the top of the anal canal, where they can be seen only with a special examining scope called an anoscope. They are usually painless, and many people are unaware that they have them unless the piles bleed. Large internal hemorrhoids can protrude outside the anus during a bowel movement. In this case, the stool may be accompanied by mucus and bright red blood, which also may appear on toilet paper and/or can be seen in the toilet bowl.

Hemorrhoids that originate at the lower end of the anal canal near the anus are referred to as external hemorrhoids. They can become quite painful and tender to the touch due to the large number of nerves in the anus. Inflamed external hemorrhoids can turn blue or purple as the veins become engorged with blood. Blood clots are more likely to occur in external hemorrhoids than in internal hemorrhoids. Clots create the sensation of a very painful lump. They're not as dangerous as blood clots in other parts of the circulatory system but still may require medical attention, including surgical removal.

CONVENTIONAL TREATMENT OPTIONS

There are a variety of conventional therapies for hemorrhoids. They include ointments, creams and suppositories, all of which provide temporary relief from rectal pain and itching. Common over-the-counter topical treatments include ointments and suppositories, such as Anusol and Preparation H, as well as Tucks medicated wipes. Stool softeners such as *docusate sodium* (Colace) are commonly recommended. These treatments can provide temporary relief, but they don't address the root causes of hemorrhoids.

Internal hemorrhoids that are confined to the anal canal become a problem if they prolapse and bulge from the anus. If this occurs, they are candidates for several procedures, each of which destroys the affected tissue and leaves a scar at the treatment site. The procedures include ligation (putting a rubber band around hemorrhoids so that the tissue dies)…sclerotherapy (injecting chemicals into the hemorrhoid, causing shrinkage)…heat coagulation (using heat from lasers to destroy hemorrhoidal tissue)…and cryotherapy (freezing of hemorrhoidal tissue).

Large hemorrhoids that protrude from the anal canal and/or cause bleeding that is difficult to control are commonly removed by surgery. Hemorrhoidectomy involves surgical removal of internal and/or external hemorrhoids from the anal canal by cutting out the hemorrhoidal tissue and stitching the site. Postsurgical pain is a major problem with this procedure, and strong pain medications are required for days to weeks. Patients are also told to sit on a large, soft "donut" to ease pressure after the surgery.

Even so, I remember one patient telling me that his postsurgical rectal pain was so intense that for two days, even with the strongest of painkillers, he lay in his bed, knocking his head against a wall. Patients don't typically return to work for two to four weeks. Other complications may include painful bowel movements, difficulty urinating, hemorrhaging, infection, narrowing of the anus (due to scarring) and bowel incontinence. Obviously, this type of surgery should be used only as a last resort.

AN IMPROVED DIET TO THE RESCUE

Hemorrhoids are yet another result of the typical Western diet. People who live in countries where fiber intake is high, such as Japan, have a very low incidence of hemorrhoids. The problem is that the average American consumes only about 15 g of fiber daily. For efficient bowel movements, a person should consume about 25 g to 30 g of fiber daily.

Insoluble fiber, which is found mainly in whole grains and vegetables, bulks up the stool and allows for better elimination. In addition to increasing your intake of these foods, it is imperative that you drink enough water, which allows for easier bowel movements by preventing dryness and adding weight to stool. If you are prone to constipation, drink 64 ounces of water daily, spread throughout the day. As I have mentioned before, ground flaxseed is an excellent source of insoluble fiber. I recommend using one to two tablespoons daily of ground flaxseed (grind fresh flaxseed in a coffee grinder for five seconds or buy preground flaxseed, known as flaxmeal) on cereal, yogurt, salads, etc. It adds a delicious, nutty flavor. Drink at least 10 ounces of water immediately after consuming flaxseed. As an alternative to flaxseed, people who are prone to hard stools or straining should use one to two tablespoons of flaxseed oil—it lubricates stool. Take flaxseed oil with meals or add it to salads or shakes.

Researchers have confirmed the importance of fiber for the treatment of hemorrhoids. A study published in the *American Journal of Gastroenterology* reviewed seven trials involving a total of 378 patients who received either fiber or a nonfiber placebo over the course of one to 18 months. Compared with people who received a placebo, the fiber group's risk of persistent hemorrhoidal symptoms decreased by 47% and their risk of bleeding decreased by 50%.

Not surprisingly, certain foods can aggravate hemorrhoids. These include coffee and other caffeine-containing products, alcohol, spicy foods and high-sugar products, such as soft drinks and candy. In addition, patients who are prone to repeated hemorrhoidal flare-ups usually do better when they reduce or eliminate their intake of tomatoes, cow's milk, citrus fruit, wheat and peanuts. No one knows exactly why these foods and drinks are problematic, but they most likely cause veins to swell.

SOOTHING SUPPLEMENTS WORK WONDERS

I consistently find the following nutritional supplements to be effective in treating and preventing hemorrhoids. If you have an acute flare-up, I recommend taking the first two or more supplements for quicker healing. After symptoms subside, continue taking them for two months to prevent a recurrence. If your symptoms don't improve after using the first two supplements for 30 days, consider taking the others listed below (individually or in a combination formula) for a more aggressive approach. All of the products are available at health-food stores and some pharmacies.

• **Horse chestnut** improves circulation to the rectal area and reduces swelling of hemorrhoidal tissue. One of the herb's most important active constituents is *aescin*. It is believed to strengthen the vein walls and capillaries—and helps with the functioning of vein valves—so that swelling is less likely to occur. Take 400 mg to 600 mg of horse chestnut three times daily. Choose a product that contains 40 mg to 120 mg of aescin per capsule.

Important: Because horse chestnut may have a mild blood-thinning effect, it should not be used by anyone taking a blood-thinner, such as *warfarin* (Coumadin).

• **Butcher's broom** is an herb that reduces hemorrhoidal symptoms, such as bleeding and pain. *Ruscogenins*, a primary constituent, are believed to have an anti-inflammatory effect on hemorrhoidal tissue. Take a total daily dose of 200 mg to 300 mg of butcher's broom with 9% to 11% ruscogenins. This supplement is very safe, with only rare reports of nausea.

• **Bilberry,** an herbal supplement that's well known for promoting eye health, also helps hemorrhoids, most likely because it strengthens blood vessel walls and improves circulation. A four-week, double-blind, placebo-controlled study of 40 hemorrhoid patients showed that bilberry significantly reduced hemorrhoidal symptoms. In my practice, I've received good results with virtually all my hemorrhoid patients who try bilberry. I recommend taking 320 mg daily of a 25% *anthocyanoside* extract. Bilberry can be used during flare-ups or on an ongoing basis for prevention.

• **Psyllium seed husks** are used as a supplement to treat constipation. Some people find that taking psyllium capsules is more convenient than adding flaxseed to food. Take 3 g to 4 g of psyllium in capsule form with 8 ounces of water twice daily. People who are prone to digestive upset should start with 1

g and slowly work up to 3 g over a period of three weeks.

Caution: Do not use psyllium within two hours of taking a pharmaceutical medication —it can hinder absorption of the drug.

•**Witch hazel,** an astringent derived from the bark of the witch hazel shrub, works well as a topical treatment to soothe inflamed, bleeding hemorrhoids. It's available in cream and liquid forms. Use a cotton ball to dab it on the hemorrhoid three or four times daily and after bowel movements during flare-ups.

A SECRET HEMORRHOID CURE

For about three decades, Steve Gardner, ND, DC, has been the nation's foremost expert in natural hemorrhoid therapies. Dr. Gardner holds degrees in naturopathic medicine and chiropractic. For more than 15 years, he has been an assistant professor at the National College of Natural Medicine in Portland, Oregon, teaching proctology. Patients with acute and chronic hemorrhoid problems come to his clinic near Portland from all over the world to benefit from his noninvasive therapy for internal and external hemorrhoids.

More than a decade ago, I treated patients with him at his clinic. Many had experienced the horrors of hemorrhoid surgery and were unwilling to go through such an ordeal again. Many patients told me of the seemingly miraculous relief they had experienced with Dr. Gardner's therapy.

Dr. Gardner and a limited number of doctors (mostly naturopathic and chiropractic physicians) use a procedure known as the Keesey Technique. Wilbur Keesey, MD, developed this technique in the 1930s and never reported a severe complication in more than 700 individual treatments. (Dr. Gardner has performed this therapy several thousand times.) The technique is not FDA approved, but it has a strong history of clinical efficacy.

During this outpatient procedure, known as *hemorrhoidolysis*, the doctor touches the protruding hemorrhoids with an electrode that conducts a galvanic (electrical) current. This type of current causes the hemorrhoids to shrink. The Keesey Technique leads to only slight discomfort, hemorrhage rarely occurs and infection is rare. Because hemorrhoidal tissue is shrunk through the use of this technique, hemorrhoid recurrence is uncommon. There is no loss of time from work, no special preoperative treatment is required, and the procedure costs about $1,500 to $2,000 less than hemorrhoid surgery.

For patients with moderate to severe hemorrhoids, Dr. Gardner usually gives a series of six to 10 treatments with one to two treatments a week. Patients typically have one or two more treatments three months later as a routine follow-up. The cost is about $95 per treatment. Dr. Gardner states that about half of his patients' health insurers cover the treatments.

The Keesey Technique offers relief even for people who have extensive hemorrhoidal swelling that does not respond to dietary changes, supplement use and regular exercise. Dr. Gardner has found that less than 5% of the patients he treats require a referral for surgery.

To find a doctor who uses the Keesey Technique, contact the American Association of Naturopathic Physicians, 866-538-2267, *www.naturopathic.org*. Or see Dr. Gardner or one of his colleagues at his Oregon Hemorrhoid Clinic in Portland, Oregon, 503-786-7272 or 888-664-6662, *www.hemorrhoidhelp.com*.

Chronic Constipation

Leo Galland, MD, director, Foundation for Integrated Medicine, New York City. He is author of *The Fat Resistance Diet* (Three Rivers). Dr. Galland is a recipient of the Linus Pauling award.

Biofeedback—which helps the mind to control involuntary body responses, such as blood pressure—can work if constipation is caused by rectal spasm or spasm of the pelvic muscles. In these cases of *dyssynergic defecation*—when muscles responsible for bowel movements don't work well due to a failure to relax pelvic floor muscles—biofeedback can retrain muscles to push more effectively.

There is as yet no home-based biofeedback program—one is under development.

To find a doctor who works with biofeedback: Contact the Biofeedback Certification International Alliance (866-908-8713, *www. bcia.org*).

Other treatments include increasing consumption of dietary fiber...use of beneficial bacteria called probiotics...and consuming supplements called prebiotics, which help good bacteria grow to aid digestion. Probiotics and prebiotics are available in health-food stores.

Why We Drool and How to Stop

The late Samuel Meyers, MD, clinical professor of medicine at Mount Sinai School of Medicine in New York City.

Salivary glands typically produce one to two quarts of saliva daily, which you automatically swallow. Drooling indicates that you are either making too much saliva or having trouble swallowing it.

Excess saliva production can occur with gastroesophageal reflux, in which stomach acids flow back into the esophagus, or with poorly fitting dentures.

It also may be a side effect of medication, such as *reserpine*, which lowers blood pressure, or *bethanechol* (Urecholine), used to treat urinary retention. Trouble swallowing saliva may signal a tonsil abscess, strep throat, Bell's palsy (temporary facial paralysis), Parkinson's or other neuromuscular problem.

What to do: See your doctor. Excessive drooling raises the risk for inhaling saliva, which could cause pneumonia...and in any event, the underlying problem still must be corrected.

Hidden Dangers of Snoring: You May Be At Increased Risk for Heart Attack or Stroke

Samuel L. Krachman, DO, professor of medicine and director of the Sleep Disorders Center at Temple University School of Medicine in Philadelphia. He was the lead author of "Sleep Abnormalities and Treatment in Emphysema," Proceedings of the American Thoracic Society, Vol. 5, 2008.

Snoring may not strike you as a serious health problem. But that belief could cause you to unwittingly increase your risk for a variety of medical conditions, including some that are life-threatening.

It's been known for some time that the sleep disorder sleep apnea—commonly marked by snoring—is associated with an increased risk for cardiovascular disease, heart failure and stroke. Recent scientific evidence now links sleep apnea to erectile dysfunction and even eye disorders, such as glaucoma.

Good news: There are improved treatments available to relieve sleep apnea symptoms.

ARE YOU AT RISK?

Up to 20 million Americans—including one in every five adults over age 60—have sleep apnea, a condition in which breathing intermittently stops and starts during sleep. Most people who have sleep apnea snore—but not all snorers have sleep apnea.

And contrary to popular belief, sleep apnea also can affect women. About 9% of middle-aged women have the disorder and 24% of middle-aged men.

EVEN MILD CASES ARE DANGEROUS

Doctors once thought that only severe forms of sleep apnea posed cardiovascular risks. Now, research shows that patients who stop breathing more than five times an hour have double or even triple the rate of hypertension as those who breathe normally. With sleep apnea, breathing may stop several dozen or even hundreds of times during the night compared with one to four times an hour during sleep in a healthy adult. The frequent interruptions in breathing that characterize sleep apnea can lead to a potentially harmful decrease in oxygen levels.

WHAT CAUSES SLEEP APNEA

It's not widely known, but there are two forms of sleep apnea…

• **Obstructive sleep apnea (OSA),** the most common form, occurs when the muscles of the throat relax and collapse during sleep, interrupting the flow of air.

Obesity is a main cause of OSA. Fatty deposits surrounding the airways may interfere with breathing, and the weight of excess tissue makes it harder for muscles to retain their normal position during sleep. People with large neck sizes (17 inches or more for men, 16 inches or more for women) are at increased risk.

• **Central apnea,** in which the brain doesn't send the appropriate signals to the respiratory muscles, is relatively rare. It is not associated with obesity and sometimes occurs in the presence of a stroke, which affects brain function.

BEST TREATMENT OPTIONS

Patients who are slightly overweight and suffer from mild OSA (defined as five to 15 interruptions in breathing per hour) may improve if they lose just a few pounds. Most patients, however, need medical help. *Best approaches for both types of apnea…*

• **Change sleep position.** Up to 50% of patients with mild OSA and 20% of those with a moderate form of the disease (16 to 30 interruptions in breathing per hour) stop breathing only when they sleep on their backs. This form of OSA, positional sleep apnea, can be completely eliminated if the sufferer sleeps on his/her side or stomach.

New development: A product called Zzoma, which is worn around the chest like a belt, has a padded back that prevents people from sleeping on their backs. Developed by researchers at Temple University School of Medicine, Zzoma has been approved by the FDA for patients diagnosed with "positional snoring." It is available with a prescription at *www.zzomaosa.com.*

Cost: $189.95.

Other treatments (all are available at medical-supply stores)…*

• **Continuous positive airway pressure (CPAP).** This is the standard treatment for OSA and central apnea.

How it works: CPAP delivers room air under pressure through a mask to a patient's nose and/or mouth. The slightly pressurized flow of air helps keep the airways open and helps prevent snoring as well as apnea.

CPAP can be uncomfortable because patients must wear a mask all night. For this reason, the device is used as prescribed—for example, worn all night, every night—only about half of the time.

Helpful: Before choosing a CPAP device, try on different masks until you find one that's comfortable enough to wear all night.

Typical cost: Starting at about $200.

Alternative: Some people with mild OSA prefer to wear a nighttime oral device, such as the Thornton Adjustable Positioner (TAP), which moves the lower jaw forward so that the tongue and throat tissue don't block the airway. The TAP is available online starting at $1,800.

• **Bi-level positive airway pressure (BiPAP)** is similar to CPAP, except the machine delivers more air pressure when patients inhale and less when they exhale. This is helpful for OSA patients who find it uncomfortable to exhale "against" air pressure—and for obese patients who tend to breathe too shallowly.

Cost: Starting at about $800.

• **Adaptive servo-ventilation (ASV)** is an air-flow approach that also involves wearing a mask. An ASV unit, which is used for central apnea, analyzes normal breathing patterns and stores the data in a computer. If a patient stops breathing, the machine automatically delivers pressurized air—and then stops when the patient's normal breathing resumes.

Cost: About $7,000.

*You should undergo a sleep evaluation at a sleep disorders clinic before buying one of these devices. Insurance won't pay for the device unless you've been diagnosed with sleep apnea by a doctor. To find a sleep disorders clinic near you, consult the American Academy of Sleep Medicine (630-737-9700, *www.aasmnet.org*).

IF YOU STILL NEED HELP

For most sleep apnea patients, surgery is a last resort. It makes a significant difference in only 20% to 30% of cases.

Common procedures...

• **Uvulopalatopharyngoplasty (UPPP)** involves removing tissue from the back of the mouth and the top of the throat. This procedure often stops snoring, but is less effective at eliminating frequent interruptions in breathing during sleep.

• **The Pillar,** a relatively new procedure, involves the placement of small synthetic rods in the soft palate in the mouth. The rods stiffen the tissue and reduce sagging during sleep. Like UPPP, it's effective primarily for snoring.

Ease the Sting of Canker Sores and Fever Blisters

Michael D. Martin, DMD, PhD, associate professor, department of oral medicine, University of Washington School of Dentistry, Seattle.

A canker sore is a shallow, painful ulcer inside the mouth, typically on the insides of the cheeks, the base of the gums or under the tongue. Canker sores, which are not contagious, usually are triggered by stress or local trauma, but also may be caused by poor nutrition, food allergies and hormonal changes (such as during menstruation). Medications for canker sores include *ibuprofen* (Advil) or *acetaminophen* (Tylenol) for pain relief...and topical medications, such as CankerMelts, an over-the-counter adhesive disk containing licorice root extract, which has been shown in clinical studies to reduce pain and speed up healing. A fever blister (also known as a cold sore) most commonly develops on or near the lips and mouth. Fever blisters are caused by the herpes simplex virus—it lies dormant in the nerve roots and can be triggered by such factors as a fever, a cold or flu, sun exposure or stress. Fever blisters typically heal then can reappear periodically. The virus can be spread from person to person by kissing, close contact with the sore or with infected saliva. For fever blisters, antiviral medications, such as *acyclovir* (Zovirax) and *valacyclovir* (Valtrex), may shorten the episodes. Ask your doctor or dentist what treatment is best for you.

Canker Sore Relief

Canker sores are painful ulcers on the inside of the cheek or lip or on the tongue or roof of the mouth that may result from an abnormal immune response. They typically take a week or two to heal. To hasten the process, dampen a black tea bag (a source of the natural anti-inflammatory *tannin*), and hold it against the sore for a few minutes...or try *Tanac,* an over-the-counter (OTC) medication.

To relieve pain, rinse your mouth for 60 seconds three times daily with one teaspoon of 3% hydrogen peroxide mixed with three ounces of milk of magnesia...or use an OTC antiseptic with *carbamide peroxide,* such as Gly-Oxide. You also can try Zilactin-B gel or Kank-A Mouth Pain Liquid, which form a protective coating over the sore. All products are sold at drugstores.

The late Ronald King, DDS, past president of the Holistic Dental Association.

Better Canker Sore Remedy

In a study of 46 people with recurrent canker sores (oral ulcers often caused by hormonal changes or food allergies), half the patients put patches containing licorice root extract over their sores for an average of 8.5 hours daily, and the others received no treatment.

Result: After seven days, the average ulcer size in the patch group was significantly smaller while the ulcer size in the no-treatment group had grown by 13%, on average.

Theory: Licorice root's anti-inflammatory and antibiotic properties help cure canker

sores. Licorice root patches are available on-line and at some drugstores.

Michael D. Martin, DMD, PhD, associate professor, department of oral medicine, University of Washington School of Dentistry, Seattle.

Are Cold Sores Hereditary?

Outbreaks of cold sores might be caused by a genetic susceptibility. Other outbreak triggers include fever, wind exposure and sunburn.

Journal of Infectious Diseases.

What You Can Do About Bunions

Michael J. Trepal, DPM, vice president for academic affairs and dean at New York College of Podiatric Medicine in New York City and a podiatrist in private practice in Brooklyn, New York.

A bunion is a foot deformity in which the bone of the big toe shifts…and painfully inflamed soft tissue forms at the joint on the inside edge of the foot. The tip of the big toe may angle toward or overlap the second toe. Blame your bunions on your genes (flat feet or lax ligaments increase your susceptibility)…gender (bunions are nine times more common in women)…and age (which loosens ligaments). While wearing too-tight, pointy-toed shoes won't cause bunions, it can worsen the condition.

If a bunion causes only mild discomfort…

• **Wear wide shoes that don't squeeze the ball of your foot.**

• **Place a foam or gel bunion pad over the joint** and/or put a bunion spacer between the big toe and second toe before putting on shoes.

• **Ask your podiatrist about custom-made orthotics** (shoe inserts) to improve foot function and keep the bunion from worsening.

• **Get a cortisone injection for temporary pain relief.**

If pain is severe, surgery may be the best option. This generally is covered by insurance and is done on an outpatient basis. *What it involves…*

• **The doctor cuts away the protruding bone and realigns the toe** using tiny screws or pins to hold it in place. Tendons and ligaments may be loosened or tightened. If the big toe joint is arthritic, it may need to be replaced.

• **Postoperative pain and inflammation are managed with prescription medication.** As with any surgery, there is a slight risk for infection.

• **Generally, patients use crutches and wear a postoperative shoe for two to eight weeks.** Swelling may persist for six to eight weeks. Range-of-motion and strengthening exercises can aid recovery, as can physical therapy.

Important: To prevent bunions from recurring, avoid narrow, pointy shoes.

The American Podiatric Medical Association, *www.apma.org.*

Avoid Foot Fungus

Never go barefoot in shared bathrooms—wear flip-flops, even when showering. Scrub your feet during a shower, then dry them thoroughly, especially between the toes. Wear socks made of cotton or other natural fibers. Change socks often if your feet sweat a lot. Avoid tight shoes—they cause excess perspiration, which can increase fungus growth. Check feet and toenails for flaky skin, itchiness between toes and/or on the bottom of feet, thickening of nails and discoloration. Have a doctor treat any of these problems.

Oliver Zong, DPM, podiatrist and foot surgeon in private practice, New York City.

To Prevent Foot Odor

Apply a natural antiperspirant that has buffered aluminum or aluminum chloride, such as Certain Dri Antiperspirant Roll-On, to the bottom of your feet. Wear natural fibers—socks made of cotton, which wicks away the moisture and allows greater circulation, and shoes made of cotton canvas or leather. Don't wear the same pair of shoes two days in a row. Go barefoot whenever possible. Cut back on caffeinated beverages—sweating can sometimes be caused by consuming too much caffeine.

Natural Health, Box 37474, Boone, Iowa 50037.

Laundry Room Cure for Stubborn Toenail Fungus

Mark A. Stengler, NMD, licensed naturopathic medical doctor in private practice, Encinitas, California... adjunct associate clinical professor at the National College of Natural Medicine, Portland, Oregon...author of *The Natural Physician's Healing Therapies* and co-author of *Prescription for Natural Cures* (both from Bottom Line Books).

When is the last time you took a good look at your toenails? If it has been a while, you may be in for an unpleasant surprise—in fungal form. Toenail fungus, also called *onychomycosis*, is a common condition that turns nails a yellow or brown color. In some cases, the nail thickens or splits and may fall off. Sufferers may experience pain around the nail and notice a foul smell. The infection is typically caused by any one of several types of fungi that feed on keratin, the protein surface of the nail. Occasionally, different kinds of yeasts and molds may cause the infection.

By age 70, almost half of Americans have had at least one affected toe. While the infection can occur in fingernails, it most often affects toenails—because feet are confined to the dark, warm environment of shoes, where fungi can thrive. The nails of the big toe and little toe are particularly susceptible, because friction from the sides of shoes can cause trauma to the nail surface, making it easier for fungi to penetrate. Nail fungus is not the same as athlete's foot—because athlete's foot affects the skin rather than the nail itself—but the two conditions may coexist and can be caused by the same type of fungus.

I find that athletes and others who commonly use gym locker rooms and showers are more likely to develop toenail fungus due to the damp floors and shared environment. Women who wear toenail polish are at increased risk because moisture can get trapped beneath the polish. Tight-fitting shoes and hosiery that rub the toenails also contribute to the problem. People with diabetes and other circulation problems that prevent infection-fighting white blood cells from adequately reaching the toes are particularly susceptible to the fungus, as are people with compromised immune systems, such as those with cancer or HIV.

Toenail fungus doesn't usually clear up on its own. In fact, it tends to get more severe over time—affecting a larger portion of the nail and spreading to adjacent toes and to the other foot. Therefore, I recommend starting treatment as early as possible.

CONVENTIONAL TREATMENTS

Medical doctors generally turn to topical and oral antifungal treatments. For mild cases that involve a small area of the nail, a medicated nail polish containing an antifungal agent, such as *ciclopirox* (Loprox), is often prescribed. For toenail fungus that covers a large portion of a nail or affects several nails, the typical medical approach is to prescribe oral antifungal medications, such as *itraconazole* (Sporanox) or *terbinafine* (Lamisil). These are quite powerful medications and may need to be taken for up to 12 weeks until the infection clears up. In 10% to 20% of cases, the fungus returns within several months.

The most worrisome side effect of oral antifungals is liver damage. To monitor the effect of these medications, liver enzyme tests should be performed before beginning treatment and every four to six weeks during treatment. An elevation in liver enzymes means that the drugs are irritating the liver and need to be discontinued. Several patients who were being treated by other doctors have come to see me after elevated liver enzymes forced them to stop this pharmaceutical treatment. As a last resort, the nail can be surgically removed—at which point the infection will clear up, and the nail will slowly grow back.

AN UNUSUAL CURE

The typical natural treatment for toenail fungus is to apply tea tree oil or oregano oil. Using a cotton swab, apply nightly to the affected area, continuing treatment for eight to 12 weeks. These oils work well to clear up mild toenail fungus, but they often are not strong enough for moderate to severe cases. So I was delighted when, 13 years ago, I learned about an unusual, yet effective, therapy for severe toenail fungus from Mark Cooper, ND, an innovative naturopathic doctor. Years ago, Dr. Cooper treated an HIV-positive patient who commented on an article he had read stating that bleach killed HIV on surfaces (not in the body). Knowing that hospital bedsheets and floor surfaces are washed with bleach to kill all types of fungi, viruses and bacteria, Dr. Cooper theorized that bleach might also kill toenail fungus and clear up persistent cases of infection.

I spoke with Dr. Cooper, who practices at Alpine Naturopathic Clinic in Colorado Springs. Over the years, hundreds of his patients have used this topical bleach treatment successfully. My patients have responded very well to it, too.

How it works: Mix one cup of household bleach with 10 cups of warm water. Soak the toes of the affected foot for three minutes, then thoroughly rinse off the bleach solution with water and dry the feet completely. Do this twice weekly, with three days between treatments. Most cases resolve in two to three months. Severe cases may take longer.

Boosting the strength of the bleach-and-water mixture beyond the one-to-10 ratio will not increase the effectiveness of the treatment—and it could irritate the skin. Nor is it wise to increase the frequency or duration of treatments. Dr. Cooper told me about a 74-year-old man who misunderstood the directions—instead of soaking his toes for three minutes, he tried to soak them for 30 minutes. The burning pain was so intense that he had to stop the soaking after 20 minutes. Obviously this treatment needs to be used with caution and should not be used when there is an open wound near the infection site.

Interesting: Bleach is composed of sodium hypochlorite (NaOCl). Household bleach usually contains 3% to 6% NaOCl, while industrial-strength bleach contains 10% to 12%. Near the end of the 19th century, after Louis Pasteur discovered its powerful effectiveness against disease-causing bacteria, bleach became popular as a disinfectant. It is still used today for household cleaning, removing laundry stains, treating waste water, sterilizing medical equipment and disinfecting hospital linens and surfaces.

FUNGUS-FIGHTING FOODS & SUPPLEMENTS

Dr. Cooper explains that the topical bleach treatment is even more effective when combined with an antifungal diet. Avoid simple sugars (white breads, pastas, cookies and soda) and alcohol—they suppress immune function and contribute to fungal growth. Eat raw or cooked onions, shallots and leeks, plus garlic (as a food or an extract) as often as possible for their antifungal action.

I also have found that severe cases of toenail fungus, especially in people with diabetes, clear up more quickly when natural antifungal supplements are taken orally. The most potent is oregano oil. It contains plant compounds, such as carvacrol and thymol, that have strong antifungal properties. I recommend taking three doses daily for four to eight weeks. Each dose equals one 500-mg capsule…or five to 15 drops of the liquid form mixed with two to four ounces of water. Some people may experience heartburn from oregano oil, so if you are prone to heartburn, you may need to reduce the dosage. Oregano oil should not be ingested by people with active stomach ulcers (since it can irritate the stomach lining) or by pregnant or nursing women (as a general precaution). It should be given to children only under the guidance of a doctor.

How will you know when the fungal infection is gone? When the discolored nail returns to its normal hue or when the damaged nail grows out and a new nail grows in normally.

More from Dr. Mark Stengler...

Fungus Prevention Strategies

Wash your feet every day using calendula soap. Made from the marigold plant, it is gentle yet antiseptic. Find it in health-food stores.

•**Always dry feet thoroughly with a clean towel.** Do not share towels with other people.

•**Keep toenails clipped short to reduce the protein surface on which fungi feed.**

•**Avoid going barefoot in public places.** Wear plastic sandals in community showers and locker rooms and at poolside.

•**Choose socks made of breathable fabrics, such as cotton.** Change socks immediately after exercising and whenever your feet perspire.

•**Be sure your shoes are not too tight.** If shoes get damp, change them promptly.

relax muscles and reduce spasms, a physical therapist may use...

•**External manipulation.** The therapist gently rubs and kneads the patient's pelvic region, hips, thighs and abdomen...and teaches the patient to do this technique herself.

•**Internal manipulation.** With a finger, the therapist gently stretches tight vaginal muscles. The patient also learns to do this herself.

•**Electrostimulation.** A device delivers an electrical current via sensors placed on the vulva or inside the vagina, producing controlled muscle contractions that ease spasms.

•**Biofeedback.** Sensors placed on the vulva help the patient recognize when she is succeeding at relaxing specific muscles.

The majority of VVD patients are treated successfully within six to 20 sessions of 30 to 50 minutes each, spread over several weeks or months. If PT is prescribed by a doctor, insurance generally covers it.

American Physical Therapy Association, 800-999-2782, *www.apta.org.*

Physical Therapy for Vulvodynia

Erin Hytrek, DPT, is a member of the American Physical Therapy Association section on women's health. A physical therapist at Advanced Physical Therapy for Women in Sioux City, Iowa, she focuses on gynecologic health.

Patients sometimes feel embarrassed at first by the hands-on physical therapy (PT) techniques used to treat vulvodynia (VVD) and other chronic pelvic pain conditions—but this fades quickly as the techniques bring significant relief. *How PT works...*

In response to the chronic pain of VVD, the muscles of the pelvic floor tighten uncontrollably and eventually go into spasm. This exhausts the muscles and allows the buildup of lactic acid, thereby causing additional discomfort. *To*

Easy Ways to Stop Vaginal Itching

Cherie A. LeFevre, MD, associate professor of gynecology and director of the vulvar and vaginal disorders specialty center, Saint Louis University School of Medicine, St. Louis.

Many people assume that the culprit in vaginal itching is a yeast infection—but this is not necessarily so. Your problem could be a sensitivity to chemical irritants in perfumed laundry detergents, fabric softeners, dryer sheets or soaps...so try fragrance-free products.

Another possible cause is pubic-hair shaving or waxing. Pubic hair serves a purpose—it absorbs potentially irritating moisture and protects the skin of the outer vaginal area.

Best: Let the hair grow naturally, or trim minimally.

Also, wear 100% cotton panties. True, nylon panties look sexier—but nylon can cause itching by trapping moisture.

Even when nylon panties have a cotton crotch sewn inside, moisture can be a problem unless you cut off the nylon that covers the cotton on the outside...which ends up looking not-so-sexy.

How to Beat Yeast Infections

Jamison Starbuck, ND, naturopathic physician in Missoula, Montana. She is past president of the American Association of Naturopathic Physicians and a contributing editor to *The Alternative Advisor: The Complete Guide to Natural Therapies and Alternative Treatments* (Time-Life).

Over the years, I've received several calls from doctors or nurses at nearby clinics concerning tricky yeast infections that affect both men and women. Even though most medical doctors don't know how to treat yeast, naturopathic medicine has answers.

Candidiasis is the medical term for an overgrowth of the fungal organism *Candida albicans*, commonly known as yeast. The overgrowth occurs most often in the digestive tract, though yeast can flourish on the skin or in ear canals, sinus cavities and the vagina. Antibiotics, birth-control pills, anti-ulcer drugs and corticosteroids are common causes of candidiasis.

Candidiasis can cause or worsen an array of conditions, including irritable bowel syndrome, vaginitis, prostatitis, eczema, psoriasis, hives, sinusitis, depression and chronic fatigue.

A stool culture is available to diagnose candidiasis, but it is often inaccurate. Therefore, I look for the cardinal signs of yeast—strong cravings for sweets (yeast feeds on sugar, so it may trigger this craving), gas, bloating, red and scaly skin rashes, rectal itching and generalized fatigue. I also review a patient's history of medication use for common candidiasis culprits. *If you have two or more candidiasis symptoms, follow these steps for one month...*

•**Improve your diet.** Avoid refined carbohydrates, including desserts, bread, pasta, chips and pretzels. Eliminate all juice, dried fruit and foods containing sugar, corn syrup, honey and maple syrup. Give up alcohol and artificial sweeteners. Curb your intake of starchy vegetables, such as white potatoes and corn. Reducing sugar and starches (which are converted in the body into sugar) starves the yeast. Eat only organic poultry, meat and dairy—other types may contain antibiotics, which worsen a yeast overgrowth. Freely consume all vegetables (excluding white potatoes and corn), protein (beans, soy and fish) and whole grains. Have two one-cup servings of fresh fruit daily.

•**Hydrate well.** Drink one-half ounce of water per pound of body weight daily, and limit caffeine to two cups of coffee or tea daily.

•**Use probiotics.** Take 4.5 billion colony-forming units (CFUs) of *L. acidophilus* and *B. bifidus* daily. These "good" bacteria, available at health-food stores, help with digestion and immune health. Antibiotics and other medications, such as antacids and corticosteroids, reduce these beneficial bacteria, allowing yeast to proliferate.

Finally, take a botanical antifungal preparation for a limited time to kill yeast and restore normal intestinal flora. Effective natural antifungals include caprylic acid, *Pau d'arco, Berberis vulgaris,* lavender and thyme. Single and combination formulas are available at health-food stores. Follow the label recommendations for daily dosing. Take the antifungal for one week, then stop it for 10 days. If your symptoms persist, repeat the antifungal for another seven days. Antifungals should be taken on an empty stomach.

If this program doesn't leave you feeling better within one month, see your doctor for an exam and evaluation.

Breakthrough Treatments for Hair Loss

Mark A. Stengler, NMD, licensed naturopathic medical doctor in private practice, Encinitas, California... adjunct associate clinical professor at the National College of Natural Medicine, Portland, Oregon...author of *The Natural Physician's Healing Therapies* and co-author of *Prescription for Natural Cures* (both from Bottom Line Books).

W hy do some women have ever-thinning hair, while others never seem to lose a single strand? Why do some men go bald in their 30s while others have a full head of hair until their final days?

Blame your genes, first of all. If your mom, dad or a grandparent had hair loss, chances are greater that you will, too. Even so, there are ways to slow hair loss and stimulate growth.

THE HORMONE FACTOR

You grow and shed hair all the time. Of the 100,000-plus strands of hair on your head, it is perfectly normal to lose 50 to 100 every day. Once a hair is shed, a new hair grows from the same follicle. Hair grows at a rate of nearly one-half inch per month (faster in warm weather, slower when frost is on the vine). Baldness results when the rate of shedding exceeds the rate of regrowth.

Hair loss usually accelerates when you're over age 50. One hormone, *dihydrotestosterone* (DHT), seems to be the chief culprit. DHT is a derivative of testosterone (the sex-determining hormone that is more abundant in men than women). In both men and women, DHT increases in the presence of the enzyme 5-alpha reductase, which is produced in the prostate, adrenal glands and the scalp. 5-alpha reductase is more likely to proliferate after age 50. When DHT is overproduced, hair follicles are damaged. Some follicles die, but most shrink and produce thinner, weaker hairs—and the weak hairs are the ones that fall out.

An oily skin substance called sebum—produced by the sebaceous glands—makes matters worse. Excess sebum clogs follicles and contributes to high 5-alpha reductase activity, which stimulates production of DHT.

STRESS

Among my own patients, stress is a factor for both men and women. I have found that highly stressed women, in particular, have higher-than-normal levels of cortisol, a stress hormone that can contribute to hair loss.

A study published in the *Journal of Clinical Biochemistry* confirms that cortisol is indeed elevated in some women who suffer hair loss—and that when they learn to cope better with stress, hair growth improves.

For stress relief, I recommend daily exercise, such as brisk walking, as well as relaxation techniques, including deep breathing and meditation. B vitamins and ashwagandha (a stress-reducing herb from India) also can help counteract the effects of cortisol.

A regular daily dose of 100 mg of a B-vitamin complex and 250 mg to 500 mg of ashwagandha can help control cortisol levels. Look for Sensoril Ashwagandha (available in a supplement formulation called GABA Soothe), a patented extract formula by Jarrow Formulas, available at many health-food stores or by calling Jarrow at 800-726-0886 or at *www.jarrow.com*.

A PROMISING FORMULA

Taking a daily multivitamin and mineral supplement as well as the herbal remedy saw palmetto also can help slow hair loss. A daily scalp massage with essential oils is beneficial, as well.

Saw palmetto helps block the effects of DHT on hair follicles, strengthening hair. In a study in the *Journal of Alternative and Complementary Medicine*, researchers used a product containing saw palmetto and a plant compound called beta-sitosterol that is found in saw palmetto and other plants. The study included 19 men between ages 23 and 64 who had mild-to-moderate hair loss. Men in one group were given a placebo daily...and men in the other group received the saw palmetto/beta-sitosterol combination (none of the participants knew which group they were in). After five months, researchers found that 60% of the men who received the saw palmetto/beta-sitosterol combination showed improvement, while only 11% of the men receiving a placebo had more hair growth.

In my clinical experience, saw palmetto is helpful for both men and women. I recommend 320 mg to 400 mg daily of an 85% liposterolic extract. It is safe to use long term but should not be taken if you are pregnant or nursing.

For a more aggressive approach, you should also take beta-sitosterol. Source Naturals (800-815-2333, *www.sourcenaturals.com*) offers a 113-mg tablet that can be taken daily. It is available at health-food stores and online at *www.iherb.com*.

The essential oils of rosemary and lavender have been shown to improve hair growth when applied to the scalp. My own belief is that they improve blood flow to the scalp, ensuring that nutrients get to the sites where they're needed.

You can purchase these essential oils in separate containers. Pour some of your regular shampoo into the lid of the shampoo bottle, then add five to 10 drops of each essential oil. Massage into the scalp and leave on three to five minutes before rinsing thoroughly.

OTHER SUPPLEMENTS

If you have tried these approaches for two to three months and still aren't satisfied with the growth of your locks, here are some other supplements that can help both men and women…

• **Biotin,** a nutrient that is required for hair growth, is particularly good for brittle hair. Food sources of biotin include brewer's yeast, soybeans, eggs, mushrooms and whole wheat. For supplementation, take 3,000 micrograms daily for at least two months or use a biotin-enriched shampoo daily.

• **MSM (methylsulfonylmethane)** is a great source of sulfur, an integral component of the amino acids that are the building blocks of hair protein. MSM improves the strength, sheen and health of hair. In one study, 21 adults (16 men and five women) who were assessed by a certified cosmetologist under the direction of a medical doctor were given MSM or a placebo and then were reassessed at the end of six weeks. The participants did not know who was given MSM and who was given a placebo.

Those given MSM showed significant improvement in hair health, while those taking a placebo showed few or no changes. I recommend a 3,000-mg daily dose of MSM. Look for Opti-MSM or Lignisul MSM, available from many manufacturers and at health-food stores.

Essential fatty acids keep hair from becoming dry and lifeless by decreasing inflammation. Inflammation worsens the quality of hair follicles, and essential fatty acids are needed for the proper development of hair. Food sources include walnuts, eggs, fish, olive oil, flaxseed and hempseed and flax oils. Or you can take a formula like Udo's Choice Oil Blend, produced by Flora (800-446-2110, *www.florahealth.com*). Follow directions on the label. The formula contains both omega-3 fatty acids (from flax oil or fish oil) and omega-6 fatty acids from evening primrose oil or borage oil. Don't expect immediate results, however. It can take four to six weeks to see improvement.

Why Women Lose Their Hair—*Alopecia* Explained

The most common type of hair loss among women is *androgenetic alopecia,* in which hair thins over several months in a predictable triangle pattern. It may be caused by a hormonal imbalance and can be treated with a hair transplant or topical medication, such as Rogaine.

Telogen effluvium occurs suddenly and strikes different parts of the scalp randomly. It often occurs after women have gone on or off hormone therapy for menopause or birth control, after pregnancy or illness, during periods of stress or when certain medications, such as blood pressure medication, are started or stopped.

Traction alopecia is caused by tight braids or ponytails that pull on the scalp.

If you notice your hair is falling out or thinning: See a dermatologist—simple diagnostic tests should reveal the problem.

Sandra M. Johnson, MD, dermatologist in private practice, Dublin, Ohio.

How to Make Thinning Hair Look Thicker

Consumers Union, nonprofit publisher of *Consumer Reports*, 110 Truman Ave., Yonkers, New York 10703.

Couvre masking lotion, applied to the scalp and the base of the hair, eliminates the contrast between hair and scalp that makes thinning hair obvious. Comes in a tube with a special applicator…eight colors… washes out with shampoo but holds through wind, sweating and swimming. One tube lasts three to four months. Toppik Inc., 800-844-2536, *www.couvre.com*. DermMatch is a hard-packed powder that coats thin hairs, thickens them and helps them to stand up and spread out for better coverage. It also colors the scalp, causing bald spots to disappear. It is available in eight colors. It withstands sweat, wind and swimming. DermMatch, Inc., 800-826-2824, *www.dermmatch.com*. Toppik consists of thousands of microfibers of keratin, the protein that hair is made of. Shaken over the thinning area, the microfibers bond via static electricity with the hair and stay in place through wind and rain—but not swimming. Toppik Inc., 800-844-2536, *www.toppik.com*.

How to Help an Itchy Head

Dandruff may cause an itchy scalp. In mild cases, minor scaling and flaking occurs, while in severe cases, the scalp can become red, irritated and itchy. Over-the-counter (OTC) shampoos, such as Head & Shoulders Dandruff Shampoo (containing zinc pyrithione), can be an effective treatment for dandruff. If the problem persists, check with your physician—certain skin diseases, such as psoriasis, allergic reactions and fungal infections of the scalp, can resemble dandruff and may need to be treated differently. For most people, though, using a gentle shampoo and

conditioner is enough to maintain healthy hair and scalp. Nutritional supplements containing biotin, zinc and B vitamins also can help. Most OTC shampoos and conditioners are safe, although fragrances and preservatives in hair products irritate the scalps of some people. In such cases, I recommend using hypoallergenic products, such as Free & Clear shampoo.

Leonid B. Trost, MD, Palm Beach Dermatology Inc., Jupiter, Florida.

Help for Dry Hair

There is a natural remedy for dry hair and dry scalp.

Put two tablespoons of olive oil in a small zippered plastic bag, then place the bag in a bowl or basin of warm water for several minutes. Dip your fingertips into the warm oil, then gently rub your scalp, continuing to apply the oil until the entire scalp is treated. Finger-comb the oil through your hair. Wrap your head in a towel…leave it on for 20 minutes…then shampoo as usual. Repeat weekly or as needed.

Dorie Byers, RN, registered nurse and herbalist in Bargersville, Indiana, and author of *Natural Beauty Basics: Create Your Own Cosmetics and Body Care Products* (Square One).

Get Rid of Unwanted Hairs

Tiny white hairs on one's chin and neck are typically caused by hormones and genetics. Try using a facial depilatory to dissolve them. Available at most drugstores, they remove hairs of all sizes.

Caution: 24 hours before applying to your face, test the product on a small patch of skin on your inner arm. If irritation develops, do not use the product.

Other methods of getting rid of unwanted hairs include shaving, plucking and waxing.

Electrolysis and laser treatment are more costly, but results are permanent. If the hairs become a real problem, ask your doctor about *eflornithine hydrochloride* (Vaniqa), a prescription cream that reduces growth of unwanted facial hair.

Neal B. Schultz, MD, dermatologist, New York City.

Hooray for Spearmint Tea

Spearmint tea may help to reduce excess body hair.

Recent finding: Spearmint tea may lower levels of free-circulating testosterone. High levels of free testosterone in women can result in *hirsutism*, characterized by hair growth on the face, breasts and stomach. Participants drank two cups of spearmint tea daily for five days.

Caution: People who have hiatal hernias or who are prone to acute gallstone attacks should not ingest spearmint.

M. Numan Tamer, MD, professor, department of internal medicine, Suleyman Demirel University, Turkey, and leader of a study of 21 hirsute women, published in *Phytotherapy Research*.

Get Rid of Razor Bumps

Razor bumps form when shaved hairs curl back on themselves and grow into the skin, sometimes becoming infected. Curly hairs, such as in the bikini area, are most susceptible.

Best: Never shave dry—instead, shower or bathe for at least five minutes—then apply shaving gel or cream that contains a silicone-based ingredient, such as *dimethicone* or *amodimethicone*, which coats the skin.

Good brands: Neutrogena Men and Philosophy Razor Sharp. Use a single- or double-blade razor. Shave in the direction of hair growth—

downward or sideways—not upward "against the grain."

Marianne O'Donoghue, MD, associate professor of dermatology at Rush University Medical Center in Chicago and past president of the Women's Dermatologic Society.

Natural Ways to Ease Psoriasis

Mark A. Stengler, NMD, licensed naturopathic medical doctor in private practice, Encinitas, California... adjunct associate clinical professor at the National College of Natural Medicine, Portland, Oregon...author of *The Natural Physician's Healing Therapies* and co-author of *Prescription for Natural Cures* (both from Bottom Line Books).

Psoriasis, a condition characterized by red, inflamed patches of skin covered with silvery or white scales, is believed to be caused when the immune system becomes overactive, stimulating an inflammatory response in the skin.

Some patients respond well to an anti-inflammatory diet consisting of mostly healthful fats (from olive oil, cold-water fish, nuts and seeds), legumes, vegetables and fruits. Foods that should be limited or avoided include saturated fat (in red meat, dairy products and fried foods) and processed carbohydrates, such as white pastas and breads. Inflammation also can result from excess consumption of the omega-6 oils found in vegetable oils, such as soy, safflower and corn oil. For some, avoiding gluten (a protein in wheat and some other grains) results in a marked improvement.

About half of patients benefit from fish oil. Try a daily supplement containing 3 grams (3,000 mg) of combined *eicosapentaenoic acid* (EPA) and *docosahexaenoic acid* (DHA). You should see an improvement in eight to 12 weeks.

A newer treatment: A whey protein isolate known as XP-828L, which is tolerated by people sensitive to cow's milk. A Canadian study published in *Journal of Cutaneous Medicine and Surgery* found that 84 people with mild-to-moderate psoriasis taking 5 g daily for 56 days showed significant improvement.

How to Erase Keratosis Pilaris

James Spencer, MD, clinical professor of medicine, department of dermatology, Mount Sinai School of Medicine, New York City.

Keratosis pilaris is an inherited condition in which small, pink or flesh-colored bumps develop around the opening of the hair follicles (sacs from which hair grows). It is a harmless skin disorder that results from a buildup of protein called keratin in the follicles. It does not have long-term health effects, but may be annoying due to its appearance. This condition may be treated topically with moisturizing lotions, over-the-counter medications containing the chemical compounds lactic acid or glycolic acid or, in some cases, a prescription topical medication, such as *tretinoin* (Retin A). Another option is microdermabrasion, in which a dermatologist uses a small machine to remove the dead, outer layer of skin. Although microdermabrasion is usually performed on facial skin to repair sun damage or the effects of aging, it is also effective for keratosis pilaris. Insurance does not cover this treatment, which costs about $100 per treatment in a series of five to 12 treatments.

Cures for Adult Acne

Richard G. Fried, MD, PhD, clinical director of Yardley Dermatology Associates, a skin-enhancement and wellness center in Yardley, Pennsylvania. He is author of *Healing Adult Acne* (New Harbinger).

Acne used to be rare in adults. No more. It can occur in people in their 20s and 30s—and some people continue to have acne into their 40s and 50s. In a recent study, 34% of participants who experienced adult-onset acne never had it during adolescence.

Doctors don't know why adult acne is on the rise, but one factor could be that we have busier lives and experience more stress than in the past. Stress triggers the release of hormones, such as testosterone (in women and men), and chemicals, such as neuropeptides, that increase skin oils and impair facial circulation. Contrary to popular belief, what you eat has little effect on acne.

Adult acne tends to affect deeper skin layers than adolescent acne. There's more inflammation and a greater risk of scarring.

THE ROOT OF ACNE

Acne occurs when hair follicles become plugged with oil and abnormally thick, sticky dead skin cells. Follicles are bulblike structures that encase hair roots and are attached to oil-producing glands. The oil travels up the hair shaft to the skin surface. Adults who produce excessive oil—due to high levels of testosterone, for example—may experience blockages in the follicles. The trapped oil (sebum) provides a haven for bacteria, which can cause inflammation and infection, resulting in acne.

About 54% of adults with acne are women, probably because their skin is more sensitive to testosterone's effects.

BEST TREATMENTS

To treat acne, start with step one below, then move on to subsequent steps if there isn't substantial clearing in two to four weeks…

Step 1. *Benzoyl peroxide* is the main ingredient in dozens of acne lotions, many of which are available over-the-counter. It has antibacterial/anti-inflammatory effects that usually work for mild acne. Use a 2.5% formula (such as PanOxyl AQ 2.5% Gel) for dry or sensitive skin…a 7% to 10% formula (such as Clearasil Maximum Strength medicated cream) for oily skin. Apply to affected areas once daily.

Helpful: Also apply a *salicylic acid* product (such as Salacid), which reduces swelling and inflammation. Use benzoyl peroxide and salicylic acid at different times of day, perhaps benzoyl peroxide at night and salicylic acid in the morning. The combination gives better results.

Step 2. *Retinoids*, prescription topical products, such as Retin-A, Renova and Avita, help unblock hair follicles. These products may cause irritation. Apply twice weekly initially, then increase to once daily as skin adjusts.

Important: Benzoyl peroxide reduces the effects of retinoids. You can use them both, but not at the same time.

Step 3. Combination ointment. Prescription products, such as Duac, contain both benzoyl peroxide and an antibiotic. Patients with mild-to-moderate acne who don't respond to other products usually do well with these.

Step 4. Periostat. Available by prescription, this oral drug contains a low dose of the antibiotic *doxycycline*. It doesn't have antibiotic properties at this dose but does act as an anti-inflammatory. When used in combination with acne ointments, such as benzoyl peroxide or topical retinoids, it is very effective in most patients (though it may need to be taken for months).

Step 5. *Isotretinoin* is a prescription vitamin-A derivative, taken in pill form, that can eliminate acne in most patients. It helps normalize hair follicles, so cells don't thicken and clog the pores, and can prevent acne from coming back.

Women who are pregnant or planning to become pregnant cannot take isotretinoin (Claravis) because it increases the risk of birth defects.

Step 6. Smoothbeam laser. About 40% of adults with severe acne experience substantial improvements with laser therapy. The 1,450-nanometer laser wavelength targets the sebaceous glands and can eliminate excess oil.

The procedure takes 15 to 20 minutes and is relatively painless—although there may be some irritation/redness for several days. Most patients require four to six treatments, usually given one month apart.

Cost: About $200/treatment, not covered by insurance.

How to (Finally!) Get Rid of Acne

Mary Ellen Brademas, MD, clinical assistant professor of dermatology at New York University School of Medicine and a dermatologist in private practice, both in New York City.

It's frustrating to battle pimples and wrinkles simultaneously—yet up to 15% of women do have acne breakouts in midlife and beyond.

Possible reason: Production of the hormone estrogen, a natural pimple suppressor, decreases at menopause—and may leave a relatively high ratio of acne-provoking hormones called androgens. Acne develops when pores get blocked with natural skin oils.

Products that helped when you were younger now may make acne worse because they're too drying for mature skin—and excessive dryness prompts the sebaceous glands to pump out even more pore-clogging oil. *What does help…*

•**Use anti-acne skin-care products.** Wash your face thoroughly with cold cream or a soapless product, such as Cetaphil Gentle Skin Cleanser. Exfoliate with a cream or gel containing salicylic acid, azelaic acid and/or glycolic acid to slough off dead skin cells that trap oil. Follow with oil-based moisturizer and makeup—water-based products are too drying.

•**Listen to your gut.** Stress activates the nervous system, which in turn triggers reactions in the digestive tract and skin. A churning stomach is a signal that you need to reduce stress if you want to protect your complexion.

Best: Do whatever relaxes you—listen to music, phone a friend, meditate.

•**Identify your personal pimple-provoking foods.** Chocolate doesn't cause breakouts—but the iodine in seafood may irritate pores, and some people are sensitive to dairy products and/or tree nuts (walnuts, cashews, almonds). Keep a food log for a few weeks, and look for patterns. If you discover that you always break out a day or two after eating strawberries, for instance, avoid them.

•**Try natural remedies.** Soak one-third of an ounce of witch hazel bark or white oak bark (sold in health-food stores) overnight in one cup of water. Strain liquid, then saturate a cotton ball and wipe it over your entire face. Let the skin dry before putting on your makeup.

Before bed: Beat an egg yolk, smooth it onto your face, let dry for 10 minutes, then remove it with cold water and a washcloth.

If your acne continues, see a dermatologist. *You may need to…*

• **Try prescription medication.** *Isotretinoin*, derived from vitamin A, reduces the oil secreted by the skin...changes the shape and texture of cells that line pores so oil is less easily trapped...and restores collagen and elastin, proteins that give skin its structure. After five months, as many as three out of four patients are cured of acne.

Caution: Isotretinoin can cause severe birth defects, so don't use it if you have any chance of getting pregnant. It can raise levels of cholesterol and triglycerides (blood fats) and cause fluctuations in blood sugar—so your doctor should conduct frequent blood tests to monitor these.

• **Consider hormone therapy.** This may combat acne (and other menopausal symptoms) by raising the body's levels of estrogen. However, it can increase the risk for breast cancer and heart disease, so talk with your doctor about the potential risks and benefits.

Stop the Hiccups

Nicholas J. Talley, MD, PhD, professor of medicine and epidemiology, Mayo Clinic College of Medicine, Jacksonville, Florida.

A hiccup is caused by an abrupt contraction of the diaphragm (the muscle that separates the chest cavity from the abdomen). This spasm pulls air into the lungs. Next, the epiglottis (a flap of tissue at the top of the windpipe) slams shut, cutting off the air and producing the "hic!" sound. Common, everyday hiccups—as opposed to chronic ones—are triggered by a number of things, such as eating or drinking too fast, drinking carbonated beverages or minor stomach disorders. While home remedies abound, there is no surefire way to get rid of hiccups. But sipping water while holding your breath is one method that has been shown to be effective.

Important: If your hiccups last for more than a day, there could be a number of underlying causes, including gastroesophageal reflux disease (GERD) or more serious disorders,

such as esophageal blockage, lung disease, kidney failure or a brain infection. See a doctor immediately if your hiccups don't go away within 24 hours.

Don't Let Heartburn Turn Deadly

Anil Minocha, MD, professor of medicine at Louisiana State University and staff gastroenterologist and director of nutrition support at Overton Brooks VA Medical Center, both in Shreveport, Louisiana. He is author of *How to Stop Heartburn* (Wiley).

N early everyone suffers from heartburn from time to time, but frequent episodes (two or more times weekly) can signal a condition that must be taken seriously. Chronic heartburn, also known as gastroesophageal reflux disease (GERD), can lead to internal bleeding and scarring—even a deadly form of cancer. More than 20 million Americans have GERD.

Alarming finding: The number of people hospitalized for conditions related to GERD doubled between 1998 and 2005, according to the US government's Agency for Healthcare Research and Quality.

WHAT GOES WRONG

When you eat or drink, food and liquid move from your mouth to the esophagus, where a valve, called the lower esophageal sphincter, relaxes to allow the food and liquid to pass into your stomach. The lower esophageal sphincter then squeezes shut to keep stomach contents from backing up (a process known as reflux) into the esophagus.

Some degree of reflux occurs normally—including after meals. But when reflux becomes excessive, causes complications or affects quality of life, it is called GERD.

Symptoms that may be misdiagnosed: GERD—with or without heartburn—also can be characterized by chronic hoarseness or cough, sore throat or asthma, conditions that occur when gastric contents come in contact with the upper respiratory tract.

A LIFE-THREATENING DANGER

No one knows exactly why some people suffer from frequent reflux. But regardless of the cause, chronic reflux can lead to injury and bleeding in the esophagus, which sometimes affects swallowing. With time (sometimes just a few years), cells lining the esophagus can become precancerous as a result of chronic inflammation. This condition, known as Barrett's esophagus, can lead to esophageal cancer, which is often fatal and is the most rapidly increasing cancer in the US.

Important: Because GERD can lead to serious, even life-threatening complications, see a doctor if you have heartburn two or more times weekly—or if you have symptoms, such as difficulty swallowing, unexplained chronic cough or hoarseness, that don't respond to standard treatment, such as medication and lifestyle changes.

GETTING THE RIGHT DIAGNOSIS

A primary care doctor or gastroenterologist usually diagnoses GERD on the basis of the symptoms described earlier. In some cases, the doctor will perform endoscopy, in which a thin, flexible, fiber-optic tube is passed through the throat to examine the esophagus and upper part of the stomach.

Ask your doctor about: An esophageal acidity test. With this procedure, a tiny device is placed in the esophagus to monitor levels of acidity for 24 hours (very high levels usually indicate GERD). This test typically is used when a patient has not responded to treatment or has atypical symptoms (such as chronic cough or hoarseness).

BEST MEDICATION CHOICES

Over-the-counter (OTC) antacids, such as TUMS, Rolaids and Maalox, neutralize stomach acid and may help relieve heartburn, but they do not heal the injury to the esophagus caused by reflux.

People who have frequent heartburn usually get better results from acid-reducing prescription medication, such as H2 blockers, including *ranitidine* (Zantac) and *famotidine* (Pepcid), or proton pump inhibitors (PPIs), including *omeprazole* (Prilosec) and *esomepra-*

zole (Nexium). Some of these medications are available OTC.

Ask your doctor about: Potential side effects of long-term use of PPIs, which include reduced absorption of vitamin B-12, calcium and magnesium, higher risk for bone fractures and increased risk for respiratory infections.

SMALL CHANGES THAT HELP

If followed conscientiously, lifestyle changes can eliminate the need for medication in up to 20% of GERD sufferers. *My advice…*

•**Check your medications.** Calcium channel blockers and beta-blockers taken for high blood pressure or heart disease, as well as some antidepressants and anti-anxiety medication, can reduce lower esophageal sphincter (LES) pressure and may worsen GERD. If you have heartburn symptoms, ask the doctor who prescribed your medication about alternatives.

•**Modify your eating habits.** Small, frequent meals leave the stomach quickly, thus providing less opportunity for reflux.

Avoid foods that may worsen GERD: Onions, chocolate and fatty foods reduce LES pressure, allowing reflux to occur.

•**Sleep right.** If you're troubled by reflux when you sleep, place a foam wedge under the mattress or wooden blocks under the bedposts to elevate the head of your bed by four to six inches.

Important: Extra pillows under your head will not do the job. They will raise your head, but won't change the angle between your stomach contents and your LES.

ALTERNATIVE APPROACHES

Stress causes the LES to relax more often, increasing reflux episodes. Practicing a regular stress-reduction technique, such as deep-breathing exercises, has been shown to reduce the amount of acid in the esophagus. *Also helpful…*

•**Acupuncture.** This ancient Chinese practice is most likely to help people diagnosed with "slow stomach"—that is, their GERD is worsened by food taking longer to leave the stomach. Acupuncture can improve the movement and emptying of stomach contents.

• **Probiotics,** such as Lactobacillus acidophilus, are "friendly" bacteria that reduce the harmful effects of acid in the esophagus.

My advice: Eat yogurt or kefir containing "live, active" cultures twice daily.

THE SURGICAL OPTION

Surgery usually is an option if drug treatment and alternative approaches have failed.

In the standard procedure, called *fundoplication*, part of the upper stomach is wrapped around the LES to strengthen it. This operation can be performed with tiny incisions (laparoscopically), rather than by opening the chest.

In one study of 100 individuals, 90% expressed overall satisfaction with the surgery. Although 80% continued to take anti-reflux medications, most took lower doses than before the surgery. Some new procedures, which involve injections or sutures to tighten the LES, are promising but unproven.

Natural Ways to Relieve Gastritis

Mark A. Stengler, NMD, licensed naturopathic medical doctor in private practice, Encinitas, California... adjunct associate clinical professor at the National College of Natural Medicine, Portland, Oregon...author of *The Natural Physician's Healing Therapies* and coauthor of *Prescription for Natural Cures* (both from Bottom Line Books).

G astritis refers to inflammation or erosion of the stomach lining, which can come on suddenly or may become chronic. The most common symptom my patients report is abdominal pain. Other complaints include nausea, indigestion, bloating and loss of appetite. This condition is confirmed by an endoscopy, in which a tiny camera at the end of a thin tube is inserted through the mouth and down into the stomach. A biopsy also may confirm gastritis. Left untreated, the condition can progress into more serious ulceration, when erosion of the stomach lining causes bleeding. To properly treat gastritis, it is necessary to first identify the cause.

Possible culprits: A bacterial infection known as *Helicobacter pylori* (H. pylori), a viral infection, stress, alcohol, smoking or pain medications, such as aspirin or *nonsteroidal anti-inflammatory drugs* (NSAIDs), including *ibuprofen*. Besides treating the cause, I have patients take natural substances that promote healing of the stomach lining. I have seen good results with a supplement known as zinc-carnosine. Used to treat gastritis and ulcers in Japan, this natural compound is available in the US and has been shown to coat the stomach and improve the health of the stomach mucosal lining. It also inhibits the growth of H. pylori. I recommend 75 mg twice daily.

Good brand: Doctor's Best, available in many health-food stores. In addition, one tablespoon of food-grade aloe vera consumed three times daily is very helpful. Avoid spicy foods and dairy products while your stomach is healing.

Soothe Your Stomach Without Drugs

Leo Galland, MD, director, Foundation for Integrated Medicine, New York City. He is author of *The Fat Resistance Diet* (Broadway). Dr. Galland is a recipient of the Linus Pauling Award.

M illions of Americans take drugs to relieve excess stomach acid. Although these drugs can relieve symptoms, such as heartburn and abdominal pain, they can have serious long-term side effects. The good news is that there are natural remedies that work even better than drugs, without the side effects.

THE DRUGS

Acid-suppressing drugs fall into two basic categories...

• **Proton-pump inhibitors (PPIs),** such as Prilosec, Prevacid, Nexium, Aciphex and Protonix, inhibit the enzymes that transport the acid from acid-secreting cells into the stomach cavity.

• **Histamine-2 (H2) blockers,** such as Zantac, Pepcid, Axid and Tagamet, inhibit the activity of *histamine* in the stomach. Histamine stimulates stomach cells to secrete more acid.

THE DANGERS

Regular use of acid-suppressing drugs is associated with increased risk of hip fractures, probably because these drugs hinder calcium absorption.

Taking acid suppressors also increases your risk of acquiring a foodborne intestinal infection or experiencing the overgrowth of bacteria in the stomach and small intestine. Bacteria overgrowth in the stomach probably explains some other risks associated with regular use of acid suppressors, including pneumonia, stomach cancer and vitamin B-12 deficiency.

Acid-suppressing therapy can be used to treat gastroesophageal reflux disease (GERD). *Here are the natural remedies…*

GERD

In GERD, the contents of the stomach flow backward up the esophagus and may reach all the way to the mouth. Symptoms include heartburn, chest pain, regurgitation of food, sore throat, hoarse voice and cough.

GERD isn't caused by excess production of acid. It is caused by failure of the muscle (called the lower esophageal sphincter, or LES) that acts like a valve and separates the esophagus from the stomach. Suppressing stomach acid doesn't prevent reflux—it merely converts acid reflux into nonacid reflux. *To prevent reflux itself…*

•**Don't stuff yourself.** Eating a lot at one time causes stomach distension, which triggers relaxation of the LES.

•**Avoid high-fat foods, including fried foods and creamy sauces.** These foods weaken the LES.

•**Don't smoke.** It weakens the LES.

•**Don't eat for three hours before lying down.** When you're upright, gravity helps to keep food down.

•**Maintain a normal weight.** Being overweight increases your risk of GERD. Excess pounds put pressure on the abdomen which pushes up the stomach and causes acid to back up.

•**Don't eat immediately before strenuous exercise.** Strenuous activity increases the likelihood of GERD.

•**Avoid foods that cause discomfort until you're better.** So-called "acidic" foods, such as oranges and tomatoes, may irritate an already inflamed esophagus.

•**Try supplements.** The simple steps already described prevent symptoms of GERD in the majority of people and may allow you to avoid the use of acid-suppressing drugs. *If not, try the following…*

•Calcium. Calcium tightens the LES. This is not an antacid effect. In fact, the best type of calcium—because it is the most soluble—is *calcium citrate,* which is itself mildly acidic. The most effective preparation is calcium citrate powder. Take 250 milligrams (mg), dissolved in water, after every meal and at bedtime (for a total daily dose of 1,000 mg). Swallowing calcium pills does not prevent reflux, because the calcium is not instantly dissolved.

•Digestive enzymes. These appear to work by decreasing distension of the stomach. The enzymes should be acid-resistant so that they work in the stomach itself, not in the small intestine. A powdered enzyme preparation (one-half teaspoon) can be mixed together with the calcium powder and taken after each meal. Digestive enzymes are available in health-food stores and pharmacies.

GO SLOWLY

People who have been taking acid-suppressing drugs daily for several weeks or more may have difficulty discontinuing them. When the stomach is deprived of acid, it compensates by producing more acid-secreting cells. The result is that even though the initial symptoms are not due to hyperacidity, attempting to stop the drug creates hyperacidity. The solution is to taper off the drug slowly, under a doctor's supervision, while taking steps to remedy the underlying cause.

Vinegar for Acid Reflux

Over the years, several patients have told me that apple cider vinegar diluted in water or juice is effective for preventing acid reflux. Acid reflux is caused by a weak or damaged esophageal sphincter (the valve between the stomach and esophagus). The sphincter is supposed to prevent the contents of the stomach from going upward. When it doesn't work properly, stomach acid flows into the esophagus. While there are no studies to prove why it works, vinegar may stimulate better digestive action and the closing of the esophageal sphincter. I recommend mixing one tablespoon of vinegar in eight ounces of water (not juice). Drink before meals or when experiencing reflux. In this small amount, vinegar is safe. Large amounts can adversely interact with certain drugs.

Mark A. Stengler, NMD, licensed naturopathic medical doctor in private practice, Encinitas, California... adjunct associate clinical professor at the National College of Natural Medicine, Portland, Oregon...author of *The Natural Physician's Healing Therapies* and co-author of *Prescription for Natural Cures* (both from Bottom Line Books).

More from Dr. Mark A. Stengler...

Try Vitamin D to Reduce Sweating

Sweating of the head is not uncommon. Excessive sweating, or *hyperhidrosis*, is a chronic medical condition that affects about 3% of the population, according to the American Academy of Dermatology. The body's temperature-regulation system produces more heat than needed.

One possible cause: Deficiency of vitamin D. I suggest that your doctor order a blood test to see if your vitamin D levels are in the low range—normal range is 20 nanograms per milliliter (ng/ml) to 100 ng/ml, with a desired amount of over 50.

Another possible cause: Low levels of the hormones estrogen and progesterone. Your physician should check these levels. If neither is the cause, seek the advice of a holistic doctor, who can recommend homeopathic or herbal treatments to normalize temperature regulation and reduce symptoms.

Another one from Dr. Mark A. Stengler...

How to Heal a Facial Wart

Warts are caused by a tenacious virus, which means that you may not be able to fully prevent them. And as you may have seen, flare-ups can last for months. Outbreaks are best treated with a homeopathic remedy (there are topical treatments for warts, but they should never be used on the face, because many are caustic and can cause scarring). Try *Thuja occidentalis*, which comes from a plant in the evergreen family. Take two pellets of a 30C potency twice daily for two weeks.

Good brand: Boiron, available in health-food stores. If the condition does not completely clear up, continue this course of treatment for four more weeks. Then, if the warts are still a problem, consult with a holistic doctor, who can prescribe an individually targeted homeopathic remedy.

New Hope for Embarrassing Warts— Green Tea Extract

Mark Blumenthal, founder and executive director, American Botanical Council (ABC), Austin, Texas, and editor, *HerbalGram* and *HerbClip*. Visit ABC's Web site at *www.herbalgram.org*.

US Food and Drug Administration, *www.fda.gov*.

From the local sushi joint to Starbucks, green tea is a health food favorite, undoubtedly one of the most popular beverages around. But a prescription drug? It is now. The US Food and Drug Administration (FDA) approved the marketing of *polyphenon E/Kunecatechins* (Veregen) ointment—derived from the leaves of the green tea plant Camellia sinensis—for the treatment of external genital and anal warts.

At first glance, this may not seem especially significant, but the fledgling botanical drug industry considers it nothing less than a milestone. Following on the heels of the release of *flavocoxid* (Limbrel)—a blend of natural ingredients including plant-derived flavonoids —as an osteoarthritis-fighting medical food, could this be a trend? Could the medical community possibly be growing more open to the use of traditional botanicals as treatments for conditions that were previously dominated by pharmaceuticals?

According to Mark Blumenthal, founder and executive director of the American Botanical Council (*www.herbalgram.org*) in Austin, Texas, the green tea extract product's approval represents a regulatory breakthrough. He said that this is the first time a chemically complex botanical preparation has come to market as a prescription botanical drug in the US in nearly half a century. He talked about green tea extract, and about what Veregen can mean for botanical drugs in general.

A DISEASE-FIGHTING ANTIOXIDANT PACKAGE

Genital warts are caused by the human papillomavirus (HPV), which is the most common sexually transmitted disease (STD) in the US. As many as one million new cases of genital warts occur in the US each year, and 20 million Americans are infected with this incurable condition. These warts can be painful and disfiguring, and also dangerous. Women who have genital warts face an increased risk of developing cervical cancer.

While green tea extract cannot be claimed to cure genital warts (new ones may still develop following treatment), it can help make a current outbreak go away. Scientists believe that the secret curing power of green tea lies in the leaves' phytochemicals, specifically in high levels of disease-fighting, antioxidant compounds called *catechins* present in the concentrated form of the new drug. In contrast to black and oolong teas, green tea leaves are not fermented, which means they are able to retain more natural catechins.

In two randomized, double-blind studies, nearly 400 adults with two to 30 external genital and/or anal warts applied green tea ointment three times a day until the warts disappeared. The median time to clear all the warts ranged from 10 and 16 weeks. Approximately 24% to 54% of the folks experienced

complete clearing with the drug compared with approximately 0% to 29% that experienced clearing with the placebo. Common side effects include local redness, itching, swelling, hardening of the wart and surrounding tissue, ulceration and pain or discomfort. Side effects are comparable with those of pharmaceutical topical treatments.

Genital warts are a serious problem that requires diagnosis by a physician, and this green tea extract product is available by prescription only. Of course, there are green tea creams available over-the-counter, as cosmetics, but they should not be used without professional oversight. This is not a condition to try to self-treat. Only time will tell if doctors also find it beneficial to prescribe green tea extract for other skin conditions.

A REGULATORY BREAKTHROUGH

Blumenthal considers Veregen's approval to be a regulatory breakthrough even though this product is a highly concentrated extract of green tea—far more powerful than its more natural forms. Blumenthal says that it is significant that the FDA recognizes that select botanicals are different from conventional synthetic or highly purified drugs, and it doesn't make sense to subject them to the same level of scrutiny in terms of safety. New drugs are almost always new chemical entities that humans have never had exposure to, while botanicals are chemically complex natural entities that have been around forever, so while many don't have large-scale preliminary research, they do have long-term experience to back up their safety.

The FDA defines a botanical as a product that contains only ingredients from plants, algae or fungi. While most conventional drugs contain one usually synthesized chemical, botanicals are comprised of a mixture of many naturally occurring compounds. According to the FDA, as most of the chemically pure new drugs are first tested in animals, many of the botanicals have a long history of human use as dietary supplements or as treatments in alternative medical systems. In a tacit recognition of the noteworthy differences between conventional chemical drugs and botanicals,

209

the FDA issued new guidelines for botanical drugs. These guidelines reduced some of the rigorous toxicology studies required for conventional non-botanical drugs when it comes to preliminary clinical testing.

In Blumenthal's view, in addition to being foods, spices, beverages (like green tea) and dietary supplements, many botanicals also potentially represent an exciting new class of "drugs." The green tea extract product may not only prove to be beneficial in and of itself, it may represent the beginning of more and more botanical drug approvals.

Chronic Bad Breath

Mark A. Stengler, NMD, licensed naturopathic medical doctor in private practice, Encinitas, California... adjunct associate clinical professor at the National College of Natural Medicine, Portland, Oregon...author of *The Natural Physician's Healing Therapies* and coauthor of *Prescription for Natural Cures* (both from Bottom Line Books).

I find that for many people, the key to resolving chronic bad breath is to address an underlying digestive problem. For example, if you are lactose intolerant, your body doesn't digest cow's milk properly. This results in the production of hydrogen and methane, which emit from the digestive tract as bad breath (and flatulence). Drinking alcohol also can lead to unpleasant mouth odors because it causes dry mouth and can create an overgrowth of yeast in the digestive tract. You can improve your breath by consuming sources of good bacteria, such as miso, tofu or natto (fermented soybeans), yogurt, kefir and sauerkraut (unpasteurized), every day or taking a daily probiotic supplement containing five billion *colony-forming units* (CFU) or more of Lactobacillus acidophilus and bifidus. Researchers also have found that overweight people are more likely to have bad breath (perhaps due to an increased risk for dry mouth), so losing weight may help as well.

Good-Bye to Fishy Burps

To prevent fish oil's aftertaste and fishy burps, take the capsules frozen—they will break down more slowly and still be fully digested.

Or: Take a capsule at the start of a meal—food mixes with the capsule in the stomach, reducing the fishy burp.

Try a capsule with enteric coating that lets it pass through the stomach and dissolve in the intestines. Switch brands—better-purified capsules have fewer side effects, although they usually cost more.

Mayo Clinic Health Letter, 200 First St. SW, Rochester, Minnesota 55905.

Best Way to Beat Bad Breath

Both antibacterial and odor-neutralizing mouth rinses are effective, but those containing *chlorhexidine* can temporarily stain the teeth and tongue.

Better: Mouth rinses, such as TheraBreath and ProFresh, with chlorine dioxide and zinc.

The Cochrane Library.

No More Raccoon Eyes

Nooshin Darvish, ND, medical director and founder of the Holistique Medical Center in Bellevue, Washington. She is a former faculty member of Bastyr University and doctor-on-call for *The Dr. Pat Show,* an internationally broadcast talk radio program.

Dark under-eye circles are not just a cosmetic concern or genetic legacy—they can signal an underlying serious health problem.

How: When veins are overtaxed, they swell and dilate. Veins beneath the eyes become visible because the area has many blood vessels and the overlying skin is thin.

Veins can be affected by sleep deprivation, dehydration, smoking and excessive alcohol or caffeine—so under-eye circles often disappear with improvements in lifestyle.

However, if dark circles persist, the culprit could be…

• **Allergies.** Sensitivities to foods (wheat, dairy), environmental triggers (pollen, dust) or chemicals (gasoline, paint) can provoke an inflammatory response from the immune system. This makes veins swell.

• **Digestive problems.** Conditions such as intestinal infections or irritable bowel syndrome can impair the digestive system's ability to fully process food.

This triggers an inflammatory immune reaction that makes veins swell.

• **Hormonal imbalance.** An underperforming thyroid or adrenal gland can affect blood circulation.

See your doctor for a check-up and follow any prescribed treatment. *Also…*

To ease inflammation: Take vitamin C at 1,000 milligrams (mg) twice daily…and drink three to six cups of green tea every day.

To improve digestion: Supplement with L-glutamine (an amino acid) at 500 mg three times daily, between meals.

Also take probiotics (beneficial digestive bacteria)—ask your doctor about the best type and dosage for you.

To balance hormones: Take selenium at 100 micrograms daily…and vitamin B-6 at 50 mg per day (with food).

Drink one cup of Panax ginseng tea each morning—but get your doctor's approval first if you use any medication.

Quick temporary fix: Chilled cucumber slices placed over the eye area for 10 minutes can reduce inflammation.

"Eye-Opening" Treatment for Droopy Lids

Neal B. Schultz, MD, cosmetic dermatologist in private practice in New York City and assistant clinical professor of dermatology, Mount Sinai School of Medicine, New York City. He is coauthor of It's Not Just About Wrinkles (Stewart, Tabori & Chang).

D rooping eyelids—a condition known as *ptosis*—often develop as people age and the tissue connected to the eyelid muscle stretches. Dermatologists can correct mild drooping with a carbon dioxide laser, which tightens the collagen in the middle layer of skin, causing the overlying skin to contract. Recuperation takes about one week, though the area may remain slightly discolored for several months. Severe drooping requires plastic surgery in which extra skin is cut out.

Botox injections in the forehead also can cause the eyelids to droop by temporarily paralyzing certain facial muscles. In that case, drooping should go away on its own within two to six weeks.

Caution: See a neurologist right away if your eyelid droops quite suddenly and you haven't had Botox within the last several days. The sudden droop can be a warning sign of a ministroke, Bell's palsy (inflammation of nerves that control facial muscles) or other neuromuscular problem.

What Your Fingernails Tell About Your Health

Jamison Starbuck, ND, naturopathic physician in Missoula, Montana. She is a past president of the American Association of Naturopathic Physicians and a contributing editor to The Alternative Advisor: The Complete Guide to Natural Therapies and Alternative Treatments (Time-Life).

S ince the time of Hippocrates, most doctors have examined patients' fingernails during routine physical exams. That's because the fingernail is an important window through which an astute physician can see signs of some diseases and even clues about a person's nutritional status, lifestyle and emotional health.

Fingernails should be strong, with a light pink color to the nail bed (the skin on which the nail rests). A few white spots and/or lines are usually due to injury to the nail bed and are harmless. However, if you have any of the conditions described below, see your physician for an evaluation and treatment, such as the use of medication and/or supplements. *What to look for...*

•**Brittle, dry, splitting nails, with deep longitudinal** (from the cuticle to the fingernail tip) ridges, can indicate thyroid disease, usually hypothyroidism (an underactive thyroid). It also can be a sign of a mineral deficiency, particularly calcium or zinc.

•**Nails loosening or separating from the nail bed can indicate hyperthyroidism** (an overactive thyroid). This condition also can be a sign of psoriasis (a chronic skin disease) or a reaction to synthetic nails or a nail injury.

•**Nail pitting** (deep depressions) can indicate psoriasis, psoriatic arthritis (a condition with symptoms of both arthritis and psoriasis) or chronic dermatitis (skin rash). Nail pitting also can be seen in people with alopecia areata, an autoimmune disease that causes sudden patchy hair loss, usually in the scalp or beard.

•**Nails curved around enlarged fingertips** (also known as clubbing) can be a harmless condition that runs in families, or it can be a sign of low oxygen in the blood, a common marker for chronic lung disease.

•**Hollowed or dipped nails** (also known as spoon nails) are often associated with an iron deficiency. A three-year-old boy I recently saw had 10 tiny scooped-out fingernails that could have each contained a drop of water.

•**Opaque (white) nails with a dark band at the fingertip** (also known as Terry's nails) can be a harmless sign of aging, or it can indicate cardiac disease, particularly congestive heart failure.

•**Yellow nails can be due to nicotine stains,** bacterial infection, fungus in the nail and nail bed, chronic bronchitis or lymphedema (swelling and congestion of the lymph system).

•**Bitten nails can indicate anxiety,** severe stress or compulsive behavior.

The best way to keep your nails healthy is to keep them clean, trim and warm. Don't pick at hangnails. Clip them. Limit nail polish remover use to twice a month (it dries nails and makes them more brittle). Protect your nails from harsh chemicals by wearing gloves and avoiding the use of synthetic nails. With normal growth, an injured nail will be replaced in four to six months.

Help for Ropy Veins On Hands

Hands have thin, delicate skin and little subcutaneous fat. That's why cosmetic procedures, such as chemical peels and injections that minimize the appearance of veins elsewhere on the body, don't work for hands.

Better: A prescription *tretinoin* cream, such as Renova, that stimulates collagen production, making skin plumper and smoother...or nonprescription Olay Regenerist Targeted Tone Enhancer.

Marianne O'Donoghue, MD, associate professor of dermatology at Rush University Medical Center in Chicago and past president of the Women's Dermatologic Society.

How to Get Rid of Spider Veins

Ronald Moy, MD, professor of dermatology at the David Geffen School of Medicine at the University of California, Los Angeles, and director of dermatology at the California Health & Longevity Institute, Westlake Village, California.

Spider veins are small blood vessels near the skin's surface that are visible as thin red, blue or purple lines. They most often appear on the legs but can occur on the face and elsewhere. In addition to being unsightly, spider veins may ache, swell or burn.

Age is one culprit—over time, veins get larger and skin gets thinner and more transparent. A propensity for spider veins runs in families, though they also can be caused by injury. Home remedies cannot get rid of spider veins, but two types of medical treatment can.

Sclerotherapy involves injecting spider veins with a salt-based solution. This collapses the veins and cuts off blood flow, causing them to fade and easing discomfort. Pain is minor because the needle is very small. A single injection can destroy many interconnected veins, though you may need several injections and/or sessions. After sclerotherapy, healthy veins take over for destroyed ones.

Cost: About $200 per treatment.

Laser treatment uses pulses of energy to heat and shrink the veins. Each laser pulse feels like a rubber band snapping on your skin, and many pulses are needed along the length of the vein. Facial spider veins generally respond best to laser treatment.

Cost: $300 or more per treatment.

Both treatments may need to be repeated if new spider veins appear. Insurance seldom covers the cost. Side effects are rare but may include sores, red marks and scarring.

To find a doctor in your area, contact the American Academy of Dermatology, 866-503-7546, *www.aad.org.*

Why Women Shouldn't Ignore Varicose Veins

Andrew Kwak, MD, past clinical assistant professor of interventional radiology and director and founder of the laser vein treatment program at University of Pennsylvania School of Medicine in Philadelphia. *www.lumenlasercenter.com*

F ar more than just a cosmetic problem, varicose veins can cause pain that interferes with daily activities—and may lead to serious health problems, such as blood clots and uncontrolled bleeding.

Good news: New treatments are safe and effective…involve minimal discomfort and downtime…and often are covered by insurance.

CONTRIBUTING FACTORS

Normally, veins carry blood back to the heart quickly, helped by tiny interior one-way valves. However, when circulation through a vein is too slow, the vein becomes enlarged, twisted and engorged with blood—a varicose vein. As the vein worsens and/or more varicose veins form, the leg may become painful and swollen. (Spider veins are similar but much smaller and do not cause pain or other health problems.)

Genetics determine in large measure who gets varicose veins. Women are most susceptible because the female hormone estrogen weakens and relaxes vein walls. Up to 25% of women and 15% of men have varicose veins. *Factors that can worsen the symptoms include…*

• **Menstrual cycle**—estrogen levels are highest midway between periods.

• **Pregnancy**—estrogen rises. Also, the growing fetus presses on a big abdominal vein, slowing blood flow out of the legs.

• **Hormone therapy or birth control pills** —estrogen is the culprit.

• **Hot weather**—heat causes blood vessels to dilate.

• **Prolonged standing**—gravity encourages blood to pool in legs.

• **Inactivity**—leg muscles don't contract enough to help pump blood onward and upward.

• **Being overweight**—this increases gravity's effects.

• **Leg injury**—veins may be damaged by any type of accident.

• **Aging**—older vein valves are more prone to malfunction.

SELF-HELP GUIDELINES

Varicose veins that do not cause discomfort or worrisome symptoms do not need to be treated—though as a general precaution, you should bring them to your doctor's attention at your next check-up. *To improve circulation and minimize symptoms…*

- **Exercise for at least 30 minutes daily.** Include a lower-body workout, such as cycling, swimming or walking.

- **Wear compression hose** (sold at drugstores and medical-supply stores). Avoid clothes that are tight at the knees, waist or groin.

- **Elevate legs above heart level for 15 minutes whenever they ache.**

- **When standing or sitting for long periods, tap your toes vigorously** every few minutes to work calf muscles. Take frequent breaks to walk around. Avoid crossing your legs—this position does not cause varicose veins, but it can aggravate symptoms.

TREATMENT OPTIONS

If you experience pain and swelling despite following the self-help guidelines, get medical treatment to close the affected veins. Afterward, your body automatically reroutes blood into healthy veins. Insurance usually covers treatment if self-help measures have failed to relieve symptoms. See a vein specialist—an interventional radiologist, vascular surgeon or dermatologist.

American College of Phlebology, 510-346-6800, *www.phlebology.org. Treatment options…*

- **Endovenous ablation.** For most patients whose varicose veins are moderate to severe, I recommend this new procedure performed with a laser or radio-frequency device. The doctor inserts a tiny tube into the vein, then heat energy from the device permanently seals the vein shut.

Cost: About $2,000 per leg. *The advantages include…*

- Success rate of about 95% with low risk for complications (such as a blood clot or excessive bleeding).

- Performed in the doctor's office in about 30 minutes for laser or 60 minutes for radio frequency.

- Requires only local anesthesia.

- Minimal discomfort, managed with nonprescription painkillers.

- Quick recovery—patients return to normal activities immediately and wear compression hose for one to two weeks.

- Good aesthetic results—bruising is minor and temporary, and veins disappear within a few weeks.

- **Sclerotherapy.** This office procedure works on small- to medium-sized varicose veins and requires no anesthesia. The doctor injects veins with a solution that causes scar tissue to form. This closes the vein, which then fades. Some veins must be injected more than once.

Cost: About $300 per leg per session.

On the horizon: Micro foam sclerotherapy. Currently undergoing FDA testing, Varisolve is a foam that is injected into varicose veins, causing them to collapse. Varisolve is a stronger sclerosant able to treat larger and more problematic veins.

Recommended: If your doctor suggests an older treatment called phlebectomy (vein stripping)—in which a long vein is removed through a series of small incisions—I suggest getting a second opinion. This in-hospital procedure involves more pain and a longer recovery time than today's advanced treatments.

More from Dr. Andrew Kwak…

Complications of Varicose Veins

Watch out for these uncommon but dangerous complications…

- **Skin sores.** The skin around a varicose vein may break down, becoming discolored and hard. Over time, an open sore (ulcer) may form and become infected. If you notice signs of skin breakdown or develop a skin ulcer, see a vein specialist without delay.

- **Blood clot.** A clot in a varicose vein (phlebitis) can make nearby skin hot and tender… create a lump…and cause sudden swelling of the leg. If an associated clot forms in a deep vein, it may break off and travel via the bloodstream to the lungs. Called a pulmonary embolism (PE), this can be fatal. If you suspect a clot in your leg, go to the emergency room. If you have symptoms of PE—chest pain, shortness of breath, light-headedness, bloody cough—call 911.

- **Bleeding.** Due to increased pressure, a varicose vein may bleed profusely from even a minor injury—for instance, if you bang your leg or cut yourself shaving. Immediately elevate the leg above heart level, cover the wound with a clean cloth and apply firm pressure. If bleeding does not stop within a few minutes, call 911—a hemorrhage can be life-threatening.

Why Folks Faint

The late Richard O'Brien, MD, former chair of the public relations committee for the American College of Emergency Physicians (*www.acep.org*) and attending emergency physician at Moses Taylor Hospital in Scranton, Pennsylvania.

Fainting usually results from a temporary reduction in blood flow to the brain, which deprives brain cells of oxygen and sugar. *Why it happens...*

•**Dehydration.** Too little fluid intake (or too much alcohol) can reduce blood volume. Drink eight cups of fluids daily.

•**Heart disease.** Clogged arteries or other cardiovascular problems can impair blood flow. If light-headedness is accompanied by signs of heart attack (pain in the chest, jaw or shoulder, nausea and/or shortness of breath), call 911.

•**Low blood sugar.** If you have diabetes, be sure to eat after taking your medication.

•**Medication.** If you use drugs to lower blood pressure or control heart rate, ask your doctor if you can take these at bedtime.

•**Menstruation.** Hormonal changes can also lead to fainting, but it usually is not cause for concern. However, fainting along with fever and vomiting can signal toxic shock syndrome—a life-threatening condition linked to tampon use—which requires emergency care.

•**Pregnancy.** The uterus can press on a major vein. Lie on your left side to shift the uterus and restore blood flow.

•**Standing up too quickly.** When rising from bed, sit up first, then point and flex your feet a few times to boost blood flow.

•**Stress.** Heart rate can drop quickly, abruptly lowering blood pressure.

If you feel faint: Lie down—or if that's not possible, sit with your head between your knees. To increase blood flow, cross your ankles, and then tense abdominal and thigh muscles.

Surprising Dangers of Gum Disease

Tom McGuire, DDS, leading authority on dental wellness. Dr. McGuire is president of the Dental Wellness Institute, founder of the International Association of Mercury Free Dentists (IAMFD), and author of *Mercury Detoxification: The Natural Way to Remove Mercury from Your Body* (The Dental Wellness Institute) *www.dentalwellness4u.com.*

Alan A. Winter, DDS, periodontist in private practice and associate clinical professor of implant dentistry at the New York University College of Dentistry, both in New York City. Dr. Winter has published several medical journal articles on gum disease.

American Dental Association, *www.ada.org.*

There's an old saying that "the eyes are the window to the soul." Based on all the news we've been reading lately, we'd like to rewrite the phrase: "the gums are the window to your health" (though it's hardly as poetic). Research is growing that shows that symptoms of periodontal disease such as inflamed or bleeding gums—and sometimes even loose teeth—raise the risk of serious health problems elsewhere in the body, including heart disease, stroke, diabetes and more.

To learn more about the connection between oral health and overall health, and to obtain advice on how to prevent or reverse periodontal disease, we consulted dental experts Alan A. Winter, DDS, and Tom McGuire, DDS.

INFLAMED GUMS = INFLAMED BODY

We asked our experts how periodontal disease leads to disease elsewhere in the body. As with many systemic problems, an inflammatory response is the underlying cause, explains Dr. Winter. In people with serious gum disease, bacteria and their irritating toxins enter into the bloodstream eliciting a systemic inflammatory response. The condition will do even more damage once the tissue that supports the tooth breaks down and the infection begins to destroy the bone. It is much less dangerous with minor gum infection/inflammation.

Many health problems, such as heart disease, are related to advanced gum disease. Inflammation triggers the liver to make C-reactive protein (CRP), which is considered a "marker" of inflammatory activity. According to Dr. McGuire, elevated CRP levels are associated with an increased risk of more serious health problems such as heart attack and stroke. Periodontal disease is also associated with an increased risk for diabetes, low birth weight and pre-term births and respiratory ailments. Evidence also links pancreatic cancer with periodontal disease. In addition, when your body has to work extra hard to fight infection and inflammation, it puts significant and undue stress on your immune system 24/7, and this constant stress can dramatically lower your resistance to other diseases.

THE COST OF IGNORING THE PROBLEM

With gum disease, it's not unusual for people to allow the infection and inflammation to go on for weeks, months or years, notes Dr. McGuire. He's surprised that people are willing to tolerate this state of affairs in their mouth, when they'd aggressively fight an equivalent infection that was eroding the soft tissue, bones and ligaments in an arm or leg. According to Dr. McGuire, a big part of this is fear—approximately 30% of the population has fear or anxiety significant enough that they avoid going to the dentist until symptoms have progressed far along and caused disease. Cost is an impediment thanks to the lack of dental insurance for many people…and cost and fear can overlap. The third major factor, he says, is that far too many people aren't aware of the serious effect on their health from gum disease.

Signs of periodontal disease are frequently ignored. This puts not just your teeth but also your overall health at risk…the body functions as an integrated system, and infection in one place leads to problems in another—and there is perhaps no more direct route than through the mouth.

How does treating periodontal disease help to prevent disease elsewhere in the body? *According to Dr. Winter, if you extrapolate current findings, here is what may be gained by improved oral care…*

- **Fewer heart attacks.**
- **Fewer strokes.**
- **Better control of type I and type II diabetes.**
- **Less respiratory disease.**
- **Lower risk of pancreatic cancer.**
- **Reduced rate of premature births.**
- **Reduced rate of underweight newborns.**

Prevention and treatment not only improve quality of life and life expectancy, they also save time and money, observes Dr. McGuire. More than 164 million work hours and 51 million school hours are lost each year due to dental disease or dental visits, according to the U.S. Department of Health and Human Services. One study, "The Effect of Periodontal Disease on Health Care Costs," showed that health care costs for people with moderate to severe gum disease were 21% higher than for those with no gum disease.

TROUBLE IS BREWING

How do you know if your gums are in trouble? Healthy gums are firm and pink. You know trouble is brewing when they grow red, tender, swollen and are prone to bleed when you brush. Even bad breath can be an early symptom. This can be early-stage gum disease, or gingivitis, and you should bring these symptoms to the attention of your dentist.

Though your personal health history (including heredity) may also be a factor, gum disease often develops due to poor oral hygiene, when a lack of brushing and flossing causes a sticky layer of bacteria or plaque to coat the teeth, and inflammation to develop along the gum lines. Certain medications, such as Dilantin for epilepsy, as well as smoking and chewing tobacco, definitely exacerbate gum disease. Left uncared for, the plaque hardens to become tartar or calculus, building up over time. If the plaque and calculus further irritate the gums and lead to nasty pockets of infection, you have a serious problem—periodontal disease, characterized by infection and inflammation that now is destroying bone and supporting tissue.

216

SOMETHING TO SMILE ABOUT

The good news is that early periodontal disease can be treated and usually reversed. Once the infection has been cleared up you can prevent any further gum disease with diligent home care and regular dental check-ups.

Andrew L. Rubman, ND, says gum hygiene should include antiseptic oral rinses such as Listerine, which is formulated to target oral bacteria. This can help prevent the plaque from further damaging the gums and leading to those pockets of infection. In many cases it is actually chronic oral yeast infection that predisposes the gum tissue to become secondarily colonized by bacteria which can produce both plaque deposits and dissolve enamel, says Dr. Rubman. He adds that Listerine and other oral rinses also effectively treat yeast and other micro-organisms.

To find out if you're facing potential problems, ask your dentist whether you have any periodontal pockets and how deep they are, advises Dr. Winter. One to three millimeters is considered normal. Once pockets reach a depth of four millimeters, you have a problem that must be attended to. Other factors your dentist may take into consideration are bleeding, loose teeth and bone loss. People with implants must be very diligent about their oral hygiene as poor oral hygiene is a leading cause of failed implants.

In Dr. Winter's opinion, in addition to twice-yearly visits to your regular dentist, your best bet is to see a periodontist for periodic exams. If you have no signs of periodontal problems, good for you—but make sure to have another check-up in five to 10 years. The severity of the disease determines the course of treatment, which may range from a thorough cleaning all the way to gum surgery. In Dr. McGuire's view, a dentist and hygienist can take care of most gum disease, although he refers patients with advanced gum disease to a periodontist (especially when surgery is required). "I also recommend a check-up at least once per year to look for symptoms of other diseases that can show up in the mouth, particularly oral cancer," says Dr. McGuire.

AS MOM ALWAYS SAID...

Regardless of whether you already have gum disease or are just doing your best to prevent it, good oral hygiene is a must. *For healthy teeth and gums, Dr. McGuire recommends...*

• **Brush.** Use a soft-bristle brush to clean teeth and gums in the morning, after eating, and before you go to bed. Replace the brush every three to four months, and soak it in an antibacterial rinse like Listerine overnight after you've been sick with a cold or flu. The brand of toothbrush does not really matter, according to Dr. McGuire. Check with your hygienist, regardless of what type of toothbrush you use, and ask her if you are getting the job done.

• **Floss.** Do this at least once a day, and always brush first.

• **Use mouthwash.** When you have gum disease, you should use an antimicrobial mouthwash, such as Listerine, after every brushing and flossing session. Once the infection has been eliminated, you can switch to a more natural product (anything you find in a health-food store that contains natural ingredients). You can also use a warm salt water rinse.

• **Consider a water irrigator.** These are especially effective at reaching between teeth to remove food. For people with severe disease, this is a must, along with brushing and flossing.

• **Stay away from sugar, refined and processed foods as much as possible.** When you allow yourself the occasional indulgence, be sure to brush, floss or at least rinse well afterward.

• **See your dentist for an exam and cleaning every six months.**

• **Avoid smoking.** It irritates gum tissue, stresses the immune system and lowers the body's resistance to infection of any kind.

Three Ways to Get Rid of Liver Spots

A cleanse will not be helpful for "liver spots"—which have nothing to do with your liver. This is a confusing term that refers to the flat, dark spots that sometimes show up on sun-exposed parts of the body—the hands, lower arms, shoulders and face. They also are called age spots, because they become more common after age 40, as you accumulate more sun damage and your skin is less able to heal. The spots are painless and harmless...and, most important, noncancerous. If they bother you for cosmetic reasons, you can reduce their appearance with bleaching, cryotherapy (freezing) or laser therapy. Consult a dermatologist for a diagnosis and a treatment plan. To prevent additional spots, do the same things you would normally do to prevent sunburn—wear sunscreen, a broad-rimmed hat and light-colored clothing with a tight weave.

Mark A. Stengler, NMD, licensed naturopathic medical doctor in private practice, Encinitas, California...adjunct associate clinical professor at the National College of Natural Medicine, Portland, Oregon...author of *The Natural Physician's Healing Therapies* and coauthor of *Prescription for Natural Cures* (both from Bottom Line Books).

Quiet the Ringing in Your Ears

Aaron G. Benson, MD, clinical adjunct professor, division of otology/neurotology (ear health), department of otolaryngology–head and neck surgery, at the University of Michigan Health System in Ann Arbor. Also in private practice in Maumee, Ohio, he specializes in hearing disorders.

Perhaps you hear a high-pitched ringing ...perhaps a buzzing, chirping, whistling or whirring. Nobody else can hear it—but the quieter it gets around you, the worse the noise in your head. This bothersome condition, *tinnitus*, afflicts an estimated 10% to 16% of Americans.

Tinnitus most often develops when a person has hearing loss caused by nerve damage from prolonged or extreme exposure to loud noise. It also can be a side effect of antibiotics, aspirin, diuretics and some cancer drugs. Tinnitus usually appears after age 50 but is increasingly common in younger people due to high-volume use of personal music players

(iPod). It can occur during pregnancy due to increased blood volume—and may or may not go away after delivery.

Tinnitus usually is not a serious health problem, but it should be evaluated—so consult an otolaryngologist.

American Tinnitus Association, (800-634-8978, *www.ata.org*). *There is no cure, but various strategies can ease symptoms and help you cope...*

•**Cut caffeine and salt.** Caffeine (in coffee, tea, cola and chocolate) constricts blood flow to the ear...and salt can raise blood pressure, aggravating tinnitus.

•**Keep ears clean.** Excessive earwax can muffle outside noises and amplify internal ringing.

Home remedy: Mix hydrogen peroxide with an equal amount of water, and place two drops in each ear weekly. Or see your doctor to have your ears irrigated.

•**Reduce stress.** Muscle relaxation, meditation, biofeedback, exercise and other stress-reducing techniques may alleviate symptoms.

•**Fill the room with white noise.** A constant low-level background sound masks the inner ringing. In a quiet room and at bedtime, turn on a fan or tabletop fountain, or use a white-noise machine (about $30 to $60 at home-products stores).

•**Wear a tinnitus masker.** This miniature white-noise device resembles a hearing aid and fits behind or in the ear.

Cost: About $2,000. To obtain one, ask your doctor for a referral to an audiologist.

•**Try a hearing aid.** This eases tinnitus for about half of people with significant hearing loss. It amplifies outside sounds, which obscures inner sounds.

•**Retrain your brain.** A new treatment provided by trained audiologists, tinnitus retraining therapy (TRT) may help up to 80% of patients. Sometimes improvement is noticed after just a few sessions. Typically, you attend weekly or monthly hour-long sessions during which you wear a special hearing aid programmed with a facsimile of your particular tinnitus sound. You are shown how to train your brain to be less sensitive to the ringing.

Rarely, tinnitus may be caused by a tumor. Call your doctor without delay if your tinnitus sounds like a pulsing or whooshing…is heard on only one side of your head…or is accompanied by dizziness or a sudden decrease in ability to discriminate between similar words, such as cat and hat.

How to Get Rid of Excessive Earwax

Mark A. Stengler, NMD, licensed naturopathic medical doctor in private practice, Encinitas, California…adjunct associate clinical professor at the National College of Natural Medicine, Portland, Oregon…author of *The Natural Physician's Healing Therapies* and coauthor of *Prescription for Natural Cures* (both from Bottom Line Books).

Earwax eliminates dirt and dead skin from the ear canal. An overabundance of earwax usually is an indication of a chronic sensitivity—either to a food or to something in the environment. Effects from common environmental causes, such as mold, dust and pollen, can be reduced by taking fish oil (1,000 mg daily of combined EPA and DHA), vitamin C (2,000 mg to 3,000 mg) and quercetin (500 mg twice daily). These supplements reduce the response of *histamine*, a chemical produced in the body that triggers allergy symptoms, including the production of earwax.

Common food sensitivities that often contribute to excessive earwax include cow's milk, wheat, soy and sugar. You can try an elimination diet—by avoiding one or more of these foods for two to three weeks—and see if the earwax production lessens.

If these supplements don't help, you should make an appointment with a holistic physician. To find one in your area, contact the American College for Advancement in Medicine (800-532-3688, *www.acam.org*).

Help for a Yucky Tongue

Black hairy tongue is an overgrowth of the tongue's normal bumps (*papillae*), making them look similar to hair. It is a harmless but embarrassing problem. The papillae can grow five to six millimeters high.

Causes: A diet of primarily soft foods, poor oral hygiene and taking antibiotics, which can disrupt the mouth's healthful bacteria. Drinking coffee and tea as well as smoking can aggravate the condition.

To get your tongue back to normal: Scrub your tongue with a toothbrush or tongue scraper twice a day, and continue to brush your tongue even when the problem goes away. Eat healthful foods, such as raw vegetables and whole-grain cereal.

Also helpful: The acid contained in fresh pineapples.

Selene Yeager, health journalist, Emmaus, Pennsylvania, and coauthor of more than two dozen health books, including *The Doctor's Book of Food Remedies* (Rodale).

Why Your Nose Runs

This kind of discharge can be caused by several conditions. If the fluid is coming from both nasal passages, you may have allergic or non-allergic *rhinitis*, a condition in which blood vessels in the nose expand, causing swelling of the lining of the nose.

As a result, the glands in the mucous membrane become overactive, producing a watery discharge. Allergic rhinitis can be caused by environmental irritants (such as pollen and dust). Nonallergic rhinitis can be triggered by many things, including outdoor temperature changes, as well as foods and beverages, especially spicy foods and alcohol.

If the discharge is dripping from only one nostril, the substance could contain cerebrospinal fluid, which cushions the brain.

Leakage of cerebrospinal fluid through the nose can occur for no apparent reason or as a result of an opening from the nose to the brain that can develop following skull or sinus surgery.

Consult an otolaryngologist (ear, nose and throat doctor) for a diagnosis.

Murray Grossan, MD, otolaryngologist, Tower Ear, Nose and Throat Clinic, Beverly Hills, California.

What Body Odor Says About Your Health

Jamison Starbuck, ND, naturopathic physician in Missoula, Montana. She is past president of the American Association of Naturopathic Physicians and a contributing editor to The Alternative Advisor: The Complete Guide to Natural Therapies and Alternative Treatments *(Time-Life).*

As a physician, I pay attention to many details about my patients, including body odor. If I detect anything other than a mild, almost neutral scent, my medical curiosity is piqued. Body odor tells me about a patient's health status, dietary habits and hygiene. People with liver disease may have a musty odor…infections anywhere on the body usually emit a foul smell…uncontrolled diabetes often creates a smell best labeled as sweet fermentation. People who are on high-protein diets or who eat a lot of fatty and/or fried foods, onions, garlic or curry, or drink coffee or alcohol excessively, also have particular body odors. Poor hygiene leads to its own recognizable scent.

If you're worried about your body odor, ask a trusted friend or a family member to perform a sniff test.

What to do: Ask the person to stand within one inch of you and inhale. If the body odor is new, quite strong or confined to a specific part of your body—for example, your mouth, ears or genitals—see your doctor for an exam and evaluation. *If body odor is a familiar, long-standing problem that's not related to an illness, try the following suggestions for 10 days (if they help, continue as needed)…*

•**Eat right.** Fresh, whole foods give your body a fresh, wholesome scent. Eat a salad daily made with dark, leafy lettuce, sprouts, raw veggies and two tablespoons of olive oil. Avoid mayonnaise and cheese-based dressings, which contain odor-producing fat. Choose brown rice or a baked potato instead of fried potatoes. Reduce protein putrification in the digestive tract by eliminating meat—or consuming no more than three ounces of red meat or poultry per day. Drink one-half ounce of water for every pound of your body weight daily.

•**Take three saunas.** Saunas make you perspire, which has a detoxifying effect that reduces body odor.

What to do: Brush your dry skin with a loofah or other skin brush. Enter the sauna and stay there until you perspire all over your body, then leave the sauna and rinse with cold water for 30 seconds. Brush your skin again and return to the sauna. End with a brisk 30-second skin brush, then wrap up in soft, warm clothing. Repeat this process two more times over the next several days.

Caution: People with high blood pressure or heart disease should avoid saunas.

•**Use chlorophyll.** This chemical compound, which is responsible for the green pigment in plants, has astringent properties and can help control the type of body odor that comes from the fermentation of food in the digestive tract. Add one tablespoon of chlorophyll (available at health-food stores) to four ounces of water and drink it at the end of each meal. If you prefer, you can eat one-eighth cup of fresh parsley daily as a substitute for liquid chlorophyll.

•**Eliminate oral bacteria.** In addition to brushing your teeth at least twice daily and flossing at least once a day, gargle each morning with a cup of warm chamomile tea mixed with one teaspoon of hydrogen peroxide. This mixture will kill bacteria living in the throat and mouth, a common cause of bad breath. After the 10-day period, gargle with the chamomile/peroxide mixture as needed for sore throats.

Save Your Money! Cellulite Creams Don't Work

C linical experiments have found that anti-cellulite formulations are no more successful than placebos at reducing cellulite, the fatty dimples that make skin on the hips and thighs appear lumpy. The only treatment that has been proven to temporarily reduce cellulite is *endermologie*—a somewhat painful process in which a suction device squeezes and kneads the affected skin between two rollers. A course of 15 to 20 treatments over several months produces a temporary visible reduction in cellulite. Monthly sessions are required to maintain results. Each treatment costs $50 to $70. Some physicians are testing a procedure called *thermage*, which attempts to eliminate cellulite by the application of heat.

Barney J. Kenet, MD, dermatologic surgeon, New York–Presbyterian Hospital/Cornell Medical Center, New York City.

Buying a Better Sports Bra

Joanna Scurr, PhD, principal lecturer, sport and exercise science, and division leader, biomechanics, University of Portsmouth, United Kingdom. She specializes in breast biomechanics research.

B reasts that bounce during workouts are uncomfortable and embarrassing. Worse, over time the uncontrolled movement causes structural damage, my research shows, stretching ligaments and other connective tissues and making breasts increasingly droopy.

Surprising: This problem affects women of all cup sizes, from A to DD to J and beyond. *What you need to know...*

•**Breasts don't just bounce up and down** —they also move side-to-side and in-and-out (toward and away from the chest wall), almost in a figure-eight pattern. Each breast moves independently from the other.

•**The typical sports bra gives limited support.** To many women, a sports bra is a compression bra—a cupless style that flattens breasts against the chest wall. This reduces up-and-down movement but is less effective at limiting side-to-side and in-and-out movements.

•**Encapsulation sports bras work better.** This style has two separate, molded cups, like an everyday bra. It provides the independent support each breast needs, as well as more all-around support.

How to choose and use a sports bra...

•**Select a style with an adjustable band and straps.** Pull-on styles lack hooks that adjust for band size, so they are unlikely to fit well enough to offer optimal support. For the same reason, opt for adjustable straps. Also, avoid stretchy straps—they have too much give.

•**Check the fit every time you buy.** Breast shape and size change over time, especially after breast-feeding, menopause or weight loss or gain...and sizing differs among manufacturers.

Good fit: The center of the bra lies flat against your sternum...the band doesn't ride up in back...breasts do not overflow the cups.

•**Make sure movement is minimal.** In the dressing room, do some jumping jacks, run in place, bend forward and sideways. If you experience any discomfort, choose a different bra until you find the right one.

•**Wear a supportive bra during all workouts**—not just the most vigorous ones. Breasts move as much during a slow jog as they do during a sprint.

•**Treat bras tenderly.** Wash them by hand and drip-dry. Never put them in the dryer—heat ruins elasticity.

•**Replace a bra as soon as it starts to wear out**—when it no longer provides enough support to prevent discomfort during exercise.

Good brands: Asics, Champion, Nike.

For full-figured women: A Big Attitude, Junonia.

Most Women Have Different-Sized Breasts

The difference, which generally is extremely small, can be due to being born with more breast tissue on one side than the other. Pregnancy, breastfeeding, weight changes and using one side of the body more than the other can make the size difference more noticeable.

Ricki Pollycove, MD, director of education, Breast Health Center, California Pacific Medical Center, San Francisco.

Sagging Breasts Are Not Caused by Nursing

Breast-feeding does not permanently affect the appearance of a woman's breasts.

What can make breasts sag: Aging, smoking, large breast size, pregnancies, significant weight fluctuations and going braless.

Brian Rinker, MD, associate professor of plastic surgery, University of Kentucky, Lexington, and leader of a study of 132 people, reported at a conference of the American Society of Plastic Surgeons.

Plantar Warts

To get rid of plantar warts, first, try an over-the-counter topical *salicylic acid* product (such as Compound W)...or moleskin, an air- and watertight adhesive-backed skin covering. If you have diabetes or poor circulation to the feet, use these products only under a doctor's supervision. If neither of these products work within a few weeks, your podiatrist or dermatologist can apply a stronger acid to the warty tissue weekly. Topical treatments are also best for *mosaic* plantar warts, which grow in tight clusters, since the medications can seep down into the warts' extensions.

Harvey Lemont, DPM, director of the Laboratory of Podiatric Pathology, CBL Path, Inc., and professor emeritus, Temple University School of Podiatric Medicine, both in Philadelphia.

Bleach Baths Ease Eczema

Twice weekly, eczema patients soaked for five to 10 minutes in a tub of water mixed with very diluted bleach. After three months, 67% showed improvement, compared with 15% of patients who bathed in plain water.

Theory: Bleach kills the staph bacteria that often accompany eczema and cause painful lesions.

Safety: Use no more than one-half cup of bleach per 40 gallons of water...do not let bleach bathwater enter the eyes or mouth... never apply undiluted bleach to skin.

Amy Paller, MD, chair, dermatology department, Northwestern University Feinberg School of Medicine, Chicago, and leader of a study of 31 eczema patients.

8

Emotions, Sleep & Stress

Easy Ways to Meditate to Relieve Stress

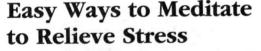We have heard all about the benefits of meditating. For decades, studies have shown that meditation helps with depression, anxiety, stress, insomnia, pain, high blood pressure, self-esteem, self-control, concentration and creativity. Yet for many people, meditation seems daunting. Maybe you find it hard to sit still…to clear your mind…to make the time…or to stick with it long enough to experience the effects.

Key to success: Choose a technique that suits your personality, schedule and level of experience, then do it consistently. Twenty minutes or more daily is a good goal, but even five minutes is helpful if you do it every day—and some techniques take almost no time at all.

IF YOU ARE A BEGINNER…

The methods below are effective yet simple enough for a novice. Start with just a few minutes, and work your way up.

• **Single-tasking.** A time-crunched society encourages multitasking—so you sort mail while on the phone and listen to audiobooks while driving.

What you may not know: The simple act of focusing fully on a single task is a meditative exercise. It improves your powers of concentration, alleviates stress and boosts mood by enhancing your appreciation of the here-and-now.

Try: Once or twice each day, give your complete attention to just one activity.

Roger N. Walsh, MD, PhD, professor of psychiatry and human behavior in the School of Medicine, and of anthropology and philosophy in the School of Humanities, both at the University of California, Irvine. He is author of *Essential Spirituality: The 7 Central Practices to Awaken Heart and Mind* (Wiley), which contains a foreword by the Dalai Lama.

Example: When you fold the laundry, don't turn on the TV—just enjoy the softness of the fabrics and the soothing rhythm of your hand motions.

•**Focused breathing.** Sit in a quiet place, on the floor or in a chair, keeping your back straight so your lungs can expand. Pay attention to your breathing.

Feel the air moving through your nostrils as you slowly inhale and exhale...feel your abdomen rise and fall. Then choose either of these sites (nostrils or abdomen) and focus fully on the sensations there.

Soon you may notice that your mind has wandered. Don't berate yourself or become discouraged and give up—this happens even to experienced meditators. Simply return your attention to the breath.

•**Centering prayer.** Choose a phrase or a word that is spiritually meaningful for you, such as *God is love* or *shalom*. With each breath, repeat it silently to yourself. Again, if your thoughts start to stray, just calmly return to your prayer.

IF YOU HATE TO SIT STILL

Some people can't stop squirming when they try to meditate.

Solution: Moving meditation.

•**Qigong, tai chi or yoga.** These practices combine specific movements with a contemplative focus on the body, so you exercise while you meditate. Many health clubs, adult-education centers and hospitals offer classes in these techniques.

Referrals: National Qigong Association (888-815-1893, *www.nqa.org*)...American Tai Chi and Qigong Association, *www.american taichi.net*...Yoga Alliance (888-921-9642, *www. yogaalliance.org*).

•**Mindful eating.** Eat a meal alone, in silence, savoring the experience. When you first sit down, spend a moment enjoying the colors and aromas of the food. Take a bite and chew slowly. How do the taste and texture change as you chew? What sensations do you perceive as you swallow?

Surprise: You are meditating. Continue to eat each bite as consciously as you can, never rushing.

IF YOU CAN'T FIND THE TIME

Some days you may not have even five minutes to meditate—but you can take just a moment.

•**Three breaths.** Whenever you feel tense, take three long, deep breaths. Even a few conscious inhalations and exhalations will calm you. Also use cues in your environment as regular reminders to focus and breathe deeply.

Example: Take three slow breaths every time you hang up the phone...walk through a doorway...or get into your car.

•**Beauty in the moment.** Three times a day, look around you and notice something lovely—the scent of someone's perfume, the happy sound of children playing. Explore the experience with your full attention.

Example: A light breeze is blowing. Watch the graceful way it makes the grass sway...listen to it whisper as it moves through the trees...feel its gentle touch on your cheeks. Notice your emotions of pleasure and appreciation—and carry them with you as you continue through your day.

More from Dr. Roger Walsh...

If You Already Love to Meditate...

If you are an accomplished meditator and want to enrich your experience, try these more advanced techniques...

•**Contemplative reading.** Select a brief passage—two or three sentences—from a philosophy book, religious text or other writing that is meaningful to you. Read it slowly and reflectively, over and over. If your reading brings up insights, ponder them. If your mind drifts to unrelated thoughts, return to reading.

•**Inquiry.** Sit and focus on your breathing. When a thought, feeling, sound or other sensation enters your awareness, instead of turning your attention back to the breath, explore the experience. Does it seem to have a shape or image associated with it? Does it change or fade away as you examine it? *Examples...*

•You notice a tickle in your shoulder. As you study it, you note that it feels diffuse...then localizes in one spot...then moves to a different area and prickles...then disappears.

• You are feeling anxious. Rather than trying to figure out what is causing this, note where the anxiety manifests in your body (a fluttery stomach, a tight muscle)...any images and thoughts associated with it...and how those images and thoughts change as you observe them.

When a particular sensation passes, return your attention to your breath until the next sensation enters your awareness...then explore this new one. Over time, this enhances awareness and acceptance.

Boost Your Mood Without Drugs

Mark A. Stengler, NMD, licensed naturopathic medical doctor in private practice, Encinitas, California...adjunct associate clinical professor at the National College of Natural Medicine, Portland, Oregon...author of *The Natural Physician's Healing Therapies* and coauthor of *Prescription for Natural Cures* (both from Bottom Line Books).
National Institute of Mental Health.

Feeling down? You're not alone. We all have gloomy moments. But if you're chronically feeling sad, apathetic, irritable or "emotionally numb," you could be suffering from chronic depression. It affects one in four women and one in eight men at some time in their lives. (For symptoms, see "Are You Depressed?" on page 227.)

Sadness is perfectly normal if you recently experienced a traumatic event, such as a loved one's death, a divorce or a job loss. Anyone who is going through such a situation should talk about it with family members, friends or a counselor. Some people come to terms with these feelings in just a few weeks. Others require months or even years. Just remember, though, that suppressed grief or anger is a common cause of depression.

If you're feeling particularly down—and everything in your life is basically fine—you could be suffering from depression that has a biochemical basis linked to genetics. If a parent or sibling has experienced depression, your risk increases by two to four times. In these cases, conventional doctors often recommend prescription antidepressants. But all antidepressants have side effects, including fatigue, weight gain, low libido, liver toxicity and/or dizziness.*

WHAT'S BRINGING YOU DOWN?

The study of brain chemistry has led to advances in the treatment of depression. We are learning more about how chemicals that are produced in the body—and even certain foods—affect our moods.

Here's why: You have trillions of nerve cells (neurons) in your nervous system. Signals pass among these cells via chemical messengers known as neurotransmitters. When neurotransmitters aren't working properly, your mood, memory and comprehension suffer.

The antidepressants that conventional doctors prescribe aim to restore balance to one or more neurotransmitters artificially. These drugs may improve symptoms of depression, but the trade-off is the risk of side effects.

The natural approach I recommend—focusing on foods and supplements—is a safe, effective way to boost the activity of the neurotransmitters that are key players in mood adjustment...

• **Serotonin,** the "feel-good neurotransmitter," is made by the body from the amino acid tryptophan, which is found in foods such as turkey and milk. If your serotonin levels are adequate, you will feel calm, sociable and relaxed much of the time. If you have depression or anxiety, your serotonin levels may be too low.

• **Norepinephrine** is produced when you're under stress, along with the hormone *adrenaline*. A low level of norepinephrine is believed to lead to depression. This neurotransmitter, also known as *noradrenaline*, is made from the amino acid *tyrosine*, which is found in dairy products, meat, fish, wheat and oats.

• **Dopamine** affects motor control (movement of body parts), motivation and your response to reward, such as winning a game or seeing a stock you own go way up. Like norepinephrine, dopamine is made from tyrosine.

*Warning: If you currently are taking an antidepressant, do not discontinue use without supervision from a doctor. If you have suicidal thoughts, seek immediate medical attention.

•**Gamma-aminobutyric acid** (GABA) has a calming effect on the brain and nervous system. A GABA deficiency is commonly associated with anxiety. This neurotransmitter is made from the amino acids *taurine* (found in meat and fish) and *glutamine* (also found in meat and fish as well as in beans and dairy products).

GET A LIFT FROM OMEGA-3s

Neurotransmitters need nutrients to function properly. One whole class of nutrients required for normal mood and alertness is omega-3 fatty acids—particularly *eicosapentaenoic acid* (EPA) and *docosahexaenoic acid* (DHA), which are found in fish and fish oil and in omega-3–fortified products, such as some eggs. Studies show that people who have low omega-3 levels are more likely to suffer from depression. This is particularly true among older adults. Studies have confirmed that depression is less prevalent in countries where the population eats a lot of fish.

Regardless of whether you're taking an anti-depressant or a supplement for depression, it's a good idea to eat at least two servings a week of omega-3–rich fish, such as salmon, sardines and trout. In addition, taking fish-oil supplements can be helpful for those prone to depression. Take a product that provides a daily dose of 1,000 mg of combined EPA and DHA. Fish-oil supplements are widely available at health-food stores.

Good brands: Nordic Naturals (800-662-2544, *www.nordicnaturals.com*) and Carlson Laboratories (888-234-5656, *www.carlsonlabs.com*).

CHECK YOUR AMINO ACIDS

Amino acids also are key to a nutrition-based approach to depression. There are 10 amino acids that are absolutely essential but that our bodies can't produce. These amino acids are found in the proteins that we eat and are converted into the neurotransmitters that affect mood. If your diet lacks protein—found in eggs, poultry, meat and fish, and, in smaller amounts, in plant foods such as soy, lentils and peanuts—these essential amino acids may be in short supply.

If you suffer from depression, get a blood or urine test that measures your amino acid levels. Tests are available through a holistic or medical doctor's office. Genova Diagnostics (800-522-4762, *www.gdx.net*) is one of several labs that offer this testing through doctors' offices. The test costs about $405 and may be covered by insurance. If an amino acid deficiency is detected, you and your doctor can decide how to correct it. Amino Acid Complex 1000 by KAL is a reliable supplement and can be found at most health-food stores.

DON'T FORGET YOUR Bs

Researchers have learned that we need plenty of B vitamins to help activate mood-regulating neurotransmitters. If you have low levels of B-12 or folic acid—two important B vitamins—you're more likely to be depressed. Deficiencies of vitamins B-1 and B-6 can affect mood as well. B-vitamin deficiencies are especially common among people in their 60s or older. Try to eat foods that are rich in B vitamins, such as whole grains and green, leafy vegetables.

Ask your doctor for a vitamin B-12 and folate blood test if you're a woman who uses oral contraceptives, you frequently consume coffee and/or alcohol or you're under extreme stress. People over age 60 should be tested annually. I advise anyone who has a B-vitamin deficiency to take a 50-mg B-complex vitamin once daily and a full-spectrum multivitamin that includes B vitamins and other important ingredients, such as selenium, inositol, iron and vitamin D. Deficiencies of these nutrients also have been linked to depression.

MOOD-LIFTING SUPPLEMENTS

The following supplements are most effective for treating depression. Start with *5-hydroxytryptophan* (5-HTP). If you don't feel better within a month, add *S-adenosylmethionine* (SAMe) and/or St. John's wort.

•**5-HTP** is made by the body from the amino acid *L-tryptophan* and converted into *serotonin*. The supplement form of 5-HTP—available at health-food stores—is naturally derived from the seeds of the West African plant *Griffonia simplicifolia*. I recommend taking 100 mg two to three times daily on an empty stomach.

Caution: Don't take 5-HTP if you're on an antidepressant, antianxiety or other psychiatric medication. Nursing and pregnant women also should avoid it.

•**SAMe,** a substance that occurs naturally in the body, helps neurotransmitters form efficiently. Studies have shown that it is as effective at reducing depression as prescription antidepressants and produces fewer side effects. In studies, people with depression have taken up to 1,600 mg of SAMe daily, but I have found that most patients benefit from 600 mg to 800 mg taken daily in two divided doses a half-hour before meals. For best results, also take a 50-mg B-complex supplement once daily. SAMe is not recommended if you have manic depression, a disorder characterized by cycles of severe highs (manias) and lows (depression)…if you're on a prescription antidepressant or psychiatric medication…or if you're a woman who is pregnant or nursing.

•**St. John's wort** is an herb that helps treat anxiety and mild-to-moderate depression. Various constituents of St. John's wort flowers and leaves have been shown to stabilize a variety of neurotransmitters, including serotonin, dopamine and norepinephrine. A study reported in the medical journal *International Clinical Psychopharmacology* found that St. John's wort given for six weeks was as effective as the prescription antidepressant *fluoxetine* (Prozac) in treating depression and caused fewer side effects. I recommend 300 mg daily of an extract containing the active ingredients *hypericin* (0.3%) and *hyperforin* (3% to 5%). Such formulations are available at health-food stores. Side effects are rare, though some people experience mild digestive upset, fatigue, sleep disturbances, itching and skin rash.

Caution: St. John's wort can interact with antidepressants and other psychiatric drugs, so seek a doctor's advice if you are taking any of these medications and want to try this herb.

GET MOVING

Exercise is another underrated treatment and prevention strategy for depression. Researchers at Duke University Medical Center found that patients with clinical depression who exercised regularly were less likely to have a relapse than those who underwent drug therapy only.

Exercise balances stress hormones, activates feel-good brain chemicals known as *endorphins* and improves blood flow to the brain. I recommend 30 to 60 minutes of exercise three times weekly.

STAY CONNECTED

Work with a licensed professional who has experience treating depression to explore possible situations or conditions that trigger your depression.

Avoid isolating yourself—this worsens depression. Research shows that people who maintain strong ties to family members and/or friends are less susceptible to depression.

For some people, proper nutrition and taking supplements don't successfully treat depression. If your symptoms don't improve with the natural therapy I have recommended above, work with your doctor to investigate other possible causes, such as hormone deficiencies, food sensitivities, hypoglycemia (low blood sugar), lack of sunlight (which leads to vitamin D deficiency and seasonal affective disorder, also known as SAD), toxic metals (such as mercury), sleep problems and candidiasis (overgrowth of *Candida albicans* yeast).

Some drugs can lead to depression. Common culprits are steroids, antihistamines, medications for high blood pressure, anti-inflammatory drugs, narcotics and—believe it or not—antidepressants, such as fluoxetine.

ARE YOU DEPRESSED?

If you have experienced two or more of the following symptoms for two consecutive weeks, you could be suffering from depression…*

•**Persistent sadness,** anxiety or "empty" mood.

•**Feelings of hopelessness,** pessimism, guilt or worthlessness.

•**Loss of interest in activities that you once enjoyed,** including sex.

•**Restlessness,** irritability or fatigue.

*If these symptoms interfere with your ability to function, you may be suffering from clinical depression. A less severe type of chronic depression is dysthymia, which can cause the same symptoms over a period of years but is less disabling.

• **Difficulty concentrating,** remembering or making decisions.

• **Insomnia,** early-morning awakening or oversleeping.

• **Loss of appetite and weight loss.**

• **Overeating and weight gain.**

• **Physical symptoms that don't respond to treatment,** such as headaches, digestive disorders and chronic pain.

• **Thoughts of death or suicide** or suicide attempts.

Foods That Lift Your Spirits...and Help You Lose Weight

Susan Kleiner, PhD, RD, a Mercer Island, Washington–based nutritionist who has worked with Olympic athletes, professional sports teams and Fortune 500 company executives. She is author of *The Good Mood Diet: Feel Great While You Lose Weight* (Springboard) and *Power Eating* (Human Kinetics). *http://drskleiner.com*

I t's long been known that our eating habits can have a dramatic effect on our overall health.

Now: A growing body of scientific evidence shows that the foods we eat can either improve —or harm—our mood.

Bonus: Mood-boosting foods will help you lose weight if you have some extra pounds to shed. They can give you the mental and physical energy to be active as well as the nutrition that best supports physical activity, muscle growth and fat burning. People of normal weight can adapt these food recommendations to their daily calorie needs.

FEEL-GREAT BUILDING BLOCKS

The basic nutrients in the food we eat each play a role in optimizing our mood and energy levels...

• **Carbohydrates** are viewed negatively by most people who are trying to eat healthfully. But, in fact, these nutrients—when eaten in the proper form—are crucial to maintaining mood.

Here's why: Your mood is largely determined by a proper balance of brain chemicals (neuro-transmitters). One key neurotransmitter, *serotonin*, is strongly linked to positive feelings.

Surprising fact: The brain uses the amino acid *tryptophan*, which is contained in most dietary proteins, to manufacture serotonin. But to cross from the bloodstream to the brain, tryptophan must compete against other amino acids. Carbohydrates help displace the other amino acids, thus increasing the amount of tryptophan that gets through—and the amount of serotonin that is produced.

A steady stream of carbohydrates will help your brain reach ample levels of tryptophan.

Best carbohydrate sources: Fruits (such as bananas, blueberries, mangoes, oranges, pome-granates and strawberries) and vegetables (such as broccoli, spinach, yams and carrots). These foods not only supply carbohydrates, but also contain water and fiber that slow the rate at which the carbohydrates are digested and absorbed into the bloodstream.

Helpful: When your favorite fruits and vegetables are out of season, frozen versions (without added sauces) are economical and convenient.

• **Fats,** like carbohydrates, have been pegged as "no-nos." But dietary fats should not be elim-inated altogether—they make foods filling and satisfying.

Surprising fact: Fats are essential in keep-ing brain-cell membranes supple and well-functioning. For example, the omega-3 fatty acids found in certain fish (such as salmon, mackerel and sardines) have been shown to improve mood in people who are depressed.

Best fat sources: In addition to fish, try olives (any type), nuts, seeds, avocados, extra virgin olive oil and cold-pressed canola oil.

• **Proteins** can be converted into blood sugar (glucose)—but slowly, to keep glu-cose on an even keel. These nutrients also help keep metabolism (the rate at which you burn calories) high.

Surprising fact: Proteins are the raw mate-rials from which neurotransmitters, including serotonin, are manufactured.

Best protein sources: Lean organic meat (beef, pork or lamb) or poultry...fish...low-fat or fat-free dairy products...eggs...and legumes (such as pinto beans or lentils).

GOOD MOOD MEALS

After three hours of not eating, glucose levels fall and so do your spirits and energy levels. To avoid "panic eating," have a meal or substantial snack every two to three hours. *For example...*

Breakfast: ½ cup of shredded wheat cereal ...2 tablespoons of raisins...1 cup of fat-free milk...1 egg (cooked without butter or margarine).

Mid-morning snack: 1 cup of fat-free milk ...omelet from 4 egg whites or 2 ounces of sliced turkey.

Lunch: 1 cup of bean soup (low-sodium canned soup is okay)...tuna salad (without mayonnaise, but with reduced-fat salad dressing made with olive oil and vinegar)...and mixed greens.

Afternoon snack: Orange...mini-carrots with 1 tablespoon of natural-style peanut butter.

Dinner: 1 cup of whole-wheat pasta tossed with 1¼ tablespoons of pesto (homemade or store-bought)...4 ounces of chicken (grilled, broiled, baked or roasted)...2 cups of sliced cucumber...at least 1 cup total of carrots and cherry tomatoes...and 1¼ cups of fresh strawberries with 1 tablespoon of full-fat dairy whipped topping (it has only a few more calories than a "lite" version).

Evening snack: 1 cup of hot cocoa made with fat-free milk, 1 to 2 rounded teaspoons of unsweetened cocoa powder and Splenda (one packet or to taste) or another sweetener, such as agave nectar (a syrup derived from a desert plant). It is sold in health-food stores.

EXERCISE-MOOD CONNECTION

Exercise not only helps control your body weight, but also has been shown to improve mood and reduce depression (as effectively as medication, in some studies). At a minimum, get 30 minutes of activity (at the level of brisk walking) five to six days a week.

How Depression Can Make You Sick... And Vice Versa

Charles Raison, PhD, associate professor in the mind-body program, department of psychiatry and behavioral sciences at Emory University in Atlanta...and Esther M. Sternberg, MD, director of the integrative neural immune program at the National Institutes of Health in Rockville, Maryland. Dr. Sternberg is author of *The Balance Within: The Science Connecting Health and Emotions* (W.H. Freeman).

It is an unfortunate double jeopardy—being sick can make you depressed...and being depressed can make you sick. New research shows that many chronic illnesses, including heart disease, diabetes and osteoporosis, have this two-way connection to depression.

Consequences can be grave. In a recent study, heart attack patients who were depressed had a two- to fourfold increased risk of dying within five years, compared with heart attack patients who were not depressed. In a global study from the World Health Organization involving 245,000 people, those with a chronic illness fared far worse if they also were depressed.

One in eight women experiences depression at some point, compared with only one in 16 men—a gender discrepancy due primarily to hormonal differences. That means it is especially important for women who are depressed to get regular checkups to screen for chronic illness... and for women who have a chronic disease to be alert for signs of depression. Self-help strategies and/or professional care can protect both your mental and physical well-being.

EXPLAINING THE CONNECTION

Scientists are trying to discover how disease and depression interact. *What the evidence suggests...*

●**How disease can lead to depression.** Common sense tells us that a woman with a chronic illness might feel sad—but physiologically speaking, the explanation may involve an overactive immune system.

Theory: Inflammation is part of the body's normal healing process...but if the immune system fails to turn off the inflammatory mechanism at the appropriate time, inflammation becomes long-lasting and widespread. This can alter metabolism and damage blood vessels, bones and other body tissues, bringing on a variety of chronic illnesses and disrupting the balance of *neurotransmitters* (brain chemicals) that affect mood, triggering depression.

Recent studies show that the following conditions may be linked to depression—cancer …heart disease…diabetes…fibromyalgia (a syndrome of widespread pain)…psoriasis (patches of scaly, red skin)…rheumatoid arthritis (an autoimmune disease)…and stroke.

• **How depression can lead to disease.** It is logical that a depressed woman may not take care of herself well enough to guard against illness, but this is only a partial explanation. Physiologically, depression is linked to high levels of stress hormones—which in turn may raise blood pressure and cholesterol levels…promote accumulation of harmful abdominal fat…impair digestion…and hamper immune function. Along with depression comes increased production of proteins called *cytokines*, which cause widespread inflammation. This can trigger changes in the brain that reduce its resistance to dementia.

Recent studies suggest that people who suffer from depression may be at increased risk for Alzheimer's disease…asthma…breast cancer …cardiovascular disease…diabetes…gastric ulcer…high blood pressure…osteoarthritis …osteoporosis…and thyroid disease.

DEFENSE AGAINST DEPRESSION

Getting relief from depression can help prevent chronic illness or make an existing illness easier to deal with. Yet even though up to 90% of depressed people can be treated effectively, only one in three seeks treatment. *To overcome depression…*

• **Develop realistic expectations.** You may pessimistically assume that your physical prognosis is worse than it really is…or you may be overly optimistic, then feel crushed if your progress is slow. Either attitude can negatively affect your motivation to participate actively in your own physical recovery.

What helps: Be proactive. Write down all of your questions about your condition, treatment and prognosis, and review them with your doctor. Use the Internet to find a national association that addresses your illness, or ask your doctor if he/she knows of one. Take medication as prescribed, and keep all of your doctor appointments.

• **Eat foods rich in omega-3 fatty acids.** Omega-3s reduce inflammation and aid neurotransmitter function. Research suggests that omega-3s may be better absorbed from food than from supplements.

What helps: Have at least four servings weekly of omega-3–rich foods.

Good choices: Two tablespoons of ground flaxseeds or flaxseed oil…one-quarter cup of walnuts…three ounces of herring, salmon or sturgeon…one cup of navy or kidney beans, cabbage, cauliflower, squash or leafy green vegetables.

• **Stay active.** Exercise releases *endorphins,* brain chemicals that lift mood and block pain.

What helps: Don't tell yourself, *I feel too lousy to work out.* Ask your doctor or physical therapist to recommend exercises that you *can* do—such as water aerobics, which is easy on joints and bones…or slow stationary cycling, which won't overtax the heart.

• **Strengthen social ties.** You may hesitate to tell loved ones how down your illness makes you feel for fear of burdening them—yet emotional support is vital to healing.

What helps: Remember that your illness affects your family and friends, too. Everyone will feel better if emotions and concerns are discussed honestly.

• **Know when to get professional help.** Many people incorrectly assume that depression is an unavoidable part of physical illness, so they don't seek treatment.

What helps: Learn the symptoms of depression—sleeping too much or too little, unintended weight gain or loss, low energy, persistent sadness, frequent crying, irritability, feelings of hopelessness, poor concentration, low libido or lack of interest in daily activities. If you have any thoughts of suicide or if you experience two or more of the symptoms above for more than two weeks, tell your doctor.

•**Consider psychotherapy.** A form called *cognitive behavioral therapy* helps depressed patients replace negative beliefs and behaviors with positive ones.

What helps: Talk to a therapist experienced in treating depression linked to chronic illness. Ask your primary care physician to refer you to a mental-health professional who meets your needs.

•**Try natural nonprescription supplements.** Sold at health-food stores, these may relieve mild-to-moderate depression. If you use pharmaceutical antidepressants or other medications, get your doctor's approval before taking natural supplements to avoid possible adverse interactions.

What helps: Ask your doctor about appropriate dosages and usage guidelines for the following…

- •**5-adenosylmethionine (SAMe)**
- •**5-hydroxytryptophan (5-HTP)**
- •**St. John's wort**
- •**Vitamin D.**

•**Consider pharmaceutical antidepressants.** These medications work by slowing the removal of neurotransmitters from the brain.

What helps: Antidepressants often are very effective, though it may take trial-and-error to find one that works for you and does not cause side effects (such as nausea, weight gain, drowsiness and low libido).

Useful: Ask your doctor about the *cytochrome P450* blood test, which helps identify genetic factors that influence your response to certain antidepressants.

The Depression–Menopause Link

As they approach menopause, women who have premenstrual syndrome (PMS) are more likely to suffer depression than women who don't suffer from PMS.

Self-defense: Seek medical treatment if you are approaching menopause and suffering from symptoms of depression.

Ellen Freeman, PhD, research professor, department of obstetrics and gynecology, University of Pennsylvania School of Medicine, Philadelphia, and leader of a study of 231 women, published in *Archives of General Psychiatry.*

The Happiness Secret

Midlife women without children are happy, generally reporting similar levels of psychological well-being as women who do have children.

Reason: Being in good health, financially stable and having a supportive husband or partner help shape the lives of women who don't have children. Mothers who are single, divorced or widowed in middle age report being the loneliest and most depressed.

Tanya Koropeckyj-Cox, PhD, sociology professor, University of Florida, Gainesville, and lead author of a study that analyzed national data on women ages 51 to 61, published in *International Journal of Aging and Human Development.*

Is Your Marriage Making You Sick?

Theodore Robles, PhD, assistant professor of health psychology in the department of psychology at the University of California, Los Angeles. Robles' research focuses on the effects of marital conflict on endocrine and immune functioning in healthy adults.

Researchers have long known that marriage can improve one's health. But only recently has scientific evidence emerged indicating that serious health consequences can result from a chronically stressful marriage.

Important recent findings…

•**Increased heart disease risk.** Negative marital interactions have been convincingly linked by studies at the University of Utah to increases in heart rate and blood pressure, coronary artery fatty deposits (plaques) and decreased elasticity in the arteries—all of which contribute to heart disease.

• **Weakened immunity.** Married couples who were more hostile or angry during a single interaction were found by an Ohio State University study to have decreased function of infection-fighting natural killer cells and, in a later study, slower rates of wound healing.

As a health risk, marital stress is on par with social isolation, high cholesterol, poor diet and lack of exercise, according to these and other findings. For unknown reasons, women seem to be particularly hard hit by marital woes—studies consistently show that wives experience stronger cardiovascular, hormonal and immunological reactions to marital stress.

Good news: While virtually all marriages endure some degree of conflict, studies suggest that it's how we *deal with* disagreements—not just whether we have them—that largely determines the effects on our health. For example, University of Utah researchers have shown that a couple's demeanor during disputes—warm, hostile, controlling, submissive—is as good an indicator of underlying heart disease as cholesterol levels.

To minimize the health impact of marital stress…

• **Break the tension.** Ohio State University researchers recently measured blood levels of the stress hormones cortisol and *adrenocorticotropic hormone* (ACTH) in 90 newlywed couples before, during and after a 30-minute discussion about sensitive marital issues. When both partners were consistently negative, the wives' cortisol and ACTH levels escalated.

However, when one or both partners were supportive and constructive—even during heated discussions—the wives' stress hormones declined throughout the discussion. (Men's hormone levels were unaffected by both the negative and supportive behaviors.)

What both spouses can do: Agree with your partner on some points…accept responsibility for your shortcomings…and propose compromises.

Research involving women with high blood pressure suggests that more hostile behaviors during marital discussions are associated with elevated blood pressure during the exchanges, and more supportive behaviors are associated with lower blood pressure during the discussions.

• **Watch your words.** While husbands appear less physiologically affected by their wives' hostility, they do react—with increased heart rate and blood pressure—to perceived challenges to their competency or skills.

What both spouses can do: Avoid controlling statements such as "You're never on time …why don't you wear your watch?" or "Why can't you just do what I ask?"

Replace comments such as: "You're spending us into bankruptcy!" with: "I know you love to shop for the grandkids, but we need to stick to a budget."

Helpful: Because we cannot control everything about our spouses, look for something to value even in those things you may not readily admire. For example, if you resent your spouse's messiness but value his/her easygoing nature, try viewing these qualities as flip sides of the same coin. You may find you have greater tolerance for—and less need to control—the clutter.

• **Trust your spouse.** In a University of Utah study involving 300 middle-aged and older couples, researchers found no correlation between self-reports of anger or antagonism and calcium buildup in their coronary arteries (a risk factor for cardiovascular disease). However, partners whose spouses had rated them high on scales of anger and antagonism were more likely to have significant calcium buildup.

What both spouses can do: Pay attention if your partner says you are being angry, hostile, unreasonable or cold. While you may be unaware of your negativity, your arteries could be paying the price.

• **Speak your mind.** In a University of Michigan study involving 192 older couples, those in which both spouses clammed up to avoid confrontation were much more likely to experience the death of one or both partners over a 17-year period. In fact, among 26 such "dual-suppressor" marriages, 27% suffered the loss of one spouse, and 23% experienced the death of both partners, while among the 166 more communicative couples, a significantly lower 19% experienced one death, and only 6% experienced the death of both partners.

Shocking recent finding: In a recent study involving nearly 4,000 married adults from Framingham, Massachusetts, women who reported regularly stifling themselves during marital disagreements were *four times* more likely than outspoken wives to die during a 10-year period.

The culprit could be stress—when husbands respond with silence to their wives' anger, studies show that wives' cortisol levels go up and stay up for the day. Chronically elevated cortisol has been linked to impaired cognitive and immune functioning, heart disease, diabetes and other ills.

What both spouses can do: Communicate openly.

• **Relax.** Studies have shown that the higher a woman's levels of stress hormones before she and her husband engage in a discussion about their relationship, the more likely she and her husband are to be critical, defensive or hostile to one another during conflict. Unfortunately, these negative behaviors only exacerbate the wife's already elevated ACTH and cortisol levels.

What both spouses can do: Make time daily to relax, whether with exercise, meditation, hobbies or spending time with friends. By lowering stress, women, in particular, may be able to keep hostility—and their stress hormones—from escalating during marital conflict.

Depression Increases Osteoporosis Risk

Women who experienced their first episode of depression before menopause had lower bone-mineral density than women who never were depressed.

Reason: Stress increases levels of the hormone cortisol, which inhibits bone-building cells and triggers bone-destroying cells.

Giovanni Cizza, MD, PhD, endocrinologist, National Institute of Mental Health, Bethesda, Maryland.

Menopause Stress Relieved by Exercise

Emotional symptoms of menopause are eased by exercising.

Recent finding: Anxiety, stress and depression are significantly lower among postmenopausal women who work out regularly.

But: Physical activity does not alleviate hot flashes.

Deborah B. Nelson, PhD, associate professor, Temple University College of Health Professions, Philadelphia, and coinvestigator of a study of 380 women, published in *Medicine & Science in Sports & Exercise*.

Insomnia Remedy

Certain aromas have a calming effect that can help bring on sleep.

Helpful: Make a sachet to place under your pillow. You'll find most of the items you need at natural-food stores.

In a bowl, toss together two tablespoons of corncob chips (sold as bedding at pet shops) and four drops each of lavender essential oil and lemon essential oil...cover and let stand overnight. Uncover and stir in one-half cup of dried hops...and one-quarter cup each of dried lavender buds and lemon verbena leaves. Place mixture inside a small fabric drawstring sack (about six inches square). Refill the sack with a fresh batch of herbal stuffing every two to three weeks or when the aromas start to fade.

Dorie Byers, RN, registered nurse and herbalist, Bargersville, Indiana, and author of *Natural Beauty Basics: Create Your Own Cosmetics and Body Care Products* (Square One).

Sleep Problems More Hazardous for Women

Among poor sleepers of both sexes, women experience more psychological symptoms (depression, anger, hostility)…and have higher blood levels of markers (including insulin, glucose, inflammatory proteins and clotting factors) linked to heart disease and diabetes risk.

Possible reason: Hormonal differences.

Self-defense: Alert your doctor if you have trouble sleeping.

Edward Suarez, MD, associate professor of psychiatry, Duke University Medical Center, Durham, North Carolina, and lead author of a study of 210 people, published in *Brain, Behavior and Immunity.*

Bedroom Makeover for More Restful Sleep

Lawrence J. Epstein, MD, instructor in medicine at Harvard Medical School in Boston and regional medical director of the Harvard–affiliated Sleep HealthCenters, a Brighton, Massachusetts–based network of specialized sleep medicine centers. He is the author of *The Harvard Medical School Guide to a Good Night's Sleep* (McGraw-Hill).

If a busy schedule prevents you from getting the full seven-and-a-half to eight hours of sleep per night that the vast majority of adults require, it's no wonder that you often feel drowsy during the day.

But what if you spend plenty of time in bed yet still never feel fully rested? Something in your sleep environment may be keeping you up or creating disturbances that, even without waking you fully, interfere with the normal progression of sleep stages that you need to feel truly rested.

Concern: Chronic sleep deprivation negatively affects virtually every aspect of life—energy, alertness, work performance, mood, sex drive.

Recent finding: Sleep deprivation also contributes to weight problems. Studies show that losing sleep for just a few nights raises levels of hormones linked with overeating and weight gain and makes a person more likely to reach for fattening comfort foods instead of nutritious fare.

Even worse: Sleep deprivation increases the risk for diabetes and heart disease as well as car crashes and other accidents.

What to do: Speak to your doctor—sleep problems sometimes signal a potentially serious condition, such as sleep apnea (repeated cessations in breathing during sleep) or depression. If you still have trouble sleeping well even after underlying medical problems are ruled out or treated, chances are that your bedroom is not offering an optimal sleep environment.

Recommended: Follow the eight simple guidelines below to create a space conducive to restful, restorative slumber…

1. Clear out clutter. Ideally, a bedroom should be simply furnished and decorated so that there isn't a lot to distract you from the primary purpose of sleep. Keeping the bedroom neat and well organized helps minimize anxiety.

Reason: A messy room often is an oppressive reminder of other things that need to be done, making it harder to fall asleep.

2. Don't work—or play—in the bedroom. Keep your computer, checkbook, to-do list, briefcase and other paraphernalia related to your chores, job or responsibilities in your home office, where they are less likely to intrude on your thoughts during the night. If you must have a phone in the bedroom, use that extension only for emergencies, not for potentially exciting or disturbing conversations.

Recreational activities (other than sex, of course) also should be done elsewhere—so remove the TV, DVD player, stereo and anything else that shifts the bedroom's focus to entertainment. If you play music in your room every night before bed, for instance, and then wake up in the middle of the night, you may be unable to fall back to sleep unless you turn on the music again.

3. Banish dust bunnies. Dust mites are microscopic creatures that provoke nasal congestion and/or asthma attacks in allergy-prone people. Because airways naturally constrict at night, allergy flare-ups are likely to interfere with sleep.

Best: Regularly wash bedding in hot water, vacuum under furniture, and dust all surfaces.

4. Block the light. Light sends a strong message to the brain to wake up. Of all the external cues that keep the body clock operating on a 24-hour cycle, light striking the eyes—even when they are closed—is the most influential. Though you may not become fully conscious, light can move you out of deep-stage sleep and into lighter, less restful stages.

Solution: Hang shades, blinds or curtains made from "blackout" material over windows. Remove or cover any electronics that light up, including your alarm clock. If you cannot block ambient light, wear a sleep mask.

For safety's sake: It is fine to use a low-level night-light—for instance, to see your way to the bathroom.

5. Hide the clock. When you have insomnia, repeatedly checking the clock only makes the problem worse by providing an unwelcome reminder of just how much rest you are missing. Turn the face of the clock away so it won't taunt you as you toss and turn.

6. Muffle or mask sounds. Noise is extremely disruptive.

Recent findings: People whose partners suffer from sleep apnea (which causes loud snoring and gasping) lose about the same amount of sleep each night as the apnea patients themselves do. Also, people who live near airports often experience blood pressure elevations and disturbances in the heart's normal resting rhythm when planes fly by.

Self-defense: Use heavy draperies, double-paned windows and rugs to muffle outside sounds. Earplugs are very effective—try an inexpensive foam or silicone drugstore product. If you find earplugs uncomfortable, turn on a fan or white-noise machine (sold at household-goods stores) to create a low, steady background sound that masks more disruptive noises.

7. Make the bed comfortable. The older the mattress, the less support it generally provides (and the more dust mites it may harbor), so if you have had yours for more than 10 years, consider getting a new one. Take your time

testing mattresses to see which brand and level of firmness feel best to you, and lie on your favorite one for as long as you need to before you buy to make sure it is comfortable.

Helpful: Replace pillows when they no longer feel comfortable. Avoid products filled with natural down if you are prone to allergies. Keep extra blankets at the foot of the bed—body temperature drops a few degrees during sleep, so you may wake up chilled during the night.

8. Keep a pen and paper on your bedside table. If you are fretting over impending tasks or feeling excited about a new idea as you're trying to fall asleep, jot down some notes about the situation. This way you won't worry about not remembering your thoughts in the morning—clearing your mind for a good night's sleep.

Solutions for a Good Night's Sleep

Lawrence J. Epstein, MD, instructor in medicine at Harvard Medical School in Boston and regional medical director of the Harvard–affiliated Sleep HealthCenters, a Brighton, Massachusetts–based network of specialized sleep medicine centers. He is author of *The Harvard Medical School Guide to a Good Night's Sleep* (Mc-Graw-Hill).

Most people assume that lack of sleep is more of an annoyance than a legitimate threat to their health. But that's a mistake. Lack of sleep—even if it's only occasional—is directly linked to poor health. If ignored, sleep problems can increase your risk for diabetes and heart disease.

About two out of every three Americans ages 55 to 84 have insomnia, but it is one of the most underdiagnosed health problems in the US. Even when insomnia is diagnosed, many doctors recommend a one-size-fits-all treatment approach (often including long-term use of sleep medication) that does not correct the underlying problem.

Everyone should have a comfortable mattress ...keep the bedroom cool (about 68°F to 72°F) ...and dim or turn out the lights (production of the sleep hormone *melatonin* can be inhibited in the presence of light). Keep TVs and computers out of the bedroom—both can be stimulating, rather than relaxing. But these basic steps may not be enough.

To treat specific sleep problems...

IF YOU WAKE UP TOO EARLY IN THE MORNING

Early risers often have *advanced sleep phase syndrome* (ASPS), which is seen most commonly in older adults. With this condition, a person's internal body clock that regulates the sleep-wake cycle (circadian rhythm) is not functioning properly. ASPS sufferers sleep best from 8 pm to 4 am.

My solutions: To reset your circadian rhythm, try a light box (a device that uses lightbulbs to simulate natural light). Light boxes don't require a doctor's prescription and are available for $100 to $500 online. Most people use a light box for 30 minutes to an hour daily at sundown. (Those with ASPS may need long-term light therapy.) If you have cataracts or glaucoma or a mood disorder (such as bipolar disorder), consult your doctor before trying light therapy. Patients with retinopathy (a disorder of the retina) should avoid light therapy.

Also helpful: To help regulate your internal clock so that you can go to bed (and get up) later, take a 3-mg to 5-mg melatonin supplement each day. A sleep specialist can advise you on when to use light therapy and melatonin for ASPS.*

IF YOU CAN'T STAY ASLEEP

Everyone wakes up several times a night, but most people fall back to sleep within seconds, so they don't remember waking up.

Trouble staying asleep is often related to *sleep apnea*, a breathing disorder that causes the sufferer to awaken repeatedly during the night and gasp for air. Another common problem among those who can't stay asleep is *periodic limb movement disorder* (PLMD), a neurological condition that causes frequent involuntary kicking or jerking movements during sleep. (Restless legs syndrome, which is similar

*To find a sleep center near you, consult the American Academy of Sleep Medicine (630-737-9700, *www.sleepcenters.org*).

to PLMD, causes an uncontrollable urge to move the legs and also can occur at night.)

My solutions: If you are unable to improve your sleep throughout the night by following the strategies already described, consult a sleep specialist to determine whether you have sleep apnea or PLMD.

Sleep apnea patients usually get relief by losing weight, if necessary...elevating the head of the bed to reduce snoring...using an oral device that positions the jaw so that the tongue cannot block the throat during sleep...or wearing a face mask that delivers oxygen to keep their airways open. PLMD is usually treated with medication.

IF YOU CAN'T GET TO SLEEP

Most people take about 20 minutes to fall asleep, but this varies with the individual. If your mind is racing due to stress (from marital strife or financial worries, for example) or if you've adopted bad habits (such as drinking caffeine late in the day), you may end up tossing and turning.

My solutions: Limit yourself to one cup of caffeinated coffee or tea daily, and do not consume any caffeine-containing beverage or food (such as chocolate) after 2 pm. If you take a caffeine-containing drug, such as Excedrin or some cold remedies, ask your doctor if it can be taken earlier in the day.

Helpful: If something is bothering you, write it down and tell yourself that you will deal with it tomorrow—this way, you can stop worrying so you can get to sleep.

Also helpful: When you go to bed, turn the clock face away from you so you don't watch the minutes pass. If you can't sleep after 20 to 30 minutes, get up and do something relaxing, such as meditating, until you begin to feel drowsy.

IF YOU CAN'T GET UP IN THE MORNING

If you can't drag your head off the pillow, sleep apnea or a *delayed sleep phase* (DSP) disorder might be to blame. DSP disorder makes it hard to fall asleep early, so you stay up late at night and then struggle to get out of bed in the morning.

My solutions: To treat DSP disorder, progressively stay up for three hours later

nightly for one week until you reach your desired bedtime. By staying up even *later* than is usual for you, you'll eventually shift your circadian rhythm. Once you find your ideal bedtime, stick to it. Also consider trying light-box therapy each morning upon arising. Light helps advance your body clock so that your bedtime should come earlier. Taking 3 mg to 5 mg of melatonin one hour before bedtime should also make you sleepy at an earlier hour.

IF YOU CAN'T STAY AWAKE DURING THE DAY

If you're getting ample rest—most people need seven and one-half to eight hours a night—and still are tired, you may have narcolepsy. This neurological disorder occurs when the brain sends out sleep-inducing signals at inappropriate times, causing you to fall asleep and even temporarily lose muscle function. Sleep apnea or periodic limb movements also can leave people feeling exhausted.

My solutions: Figure out how much sleep you need by sleeping as long as you can nightly (perhaps while on vacation) for one to two weeks. At the end of that period, you should be sleeping the number of hours you need. Give yourself that much sleep time nightly. If you remain sluggish, ask your doctor about tests for sleep apnea, PLMD—or narcolepsy, which is treated with stimulants, such as *modafinil* (Provigil), that promote wakefulness.

How to Let Go of Bad Memories for Good

Thomas H. Crook III, PhD, a psychologist in private practice in St. Petersburg, Florida. He is an affiliate professor of psychiatry and behavioral medicine at University of South Florida College of Medicine in Tampa, a former research program director for the National Institute of Mental Health and author of numerous books, including *The Memory Advantage* (Select Books).

Good or bad, happy or sad, our memories are a huge part of who we are. They can help us repeat our successes, motivate us to learn from our mistakes and provide the framework for our sense of ourselves as individuals.

But when painful or counterproductive memories echo over and over in our heads, they drain our mental energy and lessen our joy.

Self-defense: Learn how toxic memories form—then develop skills to defuse their power.

ORIGINS OF MEMORIES

Much of the way we see ourselves is rooted in childhood experiences, and the memories of those early events can be intense. Not every unpleasant childhood experience becomes a toxic memory, however. In fact, similar situations can create similar memories—yet produce very different effects.

Example: Two women remember feeling humiliated in first grade for being unable to read. Whenever the first woman thinks of this, she also reminds herself of how she excelled at math. For her, this early memory is tied to feelings of success. But when the second woman recalls her six-year-old self, she views those first failures with reading as the start of every struggle she has ever faced and every challenge she has ever avoided. For her, this unhappy memory is toxic.

Not all toxic memories are rooted in childhood. They can form at any time, especially during emotional upheaval.

For instance: The memory of losing her job turns toxic if a woman feels enraged whenever she thinks of it. The memory of a bitter divorce becomes toxic if a woman is too afraid ever to date again. The memory of her father's dying is toxic if a woman sobs uncontrollably every time she pictures his face, even years after his death.

An exceptionally traumatic event, such as being a victim of a violent crime, understandably can cause extreme fear, anger and sadness. But the memory turns especially toxic if a woman blames herself—believing, for instance, "I was sexually assaulted because I danced too provocatively"—rather than rightfully blaming the assailant.

HOW MEMORIES CAN HURT

If poisonous memories repeatedly invade our thoughts, reinforcing negative feelings about ourselves or others, we may have...

• **Diminished pleasure in life,** as even happy occasions are overshadowed by images from the past.

Example: At her daughter's wedding, a woman obsesses about how aloof her own mother was. Such thoughts increase a person's risk for depression and/or anxiety disorders.

• **Low self-esteem and missed opportunities for growth.**

Example: Having always been picked last for teams in gym class, a woman habitually labels herself as clumsy—and refuses to exercise or to socialize with friends on the golf course.

• **Inability to respond appropriately to new situations.**

Example: Continued resentment over having been laid off may negatively affect a woman's manner and the impression she makes on job interviews.

• **Chronically elevated levels of stress hormones.** These have damaging effects on blood pressure, blood sugar, digestion and immunity, increasing risk for heart disease, diabetes and gastric disorders.

BREAKING THE HABIT

A toxic memory turned constant companion is as much a bad habit as a bad memory—and like any bad habit, it can be broken. *Steps...*

1. Select a favorite positive memory. You can choose an event that specifically contradicts your toxic memory (for instance, the day you learned to ski despite being a "hopeless klutz")...or choose a completely unrelated experience, such as your first date with your husband.

2. Write down as many details as you can recall. Where did you go? What did you wear? Did you dance to a certain song or see a stunning sunset? How did that first kiss feel? Tap into all your senses.

3. Practice conjuring up this happy memory. Let this personal "movie" play inside your head during relaxed moments. Soon you'll be able to recall it vividly at will, even when stressed or depressed.

4. Mentally hit an "eject" button whenever a toxic memory pops into your head, replacing it with thoughts of the happy memory.

FULFILLING EMOTIONAL NEEDS

If the technique above isn't working, your toxic memory may be more than a bad habit —it may be fulfilling some unmet need. Ask yourself, "How am I benefiting by holding onto this painful memory?" This insight will help you explore more productive ways to meet that need, thus diminishing the power of the toxic memory. *Consider...*

• **Does thinking of yourself as unlucky let you avoid taking responsibility for your life?** On a sheet of paper, make two columns, labeled "good luck" and "bad luck," then list examples from your own life of each type of experience. You will see that your whole life hasn't been a series of misfortunes. Next, identify the role played by your own efforts— rather than good luck—in creating each positive experience...and give yourself due credit.

• **Is there a certain pleasure for you in resenting other people for past unpleasantness?** (Be honest with yourself!) Develop a habit of doing small favors that make people respond to you in a positive way. Smile at everyone you pass on the sidewalk, yield to other drivers trying to enter your lane, say a sincere "thank you" to a surly cashier. A conscious and voluntary decision to be of service to others can help you overcome old resentments, relegate toxic memories to the past and find pleasure in the here and now.

If you feel traumatized: After an extremely traumatic experience, it is normal to fixate on the event for a time. However, if you are seriously disturbed by recurrent memories of the trauma months or even years later, you may have post-traumatic stress disorder (PTSD). Symptoms include nightmares or obsessive mental reenactments of the event...frequent fear or anger...trouble concentrating...feelings of guilt, hopelessness or emotional numbness.

Defusing traumatic memories may require the help of a mental-health professional.

Recommended: Cognitive-behavioral therapy (CBT), which focuses on changing harmful thought patterns rather than on lengthy exploration of past experiences.

Referrals: National Association of Cognitive-Behavioral Therapists, *www.nacbt.org*. With CBT, even seriously toxic memories can become more manageable—and you can move on with your life.

Secondhand Stress—Don't Let It Get to You

Redford B. Williams, MD, director of the Behavioral Medicine Research Center at Duke University, Durham, North Carolina. He is coauthor of *In Control* (Rodale) and *Lifeskills* (Rodale). *www.williamslifeskills.com*

Most women are empathetic, excellent listeners and masterful interpreters of other people's emotional cues. These are admirable traits—yet they can make a woman vulnerable to feeling other people's stress so acutely that she becomes stressed herself. Thus, she falls prey to "contagious stress."

Like secondhand smoke, secondhand stress is harmful. Chronic stress weakens immunity …contributes to heart disease, depression and other health problems…and even kills brain cells.

To determine if you are prone to taking on other people's stress, consider the following scenarios.

- **The couple in the checkout line in front of you is arguing.** You begin to feel anxious.

- **Your friend is always running in 50 different directions at once.** After seeing her, you feel frazzled.

- **Your husband gripes incessantly about his bowling team's poor performance.** Whenever he mentions it, your whole body tenses up.

- **Your coworker is panicking about a team project.** Even though your part of the project is finished—and has been amply praised by the boss—you start to panic, too.

If any of these examples sounds familiar, consider these easy and effective ways to inoculate yourself against contagious stress.

THE FOUR-QUESTION TEST

Whenever you notice that you are beginning to feel tense in the company of someone who is stressed, ask yourself the following four questions.

1. Is this situation important to me?

2. Is my level of anxiety appropriate, given the facts?

3. Is the situation modifiable?

4. Considering the effort involved, is taking action worth it?

To remember these questions when you're under pressure, use the phrase "I am worth it"—a partial acronym for **I**mportant… **A**ppropriate…**M**odifiable…and **W**orth It.

IF ANY ANSWER IS NO

Often, simply answering no to the first question is enough to put the matter in perspective. You may quickly realize that the situation does not involve you personally—as in the case of the feuding couple in the checkout line, whom you don't even know.

If the answer to any of the other questions above is no—because your feelings are out of proportion to the problem, or because you cannot or choose not to change the situation —you need a strategy that deflects contagious stress. *Practical techniques you can use anywhere…*

- **Change what you say to yourself.** Cognitive therapists have discovered that it is possible to reason yourself out of anxiety. Take one of the "I am worth it" questions to which you answered no, and turn it into a statement that you repeat silently to yourself.

How this might work: You realize that a situation is not modifiable. You say to yourself, "I cannot change the fact that my friend is over-scheduled. I have suggested that she drop some of her activities, and she has chosen not to. Maybe she gets an adrenaline rush from multi-tasking—but this doesn't have to stress me."

- **Use thought-stopping.** This technique keeps you from reacting automatically or to an inappropriate degree. Every time you find

239

yourself getting pulled into someone's stress —for instance, when you tense up over a trivial matter, such as your husband's bowling complaints—silently tell yourself, "Stop!" *If that alone is not enough to change your train of thought, also use one of these strategies…*

• Add a physical cue. Place a rubber band around your wrist, and snap it as you repeat the "stop" cue. The physical sensation helps to short-circuit persistent thoughts.

• Distract yourself. Hum a favorite song… read an interesting article in a magazine…phone a friend…or make detailed plans for an activity that you're looking forward to, such as your next vacation or planting a new garden.

• Relax. Close your eyes and take four slow, deep breaths. On the first inhalation, squeeze your hands into fists…then let them go limp as you breathe out and silently say relax. On the next deep breath, shrug your shoulders as high as you can…then let them drop as you exhale slowly and focus your mind on the word *relax*. On the third inhalation, tilt your head to the right as far as you can…and on the fourth breath, tilt it to the left…each time repeating the silent mantra to relax as you exhale. This technique takes only a few moments. Practice it when you are not feeling stressed, to improve your ability to relax at will.

IF ALL ANSWERS ARE YES

When the answer to all four of the "I Am Worth It" questions is yes, you are affirming that the situation is important to you…your feelings are justified…it is within your power to improve the situation…and the rewards for doing so outweigh the effort involved. In that case, the key to reducing contagious stress is to help the other person solve her problem.

First: Make sure that the stressed-out person wants your assistance. If you just spout advice, she is likely to resist it.

Simple problem-solving techniques are effective in most situations. *The steps…*

• **Brainstorm together.** Write down all the ideas that each of you comes up with, no matter how wacky.

• **Select the best approach.** Once you've got an uncensored list of ideas, winnow them, choosing the options most likely to succeed.

• **Put the plan into action.** Periodically evaluate your progress, and adjust the plan as necessary.

Example: You can't just tune out your coworker's panic, because the project's overall success is important to you, too. Say to her, "Perhaps it would be helpful to write down every task this project requires of you, prioritize them and then set a manageable schedule for accomplishing each one. Would you like me to work with you on that?" Once your coworker feels more in control and sure of her role in the project, her panic will subside…and you will recover from your case of contagious stress.

The 3 Best Stress-Busters For Women

Alice Domar, PhD, assistant professor of obstetrics, gynecology and reproductive biology at Harvard Medical School, Boston, and executive director of the Domar Center for Mind/Body Health, Waltham, Massachusetts. She is author of several books, including *Be Happy Without Being Perfect* (Three Rivers). *www.domarcenter.com.*

On any given day, research suggests, a women is likely to feel stressed more often and more intensely than a man—and to do so in reaction to a wider variety of concerns. She even may stress out in more vivid detail, often with accompanying headaches or insomnia. One reason for these differences is hormones.

Smart: Use biology to advantage by honing three stress-relieving techniques that work especially well for women.

• **Deep breathing.** Studies suggest that, during stress, the hormone *adrenaline* may activate neurons in the part of the brain that controls emotions. This triggers strong visceral responses (racing heart, roiling stomach). Men may metabolize adrenaline more quickly, so their visceral response abates sooner. Deep breathing interrupts the visceral response, which in turn calms the mind.

What to do: Breathe in through your nose and out through your mouth, slowly and deeply, clearing your mind by focusing on your breath.

• **Challenging negative thoughts.** In times of stress, a woman's level of the stress hormone *cortisol* may remain elevated longer than a man's, according to a recent study. Cortisol affects memory formation—so a woman remembers stressful events more vividly. By challenging the validity of a habitual negative thought, you defuse the power of the stressful memory.

What to do: Identify the situation—for instance, your cousin made a crack about your cluttered house and now you keep thinking that you're a slob.

Next, ask and answer these questions: Where did this thought come from? (It made me remember how mortified I always felt when my mother criticized my messy room.) Is it logical? (Not necessarily—a house can be cluttered but clean.) Is it true? (No, I'm not a slob—I dress impeccably.)

• **Reaching out.** When women are stressed, they release the bonding hormone oxytocin, which encourages them to seek solace from other people. However, the male hormone testosterone may reduce the effects of oxytocin, so men often withdraw when stressed. Another woman may best provide comfort because she understands how you feel.

What to do: Phone or e-mail a girlfriend, and talk through your troubles. Better yet, take a walk together while you talk—exercising is also a stress antidote.

The Hidden Health Threat You Can Beat

Kathleen Hall, PhD, who has her doctorate in spirituality from Columbia University, New York City. She is author of *A Life in Balance: Nourishing the Four Roots of True Happiness* (Amacom) and *Alter Your Life: Overbooked? Overworked? Overwhelmed?* (Oak Haven). *www.stressinstitute.com*

Chronic stress is a contributing factor to all the leading causes of death, including heart disease, cancer and diabetes. Stress is behind 90% of all visits to primary care physicians.

How chronic stress leads to sickness and what you can do to ease the pressure...

THE DISEASE CONNECTION

Stress is the response to any significant change or challenge, negative or positive. Your body reacts to stress with its innate drive to survive—to maintain the life-protecting physiological, emotional and mental balance that scientists call *homeostasis*. When stress is triggered by an event—a growling dog, a deadline, a daughter's wedding—adrenaline flows, muscles tense, blood pressure rises. You're alert, motivated and primed for action. After the challenge is met, you relax. That's natural, normal and necessary.

Chronic stress—marital troubles, financial worries, an abusive boss—generates chronically high levels of the adrenal hormone *cortisol*, which takes its toll on the body. Blood pressure stays high...blood sugar levels increase...the immune system, constantly primed to counter intruders, generates chronic, low-grade inflammation that weakens cells.

Recent studies reveal that chronic stress can contribute to...

• **Heart disease.** Researchers in England studied more than 10,000 government workers and found that those who reported the highest levels of stress at work also had a 68% higher risk for heart problems. The study was reported in *European Heart Journal.*

• **Cancer.** Stress can double the speed at which cancer returns. Scientists at the University of Rochester Medical Center in New York and Stanford University School of Medicine in California studied 94 women who had been successfully treated for advanced breast cancer. After treatment, those who had experienced a lot of stress in the past—such as physical abuse or divorce—remained cancer-free for an average of 31 months. Those who hadn't experienced that level of stress remained cancer-free for 62 months, on average. The report was published in *Journal of Psychosomatic Research.*

• **Diabetes.** In a study by researchers at the University of Helsinki in Finland, women who reported feeling frequently angry, tense or stressed were 20% to 60% more likely to develop metabolic syndrome, a prediabetic condition

241

characterized by high blood sugar, high blood pressure, high triglycerides (blood fats), low HDL (good) cholesterol and being overweight. The study was reported in *Diabetes Care*.

• **Memory problems and Alzheimer's.** Researchers at the University of California, San Diego, studied 91 healthy people with an average age of 79. The higher their levels of stress, the worse their memory. Those who were stressed and who tested positive for a gene linked to Alzheimer's disease had the worst memory of all. The researchers reported their findings in *Biological Psychiatry*.

• **Weakened immunity.** Scientists at the Institute for Behavioral Medicine Research at Ohio State University reviewed decades of research on stress and the immune system. They found that stress reduces the activity of infection-fighting natural killer cells...decreases the number of white blood cells called lymphocytes...increases the production of antibodies (a risk factor for allergies and autoimmune diseases, such as rheumatoid arthritis)...and reactivates old viral infections. Weakened immunity has severe consequences for health, including slower wound healing...poor response to vaccinations against flu and other diseases...and the development and progression of cancer. The paper was published in *Cellular Immunology*.

• **Reduced life span.** The same team of researchers found that chronic stress experienced by spouses and children who care for people with Alzheimer's disease can shorten the caregivers' lives by four to eight years, compared with similar noncaregivers. The caregivers had shortened and damaged telomeres, a type of genetic material. Longer, stronger telomeres have been linked to longevity. This research appeared in the *Journal of Immunology*.

EASING STRESS

There are steps anyone can take to relieve stress. Top stress-reduction clinics in the US—at Harvard Medical School, Duke University, University of Massachusetts and Johns Hopkins University—all use a similar approach to stress relief and the treatment of stress-complicated conditions (such as high blood pressure and insomnia). It emphasizes four ways to relax and lower chronically high cortisol levels—meditation and other relaxation techniques...exercise...a healthy diet...and group support. *These four approaches can be distilled into the easy-to-remember acronym SELF...*

• **S is for serenity.** A simple technique called the "relaxation response" is one of the best and easiest ways to achieve a greater degree of stress-reducing serenity.

What to do: Find a quiet, comfortable place to sit. Close your eyes. Choose a calming word or short phrase, such as "letting go" or "all is well." As you slowly exhale, repeat the word or phrase over and over. With practice, you will be able to settle into a deeper peace with each inhalation. When you have distracting thoughts, imagine that they are clouds blowing by and focus back on the word or phrase. Repeat this process over and over for five to 10 minutes at least once a day.

Other ways you can experience more serenity: Sing...pray...pet a cat or dog...laugh (watch a DVD of your favorite comedian...or tune in to a comedy channel on cable-TV or satellite radio).

• **E is for Exercise.** Exercise doesn't have to be a sweaty workout at the gym. Stress-relieving exercise is any motion—walking your dog, going dancing, getting the tension out of your muscles with a yoga stretch.

What to do: Exercise for at least 20 minutes five times a week.

• **L is for Love.** A heartfelt connection to family and friends reduces stress.

What to do: Just as you schedule any other appointment, block out time in your calendar to spend relaxing with family and friends. Even little gestures, such as sending an e-mail to a friend asking how he/she is, can reduce stress.

• **F is for Food.** Wholesome food is medicine for stress. Healthy food helps improve your mood, sleep and health.

What to do: At least once a week, eat fish rich in omega-3 fatty acids (such as salmon, mackerel, sardines and herring, etc.), which nourish brain cells and have been shown to ease stress and reduce hostility and depression.

Other stress-reducing foods...

• **Broccoli and blueberries** and other fruits and vegetables that are rich in cell-protecting antioxidants.

• **Chicken and bananas,** high in vitamin B-6, which increases the production of the neurotransmitter *serotonin*. Serotonin helps relax and heal the body.

• **Avoid foods and beverages that aggravate stress,** including coffee and tea with caffeine...foods high in sugar...and alcohol, which may seem to de-stress you, but when the effects wear off, you tend to feel even more anxious.

When Hand Holding Helps

Did you know holding your spouse's hand reduces stress?

Recent finding: Women threatened with electric shock had reduced activity in the brain's stress-responsive regions when holding their husbands' hands. Stress increased when holding strangers' hands or not holding hands at all.

James Coan, PhD, assistant professor, department of psychology, University of Virginia, Charlottesville, and leader of a study published in *Psychological Science.*

Three Ways to Lighten Your To-Do List

Judy Kuriansky, PhD, clinical psychologist and sex therapist on the adjunct faculty of Columbia University Teachers College in New York City. She is author of several books, including *The Complete Idiot's Guide to a Healthy Relationship* (Alpha). *www.sexualtherapy.com/ therapists/jkuriansky.htm*

Are you frantic, frustrated and overloaded? Does your to-do list demand more each day than Superwoman could achieve in a week? *To stop running yourself ragged...*

• **Turn "I must" into "I want."** To be in control rather than overwhelmed, remember that you often have a choice. You might *like* to knit your new niece a sweater, but you don't *have* to. Moving nonessentials from your to-do list to your wish list transforms work into play.

• **Focus on one task at a time.** Snowed under by obligations, your brain freezes. You lurch from chore to chore, unable to persevere with any single one.

Better: Concentrate on your top-priority task, putting all others out of your mind. If a job is too big to finish in a day, divide it into several steps...focus on each step in turn...and enjoy the satisfaction that comes from completion.

• **Ask why you overburden yourself.** Perhaps it gives you a sense of importance...or a way to stay too busy to think about sorrows. For insights, try journaling until your motives are clear—then look for less taxing ways to satisfy those needs. You may realize that it's enough to do a great job as president of one club rather than three...or that sharing painful emotions brings more relief than burying them in "busyness."

High Stress Jobs Tied to Rheumatoid Arthritis

Stressful jobs increase risk for rheumatoid arthritis.

Recent finding: Your work environment can increase your chances of developing rheumatoid arthritis, especially if your job is highly stressful and you have little control over the work situation. Smoking, drinking alcohol and family history also are linked to increased rheumatoid arthritis risk.

Self-defense: Try to limit stress at work... don't smoke...drink alcohol in moderation... and talk to your doctor about reducing other risk factors.

Lars Alfredsson, PhD, professor, department of environmental medicine, Karolinska Institute, Stockholm, Sweden, and leader of a study of 2,700 patients, published in *Psychotherapy and Psychosomatics.*

Job Stress Can Make You Fat

According to a recent study, people who reported job stress on two occasions during a 10-year period were 24% more likely to become obese than people who said they were never stressed. People who reported job stress on at least three occasions were 73% more likely to become obese. Obesity contributes to heart disease and diabetes. Job stress is defined as having heavy workload demands and little decision-making power.

Self-defense: Consider how to reduce or eliminate work stress that is hurting your health.

Eric J. Brunner, PhD, reader in the department of epidemiology and public health, Royal Free and University College London Medical School, and author of a study of more than 10,000 people, published in *American Journal of Epidemiology.*

How to Keep Your Cool

Jeffrey Brantley, MD, director of the Mindfulness-based Stress-Reduction program at Duke University Center for Integrative Medicine, Durham, North Carolina, and author of *Calming Your Anxious Mind* (New Harbinger).

Ever feel like blowing up—or melting down? Whether it's due to cramped living quarters or cranky coworkers, almost everyone feels stressed occasionally.

Women are especially vulnerable: They typically feel tremendous pressure to remain calm—to serve as family peacemaker or to project professionalism at work—but physiological responses to stress make this tough.

Example: Your ex-husband threatens to boycott your son's graduation, or your department is given an impossible deadline. Your body reacts by producing the stress hormones *cortisol* and *adrenaline*, which elevate your blood pressure and flood your bloodstream with glucose (sugar). Heart racing, palms sweating and stomach churning, you feel like your body has been hijacked by your emotions. The more you worry about losing control, the more your stress hormones rise.

Solution: Practice *mindfulness*, a technique rooted in Buddhist tradition. It can calm and focus the mind, slow the heart rate, reduce the need for oxygen and quickly ease muscle tension. *The basics…*

1. Assess what's happening—not in the situation, but within yourself. Are your hands shaking? Head pounding? Recognizing these signs for what they are—normal responses to stress —reduces their power to upset you further.

2. Be compassionate toward yourself. Instead of a judgmental rebuke ("Crying again? Big baby!"), silently say, "My body is giving me a message. I will listen and learn from it."

3. Shift your focus. Rather than fretting about a physiological response that you can't control, such as a flushed face or choked voice, concentrate on one you can control—your breathing. Slow, deep, rhythmic inhalations and exhalations help you to regain a sense of mastery over your physical reactions.

4. Reconnect with your body—and disconnect from the crisis around you. Take a quick walk, do some yoga poses in the restroom, or simply close your eyes and gently massage your temples for a few moments.

5. Take action. Consciously free your mind from resentful or hopeless thoughts ("My ex is a jerk!" or "I'm just no good at this job"). Reflect calmly on specific solutions, such as family counseling or assistance from coworkers, that will allow you to regain control over the situation—and yourself.

Eating Disorder That's More Common Than Bulimia and Anorexia

Trisha Gura, PhD, author of *Lying In Weight: The Hidden Epidemic of Eating Disorders in Adult Women* (HarperCollins). Dr. Gura is a resident scholar at Brandeis University in Waltham, Massachusetts. *www.trishagura.com*

One night, Katie ate a "stew" of leftovers—stale pasta, wrinkled grapes, half a can of refried beans and week-old slices of beef. Other nights, she gnawed on frozen food without defrosting it...or microwaved it and then ate it so fast that it scalded her mouth. Sometimes she ate from the trash can. Why?

Because, she thought, if she could make food repulsive or tasteless enough—or even dangerous enough—she might not binge again. Yet more often than not, the next night she would go on another binge—alone in her kitchen, shoveling down food until she was painfully full...and completely disgusted with herself.

Katie may sound like a teenager in trouble. But, in fact, she's an adult—49 years old and suffering from binge-eating disorder (BED). Along with *bulimia* (bingeing that is followed by forced vomiting, overusing laxatives, excessive exercising or fasting) and *anorexia* (self-starvation), BED is one of three major eating disorders. Many people have never heard of BED—though it affects more than three times as many women as bulimia does and about four times as many as anorexia does. BED is widely unrecognized because people primarily binge alone, in ashamed secrecy.

Eating disorders afflict at least 10 million Americans, most of them female. While no exact figures are available, some treatment facilities report that the number of midlife women seeking help has tripled or quadrupled in the last several years. Among these women, as many as half may have BED.

HIDDEN PROBLEMS

In adult women, an eating disorder typically appears when a stressful transition—a divorce, a move, a parent's death—either triggers the recurrence of an adolescent eating disorder or launches a new one. In the face of intense or chronic stress, people are prone to return to familiar bad habits—and for many women, those involve food.

An eating disorder can have serious emotional and social consequences. A woman with BED or bulimia isolates herself because she is too embarrassed to eat in front of family or friends, so she stays home when others go out in order to be alone with her food. A woman with anorexia isolates herself because she doesn't want the temptation of being around

food and she worries that others will notice how little she eats. Among women with eating disorders, self-loathing is common.

In addition, eating disorders carry grave health risks...

•**BED can lead to obesity,** with all the accompanying health problems, including increased risk for hypertension, high cholesterol, heart disease and stroke...diabetes...gallbladder disease...sleep apnea and respiratory problems...and breast, endometrial and colon cancers.

•**Bulimia can cause nutritional deficiencies** ...weakened immunity...erosion of tooth enamel, periodontal disease and inflamed salivary glands...muscle spasms...chronic constipation ...pancreatitis...inflammation and possible rupture of the esophagus...permanent damage to the heart or kidneys...and electrolyte imbalances that can lead to heart failure and death.

•**Anorexia can lead to dehydration and malnutrition...**weakened immunity...infertility ...osteoporosis...damage to the heart and kidneys...and death from starvation.

HOPE FOR HEALING

It's never too late to develop an eating disorder —and it's never too late to seek help. Confide in your doctor, and ask for a referral to a mental-health professional.

Resource: The National Eating Disorders Association (800-931-2237, *www.national eatingdisorders.org*) provides referrals to doctors, counselors and residential treatment facilities in your area. *Approaches to treatment include...*

•**Cognitive-behavioral therapy (CBT).** There is more scientific evidence for the effectiveness of this therapy than for any other, particularly in treating BED and bulimia. CBT helps you to recognize the circumstances, emotions and thoughts that trigger a binge or other problem behavior, and then to change that behavior—for instance, by phoning a friend or going for a walk instead.

Referrals: National Association of Cognitive-Behavioral Therapists (*www.nacbt.org*).

•**Interpersonal therapy.** In one-on-one sessions with a psychologist or psychiatrist, you talk about your past and your relationships. Over time, you come to understand the underlying causes of your eating disorder so that it no longer controls you.

●**Adult in-patient treatment.** Some clinics offer programs specifically for women over age 30, including the Renfrew Center, with eight facilities on the East Coast (800-736-3739, *www.renfrewcenter.com*)...and Remuda Ranch in Wickenburg, Arizona, and Milford, Virginia (800-445-1900, *www.remudaranch.com*).

●**Support groups.** Meeting regularly with a group of adult women who also are combating eating disorders can provide a social network of sympathetic friends, practical advice for overcoming the problem and a sense of self-worth when you help another woman who is suffering.

Contact: Eating Disorder Referral and Information Center (858-792-7463, *www.edreferral. com*).

●**Medications.** Drugs appear not to be very effective in treating most eating disorders. However, if you also are depressed, antidepressant medication may help you feel more optimistic, which in turn may help you gain control over your eating. Ask your doctor or a psychiatrist about this option.

●**Creative endeavors.** Because an eating disorder keeps you isolated and secretive, healing involves projecting your voice and personality into the community. Join a writers' group, take a class in art or dance, or get involved with an organization that advocates for a better world.

If one type of therapy does not help you, don't just give up—try a different approach. With the right help, you can recover.

Stop the Obesity–Depression Cycle

In middle age, obese women are twice as likely to be depressed as non-obese women —and depressed women are twice as likely to be obese as nondepressed women.

Possible reason: The stigma of obesity damages self-esteem...which contributes to feelings of hopelessness and depression...which can make it harder to lose weight.

To break the cycle: Seek help from a mental health professional.

Gregory Simon, MD, psychiatrist and researcher, Group Health Cooperative, Seattle, and leader of a study of 4,641 women ages 40 to 65, published in *General Hospital Psychiatry.*

Brains of Bulimia Patients Wired Differently

Rachel Marsh, PhD, assistant professor, clinical psychology, division of child and adolescent psychiatry, Columbia University, New York City.

Daniel le Grange, PhD, professor, psychiatry and behavioral neuroscience, and director, Eating Disorders Program, University of Chicago.

Mary Tantillo, PhD, RN, associate professor, clinical nursing, University of Rochester School of Nursing, and director, Western New York Comprehensive Care Center for Eating Disorders.

Archives of General Psychiatry.

Brain circuitry involved in regulating impulsive behavior seems to be less active in women suffering from the eating disorder known as bulimia nervosa.

Bulimia nervosa, characterized by alternating binging and purging episodes (vomiting and taking laxatives being among the more common behaviors), primarily affects girls and women.

BACKGROUND

The frontostriatal regulatory circuits implicated in this study are mediated by both the neurotransmitter *dopamine* and the neurotransmitter *serotonin.*

So far, serotonin has been widely implicated in bulimia, which is often treated with antidepressants known as selective serotonin reuptake inhibitors (SSRIs). However, dopamine

has not been studied closely in relation to bulimia nervosa.

"These findings argue for looking more directly into dopamine systems in eating disorders," said study author Rachel Marsh, PhD, an assistant professor of clinical psychology in the division of child and adolescent psychiatry at Columbia University in New York City.

THE STUDY

The researchers compared results from functional magnetic resonance imaging (fMRI) on 20 women (average age 26) with bulimia nervosa and 20 age-matched controls.

Participants were shown pictures with arrows pointing either left or right and were asked to identify which way the arrows were pointing. In the simple version of the task, the arrows pointing left were on the left side of the screen and the right-directed arrows on the right side of the screen.

For the more difficult component of the task, the leftward-pointing arrow was positioned on the right side of the screen.

"When individuals are performing correctly, they need to engage self-regulatory control or cognitive control. They need to hold back the automatic response strategy in order to perform correctly," Dr. Marsh explained.

THE FINDINGS

Women with bulimia nervosa performed faster on the difficult trials and made more errors—and when they were performing the task, they did not engage the same brain circuitry as the controls.

Participants with the most previous bulimic episodes and the highest rates of preoccupation with shape and weight performed the worst on tasks, and engaged the frontostriatal circuits the most.

Healthy controls activated different brain circuits—the anterior cingulated cortex region of the brain more when making correct responses and the striatum more when delivering incorrect responses.

The study was published in the *Archives of General Psychiatry*.

IMPLICATIONS

At this point, it's not clear if the brain differences are a cause or an effect of the disorder.

"These were adult women who had had the illness for a median of nine years," Dr. Marsh said. "We don't know if [the changes are] the product of having the disorder for nine years, or if something determines development of the disorder."

Researchers are just beginning to untangle the neurochemistry of eating disorders.

"Patients with bulimia nervosa are very impulsive, not only in an inability to stop eating everything in front of them, but there is also a high prevalence of shoplifting and drug abuse in this population," Dr. Marsh said. Mood disorders are also common in these women, indicating that problems with behavioral self-regulation might be at play.

EXPERT REACTION

"This is pretty new stuff. We have a fair degree of understanding of the neurochemistry of eating disorders [but this study looked at] what actually happens in the brain when you engage in certain decision-making tasks or activities," said Daniel le Grange, PhD, director of the Eating Disorders Program at the University of Chicago and author of *Help Your Teenager Beat an Eating Disorder* and *Treating Bulimia in Adolescents* (both by Guilford Press). "The main interest [of the study] at this time would be to understand how these disorders develop. Does the abnormality occur because someone has bulimia nervosa, or does it contribute to developing it?"

"It's definitely preliminary…but it's not something to ignore," added Mary Tantillo, PhD, RN, director of the Western New York Comprehensive Care Center for Eating Disorders. "We need to study this on adolescents who are closer to the onset of illness [Dr. Marsh has already started such a study]."

The U.S. National Institute of Mental Health Web site has more on eating disorders at *www. nimh.nib.gov/health/topics/eating-disorders/ index.shtml*.

Caregiver's Guide to Emotional Well-Being

Barry J. Jacobs, PsyD, clinical psychologist and family therapist, and director of behavioral sciences for the Crozer-Keystone Family Medicine residency program in Springfield, Pennsylvania. He is author of *The Emotional Survival Guide for Caregivers* (Guilford). *www.emotionalsurvivalguide.com*

When a loved one is seriously ill or disabled and you take on the task of providing his/her care, it's natural to focus your energies on meeting that person's needs. The financial and physical demands you face may quickly become evident, yet the emotional impact often goes unrecognized—even though it may be the most challenging element of all. *Evidence...*

- **In a study in *Archives of Internal Medicine,*** 14% of end-of-life caregivers reported significant financial strain...18% reported significant physical strain...and 30% reported significant emotional strain.

- **Emotional stress leaves caregivers vulnerable to depression**—sometimes even more vulnerable than the person to whom they tend.

- **In another study,** caregiving spouses who reported emotional strain were 63% more likely to die within four years of the studied period than caregivers who did not feel strained.

If you're a caregiver, you need to protect yourself as well as your loved one.

Helpful: Knowing what to expect as you move through the various emotional stages of becoming a caregiver...and developing specific strategies for coping.

GETTING OVER THE SHOCK

When a loved one suffers a sudden medical crisis, such as a serious injury, a woman can be thrust into the role of caregiver with no preparation. She may assume optimistically—and often unrealistically—that things will soon return to normal as the patient recovers.

In other cases, caregiving duties grow gradually as a parent or spouse ages or develops a progressive illness, such as Parkinson's disease or Alzheimer's disease. The caregiver may not be able to admit to herself how much the loved one's condition is deteriorating.

Either way, the caregiver's instinctive reaction to the shock is denial. Initially, this tendency to minimize the impact of the illness can help give the caregiver the strength to do what needs to be done. But persistent denial can compromise a caregiver's ability to make sound decisions.

Example: If your mother can no longer walk without risking a fall, but you cannot recognize the need to insist that she use a walker or wheelchair, it jeopardizes her safety.

Support strategies: It is best to face reality. To see your loved one as she is now rather than as she used to be, keep a log of her symptoms and abilities—recording other family members' observations as well as your own. Learn enough about her medical condition so that you can understand the treatment options and prognosis. This way, you and her doctors can agree on a medical objective, such as prolonging life or, later, simply making the patient as comfortable as possible.

LIVING WITH NEGATIVE FEELINGS

Many caregivers are heartened to experience positive emotions, such as pride in their ability to help and a deepened sense of devotion. But there are bound to be negative emotions, too, such as resentment and dread. You may feel resentful about being burdened...then guilty over the resentment...then angry for having been made to feel guilty.

You also may experience conflicting emotions toward the loved one himself as you struggle with the changes in the nature of your relationship.

Example: Suppose that, after your husband's stroke, you need to feed and bathe him as you would a child—and this clashes with your longtime image of him as a partner, peer and lover.

Support strategies: Remember that negative feelings about caregiving are normal and predictable—they do not invalidate your love. To overcome resentment and restore mutual respect, it helps to promote a patient's capabilities as much as his comfort—perhaps by being

as dedicated to his physical therapy exercises as you are to his personal needs.

Strongly negative feelings also can be a helpful signal, alerting you to a need to adjust your plans. For example, taking care of an ill brother does not necessarily mean that he must live in your home forever, so stay open to all the options.

ACHIEVING BALANCE

Some caregivers worry that they're not doing enough, so they disproportionately expend time and energy on the loved one. This can be detrimental to their other relationships.

Example: If you devote yourself to taking care of an adult child with a progressive illness, you may neglect your spouse, other children, extended family and friends.

Losing ties with other people deprives you of support. The more isolated you become, the more susceptible you may be to depression and other health problems. This risk increases if you come to define yourself solely as a caregiver, losing your sense of personal identity.

Support strategies: Chronic medical conditions unfold over years, so they need to be handled much like a marathon—by pacing yourself. Talk to your doctor or a mental health professional if you show signs of burnout, such as constant fatigue, insomnia, irritability, cynicism or feelings of helplessness. Be committed to staying connected to others. Carving out time to go to dinner with your husband, play bridge with friends or attend a function at your house of worship will help replenish your spirit.

More from Dr. Barry Jacobs...

When You Need Help...

Family caregivers can get information, support and/or referrals to professional counselors through these organizations...

• **Family Caregiver Alliance,** 800-445-8106, *www.caregiver.org*.

• **National Alliance for Caregiving,** 301-718-8444, *www.caregiving.org*.

• **Caregiver Action Network,** 202-454-3970, *www.caregiveraction.org*.

• **Well Spouse Association,** 800-838-0879, *www.wellspouse.org*.

Have a Good Cry

Studies of hundreds of volunteers have found that 85% of women and 73% of men feel less sad and less angry after crying. Women cry four times as often as men—on average 5.3 times a month, while men cry only 1.4 times a month. Crying episodes in most women involve tears running down their cheeks, but most male crying episodes only result in watery eyes. Research shows that emotional tears are chemically different from other types of tears, such as those shed when cutting onions. Emotional tears have a higher protein content. Because emotional stress can increase the risk for stress-related disorders and can even contribute to constriction of the coronary artery, crying is a healthful response to emotional stress.

William H. Frey II, PhD, neuroscientist, Regions Hospital, St. Paul.

Do You Have an Undiagnosed Attention Disorder?

Kathleen G. Nadeau, PhD, director of the Chesapeake ADHD Center of Maryland, Silver Spring, *www.chesapeakeadd.com*, and cofounder of the National Center for Girls and Women with ADHD, Washington, DC. She is coeditor of *Understanding Women with ADHD* (Advantage) and author of numerous other books on adult ADHD.

Largely unheard of a generation or two ago, attention deficit hyperactivity disorder (ADHD) is now a common diagnosis for schoolchildren, especially boys. Recently, however, researchers have discovered that 4%

to 8% of adult women may have ADHD—yet most of them have never been diagnosed.

ADHD (also formerly known as attention deficit disorder, or ADD) is a neurological condition that interferes with a person's ability to concentrate, organize daily life and manage time. It can wreak havoc on all areas of life, including health. Unlike a man, a woman may develop worsening symptoms in midlife and beyond due to hormonal changes.

Fortunately, help is available. Once a woman with ADHD is diagnosed and treated, her life tends to improve dramatically.

SIGNS OF ADHD

While everyone feels frazzled at times, the typical woman with ADHD feels almost constantly overwhelmed. *Far more often than average, she…*

• **Feels rushed…**arrives late…misses deadlines.

• **Procrastinates…**gets distracted…feels like she works frantically all day but accomplishes little.

• **Has difficulty concentrating** and following directions.

• **Is easily bored…**or becomes so engrossed in an activity that she neglects other responsibilities.

• **Acts impulsively…**blurts out inappropriate remarks…makes hasty decisions.

• **Misplaces things…**forgets errands.

• **Overspends…**pays bills late.

• **Has short-lived friendships** and failed marriages.

• **Is moody…**feels ashamed…feels "different" from other women.

ADHD can be costly in myriad ways. A woman suffers financially if she impulsively buys things she can't afford. She suffers professionally due to her scattershot performance—a recent study found that, in terms of productivity, employees with ADHD do the equivalent of 22 fewer days of work per year than other employees. She suffers socially if friends and family get fed up…and psychologically if her inability to cope erodes her self-esteem.

Her physical health also is at risk—for instance, she may forget her medication or mammogram appointment. Constant stress elevates levels of the hormone *cortisol*, which can weaken the immune system and contribute to heart disease, digestive disorders, respiratory problems, infertility and fibromyalgia (widespread muscle and joint pain). ADHD even may increase her risk for depression, addiction and/or eating disorders.

WHAT'S WORSE FOR WOMEN

Because girls with ADHD generally are not as disruptive as boys, pediatricians may overlook the disorder in girls. When these girls reach adulthood, their symptoms often are wrongly attributed to depression or anxiety—misdiagnoses that are less common among men.

Gender bias plays a role, too. Women typically are expected to be the family organizers—to plan meals, put away clutter, keep track of everyone's schedule. These tasks are difficult for women with ADHD, in whom the brain's organizational functions are compromised.

Midlife's hormonal changes can worsen a woman's symptoms significantly.

Reason: As estrogen production declines, the brain's receptors for *dopamine*—a brain chemical associated with happy feelings—become less receptive.

Result: Women who used to manage their ADHD fairly well may have more trouble coping during and after menopause.

Treatment can help—but that requires a diagnosis. *There is no definitive test for ADHD, so diagnosis is based on three criteria…*

• **Symptoms began many years ago.**

• **You have at least several of the symptoms above.**

• **Symptoms are severe enough to significantly affect at least two of the three main areas of life**—home, work, social aspects.

What to do: If you suspect that you have ADHD, consult a mental-health professional who works with adult ADHD patients.

Referrals: Children and Adults with Attention Deficit/Hyperactivity Disorder, 800-233-4050, *www.chadd.org*.

HOW TO COPE

The following strategies make it much easier to live with ADHD...

•**Join a support group.** Find an online group through *www.chadd.org.*

•**Hire a professional organizer** to create systems for you for filing paperwork and storing belongings.

Referrals: National Association of Professional Organizers, 856-380-6828, *www.napo. net.*

•**Set up an automatic bill-paying system for regular expenses,** such as mortgages and car loans, through your bank's Web site.

•**Avoid food additives.** Studies suggest that artificial coloring and preservatives are linked to ADHD.

•**Supplement daily with a vitamin-B complex and with omega-3 fatty acids** (found in fish oil)—these support brain function.

•**Stabilize blood sugar.** Rapid spikes and plunges in blood sugar levels impair concentration. Include protein at every meal...avoid simple carbohydrates (white bread, cookies).

•**Get enough sleep.** Many women with ADHD are sleep-deprived because they get a "second wind" after dinner or lose track of time and stay up too late.

Helpful: Set an alarm to ring each evening to remind you when it's time for bed.

•**Practice stress-reduction techniques to clear your mind.** If it is hard to sit still for meditation or deep breathing, try yoga or tai chi.

•**Try neurofeedback,** which trains you to increase the brain-wave patterns associated with improved focus and concentration.

Referrals: The Biofeedback Certification International Alliance, 866-908-8713, *www. bcia.org.*

MEDICATION OPTIONS

If the above strategies are not sufficient to make life manageable, ask your doctor about the pros and cons of medication. ADHD drugs generally work by regulating levels of the brain chemicals *dopamine* and/or *norepinephrine,* which affect parts of the brain that control attention. Medication does not cure ADHD—when the drugs are discontinued, symptoms return.

Stimulants, such as *amphetamine* (Adderall), *methylphenidate* (Ritalin, Concerta) or *lisdexamfetamine* (Vyvanse), are most often prescribed. Fluctuations in estrogen levels may influence the effectiveness of stimulants, so women taking these drugs should be closely monitored. Side effects may include dry mouth, restlessness and high blood pressure.

Another option is an antidepressant. *Atomoxetine* (Strattera) is the first nonstimulant drug approved by the FDA for the treatment of ADHD. Other antidepressants include *bupropion* (Wellbutrin), *venlafaxine* (Effexor) and *desipramine* (Norpramin). Such drugs may be appropriate when anxiety and depression accompany ADHD. Antidepressants often are used in combination with stimulants. Side effects may include nausea, sleep problems and decreased sex drive.

If you are going through menopause and your ADHD symptoms have worsened, hormone therapy may help by balancing estrogen levels.

Downside: Increased heart disease and breast cancer risk.

Bottom line: ADHD is a legitimate medical problem, not a character flaw. Remember, the condition does have its benefits. Women with ADHD often have tremendous energy...are very creative...and have an adventurous nature that makes them great fun to be with.

Extra Help to Kick the Habit

Andrea King, PhD, associate professor of psychiatry at the University of Chicago. For information on her smoking-cessation study and links to other programs, go to *http://stopsmoking.uchicago.edu.*

Giving up cigarettes is harder for women. Studies suggest that nicotine gum doubles "quit rates" in men but seldom helps women...and that nicotine patches help 24% of men, but only 17% of women. *Reasons...*

•**Fear of fat.** Ex-smokers often put on pounds. Women are more sensitive about weight, so they're likelier to resume smoking if quitting triggers weight gain.

•**Withdrawal symptoms.** Due to hormones and/or genetics, women in withdrawal may have worse mood swings, depression, anxiety and fatigue.

•**Environmental triggers.** Women report stronger cravings when facing situations in which, back in their smoking days, they would habitually have lit up—such as after meals.

New hope: The prescription drug *naltrexone.* By inhibiting certain chemical signals in the brain, it may block nicotine's pleasurable sensations, reducing cravings and withdrawal symptoms. In a recent study of 110 smokers, half took *naltrexone* daily and half got a placebo. After eight weeks, 62% of men and 58% of women on naltrexone had quit smoking. In the placebo group, 67% of men and only 39% of women had quit.

Conclusion: Naltrexone helps women—but not men—kick the habit.

Bonus: Naltrexone users gained only 1.5 pounds on average after quitting, compared with 4.5 pounds for placebo users.

Naltrexone is FDA-approved for treating drug and alcohol addiction, but doctors can legally prescribe it off-label for smokers.

Dosage: 50 mg daily for three months. Mild, temporary side effects may include nausea, headache, dizziness and fatigue.

Birth Year and Alcoholism

Birth year affects women's risk for alcoholism. Women born between 1954 and 1983 are at least 50% more likely to become alcohol-dependent than women born between 1944 and 1953. Due to cultural changes, the younger group may be more likely to engage in behaviors—including excessive drinking—that earlier were viewed as taboo.

Wise limit: No more than one drink daily.

Richard A. Grucza, PhD, research assistant professor, department of psychiatry, Washington University School of Medicine, St. Louis, and leader of an analysis of two national surveys, published in *Alcoholism: Clinical and Experimental Research.*

Housework Can Make You Sick

A recent study shows that full-time housework can produce psycho-social stress similar to that caused by regular employment.

Main causes: Too much routine, social isolation, lack of time and lack of recognition. Women taking care of children were the most significantly affected.

Christof Wolf, PhD, sociologist, German Social Science Infrastructure, Mannheim, Germany, and leader of a study of 700 women, published in *Cologne Magazine for Sociology and Social Psychology.*

How to Let Go of Guilt

Joan Borysenko, PhD, licensed psychologist and internationally known speaker and consultant on women's health, spirituality and integrative medicine. Her books include *Guilt Is the Teacher, Love Is the Lesson* (Grand Central)...*Inner Peace for Busy Women* (Hay House)...and *Saying Yes to Change* (Hay House). *www.joanborysenko.com.*

Quick, think of three things you're feeling guilty about right now. For many women, the only hard part is limiting the list to just three. Guilt can be productive or paralyzing, justified or undeserved, healthy or unhealthy. The difference lies in the cause of the guilt feelings—and what you do about them.

Healthy guilt is a moral compass. It alerts us when we are unkind or irresponsible... and prods us when we neglect something important.

Unhealthy guilt shows up when we blame ourselves for issues outside our control...feel responsible for other people's emotions...have trouble setting boundaries...or feel overly concerned about inconveniencing others. The sense that we have to be everything to everybody affects many women. It is an exaggeration of our natural nurturing urge.

Research from the University of California, Los Angeles, reveals that, for women, tending to others is a stress reducer. Nurturing triggers the release of the hormone *oxytocin* which, in addition to promoting the bond between mothers and babies, produces a sense of peace and well-being.

Women often are so preoccupied with taking care of others that self-care suffers. We feel selfish when we turn attention to ourselves.

GOOD-FOR-YOU GUILT

To distinguish healthy guilt from unhealthy guilt, step back from your automatic reaction and analyze your role in a specific situation.

Example: Your sister is upset with you. If your knee-jerk response is, "It must be my fault—I'm a bad sister," that's unhealthy guilt. But if you have said, "Sorry, Sis, I'm too busy to talk right now," the last five times she phoned, your detachment may indeed be contributing to the problem. In that case, corrective action is called for. *Working through healthy guilt requires a series of steps...*

• **Admit to yourself that you've done wrong.** Guilt is such a powerful and unpleasant emotion that we are tempted to rationalize our behavior.

Example: At work, you took credit for a colleague's idea. You try to justify it by telling yourself, "I put more work into this project than my coworker did."

When we excuse our bad behavior, we avoid taking responsibility. An "it's not my fault" attitude makes any positive change unlikely.

• **Confide in someone.** Research suggests that keeping secrets is highly stressful and can result in stress-related disorders, such as headaches, back pain and digestive complaints. By telling someone you trust about the issue, you can start to convert immobilizing shame into constructive action.

Important: Choose a confidante who won't feel burdened by the information—for instance, a member of the clergy, a therapist or a friend who is not acquainted with the other people involved.

• **Ask yourself why.** When we wrong another person, it is often because a deep need is not being acknowledged or met. By coming to a conscious understanding of your motives, you will be less likely to repeat the action.

Example: Although your job performance is acceptable, you can't shake the feeling that you are in over your head. Once you have identified the unmet need—in this case, for a confidence boost—you can seek appropriate ways of fulfilling it, such as finding a mentor or taking a class to build your professional skills.

• **Make amends.** Apologizing to the person you wronged is a good start, but you also must take action to correct or contain the damage —if doing so will not cause additional harm.

Example: Coming clean with your colleague and boss about having taken undue credit is appropriate. Confessing a long-ago affair to your husband is not—because even if baring your soul would make you feel better, it could cause him needless pain.

If you can't make amends directly to the person you hurt, perform a service—such as volunteering at a soup kitchen or battered women's shelter—and privately dedicate it to the person you wronged.

• **Acknowledge what you've learned.** Whether or not the person you harmed forgives you, forgive yourself. Respect what you've become as a result of the experience —a more considerate and self-aware woman.

GIVE UNHEALTHY GUILT THE BOOT

When an overactive guilty conscience prevents us from setting appropriate boundaries, we can't do a good job of taking care of ourselves or others. We need to practice saying no. Setting limits is easier when we identify not just what we need to say no to, but also the deep personal needs to which we are saying yes.

Example: Your friend's birthday party is this weekend. She lives two hours away, and you are utterly exhausted—but the thought of skipping the gala fills you with guilt. Identify two vital needs—to let your friend know how much she means to you...and to take care of your own well-being. Now you can speak to your friend clearly and kindly, saying, "I love you and want to celebrate your special day, but I'm so depleted that I'm not sure I could get to the party in one piece. Let's talk about how we can celebrate together later in the month."

If unhealthy guilt is a habitual response, learn to counter that habit through repeated self-reflection. *Set aside 10 minutes every night to ask yourself two questions...*

•**Were there times today when I needed to nurture myself—but didn't do it?**

Example: "I needed to use a restroom during the drive to my in-laws' house, but I waited because my husband didn't want to stop."

•**When was I harsh with myself?**

Example: "I called myself a stupid klutz when I burned the cookies for the charity bake sale."

Write down the answers, then review the situations in which you neglected your needs. Think of an alternative response for each one and mentally rehearse it to use next time. For instance, practice saying, "Please respect my need to feel comfortable," or "It was kind of me to donate cookies to charity, even if they were crispy."

The idea is not to catch yourself "failing" at self-care, but rather to become aware of the subtle ways that guilt creeps into your life. Asking and answering these questions with compassion for yourself helps to banish unhealthy guilt—for good.

Overcome the Urge to Splurge

Judy Kuriansky, PhD, clinical psychologist and sex therapist on the faculty of Columbia University Teachers College in New York City. She is author of several books, including *The Complete Idiot's Guide to a Healthy Relationship* (Alpha). *www.sexualtherapy.com/therapists/jkuriansky.htm*

"Shop till you drop" may sound fun and funny—but compulsive overspending is no joke.

Warning signs: Hiding purchases from family...spending money when you swore you wouldn't...falling into debt. *To rein in spending...*

•**Identify underlying needs that fuel your spending**—then satisfy them in other ways. Want to impress people? Read up on current events and get noticed for your insights instead of your outfits. Feel lonesome? Phone a friend. Deprived? Buy a cappuccino, not a new purse.

•**Explore alternative activities.** To surround yourself with beautiful objects, skip stores and visit an art museum instead. If you love books, try the library, not a bookstore.

•**Get a healthful "high."** The brief thrill of the purchase often leads to buyer's remorse. Get regret-free joy from exercise—even just a brisk walk—which releases "feel-good" endorphins in the brain.

•**"Shop" in your own closets.** Pull out clothes seldom worn, pictures still unhung, cosmetics never opened. Pretend you're in the store seeing them for the first time. Invite friends to bring their own little-used stuff and have a swap, donating leftovers to charity. You'll clean your closets, rediscover previously purchased treasures, get new goods, feel generous—and won't spend a cent.

Are You Addicted to Shopping?

Money, Time-Life Bldg., Rockefeller Center, New York City 10020.

Compulsive shopping is a debilitating addiction that can undermine your emotional health...and ruin your finances.

Signs you are a compulsive shopper: You get a high from buying things...you buy items that you don't need...you lie about what you buy or how much you spend...you hide packages and receipts...you use money set aside for bills, even as your debt mounts...your shopping habits cause relationship or work problems, but you can't stop...you feel guilty or ashamed of all the shopping you do.

If you are a compulsive shopper: Keep a log of all purchases and how you feel about each one, so you learn the difference between wants and needs. Avoid places and situations in which you feel compelled to shop, including specific stores, TV channels and the Internet. Shop with a list, and stick to it. Pay for purchases with cash, checks or a debit card, not a credit card. Have only one credit card for emergencies, and leave it at home when you go shopping. Find a professional counselor or support group.

Resources: Debtors Anonymous (781-453-2743, *www.debtorsanonymous.org*)...shopping-addiction groups, which can be found through Yahoo! and other search engines.

Find Emotional Freedom

Judith Orloff, MD, assistant clinical professor of psychiatry, University of California, Los Angeles, and a psychiatrist in private practice in Los Angeles. She is author of *Emotional Freedom: Liberate Yourself from Negative Emotions and Transform Your Life* (Three Rivers Press). *www.drjudithorloff.com*

Everyone has moments of fear, flashes of anger and twinges of envy. But if your life is dominated by a painful or damaging emotion—paralyzing dread, uncontrollable fury or incessant envy—you are imprisoned by your feelings. Stress rises, self-image suffers, relationships falter...and you lose the ability to simply celebrate life.

•**You can become free.** The key is to master specific techniques that help transform negative feelings into positive ones.

What to do: Consider the three common emotional traps below. Which descriptions trigger a wince, a sigh or some other sign of self-recognition? Those are areas where you can benefit most by working toward emotional freedom. *Here's how to...*

TRANSFORM FEAR INTO COURAGE

An emotional response to real or imagined danger, fear can make you abandon good sense and hold you in a chronic state of stress.

Examples: Fear of being alone may keep you trapped in a demeaning relationship even though you know that you should get out...fear of economic insecurity may keep you awake with worry night after night.

What to do...

•**Identify the source.** Make a list of the things you are afraid of. Then ask yourself where those fears came from. Did a hypercritical parent make you fear that you were unworthy of love? Did growing up poor make you chronically anxious about money? By recognizing such origins, you can *predict* which situations set off your fear, such as arguing with your husband or incurring an unexpected expense. This helps you feel *less panicked* when your body's automatic fight-or-flight response to fear causes your heart to race and your muscles to tense.

•**Shift your internal response.** Be on the lookout for the fearful inner voice that catastrophizes every situation—*I can't afford a new roof. The water damage will ruin the house, and I'll wind up on the street.* When fear speaks, talk back to yourself with the voice of reason—*I have options. I can negotiate with the roofer or sell Aunt Jane's old silver to pay for the repairs.*

•**Take courageous action.** Identify an easy first step toward changing your situation, then do it.

Example: If you fear leaving a bad relationship, first confide in a trusted friend or therapist. After you accomplish that, take another small step—such as setting a limit on how much time you spend each week with the person you are trying to distance yourself from. Slowly but surely, you will get unstuck from fear as your confidence and courage grow.

CHANGE ANGER INTO TRANQUILITY

Occasional irritation is normal, but if you often are on the verge of a blowup, you must address the true sources of your anger. Emotional freedom comes from improving situations when possible...and accepting situations over which you have no control. *What to do...*

•**Acknowledge underlying emotions.** Anger often masks feelings of being vulnerable, unappreciated, excluded or powerless. A furious outburst ("You're a terrible friend!") makes others feel defensive or angry in return—but admitting to the deeper emotion ("I felt hurt when you invited the rest of the book club to your party but didn't include me") is likely to elicit compassion and a desire to make amends.

•**Ask specifically for what you want.** Instead of demanding, "Stop being a slob!" say to your spouse, "I'd appreciate it if you would put your dirty dishes in the dishwasher." Limit your comments to the present rather than dredging up past grievances.

•**Recognize your own role.** How are you contributing to the situations that make you angry? Perhaps you are left off of guest lists because you always argue about politics during parties. Perhaps your spouse leaves the housework to you because you are too critical. Changing your own behavior can prevent future fury.

•**Soothe yourself.** When a situation is beyond your control (the long line at the post office, the heavy traffic), giving way to anger leads only to behavior that you'll regret—such as speaking rudely to the postal clerk or endangering yourself and others by tailgating.

Better: Use a relaxation technique, such as deep breathing or listening to calming music, to safely dissipate frustration.

TURN ENVY INTO SELF-ESTEEM

Envy is the desire to have for yourself the advantages or accomplishments of another person. At the root of envy is a sense of your own inferiority.

•**Look for a pattern of putting yourself down.** Ask yourself if you habitually point out your own shortcomings ("I'm an idiot with numbers")…compare yourself negatively ("They are more outgoing than I am")…or deny your own needs ("It's okay if you smoke in the car. Don't worry about my asthma"). Like envy, these signal low self-esteem. Catch yourself when you make such remarks, and replace them with thoughts of self-affirmation—*I am well-read…I exercise and keep fit…I deserve to breathe clean air.*

•**Become the best you can be.** Look objectively at the person you envy and identify the attributes that you admire. Which of those traits can you work toward? Maybe you can't aspire to your rich cousin's designer wardrobe, but you can emulate her cheerful disposition. Rather than focusing on the ways in which you and she are different, list ways in which you are similar—you both volunteer, you both have new grandsons—and foster a positive connection by talking with the other person about the things that you have in common. Once you feel more positive about yourself, you'll be able to sincerely celebrate the successes of others.

•**Lend a hand.** Look around for people who are struggling, and use your talents to provide assistance—for instance, tutoring at a local school or organizing a charity fund-raiser. When you start to see yourself as competent and compassionate, you'll admire yourself more…be more confident of others' affections…and feel little cause for envy of anyone else.

Reiki: The Energy That Heals

Aurora Ocampo, RN, CNS, clinical nurse specialist at the Continuum Center for Health and Healing, Beth Israel Medical Center, New York City. *www.healthand healingny.org*

Reiki (pronounced RAY-key) is a healing art traced to spiritual teachings from Japan in the early 20th century. The name combines two Japanese words, *rei* (universal) and *ki* (life energy). Reiki practitioners often use the technique to help ease clients' anxiety and stress…chronic or postsurgical pain…menopausal hot flashes…menstrual cramps…migraines…and nausea and fatigue from chemotherapy.

How it works: The traditional principle is that the practitioner taps into a universal life energy that exists within and around us…then channels this energy to the client, enhancing the body's innate healing abilities. The modern scientific theory is that reiki promotes profound relaxation, increasing levels of pain-

relieving, mood-boosting brain chemicals called *endorphins.*

What to expect: During a typical 60-minute reiki session, the client (fully dressed) sits in a chair or lies on a massage table. The practitioner places his/her hands, palms down, on or just above a dozen or so different spots on the client's body, holding each position for several minutes. Clients become deeply relaxed, and some perceive sensations of warmth or tingling at the spot being treated.

Cost of treatment: About $75 to $100 per session.

How to find a practitioner: Reiki has no formal licensing process, so locating an experienced practitioner is largely a matter of word-of-mouth.

Helpful: Get a referral from a local hospital that has an integrative medicine center.

Bottom line: While no large-scale clinical trials on reiki have yet been done, studies show benefits from various touch therapies. There are no negative effects from reiki. If you have a serious health problem, try reiki as an adjunct to standard medical treatment. Some people say that reiki works only due to a placebo effect—and that may be so. However, practitioners often encounter clients who are skeptical at first…but who, after experiencing reiki firsthand, report that the therapy has helped them.

The Power of Aromatherapy

Alan Hirsch, MD, founder and neurological director of the Smell & Taste Treatment and Research Foundation in Chicago. He is a neurologist and psychiatrist, and is author of *Life's a Smelling Success* (Authors of Unity) and *What's Your Food Sign?: How to Use Food Cues to Find True Love* (Stewart, Tabori & Chang). *www.smellandtaste.org*

Aromatherapy can be a remarkable remedy. When a patient smells a particular odor, scent molecules bind to the surface of cell walls at the top of the nose. This triggers the release of neurotransmitters and other chemicals that stimulate different parts of the brain.

Scents that patients enjoy are more effective remedies than those that they find unpleasant.

Example: One study found that patients with claustrophobia who enjoyed the smell of green apple felt less anxious when they smelled it, but patients who didn't like the smell had no improvement.

Intermittent bursts of a particular scent are more effective than smelling it continuously. Patients who use aromatherapy are advised to limit their scent exposure to about three minutes or less at a time—by putting an essential oil on a handkerchief and smelling it briefly, for example, or by walking in and out of a room where an aromatherapy candle is burning. Essential oils and aromatherapy candles are available at most health food stores and many grocery stores. Or you can sniff the actual food or flower, such as green apple or jasmine.

Many health conditions can be improved with aromatherapy. Whether or not these problems can be *prevented* with aromatherapy is still being researched.

ANXIETY

Some scents appear to calm the limbic system, the "emotional" part of the brain involved in anxiety. Also, patients who smell a pleasing odor feel happy—and this crowds out feelings of anxiety and stress.

Proven effective: Green apple and/or cucumber have been shown to reduce anxiety by about 18%. Also, patients who sniff lavender have an increase in alpha waves, a sign of heightened relaxation.

MIGRAINE HEADACHE

Most migraines may be caused in part by inflammation and by dilation/constriction of blood vessels in the brain. Aromatherapy changes the electrical activity in the brain, which can reduce vascular constriction and help relieve migraines. Aromatherapy appears to be effective for other types of headaches as well, such as muscle contraction headaches. It also promotes feelings of relaxation, which can reduce both the frequency of headaches and a patient's sensitivity to pain.

Proven effective: Green apple. It has effects similar to that of *sumatriptan* (Imitrex), a leading migraine drug, and can reduce the severity and duration of migraines by about 16%.

Caution: About 15% of migraine sufferers have *osmophobia*, a hypersensitivity to odors that can make migraines worse. Also, about 18% of migraine patients have a reduced sense of smell and don't respond to aromatherapy.

CIGARETTE ADDICTION

A number of studies have shown that smokers given cigarettes infused with a pepperlike smell have reduced cravings. More recently, smokers who were exposed to both pleasant and unpleasant odors found it easier to quit smoking, but the pleasant odors were somewhat more effective.

Proven effective: Any odor that you find particularly pleasant—lavender, mint, etc. Smell the scent whenever you feel an urge to light up a cigarette.

Also helpful: People who were born prior to 1930 tend to respond better to natural smells—citrus, the odor of baking bread, etc. Younger patients often respond better to artificial smells that evoke strong positive memories, such as Play-Doh or Pez candy.

LOW ENERGY

Odors that stimulate the trigeminal nerve (which has receptors in the nose and eyes and is the same nerve that makes people cry when they cut an onion) cause increased activity in the part of the brain that is involved in wakefulness.

Proven effective: Peppermint. People who smell a peppermint scent or chew a piece of peppermint gum or candy experience a sudden burst of energy.

Also helpful: The smell of strawberries or buttered popcorn. Both cause an increase in energy as well as metabolism.

OBESITY

A number of studies have shown that particular odors can help people lose weight. Some scents stimulate the part of the hypothalamus that controls appetite. Odors also may act as

a displacement mechanism—a reminder to eat less.

Proven effective: Peppermint and green apple. One large study found that people who sniffed either one of these scents when they felt hungry lost an average of 30 pounds over a six-month period.

Also helpful: Take frequent deep sniffs of food while eating. Odor molecules, regardless of the food they come from, can fool the brain into thinking that more has been consumed, which helps suppress the appetite.

REDUCED MEMORY/CONCENTRATION

Most adults find that they don't remember new information—telephone numbers, plot twists in a novel, etc.—as well as they used to. Aromatherapy can be used to accelerate learning speed and promote better concentration and memory.

Proven effective: Floral scents. Sniffing a floral essential oil triggers the release of *norepinephrine* and *adrenocorticotropic hormone* (ACTH), hormones that increase attention. Floral scents have been shown to improve memory and learning speed by about 17%.

In one study, people were exposed to different scents prior to bowling. Those who smelled jasmine knocked down 28% more pins, probably because it improved their concentration and hand/eye coordination.

Strategy: Sniff a floral scent when the material to be learned is initially presented, and repeat exposure to the same odor when the material must be recalled.

CHEMOTHERAPY-INDUCED NAUSEA

It's common for cancer patients who are undergoing chemotherapy to develop an intense aversion to the foods they ate immediately prior to treatments. There's little evidence that aromatherapy has a direct effect on nausea, but it can help prevent patients from developing a lifelong aversion to specific foods, which they may need for good health.

Proven effective: Smelling artificial cherry flavoring prior to chemotherapy. The best way to do this is to suck on a cherry candy. (This has the added benefit of stimulating saliva and helping to reduce hunger pangs.) Some patients will later associate the smell (and taste) of cherry with the treatments, but they can avoid cherry flavoring and continue to eat healthful foods, important for maintaining good nutrition.

The Healing Magic of a Great Bath

Thomas Stearns Lee, NMD, naturopathic physician based in Kingman, Arizona.

Mary Muryn, author of *Spa Magic* (Perigee Trade). She is based in Weston, Connecticut.

Apparently, the ancient Romans knew something we are just learning—bathing is about far more than simply cleaning behind your ears. A warm bath can be a great way to relax your muscles at the end of a stressful day. A cool one might be just what you need to wake yourself up in the morning, or chill out in the middle of the scorching summer. But have you considered that bathing can be a great way to eliminate waste? Or calm down your anxious mind? Bathing can even teach your body to cope with stress *before it* occurs.

CLEANING INSIDE AND OUT

Okay, first, let's look at cleaning. You know that a bath is a pleasant way to clean yourself *off*, but it's also a great way to clean yourself out. A warm saltwater bath every three or four days can help purge toxins from within. "You are a water balloon," says Thomas Stearns Lee, NMD. Think way back to grade school science. In the process of osmosis, fluids on either side of a membrane pass through to adjust the concentration of a solution, moving from a lower concentration to a higher one. "You are filled with fluids containing salt, electrolytes and minerals. And your skin is a membrane." A saltwater bath is a mini experiment in osmosis. The saltwater against your semipermeable skin will draw out water and take toxins in your body with it in the process. You can use fancy bath salts or

simply old fashioned Epsom salts for your bath. After soaking, rinse with fresh water.

Sitting waist-deep in water is also good for pregnant women. It takes stress off the muscles and organs that are continually under pressure from the weight of a baby. Pregnant women also experience hypersensitivity, emotional stress and information overload in part due to the hormones their bodies are producing and the hormones' breakdown products. "A neutral bath, in which the temperature of the water is the same as the air in the room will act as a distraction and calm the mind."

Caution: Pregnant women should be careful not to take a bath in water higher than 102°F.

This can also be a great time to add some essential oils. "Aromatic oils impact hormones, and they have a physiological effect as well as a psychological one," Dr. Lee notes. Mary Muryn, author of the book *Spa Magic* recommends five drops each of lavender and lemon essential oils for mental clarity and balance. She says that a few drops of sandalwood also nicely complement this recipe.

Note: Since aromatic oils impact hormones, it is best—especially for pregnant women—to use them under the guidance of a trained practitioner.

HYDROTHERAPY: THE POWER OF WARMTH AND COOL

There is another aspect to bathing that most Western cultures no longer practice. It is hydrotherapy, and it can be found in bathhouses around the globe.

Our bodies react strongly to temperature. Cold is good for reducing pain and stopping inflammation. Warmth is relaxing, but will increase inflammation. The experience of moving from hot to cold is refreshing.

Hydrotherapy uses extreme temperature changes to *increase* the body's ability to adapt to stress and to help the body learn to accommodate change. It builds the immune system, and trains the body to become more efficient at balancing fluids, acquiring nutrients and eliminating waste. "It's exercise for your body's cells and systems," says Dr. Lee, who works with methods of both alternative and mainstream medicine to treat degenerative diseases and cancer. "Hydrotherapy is like strength training. It should be done gradually. Over time, you will increase the duration and extremity of the temperature changes."

Bathhouses—and some spas—that offer hydrotherapy have multiple tubs with different temperatures of water. At home, you may want to use the shower. When you are just starting off, begin with a lukewarm shower, and then switch to cool. This will enhance peripheral circulation and stimulate the nerves. Eventually, you can extend the water temperatures so that you are going from a hot shower to a cold one. Briskly dry yourself with a towel to warm up. "Ending a bath or shower with cool water closes your pores, reseals your skin and restores normal circulatory balance," says Dr. Lee.

Dr. Lee's other bath recommendations...

• **Carefully monitor your shower and bath temperatures to avoid scalding.** Baths should be no hotter than 104°F.

• **Use a natural coconut- or olive oil-based soap** in lieu of processed and synthetic soaps and shampoos.

• **Finish each bath by moisturizing with a coconut oil product.** Bathing dehydrates most adults.

• **Get a chlorine filter for your bath and shower.** Chlorine and fluorine add to the effects of aging, and are bad for the immune system. You can get a filter at most hardware stores.

Find bath recipes at *www.seasalt.com*.

The Wisdom of Native American Healing

Lewis Mehl-Madrona, MD, PhD, former associate professor of family medicine at the University of Saskatchewan College of Medicine. He is author of four books, including *Coyote Medicine: Lessons from Native American Healing* (Touchstone). *www.mehl-madrona. com*

For millennia, Native American healing has been practiced in North America. It encompasses a number of beliefs and rituals used by the more than 500 tribes of North America to treat people with emotional or physical conditions. As a medical doctor and Native American healer, I find that people often benefit from complementary care that includes these traditional practices.

Because Native American healing is so embedded in the tribal culture, it's not something an individual can dabble in on her own. However, it does include a spiritual element from which you can gain insights that promote well-being plus healing practices you can do while honoring your own traditions.

A SPIRITUAL PRACTICE

The spirit plays an integral part in Native American healing, which is as much a philosophy as a science. Typically, conventional Western medicine aims to fix the part of the body that ails. In contrast, Native American medicine considers the spirit inseparable from the healing process and so aims to heal the whole person. There is no separation between the body parts and the person...the person and the community...and the community and the natural environment.

Whereas Western medicine looks to eliminate the particular disease, Native American medicine asks, "What can the disease teach the patient?" The answers empower the patient with awareness, confidence and tools to help her take charge of her health.

Native Americans believe that many illnesses stem from spiritual problems. A person who thinks negatively, has an unhealthful lifestyle or has an imbalance of body, mind, spirit and community is more likely to become ill. Native American healing practices aim to re-establish balance and restore the patient to a healthy and spiritually pure state.

There is no scientific proof that Native American healing can cure disease. However, many people find that the practices reduce pain and stress, encourage emotional well-being and improve quality of life.

THE RITUAL RETREAT

The retreat is an essential element of Native American healing. It is vital to wellness to take

time out for a periodic respite—once a year at a minimum. A typical retreat takes place in a natural and safe environment, away from urban and residential areas. It consists of four days and nights of fasting, prayer and meditation.

Often a retreat begins and ends with a *sweat lodge ceremony*. This takes place in a dome-shaped structure made from tree branches. Inside, water is periodically poured over heated rocks to create a hot, steamy environment. The ceremony of the sweat lodge helps to purify the body's blood, heart, lungs, liver and kidneys...free the mind of distractions and bring mental clarity...and provide a sense of connection to the planet and the spirit world.

Though it's not possible to re-create the sweat lodge experience without being enmeshed in Native American culture, you can create your own personal retreat. *Whether for a few hours or a few days...*

•**Go to a place where you feel safe, protected and connected to nature**—to the open sky, towering trees, earth beneath you. This reduces stress and promotes relaxation.

•**Fast.** Most healthy people can safely go without eating or drinking for 24 hours. (If you have any medical problems, you may need to shorten your fast or avoid fasting—ask your doctor.) Longer fasts, such as the traditional four-day fast, should be done only under the supervision of an experienced healer.

•**Sit still and meditate for whatever amount of time feels right.** Even a short period of meditation helps you understand that you don't really need to do all the things you normally worry about...puts you in touch with your spiritual side...and helps you open up to whatever lesson may come. Use any meditation techniques you want—deep breathing, imagery, mantras, prayer.

The science: From the viewpoint of Western medicine, fasting and meditating can decrease the activity of the sympathetic nervous system (which controls the "fight-or-flight"

response and production of stress hormones, among other functions)...and increase the activity of the parasympathetic nervous system (which controls the body's "rest and repose" functions). The result is deep relaxation, which gives the body an opportunity to repair itself, reduce anxiety and alleviate depression.

The tradition: Nearly every culture has methods of reflection, renewal and rejuvenation. There is benefit in engaging in rituals that have been handed down for thousands of years. Honoring such traditions can provide a healing sense of connectedness, well-being and peace.

More from Dr. Mehl-Madrona...

To Experience Native American Healing

Want to learn more about Native American culture? *You can...*

•**Attend powwows.** Often open to the public, these include singing, dancing and perhaps opportunities to make initial contact with healers.

Information: *www.powwows.com* or *www.nativegatherings.com.*

•**Visit a holistic center for classes on Native American practices**...and an environment suitable for personal retreats.

Recommended: Kripalu Center for Yoga & Health, Stockbridge, Massachusetts (866-200-5203, *www.kripalu.org*)...Omega Institute, Rhinebeck, New York (877-944-2002, *www.eomega.org*).

•**Go on a retreat with a Native American healer.** For information on retreats I conduct, go to *www.mehl-madrona.com* or call 808-772-1099.

Beware of "Native Shamanism" seminars. These lump together bits of Native American ceremonies with Wicca (a pagan religion), New Age spirituality and Eastern medicine—which can trivialize and weaken the Native American healing experience.

Would Your Friends Pass The Friendship Test?

Mamta Gautam, MD, psychiatrist with a private practice in Ottawa, Ontario. She is an assistant professor in the department of psychiatry, faculty of medicine, University of Ottawa, and past president of the Ontario Psychiatric Association. This article is adapted from an essay that appeared in *The Medical Post* © Mamta Gautam.

If you have good friendships, chances are you will be healthier. A significant body of scientific research supports the health benefits of friendships.

For example…

People who have a supportive network of family and friends have less incidence of cardiac disease, as well as lower blood pressure and heart rate, according to studies conducted at the University of Chicago and the University of California at Irvine.

Social ties are even associated with a lower likelihood of premature death, based on the findings of a Yale University researcher who followed the death rate of 10,000 older adults over a five-year period. This could be because people who have social ties typically feel supported, cared for and valued. They tend to believe that their lives have more meaning, and choose to make the effort to remain healthy.

Friends also help us cope. A landmark study at the University of California at Los Angeles showed that women respond to stress by "tending and befriending." When females experience stress, a cascade of chemicals is released within their bodies, including the hormones oxytocin and estrogen—both of which compel women to bond. The increased oxytocin level suppresses the hormone cortisol, resulting in lower levels of anxiety and a sense of calm.

Friendships between women usually are based on a feeling of emotional closeness and attachment. Most women welcome the opportunity to share feelings, thoughts and experiences—and devote a great deal of time and energy to such relationships.

Friendships between men are typically quite different. A great deal of research on male friendship focuses on what are known as "activity friends"—those with whom men play sports, watch television or have a drink… "convenience friends" with whom favors can be exchanged…and "mentor friends" in which one man who has more experience and skills helps out another. In general, men's friendships focus less on communication and more on activities and companionship.

Being friends during good times is easy. What happens when there is a falling out? While it can be hard to express negative feelings of hurt or disappointment, that is exactly what we need to do. At times, we allow a friend to drift away rather than risk experiencing any conflict. A good friendship is worth the energy and risk. It takes faith to realize that a conflict is not going to break a friendship, and may actually strengthen it.

WHAT MAKES A GOOD FRIEND?

Relationship experts Drs. Les and Leslie Parrott of the Center for Relationship Development at Seattle Pacific University have created a list of traits to look for in enduring friendships.

A good friend is someone who…

1. Makes time. Whether you're in the midst of a crisis or slogging through the mundane, a friend will have time for you.

2. Keeps a secret. Trust allows you to feel emotionally safe, share feelings and explore and understand what may be bothering you.

3. Cares deeply. The ability to enter your world and feel your pain is a cornerstone of friendship.

4. Provides space. Friends will give you time alone and are there when you need them.

5. Speaks the truth. This person asks the questions you want to ignore and helps you face reality.

6. Forgives faults. Everyone has faults. A friend knows you and likes you anyway!

7. Remains faithful. You will not be deserted during bad times.

8. Laughs easily. We all enjoy the company of people who share our sense of humor.

9. Celebrates your success. Ideally, there's no jealousy, resentment or destructive competition between friends.

10. Connects strongly. Whether it's bridge, books or real estate, friends share common interests.

It's more productive to work on *being* a good friend, rather than to *look for a* good friend. Legendary self-improvement expert Dale Carnegie advised that people can make more friends in two months by simply becoming interested in other people than they can make in two years by trying to get people interested in them.

To be a good friend: Think of someone who means a lot to you, and show that person you care by contacting him/her. Schedule regular activities together, such as golf games, bike rides or lunch. If the person does not live close by, plan to meet soon, and stay connected via regular phone calls or e-mails.

Once you initiate contact, use the "Tarzan Rule"—just as Tarzan never lets go of one vine unless he's got another one at hand, do not end a contact with your friend without booking one more. Your friends may very well help keep you healthy—even keep you alive.

The Gift of Girlfriends

Joy Browne, PhD, clinical psychologist in New York City. Her internationally syndicated call-in radio show, *The Dr. Joy Browne Show*, is the longest-running of its kind (*www.drjoy.com*). She is author of many books, including *Getting Unstuck: 8 Simple Steps to Solving Any Problem* (Hay House).

Women outlive men, on average, by more than five years. I'm convinced (and numerous scientific studies back me up) that it's partly because we invest in relationships with other women—our old school friends, current pals from the office or club, even new neighbors. By sharing joys and concerns, spotting and solving problems, giving and getting comfort, we lighten our emotional load—and that helps to optimize health. So if you've moved to a new town or your empty nest feels lonely, expand your circle of friends.

• **Look for a pal, not a soul mate.** Women often long for the intense intimacy of their teens, when everyone shared concerns about boys, breast size, pimples and parents. Adult friendships have less intensity, because we have more individuality.

• **Don't target Ms. Popularity.** The woman who is center stage at the party may not be motivated to make friends. You'll get a warmer welcome from a woman who doesn't seem to know many people in the room.

• **To make a friend, be a friend.** Smile, ask questions and open up about yourself.

• **Don't compare or compete.** When it comes to your girlfriends, it doesn't matter who has the bigger house or better hair—what matters is the warmth in your hearts.

Wonderful Ways to Give Calming Comfort

Fran Dorf, author of the novels *Saving Elijah* (Putnam), inspired by the loss of her son, Michael, and *Flight* (Vivisphere). She holds a master's degree in psychology and conducts "writing for healing" workshops to help people cope with their losses, Stamford, Connecticut. *www.frandorf.com*

Thirty years after her son's death, my friend still smarts when she remembers all the people who pointed out how lucky she was to have two other children. Another friend, whose brother recently died, grumbles that everyone keeps telling her it will get better with time. Having received my share of insensitive, even hurtful, comments after my son, Michael, died 13 years ago, I certainly understand. Even people with good intentions often say and do the wrong thing.

If you want to comfort a grieving friend or relative, your primary task is to validate his/her feelings. Don't say anything that minimizes those feelings—which, in effect, "de-legitimizes" them.

WHAT NOT TO DO

I've found that "de-legitimizers" can be divided into six categories…

• **Babblers.** These people chatter on about the weather, a friend who had a heart attack and so on. But ignoring the elephant in the room just makes it bigger.

- **Advice-givers.** People often give advice, such as, "Start dating again"..."concentrate on your other children." But when we hear this advice, we may interpret it as, "If only you would take my wise counsel, you'd feel better." People advised me to take a sedative, but somehow I knew that I needed to shed a certain number of tears and that it would be counterproductive to try to mask my pain.

- **Platitude-offerers.** When you spout clichés, such as, "God must have wanted him...he's in a better place," the bereaved may feel offended. You may prefer to believe God must have wanted him, but the bereaved person may hate God at the moment and thus feel de-legitimized for feeling what he feels.

- **Pseudo-empathizers.** It's particularly distressing for those experiencing "high grief"—for example, from the loss of a child—to hear, "I know just how you feel." If you haven't experienced the same loss, you have no idea how a person feels—and maybe not even then.

- **Lesson-learners.** There may be profound lessons to be learned from tragedy, but it's best to let others learn them in their own time and ways. Don't say, "Everything happens for a reason."

- **Abandoners.** Whatever the conscious or unconscious rationalizations—such as fear of saying the wrong thing or feeling uncomfortable in the face of grief—if you walk away from a friend who needs you, you're probably walking away from the friendship permanently.

HOW TO HELP

- **Take your cues from the bereaved person.** If he's sitting quietly, sit quietly beside him. If he's using humor to cope, laugh a little.

- **Let the grieving person tell his/her story in as much detail as he chooses to,** even if he repeats it and it's hard to hear. It helps the bereaved to tell and retell the story. If you're not sure how to respond, try simply, "I'm so sorry" or even, "I don't know what to say."

- **Read a book on grief.** You honor your bereaved friend by learning all you can. Good books include *A Good Friend for Bad Times*

(Augsburg Fortress) by Deborah Bowen and Susan Strickler, and *I Wasn't Ready to Say Goodbye* (Sourcebooks) by Pamela Blair and Brook Noel. Or search online for information about grief under "grief" or "bereavement."

- **Acknowledge the deceased person.** Tell a wonderful anecdote about him. Even now, I am grateful when someone mentions my son, Michael. Just saying his name aloud brings him back into the world.

- **Contact the bereaved on significant days** —birthdays, death days, anniversaries. These are difficult, especially "firsts." Don't avoid, ignore or forget them.

- **Offer practical and specific support.** Pick up the kids from school...cook a meal... mow the lawn. Don't say, "Is there anything I can do?" or "Call me if you need me." Decide what you can do, and then do it.

- **Stay in touch.** Remember that when the formal mourning period is over and the last casserole is gone, the bereaved is still grieving. Continue to call and get together.

- **Banish the word "closure" from your vocabulary.** There is no such thing, and who would want it anyway? We incorporate our losses into our lives. Psychologists have proposed many ways to describe how we find a way to live with loss, but the one I find most useful is that we must "reinvest" in a new reality.

- **Meet us where we are.** Don't have expectations. Don't compare one grief to another. Remember that grief may take years to work through. Be prepared for tears, moaning, sighing, wailing, trembling, even screaming.

- **Don't take anger personally.** Psychiatrist Elisabeth Kübler-Ross's classic five stages of grief—denial, anger, bargaining, depression, acceptance—come not in stages but in circles and waves like a roller coaster. The best definition of compassion I've ever found is a Buddhist one—"Compassion is willingness to be close to suffering."

- **Grief support takes work, stamina and commitment.** Be present. Be humble. Be patient. Observe. Reflect. Allow silence. Don't judge. Accept. Listen.

9

Nutrition for a Slimmer, Trimmer You

How a "Foodie" Lost 42 Pounds Without Dieting

Pam Anderson, a food columnist and cookbook author, faces challenges that would tax any dieter. She tests—and tastes—every recipe that she creates. She spends two or more days a week in a test kitchen, where she might sample three dozen versions of a chocolate cake or 16 different versions of a pot roast recipe.

That led her to her top weight of 192 pounds.

Over the years, she tried dozens of different diets, including Atkins and South Beach. She lost weight initially, but the pounds always came back.

•**Her "mirror moment."** In 2002, Anderson took an exercise class that was held in a mirrored room. She didn't like the look of the overweight food writer looking back at her. At the same time, she experienced an intense longing for what she would like to become—thinner and healthier.

That morning in front of the mirror represented her first step in the healthier direction. It was another two years before she fully dedicated herself to healthier living. When she did, the results were striking. She lost 42 pounds in about eight months, without dieting, and has not gained it back.

The approach that worked for her...

•**Focus on your life, not your weight.** A few years after my "mirror moment," I saw an acupuncturist for shoulder pain. During my sessions, I would lie in a meditative state for nearly an hour. I left the sessions feeling centered and refreshed. That's when I realized

Pam Anderson, a monthly food columnist for *USA Weekend* and *Better Homes & Gardens* and a contributing editor to *Fine Cooking*. Based in Darien, Connecticut, she teaches cooking classes across the country. Her latest book is *The Perfect Recipe for Losing Weight & Eating Great* (Houghton Mifflin Harcourt).

that my weight was secondary. Changing my life was a necessary first step.

I started weekly therapy sessions with a psychologist, during which I came to understand that I have always shouldered too many responsibilities. As a working parent, I brought home a big chunk of the bacon, and I took on most of the household responsibilities. So in addition to my job, I shopped, cooked, oversaw the child care and housecleaning, took charge of the finances, planned vacations and organized the social calendar. It was too much. I unconsciously used food to build up my body to "support" the many responsibilities that I carried.

Food was one of my comforts—but the heavier I got, the more insecure I felt. So I overcompensated by taking on even more responsibilities, thinking that this would make up for my not being fit.

Therapy didn't cause me to lose weight, but it did help me to understand that my life was out of balance. It helped me feel more in control and sure of myself, which allowed me to reduce the responsibilities that I had taken on.

• **Get physical.** I never exercised regularly until my husband and I took a trip to Italy in the summer of 2004. We walked miles every day. I was surprised to discover that daily exercise made me less hungry. At the same time, those daily walks burned a lot of calories. I wasn't trying to lose weight—I ate all the bread, pasta and desserts that I wanted—but by the time we returned, after two weeks, my clothes were looser.

After that, I kept up the habit of walking every day. I would walk briskly for a few miles in the morning and sometimes again in the afternoon. As I got stronger, I alternated walking with bursts of running. I kept losing weight.

• **Opt for casual calorie counting.** Most diets incorporate nutritional rules. You're supposed to eat this many calories or limit yourself to these portion sizes. I don't bother with that. I've learned that food restriction only creates cravings and that strict portion control can leave you feeling hungry all the time.

I do have a sense of what I should and shouldn't eat and how much I should eat in a given day. I know from experience that I can maintain my current weight (about 150 pounds) on 2,000 to 2,500 calories a day. I'm in that range when I eat a big breakfast, a healthy salad for lunch and a light meal at supper, along with a few snacks. If I've been tasting a lot of new recipes, I cut back on calories somewhere else. I don't think about it very much. Calorie control becomes second nature once you know what "healthy" feels like. Now I'm rarely tempted to overindulge, because I feel so much better when I don't.

That's as specific as I get. I've developed a heightened awareness of what my body does and doesn't need at any given time. As long as I stay in this general calorie range—and burn roughly 450 calories a day with exercise—my weight naturally takes care of itself.

• **Eat often.** Most people get hungry every three to four hours. This is why doctors recommend "grazing," in which you eat five or six times a day. It's good for energy and healthy blood sugar levels, as well as appetite control.

I haven't given up my three main meals, but I supplement them with snacks whenever I'm feeling hungry. I make a ritual of afternoon tea, in which I'll have a cup of tea and something sweet, such as a small cookie. Then, before supper, I'll have an hors d'oeuvre—a deviled egg or a handful of nuts—along with a glass of wine.

• **Look good, feel good.** I got rid of the ugly sweatpants I used to exercise in. Now I have smart-looking spandex. After my workouts, I don't just shower—I fix my hair and put on makeup. The way we present ourselves indicates how we feel about ourselves. Looking good made me feel good—and the better I felt, the better I wanted to look.

I also go through my closet periodically and get rid of my "fat" clothes. I used to hang on to everything, probably because I knew in the back of my mind that my diets weren't going to stick. This new approach was different. I wasn't merely dieting, I was changing my life. I knew I wasn't going back.

• **Personalize.** One of the problems with weight-loss diets is that they force different people to follow exactly the same plan. But in fact, everyone has to figure out what works for him/her.

Example: I'm not about to give up my before-supper glass of wine, no matter how many calories it has.

I go to bed earlier than a lot of people, so I'm unlikely to snack after supper. But if you happen to be a night owl, you'll probably want to have a snack between supper and bedtime.

Similarly, we all have our own favorite foods. I love pasta and couldn't stick with a diet that forced me to give it up. Maybe you crave a daily dessert or full-fat cream in your coffee. Don't give it up! Just make the necessary adjustments.

Why Pine Nuts Help You Lose Weight...and Other Tricks to Drop Pounds

Jodi Citrin Greebel, RD, CDN, registered dietitian and president of Citrition, LLC, a nutrition consulting company in New York City. She is coauthor of *The Little Black Apron: A Single Girl's Guide to Cooking with Style & Grace* (Polka Dot).

Most weight-loss diets are hard to stick to. That's because you have to eliminate 3,500 calories to lose just one pound a week and that comes to 500 calories a day. This degree of calorie restriction can make people feel hungry all the time—and reluctant to stick with any diet for very long. That's also why it is hard for people to maintain the weight that they do lose. Roughly 95% of those who lose weight are unable to maintain the weight loss longer than a year or two.

Better: Eat foods that curtail appetite and increase feelings of fullness. People who do this naturally take in fewer calories overall and are more likely to maintain their weight loss.

What to eat...

•**Protein at every meal.** Protein is a natural appetite suppressant. People who often feel hungry probably aren't getting enough protein.

Self-test: Eat a regular meal or snack. If you're hungry again within two hours, the meal probably didn't include enough protein.

Protein should make up about 25% of every meal—three ounces to six ounces of protein is ideal. Good protein sources include chicken, seafood, lean red meats, egg whites, beans and low- or nonfat dairy.

Trap: Many traditional breakfast foods, such as a bagel or a Danish, are high in calories but low in protein. People who start the day with these foods invariably want to eat more within a few hours, adding unnecessary calories.

Always include protein with your morning meal—by spreading peanut butter on whole-wheat toast, for example.

Also helpful: High-protein snacks, such as string cheese or yogurt. They're more satisfying than carbohydrate snacks, such as pretzels or chips.

•**More fat.** Until recently, weight-loss experts advised people to eat less fat. This made intuitive sense because fat has about twice the calories as an equal amount of protein or carbohydrate. But today, after about 15 years of low-fat dieting, Americans are heavier than ever.

Reason: People who don't feel satisfied on a low-fat diet often eat excessive carbohydrates to make up the difference.

Fat is a satisfying nutrient. You may feel full after eating a lot of carbohydrates, such as pasta or bread, but you'll still want more. Fat, on the other hand, makes you crave less food, so you'll be less likely to fill up on calories from other sources.

Have a little fat with every meal. If you're having a salad, for example, use full-fat dressing in moderation rather than fat-free. Add a tablespoon of olive oil when making pasta sauce. A slice of cheese or a serving of cottage cheese also provides satisfying amounts of fat.

Easy does it: Use fats only in small amounts to avoid excess calories. One tablespoon of olive oil, for example, has about 120 calories. Small amounts curtail your appetite without adding too many calories.

•**A handful of pine nuts.** A hormone called cholecystokinin (CCK) has been found to in-

267

crease feelings of fullness. About one ounce or a small handful of pine nuts (which actually are seeds, not nuts) stimulates the body to release CCK. This reduces appetite and helps you feel fuller even when you take in fewer calories overall.

• **Fiber, especially early in the day.** High-fiber diets increase feelings of fullness and aid in weight loss. High-fiber foods also may stimulate the release of appetite-suppressing hormones.

Virtually all foods that are high in fiber, such as fruits, vegetables, legumes and whole grains, are relatively low in calories. People who eat a lot of these foods tend to feel full even when they take in fewer calories during the day.

Try to get 25 to 30 grams of fiber daily. Beans are high in fiber, with about six grams in one-half cup. Blackberries are another excellent source, with about eight grams of fiber per cup.

• **Spicy foods as often as possible.** Cayenne, jalapeños, curries and other spicy foods contain capsaicin and other compounds that may increase metabolism and cause the body to burn slightly more calories. More important, these foods appear to affect the "satiety center" in the brain, causing people to feel more satisfied and consume fewer calories.

• **Water before a meal.** Drink a full glass of water before you start eating, and keep sipping water throughout the meal. Water takes up space in the stomach. Or you can start your meal with a broth-based soup (not a cream soup, which is higher in calories). People who consume liquids before and during meals consume fewer calories than those who go straight to the main course.

Caution: Avoid high-calorie liquids. Americans consume about 20% more calories now than they did 20 years ago. Many of these calories come from soft drinks, sports drinks and coffee beverages that include sugar and cream. Some of these drinks contain 400 calories or more, which could result in almost one extra pound of weight a week if consumed daily.

Are Hormones Making You Hungry?

After a night of fasting, women and men were asked to suppress their hunger when presented with favorite foods. Brain scans showed that food-related brain activity decreased in men but not in women.

Theory: Female hormones play a role in the brain's reaction to food.

Gene-Jack Wang, MD, professor of psychiatry, Mount Sinai School of Medicine, New York City, and lead author of a study of 23 people, published in *Proceedings of the National Academy of Sciences*.

Eat What You Want, Never Feel Hungry and Still Lose Weight

Seth Roberts, PhD, professor emeritus of psychology at University of California, Berkeley, and professor of psychology at Tsinghua University in Beijing, China. Dr. Roberts is author of *The Shangri-La Diet: The No Hunger, Eat Anything Weight-Loss Plan* (Perigee) and serves on the editorial board of the journal *Nutrition*. *www.sethroberts.net*

The Shangri-la Diet (named after the mythical utopia) is a simple, effective way to adjust your natural appetite-regulation system.

How it works: Much as a thermostat maintains your house temperature at a set level, your body maintains a set point weight—the number it perceives as normal. Just as a thermostat turns a heater on and off, your body's weight-control system turns hunger on and off. If the set point is adjusted upward, your body tries to put on weight...and if the set point is adjusted downward, you naturally lose weight.

Theory: Your body regulates weight partly in response to the flavors of food. A food whose flavor is associated with calories raises your set point and increases your appetite lat-

er…a flavorless food lowers your set point and curbs appetite.

Typical result: Two 100-calorie doses of flavorless foods reduce your appetite so much that the next day you automatically consume 500 fewer calories than usual—without feeling hungry. *Flavorless foods that work best…*

• **Flavorless oil.** Choose extra-light olive oil or refined walnut oil. One dose equals one tablespoon.

• **Sugar water.** Strangely, your body doesn't count sweetness as a flavor. One dose equals two tablespoons of sugar mixed with one cup of water.

• **Daily doses.** To lose less than 20 pounds, consume one dose each of oil and sugar water daily. To lose more, double each dose. Appetite suppression usually begins within a day or so.

Essential: To prevent flavorless foods from becoming associated with other flavors, you must wait one hour after tasting anything else (including toothpaste or gum) before swallowing the oil or sugar water—then wait one hour more before eating again. Otherwise, the flavorless foods simply add to your total calorie intake without suppressing appetite at all.

Convenient: Schedule food-free intervals for mid-morning (between breakfast and lunch) and bedtime.

• **Troubleshooting.** If swallowing pure oil makes you gag, mix the oil with the sugar water, then divide into two doses. If you develop diarrhea, cut your oil dose in half for a few days. *If you have…*

• Gallbladder problems—take just one teaspoon of oil per dose…or use only the sugar water.

• Diabetes and/or recurrent yeast infections—use only the oil.

• **Reaching your goal.** Typically, people lose one to two pounds per week. Once you reach your target weight, reduce your dose of oil and/or sugar water to a level that allows you to maintain your weight loss. Don't stop altogether, or you may regain the weight.

How I Lost 172 Pounds By Eating Dinner At the "Wrong" Time

Tricia Cunningham, a former hospice nurse who is now a weight-loss coach and motivational speaker. She is coauthor of *The Reverse Diet* (Wiley), with Heidi Skolnick, MS, CDN, FACSM, a nutritionist at the Women's Sports Medicine Center at the Hospital for Special Surgery, New York City, and a sports nutrition consultant to the School of American Ballet. *www.triciacunningham.com*

In August 1999, 27-year-old Tricia Cunningham weighed 292 pounds. The mother of two had tried numerous diets without success and was becoming increasingly despondent about her size. One day that August, Cunningham decided that since everything about her relationship with food was wrong, she would completely reverse the way she ate. For starters, she would eat breakfast for dinner and dinner for breakfast.

Within one week of reversing her meals, she began losing weight. By March of the next year, she had lost more than half her body weight—and has kept the weight off ever since.

We asked Cunningham to explain how her "reverse diet" works…

REVERSING MEALS

Like most people, I used to eat my biggest meal of the day at dinner. Trouble was, I didn't burn many calories between dinner and bedtime, so my body stored most of the meal in the form of fat. Eating a large dinner also meant my body was still digesting as I tried to get to sleep at night. I didn't know this at the time, but it turns out that it's difficult to sleep soundly while digesting…and it's even harder to lose weight when we don't get enough sleep. We are less likely to remain active when we're drowsy during the day, and sleep deprivation reduces our bodies' production of the hormones that assist in weight regulation.

To compensate for a big meal at night, I ate only a small meal for breakfast, sometimes skipping breakfast entirely. But this, too, was a mistake. Skimping on breakfast left me feeling energy-deprived all day, which meant that I was less likely to exercise. Plus, I was so hungry, I ate more at lunch and dinner. Nutritionists refer to this as "residual hunger"—when we undereat early in the day, our bodies send out hunger signals with such insistence that we're prone to overeat later.

With the Reverse Diet, the first meal of my day is the largest meal, and the final meal of my day is the smallest. I feel less hungry and more energetic all day. Some people who try this diet tell me that they have so much more energy, they no longer need to drink coffee in the morning to get started.

WHAT TO EAT

The best choices are whole grains, fruits and vegetables, lean cuts of pork or beef, poultry and fish. Avoid processed foods and canned or boxed foods, which often have lots of salt and/or sugar.

Breakfast: I love to start my day with a piece of salmon and a baked potato…whole-wheat pasta with lightly sautéed shrimp…a salad… even a steak. Traditional breakfast foods, such as omelets or whole-wheat French toast, also are perfectly acceptable. Just make sure your breakfasts are high in protein and big enough so that you feel full but not stuffed.

Lunch: Eat enough at lunch so that you're not hungry in the afternoon, but eat less than you ate for breakfast. I might have a turkey breast sandwich for lunch or grilled tuna over mixed greens.

Dinner: Demote dinner from your major meal to little more than a healthy snack. Appropriate dinners include traditional breakfast foods, such as a bowl of oatmeal…two hard-boiled eggs…or a fruit smoothie made with low-fat yogurt. Or consume foods that typically are treated as a small part of a larger dinner, such as a bowl of soup or a salad.

Rule of thumb: If your caloric intake is 1,400 calories per day, then breakfast should be about 500 calories…lunch about 400…and dinner 300…with two 100-calorie snacks in between, such as one-half cup of fat-free cottage cheese with one-half cup of peaches or a handful of almonds or walnuts. Though the Reverse Diet doesn't really promote calorie counting, most people need to limit themselves to 1,400 to 1,800 calories a day to lose weight. I also walk at least 30 minutes a day.

OVERCOMING CHALLENGES

• **Late-night snacking.** If you feel the need to snack later in the evening, try increasing the size of your evening meal slightly, say, from two hard-boiled eggs to three. If that doesn't do the trick, at least favor fruits and vegetables.

Better yet, prepare yourself a cup of hot lemon water. For more flavor, add mint sprigs… vanilla and cinnamon…a touch of honey…or artificial sweetener.

• **No time in the morning.** I do most of my cooking at night, making regular dinners for my family. Then I microwave my big breakfasts in the morning. Sometimes, I cook seven meals at once and freeze them so that I'm set for the week.

• **Eating out.** Most restaurants serve large portions for dinner. I just eat a little and get the rest packed to go for my breakfast the next morning.

Belly Fat Is the Worst Fat to Have

JoAnn E. Manson, MD, DrPH, professor of medicine and women's health at Harvard Medical School and chief of the division of preventive medicine at Brigham and Women's Hospital, both in Boston. A lead investigator for two important studies on women's health, Dr. Manson is coauthor of *Hot Flashes, Hormones & Your Health* (McGraw-Hill).

To gauge whether they are a healthy size, many people rely on a scale, height-and-weight chart or mathematical formula that calculates body mass index (BMI). Yet new research reveals that a tape measure more accurately predicts a person's risk for many major health problems. That's because waist measurement indicates the amount of belly fat—the fat that accumulates deep in the abdomen, around the intestines, liver and other internal organs. Belly fat is linked to a strongly elevated risk for diabetes, heart disease, stroke, high blood pressure and abnormal cholesterol levels…some types of cancer, including breast and colorectal cancers…and dementia.

Surprising: Having a big belly is more dangerous than simply being overweight or even obese. In a 16-year study of 45,000 female nurses, women whose waists measured 35 inches or more were much more likely to die prematurely than women with waists of less than 28 inches—even when their weight was within the normal range for their height. Women in the middle range had a small-to-moderate increase in risk. *Reasons…*

• **Belly fat may be more metabolically active than other fat,** releasing free fatty acids (fat cell products that circulate in the bloodstream) directly to the liver. This can lead to insulin resistance (inability of the body's cells to use insulin properly) and widespread inflammation, both of which significantly increase diabetes and heart disease risk.

• **Belly fat may be a sign of fat deposits in the liver and around the heart,** which can impair organ function.

• **After menopause, the tendency to accumulate belly fat increases** as women produce less estrogen relative to androgens (male hormones). Androgens promote abdominal fat.

To measure: Wrap a tape measure around your torso at the level of your navel—usually slightly below the narrowest part of the abdomen. The tape should be snug but not cut into your flesh. For women of any height, a waist size of less than 30 inches is optimal…30 inches to 35 inches indicates moderately elevated health risk…and more than 35 inches indicates high risk. *To reduce belly fat…*

• **Lose weight.** Often the first fat to go is abdominal fat. Even a modest loss of 10% of your starting weight confers great health benefits.

• **Reduce stress.** Stress causes adrenal glands to release the hormone cortisol, which promotes belly fat.

• **Get the right kinds of exercise.** You cannot melt away belly fat with targeted abdominal exercises, such as sit-ups. Instead, engage in aerobic activity, such as brisk walking and racket sports. Doing three hours of aerobic exercise weekly can eliminate about 50% of the excess risk for heart disease associated with belly fat and up to 25% of the excess risk for diabetes.

Also healthful: Resistance exercises (such as using arm and leg weights).

Mint Helps You Eat Less

In a recent finding, people who sniffed peppermint oil every two hours ate almost 350 fewer calories a day than those who did not.

Possible reason: Peppermint boosts alertness, so people who smell it may be less likely to snack because of fatigue or boredom.

Bryan Raudenbush, PhD, associate professor of psychology and director of undergraduate research, Wheeling Jesuit University, Wheeling, West Virginia, and coauthor of a study of 27 adults, published in *Appetite*.

The Less You Eat, the More You Lose…and Other Diet Myths

Mark Hyman, MD, chairman of the Institute for Functional Medicine. He is author of *Ultrametabolism: The Simple Plan for Automatic Weight Loss* (Atria) and coauthor of the best-seller *Ultraprevention: The Six-Week Plan That Will Make You Healthy for Life* (Atria).

Losing weight can be hard work. People feel they have to count calories, endure hunger pangs and work up a sweat. It's no wonder so many give up and regain their hard-lost pounds. It doesn't have to be that way. The reason we are losing the battle of the bulge is that we have bought into some common myths about weight loss. *Here, six of those myths and what to do instead…*

Myth 1: **The less you eat, the more weight you'll lose.**

Our bodies are made up of hundreds of genes that protect us from starvation. That's why we end up gaining weight if we start out eating too few calories. You can starve yourself for only so long before your body engages a primitive response that compensates for starvation by making you overeat. In my experience, the average person who goes on a diet actually gains five pounds.

What to do: Never go on a diet. Instead, eat foods that turn on your metabolism. These are whole foods that come from nature, such as vegetables, fruits, whole grains, nuts, seeds, beans and lean animal protein. If you eat only these foods, you won't have trouble with your appetite—it will self-regulate, and the triggers that drive overeating will be under control.

Myth 2: **It doesn't matter what kind of exercise you do, as long as you exercise.**

It's true that any kind of exercise is better than no exercise, but interval training is the most effective for weight loss. Interval training consists of short bursts of intense activity followed by longer periods of lighter activity. This kind of training tunes up your metabolism so you burn more calories all day and while you sleep, not just when you are exercising.

What to do: Aim for 20 to 30 minutes of interval training two to three days a week. Exercise as vigorously as you can for 30 to 60 seconds, and then slow your pace for three minutes, repeating this pattern for about a half hour.

If you are over 30, have a physical before you start interval training. If you are out of shape, ease into a regular exercise routine first—you might start by walking for 30 minutes five times a week.

Myth 3: **You can control your weight by counting calories.**

Many people believe that all calories are the same when it comes to weight control—that if you substitute 100 calories' worth of, say, cookies for 100 calories of carrots, you'll come out even. But food isn't just about calories. Everything that you eat contains "instructions" for your DNA, your hormones and your metabolism. Different foods contain different information.

For instance, the sugar in soda enters your blood rapidly, increasing insulin levels. Insulin is a hormone that promotes more fat storage around the middle and raises inflammation levels in the body, which in turn promotes more weight gain.

On the other hand, the same amount of sugar from kidney beans enters your blood slowly. Because the sugar is absorbed over time, your insulin levels remain stable and more of the calories are burned and fewer are stored.

What to do: Don't focus on the number of calories you are consuming. Losing weight is not about counting calories—it's about eating the right calories.

Myth 4: **Eating fat makes you fat.**

Dietary fat does not correlate with excess body fat. Any weight-loss resulting from a low-fat diet is usually modest and temporary. The amount of fat Americans eat has dropped from 42% to 34% of total calories on average, but we still are getting fatter. That's because all fats are not created equal. There are good fats, bad fats and ugly fats. Good fats actually can help you lose weight, but many of us have nearly eliminated them from our diet.

Two examples of good fats are omega-3s and monounsaturated fats. Omega-3s are found in fish, flaxseed and flax oil, and nuts and seeds, such as walnuts and pumpkin seeds. Monounsaturated fats are found in olive oil, avocados and nuts.

Bad fats include refined polyunsaturated vegetable oil—such as corn and safflower—and most saturated fat, found in meat and animal products, such as butter.

The ugly fats are trans fats, often found in snack foods and packaged baked goods. Trans fat comes from adding hydrogen to vegetable oil through a process called hydrogenation.

What to do: Eat good fats. These improve your metabolism by activating genes that help you burn fats. Saturated and trans fats turn off fat-burning genes. The Inuit people of Greenland used to eat a diet that was very high in fat—primarily omega-3 and monounsaturated fats—and they were thin and healthy. Now they have shifted to a diet that is lower in fat and high in carbohydrates from junk food, and many are obese, with higher rates of heart disease and other illnesses.

***Myth 5:* Going low-carb will make you thin.**

Carbohydrates are the single most important food you can eat for long-term health and weight loss. They are the source of most of the vitamins, minerals and fiber in our diet—and all the phytonutrients, plant compounds that are key regulators of our health.

Phytonutrients turn on the genes that help us burn fat and age slowly. They contain disease-fighting nutrients. Some examples are the isoflavones in soy foods, polyphenols in cocoa and glucosinolates in broccoli.

However, just as there are different fats, there are different types of carbohydrates.

What to do: Eat complex carbohydrates—vegetables, fruits, nuts, seeds, beans and whole grains. These tend to have low glycemic loads, which means they are absorbed slowly and don't raise blood sugar quickly, so you feel full longer.

Refined carbs, such as white flour, rice and pasta, along with sugary foods, make your blood sugar spike so that you feel hungry sooner.

***Myth 6:* It doesn't matter what time you eat.**

Sumo wrestlers look the way they do because they fast during the day, then overeat at night and go to bed.

Like Sumo wrestlers, we eat most of our calories late in the day. When you eat late, calories are stored instead of burned.

What to do: Don't eat within two to three hours of going to bed, because you need to give your body time to digest and burn off your food.

Also, eat throughout the day to keep blood sugar levels stable. Breakfast is important. I can't tell you how many people I have helped to lose weight by having them eat breakfast. The National Weight Control Registry, which is tracking long-term weight-loss maintenance in more than 5,000 people, has found that 96% of those who have maintained weight loss for six years eat breakfast regularly.

Al Dente Pasta May Protect You From Diabetes

Slightly firm pasta has a lower Glycemic Index (GI) than pasta cooked until soft. Foods with low GIs are absorbed into the bloodstream more slowly than high-GI foods and do not cause blood sugar to rise as quickly. Slower absorption may protect against weight gain, heart disease and diabetes.

Natural Health, 70 Lincoln St., Boston, Massachusetts 02111.

Skip MSG to Stay Slim

People who used the flavor enhancer monosodium glutamate (MSG) the most were nearly three times as likely to be overweight or obese as people who did not use MSG, a recent study found—even though calorie consumption and physical activity levels were the same in both groups. MSG may affect the part of the brain that helps regulate appetite and fat metabolism. Check food labels—many processed and Asian foods contain MSG...as do the flavor-enhancing ingredients yeast extract, hydrolyzed protein and calcium caseinate.

Ka He, MD, assistant professor of nutrition and epidemiology, University of North Carolina at Chapel Hill School of Public Health, and author of a study of 752 people, published in Obesity.

Calories Don't Matter

Leo Galland, MD, director, Foundation for Integrated Medicine, New York City. He is author of The Fat Resistance Diet *(Three Rivers Press). www.drgalland.com. Dr. Galland is a recipient of the Linus Pauling award.*

Obesity continues to be rampant in America and is only getting worse. *The latest estimates of its impact are far worse than anyone had imagined...*

- **Two hundred million Americans are overweight,** and half of them are obese.

- **The rate of extreme obesity (BMI greater than 40)** is increasing twice as fast as obesity in general.

- **Forty percent of the population suffers from metabolic syndrome,** a complication of obesity and a precursor of type 2 diabetes. Having metabolic syndrome also triples the risk of developing Alzheimer's disease.

- **Osteoarthritis, a complication of obesity, is the number one cause of chronic disability.**

- **One out of three American children born in the year 2000 is predicted to develop diabetes** during his/her lifetime, a devastating long-range effect of the obesity epidemic.

- **Despite excessive caloric consumption, over three-quarters of the population has a deficient intake of one or more essential nutrients.** Greater levels of obesity are actually associated with lower nutritional status.

According to Dr. Leo Galland, "A solution to the obesity crisis is the single most important thing that needs to happen in improving the health of Americans." Dr. Galland has developed a novel and provocative theory on how to control weight, based upon recent scientific insights into the way that levels of body fat are normally controlled. The foundation of his approach, which he calls the Fat Resistance Diet, is nutrient density and control of inflammation.

"The whole premise of the Fat Resistance Diet is that we have inborn, natural regulatory systems that support a healthy weight, but our food choices and our lifestyle interfere with their functioning," he explained. Leptin, for example, is a compound that lets your brain and body know how much fat you are storing. When leptin level goes up, your appetite goes down. Leptin also speeds up your metabolism. "The problem is that overweight people have developed resistance to leptin," Dr. Galland explained. "Their leptin levels are high but it's not depressing their appetite and it's not stimulating their metabolism."

INFLAMMATION FACTOR

According to Dr. Galland, inflammation is a large part of the reason why leptin doesn't work as it should in very overweight people. "Inflammation disables the leptin signal," he told me. "It also contributes to insulin resistance, a central feature of obesity and diabetes." That's why, in Dr. Galland's program, the control of inflammation through natural anti-inflammatories found in herbs, spices and a multitude of fresh whole foods such as vegetables is so central to controlling fat. In the presence of inflammation, the fat control mechanisms simply don't work. "Inflammation is the critical link between obesity and chronic illness," Dr. Galland believes.

NUTRIENT DENSITY

The other part of the equation has to do with what's called nutrient density. "What matters most about the calories in any food are the nutrients that accompany them," he said. No one in his right mind would recommend a "calorie controlled" diet consisting of 12 packs a day of 100-calorie Oreo snack packs. "Even though the calories are on target, you'd be completely screwed up by the lack of fiber, the lack of protein and other nutrients and the resulting blood sugar roller coaster," said Dr. Galland. "That's why a weight reduction program that only looks at calories completely misses the boat."

According to Dr. Galland, the multi-billion dollar weight loss industry has failed miserably. "The whole weight loss industry has developed around the concept of calories," Dr. Galland said, "and the idea has been to find ways to decrease the number of calories that people are eating."

He's right. After all, the low-fat diets of the 1980s were based on the notion that fat has twice the amount of calories per gram as anything else, so if we cut back on fat we'll be cutting back on calories and wind up controlling weight gain. "The way that Americans have been taught to think about food is to try to find lower calorie equivalents of foods we like to eat," he said. "That hasn't worked. Some of the artificial sweeteners in low-calorie foods actually make you hungrier."

Educating people in a nutrient-dense, anti-inflammatory diet can reverse the obesity epidemic, especially when people learn how delicious this dietary approach can be. According to Dr. Galland, what we need is nothing less than a new approach to the way people actually think about food. "I think the American palate has been corrupted," he said. "We've lost the ability to really savor herbs and spices and all the subtle flavors that are so wonderful in traditional cooking. Those herbs and spices have nutritional value—they're rich in antioxidants, rich in minerals and especially rich in anti-inflammatories."

FLAVORFUL, HEALTHFUL OPTIONS

Some of the best anti-inflammatory spices and herbs include cloves, ginger, parsley, tumeric, cinnamon and basil. "We need to re-educate our palate to learn to appreciate the wonders of these foods," Dr. Galland told me. Dr. Galland has identified 12 core principles to eating for fat resistance. *These include...*

• **Choose foods that are loaded with nutrients** such as colorful vegetables and fruits, and lean, minimally processed protein. As much as possible, avoid food that has been processed.

• **Avoid trans fats.**

• **Consume foods with plenty of omega-3 content.**

• **Eat fish three times a week or more.**

• **Eat at least 25 grams of fiber per day.**

• **Eat at least nine servings of vegetables and fruits daily.**

• **Average one serving a day of alliums** (onions, scallions, garlic) and crucifers (broccoli, cabbage, kale, cauliflower).

• **No more than 10% of total calories should be from saturated fat.** This doesn't mean only 10% of total diet is from fats—it means to be careful about eating foods with saturated fats.

• **If you eat eggs, don't scramble the yolk.**

• **Don't follow a "low-fat" diet.**

• **Eat two healthy snacks a day**—such as berries, tomatoes, string cheese, organic turkey slices.

• **Eat fruit instead of sugary sweets.**

Dr. Galland's Fat Resistance Diet is a lifestyle based around healthful food rather than calorie restriction, limiting the use of artificial sweeteners, sugar substitutes and fake fats. He says, "only through education and positive reinforcement for making healthy choices will the coming health-care crisis be averted."

More from Dr. Leo Galland...

Dr. Leo Galland's Lose Weight Forever Diet

Weight loss isn't only—or even mainly—about calories. Surprisingly, we gain weight when natural weight-control mechanisms are disrupted by inflammation, a low-grade inflammatory response caused by poor diet and environmental toxins.

When people gain weight, the extra fatty tissue produces leptin, a hormone that suppresses appetite and speeds metabolism. In theory, this should cause people to lose the extra weight.

Instead, inflammation in fat tissue and blood vessels stimulates the production of anti-inflammatory chemicals. These chemicals lead to changes in the body that disable leptin's ability to suppress appetite and speed metabolism. This is called leptin resistance.

To combat leptin resistance, I have developed a fat-resistance diet based on cutting-edge research at premier institutions such as Harvard, Johns Hopkins and Rockefeller universities. Eating the proper foods can eliminate chronic inflammation and reprogram the body's weight-loss mechanisms.

ANTI-INFLAMMATORY FOODS

The focus of the diet isn't calorie control. The idea is to eat foods that supply anti-inflammatory nutrients. A major problem with most weight-loss diets is the use of artificial sweeteners and fat substitutes to reduce calories. Substituting these products for real foods deprives your body of key anti-inflammatory nutrients. *Main principles...*

• **Eat fish at least three times weekly.** The omega-3 fatty acids in fish have powerful anti-inflammatory properties. Fish that are rich in omega-3s and relatively low in mercury include anchovies, conch, herring (fresh or pickled, not creamed), mackerel (Atlantic only), sablefish, salmon (fresh, canned or smoked, wild or farmed), sardines (Atlantic), sturgeon and tuna (fresh or canned bluefin—not albacore).

•**Balance essential fatty acids.** The optimal ratio of omega-6 fatty acids to omega-3s is about 4:1. The ratio in the average American diet is closer to 20:1. A relative excess of omega-6 fats in tissues leads cells to produce excessive levels of pro-inflammatory chemicals called prostanoids. The best approach is to decrease intake of omega-6s and increase intake of omega-3s.

Foods high in omega-3s: Fish, flaxseed, walnuts and beans—navy, kidney, as well as soybeans.

Foods high in omega-6s: Red meat, chicken, milk, eggs and most vegetable oils, including corn, sunflower and safflower.

•**Cut back on unhealthy fats.** Saturated fat—primarily found in beef, pork, lamb, dairy products and poultry skin—should be limited to no more than 10% of total calories. Don't eat any trans fat—this means avoiding any foods made with hydrogenated or partially hydrogenated vegetable oil. These include most commercial baked goods and some fast foods. Both saturated fat and trans fat greatly increase levels of inflammatory chemicals.

•**Get 25 grams of fiber daily.** A high-fiber diet helps control appetite and reduce inflammation. A study by the Centers for Disease Control and Prevention found that people who consume the most fiber have lower levels of C-reactive protein (CRP), which indicates the presence of inflammatory chemicals in the body. All plant foods contain some fiber. Among the best sources are beans, whole grains and vegetables.

•**Eat colorful fruits and vegetables.** Get at least nine servings daily. Produce with deep colors and intense flavors is high in flavonoids and carotenoids, chemical compounds that have anti-inflammatory effects.

Important: Have at least one serving of blueberries, cherries or pomegranates a day.

These contain anthocyanins, which are among the most potent anti-inflammatory agents.

•**Choose alliums and crucifers.** Crucifers are strong-flavored vegetables, including broccoli, cauliflower, cabbage and kale. Alliums include onions and garlic. Both classes of vegetables reduce chronic inflammation and lower the risk of cancer, particularly breast cancer. Eat at least one serving of each daily.

•**Use only egg whites or unbroken egg yolks.** The cholesterol in yolks has relatively little effect on cholesterol in the blood—but if the yolk is broken, the cholesterol is oxidized and produces inflammatory by-products. Poached or boiled whole eggs are fine. Avoid scrambled eggs and whole-egg omelettes.

•**Favor herbs and spices that are potent anti-inflammatories.** These include basil, cardamom, cilantro, cinnamon, clove, ginger, parsley and turmeric. Use them every day. Avoid chiles, cayenne pepper and jalapeños, which can trigger inflammation.

THREE STAGES

The diet progresses in phases…

Stage 1. Eat as much as you want of such foods as arugula, bell peppers, broccoli, cabbage, carrots, leeks, onions, romaine lettuce, scallions, shiitake mushrooms, spinach and tomatoes—as well as blueberries, cherries, grapefruit and pomegranates.

Eating three four-ounce servings of high-protein foods each day helps suppress appetite and maintain muscle mass. Choose fish, egg whites, poultry and plain, fat-free yogurt. Meat lovers can eat red meat twice a week but should marinate beef with cherry or pomegranate concentrate (this reduces inflammatory chemical compounds produced during cooking). You can have a tablespoon or two each day of nuts or seeds (especially flaxseed, walnuts and almonds). During this stage, get 25 grams of fiber, primarily from vegetables.

Avoid grains, even whole grains, because they tend to raise insulin levels, increasing leptin resistance.

Most people stay in this stage for two weeks and lose six to 10 pounds.

Stage 2 is the long-term weight-loss part of the diet. Stay on this until you reach your goal weight. Expect to lose one to two pounds per week.

In addition to the Stage 1 foods, add some whole grains, such as oats and brown rice, and beans, lentils and other legumes (about two to three cups a week of each).

Stage 3 is the lifelong maintenance phase. Increase variety by adding potatoes, pasta and whole-grain breads.

Snacks That Help You Lose Weight

If you are a "night snacker" or someone for whom after-dinner snacking significantly contributes to a weight problem, eating a low-calorie snack about 90 minutes after dinner may help curtail eating and overall daily caloric intake—and promote weight loss.

Good choice: A serving of low-calorie ready-to-eat cereal with fat-free milk.

Jillon S. Vander Wal, PhD, associate professor of psychology, and director of the the Eating and Weight Studies Lab at Saint Louis University, Missouri.

The CortiSlim Phenomenon

Mark A. Stengler, NMD, licensed naturopathic medical doctor in private practice, Encinitas, California... adjunct associate clinical professor at the National College of Natural Medicine, Portland, Oregon...author of *The Natural Physician's Healing Therapies* and co-author of *Prescription for Natural Cures* (both from Bottom Line Books).

The recent claims made for CortiSlim, the once highly advertised weight-loss supplement, do not appear to be supported by scientific evidence. As the TV infomercial and radio ads declared, prolonged elevation of the stress hormone cortisol can lead to weight gain, especially around the abdomen.

It's true that many things, such as work-related stress, emotional upset and/or chronic illness, can stimulate the overproduction of cortisol by the adrenal glands.

These glands, located on top of each kidney, have the important function of producing stress hormones (such as cortisol, adrenaline, noradrenaline) that help the body deal with stressful situations.

When too much cortisol is produced, blood sugar and insulin levels rise, which increase appetite and fat storage.

The marketers of CortiSlim took this basic physiological truth and adopted it as the backbone of their infomercial. The fact is, however, there is not one published peer-reviewed study that I know of on this product.

Not surprisingly, the US Food and Drug Administration (FDA) took regulatory action against the marketers of CortiSlim, citing unsubstantiated claims made by the company, such as "eliminates cravings," "controls appetite," "diminish[es] hunger and stress eating" and "supports healthy cortisol levels." And there is a class action lawsuit pending against the makers of CortiSlim by dissatisfied customers who found the claims made by the company to be misleading.

BALANCING CORTISOL

Several herbal and mineral ingredients are found in CortiSlim, including bitter orange peel (known as *Citrus aurantium*), which contains a naturally occurring stimulant called *synephrine*.

Published peer-reviewed studies have shown that nutritional supplements not found in CortiSlim, such as *phosphatidylserine* and the herb *ashwagandha*, can reduce cortisol levels. *Dehydroepiandrosterone* (DHEA), typically used by people who suffer fatigue, low libido and depression due to low levels of this hormone, also can dramatically reduce cortisol levels.

Use of DHEA should be monitored by a physician. And we know that exercise, positive mental imagery, deep breathing and prayer are powerful methods of maintaining cortisol balance. Unlike CortiSlim, these natural approaches have been proven to be effective.

NO PLACEBOS, PLEASE

This product also concerns me because its labeling does not tell consumers how much of each herb is used in the formulation. Too often the amounts listed are too low to have significant benefits.

In reality, the amounts of the ingredients often are one-tenth or one-hundredth of what would be needed for a therapeutic effect.

The absence of published studies does not necessarily mean that the product doesn't work. What is troubling in this particular case is that the marketing hype leads the consumer to believe that CortiSlim is scientifically proven to reduce weight.

Suggestion: If you are overweight, by all means have your cortisol level tested. To do so, ask your doctor or natural health-care practitioner to order a salivary cortisol test. Leading research institutions use this type of testing, because it is convenient and accurate. If you prefer to do the testing yourself, you can order a kit from ZRT Laboratory (866-600-1636, *www.zrtlab.com*).

If your cortisol level is elevated, exercise regularly, use positive mental imagery and consider counseling. Also try the supplement ashwagandha (containing 8% withanolides) at a dose of 250 mg daily. As an alternative, you may want to try taking 300 mg to 500 mg daily of the nutritional supplement phosphatidylserine.

More from Dr. Mark Stengler...

Supplements That Suppress Appetite...Really!

Americans are in a ferocious battle with obesity. Statistics tell us that approximately 70% of the American adult population is overweight. Unfortunately, few people realize that many over-the-counter (OTC) and prescription weight-loss medications are not very effective—and that some actually can be dangerous.

When patients come to see me for guidance in achieving healthful, permanent weight loss, I approach their needs on many levels, including their diet, level of physical activity, emotional state, hormone levels and other factors that affect body weight.

There is one area in which I (and other knowledgeable natural practitioners) can add a unique weapon in the fight against excess body weight—the use of specific nutritional supplements. Plant and other natural substances in supplement form can be used to reduce a person's appetite.

I also often can help reduce a patient's food cravings and accelerate metabolism with a selection of nontoxic dietary supplements.

NO MORE OVEREATING

It doesn't take a medical degree to know that one powerful way to lose weight successfully is to eat less—but that is much easier said than done. That's why appetite suppressants are very useful—even vital—for people who have trouble reducing their caloric intake.

Reasons for overeating vary. Some people grew up in families where portions were lavish, and they are "conditioned" to consume lots of calories. For others, there seems to be an imbalance in the appetite control mechanism, whereby the brain does not reach a state of satiety (feeling satisfied) with normal caloric intake. A complex feedback mechanism between hormones released in the digestive tract and the brain controls this sensation of satiety.

While there's no "magic bullet"—you'll always need willpower to lose weight—I have found that the following supplements do help my patients, and there's good scientific data to back up their effectiveness and safety.

Begin by trying the first supplement. If it doesn't help within four to six weeks, then try the supplements that follow one at a time.

• *Caralluma fimbriata.* This roadside shrub is found throughout many parts of India, where for centuries the whole plant has been boiled like a vegetable or eaten raw in chunks. It has an interesting history as a food to suppress hunger and thirst. During long journeys, tribesmen would pack caralluma to help sustain themselves. Today, caralluma is listed as a vegetable and "famine food" (a plant that is normally not used as a food crop but is consumed in times of scarcity) in the Indian Health Ministry's compilation of medicinal plants.

Gencor Pacific, an Indian herbal product provider, has done a great deal of research on this plant. It has developed caralluma farms in India as well as a special extraction technique that can produce a therapeutic amount of this plant in capsule form. The extract is known commercially as Slimaluma. It has been studied in two double-blind, randomized, placebo-controlled trials in humans. Both studies used a 500-mg capsule taken 30 to 45 minutes before breakfast and dinner. According to Gencor's research, this is equivalent to the traditional intake of 100 g of raw caralluma consumed for an appetite- and thirst-quenching effect.

In the first study, at St. John's National Academy of Health Sciences in Bangalore, India, 50 participants walked for 30 minutes daily and took caralluma or a placebo. Those taking caralluma showed only a slightly greater average weight loss after eight weeks than a placebo group (1.94 pounds versus 1.12 pounds). However, the average loss in waist circumference was 2.75 inches in the caralluma group versus a 1.29-inch loss in the placebo group. Loss of abdominal girth correlates with reduced body fat. The appetite-suppressing effect of caralluma was confirmed in a questionnaire.

In the second study, at Western Geriatric Research Institute in Los Angeles, overweight patients took the regular dose of caralluma or a placebo for four weeks. Participants were instructed not to change their daily activity pattern (exercise) or their food intake for four weeks before starting the trial and during the trial. Out of 18 patients who took the caralluma and completed the trial, 15 lost weight. Eleven patients lost an average of six pounds, with the highest loss at nine pounds. The other four participants lost one to two pounds. Of the three others taking caralluma, one gained weight and two stayed the same. Of the six patients taking a placebo, three gained one pound each, one lost one pound and the other two dropped out due to minor digestive upset. Although it's not confirmed, researchers believe that substances in caralluma known as *pregnane glycosides* are most likely responsible for the appetite-suppressing effect.

I have recommended Slimaluma for many patients. In the informal trial I conducted at my clinic, 80% of users experienced reduced appetite. As in the formal research, I have found that side effects are rare. Occasionally, a person will notice minor digestive upset

that usually goes away when the supplement is taken with food. Caralluma does not have a stimulant effect, as do many OTC and prescription weight-loss medications. This supplement should not be used during pregnancy or by nursing mothers. Use by children should be supervised by a doctor.

A number of manufacturers of supplements containing Slimaluma:

Examples: Stop Aging Now (800-627-9721, *www.stopagingnow.com*)...NOW Foods (888-669-3663, *www.nowfoods.com*). Both are available at health-food stores.

• **Pinolenic acid.** One new dietary supplement used to suppress appetite—without acting as a stimulant—is pinolenic acid, an extract from the Korean pine nut.

At a 2006 meeting of the American Chemical Society, scientists reported the results of a study that assessed pinolenic acid's effects on hunger and satiety. In this randomized, double-blind, placebo-controlled trial, overweight women were given 3 g of pinolenic acid or a placebo (olive oil) right before eating a moderate-sized carbohydrate breakfast.

Researchers measured blood levels of hormones associated with hunger and satiety before the supplement was taken and at regular intervals for four hours thereafter. At each interval, participants reported how hungry they felt. The pinolenic acid group reported significantly less hunger than the placebo group, rating their "desire to eat" 29% lower and their planned food intake 36% lower.

The blood tests also were revealing. After four hours, the hormones cholecystokinin (CCK) and glucagon-like peptide-1 (GLP-1), produced in the small intestine, were considerably higher in the pinolenic acid group than in the placebo group. It's known that upon the consumption of food, these hormones signal satiety to the brain—so it's no surprise that the pinolenic acid group felt less hungry.

A high-quality form of pinolenic acid is available from Life Extension Foundation (800-544-4440, *www.lef.org*). The recommended dose is three 3,000-mg capsules taken 30 to 60 minutes before your highest-calorie meal of the day. Side effects are rare, but pinolenic acid is not approved for use by pregnant women or nursing mothers and should be used by children only under a doctor's supervision. A 90-softgel supply costs $28.

• **Hydroxycitric acid (HCA).** This supplement is a compound found in the rind of a Southeast Asian fruit called *Garcinia cambogia*. The fruit is about the size of an orange and is used as a condiment in Thai and Indian cuisine. It is not a citrus fruit, but the chemical structure of HCA is similar to that of the citric acid found in citrus fruits.

Animal research has shown that HCA suppresses appetite and induces weight loss. However, results of human studies with HCA have been mixed. A study published in the *International Journal of Obesity* looked at the effect of HCA on caloric intake and satiety in overweight women and men. Twelve women and 12 men consumed a placebo—100 milliliters (ml) of tomato juice (about 3.5 fluid ounces)—three times daily for two weeks, then returned to their normal diet for two weeks and, in a final two-week phase, consumed 100 ml of tomato juice that contained 300 mg of HCA three times daily. Researchers found that participants consumed 15% to 30% fewer calories daily during the final phase than they had during the placebo phase. Other studies have not found a similar benefit.

Even though study results on HCA are not conclusive, many of my patients have benefited from this inexpensive and safe supplement. The recommended dose is 500 mg taken three times daily, just before meals. Side effects, including digestive upset, are rare. HCA should not be used by pregnant women, nursing mothers or children. It is available at many health-food stores for about $15 for a one-month supply.

• **Fiber.** One of the simplest and least expensive ways to decrease your appetite is to increase the amount of fiber in your diet. This isn't high tech—but fiber really works, because it makes you feel full. I recommend that all of my overweight patients (regardless of whether or not they are taking a dietary supplement) include a good source of fiber in every meal. Insoluble fiber, the type that is not absorbed through the digestive tract, is an ex-

cellent choice. It is found in most vegetables, especially leafy, green ones, and fruits. For an easy way to increase your intake of insoluble fiber, include a salad or a variety of vegetables with lunch and dinner.

To achieve the greatest appetite suppression, eat vegetables at the start of meals so that you begin to feel full as early as possible. Since most people are not accustomed to eating vegetables with breakfast, I advise patients to take one to two tablespoons of ground flaxseed (grind flaxseed in a coffee grinder for five seconds) or flaxmeal (preground flaxseed is available at most health-food stores). Flaxseed can be added to cereal or a yogurt-and-fruit and/or protein shake. Be sure to drink eight to 10 ounces of water after consuming flaxseed.

You also can get appetite-suppressing fiber from supplements. A good choice is psyllium seed husks. Available at health-food stores and pharmacies, psyllium is commonly used to treat constipation, as it adds bulk to stool and stimulates peristalsis (contractions) of the intestines. Fiber supplements are best taken at least two hours before or after using vitamin and mineral supplements and pharmaceutical medications, as they can impair nutrient and drug absorption.

The High School Reunion Diet—Lose 20 Years in 30 Days

David A. Colbert, MD, founder and head physician of New York Dermatology Group in New York City. He is a member of American College of Physicians and Surgeons, American Academy of Dermatology and American College of Dermatological Surgeons. He is coauthor, with Terry Reed, of *The High School Reunion Diet: Lose 20 Years in 30 Days* (Simon & Schuster). *www.highschoolreuniondiet.com*

Patients who first try Botox often say that they want to look good for an upcoming wedding, high school reunion or other important event. Botox is very effective at treating some wrinkles, but it doesn't improve the aged look of skin. Nor can it reverse the aging effects of obesity, including lack of vitality.

The right diet can not only help you lose weight, it also can make you feel and look 10 to 20 years younger…

• **Eat low-glycemic carbohydrates.** The *Glycemic Index* (GI) is a measure of how quickly the carbohydrates in foods turn into *glucose* (sugar) in the blood. A food on the GI is ranked relative to pure glucose, which is given the ranking 100.

High-GI foods cause a spike in blood sugar and a consequent dip, which causes cravings for more sugar. A consistently high-GI diet not only causes weight gain and risk for insulin resistance and diabetes, it compromises the radiance and suppleness of skin.

A food with a low GI causes a more even rise and fall in blood sugar than a food with a high GI. I advise patients to eat lots of fresh, whole foods. Many green vegetables, such as spinach, broccoli and asparagus, have GI rankings under 20 and are full of the antioxidants that promote beautiful skin. Slightly higher on the GI but still wholesome are whole-grain products.

Example: Oat bran bread has a 68 GI versus a French baguette with a 136 GI.

To find the GI ratings of foods, go to *www.glycemicindex.com*.

• **Limit refined sugar.** The trick to looking years younger just by changing your daily diet is sugar control—know how sugars work in your system and where they lurk in processed foods and avoid them.

The sugars added to many packaged foods trigger a process known as *glycosylation*, which causes the skin to become stiff and discolored.

Don't buy any product that lists sugar in the top three ingredients. Be aware that sugar goes by different names including dextrose, galactose, high-fructose corn syrup and caramel.

Fruits have a lot of *fructose* (sugar), but if eaten whole, they are full of fiber that slows down the sugar. I tell patients to avoid drinking fruit juices, though, and to go for the whole fruit.

• **Eat antioxidant-rich foods.** Much of the skin damage that accompanies aging is caused by *free radicals*, oxygen-based molecules that are produced in higher-than-normal amounts when we're exposed to sun or environmental toxins (such as cigarette smoke). Free radicals damage cells and alter genetic material, leading to skin aging, including wrinkling, and skin cancer.

Antioxidants can fight free radicals. Here are a few of the powerful anti-oxidants that can help repair skin…

• Allium—in garlic, onions and scallions.

• Anthocyanin—in berries, pomegranates, cherries, blood oranges, black beans as well as soybeans.

Helpful: Blueberries are particularly good for skin. I recommend one-half cup to one cup a day. If you get tired of blueberries, switch to blackberries.

• Beta-carotene—in carrots, sweet potatoes, pumpkins and squash.

• Lutein—in spinach, kale, broccoli and brussels sprouts.

• Lycopene—in tomatoes, watermelon and pink grapefruit.

• Quercetin—in broccoli, cranberries, onions and apples.

• **Eat fish three to four times weekly.** The omega-3 fatty acids in cold-water fish, such as salmon and sardines, can help reduce acne, rosacea and other forms of skin infection and inflammation. The omega-3s also help reduce joint inflammation—important for maintaining youthful flexibility.

If you don't like fish, take a supplement of 1,000 milligrams (mg) of omega-3s daily.

• **Eat plain unsweetened yogurt.** It's high in protein as well as calcium—important for skin collagen as well as healthy muscles and joints. Yogurt also aids weight loss. One study found that people who ate one serving of yogurt with blueberries daily lost an average of 12 pounds in a year without doing anything else.

Look for Greek yogurt, which is strained longer and therefore is thicker—it delivers the highest amount of protein. You can add berries, nuts or a touch of honey.

• **Drink water**—at least eight (and preferably more) tall glasses a day. Water literally plumps the skin and makes wrinkles less apparent.

More from David A. Colbert

Youth in a Blender

This smoothie gives you—and your skin—a good start on the day...

BREAKFAST SMOOTHIE

½ cup milk (regular or skim)
½ cup plain yogurt (full-fat or low-fat)
½ cup frozen strawberries
½ cup frozen blueberries
1 teaspoon honey
4 ice cubes

Purée everything but the ice cubes in a blender. Add the ice, and purée again. Serves one.

The Latest on Calcium

JoAnn E. Manson, MD, DrPH, professor of medicine and women's health at Harvard Medical School and chief of the division of preventive medicine at Brigham and Women's Hospital, both in Boston. A lead investigator for two important studies on women's health, Dr. Manson is coauthor of *Hot Flashes, Hormones & Your Health* (McGraw-Hill).

The typical midlife woman in the US consumes about 700 milligrams (mg) of calcium daily—far less than the recommended 1,200 mg for women age 50 and older. Perhaps this would improve if more women were aware of recent research showing how directly calcium's ability to prevent bone loss translates into better health.

Until recently, there was scant evidence that calcium cut the risk for hip fracture, a common and disabling complication of thinning bones. As part of a large study called the Women's Health Initiative (WHI), my colleagues and I conducted a seven-year clinical trial of calcium and vitamin D supplementation. More than 36,000 postmenopausal women were assigned to take either placebos or daily supplements of calcium at 1,000 mg plus vitamin D at 400 international units (IU), in two divided doses. Compared with placebo users, women who consistently took their pills as prescribed decreased their hip fracture risk by 30%...

while in the 60-and-up age group, risk was reduced by 21% whether or not the pills were taken consistently. The benefit might have been even greater if higher doses of vitamin D had been tested—many experts now recommend 800 IU to 1,000 IU daily. *Calcium also may protect against...*

• **Colorectal polyps.** Small trials of calcium supplementation report reductions in risk for precancerous polyps called colorectal adenomas. In the WHI, however, calcium supplementation did not lower colorectal cancer risk. Research is ongoing.

• **Weight gain.** Although the effect was modest, WHI participants assigned to calcium supplementation were less likely to gain weight.

Theory: Calcium may positively affect fat metabolism.

The news about heart health: Although a recent small trial suggested that calcium supplements may contribute to cardiovascular problems, the much larger WHI study found that calcium plus vitamin D supplements did not increase heart attack or stroke risk.

Good dietary sources of calcium are low-fat dairy foods...canned oily fish with bones (sardines, salmon)...calcium-fortified orange juice and cereals...broccoli, collard greens and kale.

Few women get enough calcium from food alone.

Best: Take a daily calcium supplement, preferably along with vitamin D to maximize absorption. Discuss with your doctor the right dosage for you.

Options: Calcium carbonate (Caltrate, Viactiv) requires stomach acid for proper absorption, so you must take it with a meal or snack...calcium citrate (Citracal) is more convenient because it can be taken without food, but you need a higher dose to get the same amount of actual (elemental) calcium.

Excess calcium can increase kidney stone risk, impair kidney function and interfere with magnesium absorption.

National guidelines: Do not exceed 2,500 mg of calcium daily from all sources. If you supplement with more than 500 mg, take it in divided doses at least two hours apart.

Don't Mix Antibiotics And Calcium

Taking *fluoroquinolone* antibiotics, such as Cipro or Levaquin, with calcium-rich or -fortified foods, such as milk, orange juice and breakfast cereals, can reduce antibiotic absorption. This makes treatment less effective and may produce antibiotic-resistant bacteria.

Self-defense: Whenever possible, take these antibiotics with water—and either two hours before or after meals.

Ask your doctor about other antibiotics, which also may need to be taken separately from meals.

The late Guy Amsden, PharmD, Bassett Healthcare, Cooperstown, New York, and leader of a study of antibiotic absorption, reported in *Journal of Clinical Pharmacology.*

Birth Control Pills Deplete Nutrients

Mark A. Stengler, NMD, licensed naturopathic medical doctor in private practice, Encinitas, California... adjunct associate clinical professor at the National College of Natural Medicine, Portland, Oregon...author of *The Natural Physician's Healing Therapies* and coauthor of *Prescription for Natural Cures* (both from Bottom Line Books).

A study published in the *American Journal of Obstetrics and Gynecology* examined how oral contraceptives affect blood levels of fat-soluble antioxidants, including coenzyme Q10, alpha-tocopherol and gamma-tocopherol (members of the vitamin E family) and the carotenoids beta-carotene, alpha-carotene and lycopene. Nonfasting blood samples were collected randomly on any day of the menstrual cycle from 15 premenopausal women who had used oral contraceptives for at least six months and from 40 women who did not use oral contraceptives. Women who consumed coenzyme Q10 supplements and/or multivitamins and women who had irregular menstrual cycles were excluded.

Result: In the oral contraceptive users, blood levels of coenzyme Q10 were 37% lower and alpha-tocopherol levels were 23% lower than those in women who did not use contraceptives. Blood levels of the other nutrients were comparable between the two groups.

My view: An abundance of evidence has shown that most pharmaceutical drugs deplete the body of nutrients, especially when used long term (more than two months). Birth control pills are no exception. For several years, it has been documented that birth control pills deplete the body of B vitamins (B-1, B-2, B-3, B-6, B-12 and folic acid) as well as magnesium, zinc and vitamin C. This study adds coenzyme Q10 and alpha-tocopherol to the list. These nutrients help prevent damage caused by free radicals and also promote proper immune and cardiovascular system function. To guard against nutritional deficiencies in the millions of American women who use birth control pills (often for several years at a time), it should become standard practice for doctors and pharmacists to recommend a full-spectrum multivitamin along with coenzyme Q10 (25 mg to 50 mg) daily.

Are You Taking the Right Multivitamin?

Alan H. Pressman, DC, PhD, CCN, certified clinical nutritionist, director of Gramercy Health Associates, New York City. He hosts the radio show "Healthline" on Air America and is coauthor of *The Complete Idiot's Guide to Vitamins and Minerals* (Alpha).

A daily multivitamin/mineral supplement helps you meet your nutritional needs—but with so many brands available, it's not easy to select one. *What to do...*

●**Choose a multi made especially for women.** Women's multis typically provide extra folic acid, which protects against heart disease, colon cancer and birth defects...and extra bone-building calcium, magnesium and vitamin D.

●**Look for an age-appropriate formula.** Before menopause, it is common for monthly blood loss to deplete the iron that red blood cells need—which is why women's multis often contain iron. Excess iron supplementation can damage organs, however—so if you're postmenopausal and have no diagnosed iron deficiency, it is wise to take an iron-free multi. Some "50+" formulas also provide extra B vitamins because the body's ability to absorb these often declines with age...and/or even higher amounts of calcium and vitamin D.

Good brands: Nature Made Multi for Her and Multi for Her 50+...One A Day Women's and Women's 50+ Advantage.

•**Supplement your supplement.** The daily value (DV)—the government-recommended daily intake—for calcium is 1,000 milligrams (mg) for women ages 19 to 50 and 1,200 mg for women over 50...the DV for magnesium is 400 mg. But many multis provide just a fraction of those DVs—otherwise, the pills would be too big.

Another problem: The DV for vitamin D is 400 international units (IU), an amount that many multis provide—yet experts advise getting 1,000 IU to 2,000 IU of vitamin D to lower risk for osteoporosis, diabetes, heart disease and some cancers.

Best: In addition to a multi, take a supplement that helps make up for these shortfalls, such as Caltrate 600-D Plus Minerals or Schiff Super Calcium-Magnesium...take additional vitamin D if necessary.

Look for the USP on The Label

If a vitamin supplement does not disintegrate in the digestive tract, it will provide little benefit.

The best guarantee that pills will disintegrate properly is to look for the letters "USP" on the label. That means they meet the disintegration standards of US Pharmacopeia, an independent, nonprofit pharmaceutical-testing organization. Generic vitamins approved by USP meet the same test standards as more expensive name brands.

Robert Russell, MD, former director, USDA Human Nutrition Research Center on Aging, Tufts University, Boston.

Four Types of Iron Supplements That Don't Cause Constipation

Mark A. Stengler, NMD, licensed naturopathic medical doctor in private practice, Encinitas, California...adjunct associate clinical professor at the National College of Natural Medicine, Portland, Oregon...author of *The Natural Physician's Healing Therapies* and co-author of *Prescription for Natural Cures* (both from Bottom Line Books).

If you can't get enough iron from iron-rich foods such as hormone-free red meat, blackstrap molasses, almonds, raisins and brewer's yeast and you've been prescribed supplemental iron for anemia, you may be experiencing constipation. You should take a different form of iron supplement. What you've been prescribed—ferrous sulfate—is poorly absorbed, and it can cause constipation (and stomach irritation) more often than other types of iron.

Iron citrate, iron glycinate, iron fumarate and *iron gluconate* are forms of the mineral that are more easily absorbed by the body and less likely to cause constipation. Dosage generally is 50 milligrams (mg) to 100 mg per day for mild anemia or up to 200 mg for more severe anemia, as determined by blood tests. Check with your doctor about dosage.

Don't take your iron within three hours of taking any supplements containing calcium, magnesium or zinc. These minerals interfere with the absorption of iron. Vitamins C and A, however, improve iron absorption—taking your iron with a glass of orange juice, for example, is a good idea. Be sure to have your blood retested after four to six weeks.

Vitamin C to the Rescue

Vitamin C may help prevent asthma, bronchitis and other lung problems. When researchers studied the diets and lung functions of over 2,500 people, they found that the people who consumed the most vitamin C had the best-functioning lungs. The difference in lung function between those whose daily diet contained an amount of vitamin C equivalent to that contained in 10 ounces of orange juice (99 milligrams) and those who had almost none was as great as that between nonsmokers and people who smoked a pack of cigarettes every day for five years.

Scott T. Weiss, MD, professor of medicine at Harvard Medical School, Boston.

Vitamin C Helps You Burn More Fat

In a recent study, people who took 500 milligrams (mg) of vitamin C daily burned 39% more fat while exercising than people who took less. Since it is difficult to get enough vitamin C just from fruits and vegetables, take a vitamin C supplement to be sure you get at least 500 mg per day

Carol Johnston, PhD, professor and chair, department of nutrition, Arizona State University, Mesa, and leader of a study published in *Journal of the American College of Nutrition.*

Can This Patient Be Cured? Supplement Sensitivity

Mark A. Stengler, NMD, licensed naturopathic medical doctor in private practice, Encinitas, California... adjunct associate clinical professor at the National College of Natural Medicine, Portland, Oregon...author of *The Natural Physician's Healing Therapies* and co-author of *Prescription for Natural Cures* (both from Bottom Line Books).

When Carrie, a 55-year-old homemaker, first came to see me five years ago, she was experiencing a multitude of symptoms, including migraines, fatigue, mood problems with depression and irritability, hair loss and irritable bowel symptoms, including extreme bloating. I took a medical history, performed a physical exam and ordered lab tests. I took a close look at her thyroid (which regulates metabolism) and adrenal glands (which produce the hormones needed to deal with physical and mental stress). The dysfunction of either can cause fatigue and some of the other symptoms Carrie described. As it turned out, her thyroid and adrenal gland function were both deficient—so I prescribed natural hormone replacement for thyroid support and supplements to bolster the adrenal glands.

At times, Carrie thought that the hormone replacement improved her energy, but her fatigue and bloating persisted. Over the next year, we adjusted the dose of her thyroid supplement, but this did not seem to help her feel better consistently. Sometimes she felt better...sometimes, worse.

Next step: To help with her digestive problems and fatigue, I tested Carrie for sensitivity to gluten, a protein found in wheat and some other grains. It came back positive, so it seemed likely that avoiding gluten would resolve Carrie's digestion problems, but after two months, we both were disappointed in the result. I then prescribed digestive enzymes and probiotics (helpful bacteria for the gut) to help with Carrie's digestion and lack of energy, but this too resulted in only a mild benefit.

I was puzzled. Something was going on with Carrie that wasn't on my radar. The best strategy in a situation like this is to assess everything a patient is doing and taking to determine where the bottleneck might be.

In addition to the supplements I had prescribed, Carrie also was taking a multivitamin. I had her stop taking it to see what would happen. To our surprise, her energy and digestive function improved within five days. To confirm that the multivitamin had been the culprit, Carrie started taking it again—and sure enough, within three days, her fatigue and bloating returned with a vengeance.

I took a close look at her multivitamin. There was nothing out of the ordinary in its composition, but it was clear that either Carrie was having a reaction to one of the ingredients or that there was a contaminant in it. I put her on a different multivitamin and had her continue with the thyroid supplement and natural hormone replacement, and she felt much better.

Every once in a while, I have a patient who is sensitive to a supplement or a medication, and it causes unexpected symptoms (such as fatigue or depression) or mimics those of other medical conditions (such as chronic fatigue or irritable bowel syndrome). The human body can be sensitive in surprising ways.

Are You Getting Enough Vitamin D?

Reinhold Vieth, PhD, professor in the department of nutritional sciences and the department of laboratory medicine and pathobiology and director of the bone and mineral laboratory, both at Mount Sinai Hospital, University of Toronto, Canada. Dr. Vieth has written more than 70 related professional articles.

Until recently, physicians rarely diagnosed deficiencies of vitamin D except in occasional cases of childhood rickets (a disease in which the bones do not harden).

Now: One in three Americans is considered to be deficient in vitamin D—and most of them don't know it, according to the US National Center for Health Statistics.

How did vitamin D deficiency become such a widespread problem so quickly—and what should be done about it? Reinhold Vieth, PhD, a leading expert on vitamin D, provides the answers below.

NEW DISCOVERIES

To produce adequate levels of vitamin D naturally, you must expose your skin (without sunscreen) to ultraviolet B (UVB) rays from the sun for about 15 minutes, as a general guideline, twice a week. If you use sunscreen, your body makes little or no vitamin D. Generations ago, when large numbers of Americans began working indoors—thus reducing their

exposure to sunlight—their average vitamin D blood levels declined.

More recently, average blood levels of vitamin D in the US have remained fairly constant. What has changed is all the scientific research pointing to the importance of the vitamin.

An overwhelming body of evidence shows that vitamin D not only affects the bones (by facilitating the absorption of calcium), but also may play a key role in fighting a wide variety of ailments, including cardiovascular disease…autoimmune diseases (such as rheumatoid arthritis, lupus and multiple sclerosis)…chronic bone or muscle pain (including back pain)…macular degeneration…and increased susceptibility to colds and flu.

A number of studies also have shown a link between adequate blood levels of vitamin D and lower risk for some types of cancer, including colon, lung, breast and prostate cancers as well as Hodgkin's lymphoma (cancer of the lymphatic system).

Important new finding: In a study of 13,000 initially healthy men and women, researchers at Johns Hopkins found that vitamin D deficiency was associated with a 26% increase in death from any cause during a median period of nine years.

HOW VITAMIN D HELPS

Recent scientific discoveries have demonstrated that vitamin D is critical for the health of every organ in the body. By acting as a signaling molecule, vitamin D helps cells "talk" to each other, which in turn helps control how they behave. Cellular communication is essential for healthy biology.

To understand the function of vitamin D, think of paper in an office—you need paper to send memos and create reports. With enough paper, communication occurs easily. Without adequate paper supplies, the office may continue to function, but some important messages will not be communicated and mistakes will be made. Similarly, without enough vitamin D, your body is more likely to experience a breakdown of cellular communication that can lead to the conditions described above.

ARE YOU AT RISK?

Vitamin D deficiency is considered a "silent disease"—it can occur without any obvious signs. When symptoms do occur, muscle weakness and musculoskeletal pain are common.

Frightening recent study: People with a severe vitamin D deficiency were more than twice as likely to die of heart disease and other causes than people with normal levels of vitamin D.

Among those at greatest risk for a vitamin D deficiency...

• **People over age 50.** Beginning at about age 50, our skin progressively loses some of its ability to convert sunlight to the active form of vitamin D.

• **People with dark skin** (anyone who is of non-European ancestry). Dark skin pigmentation offers some protection from skin cancer because it naturally filters the sun's cancer-causing ultraviolet B (UVB) rays. However, these are the same rays that we need to produce vitamin D.

• **People with limited sun exposure.** Those who live in most parts of the US, except the extreme South, do not produce enough vitamin D from sun exposure in the winter months. Elderly people who may spend less time outdoors also are at increased risk for vitamin D deficiency.

AVOIDING A DEFICIENCY

Many doctors now advise their patients to receive a blood test that measures levels of *25-hydroxy* vitamin D—a form of the vitamin that acts as a marker for vitamin D deficiency. If you are concerned about your vitamin D levels, ask your primary care physician for the test—it typically costs $75 or more and is covered by some health insurers.

My recommendation: Get the test in the winter. If done in the summer, when you are likely to get more sun exposure, the test may reflect higher vitamin D levels than is typical for you at other times of the year.

As research confirming vitamin D's health benefits continues to mount, medical experts have raised the recommended blood levels for the vitamin—currently, levels of 30 nanograms per milliliter (ng/mL) are considered adequate—but a more desirable range for most people is 31 ng/mL to 90 ng/mL.

The US adequate intake level for vitamin D (from food and/or supplements) is 400 international units (IU) per day for adults under age 70 and 600 IU for adults age 70 and older.

However, the consensus among vitamin D researchers is that most adults should be taking vitamin D supplements totaling 1,000 IU daily...and 2,000 IU daily might be even better for meeting the body's needs. Ask your doctor what the right dosage is for you. Either dosage can be taken along with a multivitamin.

It is nearly impossible to get enough vitamin D from diet alone. In the US, milk and other dairy products and some breakfast cereals are fortified with vitamin D. Other food sources such as salmon, sardines, egg yolks and beef liver also provide small amounts.

How difficult is it to get 1,000 IU of vitamin D per day from food? You would need to drink about 10 cups of vitamin D–fortified milk or orange juice...eat 30 sardines...or eat 55 egg yolks.

Helpful: When choosing a vitamin D supplement, look for vitamin D-3 (*cholecalciferol*). It is twice as potent as vitamin D-2 (*ergocalciferol*).

Caution: Because vitamin D is fat-soluble (stored in the body), consuming more than 10,000 IU daily (or 70,000 IU weekly) can lead to toxic reactions, such as weakness, nausea and vomiting.

What Most People Still Don't Know About Omega-3s

Jonathan Goodman, ND, naturopathic physician with private practices in Bristol and Bloomfield, Connecticut. An adjunct professor at the University of Bridgeport's College of Naturopathic Medicine, Dr. Goodman is author of *The Omega Solution* (Prima Lifestyles). *www.drgoodmannd.com*

Omega-3 fatty acids have been widely studied since 2002, when the American Heart Association (AHA) linked the consumption of these healthful fats to a decreased risk for heart disease.

Now: Hundreds of scientific studies have found that omega-3s, commonly found in cold-water fish, may help prevent not only heart disease, but also cancer (including advanced prostate cancer), rheumatoid arthritis, Parkinson's disease and depression.

Scientific evidence: A diet high in omega-3–rich fish can reduce heart attack risk by 20% to 40%, for example. In countries where people eat a lot of fish, such as Japan, the rates of depression can be up to 50 times lower than in countries where fish is rarely eaten.

Even though the varied health benefits of omega-3s are becoming more widely known, many consumers still have questions about the best way to use these healthful fats. For answers, we talked to Jonathan Goodman, ND, a naturopathic physician and a leading authority on omega-3s.

•**Is fish the best source of omega-3s?** Most physicians believe that natural foods are always preferable to supplements due to the greater variety of nutrients in food. The AHA advises everyone to eat fish at least twice a week. That's considered the minimum amount for heart disease prevention.

I recommend eating fish (12 ounces weekly) that accumulate little mercury, such as salmon, sardines, herring or mackerel. These smaller fish, which are lower on the food chain, tend to accumulate less mercury than swordfish, halibut and other big fish. To avoid potentially dangerous compounds that may be created by frying or grilling, it's best to bake or steam fish.

•**What if I don't like the taste of fish?** Few of my patients eat more than a couple of ounces of fish a week, so I often suggest that they take fish oil supplements.*

For overall disease prevention, I recommend a daily supplement that provides 1,000 mg of omega-3s. It should include both *eicosapen-*

taenoic acid (EPA) and *docosahexaenoic acid* (DHA), two of the omega-3s found in fish.

If you have a specific health problem, you should work with an integrative medicine physician who is familiar with fish oil dosing for that condition. Someone with high triglycerides, for example, might need to take 4,000 mg of omega-3s daily. For a person with bipolar disorder, studies show that more than 4,000 mg of omega-3s a day are needed to ease symptoms.

•**Aren't fish oil supplements difficult to swallow?** They can be. The capsules are large because they contain only about 30% omega-3s, which are mixed with other oils. You can now buy supplements with an omega-3 concentration of 50% or even 90%. These capsules are much smaller. Fish oil liquids also are available, but some brands have an unpleasant taste. A fish oil liquid from Carlson is available in lemon and orange flavors.

•**Are there any fish oil supplements that don't have a fishy taste?** Some people find that freezing the capsules reduces the fishy taste that some fish oil supplements have.

There's also a new, phospholipid form of fish oil, known as Vectomega (manufactured by EuroPharma), that comes in a dry tablet rather than an oily capsule. Because of its molecular structure, it is more readily absorbed into the body's cells, according to studies by the manufacturer. This means you can get the same results as conventional supplements in a much smaller dose (43.2 mg per tablet).

My wife and I use Vectomega, and we've found that it doesn't cause the fishy aftertaste or burps. Vectomega is available at some health-food stores and Web sites, including *www.Amazon.com*). Typical cost is about $38 for 60 tablets.

Other good brands of fish oil supplements: Nordic Naturals and Vital Nutrients.

Supplements made from krill, a small crustacean, also are less likely to have a fishy aftertaste. Krill contain the same fatty acids as fish, but in a form that's easier to absorb than most fish oil supplements. I recommend Neptune Krill Oil (sold under many labels that are available online, including Source Naturals and Schiff MegaRed).

---

*If you have congestive heart failure (CHF) and angina (chest pain), ask your doctor whether you should avoid fish and/or fish oil supplements. People with CHF and angina may have worse cardiac function when they consume omega-3s.

Caution: Do not take krill supplements if you have a shellfish allergy.

●**Is there anyone who should not take fish oil supplements?** Some people might experience stomach upset. That's about the worst of it.

However, if you're taking medications that affect blood clotting, such as *clopidogrel* (Plavix) or *warfarin* (Coumadin), you should avoid fish oil and krill supplements because they have a blood-thinning effect.

Combining a fish oil or krill supplement with an anticlotting drug could result in gastrointestinal bleeding. Even people who take aspirin daily to help prevent heart attack or stroke should consult a doctor before adding fish oil or krill to their daily regimen.

●**Is fish the only food source of omega-3s?** No. Strict vegetarians (vegans) or those with fish allergies often eat flaxseed, or take flaxseed-oil supplements (available in capsule or liquid forms) as an alternative. Flax is one of the few plant foods that provide omega-3s, but you have to use a lot. That's because flaxseed contains short-chain fatty acids, mainly alpha-linolenic acid (ALA), that are converted to longer-chain omega-3s in the body.

The conversion process isn't efficient, so you would need to consume much more flaxseed to get the equivalent level of omega-3s found in fish oil. (For best absorption, flaxseed should be ground before consuming.)

●**Is flaxseed safe for everyone?** Flaxseed contains lignans, substances that have complicated effects on estrogen metabolism and may protect against estrogen-driven breast cancer. However, because the research is inconclusive, consult your doctor before using flax products if you have a personal or family history of breast cancer.

Because the high amounts of ALA in flaxseed oil may stimulate prostate cancer cells to grow, flaxseed oil should be avoided by men who have prostate cancer or risk factors for the disease, such as family history. However, flaxseed, which contains lower levels of ALA, appears to be safe for such men.

The Probiotic Diet

Joseph Brasco, MD, gastroenterologist at the Center for Colon and Digestive Disease, Huntsville, Alabama. Dr. Brasco is coauthor of *Restoring Your Digestive Health* (Kensington Press).

Increasing evidence is pointing to a distinct connection between maintaining a healthy balance of flora in your gut and a healthy number on your bathroom scale. The main goal in eating foods that promote digestive health is overall well being, says Joseph Brasco, MD, a gastroenterologist in private practice in Huntsville, Alabama and the coauthor of *Restoring Your Digestive Health* (Kensington). Nonetheless, he acknowledges that the weight loss that often accompanies a shift to a diet that emphasizes probiotic foods is a very attractive side benefit.

TIP THE SCALES
IN THE RIGHT DIRECTION

Probiotics are friendly bacteria that normally inhabit your intestinal tract and aid digestion. When the balance between the helpful and harmful bacteria gets out of whack, weight gain is just one of the health problems that may follow. A preponderance of harmful bacteria slows the passage of food through the digestive tract, Dr. Brasco explains, giving your body more time to absorb more calories from it. In addition, these bacteria rob your body of valuable nutrients in the food you eat, leaving you hungry and wanting to eat more.

If you are having trouble shedding unwanted pounds and you are already following a healthful diet, watching your portions and exercising regularly, your difficulty may be due to an imbalance of gut flora. *To tip the scales toward weight loss, Dr. Brasco recommends these simple probiotic strategies...*

●**Eat fermented foods every day.** Eating at least one fermented food—choose from yogurt with active cultures, sauerkraut, pickles, kimchi, kefir and miso—on a daily basis will restore proper gut balances.

●**Consume more fresh fruits and vegetables and fewer processed foods.** Fresh produce supports growth of friendly, healthful microbes, while products like breads, dough-nuts and cookies are loaded with starch and simple sugars that encourage the growth of harmful bacteria. Dr. Brasco says to remember that what you don't eat is as important as what you do.

• **Take a daily probiotic supplement.** In his practice, Dr. Brasco has seen good results with Garden of Life Primal Defense® Ultra, Align® by Procter & Gamble and Pharmax products (available through your health-care provider).

• **If you find that probiotic supplements make you gassy or bloated,** take them on an empty stomach. While doctors advise most patients to take probiotics with food, Dr. Brasco says those who get an upset stomach may do better to take them away from meals. Other solutions may include taking them every other day…or you could try a another product based on a different bacteria. If problems persist, see your health-care provider.

A RECIPE FOR EFFICIENT DIGESTION AND WEIGHT LOSS

According to Dr. Brasco, emphasizing probiotics in your diet can lead to lifetime good health. He points out that this approach is embraced around the world, from Russia and Bulgaria to India and China. Dr. Brasco's Probiotic Diet Eating Plan features plenty of advice on incorporating sprouted grains, smoothies, nuts and seeds into your diet. *Here are a few simple and healthful recipes you might enjoy…*

CREAMSICLE SMOOTHIE

Ingredients

6 oz of yogurt or kefir

4 oz freshly squeezed orange juice

1–2 raw omega-3 eggs (optional)

1 Tbsp of flaxseed oil or hemp seed oil

1–2 Tbsp unheated honey

1 Tbsp of goat's milk protein powder (optional)

1–2 fresh or frozen bananas

Vanilla extract (optional)

Directions

Combine the ingredients in a high-speed blender.

Yield: 2 servings.

TURKEY AND GOAT CHEESE WRAP

Ingredients

Sprouted grain or sprouted wheat tortilla

Mayonnaise, mustard or hummus

Turkey

Sprouts

Tomatoes

Goat cheese

Directions

Spread tortilla with your choice of mayonnaise, mustard or hummus. Top with remaining ingredients. Roll up tortilla.

Yield: 1 serving.

CREAMY HIGH-ENZYME DESSERT

Ingredients

4 oz plain goat's milk or cow's milk yogurt, or cultured cream

1 Tbsp raw, unheated honey

1 tsp flaxseed oil

½ cup fresh or frozen organic berries

Directions

Mix together yogurt, honey and flaxseed oil; top with berries.

Yield: 1 serving.

Food Combinations That Fight Disease

Joy Bauer, RD, CDN, author of several nutrition books, including *Joy's LIFE Diet: 4 Steps to Thin Forever* (Collins Living) and *Joy Bauer's Food Cures* (Rodale). Bauer is the nutrition expert for the *Today* show and has a private practice with offices in New York City and Westchester County, New York. *www.joybauer.com*

Until recently, most nutrition research has focused on the health benefits of individual nutrients. For example, it's well-established that vitamin A is good for the eyes…calcium builds stronger bones…and zinc boosts immunity.

Now there is strong scientific evidence that nutrition is much more complex than that. When certain foods are combined, their nutritional value is much greater than when the foods are eaten individually.

That's why dietitians recommend eating a varied diet with plenty of fruits, vegetables, whole grains and low-fat proteins—the greater the variety, the better your chances of maximizing the health benefits of your food.

Recent development: Scientists are beginning to understand exactly which specific food combinations are the most effective in helping the body fight common ailments.

For example…

TO FIGHT ARTHRITIS

• **Combine carotenes and spices.** Carotenes are a group of powerful antioxidants that attack toxic, cell-damaging molecules known as free radicals.

In addition to the widely known *beta-carotene*, there are other carotenes, including *beta-cryptoxanthin*, which has been shown to fight rheumatoid arthritis and osteoarthritis.

Good sources of both beta-carotene and beta-cryptoxanthin: Winter squash (especially butternut), pumpkin, red bell peppers and carrots…apricots and watermelon.

The spices turmeric (with its antioxidant oil curcumin) and ginger contain *phytochemicals* that help suppress inflammatory reactions that can lead to arthritis. Turmeric is the bright yellow, dried spice found in curry powder. Ginger is available in powdered form as a spice and also as a fresh root.

My favorite arthritis-fighting combos: Curried butternut squash soup…pumpkin-ginger muffins…Asian ginger stir-fry with red bell peppers…and curried carrots.

TO FIGHT HEART PROBLEMS

• **Combine lycopene and monounsaturated fats.** *Lycopene* is a fat-soluble antioxidant that has been shown to reduce the risk for heart disease, perhaps by stopping the process that leads to *atherosclerosis* (fatty buildup in the arteries).

Good sources of lycopene: Tomatoes, red and pink grapefruit, watermelon and guava.

Helpful: Eat cooked tomatoes—they contain three to four times more lycopene than raw tomatoes.

Monounsaturated fats are believed to protect against heart disease and have a number of cardiovascular benefits. These healthful fats help the body absorb all fat-soluble nutrients, including lycopene.

Good sources of monounsaturated fats: Olive oil and canola oil…avocado…almonds, walnuts, peanuts and cashews.

My favorite heart-healthy combos: Roasted tomatoes with a touch of olive oil…any meal made with homemade or store-bought tomato sauce that contains olive oil…a salad of grapefruit and avocado…and turkey, avocado and tomato sandwiches.

TO FIGHT MEMORY LOSS

• **Combine folic acid and anthocyanins.** One of the B vitamins, folic acid (also known as folate) helps lower blood levels of the amino acid *homocysteine*—a process that research suggests may promote blood flow to the brain. Folic acid also enhances communication between brain chemicals known as *neurotransmitters*.

Good sources of folic acid: Fortified whole-grain breakfast cereals and oatmeal…green, leafy vegetables, bok choy and broccoli… oranges (or orange juice) and berries (such as strawberries and blackberries).

Anthocyanins are antioxidant phytochemicals that have been shown to not only help prevent memory loss but also improve failing memory.

Good sources of anthocyanins: Berries (especially blueberries—their antioxidant flavonols help protect against brain degeneration), red or black grapes…red or purple cabbage, beets, red onions and eggplant.

My favorite memory-enhancing combos: Folic acid–fortified breakfast cereal with berries…coleslaw with red cabbage and bok choy …chicken-vegetable stir-fry with red onions and broccoli…and fruit salad with oranges and blueberries.

TO FIGHT FATIGUE

• **Combine iron and vitamin C.** Iron helps red blood cells carry oxygen throughout the body. Without enough iron, your cells can become starved for oxygen. This can lead to anemia, which causes listlessness, headache, irritability and general lack of energy.

Good sources of iron: Lean beef, turkey, chicken, lamb and pork...clams, oysters and shrimp...soybeans, chickpeas and lentils...spinach, asparagus and green, leafy vegetables.

Vitamin C is a powerful antioxidant, but most people don't realize that it can help fight fatigue by enhancing the body's ability to absorb iron. By adding a food that contains significant amounts of vitamin C to a meal with an iron-rich food, your body will absorb up to three times more iron.

This is especially important for vegetarians, premenopausal women (who lose iron through menstruation) and people with a genetic predisposition to anemia (determined through blood tests).

Caution: People with hemochromatosis, a dangerous disorder that causes iron to build up in the blood, should not combine foods high in iron and vitamin C.

Good sources of vitamin C: Bell and hot chili peppers, broccoli and kale...tomatoes, mangoes, oranges (or orange juice), strawberries and pineapple.

My favorite fatigue-fighting combos: Spinach salad with mandarin oranges...bean chili (such as kidney, pinto or black bean) with crushed tomatoes...steak with sautéed broccoli...and chicken cacciatore with tomatoes and peppers.

TO FIGHT MOOD SWINGS

• **Combine soluble fiber and protein.** Fluctuations in blood sugar (glucose) often cause mood swings.

Low-quality carbohydrates, such as white rice, white bread, cakes and soft drinks, cause blood sugar spikes that usually lead to a sluggish, depressed feeling when they begin to plummet about one hour after consumption of such foods.

High-quality carbohydrates, such as vegetables, fruits and whole grains, contain soluble fiber that causes a slower, less dramatic rise in glucose.

Good sources of soluble fiber: Oatmeal... barley, lentils, beans (such as kidney, lima and black) and peas...apples (all types), raisins, oranges and bananas...cauliflower and sweet potatoes.

Protein is another natural blood sugar stabilizer—it helps slow the absorption of carbohydrates in your diet. Pairing protein with soluble fiber at every meal will help keep your blood sugar as steady as possible.

Good sources of lean protein: Turkey or chicken breast...fish (all types)...pork tenderloin...lean beef...egg whites...yogurt (low-fat or fat-free)...milk (low-fat or fat-free)...and beans (such as pinto and black).

My favorite mood-stabilizing combos: Three-bean turkey chili with pinto, black and kidney beans...plain, low-fat or fat-free yogurt with fresh fruit (such as berries or peaches)... pork tenderloin with sweet potatoes and cauliflower...hard-boiled eggs with turkey bacon and fruit...and oatmeal with a hard-boiled egg.

Eight Superfoods That Won't Break the Bank

David Grotto, RD, LDN, registered dietitian and former spokesperson for the American Dietetic Association. He is author of *101 Foods That Could Save Your Life* (Bantam). *http://davidgrotto.wordpress.com.*

Food prices in the US have recently soared, increasing at the fastest rate since 1990.

Problem: You may find yourself choosing less expensive—but less nutritious—foods.

Solution: With smart food choices, you can eat well without breaking the bank or sacrificing taste.

Eight extremely nutritious yet economical foods...

ALMONDS

Rich in fiber, vitamin E and healthful monounsaturated fats, almonds are widely known to help fight heart disease. Few people are aware, however, that almonds contain more bone-building calcium than any other nut.

Recommended portion size: One ounce (about 23 nuts) daily.

Typical cost per portion: 32 to 53 cents.*

BEANS

Beans are an excellent source of fiber, protein and B vitamins—and they are rich in cancer-fighting antioxidants called *anthocyanins*.

Recommended portion size: One-half cup (cooked or canned) daily.

Typical cost per portion: 35 cents.

How to choose: All beans are similar in nutritional value, but the varieties with darker colors—such as black, red, kidney and adzuki beans—contain more disease-fighting antioxidants. Dried and canned beans have similar nutritional value. To reduce the sodium content of canned beans by about 40%, rinse them in water for 40 seconds before cooking.

CHARD

Chard is a dark green, leafy vegetable that is very low in calories but high in fiber. It is an excellent source of the antioxidants vitamin A and vitamin C...vitamin K, which promotes blood health...vitamin D and magnesium, which are necessary for bone health...and potassium, which helps minimize the negative effects of excessive sodium. Chard also contains the antioxidants *lutein* and *zeaxanthin*, which help prevent eye disease.

Recommended portion size: One cup raw...or one-half cup cooked, daily.

Typical cost per portion: 50 cents.

How to choose: All varieties—Swiss chard, red chard and rainbow chard—offer similar levels of nutrients.

EGGS

Eggs are a good source of protein, providing all the essential amino acids. They also contain vitamin D for bone health...vitamin B-12, which helps maintain energy...*choline*, which improves brain function...and eye-protecting lutein and zeaxanthin.

These important nutrients are found in egg yolks, which contain cholesterol. However, there is not a strong correlation between dietary

*Typical cost per portion is based on national food price estimates. Prices may vary.

cholesterol and blood cholesterol levels, so it's safe for most people to eat eggs every day.

Helpful: To limit saturated fat intake, cook eggs in a nonstick pan coated with vegetable spray and make scrambled eggs with nonfat milk.

Recommended portion size: One or two eggs daily. If you have heart disease, check with your doctor or a registered dietitian before eating this number of eggs.

Typical cost per portion: 15 cents per egg.

How to choose: Brown or white—free-range or not—all eggs provide similar levels of nutrients.

MUSHROOMS

Mushrooms, such as white button or cremini, are a good source of vitamin D, as well as the mineral selenium and the phytochemical *ergothionine*, both of which have cancer-fighting properties. With their meatlike texture, mushrooms are an inexpensive supplement to beef—for example, you can use mushrooms to replace some of the beef in hamburgers or meatloaf.

Recommended portion size: One-half cup (about 1.5 ounces)...or four to five small mushrooms daily.

Typical cost per portion: 25 to 50 cents.

How to choose: All edible mushrooms have nearly the same nutritional profile.

OATS

Oats can significantly reduce cholesterol—people who eat one-and-a-half cups daily for one month can lower total cholesterol by up to 14 points. In addition, oats contain healthy amounts of vitamin E, calcium, magnesium, potassium, selenium, zinc and iron.

Recommended portion size: Up to three-quarters cup dry (one-and-a-half cups cooked) daily.

Typical cost per portion: 35 cents.

How to choose: There is no health benefit to eating steel-cut oats over whole oats.

POTATOES

Of all vegetables, potatoes are among the richest sources of potassium, which is important for controlling blood pressure and reducing risk for stroke and dementia. Potatoes are highly "satiating"—meaning they effectively reduce hunger.

Important: The nutritional value of a potato is almost equally divided between the flesh and the skin, so eat the skin whenever possible.

Recommended portion size: One medium potato (about eight ounces) daily.

Typical cost per portion: 40 cents.

How to choose: Potatoes with purple or red skins and sweet potatoes have more valuable antioxidants.

PRUNES

The antioxidant compounds in prunes help prevent hardening of the arteries—perhaps by protecting the lining of the blood vessels from plaque formation. Prunes also may help lower LDL cholesterol. The laxative effect provided by prunes is due not only to their high fiber content, but also to a natural compound in the fruit called sorbitol.

Recommended portion size: Five or six prunes daily.

Typical cost per portion: 30 to 40 cents.

How to choose: Consume the dried fruit, not the juice, which contains more concentrated sugars and less fiber per serving.

Eight Simple Ways to Eat Better

Jamison Starbuck, ND, naturopathic physician in family practice in Missoula, Montana. She is past president of the American Association of Naturopathic Physicians and a contributing editor to *The Alternative Advisor: The Complete Guide to Natural Therapies and Alternative Treatments* (Time-Life).

If improving your diet has ever been a personal goal for you—or perhaps a New Year's resolution—I have good news. There are some very practical and simple steps you can take to reach this goal—and you don't have to make radical changes that are next to impossible to sustain.

Several years ago, a patient named Eugene asked me how he could improve his eating habits. As I told Eugene, the key is substituting a few healthful foods for some of the less nutritious items that most people eat. *My advice...*

1. Use plain, low-fat yogurt instead of milk, ice cream or sour cream. Yogurt offers all of the nutrition of milk plus the addition of beneficial bacteria that help improve digestion and nutrient absorption and fight overgrowth of yeast. Yogurt is an excellent choice for breakfast or a snack. It can be used on vegetables, in soup or as a healthful dessert. If you don't like the taste of plain yogurt, add your own honey, maple syrup, fresh fruit and/or nuts.

2. Replace iceberg lettuce with chopped red chard leaves. Iceberg lettuce provides few nutrients. By replacing it with red chard, you can add vitamin A, iron and fiber to your salads.

3. Try romaine lettuce leaves in place of bread. Romaine lettuce is firm enough to be filled with spreads or something more substantial, such as tuna or turkey. Simply roll up the leaf as you would a sandwich wrap. Romaine "sandwiches" will help you reduce calories, contribute to your daily fiber intake and improve your digestion.

4. Use sesame butter instead of peanut butter. Sesame butter is a richer source of calcium and healthful omega-3 fatty acids.

5. Substitute ground flaxseed for flour. Ground flaxseed is more nutritious than wheat flour and is a great source of fiber and a form of heart- and brain-healthy omega-3s. Add ground flaxseed to oatmeal or cereal or substitute ground flaxseed for one-third of the flour in recipes for muffins and breads.

6. Add a few bok choy leaves to soup. Like chard, bok choy is high in folic acid (needed for red blood cell formation) and iron—and the compounds that give the leafy, green vegetable its bitter quality aid digestion. To improve the nutritional value of even canned soup, sprinkle several coarsely chopped bok choy leaves on top when it's steaming hot and almost ready to eat. Cover and let simmer for four minutes.

7. Eat parsley regularly. It's rich in vitamin C, helps freshen your breath and reduces intestinal gas. Chop it up raw and add it to green salads or tuna. Or make a batch of parsley pesto (substitute parsley for some or all of the basil in a pesto recipe).

8. Go vegetarian one day a week. Use crumbled tempeh (fermented soy) instead of ground beef in chili or soups. Also, scramble tofu, instead of eggs, with onions and veggies for breakfast. Avoiding meat for just one day a week will help reduce your cholesterol levels.

Nutrients That Fig Cancer

Patrick Quillin, PhD, RD, clinical nutritionist in San Diego. He is author of 15 books, including *Beating Cancer with Nutrition* (Nutrition Times). *www.nutritioncancer.com*. He edited the textbook *Adjuvant Nutrition in Cancer Treatment* and organized three international symposiums on that topic.

Every year, more than 1.4 million Americans are diagnosed with cancer. Nearly half of all Americans eventually will get the disease—and about 25% of them will die from it. But there is a powerful way to reduce your risk of getting cancer.

Specific nutrients and foods can help prevent or correct cellular, hormonal and other imbalances that may lead to cancer. The supplements mentioned here are available at health-food stores and some supermarkets.

FISH OIL

The most common nutritional deficiency in Americans is low *eicosapentaenoic acid* (EPA). It is one of the omega-3 fatty acids found in the oil of fatty fish, such as salmon and tuna. A healthy diet has a 1:1 ratio of omega-3 to omega-6 fatty acids (found in vegetable oils). The typical American diet has a 1:16 ratio.

EPA helps prevent cancer by improving cell membrane dynamics—the ability of each cell to receive hormones and signals from other cells while absorbing essential nutrients and expelling waste products. EPA also boosts immune function and lowers levels of hormones that contribute to breast and other cancers, such as estradiol.

What I recommend to my patients: One tablespoon of fish oil daily. For capsules, follow dosage recommendations on labels. Carlson Laboratories, Dr. Sears, Nordic Naturals and Pharmax brands are reliable. Take it in the middle of a meal to avoid "fishy" belching or reflux.

CLA

Another fat that helps prevent cancer is *conjugated linoleic acid* (CLA), found in the meat and milk of grass-eating animals, such as cattle, deer, sheep and goats. CLA helps build healthy cell membranes, allowing cells to absorb nutrients, process hormones and expel waste. It's hard to find CLA-rich foods in markets because most livestock in America are fed grain, not grass.

What I recommend to my patients: Three grams of CLA a day. You can get that from an eight-ounce serving of grass-fed beef. Look for such brands as Lasater Grasslands Beef, available at specialty food stores. On days when you don't eat grass-fed red meat, you can take a CLA supplement—three one-gram soft-gel capsules a day.

VITAMIN D

People living in Boston have, on average, double the risk of breast, colon and prostate cancers, compared with residents of San Diego. Why? Many scientists think it's because Bostonians, like other northerners, don't get enough vitamin D, which is produced when skin is exposed to sun. Vitamin D is one of the most powerful anticancer nutrients. It facilitates the absorption of calcium, a mineral that not only builds strong bones but also is critical for "telegraphing" messages between cells. Poor cell-to-cell communication can contribute to cancer. Studies show that levels of vitamin D in fortified foods rarely equal the claims made on the labels. There is a debate as to whether synthetic vitamin D—the kind found in supplements—provides the same cancer protection as the naturally produced variety.

What I recommend to my patients: During the warmer months, get 15 minutes a day of midday sunshine with no sunscreen (without burning) on face and bare arms. The body stockpiles vitamin D in the liver for use during the rest of the year.

VITAMIN C

In a report published in *American Journal of Clinical Nutrition*, 33 of 46 studies showed that vitamin C protects against cancer. Cancer feeds on blood sugar (glucose)—and lowering chronically high blood sugar is crucial to preventing cancer. When you get enough vitamin C, you cut in half the amount of blood sugar that enters cells.

What I recommend to my patients: 500 to 1,000 milligrams (mg) of vitamin C a day, in three divided doses, taken with meals. Cancer patients may need higher doses, which usually are given intravenously.

Other ways to normalize blood sugar levels include regular exercise, weight loss and a diet that emphasizes lean meats, beans, nuts and produce. Five daily servings of fruits and vegetables nets you 300 mg of vitamin C.

SELENIUM

In the four-year Nutritional Prevention of Cancer Trial, scientists gave 1,312 participants either 200 micrograms (mcg) of the trace mineral *selenium* or a placebo. The results showed that selenium lowered the risk of prostate cancer by 63%, colon cancer by 58% and lung cancer by 46%.

Selenium strengthens the immune system, helps repair DNA damage and protects cells against toxins.

What I recommend to my patients: 200 mcg of selenium a day. Look for *selenomethionine*—selenium bound in yeast—which is absorbed the best. A particularly good food source is Brazil nuts (four nuts provide 200 mcg).

Caution: More is not better. Selenium supplements in doses of 2,000 mcg or higher can be toxic.

GREEN TEA

Literally hundreds of studies have proven that green tea and its various extracts can prevent and, in some experiments, reverse cancer. These extracts work by different mechanisms, among them *apoptosis* ("programmed cell death"). In other words, green tea orders cancer cells to commit suicide.

What I recommend to my patients: Drink three eight-ounce cups of green tea a day. If you don't like the taste, take supplements of green tea extract, available in capsules, following the dosage recommendation on the label.

KILLER CONSTIPATION

With chronic constipation, cancer-causing chemicals from the environment are ingested but not expelled quickly. Normally friendly food-digesting bacteria then produce toxins that end up in the bloodstream.

What I recommend to my patients: To ensure a daily bowel movement, get plenty of high-fiber foods…drink 64 ounces of filtered or bottled water a day…and exercise regularly. Prune juice and figs often relieve constipation. Or try a gentle herbal laxative, such as *psyllium* (Metamucil), following the dosage recommendation on the label.

Eating for Better Exercise

Heidi Skolnik, MS, CDN, certified dietitian nutritionist and senior nutritionist at the Women's Sports Medicine Center at the Hospital for Special Surgery in New York City. A guest contributor to *Good Morning America*, she also is a sports nutrition consultant to the School of American Ballet.

You already know that a regular exercise routine—ideally, at least 30 minutes of vigorous activity daily—is among the smartest steps you can take to protect your health.

What you may not know: Consuming the right foods and fluids is one of the best ways to improve your exercise performance.

If your body is not properly fueled—regardless of the type, frequency or intensity of physical activity—your energy levels are more likely to wane, your muscles will be more susceptible to fatigue and soreness, and you'll find it harder to maintain your desired weight. *My secrets…*

1. Remember to drink enough fluids before exercise. Research shows that about half of people who work out in the morning are dehydrated when they begin to exercise.

Why is fluid consumption so important? When you're dehydrated, your heart must pump harder to get blood to your muscles. Being dehydrated also impairs your ability to perspire and cool yourself.

Advice: Drink one cup of water or a sports drink, such as Gatorade, before your workout and another during your workout. If your workout is vigorous or lasts more than 60 minutes, you may need to consume more fluids.

Also remember to drink fluids throughout the day. You don't have to limit yourself to water. Milk, tea, coffee, fruit juice and carbonated beverages also count toward your daily fluid intake.

Caution: Your risk for dehydration is increased if you take a diuretic drug, have diabetes or are an older adult—the body's thirst center functions less efficiently with age.

2. Don't exercise on an empty stomach. When you don't eat for several hours—including the time when you're sleeping—your blood sugar levels decline. This can leave you with less energy for physical activity and at risk for injury.

The quickest solution is to consume carbohydrates, which are your body's primary energy source. Carbohydrates are found mainly in starchy foods, such as grains, breads and vegetables, as well as in fruit, milk and yogurt.

Advice: If you're exercising before breakfast, first have half a banana or a slice of toast. If you're exercising just before lunch, eat a healthful mid-morning snack—and a mid- to late-afternoon snack if your workout is before dinner. It's okay to eat the snack right before your workout.

3. Eat a balanced breakfast. Eating a good breakfast helps get your metabolism going—and may help you consume fewer calories during the rest of the day.

Advice: Choose whole-grain foods (such as oatmeal or whole-grain cereal or toast) to fuel your muscles…a serving of dairy (yogurt, low-fat milk or cheese) or another protein (such as eggs or Canadian bacon) to promote muscle repair…and fruit (such as a mango, berries or melon) for vitamins and disease-fighting *phytonutrients*.

4. Fill in your nutritional "gaps" with lunch. Like breakfast, your midday meal should include healthful carbohydrates and protein.

Advice: At lunch, get some of the nutrients you may not have included in your breakfast. For example, if you ate fruit in the morning, eat vegetables at lunch. If your breakfast included a dairy product as your protein source, eat lean meat or fish at lunch.

Example of a healthful lunch: A salad with grilled chicken, legumes, peppers, broccoli and an olive oil–based dressing.

5. Eat an evening meal. If you exercise late in the afternoon or after work, don't skip your evening meal. You may wake up the next morning with a "deficit" that can lead you to overeat.

Advice: Strive for a balance of unprocessed carbohydrates (such as brown rice or vegetables), lean protein (such as fish or poultry) and a little healthful fat (such as nuts or olive oil).

Example: A shrimp and vegetable stir-fry served over one-quarter cup of brown rice.

Supplement Boosts Heart Health in Women Runners

Medical College of Wisconsin, news release.

High-dose folic acid supplementation improved vascular function in young female runners who stopped menstruating (*amenorrhea*) because their caloric intake was lower than their energy output, researchers say.

BACKGROUND

"Previous studies have shown that amenorrheic women runners have decreased dilation in the main (brachial) artery of the arm in response to blood flow. Athletic amenorrhea has a hormonal profile similar to menopause, when the earliest sign of cardiovascular disease is reduced vascular dilation, which can limit oxygen uptake and affect performance," said study author Stacy Lynch, MD, a women's sports medicine fellow at the Medical College of Wisconsin in Milwaukee.

THE STUDY

The study included 16 female college or recreational runners, ages 18 to 35, who weren't on birth control pills and had been running at least 20 miles a week for the past year. All the women were healthy, but six of them had reduced vascular function and irregular or absent menstrual periods.

The researchers measured the women's vascular function before and after four to six weeks of treatment with 10 milligrams a day of folic acid. At the end of that time, vascular function had returned to normal in the amenorrheic women and remained at normal levels in the other women.

The study was presented at a meeting of the American Medical Society for Sports Medicine, in Tampa, Florida.

IMPLICATION

The findings suggest that folic acid may decrease cardiovascular risk and also improve performance in young female athletes, according to the Medical College of Wisconsin researchers.

LEARN MORE

The US National Institute of Child Health & Human Development Web site has information about amenorrhea at *www.nichd.nih.gov/health/topics*.

Age-Proof Your Muscles

Mark A. Stengler, NMD, licensed naturopathic medical doctor in private practice, Encinitas, California...adjunct associate clinical professor at the National College of Natural Medicine, Portland, Oregon...author of *The Natural Physician's Healing Therapies* and co-author of *Prescription for Natural Cures* (both from Bottom Line Books).

As we age, we steadily lose muscle mass. It's a fact that many falls and bone fractures result not from weak bones, but from insufficient muscle to support ourselves as we go about our lives.

It's easy to preserve muscle or reverse age-related muscle loss, which doctors call sarcopenia. You can do this through diet, exercise and supplements or any combination of these. The more you do, the more you will ensure that you lead an active, independent and productive life long into your 60s...70s...80s...and beyond.

THE POWER OF PROTEIN

The word *protein* comes from the Greek *proteios*, which essentially means "first and foremost." This hints at just how important protein is for life and health. In addition to forming our muscles, protein constitutes much of the tissue of the internal organs. And bone is a matrix of proteins and minerals. Proteins also are the building blocks of hormones, immune cells, neurotransmitters and thousands of other biochemicals.

For too many years now, doctors and dietitians have warned patients about the dangers of eating too much protein. That view now is changing, but too slowly in my opinion. It turns out that many people, particularly seniors, do not consume enough high-quality protein. High-quality protein foods contain all the essential amino acids, the compounds that are the building blocks of protein. Poultry is one example. Fish is another, and it has an added benefit since many cold-water types, such as salmon and sardines, are high in the healthful type of omega-3 fatty acids. Eggs, in moderation, are another option, especially those enriched with omega-3s.

Several recent articles in *The American Journal of Clinical Nutrition* have focused on ideal amounts of dietary protein. One study, conducted at Purdue University in Indiana, found that seniors actually had the same protein requirements as men and women half their age. The researchers calculated that an "adequate" daily intake is 0.39 grams (g) of protein per pound of body weight, or 64 g for a 165-pound man or woman. This is more than the current US Recommended Dietary Allowance (RDA) of 60 g daily for an adult man or woman weighing 165 pounds. I think that many seniors can benefit from as much as 25% more protein than the RDA. (To determine the amount in grams for you, take 125% of your weight and multiply by 0.39.)

Best: Eat a variety of proteins, including fish, poultry and legumes, such as kidney beans and lentils. A legume might be low in one particular amino acid, but chances are you'll eat another food rich in that amino acid that will make up for it.

Over the course of one year, one of my older patients, a 90-year-old man, lost a great deal of weight and strength. (If a person is overweight, losing weight is healthy. In his case, it wasn't.) He was able to gain weight—increasing muscle, not fat—and enhance his strength simply by consuming more protein.

Important: Protein is both essential and safe. However, people with kidney disease should consume relatively small amounts of protein daily because high amounts can stress the kidneys. If you have reduced kidney function or any type of kidney disease, speak to your physician first before changing the amount of protein you consume.

EAT MORE PROTEIN EVERY DAY

There are lots of ways to get more protein into your diet. Here are the protein amounts for some common foods. Do the math—you'll see that it's not hard to boost intake.

- **Chicken** (white meat), 3.5 oz = 31 g protein
- **Turkey,** 3 oz = 28 g protein
- **Beef round roast** (preferably grass fed), 3 oz = 25 g protein
- **Tuna,** 3 oz = 24 g protein
- **Salmon,** Chinook, 3 oz = 21 g protein
- **Pumpkin seeds,** 1/4 cup = 19 g protein
- **Pork roast,** 3 oz = 21 g protein
- **Black beans** (boiled), 1 cup = 15 g protein
- **Chickpeas** (boiled), 1 cup = 15 g protein
- **Shrimp,** 6 large = 8.5 g protein
- **Skim milk,** 1 cup = 8 g protein
- **Walnuts,** 1/4 cup = 4 g protein
- **Brown rice** (cooked), 1 cup = 4 g protein
- **Peanut butter,** 1 tbsp = 4 g protein
- **Broccoli,** 1 cup = 3 g protein

THE ROLE OF VEGETABLES

Most plant foods have less protein than fish, poultry, beef and other meats, but they are good protein sources because they are low in fat and high in fiber.

What you might not know: Vegetables and fruits help build muscle, but not because of their protein content. Plant foods are rich in potassium and bicarbonate, which result in a more alkaline pH (pH is the body's alkaline-to-acid ratio). Most other foods make your body more acidic, and acidosis triggers muscle wasting. A recent Tufts University study found that higher intake of foods rich in potassium, such as fruits and vegetables, can help preserve muscle mass in older men and women.

THE BENEFITS OF EXERCISE

I can't overstate the benefits of regular exercise, particularly resistance activities, such as weight lifting, for preserving and increasing muscle. As I have explained, muscle is mostly made of protein. Exercise stimulates the conversion of dietary protein to muscle. The more exercise you do, the better. Going for a daily brisk walk is a good way to start. Consider advancing to hand weights, larger weights, cycling or swimming. Alternate activities to avoid boredom. Resistance exercise, such as weight lifting, will reverse sarcopenia even if you consume relatively little protein, according to an article in *Journal of Physiology*, because the physical activity stimulates the conversion of protein to muscle.

TAKE VITAMIN D DAILY

Vitamin D is needed to make muscle. It ensures that calcium, which is essential for transporting proteins to muscle tissue, is absorbed. If you don't already do so, take 1,000 international units (IU) of vitamin D daily.

GETTING PROTEIN FROM SUPPLEMENTS

As I have mentioned, protein consists of compounds called amino acids, so think of taking amino acid supplements as a way to get more protein.

Some exciting recent research has focused on using amino acid supplements to increase muscle mass and strength while reducing body fat and fatigue. These supplements won't give you a bodybuilder's physique, but they can help reverse age-related muscle loss.

Beware: Not all amino acid supplements are alike. Many of the protein powder supplements that come in huge containers in health-food stores or pharmacies have poor-quality proteins (such as soy) and lots of sugar. These are not worth using.

I recommend these protein supplements…

•**Multi amino acids.** These supplements, available at most health-food stores, provide between eight and 11 different amino acids. Recent studies have shown impressive benefits in seniors after they took these supplements. One of the studies, reported in *The American Journal of Cardiology*, found that people who took daily amino acid supplements had significant increases in muscle after six months—and experienced even more of an increase after 16 months, reaching the normal levels found in peers without sarcopenia. I often recommend multi amino acids because they come closest to being a complete protein (one that contains all of the amino acids). One good example is Country Life's Max Amino Caps (800-645-5768, *www.country-life.com*). Follow instructions on the label.

Alternatives: Use supplements that contain individual amino acids. I recommend *beta-alanine*, *l-ornithine* (which seems to help women especially) and *l-leucine*, known to help convert protein to muscle. For each, follow instructions on the label.

Eat More Fruits And Veggies to Stop Muscle Loss

Muscles tend to lose mass over time, leading to frailty and an increased risk for dangerous falls. Fruits and vegetables can help slow or prevent this effect. Aim for eight to 10 servings of fruits and vegetables every day.

Bess Dawson-Hughes, MD, director, Bone Metabolism Laboratory, Jean Mayer USDA Human Nutrition Center on Aging, Tufts University, Boston.

Red Meat Linked to High Blood Pressure

When researchers followed more than 28,000 women over 10 years, those who ate more than one-and-a-half servings daily of red meat (for example, six to nine ounces of beef) were 35% more likely to develop high blood pressure than those who ate no red meat.

Researchers believe similar results would apply to men.

Theory: Saturated fats, cholesterol, animal protein and heme iron (the type in red meat) may play a role in raising blood pressure.

To lower your risk for high blood pressure: Limit your intake of red meat, and substitute other protein sources, such as fish, legumes, soy and low-fat dairy foods.

Lu Wang, MD, PhD, instructor in medicine, Brigham and Women's Hospital, Boston.

Cheers! Red Wine Blocks Toxins in Meat and Poultry

Digestion of the fat in meats, such as beef and poultry, leads to the release of toxic chemicals in the body. These chemicals have been linked to cancer and heart disease.

But: The toxins are neutralized by antioxidants called *polyphenols* in red wine.

Self-defense: Eat meat only occasionally—and have a glass of red wine with your meal when you do.

Shlomit Gorelik, MSc, department of pharmaceutics, Hebrew University of Jerusalem, and leader of a study reported in *Journal of Agricultural and Food Chemistry*.

Can Bread Make You Sick? The Answer Is Yes!

Mark A. Stengler, NMD, licensed naturopathic medical doctor in private practice, Encinitas, California... adjunct associate clinical professor at the National College of Natural Medicine, Portland, Oregon...author of *The Natural Physician's Healing Therapies* and co-author of *Prescription for Natural Cures* (both from Bottom Line Books).

Millions of people endure chronic symptoms including abdominal pain and bouts of fatigue—but they don't have to anymore.

For you (or someone you love), the solution to these and many other troubles might be shockingly simple—if you and your doctor are willing to do a little unusual sleuthing.

When Bonita, age 60, came to see me, she complained of daily abdominal pain and flatulence. She told me that she had suffered frequent waves of fatigue since she was a child. Numerous visits to doctors and specialists over the years turned up a variety of problems. Bonita had been diagnosed with chronic *anemia* (low red blood cell count) and *hypoglycemia* (low blood sugar). Those conditions could help account for her fatigue.

There were other issues as well. Osteoporosis had set in—a bone-density scan showed loss of bone mass. Bonita also had lost too much weight. Examinations revealed that she also had fatty liver (fat buildup in the liver cells) and inflammation of the pancreas. Typically, when I see such signs in the liver and pancreas, I suspect excessive alcohol consumption—but Bonita didn't touch a drop!

These signs pointed to *celiac disease* (CD), also sometimes called by its older name, sprue. If you don't know much about this condition, you're not alone. It took medical researchers many years to unravel its root cause—and even today, lots of people have it and don't know it.

When I ran some additional blood tests on Bonita, my suspicions proved correct. I immediately put her on a diet free of gluten (a protein complex found in wheat, barley and rye), meaning she could have absolutely no bread, crackers, cake, cereal or other foods containing these common grains. Within weeks, there was a noticeable improvement in Bonita's energy. Her abdominal pain diminished. Blood tests showed that her anemia was improving, as were liver and pancreatic function. She felt much better, gained some weight and looked vibrant!

THE CURSE OF THE GRAIN

Celiac disease (CD), the cause of Bonita's lifelong discomfort, is an autoimmune condition. This means that the immune system—designed to prevent infection and fight off disease—turns traitor and harms the body.

With CD, the body recognizes gluten as a harmful foreign substance. When someone with CD consumes gluten, a big problem develops in the small intestine—specifically with the multitude of soft, tiny, fingerlike projections called villi that line the intestinal walls. Villi are responsible for absorbing nutrients.

In people who have CD, the villi are damaged and can't do their job properly. They're caught in a cross fire between the immune system and the gluten that's traveling through the small intestine. For some reason, in certain people—this is the part we don't fully understand—the immune system attacks the gluten, and the fragile villi get mauled in the autoimmune battle.

When a CD sufferer stops eating foods that contain gluten, the turnaround can be remarkable. For people who have suffered with this condition for years without knowing the cause, eliminating gluten can seem like the beginning of a new life.

Many doctors don't pay much attention to CD's all-too-common signs. That's a big mistake because recent studies have shown that it is much more prevalent than previously suspected. At a conference held by the National Institutes of Health in 2004, researchers reported that CD affects as many as three million Americans, or about one out of every 100 people.

MALABSORPTION MAYHEM

CD leaves plenty of clues. When inflamed villi can no longer absorb nutrients as they should, you end up with a condition called malabsorption, which results in deficiencies of certain nutrients.

Other possible damage can occur as well, including a condition called increased intestinal permeability. This type of intestinal-wall damage can be compared with holes punched in a screen door—larger-than-normal molecules can escape through holes in the small intestine and enter the bloodstream. Among those larger molecules are portions of protein compounds (gluten fractions) that aren't supposed to penetrate the intestinal wall.

Result: The body, sensing the presence of these gluten fractions, intensifies the autoimmune reaction.

If an infant or a child has CD, malabsorption takes a cruel toll. Some infants display signs of "failure to thrive" (slowed growth in a number of the body's systems). Older children may have physical and behavioral development problems.

The longer CD goes undetected and a person continues to eat gluten, the more likely he/she is to develop other autoimmune diseases—insulin-dependent type 1 diabetes, thyroiditis (inflammation of the thyroid) and hepatitis (inflammation of the liver). People with untreated CD also have an elevated risk of certain types of cancer, especially intestinal lymphoma. While CD exists in sufferers from birth through adulthood, the symptoms may start to show up at any time.

THE TESTS—WHAT'S INVOLVED?

CD can affect anyone, but it is more prevalent in people of European (especially Northern European) descent. But studies have also shown that it affects Hispanic, black and Asian populations.

Because neglecting CD can be life-threatening, I recommend that screening begin in early childhood. If you have any of the symptoms or suffer from lupus, type 1 diabetes, rheumatoid arthritis or thyroid disease, then it is even more critical to be screened for CD. Genetics is a factor, so if a parent, sibling or child of yours tests positive for CD, I recommend that you also get screened.

CD is detected by a group of blood tests referred to as a celiac panel. These tests, which generally are covered by health insurance, measure your immune system's response to gluten in the foods you eat. If blood tests

point to a diagnosis of CD, your doctor may recommend that you see a gastroenterologist for a biopsy of the small intestine.

The biopsy involves the use of an endoscope (a long, thin tube with a tiny periscope and cutting tool at the end), which is inserted through the mouth and manipulated through the small intestine. If the extracted villi are severely damaged, it confirms CD.

Caution: Don't stop consuming gluten before a celiac blood test or biopsy. This could throw off your test results. (Fortunately, the blood tests now used to diagnose CD are so accurate that a biopsy usually isn't necessary.)

GLUTEN SENSITIVITY

If you have a number of symptoms that suggest CD but your test results are negative, there's a chance that you have a less severe form of the condition, called gluten sensitivity. In my own practice, I have found that gluten sensitivity is much more common than CD.

Some patients complain of bloating, headache, rashes or other symptoms that might be related to CD or to allergies, but traditional skin-scratch or blood antibody tests don't point to a single diagnosis. To find out whether gluten is a factor, I recommend reducing (or better, eliminating) intake of wheat and other gluten-containing grains. If symptoms improve, it's a strong indication of gluten sensitivity.

Some people with gluten sensitivity can eat grains as long as they "rotate" among different kinds—that is, consuming different grains instead of the same ones all the time—to reduce symptoms and provide a wider variety of nutrients. This plan is not appropriate for people who have CD—they must completely eliminate gluten from their diets, permanently, period.

WHAT THE FUTURE HOLDS

Continuing research shows that we still have much to learn about CD, but there is good reason to be hopeful that prevention might one day be possible. In identical twins who live in the same household, for example, sometimes only one has CD—raising the question of what role environment plays.

A study published in *American Journal of Clinical Nutrition* showed that the more gluten-containing foods introduced to an infant, the greater the risk of developing CD in childhood. However, breast-feeding during this time cuts the risk of developing CD in childhood. We don't yet know whether these findings hold true throughout life.

And, based on Dutch research, there may be a connection between the overgrowth of *Candida albicans*, a yeast normally found in the digestive tract, and the onset of CD, perhaps because of chemical similarities between Candida and gluten. The idea that infections of the gut and autoimmune conditions are linked continues to gain acceptance.

SIGNS OF CELIAC DISEASE (CD)

CD is associated with a wide range of symptoms, including…

- **Diarrhea**
- **Feeling or looking bloated**
- **Unexplained fatigue**
- **Unexplained abdominal pain**
- **Gassiness**
- **Skin redness, rash, itchy skin**
- **Loss of tooth enamel**
- **Unexpected hair loss**
- **Low body weight**
- **Infertility or irregular menses**
- **Premature osteoporosis**

If you have any of these symptoms, ask your doctor about CD—the sooner, the better.

No-Cow Milks You'll Love

Dennis A. Savaiano, PhD, dean of the College of Consumer and Family Sciences and professor in the department of foods and nutrition at Purdue University in Lafayette, Indiana. He has authored or coauthored numerous studies on lactose intolerance, published in peer-reviewed biomedical journals.

If you grew up in the US, you were probably admonished to drink cow's milk for its bone-building calcium. But do you still follow that advice?

As adults, many people give up cow's milk because they don't like its taste…don't like the way cows are raised (on "factory farms")…or have difficulty digesting lactose (the primary sugar in cow's milk and other dairy products).

Good news: There are more good-tasting milk options now available than most people realize.

MILK FROM ANIMAL SOURCES

Milk is a good source of calcium—one eight-ounce cup contains about 300 milligrams (mg) of the mineral (nearly one-third of the daily recommended intake for adults age 50 and under and about one-quarter of the daily recommended intake for adults over age 50). Milk also contains vitamin D (needed to absorb calcium) and protein, an important nutrient that helps us maintain strength and muscle tone as we age.

However, about 5% of infants are allergic to cow's milk. Symptoms include diarrhea, runny nose and hives. Most children outgrow the allergy by age two or three.

Because whole cow's milk contains saturated fat, which can contribute to obesity and heart disease, it's usually best to drink nonfat or 1% milk. *Milk options…*

- **Lactose-free cow's milk.** About one out of every four American adults has lactose intolerance. This condition, which is different from a milk allergy, causes stomach pain, diarrhea, bloating and/or gas after milk or other dairy products that contain lactose are consumed. But lactose can be removed from milk.

Examples: Lactaid and Land O Lakes Dairy Ease.

- **Cow's milk (with meals).** Studies show that many people who believe they are lactose intolerant can drink milk without suffering any symptoms as long as it's consumed with a meal, which helps slow the digestion of lactose.

If you've stopped drinking cow's milk due to lactose intolerance and would like to try reintroducing it: Drink one-quarter to one-half cup of milk with a meal twice daily. Within a few days, try drinking a full cup of milk with a meal. Most people who have identified themselves as being lactose intolerant can adapt to this level of milk consumption within two weeks—the length of time that it usually takes intestinal bacteria to activate the body's lactases (enzymes that break down lactose).

If you have gas or loose stools, reduce your milk intake to one-quarter cup daily until the symptoms subside. If this does not work, see a doctor. You may have another condition, such as irritable bowel syndrome, which causes cramping, abdominal pain, constipation and diarrhea.

•**Kefir.** Kefir is a slightly sour fermented milk drink produced by "friendly" probiotic bacteria and yeasts found in kefir grains. Kefir, which has a milkshake-like consistency, is an option for some people who are lactose intolerant.

Example: Lifeway Lowfat Kefir.

•**Goat's milk.** Like cow's milk, goat's milk contains lactose and is a good source of calcium, vitamin D and protein. Goat's milk has a refreshingly tart, almost sour taste.

Example: Meyenberg Goat Milk.

Kefir and goat's milk are available at health-food stores and some supermarkets.

PLANT-BASED MILKS

Plant-based milks are lactose-free and offer health benefits of their own. Most of these milks contain only small amounts of calcium and vitamin D, so they are usually fortified with these nutrients. Some plant-based milks are flavored (vanilla and chocolate, for example), but these varieties can contain up to 20 grams (g) of sugar per cup. Check the label for the sugar content to avoid unnecessary calories. Choose a low-fat plant-based milk whenever possible. Plant-based milks, which can be used in baking and cooking, are available at health-food stores and most supermarkets. *Choices include...*

•**Soymilk.** This milk has a mild, bean-like flavor and contains heart-healthy soy protein. In addition, some studies, though inconclusive, suggest that the *phytoestrogens* (naturally occurring compounds with estrogen-like effects) in soy may help reduce the risk for breast and prostate cancer.

Example: Silk Organic Soymilk.

Caution: Anyone who has had breast or prostate cancer or who is at high risk (due to family history, for example) should consult a doctor before consuming soy—in some cases, phytoestrogens are believed to stimulate the growth of certain hormone-dependent malignancies.

•**Nut milks.** People who don't like the taste of soy milk often prefer almond or hazelnut milk.

Examples: Blue Diamond Almond Breeze and Pacific Natural Foods Hazelnut Milk.

•**Oat milk.** The fiber in this milk, which has a mild, sweet taste, may help lower cholesterol levels.

Example: Pacific Natural Foods Oat Milk.

•**Hemp milk.** Derived from shelled hemp-seeds, this creamy, nutty milk contains a balance of fatty acids that are believed to fight heart disease and arthritis.

Example: Living Harvest Hempmilk.

•**Rice milk.** For many people, rice milk, among all the plant-based milks, tastes the most like cow's milk. Rice milk has less protein than cow's milk and soymilk, but it can be consumed by some people who are allergic to cow's milk.

Example: Rice Dream.

More from Dr. Dennis Savaiano...

Calcium in Food

Milk is not the only source of calcium. Calcium-rich foods include leafy green vegetables (one cup of cooked collard greens contains 266 milligrams [mg] of calcium)... canned sardines with bones (324 mg per three ounces)...and blackstrap molasses (274 mg per two tablespoons).

Pomegranate Juice the Healthiest Choice

In a recent test of juices, pomegranate had more antioxidants than blueberry, black cherry, concord grape, acai, cranberry, orange and apple juices. Antioxidants can reduce the risk for cardiovascular disease and prostate cancer.

Best: Buy 100% natural juice. Because juice is relatively high in calories, limit yourself to eight ounces a day—even two ounces a day has health benefits.

Keith R. Martin, PhD, MTox (master of toxicology) and assistant professor, department of nutrition, Arizona State University, Mesa.

Pumpkin Packs a Nutritious Punch

Fresh pumpkin is the most nutritious way to eat this vegetable, but if you don't have the time or inclination to cut, boil and mash fresh pumpkin, canned pumpkin certainly is a healthful option. Both fresh and canned pumpkin contain many nutrients, such as fiber, the antioxidant beta-carotene (vitamin A), vitamin K, choline (a crucial B vitamin) and potassium. Pumpkin also is low in calories (averaging about 85 calories per cup of canned pumpkin), sodium (12 mg per cup in the low-sodium varieties) and fat (about 0.7 g

per cup). But be aware that canned pumpkin may contain more sugar than fresh pumpkin (up to 6 g more per one-cup serving), as well as salt (about 10 mg per one-cup serving)…so carefully compare brands when shopping, and opt for salt-free varieties.

Bonus: If you're time-crunched this year, not making pumpkin pie and/or bread from fresh pumpkin may reduce your stress level. So grab the can opener and enjoy the holidays.

Susan Mudd, CNS, LD, clinical nutritionist, Westport, Connecticut.

A Delicious Way to Fight Heart Disease

Eating three 100-calorie servings of dark chocolate per week lowers chronic inflammation by 17% and can cut heart disease risk by 26%.

Caution: Eating more chocolate may increase risk.

Licia Iacoviello, MD, PhD, chair, Laboratory of Genetic and Environmental Epidemiology, Catholic University, Campobasso, Italy, and leader of a study of 10,994 people, published in *The Journal of Nutrition*.

10

Fit for Life

Best Workouts For Women

Exercise machines can provide excellent workouts. But unfortunately, a woman may wind up with injuries if she uses a machine improperly—or if the machine is not suitable for a person her size.

Benefits: Cardiovascular exercise helps you control or lose weight...reduces blood pressure and cholesterol...and boosts energy and mood.*

Do a cardio workout for 30 minutes or more at least three times a week. Begin with a five-minute warm-up, working up to your target speed...and end with a five-minute cooldown, gradually slowing your pace. For the 20 minutes in between, work hard enough to give

*Check with your doctor before beginning any exercise program, especially if you are pregnant, are new to exercise, have recently recovered from an injury or have a chronic disease.

your heart a workout, but not so hard that you risk overtaxing it.

To gauge effort: If you can talk normally, work harder...if you barely have the breath to get a word out, ease up. Interval workouts—alternating every few minutes between bursts of intense activity and periods of lighter activity—burn more calories than a single sustained pace.

RECOMMENDED: TREADMILL

You walk or run on a flat or inclined surface as the treadmill records your time, mileage, heart rate and/or calories burned. A preset program can automatically generate varying speeds and inclines.

Especially beneficial for: Women with or at risk for osteoporosis (brittle bone disease). Walking is a weight-bearing exercise that increases bone density...and the treadmill's

Wayne Westcott, PhD, consultant, South Shore YMCA, and adjunct professor at Quincy College, both in Quincy, Massachusetts. He is author or coauthor of more than 20 fitness books, including *Get Stronger, Feel Younger* (Rodale).

shock-absorbing platform is easier on joints than pavement.

To use: Start by setting the speed at two miles per hour, then slowly increase your pace. Move naturally, keeping your head up and staying in the center of the belt.

Safety alert: Holding the handrails while walking rapidly or running forces your body into an unnatural posture, increasing the risk for muscle strain—so once you have your balance, let go. Use a safety key with a cord that clips to your clothing and connects to the emergency "off" switch so that the treadmill belt will immediately stop moving if you fall.

RECOMMENDED: STATIONARY BICYCLE

An upright bike looks and feels like a regular road bike. With a recumbent bike, the rider sits on a wide saddle, leaning against a backrest, legs out in front. Both types give an equally good cardio workout.

Especially beneficial for: Women with balance problems, because there is no risk of falling...and overweight women, because it supports the body and allows adjustable levels of external resistance rather than working against the user's own body weight. A recumbent bike is most comfortable for people with back problems or limited mobility.

To use: Every few minutes, alternate "sprints" of fast, low-resistance pedaling..."climbs" of slow, high-resistance pedaling...and recovery intervals of moderately paced, medium-resistance pedaling. To work shin muscles, use pedal straps or toe clips so that you can pull up as well as push down while pedaling.

Safety alert: Improper seat height can lead to knee injuries. When one pedal is pushed all the way down, your knee should be slightly bent—never fully extended. If the seat adjusts forward and aft, position it so that knees align with your ankles rather than extending beyond your toes. If you have narrow hips and the distance between the pedals seems too wide, see if a different brand of bike feels more comfortable. To reduce back and shoulder strain on an upright bike, raise the handlebars.

USE WITH CAUTION: STAIR STEPPER

This machine provides a challenging workout because you work against your own body weight and your center of gravity moves up and down with every step.

Problem: Users may lean heavily on the handrails to keep their balance and to take weight off the legs. This increases the risk for injury to the wrists...and misaligns the spine, which can strain the back.

Solution: To avoid falls, keep only your fingertips on the rails, using a light touch...maintain a moderate pace that does not challenge your balance. Do not set the height of the rise too high (as if taking stairs two at a time)—the stepping motion should feel natural. For good posture, keep shoulders and hips aligned and imagine trying to touch the top of your head to the ceiling.

Note: The stair stepper may not be appropriate if you are overweight or new to exercise and feel discouraged by the difficulty of the workout...have problems with your joints... or have any trouble with balance

USE WITH CAUTION: ELLIPTICAL TRAINER

This low-impact machine combines the leg motions of stair climbing with cross-country skiing to work the lower body. Some styles include movable arm poles, adding an upper-body component.

Problem: For short-legged women, the elliptical can force a longer-than-normal stride that may strain the knees, hips and/or lower back.

Solution: The goal is to move smoothly with good posture. If your movement feels awkward or jerky, decrease the stride setting (try 16 inches). If this does not help, avoid the elliptical trainer.

STRENGTH TRAINING

Next, add strength-training machines, which build muscle...fortify tendons and ligaments... increase bone density...improve posture... boost mood...and raise metabolic rate so that you burn more fat.

Best: Do a strength-training workout two to three times per week, leaving at least one day between workouts so that muscles can recover. Start with a gentle warm-up of three to five minutes, doing an activity that involves the whole body, such as jumping jacks. Then use the machines for a total of 20 to 30 minutes.

Machine styles and weight increments vary depending on the manufacturer. If the machines in your gym do not have the same increments as the starting weight guidelines below, ask a trainer if it is possible to modify the options. *On each machine...*

• **Perform one to three sets of eight to 12 repetitions,** resting for one minute between sets.

• **If you can't complete eight repetitions using the starting guidelines,** reduce the weight. When it becomes easy to complete one set of 12 reps, try two sets, then three. When it becomes easy to do three sets, increase the weight.

• **Control the motion at all times.** Count slowly to two as you raise the weight...count to four as you lower the weight.

• **Exhale as you raise the weight...**inhale as you lower the weight. This helps keep blood pressure down.

Finish workouts with a three-minute walk to cool down. Then do three minutes of gentle stretching to maintain flexibility, holding each stretch for 15 to 30 seconds.

Recent research: Stretching promotes additional gains in strength.

Address each major muscle group to keep muscles in balance—otherwise the weaker muscles could be prone to injury. *A complete workout typically includes...*

• **Lat pull-down.**

Muscles worked: The *latissimus dorsi* (upper back) and biceps—muscles used in daily life for lifting and carrying (for example, grocery bags).

To use: Sit tall, facing the machine, with thighs tucked beneath the pads to stabilize your lower body. Reach up, palms facing you and slightly farther than shoulder-width apart, and grasp the bar hanging overhead. Squeeze shoulder blades together as you pull the bar down a few inches in front of your face... stop at chin level...then raise  the bar to starting position. Start with 35 pounds if you're in your 40s...32.5 pounds

in your 50s ...30 pounds in your 60s...27.5 pounds in your 70s...25 pounds in your 80s and beyond.

Safety alert: Don't pull the bar behind your head. This can injure the neck and shoulders. It is safe to grasp the bar with palms facing away—but muscles get a better workout when palms face you.

• **Shoulder press.**

Muscles worked: Shoulders, triceps (back of the arms) and base of the neck—used when placing items on a high shelf.

To use: Sit erect, hips and shoulder blades pressed against the backrest. With hands at  shoulder height, palms facing forward and arms bent, grasp the outer set of handles and push up until arms are nearly straight...then lower to starting position. Start with 30 pounds if you're in your 40s...27.5 pounds in your 50s...25 pounds in your 60s...22.5 pounds in your 70s...20 pounds in your 80s and beyond.

Safety alert: If you have shoulder problems, such as with your rotator cuff, use the inner handles, palms facing each other—this is easier.

• **Chest press.**

Muscles worked: Pectorals (front of the chest) and triceps—used for pushing a lawn mower or wheelchair.

To use: Sit erect with arms bent, hands at chest height, palms facing forward. Grasp handles and press forward, elbows pointing to the sides (not down), until arms are nearly straight...then bend elbows and return to starting position. Start with 35 pounds if you're in your 40s...32.5 pounds in your 50s...30 pounds in your 60s...  27.5 pounds in your 70s...25 pounds in your 80s and beyond.

Safety alert: Do not lean forward—keep head up and entire back pressed against the backrest to avoid neck and low-back strain.

• **Biceps curl.**

Muscles worked: Biceps and forearms— needed for lifting and carrying.

To use: Sit with arms out in front, elbows resting on the padded platform. Palms facing

you, grasp handles and bend elbows to bring hands toward your chest...then straighten arms to return to starting position. Start with 30 pounds if you're in your 40s...27.5 pounds in your 50s...25 pounds in your 60s... 22.5 pounds in your 70s...20 pounds in your 80s and beyond.

Safety alert: Elbows are prone to hyperextension—so to prevent joint injury when lowering the bar, stop when elbows are still slightly bent. If your lower back arches, reduce the weight to prevent back strain.

• **Leg press.**

Muscles worked: Quadriceps and hamstrings (fronts and backs of thighs), inner thighs and buttocks—vital for walking and climbing stairs.

To use: Sit and recline against the backrest, legs raised in front of you, knees at a 90-degree angle, feet flat and hip-width apart on the movable platform. Slowly straighten legs until knees are almost straight, pressing with heels to push platform

away...then bend knees to return to starting position. Start with 85 pounds if you're in your 40s...80 pounds in your 50s...75 pounds in your 60s...70 pounds in your 70s...65 pounds in your 80s and beyond.

Safety alert: To protect knees, do not straighten legs completely...keep thighs parallel to align knees.

• **Ab crunch machine.**

Muscles worked: Abdominals—which help maintain posture and combat belly bulge.

To use: Sit and place feet behind ankle pads to stabilize lower body...grip handles and place

elbows on padded rests to stabilize upper body. Using abdominal muscles, curl upper body forward to bring your chest toward your knees... then uncurl as far as possible without letting weights return

to the resting position. Start with 40 pounds if you're in your 40s...37.5 pounds in your 50s...35 pounds in your 60s...32.5 pounds in your 70s...30 pounds in your 80s and beyond.

Safety alert: Keep head and spine aligned to prevent neck injury.

Illustrations by Chris Andrews/Getty Images.

More from Dr. Wayne Westcott...

The 20-Minute Cellulite Solution

When scientists say there's "no such thing" as cellulite, they mean that cellulite is not a distinct type of body tissue, but it is ordinary fat. Yet for nearly nine out of 10 women, that unwanted dimpling on the hips and thighs is undeniably real.

How it got there: Fibrous cords connect the skin to the underlying muscle. When the fat layer that lies between the skin and the muscle is too thick, the cords are pulled tight and fat cells bulge out between them, causing that "cottage cheese" look. *And cellulite gets worse with age...*

• **The typical woman loses muscle mass at an average rate of about five pounds per decade from ages 20 to 50...**and perhaps more rapidly after menopause.

• **As muscle mass decreases, metabolism slows,** the body burns fewer calories and the ratio of fat to muscle rises.

• **Supporting connective tissues (such as collagen) break down and lose elasticity,** making cellulite more pronounced.

What doesn't help: A swarm of creams, wraps, massage techniques and mechanical devices purported to eliminate cellulite, typically by "melting away fat." None address the underlying physiological causes. Even dieting can backfire if you overdo it, because your body may break down muscle as well as fat to get the energy that it needs, raising your fat-to-muscle ratio.

What does help: Strength training, which rebuilds muscle, burns calories and boosts metabolism.

Best: Three times a week, do the following exercises. The routine takes about 20 minutes.*

You need only three simple kinds of equipment. Go to a gym or buy your own equipment at a sporting-goods store or online (try *www.spri.com*). Within four to six weeks, you should see a noticeable reduction in cellulite.

MEDICINE BALL

A medicine ball is a weighted ball about six to eight inches in diameter. Holding one while doing the following two moves adds extra weight that makes your lower body work harder—and as a bonus, tones the upper body, too. To start, choose a ball with which you can do eight to 12 repetitions per side. Once you work your way up to 15 reps, switch to a ball about one to two pounds heavier. Typically, a woman starts with a two- to four-pound ball and works up to six, eight or 10 pounds.

Cost: About $20 to $40 per ball.

Target zones: Front and back of thighs…buttocks.

• **Lunge.** Stand with feet shoulder-width apart, holding ball between hands at waist level, about six to eight inches in front of you. Bend elbows to bring ball up to chest level…at the same time, with right foot, lunge forward about two to three feet, bending right knee to a 90-degree angle so that it is directly above foot. Step out far enough so that your knee does not move past your ankle (left leg will be slightly bent, heel up).

Hold lunge position for three seconds, keeping back straight…then push off with right foot and return to standing, bringing ball back down. Do 10 to 15 reps, then repeat on left. (Avoid lunges if you have or even suspect knee problems.)

• **Knee lift.** Stand with feet shoulder-width apart, holding ball between hands at waist level.

*Check with your doctor before beginning any exercise program.

310

Step right foot back about two to two-and-a-half feet, keeping right leg straight and bending left knee slightly. Elbows straight, raise ball in front of you to head height.

Bring right knee forward and up as high as you can…bend elbows and bring ball down to touch knee…then step back again with right foot as you straighten arms and raise ball to head height. Do 10 to 15 reps, then repeat on left.

RESISTANCE TUBES

Resistance tubes are elastic tubes about four feet long with handles on each end. They vary in thickness—start with a tube with which you can do eight to 12 reps per side. When you can do 15 reps, switch to a thicker tube.

Cost: About $5 to $15 per tube.

Target zones: Inner and outer thighs.

• **Hip adduction.** Attach one handle to a secure anchor (such as around a bed leg). Loop other handle securely around your right foot (push past toes as far as possible so it doesn't fly off).

Sit on floor, with knees straight and legs spread, so tube is straight out to the right of your right foot. With hands on floor behind you, use inner thigh muscles to slide right leg in to meet left leg. Hold three seconds, then slowly slide right leg back out to spread-leg position. Do 10 to 15 reps, then repeat with left leg.

• **Hip abduction.** Attach one handle to a secure anchor, and loop other handle around right foot (as in the previous exercise).

Sit on floor, with knees straight and legs together, so tube is straight out to the left of your right foot, crossing over left ankle. With your hands on the floor behind you, use outer thigh muscles to slide right leg out to the right until legs are spread as much as possible. Hold three seconds, then slowly slide right leg back to meet left leg. Do 10 to 15 reps, then repeat with left leg.

DUMBBELLS

To start, use a pair of dumbbells (hand weights) with which you can do eight to 12 reps. When you are able to do 15 reps, switch to weights two to three pounds heavier. Typically a woman starts with five-pound weights, increasing to eight, then 10, then 12, then 15 pounds.

Cost: About $10 to $30 per pair.

Target zones: Front and back of thighs… buttocks.

• **Squat.** Stand with feet shoulder-width apart, one weight in each hand, arms down at sides. Keeping torso erect and head in line with spine, bend knees (as if sitting on a chair) until thighs are nearly parallel to floor. Do not allow knees to move forward past toes. Hold for three seconds, then return to standing. Do 10 to 15 reps.

• **Step-Up.** Stand at bottom of a stairway, facing steps, one weight in each hand, arms down at sides. (If you have balance problems, hold a weight in one hand and hold onto banister with the other hand.)

Place entire left foot flat on first step, then rise until you are standing on the stair. Step back down, again moving left foot first. Do 10 to 15 reps, then repeat on the right side.

Illustrations by Shawn Banner.

Fight Bone Loss— And Look Better, Too

Karena Thek Lineback, a master Pilates instructor and rehabilitation therapist. She is president of Pilates Teck in Newhall, California, and author of *OsteoPilates: Increase Bone Density, Reduce Fracture Risk, Look and Feel Great!* (Career Press).

Menopause and the use of steroid drugs are common causes of the bone-thinning disease known as osteoporosis. *But few people are aware of other osteoporosis risk factors, including…*

• **Hypertension,** which can increase the amount of calcium excreted in urine, possibly resulting in loss of bone mineral density.

• **Gastrointestinal disorders,** such as colitis and irritable bowel syndrome (IBS), all of which reduce absorption of dietary calcium.

It's also a big mistake to overlook bone loss in men. While eight million American women have been diagnosed with osteoporosis, two million American men also suffer from the condition—and several million additional women and men are at risk for the disease.

Both women and men can help prevent osteoporosis with a variety of bone-protecting strategies. Among the most important are eating a well-balanced diet (including calcium-rich foods, such as low-fat dairy products …almonds…and green, leafy vegetables, including broccoli and kale) and taking mineral and vitamin supplements (for example, calcium, vitamin D, magnesium, potassium, zinc and vitamin K).

WHAT IS OSTEOPILATES?

Most doctors recommend weight-bearing exercise, such as walking, stair-climbing and/or strength-training with hand weights, as part of an osteoporosis prevention program.

After eight years of working with women and men at risk for osteoporosis, I have developed a specialized form of the exercise technique known as Pilates to help fight bone loss. Pilates concentrates on strengthening the "core muscles" (in the abdomen and the back) that stabilize and support the spine, as well as the small muscles throughout the body.

I call my version OsteoPilates. The exercises of OsteoPilates are designed to stimulate bone growth in areas that are especially vulnerable to thinning (the spine, wrists and hips), while also providing the overall toning benefits of Pilates.

OsteoPilates is generally safe for people with low bone density (including those with osteoporosis) and those with normal bone density, as measured by a dual energy X-ray absorptiometry (DEXA) scan. Ask your doctor before starting the program.

The following basic workout, which takes about 15 minutes to complete, should be performed three times weekly, with at least one day of rest between sessions. (The floor exercises can be performed on a thin mat, such as a yoga mat.)

TOE TOUCHES

Purpose: Builds bone mass in the spine, thighs and knees.

What to do: Lie on your back with your bent legs in the air. Your knees should be positioned directly above your hips and your lower legs extended slightly higher than your knees. Point your toes. Next, while keeping your spine pressed to the floor and your legs slightly bent, 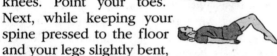 move your feet forward and downward in a rainbow-like arc until the tips of your toes touch the floor. Then slowly return to the starting position. Repeat four to 12 times.

SWAN

Purpose: Builds bone mass in the spine and wrists.

What to do: Lie on your stomach with legs squeezed together and arms crossed under your head so that your forehead rests on your hands. Keeping your forehead on your hands, lift your head, shoulders and arms off the floor. As you lower them again, lift your legs off the floor, being careful to keep them straight. Imagine that you're a seesaw—as one-half of your body goes down, the other half goes up. Repeat six to 10 times.

 Next, lie on your stomach with your hands under your shoulders and your palms flat on the floor. Slowly straighten your arms to lift your head and torso off the floor, while at the same time pulling your navel in toward your spine. Return slowly to the starting position. Repeat four to eight times.

MERMAID

Purpose: Builds bone mass in the spine.

312

What to do: While sitting on a firm chair, reach your right hand toward the ceiling, being careful to keep your shoulders level. Looking straight ahead, lean your raised arm, head and torso to the left, keeping your right hip firmly pressed down. When you've bent as far as you can, pause,  then return to the starting position. Repeat three to six times on each side.

SIDE KICK

Purpose: Builds bone mass in the hips, thighs and knees.

What to do: Lie on your right side with your torso straight and your legs angled forward, so that your body is bent in a slight "L" shape. Fold your right arm under your head, rest  your head on your forearm and place your left palm on the floor for support. Keeping your left hip directly above your right hip, lift your left leg about four inches. Flex your left foot and swing your left leg forward as far as you can (stopping when you feel your torso moving), giving a little extra kick at the end of the forward swing. Now swing the leg behind you, giving two small kicks at the end of the backward swing. Repeat eight times on each side.

Illustrations by Shawn Banner.

The Ultimate Stay-Young Workout

Joel Harper, a New York City–based certified personal trainer who designs equipment-free workouts. He created the following program for the book *YOU: Staying Young* by Dr. Mehmet Oz and Dr. Michael Roizen (Free Press).

If you would love to have strong, limber muscles but hate the idea of trudging off to the gym to lift weights or use exercise machines, there's a new no-equipment workout that uses your body to create strength-building resistance.

Muscle strength is key to staying robust as you age. In fact, research shows that building strong muscles is one of the best ways to stay out of a nursing home.

The following exercise plan should be performed three times a week, with at least one day of rest between workouts. The exercises, which take about 10 minutes to complete, are generally appropriate for people of any age or fitness level. Just be sure to check with your doctor before starting the program—especially if you have a chronic health problem. If the basic exercises seem too easy, try the advanced versions.

Important: If you catch yourself holding your breath during the workout, immediately start counting your repetitions *out loud*. This is a simple way to force yourself to breathe properly. Always count backward rather than forward—it tricks your mind into thinking that you're headed toward a finish line.

My stay-young workout…

TITANIC

Purpose: Stretches your chest, shoulders and arms.

Helps with: Maintaining good posture—especially for people who work at computers.

What to do: While standing with your feet slightly apart, hold your arms out to your sides, palms facing forward, two inches below your shoulders. Keeping your torso upright, stretch your hands back as far as you can reach. Hold for 20 seconds, while breathing deeply into your chest. This will expand your diaphragm, the large muscle that separates the chest and abdominal cavities.

Advanced version: Bend your wrists back and reach the backs of your hands toward each other.

DREAM OF JEANNIE

Purpose: Strengthens your quadricep muscles (in the fronts of the thighs), abdominals and shoulders.

Helps with: Walking up stairs.

What to do: While kneeling, cross your arms and hold them in front of your body like a genie, maintaining a straight line from the top of your head to your knees. Keeping this straight line, lean back slightly, pulling your navel in and squeezing your buttocks together. Hold for 30 seconds, while breathing deeply. If necessary, cushion your knees with a folded towel.

Advanced version: Lean back as far as possible while continuing to maintain the straight line from your head to your knees.

SUPERMAN TOE TAPS

Purpose: Strengthens your lower back and buttocks.

Helps with: Gardening, making the bed or carrying luggage.

What to do: Lie on your stomach with your head turned to the side and resting on your interlaced fingers. Keeping your legs straight, lift them off the ground and raise your knees as high as you can. Tap your toes together 40 times.

Advanced version: Reach your arms (palm side down) as far as you can in front of you. While looking down, lift your elbows as far above the ground as possible, then press your thumbs together and apart 40 times, while tapping your toes together.

HAMMOCK STRETCH

Purpose: Stretches your hips and hamstring muscles (in the backs of the thighs).

Helps with: Easing low-back tension—especially when caused by sitting for long periods, such as during an airplane flight.

What to do: Sit on the floor with your hands behind you and your palms on the floor. Keep your fingers pointing backward and your elbows slightly bent. Bend your knees and draw your heels in until they are two feet from your tailbone. Keeping the sole of your left foot flat on the ground, place your right ankle on top of your left knee and sit up as straight as possible. Focus on pressing your lower back forward toward your right calf. Resist raising your shoulders toward your ears. Hold for 15 seconds, then switch legs and repeat.

Advanced version: For a deeper stretch, gently press the knee of your crossed leg away from you while doing this exercise.

ABDOMINAL BUTTERFLY

Purpose: Strengthens your abdominals.

Helps with: Building strength in the core muscles of the trunk, which, in turn, supports the back.

What to do: Lie on your back and bring your legs into the "butterfly position"—knees  pointing out to the sides and the soles of your feet touching. Relax your legs and lace your hands behind your head, resting your thumbs on your neck to ensure that it stays relaxed. Using only your abdominals, lift your upper body two inches off the ground then lower it back down, pressing your belly button toward your lower back. Repeat 25 times. Next, hold your upper body off the ground and lift your legs two inches, then tap the sides of your feet on the ground 25 times.

Advanced version: Lift your legs as high as you can off the ground and simultaneously raise your upper body into a "crunch" 25 times, while tapping the sides of your feet on the ground after each crunch.

CROSS-LEGGED TWIST

Purpose: Stretches your back, abdominals and hips.

Helps with: Releasing low-back tension and opening up the hips—good for those who sit at a desk all day and for activities such as tennis and skiing.

What to do: Sit on the floor with your legs crossed. Keeping your torso upright and the top of your head directly above your tailbone, place your left hand on your right knee and your right hand on the ground behind you. Slowly twist to the right. Take two deep breaths while holding the stretch. Switch sides and repeat, then do once more on each side.

Advanced version: Do this in the lotus position (legs crossed with ankles on top of your crossed legs).

Illustrations by Shawn Banner.

Yoga Can Help You— But Which Kind Is Best?

Timothy McCall, MD, a board-certified internist in Oakland, California, medical editor of *Yoga Journal* and author of *Yoga as Medicine* (Bantam). Dr. McCall leads workshops and retreats on yoga around the country and worldwide. *www.drmccall.com*

Yoga is powerful medicine. It can improve balance, flexibility and posture… strengthen muscles and bones…lower blood pressure, ease pain and boost immune function…heighten sexual functioning… alleviate stress and depression…and bolster spiritual well-being.

Key: Finding a style that fits your abilities, temperament and goals. *With your doctor's okay, consider…*

• **Anusara.** This playful, warm-hearted and physically challenging style emphasizes body alignment (often with hands-on adjustments from the teacher) and a positive mindset that looks for the good in all people.

Best for: Physically fit people who want to be part of a like-minded community.

• **Ashtanga ("power" yoga).** A vigorous practice, it includes a fixed series of postures that flow rapidly and continuously, accompanied by energizing breathing techniques.

Best for: People who can handle an intense workout, want to build stamina and strength, and enjoy a set routine.

• **Bikram ("hot" yoga).** An invariable sequence of 26 poses is performed in a studio heated to at least 100°F to loosen muscles, tendons and ligaments.

Best for: People in good health who don't mind heat and want improved flexibility. Bikram, like other vigorous styles, may not be appropriate for frail or older students or those with serious illnesses.

•**Integral.** Beginning classes include gentle poses, breathing techniques, meditation and discussions of ancient yoga texts. The principle of selfless service (such as volunteer work) is emphasized. Some centers offer special classes for students with physical limitations or health problems (such as heart disease or cancer).

Best for: People interested in traditional Indian yoga that includes more than just poses.

•**Iyengar.** Emphasizing meticulous body alignment, this style makes use of blocks, straps and other props so students with limited flexibility can safely and comfortably assume poses. Teacher training requirements are among the strictest.

Best for: Anyone new to yoga or especially in need of better body alignment, such as people with arthritis or back pain.

•**Kripalu.** A blend of Western psychology and Eastern philosophy, this practice provides a safe place to explore emotional issues. Meditation and chanting accompany moderately vigorous and sometimes improvised movement.

Best for: People looking for stress relief and emotional release.

•**Kundalini.** This style includes a wide variety of breathing techniques, intense physical movements, chanting and meditation. The focus is on raising energy rather than on precise body alignment.

Best for: People who are seeking to build prana (life force) and who are open to yoga's spiritual dimensions.

•**Viniyoga.** Gentle flowing poses are held only briefly. Safety and breath work are emphasized. Teachers often focus on private one-on-one sessions rather than group classes.

Best for: People who are new to yoga or out of shape or who are looking to use yoga to help alleviate any of a variety of chronic ailments.

To find a class: Yoga Alliance (888-921-9642, *www.yogaalliance.org*) registers teachers who complete a certain number of hours of training in specific styles. If you have a medical condition, contact the International Association of Yoga Therapists (*www.iayt.org*; click on "find a member") to find an appropriate yoga therapist. Yoga therapy has been shown in studies to be effective for a wide range of conditions, from diabetes and arthritis to cancer and chronic lung disease.

Posture Perk

It has been proven that women who do yoga actually stand taller.

Recent finding: Elderly women walked more quickly, had better balance and gained an average of one centimeter in height after a nine-week yoga program—because they stood more upright as a result of practicing yoga. Twice a week, for 90 minutes each time, the women did a series of basic poses developed especially for older people. After nine weeks, participants used longer strides when walking and could stand for a longer time on one leg. They also felt more confident in their ability to balance while standing or walking.

Jinsup Song, DPM, PhD, director, Gait Study Center, Temple University School of Podiatric Medicine, Philadelphia, and principal investigator of a study of 24 women, ages 60 and older, presented at a recent meeting of the Gait and Clinical Movement Analysis Society.

Laughing Is Healthy

Laughter yoga combines traditional yoga stretches and poses with exercise designed to make people laugh. In terms of cardiovascular benefits, one minute of laughter (about 100 giggles) is the equivalent of six to 10 minutes on a rowing machine. Laughter has aerobic benefits and can help lower blood pressure, lift mood and boost immunity. To find a class near you, call 212-956-5920 or go to *www.laughteryoga.org*.

Alex Eingorn, DC, laughter-yoga instructor and director, Better Health Chiropractic, New York City.

10 Easy Ways to Sneak Exercise Into Your Day

Carol Krucoff is a registered yoga therapist at Duke Integrative Medicine in Durham, North Carolina. She is coauthor of *Healing Moves: How to Cure, Relieve, and Prevent Common Ailments with Exercise* (Healthy Learning).

Getting the recommended 30 minutes of exercise a day can be challenging during the cold, dark days of winter. But the good news is that you don't have to work out for a half-hour straight to boost your health. New guidelines from the American Heart Association and the American College of Sports Medicine state that three 10-minute bouts of moderate-intensity physical activity (such as a brisk walk) can be just as effective as exercising for 30 minutes straight. And other evidence suggests that even shorter periods of activity—in fact, every step you take—adds up to better health.

Don't let wintry weather freeze your exercise plans. *Try these simple strategies to slip exercise into your day...*

1. Break the elevator/escalator habit. Climbing stairs is a great way to strengthen your heart, muscles and bones. The Harvard Alumni Health Study, which followed 11,130 men (mean age 58 at the beginning of the study) for about 20 years, found that those who climbed 20 to 34 floors per week had about a 30% lower risk of stroke. Take the stairs at every opportunity and even look for ways to add extra flights, such as using the bathroom on a different floor. If you must take an elevator up a tall building, get off a few flights early and walk.

2. Use muscle, not machines. In our push-button world, we expend about 300 to 700 fewer calories per day than did our grandparents, who had to do things like chop wood and fetch water. Drop the "labor saving" mentality, and embrace opportunities to activate your life. Use a rake instead of a leaf blower...wash your car by hand...get up and change the TV channel.

3. Walk to a coworker's office instead of sending an e-mail. William Haskell, PhD, calculated, in *The Journal of the American Medical Association*, that the energy expenditure lost by writing e-mails for two minutes every hour for eight hours per day five days a week—instead of two minutes of slow walking around the office to deliver messages—adds up to the equivalent of 1.1 pounds of fat in one year and 11 pounds of fat in 10 years.

4. Take exercise breaks. Energize your body with movement instead of caffeine by turning your coffee break into a "walk break." Every hour or two, get up and walk around or stretch.

5. Wait actively. If you're forced to wait for an airplane, hairdresser, dentist, doctor, restaurant table, etc., take a walk. To boost the calorie burn of your walk, move purposefully—as if you're late for a meeting—rather than just strolling along.

6. Do the housework boogie. Play lively music when you're doing household chores, and dance off extra calories by moving to the beat.

7. Try aerobic shopping. Take a lap or two around the mall or grocery store before you go into a store or put anything in your cart.

8. Socialize actively. Instead of sitting and talking (or eating) with friends and/or family, do something active, such as bowling, playing Ping-Pong, shooting baskets or dancing.

9. Install a chin-up bar in a convenient doorway. Whenever you walk through, do a pull-up or simply "hang out" and stretch. Chin-up bars are available at sporting-goods stores and on-line for less than $20.

10. Practice "phone fitness." Stretch, walk or climb stairs while you're talking on your cell phone or cordless phone.

Why I Love Karate

Tamara Eberlein, former editor,, Bottom Line Inc., 3 Landmark Square., Stamford, Connecticut 06901.

Four years ago, I signed up for a free karate lesson. Within the hour, I was hooked. Three weekly classes keep me fit—but the rewards go way beyond the physical. *What I've learned…*

• **I am worth defending.** Whether fending off a mugger or insisting on a refund for flawed merchandise, I have a right to stand up for myself.

• **Brain beats brawn.** A small woman can knock down a big man if she knows the right techniques.

• **Looking goofy doesn't matter.** Who cares if I'm the oldest person in class or if my arthritic kick can't match a nimble teen's? I'm improving.

• **Cooler heads prevail.** When a sparring partner punches hard, getting mad makes me forget my skills. I'm learning to stay calm— even during tiffs with my husband.

• **Exercise doesn't have to be boring.** During a treadmill trudge, minutes crawl by. Karate engages the mind, so it's more fun—classes are over before I know it.

• **A loss is a gain.** I learn more from the matches I lose than from the ones I win.

• **Breathe.** I have asthma, so I used to panic when I couldn't catch my breath. Karate has taught me to control my breathing—whether stress is physical or emotional.

• **It's easy to make friends.** Nothing dissolves social stiffness quite like a sweaty wrestling match.

• **Persistence pays off.** Except for giving birth, I've never felt an exhausted exhilaration that matched the moment when I earned my black belt.

It's Better with a Buddy

Cedric X. Bryant, PhD, chief science officer and vice president of educational services, American Council on Exercise, San Diego. He has coauthored many books, including *Strength Training for Women* (Human Kinetics).

Whether you plan to walk briskly around the neighborhood each morning or train for a triathlon, an exercise partner may be just what you need. *Advantages of working out together…*

• **Exercising is more fun when you play, chat or engage in friendly competition with another person.**

• **You're less likely to skip a workout when someone is counting on you to show up.**

• **A partner minimizes your risk for injury** —spotting as you lift weights, correcting your body alignment in yoga poses.

• **You work muscle groups and deepen stretches in ways that are difficult to do on your own.**

• **You save money by sharing equipment, swapping fitness DVDs or carpooling to the tennis court.**

The key to success is to make a good match —so your best friend or nearest neighbor may not be the optimal choice. *Ask yourself if you and a potential partner are similar enough in these key areas…*

• **Fitness level.** Is she interested in a leisurely bike ride around the park, while you want to train for a cycling trip through France? That's not a fit.

• **Schedule.** If you're a morning exerciser and she's a night owl, can you find a compromise—such as lunch hour?

• **Temperament.** Do you both like to talk while you lift weights, or would one of you find the other's chatter distracting?

• **Commitment.** Is she game to jog in any weather, while you run for shelter when clouds roll in?

There are no right or wrong answers to the questions above—it's just a matter of compatibility. *If you have doubts, keep looking…*

• **Check the bulletin board at a local community center, spa or gym.**

• **Ask a personal trainer for a referral.** She even may offer you and your new partner a two-for-one discount.

• **Search** *www.exercisefriends.com…*or *www.craigslist.org* (look under "community" for your city) for a match.

Important: Always check with your doctor before beginning a new exercise program.

STRENGTH TRAINING FOR TWO

Many strength-training moves can be adapted for partners. Here are examples of exercises for the upper, mid and lower body. For more techniques, experiment with your buddy or consult a trainer.

•Medicine ball push.

Equipment: A four- to 10-pound medicine ball (a weighted ball about the size of a basketball, sold at most sporting-goods stores, about $20).

Partner 1: Stand facing your partner, about three feet apart. Hold the ball between your hands at chest level, a few inches in front of you, elbows bent and pointing out to the sides. Step forward with the right foot and gently throw the ball, using a pushing motion, so it arcs just above head height.

Partner 2: Extend arms to meet the ball, bending elbows as you catch it to bring the ball toward your chest.

Both partners: Take turns throwing and catching 10 to 15 times, alternating the foot that steps forward as you throw.

Modification: If you have bone loss or wrist problems, use a ball no heavier than six pounds.

•Stability ball crunches.

Equipment: A 21-inch-diameter inflatable stability ball (about $20 at sporting-goods stores). If you are shorter than five feet tall, use a 17-inch ball…if taller than five feet, seven inches, use a 25-inch ball.

Partner 1: Kneel and face your partner, one arm extended forward at chest height, palm facing away from you to create a "target" for your partner to clap. Between each of her "crunches," move your palm to a slightly different location—giving her a moving target.

Partner 2: Recline face-up, low to mid-back pressed against the ball, knees bent at

a 90-degree angle, feet shoulder-width apart and close to where your partner is kneeling. Hold your hands a few inches in front of your chest, elbows bent. Using abdominal muscles, do a crunch by lifting your upper body up and away from the ball…at the top of your crunch, straighten one arm and clap your partner's palm…lower back down. Do 10 to 15 crunches, alternating the hand that claps.

Both partners: Switch positions.

Modification: If balance is a problem, lie on the floor instead of the ball to do crunches.

•Squats.

Both partners: Stand back-to-back, keeping your torso firmly pressed against your partner's from shoulder blade to hip throughout the exercise. Together, slowly bend knees and lower hips while moving feet forward until thighs are parallel to the floor (as if sitting on a chair) and knees are directly above ankles. Hold for about 30 seconds. Then slowly straighten knees and raise hips while walking backward until you are standing once again. Rest for about 15 seconds. Repeat five to 10 times.

Caution: If you have knee problems, limit the depth of your squat to your pain-free range.

TANDEM STRETCHING

For safety, always move slowly and gently, clearly communicating when your stretch has reached the desired level of intensity. Do the stretches below after your aerobic or strength-training workout, as part of your cooldown. Finish with the breathing exercise.

•Chest-opening stretch.

Partner 1: Stand erect, arms reaching behind you, elbows straight but not locked, palms facing each other.

Partner 2: Stand facing your partner's back, just beyond her outstretched hands. Grasping her wrists, pull gently and steadily toward yourself

318

to open your partner's chest...hold for 15 to 30 seconds...rest...repeat two to four times.

Both partners: Switch positions.

• **Straddle stretch.**

Both partners: Sit on the floor facing each other. Holding hands, spread legs as wide as possible, knees straight,  toes up, feet pressed against your partner's feet. As one partner slowly leans forward, the other leans back...then switch, continuing the forward-and-backward movements. After about 30 seconds, widen your straddle if possible. Repeat several times.

• **Yoga breathing.**

Both partners: Sit on the floor cross-legged, facing away from each other, backs touching, spines straight. Breathing through the nose, inhale deeply, pause for a few seconds, then exhale slowly. Continue for one minute, matching the rhythm of your partner's breathing. Then switch, so that one partner inhales as the other exhales, continuing for another minute. Use this meditative breathing technique to calm your mind and prepare for the rest of your day.

Illustrations by Shawn Banner.

Gender Bender

Men and women tend to view their fitness levels differently.

Recent study: Men and women who practiced strength training for 12 weeks all felt better about themselves in the end—but men based their new body image on feeling thinner, while women were more focused on their strength and the size of their muscles.

Kathleen A. Martin Ginis, PhD, professor of kinesiology, McMaster University, Hamilton, Ontario, and leader of a study of body image changes in 44 men and women in a strength-training program, published in *Body Image*.

You're Probably Exercising Wrong

Edward J. Jackowski, PhD, founder and CEO of Exude, Inc., a New York City–based fitness company. He is author of *Escape Your Shape: How to Work Out Smarter, Not Harder* (Touchstone) and *Hold It! You're Exercising Wrong* (Fireside).

Little-known fact: The shape of a person's body—Hourglass, Spoon, Cone or Ruler*—dictates the type of exercise he/she should be performing to get health and fitness benefits.

Solution: A six-year medical study shows that by selecting exercises according to your body type, you can begin to address the built-in imbalances of your body.**

WHAT'S YOUR BODY TYPE?

Your body type has nothing to do with how tall, short, slim or chunky you are. It has to do with where your weight—both fat and muscle—accumulates on your body.

Your body is most likely...

• **Hourglass**—if you carry most of your weight in your upper and lower body...and there's a significant difference (six inches or more) between the circumference of your chest and waist or between your hips and waist.

• **Spoon**—if you carry most of your weight in your hips, thighs and buttocks.

• **Cone**—if you carry most of your weight in your back, chest, arms and stomach.

• **Ruler**—if there's not much difference in the circumference of your chest, waist and hips ...and you tend to put on weight around your midsection.

If you're not sure of your body type: You're probably overweight. Follow the recommendations below for the Hourglass body type until you've lost some of your extra weight. As you slim down, your natural shape will start to emerge.

*These body types are registered trademarks of Exude, Inc., and the fitness prescriptions for them are patented.

**Check with your doctor before beginning a new exercise program.

HOURGLASS

About 40% of women and 20% of men have an Hourglass body type. People with this body type require exercises that burn fat without adding muscle mass in the upper and lower body areas.

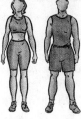

Recommended exercises...

Main aerobic exercises: Jump rope...stationary bicycling with low resistance (level 1 to 3)... jumping jacks...fast walking (a pace of 3 to 4.5 mph) on a flat surface... elliptical machines with no resistance.

Main resistance exercises: Weight machines with light weights (10 pounds or less for the upper body and less than 25 pounds for the lower body) and a high number of repetitions (25 to 50 per exercise)...upper-body exercises with a four-pound aerobic (weighted) bar (for women) or 12- to 15-pound aerobic bar (for men)...leg extensions with light weight and high repetitions (25 to 50 per exercise).

Exercises to avoid...

Aerobic: Step classes...spinning classes... high-impact aerobics.

Resistance: Any upper- or lower-body exercises using high resistance or weights...any exercise using ankle weights.

SPOON

About 30% of women and 10% of men have a Spoon body type. Spoons require exercises that quickly burn fat in the lower region of the body and build muscle in the upper region.

Recommended exercises...

Main aerobic exercises: Jump rope...stationary bicycling with low resistance (level 1 to 3) and high revolutions per minute (90 to 120)...fast walking (3 to 4.5 mph) on a flat surface.

Main resistance exercises: Upper-body exercises with moderate to heavy weights (10 pounds or more) and low repetitions (8 to 10 per exercise)...lower-body exercises with low resistance (less than 25 pounds) and high repetitions (25 to 50 per exercise).

Exercises to avoid...

Aerobic: Elliptical machines and stair climbers...rollerblading...swimming...long-distance running...spinning...step classes... high-impact aerobic classes.

Resistance: Squats...lunges...leg presses ...any lower-body exercises with moderate to high resistance or weights.

CONE

About 30% of men and 10% of women have a Cone body type. Cones need to concentrate on building bulk in the lower body and endurance in the abdomen and upper body.

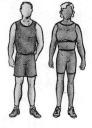

Recommended exercises...

Main aerobic exercises: Spinning...stair climbers... stationary bicycling with moderate to high resistance (level 4 or higher)...slow walking (3 mph or less) on an incline or hills...step classes.

Main resistance exercises: Leg presses, leg extensions and leg curls (done on weight machines) using moderate to heavy resistance (50 pounds or more) and low repetitions (8 to 10 per exercise)...upper-body exercises with low resistance (10 pounds or less) and high repetitions (25 to 50 per exercise)—especially push-ups, pull-ups and dips.

Main flexibility exercises: Hamstring and upper-body stretches.

Exercises to avoid...

Aerobic: Rowing...aerobic or step classes using hand weights.

Resistance: Any upper-body exercises with moderate to high resistance or weights.

RULER

Approximately 40% of men and 20% of women have a Ruler body type. Rulers need to focus on building muscle and overall strength.

Recommended exercises...

Main aerobic exercises: Step classes...spinning...stationary bicycling or elliptical machines with moderate to high resistance (level 7 to 15)...walking on an incline or hills (3.7 to 4.3 mph)...swimming.

Main resistance exercises: Squats, lunges and leg presses...all upper- and lower-body exercises using moderate to heavy resistance or weights (10 pounds or more for the upper body, 50 pounds or more for the lower body) and low repetitions (8 to 10 per exercise).

Main flexibility exercises: Hamstring and quadriceps stretches.

Exercises to avoid...None.

Illustrations by Shawn Banner.

Best Workouts for the Plus-Sized Woman

James Hagberg, PhD, professor of exercise physiology, department of kinesiology at the University of Maryland in College Park.

You begin with good intentions, determined to exercise away those excess pounds. But a workout that is too challenging for your full figure and fitness level may leave you discouraged—or possibly even injured. *Here's how heavier women can exercise safely, effectively and enjoyably...*

•**Have fun.** In school, did you dread gym because you felt self-conscious in shorts or because running laps was used as punishment? Find an activity that lets you feel good about yourself and brings you pleasure—aqua aerobics, square dancing, canoeing.

•**Start slowly.** If you're daunted by the idea of a daily half-hour hike, begin with a five-minute walk three times a week. It doesn't matter if it takes six months to work your way up. Fitness is a lifetime commitment, not a "gotta do it now" goal.

•**Protect your joints.** For heavier women, jogging and aerobics put excess stress on knees and ankles, because body weight comes down hard with each footfall.

Better: Use an elliptical machine, which simulates fast walking, stepping or running yet involves little impact because feet remain grounded on the pedals...or swim, because the water supports your weight.

•**Maintain a stable center of gravity.** Sports such as tennis require quickly shifting your center of gravity up and down and side to side. The heavier you are, the more energy this takes—and the more quickly you may become exhausted and give up. Opt instead for an activity in which your center of gravity does not have to shift much, such as bicycling or rowing.

•**Forget about "winning."** Competitive team sports that pit you against fitter people might be discouraging. If it's your dream to play basketball, go for it—but find a league that focuses on fun.

Satisfying: Try yoga or tai chi, using personal progress as your measure of success.

Busting the 6 Biggest Exercise Myths

Andrea Chernus, RD, CDE, registered dietitian, certified diabetes educator and exercise physiologist in private practice in New York City. She counsels patients on diet and exercise related to diabetes, high cholesterol, weight management and sports nutrition.

You may be surprised to learn that some of the long-held beliefs about exercise are not really true. While it's a fact that exercise is good for your health, understanding the realities behind the myths can help you get more out of your workout.

Myth: **Gaining muscle will significantly increase your metabolism and thus help keep your weight down.**

Reality: While there are many benefits to resistance (weight) training, the boost to metabolism often is overstated.

It is true that one pound of muscle burns about five to six calories per day, while one pound of body fat burns about two calories per day. But even if a person gains five pounds of muscle, it increases his/her resting metabolism by only about 25 to 30 calories per day, which is not a significant change.

Myth: **If you stop exercising, muscle turns to fat.**

Reality: Muscle and fat are two separate types of tissue—one does not become the other.

Often when a person stops exercising, his calorie needs decrease due to reduced physical activity. If his eating pattern does not decrease accordingly, body fat will increase over time. Together with a loss of muscle tone, it may appear that muscle is turning into fat, but an increase in body fat is the reality.

Myth: **You can build lots of muscle while losing pounds of fat.**

Reality: Generally, it takes an increase of calories to build muscle tissue, along with sufficient resistance exercise to stress the muscle. If you attempt to lose weight and gain muscle simultaneously, your results on either end will be minor. A very low calorie intake even can cause a substantial loss of muscle tissue—especially in people who have only a small amount of body fat to lose. Crash diets that severely restrict calories often result in losses of lean body mass.

If you have more body fat to lose and you slowly lose the weight, with a minor calorie deficit, you have a better chance of losing the fat while minimizing muscle loss.

Myth: **It takes a lot of protein to build muscle.**

Reality: While protein needs are higher if you are trying to gain muscle mass, it's not necessary for the recreational exerciser to eat pounds of meat or to drink protein shakes. Most people can get all the protein they need from a balanced diet.

Example: A 154-pound person who doesn't exercise needs 61 grams (g) of protein per day to maintain his health. If the same person were engaged in a heavy-duty weight-lifting program and was actively trying to gain muscle mass, the maximum amount of protein he would need would be 130 g, which easily could be met by food—a turkey sandwich, a bowl of bean soup, eight ounces of fish and one cup of plain yogurt.

The body cannot use more than .9 g of protein per pound of body weight. Any additional dietary protein will be turned into glucose, which is either burned for energy or stored as body fat.

Myth: **You can lose body fat in a specific part of your body by exercising that part.**

Reality: Resistance exercise on specific muscles will strengthen, tone and tighten those muscles. But if you carry body fat over those muscles, extra repetitions of a weight-lifting or toning exercise won't burn the fat in that area.

Example: Many fitness enthusiasts feel that targeting the abdominal muscles will yield flat tummies. Performing many sets of exercises will strengthen and tone these muscles but won't yield a flat stomach if body fat covers them.

To lose body fat, you need to create an overall energy deficit—burn more calories than you take in. If you do this, you may lose the fat from areas that have extra padding, but this is by no means guaranteed.

Myth: **Carrying weights while walking or running is a good way to burn some extra calories.**

Reality: Studies have shown that there are no benefits to using hand or ankle weights during cardiovascular exercise. And there are potential drawbacks to using heavy weights. The unnatural weight distribution along your arm or leg may inappropriately stress your joints (shoulder, elbow, knee, hips). The weight imbalance to your limbs also may lead to muscle injury.

Smarter, *Not Harder,* Ways to Exercise

Edward J. Jackowski, PhD, founder and CEO of Exude, Inc., a New York City–based fitness company. He is author of several books, including *Escape Your Shape: How to Work Out Smarter, Not Harder* (Touchstone) and *Hold It! You're Exercising Wrong* (Fireside).

Want to feel better? Exercise. Lose weight? Exercise. Ward off disease, prevent injuries and recover from health problems faster? Exercise, exercise, exercise.

A true health panacea, exercise is an appropriate prescription for just about everything and everyone.*

Problem: Exercise is a vague term that many women (and doctors) think they understand —but about which they get little expert guidance. As a result, women often waste time and effort on fitness regimens that offer minimal benefit and may even lead to injury.

Here are eight common mistakes that women make...plus smart and simple solutions that will help you get the most from your workouts.

Mistake: Confusing activity with exercise. You can't get fit from an occasional play-till-you-drop game of tennis or a nightly stroll around the block—yet many women convince themselves that sporadic bursts of effort or low-intensity activities fulfill their exercise needs. While it is true that some exercise is better than no exercise, true fitness comes from workouts that are consistent and challenging but not exhausting.

Smarter: *Each exercise session should include all of the following...*

- **A warm-up.**
- **Stretches** to increase flexibility.
- **Cardiovascular workout,** such as walking fast enough to raise your heart rate for 10 minutes.
- **Strengthening moves** that build muscles in your upper body, core (torso) and lower body, such as biceps curls, sit-ups and lunges.
- **A cooldown,** such as relaxed walking, to gradually lower your heart rate.

Mistake: Working out for too long a period of time. Your entire session should not exceed 60 to 75 minutes. Your body won't reap significant additional health benefits from exercising longer than this. What's more, if your body gets used to extended workouts and then you have to cut down—due to increased demands at home or at work, for instance— you'll gain weight if you don't also cut calories. This is because your body will no longer

*Always check with your doctor before beginning any exercise program.

be expending as many calories as it is accustomed to burning.

Smarter: Schedule an hour or so of exercise into your calendar three or four times per week—then stick with it. The idea is to make exercise a consistent part of your life, not an ordeal that knocks you out so much on Tuesday that you can't face the gym again until Saturday.

Mistake: Lifting weights that are too heavy. Many women believe that the heavier the weight, the better the effect on body shape. But if one of your reasons for working out is to slim down, heavy weights won't help—in fact, they'll make you bulk up.

Smarter: To reduce your size while still building strength, use lighter weights and increase the number of repetitions.

Example: Do 25 leg lifts with two-pound leg weights instead of 15 lifts with five-pound weights. The lighter weights will still challenge your muscles, but the muscles won't grow as big. If you do want to build muscle size, use heavier weights and do fewer repetitions.

Mistake: Relying on classes to keep you fit. A well-choreographed class with an excellent instructor is a good way to learn proper technique. But what will you do when you can't make it to class or the teacher is absent? You may end up skipping your workout altogether.

Smarter: Create an alternate routine for the days when you can't take a class—preferably one you can do alone, anywhere, anytime. Also create a mini version that you can do no matter what your time constraints may be.

Mistake: Working through an injury. Maintaining a consistent exercise schedule does not mean that you should keep working out when you're hurt. Doing so probably would worsen the injury and undermine your fitness goals.

Smarter: *To avoid paying the price for overworking an injury, remember the word PRICE...*

- **P is for PROTECTING** your body from further injury by laying off until you feel better.
- **R is for RESTING** the part of your body that aches.

•**I is for ICE**—apply to the painful area for 30 minutes twice daily for a few days to ease swelling and pain. Do not use heat on a new injury.

•**C is for COMPRESSION**—wrap the sore area with an Ace bandage (not too tight!) for a few days.

•**E is for ELEVATE**—to take pressure off the injured area, elevate it whenever possible.

When you are pain-free, return to your exercise regimen. If pain is severe or does not abate after several days, see your doctor.

Mistake: **Rushing to buy an exercise machine.** If you can afford it and know that you'll use it as one part of your overall routine, it's fine to buy a machine, such as a treadmill. However, most people end up stuffing that machine in a corner and forgetting about it —or overusing it and building up one particular body part while neglecting the rest.

Smarter: Use machines at a local gym... build a repertoire of exercises that need no equipment, such as running, jumping jacks and push-ups...buy only versatile, portable, low-cost gear, such as an elastic resistance band and a jump rope.

Mistake: **Extending your knees over your toes.** Lunges and squats are excellent exercises—but if you let your knees extend too far forward, you strain the knee joints and increase the risk for injury to the cartilage, tendons and ligaments.

Smarter: Keep an eye on your alignment. You always should be able to see your toes just beyond the tops of your knees.

Better: Perform these exercises in front of a mirror so that you can periodically check your form.

Mistake: **Believing that jump ropes are just for little girls.** If you haven't jumped rope since elementary school, you're missing out on one of the simplest and most effective exercises. Jumping rope is an aerobic activity, so it's good for your heart...improves all-over muscle strength by working the entire body at once... builds bones because it is weight-bearing...and is low-impact if done on a surface with natural give, such as a wood floor or a thin mat.

Smarter: To add jumping rope to your fitness routine, start slowly—try to do 20, then 50, then 100 jumps in a row. As your endurance builds, aim to jump rope for 10 minutes straight during the cardio portion of your workout two or three times per week. Even if you have problems with incontinence, keep jumping—my clients say that their symptoms improve within a few weeks, perhaps because the exercise strengthens pelvic area muscles.

Bonus: Jumping rope burns twice as many calories as playing singles tennis, but it places much less pressure on your joints.

This 7-Minute Workout Gives You Energy All Day

Lee Holden, an instructor in meditation, tai chi and qi gong and the founder of Pacific Healing Arts in Los Gatos, California. He is author of *7 Minutes of Magic* (Avery), for which companion DVDs are available at *www.exercisetoheal.com*.

L ow energy is almost an epidemic—and starting the day with an eye-opening double latte doesn't really help. The stimulating effects of caffeine wear off quickly and are invariably followed by an energy slump.

Better: This seven-minute morning routine revs you up before you leave home and keeps you energized throughout the day. You also will notice a significant increase in strength, flexibility and balance.

Bonus: Many studies have found that people with the highest energy levels tend to be healthier overall, both physically and psychologically. They experience less depression... less stress...and less illness.

THE WORKOUT

These exercises combine the best time-proven movements of Eastern fitness—from the practices of qi gong, yoga and tai chi—with the scientific principles of Western exercise physiology. This routine "opens" the lower back and abdominal area, which, according to

Eastern philosophy, is where the body stores energy. It also tones and strengthens muscles in the abdomen, back, legs and upper body.

The movements in each exercise are designed to "flow" together. Do the complete routine slowly and with control—but without stopping.

Throughout the routine, the number seven is repeated—for example, doing a movement seven times or taking seven breaths—but it doesn't need to be exactly seven. If you prefer to do, say, 10 repetitions or 10 breaths, that's fine, too. Also, try to walk at least 20 minutes, three times a week, for cardiovascular health and other benefits.

Exercise 1: **Knees to chest.** This movement works the abdominal muscles, as well as muscles in the hips and along the spine, improving joint flexibility and strength.

Lie on your back and hug your knees to your chest. Hold for about 30 seconds.

Rock slightly to your right side, then return to the center position. Repeat the rocking seven times. Then rock to your left, and repeat seven times.

Exercise 2: **Twist.** This movement flows naturally from the previous exercise—all you have to do is drop your knees to the side. The twisting motion opens up the spinal joints, which increases flexibility and can help relieve back pain.

Lie on your back with your knees bent and your feet off the ground. Place your left hand on your right knee, and pull both knees down to your left side. At the same time, twist your head, arm and upper body to the right. Hold while you take seven deep breaths.

Return to the center position, and reverse the movement. Place your right hand on your left knee, and pull both knees down to the right side. Hold while you take seven deep breaths.

Exercise 3: **Bicycle movement.** This exercise is designed to strengthen the abdominals. The rotation strengthens the oblique (side)

muscles, and moving the legs works the muscles along the spine.

 Lie on your back with your feet on the floor and your fingers interlocked behind your head. Bring your left elbow to your right knee, then your right elbow to your left knee.

Go back and forth like this at a steady pace for about 14 seconds and for a total of seven seconds a side.

Option: If the exercise is too difficult or puts too much strain on your neck, keep your head on the floor and just bicycle your legs.

Exercise 4: **Cobra and Mountain.** This combines two traditional Eastern movements. The Cobra opens the shoulders and upper back and energizes the spine. The Mountain elongates the spine and strengthens the upper body. Alternating smoothly between the two is a great way to fire up more energy.

Cobra: Start facedown on your belly, with your hands under your shoulders. Slowly press up, lifting your chest off the floor. Come up only as far as you comfortably can.

Keep your hips down on the floor, and lightly squeeze your buttocks to help support your lower back.

Mountain: Bend your body so that it forms an inverted V, with your bottom in the air and your hands and feet on the floor.

Go back and forth between the Cobra and the Mountain seven times. Synchronize your breathing with the movements. As you inhale, move into the Mountain. As you exhale, move into the Cobra.

Exercise 5: **Tiger.** This exercise strengthens the main muscles in the legs—the quadriceps, hamstrings and gluteal muscles. Do the movement in a continuous, fluid motion, and repeat seven times.

With feet shoulder-width apart, raise your hands over your head. Then slowly squat down into a deep knee bend. (If too difficult, hinge forward at the waist, only bending knees slightly.) While you lower your body, bring hands down to the floor. Then come back up.

Exercise 6: Knocking on the door of life. This is a very dynamic movement that combines a twisting motion (for spinal flexibility) with actual "knocking" on the lower back. The knocking stimulates an energy pressure point, which helps to increase the body's energy levels.

Stand with your feet shoulder-width apart. Keeping your shoulders, arms and upper back relaxed, rotate your upper body at the waist, going as far as you can to the right.

Let your arms gently knock against your lower back and abdomen while you rotate. Repeat the movement seven times in the same direction.

Then do the same movement in reverse, this time twisting to the left.

Exercise 7: Holding up the sky. Energy comes from the oxygen we breathe—but most people breathe too shallowly, particularly in response to stress. This movement floods the lungs with oxygen.

With feet shoulder-width apart, slowly bring your arms in front of your abdomen, with your palms facing up. *Then…*

While inhaling: Slowly bring your arms up, palms facing your chest. Pause. Raise your arms over your head, turning your palms upward to face the ceiling, and look up to the ceiling.

Pause and inhale.

While exhaling: Allow your arms to come back down, with your palms facing your chest, until you're back at the starting position.

Pause and relax. Repeat this exercise seven more times.

Interval Training for Peak Fitness

Jason L. Talanian, an exercise physiologist at the University of Guelph in Ontario, Canada, has coauthored several studies on exercise, training and adaptation.

There are two big challenges in sticking with an exercise regimen—keeping it interesting, since doing the same thing all the time gets so boring…and attaining the same level of health benefits from the same old workout, because your body gets more efficient as it gets increasingly fit. When you only have 30 minutes a day to exercise, it is best to try a method that meets both of those challenges. What the Swedes call "fartlek," which means "speed play," is a form of unstructured interval training that is popular with runners.

It works by alternating intervals of high-intensity exercise with periods of what's called "active recovery." For example, if you're walking for an hour, try jogging for 30 seconds every few minutes. If you're already running, sprint for a half-minute. Jason L. Talanian, an exercise physiologist at the University of Guelph in Ontario, Canada and author of several studies on exercise performance, says that these spurts of high-intensity exercise lead the body to physiological adaptations that help burn more fat. In addition, the periods of rest make it possible for the body to meet escalating levels of challenge. One measure of aerobic fitness—maximum oxygen consumption (known as VO2max)—is also notably improved by interval training. Again, by varying and increasing the challenges of your intervals, you are able to intensify your workout without adding more time.

RESEARCH FINDINGS

In his most recent study, published in the *Journal of Applied Physiology*, Talanian asked eight college-age women to work out in his lab every other day for two weeks, for a total of seven interval sessions. During each workout, they performed 10 high-intensity intervals of four minutes each, following each with two minutes of rest time. The women were all over the map when it came to fitness levels—some had been fairly sedentary, but one was a tri-athlete and another played competitive soccer. About half were of average fitness and had been exercising in a conventional manner prior to the study (three times a week or so, at moderate intensity).

To track results of fat utilization, Talanian used a measure called whole body indirect calorimetry, which uses exhaled gases to calculate carbohydrates and fats burned.

Talanian's study, which reinforces the benefits of interval training, was unusual in the duration of the "high-intensity" intervals (four minutes) and in measuring changes in fat utilization in the whole body. In previous studies, subjects ran "all out" for 30 seconds, followed by a lower intensity active rest period of two or three minutes, which he hypothesized was a key reason for the impressive results. The exact mechanism that resulted in improved fat utilization following interval training is not yet known, but Talanian says it may be the aerobic component…it may be that the fat is burned during recovery periods following exercise where the body replenishes its lost glycogen stores. "But at this time we really don't know why an exercise that requires primarily carbohydrate for energy results in improvements in fat burning," he says.

If four-minute intervals of high intensity seems daunting to you, don't despair. You can get some of the benefits of interval training with much shorter intervals. An earlier study at McMaster University found that between four and seven "all-out" bouts of 30 seconds each, alternating with a four-minute full-rest recovery period between intervals, still doubled the endurance capacity of the subjects in a mere two weeks of training.

GETTING STARTED

It's often helpful to work with a trainer for your first interval workout to get an idea of how hard you can safely push yourself. If a trainer is not for you, Talanian suggests starting your interval training by computing your maximum heart rate (subtract your age from 220). Then you multiply by a percentage to get your range or goal. For example, a 40-year-old who wants to exercise between 60% and 80% of max would subtract 40 from 220—180. Then

60% of 180 is 108 (which stands for beats-per-minute), 80 percent of 180 is 144. His range is 108 to 144 beats-per-minute (in this case 80% is his high-intensity goal). You can, of course, work up to that, and you can also start with shorter intervals of low to moderate intensity and increase to longer ones as you improve.

"Beginning with a low intensity is a good way to start exercising, and can make it more manageable for beginners," says Talanian.

Lose a Pound a Day And Keep It Off

Rob Huizenga, MD, associate professor of clinical medicine at University of California, Los Angeles. He is the medical adviser for *The Biggest Loser*, the NBC-TV reality series whose contestants compete to lose the most weight.

One of the most effective weight-loss strategies was developed for *The Biggest Loser*, the popular NBC reality show. The first 64 contestants—all of whom were obese—lost an average of about 60 pounds each over five months, three times more than most people lose on standard diets.

Admittedly, the participants were in a highly artificial environment. People in real life don't have full-time trainers, around-the-clock peer pressure and cameras recording their every move.

As an experiment, the producers arranged for 36 people who weren't on the show to follow a similar program.

Result: The participants lost nearly as much as those who were on the show.

The secret: Less emphasis on calories and more on hard exercise.

Important: To be safe, get a medical checkup before starting any intense exercise program and tell your doctor what you intend to do.

EXERCISE LONG

The Surgeon General advises overweight individuals to lose weight by walking for 10 minutes three times a week, gradually increasing the amount to 150 minutes a week. Unless you're a racewalker, this level of exercise burns only about 525 calories. It takes nearly a week to lose just one pound.

Better: Prolonged, vigorous exercise. Working out intensely for one hour, twice a day, burns up to 2,500 calories in obese women and 3,000 to 4,000 in obese men. That adds up, on average, to about one pound a day.

Important: The assumption has always been that obese men and women are incapable of long exercise. Not true. Many of our participants were morbidly obese and had been completely sedentary. They struggled at first, but nearly all completed the program.

EXERCISE HARD

It's the only way to lose appreciable amounts of weight. Suppose that your only exercise is walking. You would have to do it for 5.5 hours a day in order to lose 1% of your body weight in a week. Those who exercise more intensely can get the same results in a day. The average woman who goes from sedentary to very fit with vigorous exercise gains six to seven pounds of muscle. Each pound of muscle burns at least an extra 30 calories a day.

STAY ON SCHEDULE

People who work out at the same times every day—once in the morning and again in the afternoon or evening—tend to stick with it more reliably than those who "get around to it."

Also important: Do not quit exercising if you get hurt. Doctors used to tell people to curtail their workouts after injuries. Now we know that injuries heal faster when people keep moving—although you might need to switch to a different exercise. If you hurt your ankle, for example, you might need to swim for a few weeks instead of jog. However, if the pain is worse the next day, even after you changed the exercise, see your doctor.

FUEL UP AFTER WORKOUTS

Muscle cells are more responsive to insulin in the 30 minutes following a workout. People who have a high-protein, high-carbohydrate drink during this period absorb more nutrients into muscle cells and speed muscle growth.

You can use a commercially made muscle-recovery drink, such as Endurox (available online and at health-food stores). Or make your own by blending about a cup of skim milk with fresh or frozen fruit and a high-protein powder, such as whey (follow directions on the label).

YOU STILL CAN EAT

The good thing about this plan is that you don't have to avoid anything. Healthy foods, such as fresh produce, fish and whole grains, are important, but you don't need to be fanatical.

Even the quantities aren't that important. The participants in our program lost dramatic amounts of weight, even though they practiced only modest calorie restriction—the women consumed an average of about 1,400 calories a day and the men had about 1,800.

The program works because people who slightly curtail calories and exercise vigorously gain the necessary muscle to burn even more fat. Just as important, eating an almost-normal diet prevents the body from shifting into "starvation mode," in which it tries to conserve calories—the point at which weight loss slows or stops altogether.

Walk Off Your Chocolate Cravings

Up to 97% of women get food cravings, as do 68% of men—most commonly for chocolate.

Recent study: People who habitually ate at least 3.5 ounces of chocolate daily abstained for two days. Next they took either a 15-minute brisk walk or a 15-minute rest, then unwrapped but were not allowed to eat chocolate. Participants reported fewer and less intense cravings for chocolate after walking than after resting.

Best: An occasional piece of chocolate is fine—but for frequent cravings, take regular walks to relieve the urge to overindulge.

Adrian Taylor, PhD, professor of exercise and health psychology, School of Sport and Health Sciences, University of Exeter, England, and head of a study published in *Appetite*.

Protect Your Knees

Reduce risk of runner's knee by running on a variety of surfaces and inclines. This forces you to constantly adjust the length of your stride, which may help to avoid overuse injuries by varying the force and frequency of the foot's impact with the ground.

John Mercer, PhD, associate professor of biomechanics, department of kinesiology, University of Nevada, Las Vegas.

Better Than Walking

Gabe Mirkin, MD, a Chevy Chase, Maryland–based physician who specializes in sports medicine, allergy and immuniology, pediatrics, and pediatric immuniology. He is author of a number of books, including *The Healthy Heart Miracle* (HarperCollins). *www. drmirkin.com*

Physical activity has unequivocally been shown to be one of the best ways to ensure a long, healthy life. But which type of activity is best?

Walking is ideal, according to many medical experts. But for many people, cycling may be even better. Like vigorous walking, cycling reduces risk for heart attack and stroke. However, cycling is generally much easier on a person's joints—so it's an excellent choice if you are overweight or have back problems or arthritis.

If you're age 50 or older: Get an exercise stress test (to measure the heart's electrical impulses during physical activity) before beginning any new exercise program.

HOW TO START

I tell my patients to start with a stationary "spinning-based" bike (now available at many health clubs), in which the resistance comes from a weighted flywheel. This type of bike lets you control the pedaling resistance manually (by changing tension on the flywheel), which is more precise and gradual than the control you have when using a computerized bike. This allows you to better control the degree to which your leg muscles are taxed.

If you want to buy a spinning-based bike for home use, dozens of good models are available, starting at about $500. The best ones have at least a 40-pound flywheel. Stationary flywheel bikes are available in recumbent (with back support) as well as upright models.

Stationary bike workouts…

•**Beginner.** Start by pedaling for 10 minutes at a very low resistance (one that requires you to exert little pressure on the pedals). Next, increase your workout by five minutes per week until you can ride comfortably for 30 minutes uninterrupted.

•**Intermediate.** Once you can ride for 30 minutes at more than 60 revolutions per minute, consider adding fitness-building workouts to your program. Start with five to 10 minutes of easy cycling, then gradually increase the resistance until you feel a burning sensation in your leg muscles (due to a buildup of lactic acid in the muscles).

When you feel the "burn," immediately turn the resistance down so that you're pedaling very easily. Continue pedaling at a low resistance until your muscles are recovered, then repeat the process. Continue for 10 to 20 minutes, then finish by pedaling at a low resistance for a five-minute cooldown. Each fitness-building workout should be followed by as many easy "recovery" workouts (entire sessions that consist of low-resistance cycling) as needed on subsequent days.

How this process works: By bringing your leg muscles to the brink of fatigue (with the "burn"), you're actually damaging your muscle fibers slightly. Your muscle fibers then repair themselves and become stronger during recovery days. Many people perform one hard workout per week followed by six easy recovery workouts.

•**Advanced.** As you become more fit, you can gradually increase the length of your workouts to 60 minutes or more. Be sure that your muscles are fully recovered before each fitness-building workout.

A CYCLING PROGRAM

After you reach an intermediate level of stationary cycling, you'll be ready to also bike outdoors. Outdoor cycling should follow the steps used for stationary cycling—whenever your pedaling rate becomes slower than one full revolution per second, switch immediately to a lower gear.

Helpful: For people who don't want to share the road with cars, many communities now have cycling trails. Never ride a bike without wearing a bike helmet.

Ideally, your bike should have at least 14 gears.

Reason: As with stationary cycling, you want to be able to adjust your resistance level. More gears allow you to do this more precisely.

Hundreds of good bike models are available, starting at prices as low as $200. To avoid injuring your knees, make sure that your seat is adjusted so that the knee is slightly bent when the corresponding pedal is at its lowest point.

Smart idea: If you plan to ride primarily with your spouse or another partner, consider purchasing a tandem bike that both riders pedal at the same rate. My wife, who is age 66, and I, at 73, have been riding a tandem for years and love it. You can get a good tandem bike for less than $2,000.

The Power Plate Workout

Dan Hamner, MD, physiatrist and sports medicine physician in New York City. A world-class runner, he is medical director of Gleason's Gym, New York City, and coauthor of *Peak Energy: The High-Oxygen Program for More Energy Now!* (available at many libraries).

The Power Plate, which offers a moderate aerobic workout, is used mainly to develop strength, condition and balance. It looks like a large scale or a treadmill with a shortened platform (the plate). The plate vibrates at different frequencies in three directions—horizontally, vertically and transversely. The user stands or sits on the plate, and the vibrations disrupt his/her stability, which causes muscle fibers to contract to maintain his/her balance anywhere from 40 to 60 times a second.

Workouts involve performing specific exercises—such as neck stretches, shoulder presses, push-ups, abdominal crunches and abductor stretches—while standing, sitting or resting part of the body on the plate.

Power Plate sessions are short—novices work out for about 10 minutes three times a week and then gradually increase the intensity and duration. Experienced "Power Platers" go for up to about 25 minutes—which is the equivalent of about 90 minutes at the gym.

Power Plate users include athletes...runners training for marathons...obese people whose weight precludes other types of exercise...and people who lack the time or motivation to exercise. The Power Plate also can help people with arthritis, knee problems, multiple sclerosis, osteoporosis, Parkinson's disease and certain other conditions. It is not recommended for pregnant women, postsurgery patients or people who have pacemakers or seizure disorders. As with all exercise programs, check with your doctor before starting.

Professional Power Plates cost about $9,500. Home models, which are smaller and have fewer settings, range in price from about $2,600 to $4,700. If properly used, either type can give a powerful workout—but it is best to first try one out at a fitness center or spa. The equipment comes with instructions and exercise diagrams, but it is best to ask a trained instructor to help you the first time or two.

For a list of gyms that have Power Plates, go to *www.powerplate.com* or call the company at 877-877-5283.

11

Healthy Beauty Secrets

Look Years Younger With Lunchtime "Face-Lifts"

About a decade ago, aggressive cosmetic surgery was the main treatment for wrinkles, sagging jowls and other signs of aging. Patients experienced significant bruising and swelling, and the full effects of the procedures weren't visible for at least six months.

Today, cosmetic surgeons perform three times as many noninvasive cosmetic procedures as aggressive surgeries. More than half of the procedures are done in doctors' offices instead of hospitals—and some can be completed during a lunch break. In many cases, patients see the final results immediately.

Botox has gotten most of the headlines, but there are a number of other "instant" cosmetic procedures. All of the following procedures are safe for most people and cause no scarring.

VOLUME FILLING FOR WRINKLES AND LINES

Synthetic collagen-like substances are injected into the skin to plump up depressed areas, including wrinkles and worry and smile lines. Collagen itself, one of the first filling agents, rarely lasted more than three to six months and sometimes caused allergic reactions. The new synthetic fillers last longer and are hypoallergenic.

The patient is given a local anesthetic, then fillers are injected into the problem spots. One syringe usually can treat the entire face. It only takes a few minutes, and changes in appearance are immediately apparent.

Different fillers...

• **Restylane** is chemically similar to the gelatinous material that supports skin collagen and elastic fibers. It retains water and plumps skin. It is especially good for smile

Nelson Lee Novick, MD, clinical professor of dermatology, Mount Sinai Medical Center, New York City. He is author of *Super Skin: A Leading Dermatologist's Guide to the Latest Breakthroughs in Skin Care* (iUniverse.com).

lines, lips that have gotten thinner with age and "smoker's lines" on the upper lip. One treatment usually lasts eight to 18 months.

Approximate cost: $350 to $800 per syringe.*

•**Perlane** is similar to Restylane. It's used for deeper depressions and furrows, costs about the same as Restylane and lasts about six months.

•**Radiesse** (formerly Radiance) is the newest filler. It's made of *calcium hydroxylapatite*, the same material that makes up teeth and bone. It is ideal for deeper smile lines and sunken cheeks. One treatment may last two to five years. It is slightly more likely than other fillers to cause temporary bruising.

Approximate cost: $650 to $800 per syringe.*

DERMASPACING FOR
ACNE SCARS AND FURROWS

This new technique uses the body's natural healing mechanisms to add volume to depressed areas such as acne scars and furrows. It also is effective for cellulite on other parts of the body.

The patient is given a local anesthetic. A needle-like cutting instrument is used to break up fibrous bands and create a hollow area beneath the skin. The area fills with body fluids, and within a few weeks, natural collagen is created that fills the pocket and plumps and smoothes the skin surface.

•**Dermaspacing,** also called subcision, may be enough to restore younger-looking skin, or it can be used in combination with fillers.

Approximate cost: $400 per treatment.*

Dermaspacing causes minor bruising that can last several weeks. Also, some patients need more than one treatment. It takes about a month to gauge how effectively the body will repair the area. For acne and other scars, the results may be permanent. For furrows, the results may last several months.

CHEMICAL PEEL FOR LEATHERY SKIN

Skin loses luster and gets leathery with age, especially in people who spend a lot of time in the sun. Resurfacing uses concentrated acids to restore youthful luster and texture to skin. *Main approaches...*

*All prices subject to change.

•**Alpha hydroxy acids,** also called *fruit washes*, are applied to the skin. Dermatologists use products with a 70% concentration—home-use chemical peels usually don't exceed 15%. These acids diminish mottling as well as fine wrinkles, in part by stimulating the production of gelatinous tissue under the skin. Most patients require six to 12 treatments (two to four weeks apart), with occasional touch-ups.

Approximate cost: $150 for 10 minutes.*

•**Beta hydroxy acids** are used in the same way, but they are somewhat more effective. Most patients require two to four treatments.

Approximate cost: $500 per treatment.*

RADIOSURGERY FOR
VISIBLE BLOOD VESSELS

A small wand directs high-energy radio waves through the skin to eliminate the tiny networks of blood vessels that appear on the cheeks or around the nose, mostly in people who have rosacea or those exposed to too much sun.

The patient is given a topical anesthetic, then radio waves penetrate deeply into the skin without damaging the surface or adjoining tissues. The treatment takes about five minutes.

Approximate cost: $300 for the entire face.*

SCALPEL SCULPTING FOR
REMOVING MOLES

In the past, moles were excised from the skin and the resulting wound was sutured. The wound could take weeks to heal, and many patients were left with small scars from the stitches.

Scalpel sculpting doesn't require stitches. A drop of local anesthetic is placed on the mole. The mole is then "sculpted"—cut flush with the face. Normal skin grows to cover the area, usually with no scarring. In 90% of cases, the mole never comes back.

Approximate cost: $300.*

There may be a darkening (repigmenting) of the area. Radio waves can eliminate this in most cases.

SANDING FOR SCARS
AND FINE WRINKLES

A sterilized sanding material is used to buff away scars—from acne, injuries, etc.—as well

*All prices subject to change.

as fine wrinkles. Normal skin covers the area once the scar tissue is removed.

Approximate cost: $400.*

Scar abrasion can be combined with dermaspacing or filling. One patient had a deep scar between his eyes after being hit by a crate. I did dermaspacing to fill the area, then buffed the surface. Now he has no visible mark.

Important: Scar abrasion is most effective when performed within eight to 12 weeks after an injury/surgery to prevent long-term scarring.

*All prices subject to change.

has board certification, plus a cosmetic-surgery fellowship, and a practice that is 100% cosmetic surgery...an option for a virtual consultation—you send in photos, which the surgeon then alters using a computer to show how you could look, then have a discussion by phone...plenty of patient histories, including at least one or two that match yours closely...video of the doctor and information about the staff, so you can get a sense of the practice even before you visit the office for a consultation.

Robert Kotler, MD, FACS, clinical instructor, UCLA Medical School, and author of *Secrets of a Beverly Hills Cosmetic Surgeon* (Ernest Mitchell).

Preparing for Plastic Surgery

Get better cosmetic surgery results by following presurgery instructions. Bring a notepad or tape recorder to doctor visits—or take a friend—to help you remember instructions. Before surgery, tell the doctor all the medicines you take and whether you smoke. Get to know the nurse or office manager so you will get better answers to questions after surgery. Don't take aspirin for two weeks before and after the procedure—it can cause bleeding. Eat a low-salt diet for one week before surgery and during recovery to help reduce swelling.

Joan Kron, contributing editor-at-large, *Allure*, where she covered plastic surgery for seven years, and New York City–based author of *Lift: Wanting, Fearing, and Having a Face-Lift* (Penguin).

Research Your Surgeon

You can evaluate cosmetic surgeons online. With elective surgery, it is particularly important to do your research.

How: Look for dozens of before-and-after photos, not just two or three per procedure... a detailed professional biography of the cosmetic surgeon—which should show that he/she

Keep Hands Looking Young

You work hard to keep the skin on your face young and smooth, so don't let your hands give away your age...

• **Apply sunscreen** of SPF 30 or higher on hands every day. Use products with Z-Cote, a microfine zinc oxide. Reapply after washing, swimming or perspiring.

• **Use a bleaching product** to fade brown spots (age, sun or liver spots). Your dermatologist can give you a prescription for one, or you can try one of the milder over-the-counter products.

• **Wear gloves** whenever possible.

• **Have bulging blue veins** removed by a dermatologist with a laser, or have a dermatologist inject a sclerosing agent, which causes veins to collapse and fade.

Approximate cost: $300 or more.*

• **Remove fine lines** and improve the paper-like quality of aging skin with laser treatments that generate collagen—also available from a dermatologist.

Approximate cost: $2,000 to $4,000.*

Neal Schultz, MD, dermatologist in private practice, New York City, and author of *It's Not Just About Wrinkles* (Stewart, Tabori & Chang).

*Prices subject to change.

More from Dr. Neal Schultz...

Manicure Warning

Manicures at nail salons can result in infections, allergic reactions and injuries to the nail plate and cuticle.

Self-defense: Bring your own manicure tools. Cuticles should be trimmed, not removed with chemicals. Fingernails should be trimmed and filed in the same shape as toenails—flat tips with rounded corners. Periodically clean manicure tools with 70% isopropyl alcohol. Use nail polish remover only as needed—whenever possible, recoat chips with polish.

Cuticle Care

The cuticle protects the nail matrix—the nail's growth center—from irritants and germs. Cutting it or vigorously pushing it back injures the growth center, weakening the nail and creating opportunities for infection.

Better: If you do not like the way cuticles look, soften them by soaking your fingertips in warm water for five minutes, then gently push the cuticles back with a moist washcloth every 10 to 14 days.

Richard K. Scher, professor of dermatology and head of the nail disorders clinic at the University of North Carolina, Chapel Hill. He is coauthor of the textbook *Nails: Therapy, Diagnosis, Surgery* (W.B. Saunders).

Hand Soaps and Moisturizers That You Should Avoid

Marianne O'Donoghue, MD, associate professor of dermatology at Rush University Medical Center in Chicago, and past president of the Women's Dermatologic Society.

Did you know that many common soaps and moisturizers can make hands dry and itchy? Liquid soap is a common culprit because it is water-based and so must contain a preservative to prevent bacterial growth and boost shelf life.

The preservative commonly used is a cousin of formaldehyde called *Quaternium-15*. It can trigger an allergic reaction that causes eczema—an inflammatory condition characterized by dry, cracked skin, redness and/or itching. As liquid soaps have become more popular, I've seen a marked increase in the number of cases of hand eczema among my patients.

Better: It is my experience that bar soaps—which contain little or no water and hence need fewer preservatives—are far less likely to irritate hands. I especially like to use moisturizing products, such as Aveeno, Cetaphil, Dove and Olay.

Also helpful: Gel cleaners are a good alternative. Alcohol-based gels with emollients are less irritating and allergy-provoking than soap, particularly for people who must clean their hands frequently (such as health-care providers and restaurant workers).

Although rubbing alcohol will typically dry out skin when used alone, it is not drying when used in a gel with an emollient, such as aloe.

Moisturizer warning: Water-based liquid moisturizers also may contain preservatives that can dry and damage skin. Instead, use a waterless ointment, such as Vaseline or Aquaphor. Rub one-half teaspoon into hands before going to bed.

Note: Wearing cotton gloves over the ointment while you are sleeping is not necessary if you use it sparingly, though doing so may help the moisturizer to soak in more effectively.

Infection control: If you do have eczema, proper cleansing and moisturizing is vital because germs can enter the bloodstream through cracks in the skin. Washing with bar soap or gel and applying ointment four times daily should smooth cracks within a few days.

Note: If eczema does not improve, consult a dermatologist—he/she can prescribe a topical steroid ointment, such as *triamcinolone*, which should do the trick.

Retinol Fights Wrinkles

Retinol reduces wrinkles in aging skin and in skin damaged by the sun.

Recent finding: People 80 years old and older who applied a retinol-containing lotion to their upper inner arm up to three times a week had significantly fewer wrinkles and less roughness and aged appearance after 24 weeks than people using similar lotions not containing retinol.

Reason: Retinol (vitamin A) increases collagen production and boosts water-retaining molecules. Available over-the-counter and by prescription. Prices vary widely.

Sewon Kang, MD, professor, department of dermatology, University of Michigan Medical Center, Ann Arbor, and leader of a study published in *Archives of Dermatology*.

You Can Look Younger Without Surgery

Barry DiBernardo, MD, a board-certified plastic surgeon and chief of aesthetic surgery program, Mountainside Hospital, Montclair, New Jersey. He is a spokesperson for the American Society for Aesthetic Plastic Surgery, where he is on the nonsurgical procedures committee.

Recently, the science of reducing wrinkles has been transformed by the introduction of remarkable new devices and treatments that don't involve surgery. *Here are the latest developments that could help men and women alike look and feel better if they are concerned about wrinkles...*

•**Digital imaging** machine that provides a computerized analysis of your skin. A device called VISIA, made by Canfield Clinical Systems, uses a computer-aided digital camera to analyze facial skin in minute detail. It gives doctors an unprecedented ability to diagnose skin conditions and monitor the effectiveness of various treatments.

How it works: While the patient's head is immobilized, digital photographs are taken under different types of light to identify the precise location and depth of various skin features, including wrinkles, brown spots, enlarged pores and acne. Ultraviolet light is used to scan for latent sun damage, which will emerge as the patient gets older.

When the analysis is complete, the patient's profile is matched against a database containing thousands of profiles. A percentile score shows how the patient's skin compares with that of people of similar age, gender and skin type. This analysis can then be used to guide doctors in prescribing and administering treatments. On subsequent visits, new digital images are taken to measure how well the skin is responding.

•**Laser treatment** that stimulates skin to renew itself. *Intense pulsed light* (IPL) *photorejuvenation* is becoming the treatment of choice for eliminating fine wrinkles, brown spots, broken capillaries and birthmarks—all without any recovery time.

How it works: This non-invasive treatment produces light pulses at a variety of wavelengths, which penetrate the skin to different depths, depending on the problem being treated (brown spots tend to lie near the surface, for example, while broken capillaries are slightly below). This allows blemishes to be treated precisely without damaging surrounding tissue. Even better, IPL can penetrate below the top layer of skin (epidermis) to stimulate the cells that produce *collagen* and *elastin*—naturally occurring tissues that make skin more firm and elastic, and which we all tend to lose as we get older. IPL photorejuvenation reverses this aging effect, making skin tighter and plumper.

While IPL has been around for a number of years, a newer machine called the Lumenis One (manufactured by Lumenis) represents a significant advance over previous IPL devices. Among other things, its computer has an improved ability to deliver light at exactly the right location. This new device is so good at removing difficult-to-treat blemishes—and rejuvenating the skin—that even longtime patients praise its effectiveness. This treatment is available in most states. To find a practitioner in your area, visit *www.aesthetipedia. com/find-a-center.*

Sessions last approximately 20 minutes. Typically, patients undergo a series of IPL treatments over several weeks, followed by a maintenance treatment every six months. With older IPL technology, treatments lasted 45 minutes, but the maintenance intervals were the same.

Approximate cost: $200 to $500 per treatment.*

• **Radio frequency devices** that use radio frequency to tighten the skin have been available for several years, but a new device called Titan (manufactured by Cutera) represents a big improvement over previous machines—it is safer, more effective and less costly. It is available throughout the US and abroad. Radio frequency devices operate in the infrared range to heat the tissue under the skin surface, causing loose skin and its underlying collagen to contract and tighten. The treatment is effective even on large wrinkles. Since it doesn't remove any layers of skin, there is no flaking or redness following the treatment, eliminating the need for recovery time.

Radio frequency treatment is currently approved by the US Food and Drug Administration (FDA) for use on the forehead and around the eyes. Approval is pending for use on cheek folds and the neck area. A series of treatments may be needed for optimal results. It is not yet known how long results last.

Approximate cost: $550 to $2,500 per treatment, depending on the area covered and the amount of time involved.*

• **Hyaluronic filler** that replaces collagen. Deeper lines can be temporarily eliminated by injecting a filler material into the fat layer directly beneath the depressed area. Until recently, the only filler approved for use in the US was *bovine collagen*, derived from cattle. Collagen injections last approximately three months and require allergy testing before use.

Now Restylane, a hyaluronic acid product, is already available in approximately 60 countries. Since hyaluronic acid occurs naturally in humans, it's nonallergenic, and no skin test is needed. In addition, Restylane injections last much longer than collagen injections—typically up to a year. Many dermatologists and aesthetic

*All prices subject to change.

surgeons now use Restylane exclusively, while others continue to offer both Restylane and collagen.

Approximate cost: $350 to $800 per syringe.*

MULTI-TREATMENT SKIN MAINTENANCE

Taking advantage of the array of new tools described above, many people are now adopting a maintenance program where they see a doctor (either a plastic surgeon, dermatologist or other medical doctor who has been trained to perform aesthetic services) every six months for IPL treatment and Botox® injections, and on every second visit—once a year—they get a Restylane touch-up. Other procedures are done as needed, including radio frequency treatment and *CO_2 laser resurfacing* (which produces more dramatic results than IPL, but also requires recovery time).

The final component of the program is a good home-care regimen—including regular use of sunblock to prevent ultraviolet (UV) damage, as well as products that speed up the turnover of the skin cells.

Bottom line: People who decide to follow this skin rejuvenation program not only have great-looking skin, but also have a less invasive alternative to cosmetic surgery as they get older.

*All prices subject to change.

Skin Care from The Inside Out

Joy Bauer, RD, CDN, author of several nutrition books, including *Joy's LIFE Diet: 4 Steps to Thin Forever* (Collins Living) and *Joy Bauer's Food Cures* (Rodale). Bauer is the nutrition expert for the *Today* show and has a private practice with offices in New York City and Westchester County, New York. *www.joybauer.com*

To take care of their skin, most people reach for sunscreen, lotions and creams to protect, smooth and moisturize. These products can help, but beautiful, healthy skin starts with what goes *into* your body, not what you rub on it. Research shows that good nutrition may reduce the effects of sun damage

…minimize redness and wrinkling…and even protect against some skin cancers.

FIRST STEP: HYDRATE

The single most important nutritional factor for keeping skin healthy is water. Staying hydrated keeps cells plump, making skin look firmer and clearer. When cells are dehydrated, they shrivel and can make your skin look wrinkled. Think of it this way—when you dehydrate a juicy grape, you get a raisin. In addition, water transports nutrients into skin cells and helps flush toxins out of the body.

To stay hydrated, drink whenever you feel thirsty.

Helpful sign: If your urine is pale yellow, you are adequately hydrated—but if it is bright or dark yellow, you may need to boost your fluid intake.

Good news: Drinking unsweetened tea helps keep you hydrated, plus you get the benefit of antioxidant nutrients called *polyphenols*, which may help prevent sun-related skin cancers. Green, white, black and oolong teas provide more polyphenols than herbal teas. It is your choice whether to drink caffeinated or decaffeinated tea. Although caffeine is a mild diuretic (increasing the amount of urine that is passed from the body), the relatively small amount in tea doesn't affect its ability to keep skin hydrated and healthy.

Avoid: Teas sweetened with a lot of sugar—excess sugar can make skin dull and wrinkled.

For extra hydration: Eat "juicy foods" that are at least 75% water by weight—fruits such as apples, berries, cherries, grapes, grapefruit, mangoes, melons, oranges, peaches, plums…and vegetables such as asparagus, beets, carrots, celery, cucumbers and tomatoes.

SKIN-HEALTHY FOODS

Everything we eat is reflected in the health of our skin—for better or for worse. *Among the best nutrients for the skin…*

• **Beta-carotene,** a powerful antioxidant which, once ingested, is converted to vitamin A, a nutrient necessary for skin tissue growth and repair.

Skin-smart: Have at least one serving per day of beta-carotene–rich foods—for instance, orange carrots, sweet potatoes and tomatoes …green arugula, asparagus and spinach…and fruits such as cherries, grapefruit, mangoes and watermelon.

• **Omega-3 fatty acids,** healthful fats that are important building blocks of the membranes that make up cell walls, allowing water and nutrients to enter and keeping out waste and toxins.

Skin-smart: Eat at least three servings of omega-3–rich foods each week—such as wild salmon (farm-raised salmon may have higher levels of potentially dangerous contaminants) …mackerel (not king mackerel, which has too much mercury)…anchovies, herring and sardines. Good fats also are found in smaller amounts in flaxseed, soybeans and walnuts. If you don't eat enough of these omega-3 foods, consider taking daily supplements of fish oil providing 1,000 mg of combined e*icosapentaenoic acid* (EPA) and *docosahexaenoic acid* (DHA), the most biologically active and beneficial components. Look for brands that have been tested for purity, such as VitalOils 1000 (877-342-3721, *www.vitalremedymd.com*) and Ultimate Omega by Nordic Naturals (800-662-2544, *www.nordicnaturals.com*).

• **Selenium,** a mineral with antioxidant activity thought to help skin elasticity (which means you'll look younger longer) and prevent sun-related skin damage and cancers.

Skin-smart: Eat at least one serving a day of a selenium-rich food—canned light tuna (which has less mercury than canned albacore or white tuna), crab, tilapia…whole-wheat breads and pasta…lean beef…chicken and turkey (breast meat is lowest in fat).

Caution: Taking selenium in supplement form may increase the risk for squamous cell skin cancer in people with a personal or family history of the disease. Selenium in food is safe and healthful.

• **Vitamin C,** an antioxidant that helps build collagen and elastin (proteins that comprise the skin's underlying structure)…and also protects against free radicals (molecules in the body that damage cells) when the skin is exposed to sunlight.

Skin-smart: Eat at least one serving a day of any of these vitamin C-rich foods—cantaloupe, citrus fruits, kiwifruit, papaya, pineapple, strawberries, watermelon…and bell peppers, broccoli, brussels sprouts, cabbage, cauliflower, kale and kidney beans.

•**Zinc,** a mineral that helps maintain collagen. People with zinc deficiencies often develop skin redness and lesions.

Skin-smart: Eat at least one serving of a zinc-rich food daily—chicken or turkey breast, crab, lean beef, pork tenderloin (lower in fat than other cuts)…peanuts and peanut butter …fat-free dairy products (cheese, milk and yogurt).

Wise for everyone: A daily multivitamin that contains 100% of the daily value for vitamins A, C, E and zinc and no more than 70 mcg of selenium.

WHAT TO AVOID

•**Sugar.** Research suggests that sugary foods (such as soda and cookies) may contribute to skin blemishes. These "bad carbs" may promote harmful inflammation throughout the body, which can trigger breakouts. Limit your indulgence in sweet treats to no more than one small serving per day.

•**White flour.** Minimize white-flour foods (such as white bread and pasta) in your diet by choosing whole-grain breads and rolls, cereals, crackers and pasta.

•**Dairy foods.** Milk may contain hormones (especially if cows are pregnant) and iodine from iodine-fortified feed. Although uncommon, both of these components can cause pimples. If you are prone to acne, try going off dairy for a while to see if your skin shows signs of improvement.

•**Cigarette smoke,** including secondhand smoke. It fills your body with toxins, inflammation causing irritants and free radicals that damage every cell they touch…and also limits blood flow, so skin cells don't receive the oxygen and nutrients they need.

More from Joy Bauer…

Hair Care from the Inside Out

Foods that are healthy for skin also are healthy for hair. *In addition, hair requires…*

•**Iron-rich protein.** Hair is made primarily of protein. Without enough of it, hair can weaken, grow more slowly or fall out. Iron helps red blood cells carry oxygen throughout the body, including to hair-growth cells. Eat at least one serving per day of protein foods high in iron, such as clams, oysters, shrimp…duck, lamb, lean beef, pork, turkey…eggs…fortified whole-grain breads and cereals…tofu and legumes (beans, peas, etc.).

•**B vitamins.** Folate, biotin, vitamin B-6 and vitamin B-12 are needed to make red blood cells. Without enough of these vitamins, hair follicles can become starved for nutrients and oxygen, and your hair can fall out. Eat two servings a day of foods that contain one or more of these nutrients.

Good choices: Fortified whole-grain breads and cereals…broccoli, leafy dark green vegetables and legumes…eggs and fat-free dairy products…peanut butter…and wild salmon.

Omega-3s Keep Hair Healthy

Hair follicles need nutrient-rich blood. This requires consuming enough essential fatty acids, especially the omega-3s found in flaxseeds and wild-caught, cold-water fish, such as salmon and trout.

Best: Ingest four to six tablespoons of ground flaxseeds per day in yogurt, cereal, smoothies and salads, along with plenty of water. Eat fish at least three times a week.

Susan M. Lark, MD, editor, *Women's Wellness Today,* P.O. Box 3265, Lancaster, Pennsylvania 17604-9916.

The Root Cause Of Hair Loss

Al Sears, MD, adjunct professor, Barry University, and founder and director of Wellness Research Foundation, Wellington, Florida. *www.alsearsmd.com.*

Many women are living with a secret—they're losing their hair. We explain the reason why and what women can do to solve the problem.

In recent years, baldness has become a fashion statement for many men—but it's traumatic for women when they experience hair loss. Is there anything that can be done about it?

To find out, we spoke with Al Sears, MD, an adjunct professor at Barry University in Miami Shores, Florida, and founder and director of the Wellness Research Foundation, an integrative medicine and anti-aging clinic in south Florida. "Hair loss in women is quite common," said Dr. Sears.

HORMONALLY DRIVEN

Dr. Sears explained that baldness in men tends to follow specific patterns, while in women it tends to be more global. We asked him what causes it and if there is a cure. "Female hair loss almost always is hormonally driven," said Dr. Sears. So he generally checks thyroid, progesterone and *dihydrotestosterone* (DHT) levels—the three principal hormonal centers that cause hair loss—all at once.

When checking for thyroid abnormalities, Dr. Sears measures thyroid-stimulating hormone (TSH) as well as T3 and T4. "Low levels of any one of them could be a cause of hair loss," he said, "and if any one of them is low, you have to treat it through a combination of methods, such as changes in diet or nutritional supplements."

OTHER HORMONE CULPRITS

If thyroid hormones are not to blame, then the pattern of hair loss will be a significant clue as to what other hormones might be involved. "If it's male pattern baldness—receding hairline with thinning on the crown—it's probably associated with male hormones such as testosterone and its metabolite DHT, which is thought to be a culprit in baldness," Dr.

Sears explained. Women who have too much of their testosterone metabolized into DHT may experience hair loss, frequently in the familiar male pattern.

If tests show that a woman has high levels of DHT, then you've identified a likely cause of her thinning hair. High DHT can be treated with the same kinds of herbal remedies that have been found to be helpful in men. Saw palmetto (320 mg per day) along with pumpkin seed and pygeum, a popular herbal supplement made from the bark of a tall evergreen tree and frequently used to treat benign conditions in the prostate, are used most often to "discourage" the production of DHT from testosterone.

Beta-sitosterol, a plant sterol, also works synergistically with the saw palmetto, pumpkin and pygeum by decreasing the negative impact of the hormones. Saw palmetto formulas are widely available over the counter and are extremely safe and effective. If DHT is very high, Dr. Sears uses the drug *finasteride* (Proscar, Propecia). Proscar prevents the conversion of testosterone to DHT. Proscar is most commonly used with men but is frequently used with women as well.

Note: Women who are pregnant should not take Propecia.

MAJORITY RULES: PROGESTERONE

"I'm convinced that most hair loss in women is due to low levels of progesterone," Dr. Sears said, "because progesterone fights the effects of DHT. If a woman's DHT is normal but her progesterone is low, then even that normal level of DHT will be too much for her. She doesn't have enough progesterone to counter its effects.

"If your hair loss occurred after pregnancy, for example," he said, "it's most likely that progesterone is the culprit. Progesterone goes up like crazy during pregnancy and then frequently drops like a rock afterward. Though there's no positive research on this yet, I'm confident that low progesterone is the number one cause of hair loss that occurs after pregnancy."

HIGH INCIDENCE OF LOW PROGESTERONE

In fact, Dr. Sears believes low progesterone is very common. In his clinic, 75% of the women he measures have low progesterone levels. We asked him to speculate as to why this might be so. Though he cautioned us that what he was about to say was still only a theory, it turned out to be a theory we have heard from some very smart doctors in alternative and integrative medicine many times over the last few years.

"We have in our environment," said Dr. Sears, "estrogen-mimicking compounds. The air we breathe, the water we drink, all contain leaks from plastics and industrial solvents in the environment that literally mimic the effects of estrogen in the system. The food we eat is filled with estrogens. When I was a kid in Kentucky, it used to take one year for a chicken to mature enough to go to market. Now it takes 12 weeks. These chickens are 'steroid puff balls.' They're fed estrogens to fatten them up more quickly, and all these estrogens—plus estrogen mimickers from the environment—get into our system."

"When you have so much estrogen and estrogen mimickers, the body tries to cut back on its own production, so it decreases the production of two hormones that regulate estrogen production—*luteinizing hormone* (LH) and follicle-stimulating hormone. The problem is, those two hormones control both estrogen and progesterone. So when the body lowers production of them, it lowers estrogen production. When it turns down estrogen production, it also turns down progesterone production. The result? Plenty of estrogen but very little progesterone. These women are what we call 'estrogen dominant.'"

Dr. Sears explained that although some doctors measure progesterone with blood tests, it is more effective to measure it with a 24-hour urine test. Unfortunately, many conventional doctors don't bother to measure progesterone levels, even when they put women on hormone-replacement therapy.

Important: Progesterone cream is available by prescription from a compounding pharmacy but should not be used without professional guidance.

Best: Dr. Sears recommends the "natural" bio-identical kind.

"Progesterone supplementation provides a very slow-acting solution to hair loss. It has its effects over months and years. But it *will* rebuild the follicle and the mechanisms regulating its function, and the situation can be corrected."

Getting Rid of Unwanted Hair

David J. Goldberg, MD, clinical professor and director of laser research, department of dermatology, Mount Sinai School of Medicine, New York City. He is director of Skin Laser & Surgery Specialists of New York & New Jersey, in New York City, Boston, Hackensack and Hillsborough, New Jersey and Boca Raton, Florida.

When my patients say they are tired of tweezing and other temporary fixes for unwanted facial or body hair, I suggest these permanent solutions…

• **Laser hair removal** uses a special pulsed light. *Melanin* (pigment) in hair strands absorbs the light, heating up and destroying hair follicles.

Pros: Discomfort is minimal—each pulse feels like the snap of a rubber band—so it's excellent for sensitive areas, such as the upper lip and between the eyes. One pulse treats an area from the size of a dime to a silver dollar. Laser works best on brown or black hairs.

Cons: White, gray or blond hairs may not absorb enough laser light to destroy the follicle. Laser cannot be used on eyebrows because the light could damage eyes. In very rare cases, laser can cause scarring of the treated skin.

Where to go: Laser hair removal is best done by a cosmetic dermatologist.

What to ask: "Do you have more than one laser machine?" Different lasers are needed for dark skin and for light skin.

Approximate cost: $200 or more per laser treatment.*

• **Electrolysis** uses a handheld instrument to deliver an electrical current that destroys follicles one by one.

Pros: Electrolysis can be used almost anywhere on the body, including eyebrows (though

*All prices subject to change.

brows may require 10 or more sessions). It works on all hair colors.

Cons: Each zap creates a burning sensation (nonprescription numbing cream can help). Numerous zaps may be needed per follicle. Only small areas are treated at each visit. Uncommon side effects include scarring and discoloration.

Where to go: Many spas and salons offer electrolysis. Choose an electrologist who belongs to the American Electrology Association (*www.electrology.com*).

Approximate cost: $25 to $250 per electrolysis session.*

*Price subject to change.

Reverse Gray Hair With Hormones

Genetics generally determine if and when hair turns gray, and nothing can alter that. However, studies suggest that graying is occasionally linked to an under- or overactive thyroid gland, pernicious anemia (due to impaired absorption of the vitamin B-12 necessary to produce red blood cells), smoking or extreme stress.

Treating the underlying problem may slow the graying process.

For a few of my female patients who had just begun to go gray, new hair growth resumed its normal color when they used hormone-balancing treatments, such as over-the-counter homeopathic *Sepia*...and/or prescription bioidentical (natural) estrogen and progesterone hormone replacement.

Note: These therapies would not be appropriate for men, and should be used by women only when a hormonal deficiency has been officially diagnosed and only under a doctor's supervision.

Mark A. Stengler, NMD, licensed naturopathic medical doctor in private practice, Encinitas, California... adjunct associate clinical professor at the National College of Natural Medicine, Portland, Oregon...author of *The Natural Physician's Healing Therapies* and co-author of *Prescription for Natural Cures* (both from Bottom Line Books).

Gray Hair Alert

Drugs may cause hair to turn gray. People with substance abuse problems are twice as likely to prematurely gray as people who do not overindulge. Along with illegal drugs, alcohol can damage the production of melanocytes, the cells that give hair its color.

Stuart Reece, MD, University of Queensland Medical School, Brisbane, Australia, and leader of a study of the effect of drug consumption on hair color, published in *Archives of Dermatology.*

Hair-Dye Danger

Women who color their hair have a 50% to 70% higher risk of developing non-Hodgkin's lymphoma, compared with women who go natural. The cancer may be linked to a chemical called paraphenylenediamine (PPD).

Alternative: Shiseido Re:nual Serum. To find a distributor, go to *www.joico.com*.

Yawei Zhang, MD, PhD, associate professor, division of environmental health sciences, Yale School of Public Health, New Haven, Connecticut, and author of a study, published in *American Journal of Epidemiology.*

Lead in Lipsticks

Many lipsticks contain lead. Of 33 tested, 20 had measurable lead levels. Lead is a neurotoxin that builds up in the body over time. It can cause memory and concentration problems, miscarriage in pregnant women and lowered IQ and behavioral problems in children.

Stacy Malkan, cofounder, Campaign for Safe Cosmetics (*www.safecosmetics.org*), a national coalition of health and environmental groups working to eliminate toxic chemicals from personal-care products, San Francisco.

Makeup Without Risky Chemicals

Find out which cosmetics have chemicals linked to cancer, allergies or other harmful substances.

You can browse lists of lipsticks, nail polishes, etc., and sort the lists by product name or level of hazard, or search for a specific manufacturer, ingredient or product. The site also maintains databases on baby-care and oral-care products. Visit Environmental Working Group's Skin Deep database at *www.ewg.org* for these features or to join the Campaign for Safe Cosmetics.

Money, Time & Life Building, Rockefeller Center, New York City 10020.

Is It Safe to Apply Bug Repellent and Sunscreen At the Same Time?

Recent research advises against that practice. Researchers recently applied sunscreen containing oxybenzone (an organic compound that absorbs UVA rays) plus an insect repellent spray containing the chemical DEET to human skin samples.

Result: With this combination, the skin absorption rate was unnecessarily increased—specifically, threefold for oxybenzone and elevenfold for DEET.

Theory: Oxybenzone and DEET work in combination to enhance skin absorption of these substances.

Research is under way on the effects of combining other sunscreen ingredients with non-DEET bug repellents.

Self-defense: After you apply a sunscreen containing oxybenzone, wait at least 30 minutes before using an insect repellent containing DEET.

Caution: Never apply a DEET repellent before a sunscreen containing oxybenzone...

and do not use combination products containing both of these substances.

Xiaochen Gu, PhD, associate professor of pharmacy, Faculty of Pharmacy, University of Manitoba, Winnipeg, Canada.

Sunscreen vs. Sunblock

Sunscreen and sunblock are not the same. Sunblock, which is opaque, blocks almost all of the sun's UVA and UVB rays. It consists largely of zinc oxide and titanium dioxide. Sunblock does not have to be reapplied every few hours. Sunscreens are less visible on the skin and are designed to protect against UVA, UVB or both types of ultraviolet rays. However, they do allow some radiation through and need to be reapplied every few hours, because their ingredients break down after exposure to sunlight. If you use sunscreen, choose one with a high SPF, apply generously and reapply every two to three hours.

*Kenneth A. Arndt, MD, clinical professor of dermatology, Harvard Medical School, Boston, and editor of the report "Skin Care and Repair," published by *Harvard Health Publications*.*

More from Dr. Kenneth A. Arndt...

Hope for Sun-Damaged Skin

Topical retinoids (creams and gels containing chemicals derived from vitamin A) first developed to treat acne and psoriasis have proved effective at repairing skin—beyond improving appearance—that's been damaged by long sun exposure.

How they work: Topical retinoids lighten freckles and spots and improve skin's appearance. They also increase collagen production to help make small wrinkles disappear. Retinoids improve the quality of skin growth and decrease the number of atypical skin cells.

Topical retinoids are a prescription drug, so consult your doctor. They are safe for everyone (except during pregnancy), but may cause skin irritation.

A Non-Prescription Solution to Raised Scars

Try flattening a raised scar with a soft silicone gel sheet, which looks like plastic food wrap and is sold at most drugstores and online.

Recommended: Epi-Derm is affordable ($45 for a 4.7- by-5.7-inch sheet, 800-322-3729, *www. biodermis.com*) and easy to apply. The sheet lets oxygen in but keeps excess moisture out, providing a good healing environment.

Cut the sheet slightly larger than the scar, and press the tacky side onto skin. It should be worn for at least 12 hours and preferably 24 hours per day. Remove the sheet once a day to clean it.

Each sheet lasts about 10 to 15 days. Within two months, you should see improvement.

James Spencer, MD, spokesperson for the American Academy of Dermatology and director of the Spencer Dermatology & Skin Surgery Center, St. Petersburg, Florida.

More from Dr. James Spencer...

Cream for Dark Scars

A hydroquinone cream, such as Esotérica or Melquin HP, helps to lighten scars that are darker than the rest of your skin by decreasing formation of the skin pigment melanin.

A 2% formulation is sold over the counter... a stronger 4% formulation is readily available by prescription. Apply hydroquinone cream to the scar twice daily.

Important: Do not exceed the recommended amount—in animal studies, very high dosages have been linked to skin disfiguration and kidney and liver tumors. Do not use hydroquinone in the same area where you use topical skin medications containing *benzoyl peroxide* or *hydrogen peroxide*—the combination can discolor skin. Minimize sun exposure, or dark spots may return. Do not use hydroquinone during pregnancy—it may adversely affect the fetus.

Birthmark Danger

If a birthmark is getting darker, you should have a dermatologist look at it. Any change in anything on your skin could be an early sign of a serious type of skin cancer called melanoma. The five characteristics to watch for are referred to as ABCDE—Asymmetry, Border irregularity, Color, Diameter and Elevation. See a dermatologist even if a change is not on the official ABCDE list—for example, a change in sensation, in which something that has never bothered you before begins to itch or hurt.

Barney Kenet, MD, dermatologist specializing in skin cancer, New York City, and cofounder, American Melanoma Foundation.

Summer Skin Protection

Mark A. Stengler, NMD, licensed naturopathic medical doctor in private practice, Encinitas, California... adjunct associate clinical professor at the National College of Natural Medicine, Portland, Oregon...author of *The Natural Physician's Healing Therapies* and coauthor of *Prescription for Natural Cures* (both from Bottom Line Books).

For years, dermatologists have advised us to limit our sun exposure and cover our skin with sunscreen, clothing and protective gear, such as hats. However, some people are terrified of exposing their skin to sunlight —even for only a few minutes. This can be a major problem, since sunlight activates the formation of vitamin D.

THE IMPORTANCE OF VITAMIN D

Most people associate vitamin D with healthy bones, because it aids the absorption of bone-building calcium. However, researchers recently have also discovered that vitamin D plays a key role in preventing a wide range of serious diseases, including many types of cancer (most notably lung, colon, breast and prostate), diabetes, multiple sclerosis and asthma.

Vitamin D actually functions as a hormone in the body. While all other vitamins are used for normal growth and metabolism, vitamin D acts as a chemical messenger from one cell to

343

another. Many cells in the body have vitamin D receptors, which influence the behavior of genes that affect cell replication, immunity and bone development. These vitamin D receptors are controlled by a single gene, known as the vitamin D receptor gene, or VDR gene. Researchers have found that this gene is defective in many people, which prevents their cells from using vitamin D efficiently.

When this genetic defect is combined with a vitamin D deficiency resulting from a lack of sun exposure or a poor diet, there is cause for even more concern. Researchers have found that vitamin D deficiency is more prevalent than was once thought. A study by Harvard Medical School found that vitamin D deficiencies were common among a group of 290 patients hospitalized for a variety of disorders, including hypertension and diabetes. Fifty-seven percent were considered deficient, and 22% were "severely" deficient as measured by vitamin D levels in the blood.

The current federal guideline for an adequate intake of vitamin D is 200 international units (IU) daily through age 50…400 IU daily for those ages 51 to 70…and 600 IU after age 70. Most nutrition-oriented doctors like myself believe that these recommended levels are too low. Instead, I encourage all adults to get 800 IU to 1,000 IU of vitamin D daily.

SUNSCREEN: FRIEND OR FOE?

While sunscreens help prevent sunburn and skin damage, they also block the ultraviolet (UV) rays that are needed for the production of vitamin D. The human body can produce 10,000 IU to 12,000 IU of vitamin D from 30 minutes of sun exposure during summertime, when the sun's rays are most intense. Sunscreen interferes with this process. For adequate vitamin D production, aim for 10 to 15 minutes of sun exposure without sunscreen daily. (The sun-derived form of vitamin D never causes toxicity. When taken in doses above 2,000 IU daily, the supplement form can cause headaches, weight loss and kidney stones.)

Sun protection factor (SPF) is one of the most misunderstood issues related to sunscreen. SPF numbers range from 2 to 50 and higher. These numbers refer to the sunscreen's ability to deflect the sun's burning rays. The SPF rating is calculated by comparing the amount of time that's needed to produce sunburn on sunscreen-protected skin with the amount of time needed to cause sunburn on unprotected skin.

For example, if a fair-skinned person who develops red skin after 20 minutes of sun exposure uses a sunscreen with an SPF of 3, he/she could stay in the sun three times as long—for 60 minutes—before skin redness would begin to occur. With an SPF of 10, it would take 10 times longer to burn, or 200 minutes (although sunscreen should be reapplied at least every two hours). What most people don't realize is that sun protection does not increase proportionately in products with an SPF above 15. For example, an SPF of 2 provides 50% deflection, an SPF of 15 provides 93% deflection and an SPF of 30 provides 97% deflection.

The American Academy of Dermatology recommends the use of sunscreen year-round for people of all skin types if they are going to be in the sun for more than 20 minutes. Contrary to what many believe, sunscreen *should* be used on cloudy days—80% of the sun's UV rays pass through the clouds.

Sun exposure occurs all the time, even while you're taking a short walk on a cloudy day. Sunscreen should be applied liberally to exposed, dry skin 15 to 30 minutes before going outdoors. Areas that are most vulnerable to the sun, including the face, ears, upper chest, hands, arms—and even the fingernails—should be covered evenly with sunscreen.

Regardless of your skin type, use a sunscreen with an SPF of 15 or higher. Also, protect your lips by using a lip balm that contains sunscreen with an SPF of 15 or higher. No matter what the SPF is, sunscreen should be reapplied every two hours as well as after swimming or perspiring heavily.

Even so-called water-resistant sunscreens may lose effectiveness after 80 minutes in the water. Sunscreens also rub off, so if you've towel-dried, reapply waterproof sunscreen. In addition to using sunscreen, if you are prone to sunburn, avoid spending more than 20 minutes outside during "peak" sunlight hours—between 10 am to 4 pm—when the sun's rays are the strongest.

SUNSCREENS ARE NOT FOOLPROOF

The two types of UV light that we are exposed to are classified according to their wavelengths. UVA, which has a longer wavelength, accounts for up to 95% of the solar UV radiation reaching the Earth's surface and can penetrate clouds and glass. UVA also can penetrate the deeper layers of the skin, and it plays a major role in skin aging and wrinkling. Recent studies strongly suggest that it also may promote the development of skin cancers. UVB causes skin tanning, burning and aging of the skin and triggers the development of skin cancers. It does not penetrate glass but does penetrate clouds and superficial skin layers.

For years, people have assumed that sunscreen not only prevents sunburn, but also skin cancer, particularly melanoma. However, sunscreen is not an absolute safeguard against this deadly disease. According to the Centers for Disease Control and Prevention, the death rate from melanoma in the US has increased by about 4% a year since 1973. Melanoma represents about 47,000 of the 1.8 million cases of skin cancer diagnosed each year. According to the American Cancer Society, it causes 79% of skin cancer deaths.

Sunscreens mainly block UVB wavelengths. Most sunscreens don't *fully* protect skin from UVA wavelengths, and this may be a primary reason why deadly melanoma and other skin cancers are on the rise among sunscreen users. The SPF number on sunscreens provides only the products' UVB ray screening ability.

There is no FDA-approved rating system that identifies UVA protection, and sunscreen manufacturers still need to develop sunscreens that guarantee UVA protection. The only sunscreens that offer both UVA and UVB protection are "broad-spectrum" formulas, especially those containing *zinc oxide* or *titanium dioxide*, but even with these products, there is no accepted rating of the UVA protection they provide.

Researchers at Queensland Institute for Medical Research in Brisbane, Australia, tracked 1,383 adults for four-and-a-half years. They reported that normal UVB-protecting sunscreen reduces risk for squamous cell carcinoma (the second most common skin cancer —it spreads quickly and is mainly found on the face and ears) by 40%. Using sunscreen did not reduce risk of melanoma or basal cell carcinoma (the most common type of skin cancer—it is slow to spread and generally appears as a nodule-like lesion that develops on the head, including the scalp, or neck).

In addition, some sunscreens contain potentially dangerous ingredients, such as parabens, which mimic estrogen in the body. Excessive levels of this hormone have been linked to some breast malignancies.

Sunscreen I recommend most often…

• **Mineral Sunscreen Broad Spectrum SPF 30** blocks UVA and UVB rays without parabens or harmful chemicals. It is made by JASON Natural Cosmetics (888-659-7730, *www. jason-natural.com*). A four-ounce tube costs $9 at most health food stores.

Cold-Weather Skin Care

Brandith Irwin, MD, a board-certified dermatologist and internist, and director of the Madison Skin & Laser Center in Seattle. She has been a guest medical expert on *The Oprah Winfrey Show* and is author of *The Surgery-Free Makeover* (Da Capo).

Winter is lizard-skin season—when skin turns dry, scaly, itchy and flaky. But don't blame the cold weather.

Real culprits: Low humidity outdoors…and dry, heated air indoors, which draws moisture out of the inner layers of skin. In addition, normal shedding of skin cells slows with age because cells become less active. As a result, you end up with visible layers of dead, scaly skin. *What helps…*

• **Shorten your shower.** Though it seems counterintuitive, excess water dries out skin by breaking down its natural oils. The hotter the water, the worse it is.

Best: Use lukewarm water, and limit showers to no more than five minutes.

• **Take an Epsom salt bath.** Epsom salts contain magnesium, which helps slough off dead skin cells. Once or twice a week, add one to two cups of Epsom salts to a tubful of luke-warm water and soak for 10 to 15 minutes.

• **Use cleansing lotion, not soap.** Soap is alkaline and can strip skin of moisture.

For face and body: Try Cetaphil Gentle Skin Cleanser or Purpose Gentle Cleansing Wash.

• **Exfoliate—gently.** Use a loofah in the shower or bath to manually remove dead skin cells from your body.

Note: Allow the loofah to dry completely after each use to minimize bacteria.

Recommended: On your face, use a mildly abrasive exfoliating cream for all skin types, such as Dermalogica Daily Microfoliant (800-345-2761, *www.dermalogica.com*).

Best: I recommend exfoliating no more than twice every week to avoid irritating the skin.

• **Slather on a body moisturizer with a high oil-to-water ratio.** Choose a brand for all skin types that feels rich and slick.

Recommended: Éminence Honeydew Body Lotion (888-747-6342, *www.eminenceorganics.com*). Apply liberally while skin is still damp from your shower or bath.

Helpful: Reapply the lotion at least once more per day, first dampening skin with a wet washcloth.

• **Spritz your face with water.** Do this be-fore applying makeup and again before bed. Follow with moisturizer, such as Cetaphil Daily Facial Moisturizer.

• **Avoid irritating laundry products.** Use detergent that has no bleach or fragrances, such as All Free or Cheer Free.

Important: Never use dryer sheets—even the unscented ones leave tiny irritating fibers on clothes.

Tender Care for Healthier, Lovelier Lips

Margaret E. Parsons, MD, assistant clinical professor of dermatology at University of California, Davis, and a der-matologist in private practice in Sacramento, California.

Chapped, irritated lips look bad and feel worse. You lick them for relief—but that only exacerbates the problem because saliva evaporates quickly, leaving lips even drier than before. *For supple lips…*

• **Lock in moisture.** Apply a protective layer of lip balm or lipstick that contains sunscreen with SPF 15 or higher…reapply often, espe-cially outdoors. Before bed, grease up with petroleum jelly—especially if you take an-tihistamines (which dry you out) or mouth-breathe due to a stuffy nose.

• **Avoid plumpers.** Products that promise a fashionably full, pouty mouth are irritants—literally—that work by causing lips to swell. Plumpers contain *capsaicin* (from chili pep-pers), mint or menthol, which cause reactions ranging from mild to painful.

Best: Skip plumpers, and stick to lip prod-ucts with the shortest ingredient lists, which are least likely to contain irritating additives.

• **Beware of unfriendly foods.** Citrus fruits and spicy foods make chapped lips sting or burn and worsen irritation. Peel mangoes be-fore eating—the cut edges of mango skin re-lease a chemical also found in poison ivy.

• **Keep facial products away from lips.** When used too near the mouth, topical acne products with *benzoyl peroxide* and anti-wrinkle creams with retinoids or alpha hy-droxy acids cause chapping.

• **Combat cold sores.** Sun exposure and dry-ness can trigger flare-ups of the herpes simplex virus that causes cold sores.

To treat: Prescription oral medication, such as *acyclovir* (Zovirax) or *valacyclovir* (Valtrex), speeds healing. Some people say that supple-menting with the amino acid *lysine* heals cold sores—and though not proven to be effective, lysine generally is safe, so there is no harm in trying it if you want to.

Soothing: Apply a dab of a product that contains petroleum jelly plus mineral oil, such as Aquaphor.

Poison Ivy Survival Guide: How to Treat It Now—And Avoid It in the Future

Chris Meletis, ND, a naturopathic physician in Beaverton, Oregon, and executive director, the Institute for Healthy Aging.

Andrew L. Rubman, ND, director, Southbury Clinic for Traditional Medicines, Southbury, Connecticut

---

Beware of poison ivy—it's not just a summer problem and you don't even have to touch it directly to get it. In most people, poison ivy shows up as a rash consisting of small bumps, blisters or swelling. The rash might appear in streaks, reflecting how you brushed by the plant or its oil, called urushiol. Unfortunately, for some people who are highly sensitive to it, even limited exposure results in a full body breakout, as the toxins get deep into their system. Mainstream doctors tend to prescribe repeated doses of prednisone to ease the inflammation…but even prednisone doesn't always prevent new skin eruptions, since it doesn't stop immune system activity. How to minimize the misery—offer systemic support and quiet the histamine response—when suffering from poison ivy?

According to Chris Meletis, ND, a naturopathic physician in Beaverton, Oregon, and executive director for the Institute for Healthy Aging, about 85% of people develop an urushiol allergy, though older adults tend to be more resistant. However, about 10% of people get particularly nasty reactions to it—people whose skin is especially thin, if their skin is more reactive in general or if they have any kind of abrasions on their skin. Such people also tend to be the ones whose rash lasts longer than it does in others. The rash itself isn't dangerous, but given the amount of discomfort it causes, the challenge is to find how to treat it so that it becomes more bearable.

WASH FAST AND THOROUGHLY

Dr. Meletis says to take immediate action if you know you have come in contact with poison ivy. Wash the affected area thoroughly and as soon as possible to remove all traces of urushiol from your skin.

Take care before you wash or shower that you don't cross-contaminate by touching the affected area and then another part of your body. Should you get urushiol on your hands, any other place on your body that you touched with them—including your face or even your eyes if you rubbed them—will break out. The palms of the hands and the soles of the feet, where skin is thick, are usually spared. Use mild soap and cool water to wash and wash and wash, he says, because hot water can aggravate the rash and spread the irritants that contribute to the spread of the rash.

But, if like many people, you weren't aware of the contact and so didn't wash the urushiol off in time, you will need to prepare for battle. *Dr. Meletis recommends adding the following to your medicine chest to use for the duration (follow label directions carefully)…*

●**Hydrocortisone cream**—a number of brands are available in your drugstore.

●**Calamine lotion**—the pink stuff used for chicken pox before vaccination was available.

●**Antihistamine**—anything with Benadryl (*diphenhydramine*), such as Tylenol PM, will do, but be warned that Benadryl causes sleepiness.

●**Cool-water oatmeal baths**—Aveeno and similar products are good…or make your own by mixing a cup of oatmeal with three cups of cold water and adding it to the bath.

●**Calendula salve**—an ancient remedy made from marigolds, is excellent for poison ivy and also other kinds of skin irritation, including sunburn.

●**Rhus tox** (a homeopathic preparation, Rhus toxicodendron)—talk to a trained professional about proper dose…but you can also use over-the-counter poison ivy homeopathics.

●**Whole-milk compress.** Use whole milk, not skim. It is the fat in the milk that brings relief.

DEEP-SEATED POISON IVY

Although rare, it is possible to have a "super-sized" case of poison ivy. In these instances, the rash goes deep into the tissue, is resistant to ordinary treatments and hangs on, making the afflicted person miserable sometimes for several months. Who is vulnerable to severe cases and what should he/she do? Dr. Andrew L. Rubman, ND, director of the Southbury Clinic for Traditional Medicines in Southbury, Connecticut, explains that some people are simply more sensitive to poison ivy. Those who are immune-compromised or who are taking medications that compromise the digestive process, including proton pump inhibitors, beta blockers and chemotherapy drugs, are more susceptible.

Since the inflammatory response is at the core of severe poison ivy reactions, Dr. Rubman says that strengthening the digestive system will help reduce the allergic reaction. But poison ivy doesn't come in through food, right? True. However, healthy digestion removes many inflammation inducers and prevents others that are in foods from entering the tissues. This in turn may help prevent the poison ivy response from triggering the deep tissue reaction that is seen in severe cases. The treatment challenge, he says, is to limit the inflammatory response while at the same time build up the body's ability to fight off the poison ivy "infestation." This requires natural anti-inflammatory medications, including leukotriene mediators such as beta-carotene and fish oils that help the tissues regenerate and strengthen. However, Dr. Rubman cautions that this is too complex to do on your own and requires the supervision of a knowledgeable naturopathic physician or other health-care professional trained in these areas.

The urge to scratch poison ivy is great, and many people give in. Scratching doesn't spread the rash further, but it can cause a different problem—bacterial infection. Should a fever of more than 100 degrees develop or the blisters start to ooze pus instead of blister fluid, call the doctor, who will probably start you on a course of antibiotics.

PREVENTION IS EVERYTHING

Clearly the best way to handle poison ivy, so to speak, is to avoid any contact with it. That includes your clothes and other objects as well.

Even if you don't touch the plant, but your clothes do, you can still get infected later when removing your clothes. You can even get poison ivy from your pet after he/she romps outside. So be alert. For people who have poison ivy on their property, clear it by wearing gloves and protective clothing and wash all items, along with any garden tools, you used right away, preferably in old-fashioned brown lye soap. If you can't wash immediately, put the contaminated items in plastic bags or sealed containers to prevent cross-contamination of other clothes. Urushiol can remain active for years, including on that jacket in your closet. Never burn poison ivy—burning the plant releases urushiol into the air, where it can be carried by the smoke and cause a skin reaction or lung irritation.

And, a word of warning…poison ivy knows no seasons. You can still get it in the winter if you come into contact with the vine or plant.

The Health Benefits Of a Sauna

Mark A. Stengler, NMD, licensed naturopathic medical doctor in private practice, Encinitas, California… adjunct associate clinical professor at the National College of Natural Medicine, Portland, Oregon…author of *The Natural Physician's Healing Therapies* and co-author of *Prescription for Natural Cures* (both from Bottom Line Books).

Saunas are an excellent way to increase circulation and eliminate toxins from the bloodstream and fatty tissues through sweating. Saunas may alleviate nasal congestion, clear the complexion, ease muscle soreness and promote relaxation. For maximum benefit, exercise for 30 minutes beforehand to stimulate circulation of the blood and *lymph* (fluid that carries infection-fighting cells via the lymphatic vessels).

A traditional *European-style sauna* produces dry heat followed by wet heat (as water is splashed on hot rocks or a stove to create

steam). An *electric sauna* provides dry heat. A *steam room* creates intense moist heat.

A newcomer on the sauna scene is the *infrared sauna*—which uses infrared radiation to heat the skin without warming the air. Which is best? It's a matter of personal preference—they all do the job.

A sauna can feel wonderful—but precautions should be followed. Check with a physician before beginning sauna treatments if you have high blood pressure, heart disease, diabetes or any other chronic health problem …are pregnant…or are under age 13. Do not visit the steam room or sauna if you're not feeling well or have been drinking alcohol. Leave the sauna at once if you begin to feel nauseated or dizzy.

Even a short sauna session can result in significant fluid loss, so drink 12 to 24 ounces of water before and afterward, and sip water while inside.

Helpful: Sports drinks or electrolyte-replacing bottled waters (sold at grocery and health-food stores) replenish sodium and potassium lost through perspiration.

As a general rule, I recommend spending no more than 10 to 15 minutes in the steam room…20 to 30 minutes in the European or electric sauna…or 25 to 30 minutes in the infrared sauna. Aim for one or two sessions weekly to detoxify, relax and rejuvenate.

Love Your Looks…No Matter What Your Age

Pamela D. Blair, PhD, holistic psychotherapist in private practice, life coach and motivational speaker in Hawthorne, New York and Wilton, Connecticut. She coordinated the Institute for Spiritual Development at Wainwright House, a learning center in Rye, New York. *www.pamblair.com*

Do you catch your reflection in a mirror and feel shock when you see an "old woman" gazing back, because inside you still feel so young?

Coping with our changing appearance requires looking inward. Coming to rely on who we are rather than what we look like yields profound confidence, strength and self-assurance that often elude younger people.

Paradoxically, self-knowledge creates a magnetism that also is deeply attractive. *To nourish healthy self-acceptance…*

• **Savor each day.** Perhaps more than any other quality, being able to take pleasure in life makes a woman beautiful.

• **Pay attention to your senses.** Really taste the food you eat. Feel the fresh air on your skin as you walk outdoors. Relish the touch of a loved one. Some attractive qualities we tend to associate with youth—eagerness, curiosity, openness—can become stronger with age if we take time to appreciate the world around us.

• **Reexamine your goals.** Does your life now reflect your true values? Or are you investing time in relationships that are no longer fulfilling …activities that are no longer interesting… surroundings that no longer meet your needs?

Each morning, try this affirmation exercise. Say, "I am a woman who…" 10 times, and finish the sentence with a different ending each time, specifying goals you are striving for.

Examples: "I am a woman who is free of back pain…likes a gentle, relaxed pace to her life…has all the financial rewards she wants and needs…takes pleasure in her work."

After several weeks, notice what has shifted in your life. Even if these dreams have not yet come true for you, the power of positive thought can help bring about profound changes in the choices you make and in the way you live.

Example: If I am a woman who is free of back pain, I will choose not to lift that heavy box, and I will ask for help instead. I will choose not to skip yoga class. I will take actions that support who I want to be.

• **Reclaim beauty.** We all know that the media promotes an impossible standard of beauty. A recent study at the University of Missouri-Columbia found that women felt worse about their bodies after viewing photos of models in ads.

We do not need to accept the media's definition of beauty. I've stopped reading magazines that show only young, implausibly perfect models in their articles and ads. These pictures are not real. My former husband was an art director for a major fashion magazine, so I often saw the "before" photos of models with wrinkles, crooked noses and large hips —all of which were airbrushed away.

I am learning to be proud of my wrinkles. They represent laughter, conversation, concern for others and the hard work to become a good writer, mother, therapist, gardener. They are symbols of a beautiful life.

Find role models who exemplify a more enlightened beauty. My idol is the actress Tyne Daly—a little overweight, gray-haired, strong-willed, absolutely beautiful and unapologetically not "young." Many European actresses, such as Helen Mirren and Judi Dench, proudly look their age and remain elegant and desirable. I enjoy watching their films and reading about their personal and professional successes. If they can pursue their dreams and not be ashamed of their aging faces, then so can I.

• **Revisit your beauty rituals.** Valuing inner beauty doesn't mean ignoring your appearance. Decide which maintenance routines are worth keeping and which ones you can let go. By fighting the aging process a little less, you gain time and energy that you can put into other fulfilling pursuits. You also will become more relaxed, which is an attractive quality.

Example: I get manicures and pedicures because they make me feel pampered and cared for. They are a source of energy for me, rather than an energy drain. On the other hand, this past year I chose to stop dying my hair. I have gained many hours, and my skin looks better, too—the natural gray provides a softer contrast than the dyed color did. My choice wouldn't work for everyone. Someone who loves dying her hair should keep doing it.

Also experiment with new styles and products that acknowledge your changing body.

Helpful: Make an appointment with an image consultant to find out which clothing styles and colors complement your skin, hair and body shape now. Find a consultant through the Association of Image Consultants International (651-290-7468, *www.aici.org*).

Cost: $75 to $350 per hour, depending on your location and the extent of services provided.

Alternative: Get a free makeover at a department store cosmetics counter.

Example: I learned to switch to a lighter-consistency foundation and to stop using powder, which can emphasize imperfections in skin. My image consultant also suggested V-necklines to draw attention away from my filled-out chin…and pants that drop gently from my wider hips. I look and feel more elegant.

• **Pace yourself to allow for physical changes.** Your strength may be slightly less, your reaction time a bit longer. I have been doing Pilates exercises, which have increased my muscle strength, bone density and energy as well as decreased my arthritis pain.

• **Increase your serenity by taking a meditative approach.** Before you start your day, sit quietly and visualize what you need to accomplish that day. Pick no more than three major tasks, and go about them with full attention.

Once you've completed those tasks, you can add one or two more. Notice how much calmer and more graceful you feel than when you race around trying to cross 20 items off your to-do list yet give them all short shrift. Enjoy the alertness that comes from being fully present with one task at a time. Your increasing serenity will radiate outward, assuredly making you feel and look more beautiful.

12

Aging Gracefully

The Science of Staying Young

If someone asked you to predict how long you will live, chances are you would base your answer, in part, on the life span of your parents. Undoubtedly, genetics do play a powerful role in longevity.

What you may not realize: Anywhere from 50% to 80% of a person's longevity is determined by factors within our control.

Even though you may be surprised to learn that the lifestyle choices you make each day have such a profound impact on how long you live, there is a simple principle to keep in mind if you want to extend your life span.

How to live as long as possible: Improve the health of the cells in your body. With each decade we live, our cells divide less rapidly. This slowdown is associated with declines in muscle mass and bone strength and with the onset of chronic diseases, such as heart disease.

We can't stop this process altogether, but we can slow the rate at which it occurs. Research shows that by eating a healthful diet, exercising regularly, avoiding dangerous behaviors (such as smoking) and taking certain steps to protect general health, many people could add a decade or even more to their lives.

Specific actions that can give you a longer —and healthier—life...

1. Keep your balance. Falling is among the strongest predictors of premature disability and death. Most falls are due to impaired balance, which is caused by declines in muscle strength, decreased flexibility and nerve degeneration.

Try the dance test: To assess a patient's balance, I dance with him/her in my office. If the

John E. Morley, MD, Dammert Professor of Gerontology and director of the division of geriatric medicine at Saint Louis University School of Medicine. He also is director of geriatric research at the Saint Louis Veterans Affairs Medical Center and is coauthor of *The Science of Staying Young* (McGraw-Hill).

patient has trouble following dance steps…can't lift his feet off the ground…or has trouble balancing during turns, there may be a potentially dangerous problem with gait and/or balance.

My recommendation: Perform balance-specific exercises once a day (for 15 to 30 seconds per exercise).* *Examples…*

• Stand in different ways—with your eyes closed…with your head tilted to one side…or with your hands held away from your body.

• While standing in bare feet, put a towel on the floor and practice gripping it with the toes of one foot, and then the other.

2. Increase your "SPA." People who exercise tend to live longer and remain healthier—but it's possible to gain even greater benefits by getting more spontaneous physical activity (SPA), daily physical exertions that complement "formal" exercise routines.

Suppose you burn 200 calories daily by walking about an hour at a leisurely pace. That's a good start, but you'll do better if you find ways to stay active the rest of the time. A study of older adults ages 70 to 82 found that for every 287 calories expended per day during physical activities (primarily SPA), they increased their chances of living longer by 68%.

My recommendation: Boost your SPA by doing housework, for example, or gardening.

3. Supplement with testosterone. Traditionally, testosterone replacement has been recommended only for men with extremely low levels of the hormone. Yet there's good evidence that millions of American men—and women—with even slightly low testosterone levels could benefit from replacement therapy.

Men with low testosterone have an increased risk for cardiovascular disease and are more likely to suffer from depression and fatigue. In addition, there appears to be a link between low testosterone and Alzheimer's disease. In women, low testosterone is a leading cause of low libido along with declines in muscle mass and bone density.

My recommendation: Get tested for bio-available testosterone (the form that's available to the body's tissues) if you suffer from chronic

*Make sure that someone is with you to monitor your balance when you first try these exercises.

fatigue, moodiness or depression—or if you've noticed a decline in libido and/or sexual function. Low testosterone can be treated with a gel or patch (usually at a starting dose of 5 mg for men) or with twice-monthly injections. (Women typically are prescribed a lower dose.)

New alternative for men: A small, tablet-like testosterone-replacement product that is held between the cheek and gum.

Important: There's been some concern that long-term testosterone replacement might increase the risk for prostate cancer in some men. Although the research has not definitively found this association, I suggest that men using testosterone play it safe and get an annual prostate examination and prostate-specific antigen (PSA) blood test.

The safety of long-term testosterone use in women is also of concern. Patients who choose this treatment should be closely monitored by a doctor.

4. Get more alpha lipoic acid. It's a very powerful antioxidant (more potent than vitamin E) that reduces free-radical damage within the mitochondria, the energy-producing parts of cells. Damage to the mitochondria is thought to be a main cause of cellular aging.

My recommendation: Eat more foods that are high in alpha lipoic acid (such as spinach, broccoli, tomatoes, potatoes, green peas and brussels sprouts). If you have diabetic neuropathy, painful nerve damage that often occurs in people with diabetes, take 600 mg of alpha lipoic acid daily. The same dose also may improve memory and slow the progression of Alzheimer's disease.

5. Consume alcohol. Red wine is widely recognized for its heart-protective effects, but recent research has found that any alcoholic beverage, including hard liquor (such as vodka or whiskey) and beer, can help you live longer.

Why is this so? Cell membranes get more rigid with age, impairing the ability of molecules to effectively communicate with one another. Alcohol is thought to make the cell membranes less rigid and to improve cellular functions.

My recommendation: Men should consume no more than two drinks daily...and women no more than one drink daily.

Important: Even one daily drink has been associated with increased risk of breast cancer.

6. Drink green tea. It has a five- to tenfold higher concentration of polyphenol antioxidants than black tea. One such antioxidant, *epigallocatechin*, improves the liver's ability to break down potential carcinogens, potentially reducing cancer risk. People who drink three or more cups of green tea daily also are less likely to experience age-related cognitive declines.

My recommendation: For cancer-fighting and brain-protective effects, drink three or more cups of green tea daily.

A Surprising New Key To Longevity: Good Oral Health Lowers Disease Risk

Robert J. Genco, DDS, PhD, distinguished professor in the department of oral biology, School of Dental Medicine, and in the department of microbiology, School of Medicine and Biomedical Sciences at the State University of New York at Buffalo. He is also a professor in the department of immunology at the Roswell Park Cancer Institute.

Until recently, most people who took good care of their teeth and gums did so to ensure appealing smiles and to perhaps avoid dentures. Now, a significant body of research shows that oral health may play a key role in preventing a wide range of serious health conditions, including heart disease, diabetes, some types of cancer and perhaps even dementia.

Healthy teeth and gums also may improve longevity. Swedish scientists recently tracked 3,273 adults for 16 years and found that those with chronic gum infections were significantly more likely to die before age 50, on average, than were people without gum disease.

What's the connection? Periodontal disease (called gingivitis in mild stages...and periodontitis when it becomes more severe) is caused mainly by bacteria that accumulate on the teeth and gums. As the body attempts to battle the bacteria, inflammatory molecules are released (as demonstrated by redness and swelling of the gums). Over time, this complex biological response affects the entire body, causing systemic inflammation that promotes the development of many serious diseases. *Scientific evidence links poor oral health to...*

- **Heart disease.** At least 20 scientific studies have shown links between chronic periodontal disease and an increased risk for heart disease. Most recently, Boston University researchers found that periodontal disease in men younger than age 60 was associated with a twofold increase in angina (chest pain), or nonfatal or fatal heart attack, when compared with men whose teeth and gums are healthy.

- **Diabetes.** State University of New York at Buffalo studies and other research show that people with diabetes have an associated risk for periodontitis that is two to three times greater than that of people without diabetes. Conversely, diabetics with periodontal disease generally have poorer control of their blood sugar than diabetics without periodontal disease—a factor that contributes to their having twice the risk of dying of a heart attack and three times the risk of dying of kidney failure.

- **Cancer.** Chronic gum disease may raise your risk for tongue cancer. State University of New York at Buffalo researchers recently compared men with and without tongue cancer and found that those with cancer had a 65% greater loss of alveolar bone (which supports the teeth)—a common measure of periodontitis. Meanwhile, a Harvard School of Public Health study shows that periodontal disease is associated with a 63% higher risk for pancreatic cancer.

- **Rheumatoid arthritis.** In people with rheumatoid arthritis, the condition is linked to an 82% increased risk for periodontal disease, compared with people who do not have rheumatoid arthritis.

Good news: Treating the periodontitis appears to ease rheumatoid arthritis symptoms. In a recent study, nearly 59% of patients with rheumatoid arthritis and chronic periodontal disease who had their gums treated experienced less severe arthritis symptoms—possibly because eliminating the periodontitis reduced their systemic inflammation.

• **Dementia.** When Swedish researchers recently reviewed dental and cognitive records for 638 women, they found that tooth loss (a sign of severe gum disease) was linked to a 30% to 40% increased risk for dementia over a 32-year period, with the highest dementia rates suffered by women who had the fewest teeth at middle age. More research is needed to confirm and explain this link.

STEPS TO IMPROVE YOUR ORAL HEALTH

Even though the rate of gum disease significantly increases with age, it's not inevitable. To promote oral health, brush (twice daily with a soft-bristled brush, using gentle, short strokes starting at a 45-degree angle to the gums) and floss (once daily, using gentle rubbing motions—do not snap against the gums). *In addition…*

• **See your dentist at least twice yearly.** Ask at every exam, "Do I have gum disease?" This will serve as a gentle reminder to dentists that you want to be carefully screened for the condition. Most mild-to-moderate infections can be treated with a nonsurgical procedure that removes plaque and tartar from tooth pockets and smooths the root surfaces. For more severe periodontal disease, your dentist may refer you to a periodontist (a dentist who specializes in the treatment of gum disease).

Note: Patients with gum disease often need to see a dentist three to four times a year to prevent recurrence of gum disease after the initial treatment.

Good news: Modern techniques to regenerate bone and soft tissue can reverse much of the damage and halt progression of periodontitis, particularly in patients who have lost no more than 30% of the bone to which the teeth are attached.

354

• **Boost your calcium intake.** Research conducted at the State University of New York at Buffalo has shown that postmenopausal women with osteoporosis typically have more alveolar bone loss and weaker attachments between their teeth and bone, putting them at substantially higher risk for periodontal disease. Other studies have linked low dietary calcium with heightened periodontal risk in both men and women.

Self-defense: Postmenopausal women, and men over age 65, should consume 1,000 milligrams (mg) to 1,200 mg of calcium daily to preserve teeth and bones. Aim for two to three daily servings of dairy products (providing a total of 600 mg of calcium), plus a 600-mg calcium supplement with added vitamin D for maximum absorption.

Helpful: Yogurt may offer an edge over other calcium sources. In a recent Japanese study involving 942 adults, ages 40 to 79, those who ate at least 55 grams (about two ounces) of yogurt daily were 40% less likely to suffer from severe periodontal disease—perhaps because the "friendly" bacteria and calcium in yogurt make a powerful combination against the infection-causing bacteria of dental disease.

• **Control your weight.** Obesity is also associated with periodontitis, probably because fat cells release chemicals that may contribute to inflammatory conditions anywhere in the body, including the gums.

• **Don't ignore dry mouth.** Aging and many medications, including some antidepressants, antihistamines, high blood pressure drugs and steroids, can decrease saliva flow, allowing plaque to build up on teeth and gums. If you're taking a drug that leaves your mouth dry, talk to your doctor about possible alternatives. Prescription artificial saliva products— for example, Caphosol or Numoisyn—also can provide some temporary moistening, as can chewing sugarless gum.

• **Relax.** Recent studies reveal a strong link between periodontal disease and stress, depression, anxiety and loneliness. Researchers are focusing on the stress hormone cortisol as a possible culprit—high levels of cortisol may exacerbate the gum and jawbone destruction caused by oral infections.

•**Sleep.** Japanese researchers studied 219 factory workers for four years and found that those who slept seven to eight hours nightly suffered significantly less periodontal disease progression than those who slept six hours or less.

Push-Ups Great for Seniors

Push-ups are excellent exercise for seniors. The ability to do them is more than an indicator of fitness—the exercise increases upper-body strength, which helps protect against injury from falls.

Why: When people fall, they instinctively reach out to catch themselves in a manner similar to the push-up motion. Upper-body strength helps break the weight of a fall safely. Those who don't have the strength to do a push-up are at heightened risk of suffering a broken wrist or other injury in a fall—and of not being able to push or lift themselves up, even if not injured.

Fitness: At age 60, men should be able to do 17 push-ups…women should be able to do six of them.

James Ashton-Miller, PhD, director, biomechanics research laboratory, University of Michigan, Ann Arbor.

Easy Ways to Prevent Falls

Rosanne M. Leipzig, MD, PhD, vice chair for education and Gerald and Mary Ellen Ritter Professor of Geriatrics in the Brookdale Department of Geriatrics and Adult Development at Mount Sinai School of Medicine in New York City.

Anyone can trip and be thrown momentarily off balance. But can you regain your balance—or do you go down? Anything that makes an initial misstep more likely or interferes with a person's ability to self-correct increases the risk for falls. And many such factors become more common with age. *For example…*

•**Muscle weakness.** If you stumble, it requires coordinated actions of your feet, ankles, knees and hips to prevent a fall. Muscle weakness in any of those areas impairs this ability. That's why physical inactivity is a common—though often unrecognized—cause of falls.

Exercise helps slow the loss of muscle mass that occurs with aging. Stair-climbing is an excellent way to strengthen critical thigh muscles.

Also helpful: Leg extensions—while sitting in a chair, raise your lower leg until it is in line with the thigh. Repeat 10 times and switch legs. Perform this exercise three times a day.

•**Impaired nerve function.** The nervous system plays a part in sensing loss of balance early and guiding the self-correction process. Blunted nerve function in the feet often is due to peripheral neuropathy, which can be caused by diabetes, vitamin B-12 deficiency or low thyroid levels (hypothyroidism).

•**Thinning bones.** Bone mass declines with age. If the thinning process goes far enough, osteoporosis can develop—in both women and men—and those dangerously fragile bones are liable to fracture. Osteoporosis can worsen the consequences of a fall, but in some cases, weakened bones are the cause, rather than the effect.

Here's what happens: As bones lose density, the body's center of gravity shifts forward, causing an older person to lean progressively forward. Balance becomes more precarious, so a slip is more likely to become a fall. Small fractures of the vertebrae caused by osteoporosis accentuate the forward shift.

•**Low vitamin D levels.** A 2005 analysis of five studies published in *The Journal of the American Medical Association* found a more than 20% reduction in falls in healthy older people who took vitamin D supplements, compared with those who didn't.

Researchers theorize that vitamin D may have an effect on muscle that helps reduce falls. Although the Daily Value (the FDA's reference guideline for daily nutrient intake) for vitamin D is 400 international units (IU), most studies have found that daily doses of 700 IU to 800 IU are needed to prevent falls and fractures.

Vitamin D deficiency is more common than previously believed—it's often due to a lack of regular sun exposure and/or a low intake of foods containing or fortified with vitamin D. If either of these factors applies to you, ask your doctor to check your blood level of vitamin D.

VISION AND HEARING LOSS

"Silent" vision problems, such as cataracts and glaucoma that have not yet caused difficulties in reading or other activities, can increase a person's risk for falls. Subtle vision changes, such as a decline in the ability to see contrasts in color or light and dark, can be missed as well. This makes tripping over curbs and on stairs or escalators more of a danger.

Correcting nearsightedness or farsightedness with glasses will help but initially can be risky. It takes time to adjust to new glasses—particularly when they have multifocal (bifocal, trifocal or variable) lenses. An Australian study found that in the period just after patients got new glasses, they were more likely to fall.

Even hearing loss may be linked to increased falls—possibly because some hearing problems reflect damage to the eighth cranial nerve, which also controls the inner-ear system that maintains balance.

DANGEROUS MEDICATIONS

Any drug that causes sedation can impair alertness, slow reaction time and disable the coordinated interplay of nerves and muscles that protects against falls. Some medications lower blood pressure when you stand up—these can cause weakness and light-headedness that can lead to a fall.

Among the most common culprits: Some antidepressants and anti-anxiety drugs...medications taken for enlarged prostate...painkillers, such as the combination of codeine and *oxycodone* (OxyContin)...and pills for high blood pressure.

Important: The more medications you take, the higher your risk of falling.

Hidden menace: Over-the-counter (OTC) drugs. For example, older OTC antihistamines that can have sedating effects, such as *diphenhydramine* (Benadryl), should not be used by older adults, who may experience confusion when taking such drugs. First try a nonsedating antihistamine, such as *loratadine* (Claritin).

SLEEP PROBLEMS

Lack of sleep can increase fall risk by impairing alertness and slowing reaction time. However, sleeping pills aren't the solution—their effects often linger, dulling the senses and slowing reaction time. Even newer sleep medications, such as *zolpidem* (Ambien), which are designed to be shorter acting, keep working longer in older people, possibly contributing to falls.

Anything that gets you out of bed in the middle of the night—such as an urgent need to urinate—also increases your fall risk. Keep a clear path to the bathroom, use night-lights and keep a cane or walker easily accessible, if necessary.

UNDIAGNOSED ILLNESS

Falls also can be a harbinger of a new health problem, such as pneumonia, a urinary tract infection, heart attack or heart failure. In some cases, weakness that can lead to a fall is more evident than the usual symptoms for these illnesses.

SMALL CHANGES THAT HELP

The exact cause of a fall is often impossible to pin down and may actually be due to several subtle factors working together—such as a slight loss of sensation in the feet, mild sedation due to medication and minor difficulty with balance.

Fortunately, safety is cumulative, too. Slight adjustments can be lifesaving. For example, avoid shoes that don't fit snugly or have slippery soles...instead, wear sneakers or walking shoes. In addition, get rid of any throw rugs...make sure that lighting is adequate and handrails are available where needed...and don't be vain about using a cane or walker if it helps you move about safely.

Falls More Likely for Sleep-Deprived Older Women

A recent study shows that women over age 70 who get five hours of sleep or less on a regular basis are 47% more likely to fall than those women who get seven to eight hours of sleep. Talk to your doctor if you have trouble getting enough sleep—there are several treatment options, including medication and environmental changes, such as darkening the room, eliminating noise, etc.

Katie L. Stone, principal investigator, California Pacific Medical Center Research Institute, San Francisco.

Secrets for a Great Night's Sleep

Meir H. Kryger, MD, director of research and education at the Gaylord Sleep Center of Gaylord Hospital in Wallingford, Connecticut. The author of *A Woman's Guide to Sleep Disorders* (McGraw-Hill), he has been researching and treating women's sleep problems for more than 25 years.

Have you ever felt frustrated watching a man sleep like a baby while you tossed and turned? Do the strategies that used to help you sleep no longer seem to work? Blame biology, at least in part.

As early as adolescence, gender-based differences in physiology and lifestyle make sleep disorders far more common in women than in men. Because these factors change over time, a woman's sleep problems also change—usually for the worse. So it is no surprise that a 2007 poll from the National Sleep Foundation reported that 67% of American women frequently experience sleep problems.

Fortunately, once you understand what triggers your sleep problems, you can take steps toward a better night's rest.

THE CHILDBEARING YEARS

Some women don't need a calendar to remind them when their period is due. A group of symptoms called premenstrual syndrome (PMS)—including breast tenderness, headaches and joint and muscle pains—can cause sufficient discomfort to interfere with rest. A more severe form is premenstrual dysphoric disorder (PMDD), which can cause insomnia, depression, anxiety and fatigue.

Polycystic ovary syndrome is an endocrine disorder in which the ovaries are enlarged and have multiple cysts. Symptoms include infrequent or irregular periods, weight gain, excessive hair growth, prediabetes and infertility. About 30% to 40% of women with this syndrome experience sleep apnea, in which breathing repeatedly stops during sleep. Sleep apnea causes persistent fatigue and raises a person's risk for cardiovascular disease by increasing blood pressure and decreasing oxygen going to the heart.

During pregnancy, the quality of sleep worsens for more than 80% of women. The uterus presses on the bladder (so you wake up often to urinate) and on the stomach (causing heartburn that can keep you awake). Pregnant women also are prone to restless legs syndrome (RLS), an irresistible urge to move the legs, which interferes with sleep.

Sleep disturbances worsen after the baby is born, thanks to nighttime feedings. For the 10% to 15% of women who develop postpartum depression in response to the hormonal fluctuations that follow childbirth, sleeplessness often accompanies depression.

MIDLIFE AND BEYOND

The transition to menopause can be brief or may last as long as seven years. During this stage, called perimenopause, periods become irregular. Due to fluctuating hormone levels, many women experience hot flashes and night sweats caused by dilating blood vessels. These rapid changes in body temperature can awaken women repeatedly.

Menopause typically occurs between ages 48 and 55. One in two postmenopausal women experience a sleep disorder, such as sleep apnea or RLS, while nearly two in three have insomnia at least a few nights each week. One culprit is excess weight, particularly in the neck area. The average woman gains eight pounds after menopause, increasing her risk for sleep apnea.

Another sleep-disturbing factor may be the worry that accompanies caregiving, as women in midlife assume responsibility for aging parents and/or ailing husbands.

Advancing age increases a woman's risk for arthritis, diabetes, cardiovascular disease, depression and other chronic conditions. In addition to the discomforts of the diseases themselves, the medications used to treat such conditions can affect sleep.

FOR BETTER SLUMBER...

The good news: Several simple steps can yield big improvements.

•**Eat light—and early—in the evening.** A heavy, spicy or late-night dinner may trigger heartburn that keeps you awake.

Better: A light dinner two to four hours before bedtime. Limit beverages to avoid middle-of-the-night trips to the toilet.

•**Skip the buzz.** Limit caffeinated beverages to two per day, both before lunch. Have no more than one alcoholic drink per evening, at least three to four hours before bed. When you drink too much or too late, your blood alcohol level drops in the middle of the night, causing brain arousal that wakes you up.

•**Quit smoking.** Many smokers wake at night when blood levels of nicotine fall.

•**Argue in the morning (or not at all).** Evenings should be free from confrontations, strenuous workouts and heart-stopping action films that rev you up when you need to wind down.

Exception: Sex, which promotes sound sleep.

•**Avoid evening naps.** Nap only in the afternoon—and for no more than 45 minutes—to minimize disruptions of your nighttime sleep cycle.

•**Create a relaxing bedtime ritual.** Light reading or soothing music tells your brain it's almost bedtime. A warm bath is especially

good because raising the body temperature promotes deep sleep.

•**Don't push back your bedtime.** Your body clock works best when bedtimes and awakening times are consistent.

•**Don't lie there staring at the clock if you can't sleep—get up and do something boring.** Tossing and turning is futile and frustrating. Fold some laundry or read something dull until you feel sleepy.

•**Get help for hormonal problems.** Consult your doctor if you suffer from PMS, PMDD or hot flashes.

•**Don't suffer in silence.** Talk to your doctor if your sleep disturbances are due to illness, stress or the side effects of drugs.

•**See a sleep specialist** if you have insomnia more than three times per week for more than a month...if you think you have RLS...or if reports of your snoring and gasping lead you to suspect sleep apnea. You may need an overnight evaluation in a sleep clinic. Your doctor can provide a referral.

Feeling "Old"? It Could Be a Vitamin B-12 Deficiency

Sally M. Pacholok, RN, and Jeffrey J. Stuart, DO, co-authors of *Could It Be B-12?* (Linden). Ms. Pacholok has studied vitamin B-12 deficiency for more than 20 years. Dr. Stuart is a board-certified emergency medicine physician. Both are based in Rochester, Michigan.

Millions of Americans suffer tingling, numbness or pain in their hands or feet...dizziness...balance problems...depression...and/or memory loss because they are deficient in vitamin B-12, a nutrient that most of us—including many doctors—rarely think about. Low levels of vitamin B-12 can even raise the risk for heart disease and osteoporosis, according to research.

Good news: You can avoid the potentially serious complications of vitamin B-12 deficiency with simple, inexpensive treatment—if the problem is identified soon enough. Permanent damage can occur if the deficiency is not treated within a year of the development of symptoms.

What you need to know...

A KEY TO PROPER NERVE FUNCTION

Vitamin B-12 is needed to maintain the layers of tissue, called the myelin sheath, that insulate each nerve cell. We need only a very tiny amount of the vitamin each day—2.4 micrograms (mcg).

The vitamin is abundant in meats (such as red meat, poultry and liver), shellfish, eggs and dairy products. Because vitamin B-12 is readily stored by the body (mainly in the liver), doctors have long assumed that deficiency is rare.

But a complex process must occur before vitamin B-12 can do its job. When it is consumed, the vitamin must be split from the proteins to which it is attached, carried into the small intestine and transported throughout the body with the help of other proteins.

If there is a problem—for example, a person takes a drug that interferes with vitamin B-12 absorption—a potentially dangerous deficiency can result. Among adults over age 65, up to 25% have been found in studies to have a clear B-12 deficiency (blood levels of less than 225).

THE TOLL OF B-12 DEFICIENCY

Many so-called symptoms of aging—both physical and mental—actually could be the result of B-12 deficiency. When a lack of this vitamin impairs the nervous system, a variety of problems can result, including weakness, dizziness and tremor—all of which can be mistaken for signs of neurological disorders, such as Parkinson's disease, multiple sclerosis, vertigo or neuropathy (nerve damage that causes pain or numbness).

A B-12 deficiency also can affect how you think, feel and act, resulting in irritability, apathy, confusion, forgetfulness—even serious depression, dementia, paranoia and/or hallucinations. Vitamin B-12 deficiency can lead to symptoms that are sometimes mistaken for Alzheimer's disease.

The cardiovascular system also can be affected. Vitamin B-12—along with vitamin B-6 and folic acid (another B vitamin)—plays a key role in the breakdown of homocysteine, a naturally occurring amino acid. Elevated levels of homocysteine damage blood vessels and promote the buildup of fatty deposits in the arteries (atherosclerosis) as well as abnormal blood clotting. Several studies have linked high blood levels of homocysteine to significantly increased risk for heart disease, heart attack, stroke and blood clots in the lungs and/or extremities.

The dangers of elevated homocysteine are widely known, but many doctors—cardiologists among them—simply prescribe high doses of folic acid to lower levels of the amino acid, ignoring the need to test for and possibly correct vitamin B-12 deficiency as well.

Also linked to B-12 deficiency...

•**Breast cancer.** A Johns Hopkins study of 390 women found that those with the lowest levels of B-12 were two to four times more likely to develop breast cancer than those with healthier levels.

•**Infections.** In another study, 30 older adults who had very low levels of B-12 produced fewer antibodies when vaccinated against pneumonia—leaving them with less protection against this potentially fatal infection than adults with adequate levels of B-12.

•**Osteoporosis.** Research shows that B-12 deficiency is linked to osteoporosis—in part, because B-12 is crucial to the function of osteoblasts (bone-forming cells).

ARE YOU AT RISK?

Aging is a primary risk factor for B-12 deficiency. That's because 30% to 40% of people over age 50 suffer from atrophic gastritis, which damages the stomach lining, markedly reducing production of the stomach acid needed to absorb vitamin B-12. Many older adults also fail to eat vitamin B-12-rich foods.

Another cause of B-12 deficiency is pernicious anemia—an autoimmune disorder in which the body does not produce a substance called intrinsic factor, which is necessary for the vitamin's absorption. Pernicious anemia is more common among people who have other autoimmune diseases, such as rheumatoid arthritis, lupus, thyroid disease and type 1 diabetes.

It's now recognized that Crohn's disease (chronic inflammation of the intestinal wall) and celiac disease (intolerance to gluten, a protein found in wheat, barley and rye) can impede absorption of vitamin B-12. So can gastrointestinal surgery—particularly gastric bypass.

In addition, commonly used medications—such as the heartburn drugs known as proton pump inhibitors, including *omeprazole* (Prilosec) and *lansoprazole* (Prevacid)…and H2 blockers, including *ranitidine* (Zantac) and *famotidine* (Pepcid)…as well as the oral diabetes drug *metformin* (Glucophage, Glucovance) —can interfere with B-12 absorption.

Because vitamin B-12 is found only in animal products, strict vegetarians are at high risk for a deficiency. Some research shows that 80% of people who do not eat animal products and fail to take a B-12 supplement have a deficiency of the vitamin.

GET THE RIGHT TEST

When doctors order a complete blood count (CBC), among the abnormalities they look for is macrocytic anemia, a condition in which red blood cells are abnormally large. This can be a sign of vitamin B-12 deficiency. But in people who take supplements that contain folic acid —as do most multivitamins—blood test results may appear normal even when there is a vitamin B-12 deficiency. (Folic acid can "mask" such a deficiency.) A blood test that specifically measures B-12 levels also is available. However, this test is not always accurate—it has a wide "normal" range and can be inconsistent in its sensitivity.

The most sensitive B-12 test measures the amount of *methylmalonic acid* (MMA) in the urine. Because vitamin B-12 plays a key role in the production of MMA, results of this test can conclusively diagnose or rule out B-12 deficiency. Health insurance will pay for the test if the patient has symptoms of B-12 deficiency or is at high risk for deficiency.

BEST TREATMENT OPTIONS

If you have a B-12 deficiency, injections of 1,000 mcg—daily at first, then weekly, then monthly—are the most dependable solution,

especially if neurologic symptoms are present. Sublingual (under-the-tongue) doses may be an alternative for some people. Ask your doctor. The MMA test should be repeated in three months to check the sublingual supplement's effectiveness.

If you have a B-12 deficiency, it's also wise to receive a homocysteine blood test before treatment to determine whether inadequate B-12 has raised your homocysteine levels, thus increasing your risk for vascular disease.

Why Rheumatoid Arthritis Is on The Rise in Women

Eric L. Matteson, MD, chair of rheumatology, Mayo Clinic, Rochester, Minnesota.

When most people hear the word "arthritis," what comes to mind is osteoarthritis, the seemingly ubiquitous aching-joint condition suffered by more than a third of people over age 65. Much less common, but often more devastating, is rheumatoid arthritis (RA), an autoimmune disease that also attacks the joints affecting many in the prime of life. About three-fourths of patients with rheumatoid arthritis are women. Where incidence had been declining for nearly 40 years, researchers from the Mayo Clinic announced that it is again on the upswing, specifically among women. Between 1995 and 2005, the number of female patients diagnosed with rheumatoid arthritis climbed 50% from 36 new female patients per 100,000 to 54 per 100,000.

WHAT'S BEHIND THE INCREASE?

Why the increase? Some of the growth can be accounted for by the fact that doctors now have more awareness of how to diagnose the disease. Other factors are at work too, we learned from Eric L. Matteson, MD, chair of rheumatology at the Mayo Clinic in Rochester, Minnesota. Hormones are known to play a role (since RA typically improves with pregnancy but comes back after delivery) but researchers are examining possible environmental explanations as well. For instance, researchers recently learned that there is an association between living near busy highways and development of RA.

Here's another theory: For unknown reasons, some people are prone to develop RA after exposure to particular viruses. After a virus has made the rounds and exposed large numbers of people, it may be dormant for a long period, since many people have built immunity. That immunity eventually fades—then, if the same virus returns, it once more affects many people, including some who are susceptible to developing RA. Dr. Matteson noted that such a swell in chronic diseases due to reemergence of a triggering cause, such as virus, is not uncommon.

A recent discovery is that people with RA are at higher risk for heart disease. However, this is not much of a surprise, says Dr. Matteson, since RA is an inflammatory disease—increased inflammation in the body causes more inflammation in the lining (endothelium) of the arteries including those into the heart, which leads to greater cardiovascular risk. Researchers are at work trying to identify more sophisticated inflammation biomarkers to learn more about this and other health risks that may coexist with RA.

MAINSTREAM TREATMENT

Doctors used to wait until joint damage showed up on X-rays before they would prescribe drugs for RA to hold off further harm. Now, doctors prescribe these drugs as soon as the diagnosis is recognized, so patients can live longer with less pain and permanent damage. It's important to be aware of the symptoms that could indicate a diagnosis of RA and treat them early on.

While several drugs are effective, *methotrexate* is the anchor drug for most RA patients, Dr. Matteson said. All treatments have the same goal—to reduce signs of inflammation and free patients from joint swelling discomfort. RA drugs have many toxic side effects, so doctors typically try to find the lowest effective dose.

NATURAL TREATMENT

Dr. Matteson said there are a number of ways to ease RA through natural treatment. Since omega-3 fatty acids reduce inflammation and its associated pain, he recommends a large dosage—perhaps two to three grams per day. Exercise keeps the joints limber, increases range of motion and strengthens supporting muscle and keeps the bones strong. Research shows that yoga may be helpful in reducing discomfort, but Dr. Matteson cautions against more active and intense forms of power yoga, which can stress the joints. In his view, gentle tai chi is ideal—patients report that it helps reduce pain and creates more comfortable stretching.

Dr. Matteson advises following a healthy diet, including avoiding foods that may provoke inflammation and choosing fresh fruits and vegetables. Turmeric has some anti-inflammatory properties and may help somewhat. While some people believe that nightshade vegetables—primarily eggplant, tomatoes, white potatoes and peppers—can exacerbate discomfort in certain sensitive patients, Dr. Matteson says he hasn't found that to be true for most of his patients.

His advice: Watch to see if these or other foods trigger discomfort and, of course, avoid any that do.

Finally, it is also important to stop smoking if you smoke, because smoking is associated with an increased risk of RA, and people who smoke and have RA tend to have worse disease than those who do not.

DIAGNOSIS CAN BE TRICKY

Typical RA symptoms include joint pain on motion, swelling, reddening and decreased range of motion of the joints of hands, especially the wrists and fingers. Also affected are the *metacarpophalangeal* joints—where the fingers meet the palm—and the middle finger joints (the *proximal interphalangeal* joints). Rheumatoid arthritis also often affects the feet and ankles, as well as other joints. The disease can arise in children or the very old, but the median age is 56. Anyone who experiences an increase of small joint discomfort and especially with swelling in the joints and symptoms that continue for six weeks, should get an evaluation from his/her doctor or a rheumatologist.

Natural Cures for Cold Fingers and Toes

Jamison Starbuck, ND, naturopathic physician in family practice in Missoula, Montana. She is past president of the American Association of Naturopathic Physicians and a contributing editor to The Alternative Advisor: The Complete Guide to Natural Therapies and Alternative Treatments *(Time-Life).*

Cold extremities are not always just about the weather. Whenever a patient of mine complains of cold hands and feet, I consider whether it could be related to poor thyroid function, anemia or Raynaud's disease (a condition in which small arteries, usually in the fingers or toes, constrict in response to exposure to cold). Cold extremities are a primary symptom of all these conditions. Cold hands and feet can also be a secondary symptom of other conditions that affect circulation. These include rheumatoid arthritis, lupus, arterial disease and high blood pressure.

If you have chronically cold hands and feet, see your doctor. Ask for a screening physical and get blood tests—a complete blood count (CBC), as well as a thyroid profile, lipid panel and C-reactive protein test—to determine if your symptoms may be caused by anemia, a thyroid disorder or heart disease.

If your physician finds no physical cause for your problem, here's my advice…

• **Bundle up!** This seems obvious, but you'd be amazed at how many of my patients who complain of cold hands and feet fail to wear proper clothing in cold weather. When you are outdoors, wear thick, lined wool mittens (not gloves), wool socks and insulated shoes or boots.

• **Eat warm food.** In the coldest months, choose soups, stews, roasts and hot cereal over salads, sandwiches and cold cereal. Cooked food already has begun to be broken down, requiring less work than cold food to digest.

This leaves your body with more energy to keep you warm.

• **Drink tea.** Although all hot beverages are temporarily warming, caffeine and other components of coffee constrict blood vessels, which promotes cold extremities. Green and black teas contain flavonoids, which promote blood vessel health and support good circulation.

• **Take supplements.** In addition to a multivitamin, be sure to get 50 milligrams (mg) of B-6 as well as 300 mg of magnesium. Vitamin B-6 promotes blood vessel health. And, magnesium helps prevent muscle spasms and encourages blood flow to hands and feet.

• **Keep moving.** Regular aerobic exercise is one of the best cures.

What to Do When You Can't Lose Weight

Mark A. Stengler, NMD, licensed naturopathic medical doctor in private practice, Encinitas, California… adjunct associate clinical professor at the National College of Natural Medicine, Portland, Oregon…author of The Natural Physician's Healing Therapies *and co-author of* Prescription for Natural Cures *(both from Bottom Line Books).*

Are you fighting a weight-loss battle? By eating a healthful diet and exercising regularly, you can shed some weight—but then it's common to "get stuck." No matter how you modify your diet and exercise regimen, the pounds just stop coming off. What's going on?

Your hormones might be the key. They influence appetite (when and to what degree you desire food)…metabolism (how you convert food to energy)…and insulin sensitivity (the degree to which your cells respond to insulin, which allows your body to use glucose).

If you have hit a plateau—or even have had a reversal—in your weight-loss efforts, it may be time for you to look more closely at your hormone levels.

To start, have them tested by a physician. Hormone levels can be detected from samples of blood, saliva and urine. A knowledgeable holistic doctor will help you interpret the results and choose supplements or other natural solutions that will allow you to lose those additional pounds.

Important factors to consider…

HOW ACTIVE IS YOUR THYROID?

Your body depends on thyroid hormones to regulate your metabolism. These hormones are produced in the butterfly-shaped gland just below your voice box. If thyroid hormones are in short supply, you can expect to gain weight. Assuming that your physician has ruled out any serious thyroid disease that must be treated in its own right, you can start to beat your weight problem by optimizing your thyroid function.

Natural solutions: For mild deficiencies—perhaps your levels are just a little off or are normal but you still have classic low thyroid symptoms, such as weight gain, fatigue, cold hands and feet, poor memory—look into one of these daily supplements or, even better, a formula that combines several of them. Take them until symptoms are better, and then taper off. If symptoms return, start taking them again—or have a doctor monitor you. If there is no improvement within four weeks, stop taking the supplements.

• **Bladderwrack** (a type of algae) contains iodine, which the thyroid requires for optimal functioning.

Typical dose: Two or three 500-mg capsules, in divided doses, for a total of 1,000 to 1,500 mg per day.

• **L-tyrosine** (an amino acid) helps the thyroid to manufacture hormones.

Typical dose: 500 mg twice daily on an empty stomach.

• **Homeopathic thyroid** (a minute dose of thyroid hormone or animal thyroid gland) stimulates your thyroid gland to produce hormones. Follow label directions.

• **Thyroid glandular** (an extract derived from animal thyroid tissue, typically that of a sheep) contains amino acids, vitamins and minerals that stimulate hormone production.

Typical dose: One to two capsules or tablets twice daily on an empty stomach.

Best formulas: I recommend Thyroid Support Liquid Phyto-Caps containing Bladderwrack and L-tyrosine from Gaia Herbs (800-831-7780, *www.gaiaherbs.com*) or Solaray's Thyroid Caps, which has L-tyrosine, iodine and thyroid glandular (800-669-8877, *www.nutraceutical.com*).

If your lab tests reveal a severe deficiency, you will be prescribed a thyroid hormone replacement program. Ask your doctor about natural thyroid replacement treatments, such as Armour Thyroid, Westhroid, Nature-Throid and compounded thyroid tablets.

THE CORTISOL FACTOR

Prolonged elevation of the stress hormone cortisol can contribute to weight gain. High cortisol levels can interfere with normal thyroid function and decrease insulin sensitivity, both of which lead to weight gain.

Natural solutions: Stress-reduction techniques curb your production of stress hormones. My favorite stress relievers include regular exercise, positive mental imagery and prayer.

Your doctor can order a saliva test to measure your cortisol level. *If yours is elevated, consider…*

• **Ashwagandha** (an herb) reduces cortisol levels when taken daily. Look for products containing the patented ingredient Sensoril, which provides optimal concentrations of ashwagandha. Widely available brands include Liquid Anti-Stress Plus Adrenal Support from Life Solutions Natural Products (a company in which I have a financial interest, 800-914-8771, *www.lifesolutionsnp.com*) and GABA Soothe from Jarrow Formulas (800-726-0886, *www.jarrow.com*).

Important: Ashwagandha may lower blood sugar levels as well as blood pressure. It may also interact with sedatives. Discuss ashwagandha use with your doctor first.

ESTROGEN DOMINANCE

Most women understand the importance of estrogen, but they might not realize that excessive amounts of this hormone can increase body fat and promote fluid retention. Estrogen in women needs to be "balanced out" with progesterone, which has a diuretic (water-excreting) effect. Premenopause, menopause and any health condition that interferes with ovulation (such as polycystic ovarian syndrome) will reduce levels of progesterone and give fat-building estrogen the upper hand. This is one reason why some women gain weight for no apparent reason.

Natural solutions: The nutrient indole 3-carbinol helps the liver metabolize estrogen. It is found in cruciferous vegetables—broccoli, cauliflower, cabbage and kale. I recommend eating at least one plentiful helping of any of these foods each day.

If a saliva, blood or urine test shows that your estrogen level is elevated even after you adopt an indole 3-carbinol–rich diet or if you just don't like to eat the above foods, try these daily supplements…

•**Indole 3-carbinol** helps the body metabolize estrogen.

Typical dose: 300 mg to 400 mg a day.

•**Vitex** (also called chasteberry, derived from the berries grown on the *Vitex agnus castus* tree) has been shown to improve the regularity of ovulation and raise progesterone levels.

Typical dose: 120 mg of a product standardized to 0.6% *aucubine* or 0.5% *agnuside* twice daily…or 800 mg of a nonstandardized supplement. Vitex is available from Nature's Way (to find a retailer, call 800-962-8873 or go to *www.naturesway.com*) and Enzymatic Therapy (800-783-2286, *www.enzymatictherapy.com*).

•**Natural progesterone cream** should be used as directed by your doctor for extreme progesterone deficiencies.

Typical dose: One-quarter teaspoon (20 mg) applied to the skin one or two times daily for two weeks before menstruation (stop when menses begin) or, if menopausal or postmenopausal, applied once daily. Consider Emerita Pro-Gest (800-888-6041 or go to *www.emerita. com*), a good brand that is commonly available in health-food stores.

THE TESTOSTERONE FACTOR

Testosterone, a powerful hormone found in women and men, affects the body's ability to maintain lean muscle mass. It is mainly produced by the ovaries in women and the testes in men. A low level makes it more difficult to tone muscles and lose weight.

Natural solutions…

•***Panax ginseng*** may help boost slightly low levels of testosterone in men and women.

Typical dose: 200 mg daily of a product standardized to 5% ginsenosides.

•***Tribulus terrestris*** is a plant whose extract may increase testosterone levels in men and women. So far, research has been done mainly with animals, but this herb appears to be safe. Tribulus Extract by Source Naturals (for a retailer, call 800-815-2333 or go to *www. sourcenaturals.com*) is a good choice.

•**Natural testosterone** is available by prescription only and should be used when there is a moderate to severe deficiency. I prefer the transdermal gel or cream form, which is applied to the skin, because it requires less metabolism by the liver than pills.

IS INSULIN ON YOUR TEAM?

Blood sugar (glucose) is terrific fuel for an active person, but you need the right level of insulin to transport the sugar from your bloodstream into tissue. A condition known as insulin resistance occurs when cells take up less glucose, causing insulin levels to spike. It is one factor that sets the stage for weight gain.

Natural solutions…

•**High-fiber diet that includes seven to nine daily servings of fresh vegetables** as well as three servings of whole-grain breads and cereals. Nuts, seeds and raw vegetables are especially good to help balance insulin levels. Stay away from simple-sugar food products, such as white breads, pasta, soft drinks, cookies and other sweets. For protein, avoid fatty red meats and favor quality sources, such as legumes, nuts, eggs, fish and poultry.

•**Help yourself to cinnamon!** Research shows that it helps balance blood sugar levels.

• **Eat smaller servings throughout the day rather than three big meals,** so your body metabolizes food more effectively.

• **High-potency multivitamin/mineral supplement.** Everyone should take one daily for general health—it provides nutrients that, among other things, balance insulin levels.

If tests for fasting blood glucose and insulin indicate that you have insulin resistance, try taking all three of these additional supplements daily...

• **Chromium** (a mineral) is particularly important to balance blood sugar levels.

Typical dose: 400 mcg.

• **Alpha lipoic acid** (an enzyme that acts as a powerful antioxidant) reduces levels of insulin and blood sugar.

Typical dose: Up to 200 mg.

• **Fish oil (**an essential fatty acid supplement) improves insulin sensitivity.

Typical dose: One teaspoon daily or a one-gram capsule, three times a day. Nordic Naturals fish oil supplements are widely available and free of mercury and other toxins (to locate a retailer, call 800-662-2544 or go to *www.nor dicnaturals.com*).

Caution: If you are on a blood-thinning medication, such as *warfarin* (Coumadin), check with your doctor before taking fish oil.

ROOT CAUSES OF WEIGHT GAIN

• **Poor diet**

• **Lack of exercise**

• **Genetic predisposition**

• **Hormone imbalance**

• **Neurotransmitter imbalance,** such as serotonin deficiency

• **Side effects of drugs**

• **Toxins,** such as chemicals (pesticides)

• **Psychological reasons,** such as stress, anxiety and depression.

More from Dr. Mark Stengler...

The Spice That May Prevent Alzheimer's

In India, the smell of turmeric, the bright yellow spice used in curries, fills almost every restaurant and home. Indians eat turmeric because they like it, but rapidly growing evidence indicates that the spice is giving them much more than flavor.

Thousands of years ago, Ayurvedic and traditional Chinese medicine recognized turmeric as a healing agent for everything from flatulence to liver disease. Now modern research demonstrates that properties in this zesty spice may be useful for lowering rates of breast, prostate, lung and colon cancers, and also for treating breast cancer, inflammatory bowel disease, Crohn's disease and possibly cystic fibrosis.

But even newer and especially exciting research concerns the relationship between turmeric and Alzheimer's disease. Nearly 10 years ago, researchers in India became curious about the influence turmeric might have on rates of Alzheimer's. They looked to see how many people over age 65 in a town in India had signs of the disease, versus a similar group of people in a similar-sized Pennsylvania town, where most people eat little—or no—turmeric.

What they found: In India, just 4.7 per 1,000 person-years (a common measure of incidence rate) showed signs of Alzheimer's, compared with a rate of 17.5 per 1,000 person-years in Pennsylvania. In fact, India has among the lowest rates of Alzheimer's disease in the world. Another study, from the National University of Singapore, involved 1,010 people over age 60. Those who reported that they ate curry "often or very often" or even "occasionally" scored higher on mental performance tests than those who rarely or never consumed it.

WHAT IS TURMERIC?

Turmeric is a powder made from the root of the plant *Curcuma longa*, which grows in southern Asia. The part of the plant that is responsible for healing is the yellow pigment, called curcumin.

When it comes to health-giving properties, curcumin gives twice. It is a potent anti-inflammatory agent, without the potential side effects of anti-inflammatory drugs. These include damage to the lining of the stomach and intestines and a greater risk for kidney and liver problems, heart attack and stroke. Next, curcumin is a powerful antioxidant—it tracks down and reduces free radicals, insidious molecules that otherwise would cause damage in the body. Both of these properties are important when it comes to preventing or slowing the progression of Alzheimer's disease.

In healthy people, immune cells attack and destroy amyloid-beta plaques—a buildup of proteins between neurons in the brain. But in people with Alzheimer's, this immune response is less efficient and allows plaques to form. Plaque triggers inflammation and free radicals, both of which cause cell damage in the brain. Curcumin slows this harmful process in a number of ways—it forms a powerful bond with the amyloid protein that prevents the protein from clumping…it may break down plaques as well, preliminary research demonstrates…and finally, as I noted before, curcumin reduces the oxidative damage and brain inflammation that are linked to Alzheimer's disease.

CHOLESTEROL BLASTER

There is yet more good news about curcumin's power to prevent and even fight Alzheimer's disease. Elevated cholesterol is thought to be involved in the development of Alzheimer's—and studies demonstrate that curcumin reduces cholesterol. In one study, healthy volunteers took 500 mg of curcumin supplements every day for one week.

Result: Reduced levels of total cholesterol and also lipid peroxides (markers of free radical damage to fats).

SPICE UP YOUR DIET

In the meantime, I encourage all my patients, especially those over age 50, to consume one or two teaspoons a day of turmeric. There are many ways to incorporate this spice into your regular diet. You can sprinkle it into egg salad or over vegetables while sautéing…

add it to soups or broths…put it on fish or meat…and use it to flavor rice or a creamy vegetable dip. And of course, turmeric adds zing to curries. If you want to make the most healthful curry dishes, it is important to purchase turmeric as a separate spice—lab tests show that many curry powders in this country contain almost no turmeric.

Good brand: Indus Organics (*www.indus organics.com,* $7.99 for eight ounces).

Those who don't love turmeric—or those who want to get even more of its protective effects—can take curcumin in supplement form. I prescribe 2,000 milligrams (mg) a day for those with a family history of Alzheimer's disease or who show signs of dementia.

Good brands: New Chapter Turmeric Force (for store locator, call 800-543-7279, or go to *www.newchapter.com,* $28.82 for 60 400-mg softgels) and Life Extension Super Bio-Curcumin with Bioperine (800-544-4440, *www. lef.org,* $38 for 60 400-mg capsules).

Anyone taking blood-thinning drugs should discuss using turmeric or curcumin supplements with a doctor, because curcumin is a natural blood thinner. Turmeric can also cause gallbladder contractions, so those with a history of gallstones or gallbladder problems should also consult a doctor. There is no risk in mixing curcumin with pharmaceutical drugs for Alzheimer's disease.

Try Tai Chi for Better Memory

Early-stage dementia patients attended sessions of tai chi (gentle martial arts movements with meditation) three times weekly… plus biweekly support groups, mental exercise sessions and cognitive behavioral therapy (which bolsters positive thoughts and behaviors). After 20 weeks, patients showed improved self-esteem and cognitive function. A control group that did not attend showed no improvement.

Referrals: American Tai Chi and Qigong Association (*www.americantaichi.net*)...Association for Behavioral and Cognitive Therapies (212-647-1890, *www.abct.org*).

Sandy Burgener, PhD, associate professor, University of Illinois, Urbana, and leader of a study of 46 people published in *American Journal of Alzheimer's Disease and Other Dementias.*

Reduce Alzheimer's Risk by 60%

Marwan Sabbagh, MD, director of clinical research and senior scientist at Sun Health Research Institute in Sun City, Arizona, and adjunct professor at Arizona State University in Tempe. Dr. Sabbagh is author or co-author of more than 70 scientific articles on Alzheimer's and author of *The Alzheimer's Answer* (Wiley).

The Alzheimer's Association recently reported that one in six women and one in 10 men age 55 and older in the US will develop Alzheimer's disease. (More women get Alzheimer's, in part, because they tend to live longer.) Many people think that not getting Alzheimer's is more about good genes than good health, but new research suggests that lifestyle factors, such as diet and exercise, play key roles.

Here's what you need to know about the latest scientific advances in the battle against Alzheimer's disease...

PREVENTION

New research shows that the primary feature of Alzheimer's—the accumulation of beta-amyloid, a protein by-product that wrecks brain cells—starts decades before symptoms begin, perhaps even in a person's 30s.

How to help prevent or slow that process...

•**Statins.** Researchers from the Netherlands studied nearly 7,000 people age 55 and older. They found that those who regularly took a cholesterol-lowering statin drug had a 43% lower risk for developing Alzheimer's than those who didn't take the drug.

Theory: Cholesterol may be a "cofactor" in beta-amyloid production.

Bottom line: More studies are needed to show that taking a statin can prevent Alzheimer's, so it's premature for your doctor to prescribe the drug for that purpose. But if you take a statin to control cholesterol, you may experience this very positive "side effect."

•**Weight control.** Researchers at the National Institutes of Health analyzed 23 years of data from more than 2,300 people. Women who were obese at ages 30, 35 or 50, with excess belly fat, had a nearly seven times higher risk for developing Alzheimer's. Men who gained a lot of weight between ages 30 and 50 had a nearly four times higher risk.

Theory: Excess pounds increase chronic low-grade inflammation...increase insulin resistance (prediabetes)...and may increase production of amyloid precursor protein—all factors that may increase the likelihood of Alzheimer's.

Bottom line: Keep your body weight within a healthy range by controlling calories and exercising regularly.

•**Fruits and vegetables.** Oxidative stress—a kind of "internal rust" caused by factors such as a diet loaded with fat and refined carbohydrates...air pollution...and hormones triggered by stress—is believed to play a role in the development of Alzheimer's. In the laboratory, researchers at Cornell University exposed brain cells to oxidative stress and added extracts of apples, bananas and oranges to the mix. The extracts reduced neurotoxicity—damage to brain cells.

Theory: Fruits and vegetables are rich in cell-protecting and strengthening antioxidants that fight the oxidative stress that contributes to Alzheimer's.

Bottom line: Fruits that deliver the most antioxidants include blueberries, blackberries, cherries, red grapes, oranges, plums, raspberries and strawberries. Best vegetables include arugula, bell peppers, broccoli, bok choy, cabbage, collard greens, kale and spinach.

•**Alcohol.** Researchers at Stritch School of Medicine at Loyola University in Chicago reviewed data on alcohol intake and health and found that more than half the studies showed that a moderate intake of alcohol (one drink a day for women, one to two drinks a day for men) was associated with a lower risk for cognitive decline and dementia, including Alzheimer's.

Theory: Alcohol delivers potent antioxidants, and moderate intake reduces inflammation.

Bottom line: One to two drinks a day may slightly decrease Alzheimer's risk. One drink is five ounces of wine, 12 ounces of beer or 1.5 ounces of an 80-proof liquor, such as vodka or gin.

• **Exercise.** Research shows that regular exercise can reduce Alzheimer's risk by up to 60%. A new study shows that it also may help slow the progression of the disease. Scientists at University of Kansas School of Medicine studied 57 people with early-stage Alzheimer's disease and found that those who were sedentary had four times more brain shrinkage (a sign of Alzheimer's) than those who were physically fit.

Bottom line: Aim for 30 minutes a day of exercise, such as brisk walking outdoors or on a treadmill.

COMBINATION TREATMENT

Medications can slow the development of Alzheimer's symptoms. Research now shows that combining certain drugs maximizes their effectiveness. The FDA has approved two types of drugs to treat Alzheimer's—cholinesterase inhibitors, such as *donepezil* (Aricept), which work by slowing the breakdown of acetylcholine, a neurotransmitter that helps brain cells communicate…and *memantine* (Namenda), which calms *excitotoxicity*, a type of cellular hyperactivity that harms neurons.

In a 30-month study of nearly 400 people with Alzheimer's, researchers at Harvard Medical School found that taking both drugs together is more effective in reducing Alzheimer's symptoms than taking either a cholinesterase inhibitor alone or a placebo.

Bottom line: Patients who start both drugs at the time of diagnosis may significantly slow the progress of Alzheimer's disease.

WHAT DOESN'T WORK

The following do not seem to be effective against Alzheimer's…

• **NSAIDs.** Some studies have linked regular intake of a nonsteroidal anti-inflammatory drug (NSAID)—such as aspirin, *ibuprofen* (Advil), *naproxen* (Aleve) and *celecoxib* (Celebrex)—with lower rates of Alzheimer's. But in the Alzheimer's Disease Anti-Inflammatory Prevention Trial (ADAPT)—a study conducted by more than 125 researchers, involving more than 2,000 people age 70 and older—celecoxib didn't reduce the risk for developing Alzheimer's. Naproxen had a minor effect that was outweighed by the fact that it increased the rate of heart attacks and strokes.

• ***Ginkgo biloba.*** A team of dozens of researchers led by scientists at University of Pittsburgh studied more than 3,000 people age 75 and older, dividing them into two groups. One group took a daily dose of 240 milligrams (mg) of ginkgo biloba extract, which is widely touted for invigorating the brain and improving memory. A second group took a placebo. Those taking ginkgo did not have a lower rate of developing Alzheimer's.

• **B vitamins.** Elevated blood levels of the amino acid homocysteine have been linked to Alzheimer's. Because B vitamins can lower homocysteine, scientists wondered if B vitamins could slow the development of Alzheimer's.

Researchers in the department of neurosciences at University of California, San Diego, studied 340 people with mild-to-moderate Alzheimer's disease for about four years and found that B vitamins reduced homocysteine levels but didn't slow the progression of Alzheimer's disease.

• **Antipsychotics.** Alzheimer's patients often develop behavioral disturbances, such as wandering, agitation, aggression, paranoia, delusions, anxiety and hallucinations. A standard treatment is an antipsychotic drug, such as *risperidone* (Risperdal), *ziprasidone* (Geodon), *olanzapine* (Zyprexa), *quetiapine* (Seroquel) or *aripiprazole* (Abilify).

New danger: For three years, researchers in England studied 165 Alzheimer's patients who had taken antipsychotics—continuing the drug in half the patients and switching the other half to placebos. After three years, 59% of those on the placebo were alive, compared with 30% on the medication. In other words, those who continued the drug had twice the risk of dying.

New approach: Researchers at Indiana University Center for Aging Research reviewed nine studies on the use of a cholinesterase inhibitor to manage behavioral symptoms and found it to be a "safe and effective alternative" to antipsychotics.

Alzheimer's Self-Defense

In a recent study, people who consumed less than 14 milligrams (mg) of the B vitamin niacin per day were three times more likely to develop Alzheimer's disease.

Theory: Niacin helps maintain normal neural function.

Helpful: Strive for the recommended daily intake of 14 mg for women and 16 mg for men from niacin-rich foods, including fortified cereal (20 mg per cupful)...lean poultry (11.8 mg per each half breast)...and canned tuna (11.3 mg per three ounces).

Martha C. Morris, ScD, professor of internal medicine and preventive medicine, Rush Institute for Healthy Aging, Chicago.

Brain-Boosting Nutrients Women Need

JoAnn E. Manson, MD, DrPH, professor of medicine and women's health at Harvard Medical School and chair of the division of preventive medicine at Brigham and Women's Hospital, both in Boston. A lead investigator for two important studies on women's health, Dr. Manson is coauthor of *Hot Flashes, Hormones & Your Health* (McGraw-Hill).

Certain foods may help ward off subtle age-related cognitive decline or even full-blown dementia, recent research suggests. *Nutrients linked to a clear mind and sharp memory...*

• **Folate.** In studies of people age 70 and older, those with low blood levels of folate had about twice the risk for Alzheimer's disease as those with normal levels. Folate reduces homocysteine, a dietary by-product linked to inflammation, blood clots and small blood vessel damage.

Best: Each day, eat two or more servings of folate-rich dark green leafy or cruciferous vegetables, such as spinach, romaine lettuce, broccoli and brussels sprouts. As insurance, consider taking a daily multivitamin that provides 400 micrograms (mcg) of folic acid (synthetic folate). Many doctors recommend taking up to 1000 mcg.

• **Marine omega-3 fatty acids.** Fish provide the omega-3s eicosapentaenoic acid (EPA) and docosahexaenoic acid (DHA). Studies show that people who eat fish five or more times weekly are 30% less likely to suffer a stroke than those who rarely eat fish. Frequent fish consumption also is associated with fewer "silent" (symptomless) brain lesions, as seen on imaging tests... and may reduce Alzheimer's risk. Fish oil also improves function of nerve cell membranes and boosts production of brain chemicals that allow nerve cells to communicate.

Wise: Eat salmon, tuna, herring, sardines or mackerel at least twice weekly...or take daily fish oil supplements with 400 milligrams (mg) to 1,000 mg of combined EPA and DHA.

Important: Watch consumption of large fish such as tuna and salmon. These may have higher levels of mercury and PCBs.

• **Flavonoids.** Oxidation, a chemical reaction that can damage blood vessels, may be a key contributor to brain aging. Antioxidant plant pigments called flavonoids may counteract this—particularly the anthocyanins in deep-colored fruits such as berries, cherries and Concord grapes. In animal studies, berry extracts reversed age-related declines in spatial learning and memory as measured by how quickly the animals learned to navigate a maze.

Goal: Eat berries or deep-colored fruit at least two to three times per week.

• **Coffee.** In a study of 7,017 people age 65 and older, women who drank three cups of caffeinated coffee or six cups of caffeinated tea per day experienced less decline in memory over four years than those who drank one cup or less. However, caffeine can trigger digestive upset, insomnia and migraine.

Advised: Have no more than four eight-ounce cups of coffee daily.

The alcohol question: Moderate alcohol intake is linked with less cognitive decline—though this may simply reflect that people who already have cognitive problems are less likely to imbibe.

Recommended: Do not start drinking alcohol specifically to prevent cognitive decline. If you already drink, limit consumption to no more than one alcoholic beverage daily.

Protect Your Brain Power Now!

Vincent M. Fortanasce, MD, assistant clinical professor, department of neurology and School of Biokinesiology, University of Southern California, Los Angeles. He is founder and medical director of Fortanasce Anti-Alzheimer's Clinic in Arcadia, California, and author of four books, including *The Anti-Alzheimer's Prescription* (Gotham). *www.healthybrainmd.com*

American women live, on average, to age 79—but by age 75, one-fifth of them may not be able to remember how old they are. By 85, the rate of memory-destroying Alzheimer's disease climbs to almost 50%. Younger people are at risk, too. In the past five decades, the incidence of Alzheimer's disease —which accounts for 60% to 80% of all cases of dementia (loss of mental functioning)—has increased dramatically among people under age 75. Overall, the rate of Alzheimer's is expected to increase by 70% by the year 2030.

Alzheimer's disease is characterized by increasingly severe problems with memory and speech and impairment of the ability to recognize familiar people and places. It is caused by a type of brain aging in which plaques of amyloid—a waxy protein—build up in the brain, destroying impulse-conducting neurons (nerve cells). Women are more likely than men to develop Alzheimer's disease.

Good news: New studies suggest that up to 70% of people can prevent Alzheimer's...and that even those with strong genetic risk factors, such as having a parent who has or had the disease, can delay its onset by up to 20 years. How? By controlling factors that cause brain aging. *What you need, starting today...*

LESS STRESS, MORE SLEEP

Long-term sleep deprivation coupled with chronic stress lowers levels of the mood-regulating brain chemicals dopamine and serotonin. This in turn may rob you of the willpower needed to maintain brain-protecting habits, such as exercising regularly and eating healthfully.

Crucial point: Preliminary studies suggest that chronic stress may quadruple a person's risk for Alzheimer's disease. *Self-defense...*

• **Cut back on responsibilities.** When asked to take on yet another task, consider whether it would contribute to your stress. If so, say no. Reevaluate all your commitments weekly, continuing only with those that are most important to you.

• **Meditate for 15 minutes daily**—and any time that you feel stressed.

Easy technique: Focus on the sensation of each breath as it moves in and out of your body...when your attention wanders, simply refocus on your breath.

Crucial point: A century ago, the average American slept nine hours per night. Now some research suggests that the average is less than 6.5 hours. *What you can do...*

• **Take a 10- to 30-minute nap daily**—during your lunch break or preferably in midafternoon, when sleep-inducing hormones typically are elevated.

• **Clear your mind at bedtime.** As you're falling asleep (or if you wake up during the night), again focus on your breath. Let go of intrusive thoughts about the day that is ending and what's to come the next day.

• **Reduce bedroom light and noise.** A small night-light is fine—but bright or flickering lights disrupt sleep. Wear earplugs to bed if you often are awakened by noises.

THE BRAIN BANK

The brain is like a bank account that pays interest—if you make regular deposits by doing brain-building mental exercises.

Crucial point: A key to building neuron-to-neuron connections that strengthen the brain is novelty—doing things that you're not used to doing. *Examples…*

• **Build brainpower during dinner.** If you're right-handed, try eating with your left hand …or use chopsticks instead of silverware… or if you always eat in the kitchen, try dining in a different room.

• **Learn a new word daily**—in a new language. Pick an object that you see often…look up how to say it in a foreign language…then say the word aloud throughout the day whenever you see that object. For instance, "car" is *coche* in Spanish…*voiture* in French…*auto* in German.

Resource: Use the free translator at *www. freetranslation.com.*

• **Search your memory.** Several times a day, select an image from the scene around you, then think of a pleasant memory you can associate with it.

Example: Seeing a tractor might remind you of childhood summers at your uncle's farm.

• **Play games that challenge your brain**—such as Scrabble, Boggle, bridge or charades. When you don't have a partner, do a crossword or Sudoku puzzle (visit *www.bestcrosswords. com* and *www.websudoku.com*)…or play chess online at *www.chessmaniac.com.*

STRONG BODY, STRONG MIND

Hormones can be classified as either youthful or aging. Youthful hormones include estrogen, thyroid hormone, growth hormone and testosterone. From ages 20 to 70, levels of each of these hormones plummet by about 90%. Aging hormones are cortisol and adrenaline… and the detrimental effects of these increase as you get older.

Crucial point: Physical exercise helps reduce aging hormones and boost youthful ones …strengthens connections between neurons …increases brain size…and improves blood flow to the brain. *Best…*

• **Take at least 8,000 steps each day.** A six-year study of nearly 2,000 people age 65 and older found that those who took a walk three times or more weekly—even for as little as 15 minutes each time—reduced their Alzheimer's risk by up to 38%, compared with nonwalkers.

Motivating: Wear a pedometer to count steps. To accrue extra steps, get up from your desk hourly and walk in place for several minutes…get off the bus one stop ahead of your destination…use stairs, not elevators.

• **Vary your workout**—to exercise body and brain simultaneously. Take a dance class to learn new choreography…try squash instead of your usual tennis…bike around town instead of using a stationary cycle.

• **Do isometric strength-training exercises,** which may quickly strengthen muscles and neurons. With these, your body remains in a static position throughout the exercise.

Example: Get into a push-up position and start lowering yourself as if doing a regular push-up, but stop halfway down…then remain there, without moving, for as long as possible.

Crucial point: Diet has an enormous effect on hormone balance. Certain foods trigger spikes and drops in blood sugar, leading to elevated levels of insulin. This makes the insulin-degrading enzyme in the brain work overtime to remove excess insulin rather than doing its other job of removing amyloid plaques. *To protect yourself…*

• **Stay away from simple carbohydrates.** Among the worst offenders in triggering blood sugar fluctuations are white sugar, white flour and white rice.

• **Follow the "one-thirds" diet.** Get one-third of your daily calories from complex carbohydrates (fruits, vegetables, high-fiber whole grains)…one-third from protein (fish, poultry, lean meats, soy, eggs, nuts, seeds, low-fat dairy)…and one-third from healthful fats (olive, grape seed and flaxseed oils, nuts, avocados). This keeps blood sugar and insulin levels stable, helping to minimize amyloid buildup and protect brain power.

Memory Boosters for Busy Women

Cynthia R. Green, PhD, founder and director of the Memory-Enhancement Program at Mount Sinai School of Medicine, New York City. She is author of *Total Memory Workout: 8 Easy Steps to Maximum Memory Fitness* (Bantam). *www.totalbrainhealth.com*

Have you misplaced your keys…again? Forgotten your best friend's phone number? You may blame age for these memory lapses, but for most people, the real culprit is a hyperactive life. Having too much competing for your attention is challenging no matter what your age—and attention is a key component in memory.

To improve your focus, organize your life in memory-boosting ways…

• **Build new brain cells by squeezing exercise into your schedule**—walk while you talk on the phone, do leg lifts while stirring a pot on the stove. Exercise increases blood flow to the brain, including the hippocampus, which processes memories. Exercise also appears to promote neurogenesis—the creation of new brain cells—and to combat the normal age-related memory decline that typically begins around age 30. This may explain why people who work out regularly do better on memory tests.

• **Don't stay up late or wake up too early to get more done.** This is necessary sometimes, but as a regular coping strategy, it is counterproductive. One function of sleep is to consolidate memory—to convert new memories into long-term ones. Lack of sleep also dulls concentration, which is critical to memory.

• **Use mindfulness meditation, in which you focus on the here and now.** Just remind yourself while walking, dining or at the supermarket to pay close attention to what's around you. Focus on the beauty of the trees or the cool breeze on your skin. Revel in awareness of what is happening at this moment. This lowers stress and helps you feel less overwhelmed. Prolonged stress may alter brain cells and structure, contributing to memory problems.

• **Teach yourself to pay attention.** Often the problem is not that we've forgotten something, but that we didn't focus on acquiring the information in the first place. Did you "forget" where you put your glasses, or did your mind wander as you were setting them down?

• **Devise a system to make remembering automatic.** Learn to routinely put your car keys in one place—on a hook in the garage, for instance. Make sure the system fits your habits. You may think it is wise to hang a cute key holder in your kitchen, but if you always enter the house through the garage, take off your coat in the mudroom and enjoy an enthusiastic reunion with your dog, the keys will get dropped elsewhere long before you reach the kitchen.

• **Free your mind of clutter by using memory tools.** Ask yourself, "Do I need to memorize this information or merely record it so I know where to find it?" Most of life's details (grocery lists, dinner dates) can be jotted down for reference when you need the information. Calendars, personal digital assistants and "to do" lists are excellent memory devices. Choose a memory aid that is compatible with your lifestyle. A wall calendar won't work if you're always on the go.

• **Make organizing yourself a habit.** On Sundays, list and prioritize tasks for the coming week on your calendar. Every morning, review what's coming up. Each evening, reevaluate tasks that didn't get done. Reschedule the important ones—and give yourself permission to forget about the rest.

New Treatments Help Protect Against Macular Degeneration

Rishi Singh, MD, associate staff physician at the Cole Eye Institute of the Cleveland Clinic. He has published numerous articles in peer-reviewed journals and currently is leading four clinical trials on treatment for eye conditions, including age-related macular degeneration.

The eye condition known as age-related macular degeneration (AMD) has long been associated with blindness, since no drug or surgical procedure has been able to halt the disease's progression.

Now: New treatments, including a simple nutritional therapy, have given hope to the up to 10 million Americans who suffer from the early stages of AMD.

If caught before permanent damage has occurred, the most serious form of AMD can be stabilized in 90% of people with the condition —and one-third even may experience improved vision.

ARE YOU AT RISK?

The incidence of AMD is on the rise— primarily due to the "graying" of America. As Americans live longer, AMD, which grows more common with age, affects increasing numbers of adults. Almost one in three Americans over age 75 has it. Obesity, which is strongly linked to increased risk, also remains high. *Other risk factors…*

• **Family history,** which increases risk due to a likely genetic component to AMD. If a close relative (parent or sibling) has had AMD, your own risk is greater.

• **Stroke and "mini" strokes,** which often are referred to as transient ischemic attacks (TIAs). Both result in a substantially higher risk for AMD. This increased risk is thought to be due to injury to the blood vessels, which occurs with strokes, TIAs—and AMD.

• **Cigarette smoking,** which increases oxidative stress throughout the body. It can quadruple the chance of developing AMD. Quitting will reduce the danger, but you're still at higher risk than people who never smoked.

DAMAGE IS PROGRESSIVE

AMD occurs when there is a deterioration of the tissue in the macula, the central area of the light-sensitive retina.

There are two forms of AMD…

• **Dry macular degeneration.** In up to 85% of AMD cases, deposits of protein and cholesterol called *drusen* develop among the pigmented cells behind the macula. These deposits cut retinal cells off from their blood supply, depriving them of nutrients and oxygen, leading to the accumulation of waste products.

As the drusen grow, central vision gets blurry. If the degenerative process continues, a blind spot may develop in your central vision.

• **Wet macular degeneration.** This form of AMD, which typically develops from the dry form, is responsible for the bulk of serious vision loss. Damage to the retina spurs the formation of fragile new blood vessels that often leak fluid or blood into the area around the macula. If untreated, wet macular degeneration often progresses rapidly—and within weeks or months, sight may deteriorate to the point of legal blindness.

Don't ignore the red flags: Because the progressive vision loss of AMD often can be halted, it is essential to spot the disease and start treatment as early as possible. If you notice changes in central vision (such as difficulty recognizing faces)…a decline in your ability to distinguish colors and details…and/or night blindness (inability to see in very dim light), see an eye specialist (ophthalmologist or optometrist) promptly.

Important: AMD can start in one eye while the other remains normal. This can make changes in vision difficult to notice until they become pronounced and affect both eyes.

Best approach: Schedule a yearly eye exam, particularly after age 65, to spot early signs of AMD. The doctor should use drops to dilate the pupils so he/she can see the retinas clearly with a magnifying instrument. To monitor your eyesight between visits to your doctor, check your vision daily with an Amsler grid.

NUTRITIONAL THERAPY

A large clinical trial sponsored by the National Eye Institute found that a high-dose mixture of antioxidants and zinc could slow the disease in a substantial number of people with dry AMD.

For patients with varying stages of AMD, a supplement containing vitamin C—500 mg… vitamin E—400 international units (IU)…beta-carotene—15 mg…and zinc—80 mg, with 2 mg of copper to prevent deficiency of that mineral, reduced the risk for progression to an advanced stage of the disease by about 25%, compared with a placebo. This formulation, known as AREDS (Age-Related Eye Disease

Study), can be found in a single supplement at drugstores.

If you have early AMD: Increase your dietary intake of dark green, leafy vegetables, which contain the nutrients described above… and cold-water fish, for their omega-3 fatty acids. Red wine, which contains antioxidants, also may protect against AMD. If you smoke, it's crucial that you stop.

If you have intermediate AMD or advanced AMD in one eye: Take the supplement combination described above (along with a daily multivitamin, if you like). In addition, follow the dietary guidelines described above.

NEW DRUG TREATMENTS

Until fairly recently, wet AMD made severe vision loss a near certainty, but new medications have enabled many people to preserve their sight. Anti-VEGF (vascular endothelial growth factor) drugs stop production of fragile new blood vessels by blocking the action of a protein that blood vessels need to develop. These drugs are injected into the eye monthly.

•*Ranibizumab* (**Lucentis**) is the first anti-VEGF drug to receive FDA approval for AMD. In clinical trials, it stabilized vision in nearly all the patients who used it for a year…and up to 34% registered significant improvements in sight. The effects appear to increase over time.

•*Bevacizumab* (**Avastin**) has been approved for the treatment of colorectal cancer, but appears to be equally effective when administered intravenously for wet AMD.

•*Aflibercept,* another anti-VEGF drug, is now on the market under the brand name Eylea for treatment of AMD. It is given every other month.

•**Photodynamic therapy is an older approach that involves the injection of the drug *verteporfin* (Visudyne)** into the bloodstream. When a laser beam activates the chemical within the eye, it seals off abnormal blood vessels. Photodynamic therapy is less effective than anti-VEGF drugs and will slow—but may not stop—vision decline. Nowadays, photodynamic therapy has mostly been supplanted by anti-VEGF drugs. A study is under way to

determine whether combining the two will be more effective than either alone.

ON THE HORIZON

Scientific research is focusing on AMD prevention. *For example, one recent study suggests that a protective effect may be offered by…*

•**Lutein and zeaxanthin.** Research has found that the plant-based antioxidants lutein and zeaxanthin may reduce the risk for intermediate and advanced AMD in women under age 75. It is believed that these antioxidants provide protective effects for men as well.

A major trial is currently under way to determine if a supplement with these nutrients and omega-3s might halt progression of the disease.

If you are age 65 or older, go to the Web site of the Foundation of the American Academy of Ophthalmology's EyeCare America at *www.eyecareamerica.org* to see if you qualify for a free eye exam in your area.

Little-Known Signs You've Got Cataracts

David F. Chang, MD, clinical professor of ophthalmology at the University of California, San Francisco. Dr. Chang codiscovered intraoperative floppy iris syndrome (IFIS), an iris problem that can complicate cataract surgery. He is coauthor of *Cataracts: A Patient's Guide to Treatment* (Slack).

Cataracts can develop so slowly in some people that they do not even realize they have an eye problem.

A cataract is a clouding of the eye's lens that leads to progressive loss of vision. Ordinarily, the lens, which is located behind the pupil, is clear—light passes through it. Cataracts most often are a normal result of aging, but can also result from eye injury, certain eye diseases and drugs, and some medical disorders, including diabetes. In the early stages of a cataract, just a small portion of the eye's lens may become cloudy. Only when the cloudiness of the eye's lens increases over time—sometimes over a period of years—does the person's vision worsen.

Even though cataracts are quite common—about half of people over age 65 have some signs of the condition—few people are aware that many common vision problems actually can be the result of cataracts.

To learn more about diagnosis and the latest treatment options, we spoke with internationally recognized cataract surgeon and researcher David F. Chang, MD…

SYMPTOMS THAT CAN BE MISSED

If your vision starts to appear cloudy or blurry, you might suspect a cataract—these are among the most widely recognized symptoms. But there are many other symptoms that are not nearly as well-known and that can prevent people from getting proper eye care. Symptoms can vary greatly, depending on the location, severity and type of cataract. Cataracts may be age-related, due to an eye injury, congenital (present at birth) or appearing in childhood. *Questions to ask yourself…*

• **Do colors appear faded or washed out?**

• **Do I have trouble seeing distant objects,** such as highway signs, while wearing eyeglasses?

• **Do I need more light than I used to for close work,** such as reading small print and sewing? Do my eyes tire more easily when I'm engaged in these activities?

• **Does glare make it much harder for me to drive at night or see well in bright sunlight?**

• **Do I ever experience "ghost images,"** such as seeing multiple moons at night?

If you answered "yes" to several of these questions, consult an ophthalmologist (a physician who specializes in medical and surgical eye care) or an optometrist (a nonphysician who can test for common eye problems, such as nearsightedness and cataracts, but who does not perform surgery).

A doctor can identify a cataract by dilating a patient's pupil and examining the eye with a table-mounted microscope called a slit lamp.

Important: Even if you do not experience any of the symptoms described above, get your eyes checked regularly after age 40 to help identify any treatable eye problems, such as glaucoma, a vision-robbing eye disease marked by increased pressure within the eyeball.

ARE YOU AT INCREASED RISK?

Age is a primary risk factor for cataracts. After age 50, cataracts are the most common cause of decreased vision. *Other risk factors…*

• **Family history.** In some families, cataracts tend to occur at an earlier age. If a family member, such as a parent or sibling, developed cataracts before age 60, you also may be at increased risk of developing cataracts at around the same age.

• **Medical conditions.** Diabetes increases the risk for cataracts three- to fourfold. This is because elevated blood sugar levels can cause changes in the lens that, in turn, can lead to cataracts.

Self-defense: Work with your doctor to manage your blood sugar levels.

• **Nearsightedness.** For reasons that are not yet understood, severely nearsighted people often develop cataracts at an earlier age.

• **Steroid use.** Long-term (one year or more) oral steroid use can increase risk for cataracts. Long-term use of inhaled steroids, taken at high doses, also may increase risk.

• **Eye diseases.** Some eye diseases, such as chronic eye inflammation (uveitis), increase risk for cataracts. Prior eye surgery—for retinal problems, for example—also raises risk.

• **Eye injuries.** Cataracts may develop, sometimes years later, as a result of eye injuries, such as those that can occur when being struck by a blunt object (like a ball).

Self-defense: Wear polycarbonate safety goggles (available at sporting-goods stores) when playing sports such as squash and racketball.

• **Sun exposure.** The sun's ultraviolet rays also can increase cataract risk. Wear a broad-brimmed hat and UV-blocking sunglasses.

DO YOU NEED SURGERY?

If cataracts interfere with your ability to read, drive, work or enjoy a hobby, you may need surgery.

Most ophthalmologists in the US perform "small-incision" surgery, a 20- to 30-minute outpatient procedure in which the surgeon uses an ultrathin blade to make an incision of about one-eighth inch in the cornea. The cataract is removed with ultrasound wave technology, vibrating at 40,000 times per second, to break up the cloudy lens into smaller fragments.

After these pieces of the lens are gently suctioned out, an artificial lens, called an intraocular lens, is permanently implanted in place of the natural lens. Once removed, cataracts will never recur, and the artificial lens will last for the patient's lifetime.

Small-incision surgery can be performed with topical anesthesia (eyedrops) and usually requires no sutures. (A tiny flap is created that closes on its own.) The success rate of cataract surgery in otherwise healthy eyes approaches 98%. Severe complications, such as infection or bleeding in the eye, are rare.

Latest development: New artificial lens implants that can reduce a patient's dependence on eyeglasses are now available. These multifocal lenses may provide focus for both near and far distances, allowing many patients to read without eyeglasses.

Because multifocal lenses are considered a convenience—rather than a medical necessity—patients must pay an additional out-of-pocket cost ($2,000 to $3,000 per lens) under Medicare and private insurance plans.

Important recent finding: Recent research has shown that use of drugs called alphablockers, such as *tamsulosin* (Flomax) taken for an enlarged prostate, can interfere with the necessary dilation of the pupil during surgery. Known as intraoperative floppy iris syndrome, this condition can make cataract surgery more difficult for your surgeon.

If you are planning to have cataract surgery, tell your doctor if you are taking an alpha-blocker, such as tamsulosin. Patients with cataracts or symptoms of poor vision should have an eye exam before starting to take an alpha-blocker.

The High Blood Pressure–Hot Flash Link

Women who experience hot flashes have much higher blood pressure, on average, than women who don't.

Hot flashes—a symptom of menopause—are feelings of intense heat along with sweating and rapid heartbeat. Flashes usually last from two to 30 minutes each and may occur as often as a dozen times a day. Women who have hot flashes should have their blood pressure monitored closely.

Linda Gerber, PhD, professor of public health and medicine and director of the biostatistics and research methodology core, Weill Medical College of Cornell University, New York City, and author of a study on hot flashes and blood pressure, published in *Menopause.*

Acupuncture Cools Common Menopause Symptom

After seven weeks, postmenopausal women who had acupuncture twice a week for the first two weeks and once a week thereafter had a greater reduction in nocturnal hot flashes than women who had a treatment that felt like acupuncture but wasn't.

Some women getting acupuncture had minor side effects, such as pain, redness and itching where needles were inserted.

Mary I. Huang, MS, clinical research coordinator of a Stanford University School of Medicine study, led by Rachel Manber, PhD, of the effectiveness of acupuncture for nocturnal hot flashes, published in *Fertility and Sterility.*

What Really Works to Ease Hot Flashes

Andrea Sikon, MD, board-certified internist and director of primary care/women's health for the Medicine Institute at the Cleveland Clinic in Cleveland. She is certified as a menopause practitioner by the North American Menopause Society.

As many as 75% of menopausal women experience the sudden waves of body heat known as hot flashes. Episodes can be mild, causing just a few moments of discomfort...or intense enough to make a woman drip with perspiration.

Hot flashes and night sweats (which come on during sleep) are triggered by fluctuating levels of the hormone estrogen, affecting a woman's inner thermostat and causing blood vessels near the skin's surface to dilate. Typically, a hot flash ends after several minutes, though it can last a half-hour or more. Episodes generally abate after a few years—but some women continue to have hot flashes for the rest of their lives.

Here's what you should know about which remedies help...which are of questionable value...and which are downright dangerous.

Important: Before beginning any therapy, talk to your doctor about its pros and cons and how they relate to your individual risk factors.

PRESCRIPTION DRUGS

Estrogen is the only prescription medication currently FDA-approved specifically for hot flashes, but others can be prescribed "off-label."

Most effective...

• **Estrogen therapy.** This reduces hot flashes by making up for a woman's own diminishing production of the hormone. It also eases other menopausal symptoms, such as mood swings, vaginal dryness, thinning skin and bone loss...and may reduce risk for hip fracture and colon cancer.

Caution: Estrogen therapy can increase risk for heart disease, stroke, blood clots, breast cancer and possibly Alzheimer's disease. The more time that has passed since a woman reached menopause and/or the longer she takes estrogen, the greater the risks may be.

Consider estrogen if: Hot flashes reduce your quality of life...you have additional menopausal symptoms...and your doctor says that you have no increased cardiovascular or breast cancer risk. If you have not had a hysterectomy, you also must take *progestogen* (a drug similar to the hormone progesterone) to guard against uterine cancer.

Sometimes helpful...

• **Antidepressants.** Selective serotonin reuptake inhibitors (SSRIs), such as *paroxetine* (Paxil), and serotonin/norepinephrine reuptake inhibitors (SNRIs), such as *venlafaxine* (Effexor), may relieve hot flashes by stabilizing the body's temperature-control mechanism.

New: The manufacturer of the SNRI *desvenlafaxine* (Pristiq) has applied for FDA approval of the drug as a treatment for hot flashes.

SSRIs can cause weight gain, dry mouth and decreased sex drive...and may interfere with the breast cancer drug tamoxifen in some women. SNRIs can cause insomnia, dry mouth, constipation or diarrhea, and perhaps high blood pressure.

Consider an antidepressant if: You cannot or do not want to use estrogen therapy and/or hot flashes are accompanied by mood swings.

• *Gabapentin* (Neurontin). In one study, this antiseizure drug was as effective against hot flashes as estrogen. Side effects may include sedation, dizziness and mild or widespread swelling.

Consider gabapentin if: You also have insomnia and do not have additional symptoms better treated by estrogen or antidepressants.

• *Clonidine* (Catapres). This blood pressure drug affects the central nervous system. In some small studies, it reduced hot flashes. Clonidine can cause dizziness, fatigue, dry mouth and constipation.

Consider clonidine if: Other therapies have failed to relieve hot flashes, and you also require treatment for high blood pressure.

ALTERNATIVE THERAPIES

The FDA does not test herbs or dietary supplements. Nonprescription products labeled "natural" are not necessarily effective or even safe. If you try them, choose brands that have the United States Pharmacopeia (USP) seal to ensure purity.

Perhaps helpful...

•**Supplements of soy and black cohosh.** These have phytoestrogens, plant compounds with estrogen-like effects. Theoretically, they could ease hot flashes via the same mechanism as estrogen—but they also may carry similar risks.

Caution: Women who ought not take prescription estrogen (for instance, due to elevated risk for heart disease or breast cancer) should use these products only with their doctors' approval.

•**Flaxseeds.** One small Mayo Clinic study found that hot flash frequency was reduced by half in women who consumed two tablespoons of ground flaxseeds twice daily for six weeks.

Possible reason: Flaxseeds contain lignans, antioxidants with estrogenic effects. Get your doctor's approval before using. Drink lots of water with flaxseeds to prevent gas and constipation.

•**Acupuncture.** A few studies suggest that this is somewhat effective for hot flashes.

Best: Use an acupuncturist certified by the National Certification Commission for Acupuncture and Oriental Medicine (904-598-1005, *www.nccaom.org*).

Probably not helpful...

•**Evening primrose oil...ginseng... vitamins B, C and E.** These fared no better than placebos in studies.

Ginseng should not be used with blood thinners, stimulants or antidepressant MAO inhibitors...vitamins C and E can cause bleeding in people who take blood thinners.

•**Magnets.** Supporters claim that magnetic fields have healing powers. However, in an Indiana University study, sham magnets eased hot flashes better than real magnets.

Dangerous...

•**Over-the-counter topical progestogen cream.** Absorption varies dramatically from woman to woman—so using these without a doctor's supervision can lead to hormone imbalances.

•**Dong quai.** This herb can interfere with medications and may contain a potential carcinogen.

•**Kava.** This herb is intoxicating and can damage the liver.

•**Licorice extract.** In large doses, it can cause leg edema (swelling), high blood pressure and dangerously low potassium levels.

Stress Hastens Menopause

Menopause started one year earlier, on average, among women who had "high strain" jobs than it did among women whose jobs were less stressful. (The average age of menopause in the US is 51.) High-strain jobs require employees to rush, perform several tasks at once and/or deal with interruptions.

Theory: Stress may upset a woman's hormone balance, which may expedite the aging of ovaries.

Bernard Cassou, MD, professor, Center of Gerontology, Université Versailles-Saint Quentin, Hôpital Sainte Périne, and lead researcher of a study of 1,594 women, published in *American Journal of Epidemiology*.

What You Need to Know About Hormone Therapy

JoAnn E. Manson, MD, DrPH, professor of medicine and women's health at Harvard Medical School and chair of the division of preventive medicine at Brigham and Women's Hospital, both in Boston. A lead investigator for two important studies on women's health, Dr. Manson is author of *Hot Flashes, Hormones & Your Health* (McGraw-Hill).

What happens to a woman's health risks after she stops using hormone therapy (HT) following five to seven years of use? Until recently, there was little rigorous scientific data to address this question.

Now: New findings from the Women's Health Initiative (WHI) study provide an answer.

At the start of the WHI, in the mid-1990s, more than 16,000 women ages 50 to 79 were assigned to take either a combination of estrogen plus progestin (Prempro) or a placebo for 5.6 years. After they stopped taking the pills, the women were tracked for three more years.

Good news: The risks for heart attack, stroke and blood clots, which rose while women were taking HT, quickly dropped back toward normal after HT was stopped.

Bad news: Benefits of HT—relief from hot flashes, protection against bone loss and fractures—also dissipated quickly…a slightly higher risk for breast cancer persisted…and there was a suggestion of a higher risk for various cancers and for death in the post-HT years.

Significance: These findings reinforce current guidelines advising women to consider HT only for short-term relief from moderate-to-severe menopausal hot flashes or night sweats that significantly disrupt their quality of life and/or sleep. Ideally, treatment should be limited to two to three years or, at most, five years.

Although HT does help prevent fractures, it is no longer recommended as a first line of defense against osteoporosis.

Reason: The average age of women who break a hip is close to 80 years, so women would need to take HT for many, many years to maintain bone protection when fracture risk is greatest.

Keys to safety: Health status and timing. HT-related heart attack, stroke and blood clot risks are low for women in good cardiovascular health whose periods ended less than 10 years ago, but higher in those who are older and/or in poorer cardiovascular health.

Example: Among women who entered the WHI trial with better cholesterol levels, those assigned to HT had a 40% lower risk for coronary heart disease than those on a placebo…but among women who entered with worse cholesterol levels, HT users had a 73% higher risk.

The balance of benefits and risks of HT appears quite favorable for younger women. Among WHI participants in their 50s, HT use was linked to a 30% reduction in mortality. This does not mean that healthy, recently menopausal women should take HT specifically to prevent health problems—rather, when taking HT for short-term symptom management, such women need not be overly concerned about risks.

What's next: More research is needed to determine if lower doses of oral HT or transdermal patches or gels can further minimize risk.

Cholesterol Predicts Hormone Therapy Risk

Hormone therapy (HT) eases menopausal hot flashes but may raise heart attack and stroke risk.

Recent study: Women whose ratio of LDL (bad) to HDL (good) cholesterol was below 2.5 had no increased cardiovascular risk from HT. For women with ratios of 2.5 or higher, HT did magnify cardiovascular risk.

Recommended: Discuss your ratio with your doctor if you are considering HT.

Paul F. Bray, MD, professor of medicine and director of hematology, Jefferson Medical College, Philadelphia, and leader of a study of 978 women, published in *The American Journal of Cardiology.*

Hormone Therapy (HT) May Affect Your Hearing

Women who are taking progestin have 10% to 30% higher risk of hearing loss than women taking estrogen alone or not using hormone therapy (HT) at all.

If you are taking progestin: Have your hearing checked every six months.

Robert D. Frisina, PhD, University of Rochester Medical Center, Rochester, New York, and senior author of a study of 124 women, published in *The Proceedings of the National Academy of Sciences.*

Why Women Get Shorter...and How To Stand Tall

Arthur H. White, MD, retired orthopedic spine surgeon, Walnut Creek, California. He is author of *The Posture Prescription: The Doctor's Rx for Eliminating Back, Muscle, and Joint Pain* (Three Rivers). He has published more than 200 medical journal articles related to spinal health.

The cliché of the hunched-over "little old lady" may seem outdated, yet it's true—we all get shorter as we age. However, a good portion of this shrinkage can be prevented or corrected. The following steps can help you stand tall...plus reduce your risk for back pain and slim your silhouette.

PROTECT YOUR SPINE

Each vertebra (an individual segment of the spine) is separated from adjoining ones by water-filled cushions called disks. In young adults, each disk is about one inch thick.

After about age 40, these disks begin to crack and tear, which causes them to dehydrate and flatten. Over two decades or so, each disk loses about one-twelfth of an inch of thickness—and with 23 disks, that equates to a loss of nearly two inches of height.

Any uncontrolled motion that stresses your back can increase the risk for disk damage. Activities that involve abrupt twisting—racket sports, skating, roughhousing with kids—can tear the disks, hastening dehydration. There is no need to quit these activities, but do try to avoid wrenching twists.

Three other reasons we shrink as we get older are poor posture, loss of abdominal muscle tone and reduced bone density. These problems tend to worsen over time. The humpback seen in many older women is an obvious manifestation of this, but there also are more subtle warning signs that you may be aging yourself prematurely.

PERFECT YOUR POSTURE

Poor attention to posture may be to blame for height loss if you...

• **Slump forward when sitting.**

• **Drive, watch TV or work at a computer with your head jutting forward** (instead of centered over your torso).

• **Experience back or neck pain.**

• **Have frequent headaches.**

• **Have pain in your arms or hands (pain radiates from the spine).**

Chronic slouching weakens back and chest muscles, so you eventually may find it difficult to stand up straight even when you try. Large-breasted women are particularly prone to slouching. The extra weight they carry in front places more strain on the back muscles.

Simple steps to stand tall...

• **First, check your posture.** Have someone take your picture while you stand sideways in a doorway. Stand as you normally do—if you don't, you'll only be fooling yourself. The door frame provides a visual guide to what is straight.

• **Second, stay aware.** Whenever you pass a mirror or window, notice the position of your neck, shoulders and back. If your head juts forward, pull it back in line with your shoulders ...roll your shoulders back...squeeze your shoulder blades together more...draw in your tummy...and tuck your rear end under. Even if you can't remain that straight for long, these brief moments of awareness will help to realign your spine and strengthen your muscles.

• **Third, stretch and strengthen.** When muscles are not used, they get smaller and weaker. Prevent or reverse problem posture with a few simple exercises. These are generally safe for everyone, though it is best to check with your doctor before beginning any new type of workout.

• **Secret stretch can be done anywhere.** It returns shoulders to their proper position and strengthens muscles between shoulder blades. Clasp your hands behind your back at the level of your buttocks. Push your hands down and roll your shoulders back (don't arch your back). Hold for 30 seconds. Repeat several times daily—while waiting for an elevator, watching TV or anytime you are idle.

Advanced: With hands clasped behind you and arms straight, raise arms up and away from you.

•**Doorway stretch strengthens your shoulders and back and stretches chest muscles.** Stand in a doorway, a few inches behind the threshold, feet shoulder-width apart. Place one hand on each side of the doorjamb, level with your shoulders. Keeping your back straight, lean forward, feeling the stretch across your upper chest as your back muscles work to draw your shoulder blades together. Hold for 30 seconds...repeat five times. Do every other day or whenever you feel upper-back tension.

FABULOUS ABS HELP

When tightened, abdominal muscles act as a muscular corset, supporting the vertebrae and protecting them from injury. Strong abs allow you to stand tall by preventing your rib cage from slumping down toward your pelvis.

Women generally have a more difficult time maintaining abdominal strength than men because pregnancy overstretches the belly muscles. A little effort goes a long way, however, in restoring the strength of the abs. *To try...*

•**Isometric crunch and hold.** Lie with knees bent and feet flat on the floor. Cross arms across your chest. Tuck chin slightly... then raise your head and shoulders (not your entire back) off the floor by tightening your belly muscles. Keep your head in line with your shoulders, and leave enough space to fit a tennis ball between your chin and chest. Hold the position as long as possible, then slowly lower down to the starting position. Repeat, continuing for three to five minutes. At first, you may be able to hold the pose for only a second or two and may need to rest between each crunch. Keep at it daily—soon your abs will get stronger.

BUILD STRONGER BONES

Osteoporosis is a disease in which bones become so fragile that even the jolt of slipping off a curb can fracture the spine. In severe cases, the weight of the person's own body can slowly crush vertebrae, producing a rounded humpback that steals as much as four inches of height.

Because estrogen helps to build bone, women are susceptible to osteoporosis after menopause, when estrogen levels drop. Ask your doctor about taking supplements of calcium and vitamin D. *Also...*

•**Go for a walk.** Every time your foot hits the ground, the impact sends a vibration through your bones. This produces an electrical force (the piezoelectric effect) that strengthens bones by encouraging calcium deposits throughout the skeleton.

Alternatives: Running builds even more bone density but may injure joints—so stick to brisk walking unless you're already an accomplished runner. Weight lifting also builds bone through similar forces, but the effect is less because there is no impact or vibration.

Fight Osteoporosis the Natural Way

Mark A. Stengler, NMD, licensed naturopathic medical doctor in private practice, Encinitas, California... adjunct associate clinical professor at the National College of Natural Medicine, Portland, Oregon...author of *The Natural Physician's Healing Therapies* and co-author of *Prescription for Natural Cures* (both from Bottom Line Books).

Misconceptions abound when it comes to osteoporosis, a dreaded disease marked by porous, brittle bones and hunched backs. Most people think of osteoporosis as a women's disease, but it's more than that. While 8 million American women have been diagnosed with osteoporosis, more than 2 million men also are affected by it.

OSTEOPOROSIS: A SILENT PROBLEM

Osteoporosis can develop because, starting at about age 35, our bone cells do not make new bone as fast as it is broken down. Our bones become more frail and fracture more easily. Fractures, especially of the hip, spine and wrist, are more likely to occur, even without trauma. Osteoporosis has no symptoms until a bone is fractured. Many people go for decades without a diagnosis of osteoporosis—until they fall and an X-ray reveals porous bones.

Bone density can be measured with a dual-energy X-ray absorptiometry (DEXA) scan, but many people don't get this test. I recommend a baseline DEXA scan by age 50, and if results are normal, follow-ups every three to five years.

The most worrisome risk for a person with osteoporosis is a hip fracture. According to the National Osteoporosis Foundation (*www. nof.org*), an average of 24% of hip-fracture patients age 50 or older die in the year following their fractures, often as a result of long-term immobilization that leads to blood clots or infection. Six months after a hip fracture, only 15% of patients can walk across a room without any help.

Virtually every person with osteoporosis who has come to my clinic is confused about the best way to promote bone health. Conventional doctors typically prescribe osteoporosis medication, such as *alendronate* (Fosamax) and *ibandronate* (Boniva). However, these drugs can cause side effects, such as digestive upset and blood clots, and they don't address the underlying nutritional deficiencies that promote bone loss.

The natural protocol I recommend includes a healthful diet (rich in vegetables, fruit and fish and low in refined-sugar products and red meat)…weight-bearing exercise (such as walking and stair-climbing)…and good hormone balance (deficiencies of some hormones, such as testosterone, accelerate bone loss). I also suggest certain bone-protecting supplements.

Caution: People with kidney disease should not take supplements without consulting a doctor. With kidney disease, the kidneys cannot process high doses of many nutrients.

My recommendations for women and men: To help prevent osteoporosis, take the first three supplements listed below. If you have osteoporosis or osteopenia (mild bone loss that can be diagnosed with a DEXA scan), take the first three supplements listed and as

many of the others as you're willing to try, in the dosages recommended…

SUPER TRIO PREVENTS AND TREATS OSTEOPOROSIS

Calcium is the most prevalent mineral in bone tissue. Taking supplements helps prevent a deficiency. Most studies have found that calcium slows bone loss but does not increase bone density when used alone. Women with osteoporosis should take 500 milligrams (mg) of calcium twice daily with meals. It should be a well-absorbed form, such as citrate, citrate-malate, amino acid chelate or hydroxyapatite. To boost absorption, take no more than 500 mg per dose. Calcium carbonate, which is widely used, is not well-absorbed. For osteoporosis prevention, men and women, as well as boys and girls starting at age 13, should take 500 mg daily.

Calcium supplementation for men with osteoporosis is more complicated. Some recent research has identified a link between high calcium intake (from dairy products) and increased prostate cancer risk. A meta-analysis in the *Journal of the National Cancer Institute* that reviewed 12 studies on this association concluded, "High intake of dairy products and calcium may be associated with an increased risk for prostate cancer, although the increase appears to be small." A recent study found that calcium intake exceeding 1,500 mg a day (from food and supplements) may be associated with a higher risk of advanced, and potentially fatal, prostate cancer. The saturated fat in dairy products may raise prostate cancer risk.

Until there is more definitive information, I recommend that men who have osteoporosis, regardless of whether they have eliminated calcium-rich foods from their diets, take no more than a 500-mg calcium supplement daily. Men with prostate cancer should consult their doctors before using calcium supplements.

Vitamin D promotes absorption of calcium. Deficiencies of this vitamin are more common in Americans over age 50 than in younger adults. Sun exposure prompts the body to produce vitamin D, and the kidneys help convert it to its active form. As we age, our skin cannot synthesize vitamin D as effectively from sunlight, and our kidneys become less efficient.

People with darker skin, those with digestive problems (due to malabsorption conditions, such as Crohn's disease) and those with limited exposure to sunlight are also at greater risk for vitamin D deficiency. Preliminary studies indicate that an inadequate intake of vitamin D is associated with an increased risk of fractures.

For the prevention of osteoporosis, I recommend 600 international units (IU) to 800 IU of vitamin D daily. People with osteoporosis should take 800 IU to 1,200 IU daily. Vitamin D is fat soluble, meaning it is better absorbed when taken with meals (containing small amounts of fat).

For many patients with low vitamin D levels, I recommend 2,000 IU of vitamin D daily. To ensure that vitamin D levels are optimal, I monitor blood levels once or twice a year. Overdosing can lead to heart arrhythmia, anorexia, nausea and other ill effects.

Magnesium, an important constituent of bone crystals, is crucial for the proper metabolism of calcium. A deficiency of magnesium impairs bone-building cells known as osteoblasts. Like calcium, magnesium requires vitamin D for absorption.

Researchers at Tel Aviv University in Israel looked at the effect of magnesium supplementation on bone density in 31 postmenopausal women with osteoporosis. This two-year, open, controlled trial (both the researchers and patients knew who was receiving the placebo or the supplement) involved giving the participants 250 mg to 750 mg of magnesium daily for six months and 250 mg for another 18 months. Twenty-two patients (71%) experienced a 1% to 8% increase in bone density. The mean bone density of all treated patients increased significantly after one year and remained at that level after two years. Among an additional 23 postmenopausal women not receiving magnesium, mean bone density decreased significantly.

For osteoporosis prevention, take 400 mg to 500 mg of magnesium daily...for osteoporosis, take 500 mg to 750 mg daily. In both cases, take in divided doses.

IF YOU HAVE BONE-LOSS DISEASE

Vitamin K has received attention in recent years for its role in treating osteoporosis. It activates *osteocalcin*, a bone protein that regulates calcium metabolism in the bones and helps calcium bind to the tissues that make up the bone. It also has been shown to inhibit inflammatory chemicals that cause bone breakdown.

Studies have shown that low vitamin K intake and blood levels are associated with reduced bone density and fractures in people who have osteoporosis. A recent meta-analysis published in the American Medical Association's *Archives of Internal Medicine* found that vitamin K supplements were associated with a consistent reduction in all types of fractures. Leafy, green vegetables, such as spinach, kale, collard greens and broccoli, are the best sources of vitamin K, yet many people do not consume these vitamin K–rich foods on a regular basis. High-dose vitamin K (above 2 mg) should be used only under the supervision of a doctor, because excess vitamin K may increase blood clotting. Vitamin K supplements should not be used by people who take blood-thinning medication, such as *warfarin* (Coumadin) or *heparin,* or by pregnant women or nursing mothers. I typically recommend 2 mg to 10 mg daily of vitamin K for people who have osteoporosis to help increase their bone density.

Essential fatty acids (EFAs) have been shown to improve bone density in older women and are believed also to promote bone health in men. Many researchers theorize that osteoporosis develops because of chronic inflammation of bone tissue (due to stress, toxins, poor diet and infection). EFAs, especially those found in fish oil, reduce inflammation. Some studies show that EFAs also improve calcium absorption. I recommend that people with osteoporosis take fish oil daily (containing about 480 mg of EPA and 320 mg of DHA), along with 3,000 mg of evening primrose oil, which contains inflammation-fighting gamma-linolenic acid (GLA). Because EFAs have a blood-thinning effect, check with your doctor if you are taking a blood thinner.

Strontium is a mineral that doesn't get much attention, because it is not regarded as essential for the human body. However, 99%

of the total amount of strontium found in the body is located in the teeth and bones. Supplemental strontium is not the radioactive type that you may have heard about in relation to nuclear facilities. Strontium is a valuable mineral for people with osteoporosis, and I often recommend it.

A 2004 clinical trial in *The New England Journal of Medicine* found that strontium prevents vertebral fractures and increases bone density. The most common supplemental forms are strontium chloride and strontium citrate. I suggest a supplement that contains 680 mg of elemental strontium daily (similar to the dose used in most studies). Because calcium inhibits strontium absorption, strontium should be taken at least four hours before or after calcium is taken. Strontium should not be taken by pregnant women and nursing mothers. It is not available at most health-food stores, but you can buy it from Vitacost (800-381-0759, *www.vitacost.com*). A 120-capsule supply costs about $13.

Soy, as a supplement and/or food, has been shown in several studies to improve bone density. Soy contains isoflavones, estrogen-like constituents that support bone mass and relieve menopausal symptoms in women. Women and men with osteoporosis or osteopenia should take 125 mg of soy isoflavones daily in soy protein powder or supplement form and consume three to five servings of soy foods weekly. (One serving equals one-half cup of tofu...one-half cup of soy beans...or one cup of soy milk.)

Caution: Soy supplements are not well studied in women who have had breast cancer, so they should avoid supplements and nonfermented soy products.

Vitamin C is required for the production of the protein collagen, a component of bone tissue. I recommend that people with osteoporosis take 1,000 mg twice daily. Reduce the dosage if loose stools develop.

Silicon is a trace mineral required for bone formation. I recommend 2 mg to 5 mg daily.

BEST OSTEOPOROSIS FORMULAS

These products contain all the vitamins and minerals described in this article, in the therapeutic doses used for osteoporosis treatment...

- **Bone-Up by Jarrow.** To find an online retailer, call 800-726-0886 or go to *www.jarrow.com.*

- **OsteoPrime by Enzymatic Therapy.** To find a retailer, call 800-783-2286 or go to *www.enzymatictherapy.com.*

- **Bone Plus.** It is available from my clinic at 855-362-6275, *http://markstengler.com.*

Are Osteoporosis Drugs Killing Your Bones?

Andrew L. Rubman, ND, director, Southbury Clinic for Traditional Medicines, Southbury, Connecticut.

Salvatore Ruggiero, DMD, MD, former chief of oral and maxillofacial surgery at Long Island Jewish Medical Center and currently an oral surgeon at the New York Center for Orthognathic & Maxillofacial Surgery, West Islip, New York.

Salvatore Ruggiero, DMD, MD, former chief of oral and maxillofacial surgery at Long Island Jewish Medical Center in New Hyde Park, New York, was astonished to see a rare condition develop with the jaw bone in a particular set of female patients. The condition, called osteonecrosis of the jaw (ONJ), is a condition that tends to occur after dental work that causes trauma to the jaw. Doctors often detect it when the jawbone becomes exposed and sometimes an infection has set in. ONJ had been associated with bisphosphonates before *alendronate* (Fosamax), but previous to this, patients were those who had been administered bisphosphonates as IV treatment for cancer. What Dr. Ruggiero observed was ONJ had also developed in another group of patients who had undergone oral surgery at his hospital over a three-year period. These women were taking bisphosphonates orally for the treatment of osteoporosis. (Besides Fosamax, other bisphosphonates for osteoporosis include Boniva and Actonel.)

We called Dr. Ruggiero to discuss what millions of women currently taking bisphosphonates should do in response to this finding. He stresses that while the Food and Drug Administration (FDA) now requires that drug manufacturers add labeling stating that ONJ is a potential side effect of bisphosphonates, the condition as associated with osteoporosis is rare. Of the 159 ONJ patients from his medical center, just 25 had taken the medication orally and the overall percentage of women on oral bisphosphonates who develop ONJ is much smaller than that—well under 1% of all patients, he says. That said, there are those who theorize, including director of the Southbury (Connecticut) Clinic for Traditional Medicines Andrew L. Rubman, ND, that ONJ is just the first sign of a broader bone deterioration problem. He explains that the long-term survival of bone is dependant on ongoing activity of both bone formation by osteoblast cells and bone resorption (removal or breakdown of micro-damaged or old bone) by osteoclast cells. Inhibiting osteoclast function with bisphosphonates has the effect of slowing and eventually stopping the other over time, believes Dr. Rubman. Risk ONJ or spend elderly years with dead bones?

STEPS TO TAKE

Prior to this disclosure, the main reported side effects of bisphosphonates were a bevy of gastrointestinal problems. As long as women's "tummies didn't rumble" they saw no reason to suspend use of the medication. Besides, *ibandronate* (Boniva), a newer bisphosphonate drug that requires taking just once a month rather than daily or weekly, as with Fosamax, seemed to help with GI side effects. However, Dr. Ruggiero feels it is time to rethink the length of time osteoporosis patients are allowed to stay on any of these drugs. He anticipates that the next step may be to have "drug holidays" in which women go off the medication for several years at a time, and then return to it for the same period before suspending its use once again. Women would need to be monitored in this period for any bone deterioration with bone density scans… and they must also be careful to continue vigi-lance about protecting their bone strength in more traditional ways, such as taking their calcium and vitamin D, exercising regularly, limiting alcohol and not smoking.

ONJ AND DENTAL CARE

Dr. Ruggiero is extremely concerned about some of the over-reaction he is seeing among patients who are shying away from routine dental care and even among dentists who are reluctant to treat this group of patients. He stresses that routine dental care is not likely to open the gates to ONJ—it is bone that was once traumatized that fails to heal properly that causes the problem, for example, work that involves trauma to the jaw including extractions and implants. Furthermore, he says it is critical for all women on bisphosphonates to get regular careful dental care. That is how they can be sure their teeth will stay strong so they will not end up needing extractions or implants. He says for those women who do have to have dental work that will involve jaw bone healing, information to date shows that there is nothing to worry about if they have been on oral bisphosphonates for up to five years.

The exception: For those patients taking steroids and a bisphosphonate, the time frame is much less, or as little as two years. For those who have taken them longer, he suggests going off the medication for at least a few months before elective dental work. Even though these drugs stay in the bones for an extremely long time, he says that a year off them does seem to make ONJ more manageable—assuming that normal bone cell function can be restored and metabolically supported, based on the ebb and flow of bone cell formation and resorption.

TELLTALE SIGNS OF ONJ

Symptoms of ONJ are pain and/or numbness in the jaw, swelling, loosened teeth, gum infections and exposure of bone within the oral cavity. Women who experience any of those should see their doctor right away.

Dr. Ruggiero says not to be alarmed about the possibility that problems like this could develop in other bones in the body, from bisphosphonates. To date, there has been no reports of this complication occurring anywhere other than the jaw, he added. Dr. Rubman feels somewhat otherwise, given that maintaining the drug is necessary to maintain any bone density gains and the fact that studies have yet to be done to show the effects of discontinuing the drug and the ability of the natural bone turnover process to restart itself. Thus he fears that we may be creating bone that lacks vitality and survivability over time. Dr. Rubman is a strong proponent of doing everything possible to support healthy bone density.

Need a New Knee? Now There's One Made for Women

Aaron G. Rosenberg, MD, professor of orthopedic surgery and director of the Center for Adult Reconstruction and Joint Replacement at Rush University Medical Center in Chicago. He is coeditor of *The Adult Hip* and *The Adult Knee* (both published by Lippincott Williams and Wilkins).

Women are not built like men—obviously. So why expect a knee replacement designed for a man to work equally well for a woman?

Fact is, two-thirds of all knee replacement surgeries are performed on women. Yet until now, female patients have received prosthetic knees that are just smaller versions of the men's—and that don't address women's anatomical differences.

Result: While most knee replacement patients do fine, some do not...and of those who are dissatisfied, a higher percentage are women. Their problems include stiffness, pain, difficulty bending, and an inability to move naturally.

When an injury, infection or arthritis causes deterioration of the knee's cartilage, the bones are left unprotected as they grind against each other. When pain and loss of mobility progress to the point that the patient's lifestyle is compromised, knee replacement surgery may be the best option.

As a member of a team of orthopedic surgeons and medical engineers, I helped to devise the first knee implant specifically designed to fit a woman's anatomy. Called the Zimmer Gender Solutions Knee, it is now widely available. *The device is based on three differences between men and women at the knee joint...*

•**A woman's knee is narrower from side to side,** and her distal femur (the end of the thighbone nearest the knee) tends to be trapezoidal, whereas a man's is more rectangular. Using a traditional implant, a female patient may end up with a joint that has a front-to-back dimension that is too wide, so it presses painfully on the surrounding soft tissues.

•**The bone in the front of a man's knee usually is thicker than a woman's.** Because of this, some women find that the traditional male-oriented implant feels stiff.

•**The female pelvis is wider,** so a woman is more likely to be slightly knock-kneed. Also, a woman has more forward rotation of the hip. These differences affect how well the kneecap tracks over the end of the thighbone as the knee moves through a range of motion.

Some people suggest that the new knee implant for women is just a marketing gimmick. But many orthopedic surgeons recognize the solid science behind it, appreciating that we now have a greater inventory to choose from for each individual patient.

Surgeons who have been using the new implant with female patients report that it requires fewer compromises—such as cutting a patient's bone to make the implant fit—during surgery. And while solid statistics aren't as yet available, anecdotal reports by surgeons indicate that female patients are more satisfied with the new implant.

It's satisfying for me, too, when I hear that the new implant is helping women get back to gardening, golfing or whatever activities bring more enjoyment to their lives.

Overactive Bladder

Rebecca G. Rogers, MD, director of the division of urogynecology at the University of New Mexico Health Sciences Center, and associate professor of obstetrics/gynecology at the University of New Mexico School of Medicine, both in Albuquerque. She is author of *Regaining Bladder Control* (Prometheus).

People with bladder problems are often too embarrassed to report their symptoms to their doctors—and feel that it is just a problem they must learn to live with. Not true.

Bladder problems aren't life-threatening, but they can be life-altering. Patients with overactive bladder (OAB)—increased urinary urgency and/or frequency with or without incontinence—often are ashamed…and they're *always* uncomfortable.

An estimated 34 million American adults have OAB (it affects men and women equally), yet only one in 25 sufferers seeks medical treatment.

Good news: Up to 85% of patients who undergo OAB treatment experience significant improvement or are cured.

BRAIN-BLADDER DISCONNECT

The bladder normally holds approximately eight to 12 ounces of urine before it sends the "have to go" message to the brain. In patients with OAB, as little as a few ounces can trigger the urge to urinate.

Patients with OAB have one or more of the following symptoms…

•**Frequency**—the need to urinate more than eight to 10 times in a 24-hour period.

•**Urgency**—an extremely strong need to urinate immediately.

•**Nocturia**—the complaint that one has to wake more than one time at night to urinate.

About 90% of cases of OAB are idiopathic, meaning the cause is unknown. The remaining cases may be due to spinal cord injuries, neurological diseases (such as Parkinson's), interstitial cystitis (irritation of the bladder wall), a urinary tract infection or a prolapsed (dropped) uterus in women or an enlarged prostate gland in men.

DIAGNOSING OAB

Most cases of OAB can be diagnosed with a medical history. The doctor will ask questions about the frequency of urination, the urgency of sensations, etc. In addition, he/she will diagnose or rule out any identifiable underlying causes for the symptoms.

Tests may include…

•**Urinalysis** to identify a urinary tract infection.

•**Abdominal and/or vaginal or rectal exam** to identify possible obstructions, such as uterine prolapse (descent of the uterus into the vagina) or an enlarged prostate gland.

•**Postvoid residual volume measurement** to determine how completely a patient's bladder empties. Incomplete emptying can result in excessive urinary frequency/urgency. For this outpatient test, the doctor uses a catheter or ultrasound wand to measure the volume of residual urine in the bladder after the patient urinates. A large volume of residual urine could indicate an obstruction or problems with the nerves/muscles in the spine or bladder.

TREATMENTS

Most patients with OAB improve with a combination of behavioral and physical therapies, plus medication in some cases.

Important: Patients with OAB symptoms should keep a voiding diary for at least three days. The diary should include how much you drink…how much and when you urinate (your doctor can provide a plastic "hat," which attaches under the toilet seat, or a urinal, to measure urine output)…whether you've had incontinence episodes, etc. This diary can aid your doctor in making an accurate diagnosis. Also, many patients naturally improve once they become more aware of their urinary habits and may modify the volume and timing of fluid intake and other behaviors.

Best treatment choices for men and women who suffer from OAB…

•**Dietary changes.** Alcohol as well as caffeine, including that found in chocolate, tea and cola, can trigger symptoms in some people. Eliminate these offenders one by one to see if symptoms improve.

•**Pelvic-floor exercises.** Known as Kegels, these simple exercises reduce OAB by strengthening the urinary sphincter (a circular muscle that constricts to retain urine or relaxes to allow urine to pass from the urethra to outside the body) as well as the muscles of the pelvic floor. Contracting pelvic-floor muscles prompts the spinal column to send a message to the bladder to stop contracting.

What to do: Imagine that you're trying to stop the urine flow in midstream. Tightly squeeze the muscles that control urine flow …hold for a count of three…relax for a count of 10…repeat. Do the exercise for five minutes twice daily.

Helpful: Perform Kegels when you feel a sudden sense of urgency. They can help prevent urine leakage on your way to a bathroom.

•**Timed voiding.** Urinate "by the clock" instead of in response to internal signals. Your doctor might advise you to urinate every hour for several days…then every two hours…working up to every two and a half to three hours during the day. Timed voiding trains the bladder to hold more urine for longer periods of time.

•**Medications.** They're often used when behavioral techniques do not work or as an adjunct to these therapies to help patients gain better control—and may be the first choice for some patients with nocturia (since behavioral therapies cannot be used while sleeping). OAB medications include…

•Anticholinergic and antispasmodic drugs, such as *tolterodine* (Detrol), *oxybutynin*, *solifenacin* (Vesicare) and *trospium*. These medications relax the bladder and reduce sensations of urgency. Some studies have found tolterodine to be slightly more effective than the other drugs. *Main side effects:* Dry mouth and constipation. Some older patients may suffer temporary cognitive impairment. Newer drugs in this class, such as solifenacin and trospium, may be less likely to cause cognitive difficulties.

•*Imipramine* (Tofranil). This anti-depressant reduces bladder contractions and also increases the "holding power" of the urethra. Imipramine is typically used to treat nocturia. *Main side effects:* Extreme sedation. When used by older patients, it may increase the risk for low blood pressure and falls.

TREATMENTS ON THE HORIZON

Preliminary studies indicate that inserting a cystoscope into the bladder to inject Botox (normally used to treat wrinkles) in the bladder wall blocks the release of chemicals that cause the bladder to contract. The procedure involves 20 to 30 injection sites and may require anesthesia. Risks include urinary retention.

•**Electrical stimulation.** Electrodes temporarily placed in the vagina or rectum deliver electrical impulses that inhibit nerves in the bladder wall from firing inappropriately. Most patients receive the treatments in a doctor's office once weekly for six to eight weeks. I recommend electrical stimulation, but it has not been well studied and the long-term effects are not known. It's mainly used as a last resort for patients who don't respond to other methods.

Urinary Incontinence Common Among Postmenopausal Women

Postmenopausal women have a high prevalence of urinary incontinence.

Recent finding: 60% of postmenopausal women experience one or more episodes of incontinence in a month. Postmenopausal women with diabetes are more likely to report severe incontinence—difficulty controlling urination, inability to completely empty the bladder and discomfort during urination. Treatment options for incontinence include Kegel (pelvic floor) exercises, medication and surgery.

Sara Jackson, MD, MPH, senior fellow, VA Puget Sound Health Care Center, department of medicine, University of Washington, Seattle, and lead author of a study of 1,017 postmenopausal women, published in *Diabetes Care*.

Should Postmenopausal Women Avoid Extra Iron?

Because postmenopausal women no longer lose blood through menstruation, they tend to build up iron in their body tissue. High levels of iron can lead to a number of problems, including increased risk for infections and inflammatory conditions such as arthritis, fibromyalgia, diabetes and even cancer. About 1% of the world's population has hemochromatosis, a hereditary condition that causes an increased storage of iron that can lead to organ or tissue damage. Men of any age and postmenopausal women who have hemochromatosis are at risk of building up too much iron if they take iron supplements...regularly eat foods rich in iron, especially animal foods, such as liver...and/or use cast-iron cookware. Even if you do not have hemochromatosis, it is best to avoid taking any iron supplements unless you are certain that you have low levels of iron. Ask your physician for a test to determine the iron levels in your body tissue.

Russell B. Marz, ND, assistant professor, department of nutrition, National College of Natural Medicine, Portland, Oregon.

13

Manage Pain

One Woman's Migraine Cure

Migraine headaches had plagued Allison, 35, for 20 years. By the time she came to see me, she was experiencing low-grade headaches daily and full-blown migraines about twice a week. Her head pain always worsened right before her menstrual cycle. Pharmaceutical pain medications, including the potent Vicodin, were no longer effective. A magnetic resonance imaging (MRI) scan ruled out a tumor. The next step, according to conventional treatment, was to try anti-seizure medications. Allison didn't want to go that route, as it became increasingly clear that pharmaceuticals were not treating the cause of her headaches.

IDENTIFYING HIDDEN TRIGGERS

When I questioned Allison, the causes of her headaches quickly became apparent. She told me that her stomach often was painful and bloated, a sign that food allergies and poor digestion were involved. Hypoglycemia (low blood sugar) was a factor, too. Allison needed to eat every few hours or a headache would develop. As I also suspected, her water intake was minimal—about two eight-ounce glasses a day. I often find low-level dehydration in people with chronic headaches.

I ordered a routine blood screen test, which came back normal. Food-sensitivity testing showed a reaction to dairy products and artificial sweeteners.

THE HEALING PROCESS

I advised Allison to eat three meals and two snacks daily. Frequent eating helps prevent low blood sugar, which triggers headaches. To maintain her blood sugar balance, she needed

Mark A. Stengler, NMD, licensed naturopathic medical doctor in private practice, Encinitas, California...adjunct associate clinical professor at the National College of Natural Medicine, Portland, Oregon...author of *The Natural Physician's Healing Therapies* and coauthor of *Prescription for Natural Cures* (both from Bottom Line Books).

a serving of protein with each meal—poultry, fish, eggs or legumes. In addition, I suggested that for dinner she eat a salad or large serving of vegetables and a medium portion of complex carbohydrates, such as potatoes or carrots, whole-grain bread or brown rice. For snacks, she could have a handful of almonds or walnuts, a protein shake or a protein bar.

I also emphasized the importance of tripling her water intake to at least six eight-ounce glasses a day. I asked her to reduce her intake of cow's milk and cheese products and avoid anything with artificial sweeteners, particularly the diet soda she was drinking daily.

In addition, I suggested she take a full-spectrum digestive enzyme (available at health food stores and some pharmacies) at the end of each meal to improve her breakdown of food. I also suggested that she take 500 mg of *calcium citrate* and 200 mg of *magnesium glycinate* twice daily. These minerals help prevent migraine and tension headaches by improving blood flow and relaxing muscular tension. Finally, I prescribed homeopathic *pulsatilla* (30C daily). This preparation helps balance the ratio of progesterone and estrogen and acts as a stress reducer for women.

One week after making these changes, Allison called my clinic to say that she hadn't suffered a single headache. I saw her two and a half weeks later, and she was still headache-free. It has now been more than four months, and Allison has headaches only when she eats poorly—and even then, they are mild.

containing barbiturates, such as *Fiorinal*, or narcotics, such as codeine, are associated with increasing headache frequency, perhaps because they make the brain more sensitive to pain.

Self-defense for migraine sufferers: Talk with your physician about other ways to treat migraine attacks, such as nonsteroidal anti-inflammatory drugs,* including Motrin and Advil (although these drugs can cause rebound headaches) and triptans, such as *Imitrex*. Also ask about preventives, including beta-blockers, epilepsy drugs and certain antidepressants, as well as natural products, such as vitamin B-2. Do not take barbiturate or narcotic painkillers more than two days per week.

*Beware of chronic use of NSAIDs because they often cause "rebound" headaches or "withdrawal" headaches.

Relief for Cluster Headaches

Deep brain stimulation may relieve cluster headaches. These headaches cause sudden, intense pain and can last up to three hours.

Recent study: Patients received surgically implanted electrodes that directed electric current to the brain's hypothalamus. Of six patients who received the implants, three had fewer headaches and less pain in the first six months.

Thorsten Bartsch, MD, department of neurology, University Hospital Schleswig-Holstein, Kiel, Germany, and leader of a study published in *Cephalalgia*.

Ouch! Migraine Medications that Make Pain Worse

Richard Lipton, MD, vice-chair, professor of neurology, Albert Einstein College of Medicine, and director, Montefiore Headache Center, both in Bronx, New York, and leader of a study of 8,200 migraine sufferers, published in *Headache*.

Medications that relieve migraines may make headaches more frequent over time. Prescription pain medication

No More Headaches

Alan M. Rapoport, MD, neurologist and clinical professor, of neurology, David Geffen School of Medicine at University of California, Los Angeles and cofounder and director emeritus, New England Center for Headache in Stamford, Connecticut.

If your doctor hasn't been able to relieve your headaches, don't give up. Most headaches persist because they're misdiagnosed or improperly treated.

What your neurologist or headache specialist should look for to establish a telltale pattern...*

• **Where does it hurt** (on one or both sides of your head, in the front or the back)?

• **How does it hurt** (throbbing, jabbing, steady pain, pressure, etc.)?

• **How frequent** (twice per month, daily, etc.) and how intense (mild, moderate, severe) are your headaches?

• **What triggers your headaches** (diet, poor sleep, psychological stress, etc.)?

• **What other symptoms** (dizziness, nausea, vomiting, sensitivity to light and sound, worse with exercise, visual disturbance, etc.) accompany them?

• **Who else in your family gets headaches?**

Your evaluation also should include appropriate blood tests to see if a thyroid condition, Lyme disease, infection or other illness is responsible for your headache.

More advanced tests, such as magnetic resonance imaging (MRI) and computed tomography (CT), scan the brain for tumors, bleeding or other serious problems. These tests are necessary only when the examination or symptoms suggest cause for concern.

Headaches that are not caused by illness, injury or other conditions are called "primary headache disorders." *Most common types...*

TENSION-TYPE HEADACHE

Tension-type headache (TTH) affects about 90% of people over the course of their lifetimes. It causes a tight, squeezing sensation on both sides of the head. This used to be called "tension" headache because it was thought to be caused by emotional upset or muscle tension in the scalp or neck. Doctors recently have established that the same headache can occur without psychological stress or muscle tightness. It is not known what causes TTH, but it may result from an abnormality in the brain and/or be related to migraine. TTH is usually mild to moderate.

*To locate a headache specialist in your area, contact the American Migraine Foundation, 856-423-0043, *www.americanmigrainefoundation.org*.

MIGRAINE

Migraine is the second most common kind of primary headache, affecting about 28 million Americans. The condition tends to run in families, although the genes responsible haven't been completely identified. If one parent had migraines, you have a 40% chance of having them, too...if both did, the odds rise to 75%.

Migraines are generally more severe than TTH—in fact, they can be disabling—and last for four to 72 hours.

The diagnosis is made by physicians when recurrent episodes have two out of four basic characteristics (pain that is moderate to severe...throbbing...on one side of the head ...worsened by activity) and one out of three other characteristics (nausea...vomiting... sensitivity to both light and sound).

Fifteen percent to 20% of people with migraine experience an "aura" that occurs just before or at the start of the headache itself and lasts 20 to 30 minutes. This is primarily a visual disturbance—flashing lights, multicolored spots and zigzag lines are common.

Important: Most people mistakenly believe that "sinus headaches" are common. In reality, 90% of people who think they suffer from sinus headaches actually have migraines. When your headache is the result of acute sinus infection, you'll also have other symptoms, such as fever...red-hot skin in the sinus area...and/or a yellow-green, bad-tasting nasal or throat discharge.

CLUSTER HEADACHE

Cluster headache, the least common kind of primary headache, afflicts about two million Americans.

The pain of cluster headache is steady and severe—often excruciating—in or around one eye. Sufferers say it feels like a tremendous pressure on the eyeball.

The pain is accompanied by one or more other symptoms, such as tearing, a drooping eyelid, a stuffed or runny nostril or sweating over the eyebrow—always on the same side as the headache.

Besides the pain itself, the pattern is distinctive. The attacks last 45 minutes to two hours, in "clusters" of one to three a day, for a period of four to eight weeks. Typically, the headaches then go away until the following year—often around the same time—when a new cluster begins.

GETTING THE RIGHT TREATMENT

Few general physicians take the time to deploy the entire arsenal of available headache weapons. *Even a specialist may leave out some crucial steps…*

•**Elimination of triggers.** Migraines can be set off by a number of triggers, including bright sun, high altitude, skipped meals, too little or too much sleep, alcohol, certain foods (such as chocolate and aged cheeses), hormonal fluctuations and psychological stress. Keep track of your migraines to identify your personal triggers.

TTH also can be triggered by psychological stress, and cluster headaches by alcohol.

•**Behavioral medicine procedures.** Biofeedback training, which helps sufferers recognize changes in muscle tension, heart rate and/or temperature, has been found helpful for TTH and migraine.

Deep breathing, guided imagery and progressive muscle relaxation techniques tone down the "fight or flight" response that can cause or worsen headaches.

•**Vitamins, minerals and herbs.** For migraine prevention, the strongest scientific evidence supports the use of magnesium (400 mg daily) and vitamin B-2 (400 mg daily). A recent study conducted in Switzerland and presented at the American Academy of Neurology annual meeting found that 100 mg of the dietary supplement coenzyme Q10 taken three times daily helps prevent migraines. Consult your doctor.

MEDICATION

For TTH and mild migraine, OTC painkillers may suffice if taken at the onset of pain. These include *acetaminophen* (Tylenol) and nonsteroidal anti-inflammatory drugs (NSAIDs), such as *ibuprofen* (Motrin).

If OTC painkillers don't help, you may need prescription medication. A drug that combines aspirin or acetaminophen with a prescription pain reliever, such as Fiorinal, may help if TTH or migraine is mild and the drug is taken within 30 to 60 minutes of the onset of pain.

Triptans are the most effective drugs against migraine. If taken early, they can stop an attack before it becomes severe. Side effects may include dizziness and tingling in the fingers. Triptans are available in tablets, nasal spray and injectable forms. They include *sumatriptan* (Imitrex), *zolmitriptan* (Zomig) and *eletriptan* (Relpax).

Caution: When medications are overused, they can make headaches more frequent and more severe. Do not take analgesics or use triptans for headache more than two days per week. Also, do not take a triptan if you have uncontrolled high blood pressure, previous stroke or serious heart problems.

Daily preventive medications decrease the frequency, duration and intensity of headaches. They include antidepressants, such as *amitriptyline*…calcium channel blockers, such as *verapamil* (Calan)…beta-blockers, such as *propranolol* (Inderal)…and antiseizure drugs, such as *topiramate* (Topamax).

Helpful: If you have daily headaches and are overusing analgesics, start on preventive medication one month before cutting down on painkillers. Then gradually reduce the amount of painkillers you use over a two-week period to avoid worsening headache symptoms and withdrawal effects, such as anxiety and insomnia.

WHEN HEADACHES DON'T GET BETTER

If headaches persist, despite your best efforts, you and your doctor may have overlooked some of the basic tools outlined above. Many doctors do prescribe appropriate preventive drugs, but even the right ones don't always work. Why? The headache sufferer may have given up too soon. It may take up to three months for preventive drugs to help. If you still have headaches and now also suffer side effects, such as dizziness or sleepiness, you're unlikely to want to persevere and increase the dose. But you may need to do so for relief.

Example: A patient with migraines had been prescribed 60 mg of the beta-blocker propranolol. After three weeks, she still had severe headaches several times a week, so she stopped taking the drug.

Solution: Beta-blockers and other preventive medications may need to be taken for two to three months before they reduce headache frequency.

Neck-Pain Breakthrough Research Brings Surprises

Scott Haldeman, DC, MD, PhD, a clinical professor of neurology at the University of California, Irvine, an adjunct professor of epidemiology and public health at the University of California at Los Angeles, and an adjunct professor of research at Southern California University of Health Sciences in Whittier, California.

Neck pain is one of the most common of all ailments—affecting 30% to 50% of Americans each year—but it's also one of the least understood by medical professionals. As a result, anyone who suffers from neck pain is likely to be offered an array of different treatments—most of them unproven.

Latest development: Recently, an international task force published in the peer-reviewed medical journal *Spine* one of the most extensive reports ever created on the diagnosis and treatment of neck pain. The task force, which I led, was comprised of 50 researchers from nine countries whose specialties ranged from neurology and chiropractic to orthopedic surgery and physical therapy.

We analyzed more than 1,000 studies to create the most up-to-date recommendations about which neck pain treatments are truly effective—and which are not. In the process, the task force uncovered some surprising facts that dispel many popular myths about neck pain. *For example...*

Myth 1: **To successfully treat neck pain, you must know its exact cause.**

Reality: The evidence shows that it's virtually impossible to identify a specific cause for most cases of neck pain. Instead, it appears to be a very complex phenomenon that is affected by the neck pain sufferer's overall physical and mental health and daily physical and emotional stresses.

If your doctor or health-care provider says he/she doesn't know the exact cause of your neck pain, don't think less of him—he's just being honest.

Myth 2: **Seeing more than one doctor will increase your odds of getting relief for your neck pain.**

Reality: The evidence shows just the opposite—the more doctors you see, the longer your neck pain is likely to last. How could this be true? The most likely explanation is that patients who see multiple doctors end up focusing excessively on their pain, which ultimately creates psychological stress that makes the pain worse.

Also, by relying on others to "cure" them, these neck pain sufferers often take less responsibility for doing things that will actually make them feel better. The same is true for people who get neck X-rays or magnetic resonance imaging (MRI) scans. Research shows that these scans usually have no value in determining the cause of neck pain and even can be misleading, since they often detect changes, such as small disk bulges or misalignments, that are also seen in patients who do not have neck pain. However, imaging tests (such as X-rays) may be necessary to check for fractures if the patient has suffered serious trauma, such as in a car accident.

Important: Even though trips to multiple doctors are not helpful when you have neck pain, you should at least get screened by a physician who is experienced in treating neck pain (ask your primary care doctor for a referral) to rule out infection, a tumor or serious trauma such as a fracture (these conditions collectively account for 1% of neck pain cases). Initial screening also should include tests for *cervical radiculopathy,* a condition in which pressure on a nerve in the neck (due to a herniated disk) causes pain, numbness or weakness down the arm. About 5% of neck pain is due to cervical radiculopathy.

For the 94% of patients with ordinary neck pain, the best next step is to begin treating the pain with therapies that are proven to have some effectiveness (such as those described below), rather than seeing more doctors.

Myth 3: **Surgery is often effective for ordinary neck pain.**

Reality: There's no research showing that surgery has any positive impact on ordinary cases of neck pain. The only time that surgery is useful is in treating cervical radiculopathy. This operation involves removing the herniated disk to take pressure off the compressed nerve. Surgery also may be needed if a tumor or infection is present.

Myth 4: **Rest is one of the best treatments for neck pain.**

Reality: Our review found that any treatment that reduces activity and mobility in the neck actually delays recovery. This includes bed rest (even a day or two), neck collars and stopping work and other ordinary activities. If you exercise regularly or have a physically demanding job, you may need to reduce your activity level somewhat—but you should remain active.

Myth 5: **Heating pads, cold packs and other such treatments speed neck pain recovery.**

Reality: The medical evidence shows that "passive" treatments, such as heating pads, cold packs, ultrasound, electrical stimulation and injecting medication, including steroids or anesthetics, into "trigger points" have no effect on the duration of neck pain. In some patients, however, such therapies may offer temporary relief from neck pain. If so, they should use these therapies as necessary to improve their ability to function.

Myth 6: **Some treatments for neck pain should be used indefinitely.**

Reality: Just as there is no single cause of neck pain, there is no single "magic bullet" for treating it either. Our review found that certain therapies designed to increase mobility of the neck appeared to help in many cases, but that patients often had to try several treatments before finding one that worked for them.

Treatments found to be effective were chiropractic manipulation...active physical therapy (in which the patient is given movement exercises rather than simply being treated with ultrasound and/or heat)...and exercise such as walking, swimming or low-impact aerobics.

Patients also improved when they combined these therapies with other treatments that reduce inflammation and stiffness. Among the most effective were acupuncture...massage... and over-the-counter anti-inflammatory medication, such as *ibuprofen* (Advil) or *naproxen* (Aleve). There's very little research on whether preventive steps, such as ergonomic adjustments to chairs, improving posture or using a cervical foam pillow, have any effect, but these approaches may be helpful for some people.

Whichever approach you choose, try it for two weeks. If your condition hasn't improved by then, stop it and try another approach. If the treatment is helping, four weeks of the therapy should be enough—research shows that treating neck pain any longer than this won't offer additional improvement.

Myth 7: **Stress does not play a significant role in neck pain.**

Reality: Studies clearly show that stress and anxiety make neck pain worse. Our review also found that people who take charge of their own treatment—by trying different therapies and/or activities that provide pain relief—tend to recover faster. This is your best hope for relieving neck pain.

Are Big Breasts Causing You Pain?

Jason A. Spector, MD, associate professor of plastic surgery at Weill Medical College of Cornell University, in New York City. He is a member of the Plastic Surgery Research Council and a diplomate of the American Board of Surgery.

L arge-breasted women often have chronic back and neck pain from the sheer weight of their breasts...gouged shoulders from bra straps...discomfort during exercise...and feelings of self-consciousness. Breast reduction can provide relief.

• **Surgical techniques.** Surgery is done under general anesthesia and takes two to three hours. The "anchor" or "inverted T" technique typically is used when more than 1,000 grams (about two pounds) of tissue are removed from each breast. An incision is made around the areola...down the front of the breast and under the breast. Excess tissue, fat and skin are then removed. Nipples may be repositioned to give a natural appearance. When removing less than two pounds from each breast, the vertical or short-scar technique is used. This incision runs around the areola and down the front of the breast only, resulting in less scarring.

• **Risks.** Breast reduction usually involves minimal blood loss. As with any surgery, there are risks from general anesthesia and possible infection. Complication rates generally are low, but can be higher for women who smoke, have diabetes or are overweight.

• **Postoperative care.** The patient usually goes home the same day, with a dressing over each incision. Sometimes small tubes are attached to the incision to drain fluid. These are removed after a few days. Discomfort can be managed with prescription or nonprescription pain medicine.

• **Recovery.** A supportive sports bra worn constantly for one month minimizes swelling. After one week or so, you can return to work and do moderate, low-impact exercise. You can resume all normal activities after a month.

• **Appearance.** Your age, your skin condition and breast size and shape affect results. At your initial consultation, ask the surgeon how your breasts will look after surgery. Generally, they will be smaller, rounder, higher and more symmetrical. Typically some scarring is visible.

• **Sensation.** Breasts usually feel numb overall for up to three months but return to normal within six months. It may take a year to regain normal nipple sensation, and in 10% to 15% of cases, it does not return completely. In some cases, if nipples were repositioned, they lose all sensation.

• **Cost.** Breast reduction ranges from $4,000 to $12,000. Usually health insurance covers reduction when medically necessary (for instance, to ease pain).

• **Breast-feeding.** Most women can nurse after reduction—but if breast-feeding is vital to you, delay surgery until you are done having children.

• **Cancer concerns.** Women age 40 or older and those at high risk for breast cancer due to family history should have a baseline mammogram first. Among high-risk women, reduction may diminish breast cancer risk. Breast reduction does not interfere with breast cancer detection or treatment.

For referrals: American Society of Plastic Surgeons, *www.plasticsurgery.org*.

Quick Relief for Jaw Pain

Rob E. Sable, DDS, a restorative dentist in private practice in Alpharetta, Georgia.

Waking up with a sore jaw or a headache may indicate that you grind your teeth in your sleep. This condition, called *bruxism,* is primarily caused by stress. Symptoms include tooth sensitivity to hot and cold food and drinks as well as pain while chewing. Sinus congestion can cause severe pressure on dental roots, leading sufferers to grind their teeth or clench the jaw. Misaligned dental work can also trigger bruxism, leading to unconscious grinding. This grinding causes noticeable noise in only 30% of patients.

Your dentist can diagnose the problem by feeling muscle tension in the jaw and face... observing if teeth are worn or cracked...and viewing X rays. Treatments include reshaping and polishing of tooth enamel to improve tooth alignment and/or the use of a mouth guard during periods of excessive grinding.

To ease jaw pain: Place your palm or fist under your chin and push up while barely opening your jaw against resistance. Hold for one to two seconds. Repeat 30 times, twice a day. This will stretch and strengthen jaw muscles, which helps alleviate pain.

Cod Liver Oil

Mark A. Stengler, NMD, licensed naturopathic medical doctor in private practice, Encinitas, California... adjunct associate clinical professor at the National College of Natural Medicine, Portland, Oregon...author of *The Natural Physician's Healing Therapies* and co-author of *Prescription for Natural Cures* (both from Bottom Line Books).

Reduce the need for painkillers with cod-liver oil. Researchers from Ninewells Hospital and Medical School in Dundee, Scotland, analyzed 58 rheumatoid arthritis (RA) patients and discovered that cod-liver oil reduced the need for nonsteroidal anti-inflammatory drugs (NSAIDs). Patients were given 10 grams (g) of the oil or a placebo daily for nine months.

Result: Of patients taking cod-liver oil, 39% reduced their NSAID intake by one-third without increased pain, compared with 10% of the placebo group.

My view: High-dose fish oils, rich in omega-3 fatty acids, naturally reduce inflammation. RA patients should take a supplement of cod-liver or other fish oil containing 2.2 g of omega-3 fatty acids daily.

Note: Cod-liver oil contains vitamin D, which also reduces inflammation. If you take any other fish oil, also take 2,000 international units (IU) of vitamin D daily. In eight to 12 weeks, talk to your doctor about reducing your NSAID dosage. If you take *warfarin* (Coumadin) or another blood thinner, consult your doctor before taking fish oil. Women of childbearing age should check the amount of vitamin A in cod-liver oil and other supplements and take care not to exceed 8,000 IU daily.

Foot Pain

Neil Campbell, DPM, spokesperson for the American College of Foot and Ankle Surgeons, Chicago, and a podiatrist in Yoakum, Texas.

Plantar fasciitis is an inflammation of the ligament along the bottom of the foot connecting the heel bone and the toes. It can cause stabbing or burning pain, especially after periods of inactivity.

To relieve pain, hold an ice pack on the area for 15 to 20 minutes several times a day or after exercise and/or take *ibuprofen* or another anti-inflammatory as directed by your doctor. To treat the condition and lessen the chance of recurrence, stretch the Achilles tendon—stand on the edge of a step with heels off the edge. Lower heels together or one at a time...hold the stretch for one minute...repeat as many times as feels comfortable.

Insoles also may be prescribed if the pain continues...or the doctor may inject the area with corticosteroids. If symptoms persist, surgery may release the ligament.

Big Toe Woe

Mark A. Stengler, NMD, licensed naturopathic medical doctor in private practice, Encinitas, California... adjunct associate clinical professor at the National College of Natural Medicine, Portland, Oregon...author of *The Natural Physician's Healing Therapies* and co-author of *Prescription for Natural Cures* (both from Bottom Line Books).

Stiff big toe," or *hallux rigidus,* affects the metatarsophalangeal joint, which bends with every step. An abnormal biomechanical stress on the toe—from an injury or arch problem, for example—wears away cartilage and creates bone spurs (bony growths). A cortisone injection may give temporary relief but does not fix the underlying problem, and it may suppress the immune system. Surgery is not always successful and involves a risk of infection or adverse reaction to anesthesia.

Safer: A podiatrist (foot doctor) or chiropractor can create an orthotic—a customized plastic insert for your shoe—to support your arch and minimize stress on your toe. Select shoes with good cushioning and support and a thick but flexible sole. (No high heels!) To reduce inflammation, take the natural compound *methylsulfonylmethane* (MSM) at 6,000 mg daily in divided doses (decrease to 2,000 mg to 3,000 mg if stools are loose)...and apply the homeopathic cream arnica to the toe twice daily. To improve circulation, soak the affected foot daily in comfortably hot water for 30 seconds…switch to cold water for 30 seconds… and continue alternating for five minutes. Acupuncture may help to alleviate pain. To find an acupuncturist, contact the American Association of Acupuncture & Oriental Medicine (866-455-7999, *www.aaaomonline.org*).

Do You Have Aching or Numb Hands?

Terry R. Light, MD, the Dr. William M. Scholl professor and chairman of the department of orthopedic surgery and rehabilitation, Loyola University Chicago, Stritch School of Medicine in Maywood, Illinois…and author of more than 50 medical journal articles.

Hands are vulnerable to mechanical difficulties because of their intricate networks of bones, nerves, muscles, ligaments and tendons—all of which are located in the narrow, relatively unprotected areas of the wrist, palm and fingers.

Each year, about 17% of Americans over age 55 report having hand pain. But if you count the full range of potential symptoms —including numbness, tingling, burning sensations and "frozen" fingers—the number of hand problems is much higher. *Common hand disorders…*

ARTHRITIS

Although arthritis can occur in any hand joint, one of the most frequently affected locations is at the base of the thumb, where the thumb bones connect to the trapezium bone in the wrist. This very flexible joint is in constant use and takes the most stress of any hand joint—the thumb is used anytime we need to hold an object.

Symptoms: Mild or severe pain, usually at the base of the hand between the thumb and the wrist.

First treatment step: Use a brace that surrounds the thumb and connects to the hand. This reduces stress on the joint and may decrease the painful joint inflammation associated with arthritis. Such braces are available at drugstores. Your doctor also may recommend prescription anti-inflammatory medications or over-the-counter (OTC) painkillers, such as *ibuprofen* (Advil) or buffered aspirin (to prevent gastrointestinal upset). If two or three weeks of bracing quiets the pain, this treatment can be repeated as needed.

If symptoms continue or worsen: Pain can be relieved with injections of cortisone, a powerful anti-inflammatory, into the arthritic joint at the base of the thumb. Although frequent cortisone injections can cause thinning of joint cartilage and weakening of joint ligaments, injections can be given for as long as they work. That's because cartilage is already destroyed by the arthritis, so the injections do more good than harm.

If all else fails: Surgery offers a permanent solution.* The most popular involves removing the affected joint by taking out the trapezium wrist bone, which is about the size of a sugar cube. Once this bone is removed, the thumb can be anchored and cushioned by a piece of tendon taken from the forearm.

Within a year after surgery, most patients report good pain relief and enough range of motion to allow normal daily activities. Common risks associated with this surgery include sensory nerve damage, scar tenderness and persistent pain.

CARPAL TUNNEL SYNDROME

The median nerve runs from the neck, arm and forearm to the hand, passing a "tunnel" formed by the bones of the wrist and a thick band of tissue called the transverse carpal ligament. Anything that narrows the tunnel, such as a fracture or swelling of the surrounding tissue, can pinch the nerve, causing carpal tunnel syndrome (CTS).

No one knows what causes CTS. Now experts even question the common assumption that it is due to repetitive strain, which can occur during typing or using machinery. CTS is more common in people with diabetes, rheumatoid arthritis and thyroid disease—perhaps because these conditions are often linked to inflammation.

•**Symptoms.** Numbness in the fingers nearest your thumb, especially at night. You also

*To find a hand surgeon in your area, contact the American Society for Surgery of the Hand (312-880-1900, *www.assh.org*).

may experience tingling, burning, or mild or severe pain in the fingers.

First treatment step: Use a custom-made wrist brace (available from hand therapists) or a store-bought brace at night. Both relieve nerve pressure. If symptoms improve within six weeks, no other treatment is needed.

If symptoms continue or worsen: An injection of cortisone can eliminate pain and numbness for about three months. Because cortisone can harm soft tissue, additional injections are rarely given.

If all else fails: A surgeon can cut the transverse carpal ligament, making room for the nerve, which reduces pain and improves strength and sensation. Full recovery usually takes about three months.

This surgery is successful in about 90% of cases, and it carries a low risk for complications, such as nerve damage.

TRIGGER FINGER

Each finger has one or two tendons that slide through a tunnel formed by a series of fibrous bands. The tendons normally glide smoothly as you flex your fingers. If the band at the base of the finger narrows or the tendons thicken or swell, the tendons may catch or become stuck. The cause of trigger finger is unknown, but it is more common in people with diabetes and rheumatoid arthritis.

Symptoms: Mild pain or tenderness in the palm at the base of one or more fingers. There may be a popping or clicking sensation while opening and closing the hand.

First treatment step: Rest the affected finger—using a brace to limit its use. Cut back on hand-related activities for two to four weeks.

If symptoms continue or worsen: Cortisone injections into the band at the base of the finger can relieve inflammation. Up to three injections (over a lifetime) may be given.

If all else fails: A surgeon can make a small incision at the base of the finger and cut the fibrous band, freeing the tendon. Normal activity can be resumed within two weeks. Nerve injury, though rare, is a possible complication of this surgery.

DUPUYTREN'S CONTRACTURE

This disorder causes abnormal tissue growth in the palm and the fingers, eventually causing the fingers to flex or curl. It is seen mainly in men of Northern European ancestry, but its causes are unknown.

Symptoms: The first sign is usually a small lump or nodule in the palm. Later, patients are unable to completely straighten the fingers.

First treatment step: This disorder is not dangerous, and it may take years before hand function is affected. Diagnosis is based on a physical exam.

If symptoms continue or worsen: In some cases, cortisone injections may be given if the nodule becomes painful.

If the contracture is keeping you from doing things you love, a surgeon can remove the abnormal tissue. The success rate for the surgery depends on the extent of the disorder, and risks can include nerve damage, blood vessel damage, skin healing problems and infection.

Get Sciatica Relief

Sciatica pain often gets better on its own. There is no evidence that spinal decompression does any good. Anti-inflammatory drugs, cortisone shots and exercises that strengthen abdominal and back muscles may speed healing.

Also useful: Place a pillow behind your lower back while driving. Place a pillow under your knees when sleeping on your back—or between your knees when you are sleeping on your side.

Joel M. Press, MD, medical director, Spine and Sports Rehabilitation Center, Rehabilitation Institute of Chicago, and professor of physical medicine and rehabilitation, Northwestern University Medical School, Chicago.

What Is Sciatica?

Sciatica is a common form of low back pain that radiates along one of the two sciatic nerves, each of which runs down the back of the thigh and calf and into the foot. Most cases of sciatica occur when one of the spinal disks—gel-filled pancakes of cartilage between the vertebrae—swells, tears (ruptures) or herniates (part of the interior of the disk bulges out), exerting painful pressure on a sciatic nerve. About 1 million Americans suffer from sciatica, and up to 300,000 a year have surgery to relieve the pain.

Eugene Carragee, MD, professor of orthopedic surgery and director of the Orthopedic Spine Center at Stanford University School of Medicine in Stanford, California.

Relieve the Pain of a Pinched Nerve

David Borenstein, MD, clinical professor of medicine at George Washington University Medical Center, Washington, DC. He maintains a private practice at Arthritis and Rheumatism Associates in Washington, DC, and is author of *Back In Control: Your Complete Prescription for Preventing, Treating and Eliminating Back Pain from Your Life* (M. Evans and Company).

N erve pain is one of the worst kinds of pain. People with a pinched nerve (sometimes called a "stinger") may experience sharp, burning pain for anywhere from a few seconds to a few days or longer. The pain usually comes on suddenly and may disappear just as fast—only to return. There also might be temporary numbness or slight weakness.

A nerve gets "pinched" when surrounding tissue presses against it and causes inflammation of the nerve. Causes include repetitive motions, traumatic injuries and joint diseases, such as rheumatoid arthritis. The most common pinched nerves occur in the wrist, elbow, shoulder and foot. Nerve roots in the spinal canal also are vulnerable.

Red flag: Nerve pain that is accompanied by significant weakness or that doesn't improve within a few days needs to be checked by a physician. Excessive pressure on—or inflammation of—a nerve can result in loss of function and permanent damage.

SELF-HELP

To reduce the pain…

• **Stop repetitive movements.** A pinched nerve that's caused by performing the same movements over and over again usually will improve once the offending activity—leaning with your elbows on a counter, typing, working a cash register, etc.—is stopped for a few days. Avoiding these activities is also the best way to prevent a pinched nerve.

However, patients with job-related pain can't always afford to take time off. In that case, they should attempt to change their body position when doing the activity.

Example: Raising the back of a computer keyboard (most are adjustable) will enlarge the carpal tunnel in the wrist and reduce pressure on the nerve.

• **Ice the area.** Applying cold in the first 24 to 48 hours after nerve pain starts can reduce tissue swelling and nerve pressure. Use a cold pack or ice cubes wrapped in a towel. Hold cold against the affected area for about 15 minutes. Repeat every hour or two for a day or two.

• **Take an anti-inflammatory.** Over-the-counter analgesics that have anti-inflammatory properties, such as aspirin, *ibuprofen* and *naproxen*, reduce the body's production of chemicals that cause inflammation and swelling. Don't use *acetaminophen*. It will reduce pain but has little effect on inflammation.

• **Wear looser clothes.** It's fairly common for women to experience a pinched nerve in the outer thigh (*meralgia paresthetica*) from too-tight jeans or skirts…or foot pain (tarsal tunnel syndrome) from tight shoes.

MEDICAL CARE

• **Nerve pain that's severe or keeps coming back**—or that's accompanied by other symptoms, such as a loss of bowel or bladder control—requires immediate medical care. Customized splints or braces can be used to minimize pressure on a nerve from repetitive movements. *Also helpful…*

• An injection of a corticosteroid into the painful area—or a short course of oral steroid therapy. These drugs reduce inflammation very quickly and provide short-term relief. The pain may disappear after a single treatment, but most patients need repeated courses. Sometimes, if pain is not relieved, acupuncture may be used in addition to medication and physical therapy.

•Surgery is recommended when the pain is severe or keeps coming back. The procedures vary depending on the part of the body affected.

Why Your Joints Hurt

Beth E. Shubin Stein, MD, an orthopaedic surgeon and sports medicine specialist at the Women's Sports Medicine Center at the Hospital for Special Surgery and an assistant professor at Weill Medical College of Cornell University, both in New York City.

We women have lots of joint pain. A study by the Centers for Disease Control and Prevention found that nearly one-third of adult women in the US have some type of chronic joint pain or have been diagnosed with arthritis.

Despite what's commonly believed, it's not that women have more trouble with their joints than men, but that they tend to have different types of problems.

Example: In general, women's joints tend to be looser than men's joints, particularly the knees and shoulders, which can reduce stability and lead to damaging wear patterns and pain. *What you need to know to protect and soothe your joints...*

TROUBLE SPOT #1: KNEES

Women have inherent difficulties with their *patellofemoral* joints—or kneecaps—and how they join with the thigh bone. Because women have wider pelvises than men, the hip-to-knee line is less vertical than it is in men, which places more stress across women's knees.

Another reason for knee pain in women is that their soft tissue, including ligaments, is often more lax than that in men.

A third cause of female-specific problems is muscular imbalance. The muscles that support and control the knees include the quadriceps (front of the thighs), the hamstrings (back of the thighs) and the gluteal (buttocks) muscles. Many women do not have the proper balance of strength among these muscles to support and protect knees.

Weakness in the hamstrings may increase risk for traumatic injuries, such as tears to a ligament when jumping or turning quickly. Weakness in the quadriceps or gluteals may predispose a woman to "overuse" problems, such as pain in the kneecap area due to pressure from body weight on the knee.

What to do: Knee pain often can be treated with physical therapy to strengthen the proper muscles, including the quadriceps, hamstrings and gluteals—and followed up with a long-term exercise program incorporating the fundamentals learned in physical therapy. You can't change the alignment of your hips and knees or the laxity of your ligaments, but how strong you are is something you can control with exercise.

Also helpful: Don't wear high heels more often than necessary. They worsen knee pain by increasing pressure behind the kneecap.

For mild-to-moderate arthritis in the knee that doesn't respond well to physical therapy and home exercise, your doctor may want to try *viscosupplementation,* in which a lubricant based on *hyaluronic acid,* a substance that occurs naturally in the body, is injected into the knee. This procedure doesn't build back cartilage or bone damaged by injury or arthritis, but it can reduce pain for six months or more and it is safe.

TROUBLE SPOT #2: SHOULDERS

The rotator cuff, a group of muscles and tendons that attaches the arm to the shoulder joint and lets the arm rotate up and around, can become irritated and/or inflamed. Continued irritation can cause tendonitis and bursitis.

What to do: A physical therapist can help you strengthen muscles, often using a stretchy exercise band. It's a good idea to fortify the *scapulothoracic* muscles of the back (they come into play when you squeeze your shoulder blades together).

Smart: Don't carry a heavy purse or other bag on one side of your body—it will promote shoulder and back pain. Instead, distribute weight evenly across your body, such as with a backpack-style purse.

Best of all: A small bag on wheels with an extendable handle. That's what I use to take my patients' charts between my office and the hospital.

TROUBLE SPOT #3: THUMBS

The base of the thumb, called the *carpometacarpal* (CMC) joint, is prone to pain from arthritis in women. We aren't sure why, but it may have something to do with the fact that this joint is smaller in women than in men, yet women must bear the same loads while pinching and grasping as men do. With CMC arthritis, a simple activity like holding a fork can be painful.

What to do: A special splint fitted by an occupational therapist can support your thumb joint and limit the movement of your thumb and wrist. If a splint is going to help, you should start to feel relief within a few days to a week.

If a splint isn't effective, you may need an injection of a steroid into the thumb, which can reduce pain and inflammation. Although most such injections help for only six to eight weeks, that sometimes lets the joint heal enough to stay pain free.

If a steroid injection doesn't solve the problem and arthritis progresses to an advanced stage, you may require one of two kinds of surgery...

Replacement of damaged portions of the joint with tendon from the wrist. This preserves mobility but usually results in a loss of strength.

Fusing together of bones in your thumb. This maximizes strength but limits mobility.

AEROBICS–PLUS

It's important to get aerobic exercise at least several days a week. Besides improving your cardiovascular health, it will help keep your weight down—and excess weight is an enemy of your joints, especially your weight-bearing joints, such as the knees and ankles.

Best: Aerobic activities that also put joints through ranges of different motion, such as using an elliptical training machine, swimming and cycling.

However, to slow age-related bone loss, it's vital to do weightbearing exercise, which stimulates growth of new bone. The easiest way for most people is to walk a lot. To involve the upper body, use a variety of weight-lifting machines or handheld weights.

More from Dr. Beth E. Shubin Stein...

Rub Out the Ache!

If you suffer from chronic arthritis pain or have aching muscle strains or spasms after exercising, chances are you regularly take aspirin or another nonsteroidal anti-inflammatory drug (NSAID), such as *ibuprofen* (Advil) or *naproxen* (Aleve).

There is another option. Over-the-counter (OTC) topical pain relievers can be very effective without causing the stomach upset or gastrointestinal bleeding that may accompany oral pain medication.

Latest development: A topical form of the oral prescription NSAID *diclofenac* (Voltaren Gel) is available in the United States.

Meanwhile, a variety of OTC topical pain relievers are available now. The products below relieve arthritis, backache and muscle strain. Most are used three to four times daily. Follow label instructions.

Helpful: If one type of topical pain reliever doesn't work for you, try one from another class until you find a product that provides relief.

Caution: Keep these products away from your eyes, nose and other mucous membranes.

SALICYLATES

These aspirin-based products dull pain and curb the inflammation that often accompanies and worsens pain.

How they work: Topical salicylates inhibit the production of prostaglandins, substances in the body that cause pain and swelling when they are released in response to strains, sprains and other injuries. *Salicylates include...*

•**BENGAY® Ultra Strength Pain Relieving Cream.**

•**Aspercreme Analgesic Creme Rub with Aloe.**

•**Sportscreme Deep Penetrating Pain Relieving Rub.**

• **Flexall Maximum Strength Pain Relieving Gel.**

Warning: Do not use salicylates if you are sensitive or allergic to aspirin or take blood-thinning medication that might interact with them. Consult a doctor before applying a salicylate to a large area several times a day.

COUNTERIRRITANTS

These pain relievers give the sensation of warmth or coolness to mask pain.

How they work: Creating a secondary stimulus to diminish the feeling of pain reduces physical discomfort. It's what you do instinctively when you stub your toe, then grab it to apply pressure. Both competing sensations travel to your brain at the same time—but because only a limited number of messages can be processed at one time, the initial feeling of pain is diminished. *Counterirritants include…*

• **Icy Hot Pain Relieving Balm, Extra Strength.**

• **Tiger Balm Extra Strength Pain Relieving Ointment.**

• **Therapeutic Mineral Ice.**

In most cases, coolness is beneficial for acute injuries, such as sprains, while warmth eases stiffness.

Caution: People sensitive to heat or cold should avoid counterirritants.

CAPSAICINS

These products, which are a type of counterirritant, contain capsaicin, an extract of hot peppers that causes a burning sensation.

How they work: Unlike most other counterirritants, capsaicin inhibits the production of substance P, a chemical that sends pain messages to the brain via the nervous system. *Capsaicins include…*

• **Zostrix Arthritis Pain Relief Cream.**

• **Capzasin HP Arthritis Pain Relief Creme.**

LIDOCAINE

Lidoderm is a prescription-only patch that contains *lidocaine*, a topical anesthetic similar to the novocaine that dentists often use to numb the gums.

How it works: Lidocaine blocks signals at the skin's nerve endings. The Lidoderm patch (lidocaine 5%) is worn for 12 hours a day over a period of days. It slowly releases medication, so it has longer-lasting effects than other pain relievers and helps with pain that emanates from nerves near the surface of your skin, such as that caused by shingles or diabetic neuropathy.

Caution: Side effects include dizziness, headache and nausea. Allergic reactions are rare but may occur.

Finally…an Arthritis Therapy that Works

Vijay Vad, MD, sports medicine physician specializing in minimally invasive arthritis therapies at the Hospital for Special Surgery in New York City. He is a professor of rehabilitation medicine at Weill Medical College of Cornell University, also in New York City, and author of *Arthritis Rx* (Gotham).

Only about half of the people who suffer from osteoarthritis pain obtain significant relief from aspirin, *ibuprofen* (Advil, etc.) or other nonsteroidal anti-inflammatory drugs (NSAIDs)—and each year, an estimated 16,000 Americans die from gastrointestinal bleeding or other side effects from these medications.

New approach: Up to 80% of people who have osteoarthritis can experience a significant improvement in pain and mobility—and reduce their need for medication and surgery—when they combine dietary changes, supplement use and the right kind of exercise. This program provides significant relief within six weeks.

DIET Rx

Inflammation in the body has been implicated in heart disease, diabetes and kidney disease—and it also contributes to osteoarthritis.

The incidence of arthritis has steadily risen since the early 1900s, when processed foods, such as packaged crackers, cereals, bread and snack foods, began to dominate the American diet—and more people started becoming obese. Most of these foods actually promote inflammation, which can cause joint and cartilage damage and aggravate arthritis pain.

Studies suggest that by adding more foods with anti-inflammatory effects to the average American diet—and reducing the foods that promote inflammation—can reduce inflammation by approximately 20% to 40%.

Best anti-inflammatory foods...

•**Apricots and berries contain large amounts of antioxidants,** chemical compounds that reduce inflammation.

•**Almonds have fiber,** vitamin E and monounsaturated fats to curb inflammation.

Other important steps...

•**Increase omega-3s.** These inflammation-fighting essential fatty acids are mainly found in cold-water fish, such as salmon, tuna, mackerel and sardines. At least three three-ounce servings of fish per week provide adequate levels of omega-3s.

People who don't like fish, or don't eat it often, can take fish-oil supplements or flaxseed oil.

My advice: Use 2 to 3 grams (g) daily of a fish-oil supplement which contains *eicosapentaenoic* acid (EPA) and *docosahexaenoic acid* (DHA)...or one to three tablespoons daily of flaxseed oil.

Caution: Because fish oil taken at this dosage can trigger a blood-thinning effect, check with your doctor if you take a blood-thinning medication, such as *warfarin* (Coumadin).

•**Reduce omega-6s.** Most Americans get far too many of these inflammation-promoting fatty acids in their diets. A century ago, the ratio of omega-6 to omega-3 fatty acids was about 2:1 for the typical American. Today, it's about 20:1. This imbalance boosts levels of a chemical by-product, *arachidonic acid,* that triggers inflammation.

My advice: Because the omega-6s are found primarily in red meats, commercially processed foods (described earlier) and fast foods, anyone with arthritis should avoid these foods as much as possible.

•**Give up nightshades.** Although the reason is unknown, tomatoes, white potatoes, eggplant and other foods in the nightshade family have been found to increase arthritis pain. It has been estimated that up to 20% of arthritis patients get worse when they eat these foods.

My advice: If you eat these foods and have arthritis pain, give them up completely for six months to see if there's an improvement.

SUPPLEMENT Rx

Americans spend billions of dollars annually on supplements to ease arthritis pain, but many of them are ineffective. *Best choices...*

•**Ginger.** The biochemical structure of this herb (commonly used as a spice) is similar to that of NSAIDs, making it a powerful anti-inflammatory agent. A study of 250 patients at the University of Miami School of Medicine found that ginger, taken twice daily, was as effective as prescription and over-the-counter drugs at controlling arthritis pain.

My advice: Add several teaspoons of fresh ginger to vegetables, salads, etc., daily or take a daily supplement containing 510 milligrams (mg) of ginger.

Caution: Ginger thins the blood, so consult with your physician if you take blood-thinning medication.

•**Glucosamine and chondroitin.** Taken in a combination supplement, such as Cosamin DS, these natural anti-inflammatories inhibit enzymes that break down cartilage and enhance the production of *glycosaminoglycans,* molecules that stimulate cartilage growth.

My advice: Take 1,500 mg of glucosamine and 1,200 mg of chondroitin daily. Or consider using a product called Gingerflex (formerly Zingerflex), which contains both glucosamine and chondroitin as well as ginger.

Caution: If you have diabetes, consult your doctor before using glucosamine. It can raise blood sugar. Do not take glucosamine if you are allergic to shellfish.

EXERCISE Rx

Osteoarthritis pain weakens muscles, which diminishes joint support. The result is more inflammation and pain, and faster progression of the underlying disease.

Common exercises, including both running and traditional forms of yoga, actually can increase pain by putting too much pressure on the joints. Patients will benefit most from medical exercise, which includes modified variations of common strengthening and stretching exercises, supervised by a physical therapist.*

It's best to perform medical exercises under the guidance of a physical therapist for one to two months before beginning an exercise program at home. *Best choices...*

• **Medical yoga improves joint strength and flexibility** by strengthening muscles and moving joints through their full range of motion. Unlike conventional yoga, it does not require poses that put undue stress on the joints.

• **Pilates combines yoga-like stretching and breathing control to strengthen the "core" muscles** in the lower back and abdomen, as well as muscles in the hips. Like medical yoga, it puts very little pressure on the joints.

• **Healthy breathing.** Most of us take shallow breaths from the upper lungs—a breathing pattern that increases levels of stress hormones and heightens pain.

Better: Deep breathing, which promotes the release of pain-relieving chemicals known as endorphins. Patients who breathe deeply for five minutes daily have less pain for several hours afterward. Practice deep breathing in addition to a regular exercise program.

Here's how...

• **Sit in a chair with both feet flat on the floor.** Close your mouth, place one hand on your stomach and inhale deeply through your nose until you can feel your stomach expanding. Hold your breath for five to 10 seconds.

• **Exhale through your nose,** contracting your stomach until you've expelled as much air as possible. Hold the "emptiness" for a moment before inhaling again.

• **Repeat the cycle for at least five consecutive minutes daily.**

*To locate a physical therapist in your area, contact the American Physical Therapy Association at 800-999-2782 or *www.apta.org.*

Soothing Your Sore Muscles—Most Popular Cures Don't Work...

Stephen P. Sayers, PhD, department of physical therapy, University of Missouri-Columbia.

It's unlikely you know what "DOMS" stands for but very likely you know well how it feels. DOMS is the acronym for "Delayed Onset Muscle Soreness"—the pain that peaks in overused muscles a day or two after you thought it would be a good idea to exercise really hard. We used to think the culprit behind DOMS was lactic acid buildup, but now that scientists have dispelled that popular notion, we wanted to find out what does cause the soreness. Even more to the point, we sought advice about how to avoid it if possible. To get this information, we called Stephen P. Sayers, PhD, at the department of physical therapy, University of Missouri-Columbia, who has spent years researching exercise and its aftermath.

SURPRISING REASON WHY IT HURTS

Dr. Sayers first explained what's actually behind DOMS. When you exercise harder than usual or in a new way, the unusual strain creates tiny tears in the muscles, but, nope, that isn't what causes pain. (If it were, the pain would start immediately, not later.) Rather, the muscle damage puts in motion a delayed inflammatory response that releases chemicals that sensitize nerve endings—in time these send messages to the brain that say "ouch." And it gets even more complicated. The cells that go into action to attend to the inflammation are good guys called *neutrophils* (white blood cells), but they generate free radicals that further damage the same muscles. Then helpful cells, called *macrophages,* chomp away on the inflammatory debris and stimulate healing. Yes, the system might seem a bit odd, but that's how it works and it leaves you with muscles that hurt.

The type of exercise that especially triggers DOMS is eccentric movement, which, curiously, feels the least stressful as you are doing it (running down a hill, lowering a weight, walking down stairs).

To explain: When you lift a weight your biceps muscle brings it toward you and the muscle shortens—a contraction called concentric. But as you slowly lower it and lengthen the bicep, you are making an eccentric contraction. Same thing when you are climbing stairs or hiking up terrain—going up shortens muscles and is concentric, while going down lengthens muscles and is eccentric. Dr. Sayers says eccentric motions trigger more damage, which can lead to soreness because fewer muscle fibers are available to help eccentric actions…with fewer fibers pitching in to lighten the load, there is more stress on the muscles involved, therefore greater soreness.

DOES THIS HAVE TO HAPPEN?

So the question is, can one get fit without suffering DOMS? Some exercise professionals say no, DOMS is simply part of building strength. Dr. Sayers agrees, but says it does not have to be debilitating if you use caution. He is convinced that you can do any kind of exercise routine or sport, and suffer few if any sore muscles in the process. The key, he says, is to always start slowly and give your muscles time to gradually adjust.

Because strength training is the most frequent cause of DOMS, it is a good way to illustrate this approach. Using weights that are low enough not to overly stress your muscles, perform three sets of eight to 12 reps per exercise for your upper and lower body, three times a week on nonconsecutive days. (These rules change once you have reached a certain fitness level, as you will read in a moment.) As your muscles adjust to the weights you have been using, move up gradually to heavier weights. According to Dr. Sayers, "The greatest gains in strength seem to occur in the first eight to 12 weeks of resistance training. Gains can occur after that point of course, but they occur at a slower rate." Once you have achieved your goal, he says you can maintain it by using heavier weights and training just twice a week. Similarly when you're starting a new season's sport (skiing or tennis for example), if you haven't been working those muscles in the off season, then start gradually.

Don't go from doing nothing to playing three sets of tennis…or heading out for a week of skiing the moguls.

THE WARM-UP, COOL-DOWN MYTH

The other area of chronic confusion concerns the need to warm up and cool down as a way to prevent injury to the muscles. Stretching is the usual approach to warming up, but alas, it does not prevent injury like people think it does, says Dr. Sayers, although it does enhance flexibility. A warm-up is definitely required, though, because cold muscles are vulnerable to injury. The way to do this is with a brief cardio spurt at low resistance, such as on the bike or treadmill or walking briskly for a few minutes—anything that brings blood to your muscles, increases your body temperature and revs your metabolism slightly in preparation for the session to come. A cool-down is to reverse the body changes you put into motion with your warm-up…just continue your exercise but slow the pace. Weekend warriors planning a hike or sports outing can reduce or prevent soreness by preparing with a few eccentric movements such as squats (for quads—using only your body weight) or sit-ups for several days beforehand. Stretching after exercise does not reduce DOMS.

Unfortunately, once DOMS sets in, there is little you can do to relieve it, though according to naturopathic physician Andrew L. Rubman, ND, a hot bath with Epsom salts is somewhat helpful.

A recent study indicated that drinking tart cherry juice, with its ample antioxidants, might be useful, but the research is preliminary, says Dr. Sayers. Plenty of studies have focused on other sorts of treatments, including acupuncture, yoga, massage, icing, stretching and vitamin C, but to little effect. Nonsteroidal anti-inflammatory drugs (NSAIDs) have been the subject of multiple studies for DOMS relief, but Dr. Sayers notes that the results are split right in the middle as to whether or not they help. He wants us to remember, however, that our body's inflammation response is important to muscle repair and it probably isn't a good idea to routinely take NSAIDs before exercise, because they might slow the inflammation that is part of repairing muscle damage.

Dr. Sayers does offer one way to feel better, though.

For a quick but short-acting fix, try this: Simulate the very exercise that caused your soreness, but do it lightly, just enough to get some blood flow to the muscles and release endorphins. No, the relief you get won't last long, but for a few minutes or hours, it may feel better.

Diet for a Pain-Free Life

Harris H. McIlwain, MD, rheumatologist and pain specialist with Florida's largest rheumatology practice, and adjunct professor at University of South Florida College of Public Health, both in Tampa. He is coauthor, with Debra Fulghum Bruce, PhD, of *Diet for a Pain-Free Life* (Marlowe).

As many as 150 million Americans live with ongoing pain. This usually is caused by such problems as arthritis or injuries to the neck or back.

Being overweight and having a poor diet are crucial factors, too. Fatty tissue is an endocrine (hormone-producing) organ, just like other organs in the body. Studies show that patients who are overweight produce high levels of cytokines, C-reactive protein and other proinflammatory chemicals—substances that promote joint and tissue damage and increase pain.

Good news: Losing as little as 10 pounds can significantly reduce inflammation, pain and stiffness—regardless of the underlying cause of the discomfort. People who combine weight loss with a diet that includes anti-inflammatory foods (and excludes proinflammatory ones) can reduce pain by up to 90%. The effect rivals that of *ibuprofen* and similar painkillers—without gastrointestinal upset or other side effects.

PAIN-FREE DIET

The saturated fat in beef, pork, lamb and other meats is among the main causes of painful inflammation. People who eat a lot of meat (including poultry) consume *arachidonic acid,* an essential fatty acid that is converted into inflammatory chemicals in the body.

Although a vegetarian diet is ideal for reducing inflammation and promoting weight loss (no more than 6% of vegetarians are obese), few Americans are willing to give up meat altogether.

Recommended: A plant-based diet that includes little (or no) meat and poultry…at least two to four weekly servings of fish…and plenty of fiber and anti-inflammatory foods. Patients who follow this diet and limit daily calories to about 1,400 can lose 10 to 25 excess pounds within three months.

Helpful: It takes at least two to three weeks to establish new dietary habits. People who give up meat entirely usually find that they don't miss it after a few weeks—while those who continue to eat some meat may find the cravings harder to resist.

My favorite cookbooks: *Vegan with a Vengeance* by Isa Chandra Moskowitz (Da Capo) and *Pike Place Public Market Seafood Cookbook* by Braiden Rex-Johnson (Ten Speed).

Here are the best painkilling foods and beverages. *Include as many of these in your diet as possible…*

RED WINE

Red wine contains *resveratrol,* a chemical compound that blocks the activation of the COX-2 enzyme, one of the main substances responsible for pain and inflammation. Resveratrol may be more effective than aspirin at relieving pain from osteoarthritis and other inflammatory conditions.

Other beverages made from grapes, such as white wine and grape juice, contain some resveratrol, but not as much as red wine.

Servings: No more than two glasses daily for men, and no more than one glass for women.

Alternative source of antioxidants for nondrinkers: Two or more cups of tea daily. Both green and black teas contain *epigallocatechin-3-gallate* (EGCG), a chemical that blocks the COX-2 enzyme.

BERRIES

Virtually all fruits contain significant amounts of antioxidants, which prevent free radical molecules from damaging cell membranes and causing inflammation. Berries—particularly

407

blueberries, cranberries and blackberries—are among the most powerful analgesic fruits because they're high in *anthocyanins,* some of the most effective antioxidants. One-half cup of blueberries, for example, has more antioxidant power than five servings of green peas or broccoli.

Servings: One-half cup of berries daily, fresh or frozen.

Bonus: Berries are very high in the antioxidant vitamin C, a nutrient that builds and protects joint cartilage.

PINEAPPLE

Fresh pineapple contains the enzyme *bromelain,* which is in the stem and fruit of the pineapple and inhibits the release of inflammatory chemicals. It has been shown in some studies to reduce arthritic pain. I advise patients with sports injuries to eat pineapple because of its healing powers.

Servings: At least two half-cup servings weekly, more if you're suffering from injuries or an arthritis flare-up. Bromelain also can be taken in supplement form—200 milligrams (mg) to 300 mg, three times daily before meals.

GINGER

Ginger contains potent anti-inflammatory substances and was found in one study to reduce knee pain in 63% of patients.

Servings: One teaspoon of ginger daily. Fresh and powdered ginger are equally effective and can be added to food.

FISH

I advise patients to substitute oily fish (such as salmon, tuna and sardines) for meat. Fish has little saturated fat (the main proinflammatory nutrient in the American diet) and is high in omega-3 fatty acids. Omega-3s increase the body's production of inhibitory prostaglandins, substances that lower levels of inflammatory chemicals and can reduce arthritis pain.

Servings: Two to four three-ounce servings of fish weekly or 1,000 to 2,000 mg of fish oil (available in capsule form) daily. If you don't like fish, omega-3s also are found in flaxseed, walnuts and soy foods.

408

WHOLE GRAINS AND BEANS

These are among the best sources of B vitamins—especially important for people who eat a lot of processed foods, which are usually deficient in these nutrients. Studies suggest that vitamins B-1 (*thiamin*), B-6 (*pyridoxine*) and B-12 (*cyanocobalamin*) may reduce inflammation.

Other B vitamins, such as B-3 (*niacin*), also reduce inflammation and may increase natural steroid levels and reduce the risk of osteoarthritis.

Servings: At least one-half cup of whole grains and/or beans daily.

Good choices: Brown rice, lentils, chickpeas, black beans and kidney beans.

Bonus: Grains and beans are high in fiber. High-fiber foods promote weight loss by increasing a sense of fullness and maintaining optimal blood sugar levels.

Natural Rx for Shingles

Chris Meletis, ND, executive director, the Institute for Healthy Aging. He is author of several books including *Better Sex Naturally* (Harper Resource), *Complete Guide to Safe Herbs* (DK Publishing) and *Instant Guide to Drug-Herb Interactions* (DK Publishing).

Approximately one million—mostly older—Americans get shingles (*herpes zoster*) each year as the *varicella-zoster virus* reactivates from a childhood chickenpox (*variella*) infection. The virus typically travels along one nerve to one part of the body to the skin's surface where it eventually erupts into another rash with blisters. Before that happens, though, other symptoms may appear, including tingling, itching and sometimes pain or a burning sensation that can be so intense it has been confused with that of kidney stones, appendicitis or even a heart attack, depending on the location of the affected nerve. Once the rash does appear, typically on one side of the torso or face, it brings fresh misery with more pain and blisters. Patients are warned not to scratch because that might increase the potential for a secondary bacterial infection.

In most people, shingles resolves itself by five or six very uncomfortable weeks... although, for a few patients, a painful and debilitating complication called *postherpetic neuralgia* (PHN) can linger for many more months and even years. In fact, the development of a vaccine for shingles was partly to shield people from the possibility of PHN. While the vaccination is a reality and is available to people ages 60 and over, we wondered about natural treatments that might both ease the discomfort of shingles and possibly reduce the amount of time it normally takes to run its course, as well as develop PHN. To find out, we called naturopathic physician Chris Meletis, ND, executive director of education for the Institute for Healthy Aging. Dr. Meletis often treats patients with shingles.

NATURAL Rx FOR SHINGLES

Dr. Meletis says that his first recommendation for shingles patients is to take vitamin B-12. The reason, most importantly, is that B-12 has been shown to help prevent PHN. He says that it also helps bolster energy levels and eases the discomfort of the outbreak. Dr. Meletis often prescribes 1 mg of B-12 in the form of *methylcobalamin* twice a day, preferably under the tongue (sublingually). Continue this for the duration of the outbreak and for two to three months after the resolution of the rash and other symptoms. Another useful vitamin for combating shingles is vitamin C. A potent antioxidant, vitamin C bolsters the immune system and helps patients cope with the stress of the disease. Some people find that vitamin C helps dry blisters as well and reduces pain to some degree and it may also hinder development of PHN. The dosage for many of Dr. Meletis' patients is 1,000 mg two to three times a day with meals. Vitamin C can cause diarrhea, in which case patients are directed to ease up slightly on dosage until they find the maximum level that is tolerated. If nerve pain does remain after the lesions have resolved, lipoic acid at a dose of 300 mg two to three times a day can be helpful.

One amino acid plays a particularly interesting role in shingles. *L-lysine* has been shown to be helpful in combating viruses, including another type of herpes virus called herpes simplex-1 that typically causes so-called fever blisters on the lips and herpes-simplex 2, which typically causes outbreaks of lesions on the genitalia. Use of L-lysine, however, must be prescribed and monitored carefully by a trained professional. L-lysine is contraindicated in pregnant women and those with elevated cholesterol or triglyceride levels.

TOPICAL RELIEF

Of course it is important to have topical balms and creams to soothe the itching and pain of the rash. There are several available that Dr. Meletis has found to be helpful. Lysine cream is one (but do not put on open sores) and lemon balm is another. After the sores heal, a variety of capsaicin-containing creams on the market may provide pain relief. Capsaicin, the substance that adds heat to hot peppers, is said to inhibit nerve cells from sending pain messages to the brain. Capsaicin creams come in a variety of strengths. Whichever one you select, start small by using just a dab and apply four times a day. It will sting when you first put it on, but don't let that fool you. Stick with it since it will help. After applying, wash hands with soap and water to avoid irritation on other parts of your skin.

Finally, Dr. Meletis reminds all shingles patients that your body needs time to restore itself. You may not feel inclined to do much else as you battle shingles, so use the time to take it easy and get lots of rest.

Therapeutic Magnets... Help or Hype?

Marjory Abrams, chief content officer, *Bottom Line* newsletters, Bottom Line Inc., 3 Landmark Square, Stamford, Connecticut 06901.

Oh, my aching feet! The hard floors at the local mall—combined with old walking shoes—really got to me during a recent shopping expedition. As the pain intensified, I noticed there was a display of magnetic shoe inserts promising fast relief for sore feet. But my natural skepticism kicked in and, instead of buying the insoles, I went home.

"Just as well," says Michael Weintraub, MD, clinical professor of neurology at New York Medical College in Valhalla, and Mount Sinai School of Medicine in New York City. "Most 'therapeutic' magnets sold in malls and supermarkets don't work—but that doesn't mean magnet therapy is bunk."

In a landmark study of 375 people published in *Archives of Physical Medicine and Rehabilitation*, Dr. Weintraub showed that wearing magnetic insoles constantly for four months provided significant relief for many people with diabetic foot pain and numbness.

Medical magnets also help some individuals with finger, wrist, neck or back pain, Dr. Weintraub reports. According to a Mount Sinai/University of Tennessee study, magnets worn on the abdomen can lessen disability from chronic pelvic pain in women. Magnets come in many different forms, including knee braces, wrist wraps and bracelets.

No one knows why magnets often are effective in relieving pain.

One popular theory: Magnets increase blood flow, boosting the delivery of oxygen and nutrients to the affected tissues. The stronger the magnet (measured in a unit called a *gauss*), the better the relief. A typical refrigerator magnet measures 10 gauss and has no effect on pain. Effective therapeutic magnets seem to range in strength from 450 gauss to more than 10,000 gauss. However, Dr. Weintraub points out that manufacturers usually do not list the strength of magnets and, when they do, the numbers often are wrong. Two reputable brands—Nikken (800-669-8859, *www.nikken.com*) and Bioflex Medical Magnets, Inc. (864-310-6370, *www.bioflexmagnets.com*).

Use magnets throughout the day for several weeks to see whether they work for you.

Helpful: Keep a pain journal to gauge their effect over time.

Although therapeutic magnets have no known side effects, Dr. Weintraub suggests consulting your doctor before treating pain with magnets. They usually are not recommended for pregnant women or people with internal defibrillators, pacemakers or insulin pumps. Nor should they be placed over drug-delivery patches or open wounds.

More will be learned about magnet therapy as time goes by—but for now, it's at least worth considering.

The Key to Healing Your Aches and Pains—Without Surgery or Drugs

Ming Chew, PT, a physical therapist with a private practice in New York City, *www.mingmethod.com*. He is author of *The Permanent Pain Cure* (McGraw-Hill).

Most conventional doctors' approach to orthopedic pain and injuries is "medicate or cut." But there are alternatives.

Before resorting to powerful drugs or surgery, people who suffer from aching knees, backs, shoulders, hips or necks owe it to themselves to first try physical therapy.

Secret to permanent pain relief: A specialized form of physical therapy that focuses on *fascia* (the tough sheet of connective tissue found in all parts of your body) is one of the most effective—yet underused—cures for joint pain.

WHY DOES IT WORK?

Over time, the fascia (pronounced *fash*-ee-uh) throughout your body can become less flexible from lack of exercise. Repetitive movements, such as typing, knitting, golfing or tennis playing…bad posture…or trauma, including bruising or surgery, also affect the fascia. When the fascia tightens, your muscles no longer contract properly. This results in muscle weakness that can lead to aches and pains in other parts of the body.

Important: If the fascia is injured, it won't show up on a magnetic resonance imaging (MRI) scan, which doctors routinely use to diagnose orthopedic problems. But unhealthy

fascia often is the underlying cause of joint and muscle pain.

THE KEY TO HEALTHY FASCIA

To check the resilience of your fascia, place your palm flat on a table and spread your fingers as wide as possible. Using the thumb and index finger of your other hand, pinch a fold of skin on the back of your flattened hand. Pull it up and hold it for five seconds. Then let go. If the skin snaps back and becomes completely flat instantaneously, your fascia is highly elastic and healthy. If it takes longer than two seconds, your fascia has lost some elasticity.

For the health of your fascia…

• **Stay hydrated.** The fascia in your body is 70% water. For proper hydration, drink *at least* 64 ounces of filtered water or purified bottled water per day if you're male or 48 ounces daily if you're female.

Eat an anti-inflammatory diet by limiting sugar consumption (including fruit juices and sweets), trans fats ("partially hydrogenated oils" found in many packaged and fast foods) and fried foods.

Take supplements to further reduce inflammation. For example, ask your doctor about taking 1.5 g to 2.5 g of fish oil per day (taken with meals)…and a daily joint-support supplement that combines glucosamine and chondroitin (components of joint tissue and cartilage, respectively)—consult a naturopathic or integrative medicine physician for advice on specific dosages and any precautions that should be taken when using these supplements.

STRETCHING TIGHT FASCIA

The following three fascial stretches address some especially common problem areas.

Important: Always warm up with two minutes of continuous movement, such as jogging in place or performing arm circles, before stretching.*

• **Hip flexor stretch.** This stretch affects the *psoas*, a muscle that runs down either side of the pelvis, connecting the base of the spine to the hip bones. Tight psoas muscles are a

*These stretches should not be performed by pregnant women or people with bone cancer, acute pain or recent muscle tears or strains.

major—and under-recognized—cause of low-back pain as well as hip and knee pain.

What to do: Place a chair on each side of your body. Kneel on your right knee and place your left leg in front of you with your left foot flat on the ground and your left knee bent 90 degrees. Place the palm of each hand on the seat of each chair.

Next, tilt your entire torso to the left. While maintaining this tilt, rotate your torso to the right.

Lift your chest and tuck your chin to your chest. Clench your buttocks to press your right hip forward. To avoid arching your back, contract your abdominal muscles.

Finally, while pressing your right foot downward, imagine that you're dragging your right knee forward and contract the muscles you would use to do this. You should feel a deep stretch in the front of your right hip. Hold for 20 seconds, keeping your buttocks firmly contracted. Relax for 10 seconds, then hold for 30 seconds more. Switch legs and repeat on the other side.

• **Shrug muscle stretch.** This stretch affects the *trapezius* muscle, which runs from the lower back to the outer shoulder and base of the skull. The stretch can help relieve neck stiffness, which is often due to a tight trapezius.

What to do: While seated or standing, hold your right arm five inches out from your hip, elbow straight. Bend your wrist slightly behind your body and drop your chin to your chest. Rotate your chin to the right about 30 degrees, and hold it there while you tilt the upper part of your head to the left. Press your right shoulder down hard, away from your ear and hold for 20 seconds. You should feel a stretch from the back of your head to the outer edge of your right shoulder. Rest for 10 seconds, then hold for 30 seconds more. Repeat on the left side.

• **Biceps stretch.** This stretch helps with a range of problems, including shoulder pain, tennis elbow as well as golfer's elbow. It also

411

strengthens muscles in the mid-back, which helps improve posture. For this stretch, you'll need a chair and a low table.

What to do: Place the chair back against the table and sit with your feet flat on the floor. Put both arms on the table behind you with the backs of your hands facing down. Pull both shoulders backward and lift your chest. Next, walk both feet slightly leftward so your torso is rotated to the left. Straighten your right elbow and bend your right wrist up, touching the fingers and thumb of your right hand together in a point (your left hand should remain flat on the table).

Next, tilt your head to the left, and rotate it to the left so that the right side of your neck feels a stretch. Then drop your chin to your left collarbone. It should feel like a strap is being pulled from the top front of your shoulder to your elbow. Hold for 20 seconds. Rest for 10 seconds, then hold for 30 seconds more. Switch sides and repeat.

Illustrations by Shawn Banner.

Skin Infections that Are Often Overlooked

Lawrence Eron, MD, an associate professor of medicine at the John A. Burns School of Medicine at the University of Hawaii in Honolulu. An infectious disease consultant at Kaiser Foundation Hospital, also in Honolulu, Dr. Eron is a specialist in skin and soft tissue infections. He is author of an article on cellulitis in the *Annals of Internal Medicine.*

The dangers associated with the highly drug-resistant, sometimes fatal "superbug" known as MRSA (*methicillin-resistant Staphylococcus aureus*) have been widely publicized.

MRSA, once a threat primarily in hospitals, long-term-care facilities and other health-care settings, is now appearing in a slightly mutated form in gyms, schools, military barracks and other settings where people may have skin-to-skin contact and/or share towels, linens or other items that can become contaminated. MRSA may turn life-threatening if the bacteria penetrate the skin, become bloodborne and reach other areas of the body, such as the heart or lungs.

What most people don't realize: The skin can harbor *dozens* of infectious organisms.

Example: The average handprint on a dinner plate might contain up to 35 species of bacteria, viruses or fungi.

Most of these organisms are harmless—and even those that are capable of causing disease are usually blocked from entering the body by the skin's protective barrier and/or destroyed by immune cells just beneath the skin's surface.

Danger: The skin typically has thousands of microscopic nicks or other openings that provide entry points for harmful germs—even if you don't have an obvious cut. To help prevent harmful bacteria from entering these tiny openings, wash your hands often with mild soap and warm water, and shave carefully. *Infections to avoid...**

CELLULITIS

This skin infection, which can be mistaken for a scrape, bruise or spider bite, is caused by bacteria that enter the body through dry, flaky and/or cracked skin or other skin openings such as those caused by a cut, splinter or surgical wound.

Cellulitis typically occurs on the legs but can occur anywhere on the body—even on your hand. The infection usually originates in the upper layers (the dermis and epidermis) of the skin but can also occur in deeper (subcutaneous) tissues, including the muscles and muscle linings. Infections in deeper tissues are more likely to cause serious symptoms and extensive tissue damage, such as severe swelling and pain, and formation of abscesses. Everyone is at risk for cellulitis, but those with weakened immunity (such as diabetes and dialysis patients) are at greatest risk.

*To see examples of the many ways these infections can appear on the body, go to *www.images.google.com* and type in the name of each infection. *Beware:* Many of the images are graphic.

What to look for: The affected area will be red, hot and tender. The redness spreads very quickly, and you may develop a fever (101°F or higher) and body aches. If the infection is severe, confusion or fecal incontinence also may occur. People with any of the severe symptoms described earlier should seek immediate medical care at a hospital emergency department.

Treatment: Oral antibiotics, such as *dicloxacillin* or *cephalexin* (Keflex). These are effective against *Streptococcus* and about half of the *Staphylococcus* organisms—common causes of cellulitis—and usually start to relieve symptoms within two days. Patients with more severe infections may require hospitalization and intravenous antibiotics.

To reduce your risk of developing cellulitis: Take a daily shower or bath. People who wash often and use plenty of mild soap are less likely to develop cellulitis or other skin infections.

NECROTIZING INFECTIONS

The media often refer to these infections as "flesh-eating." This isn't entirely accurate. Several bacterial species can cause the necrosis (death) of infected tissue, but the bacteria don't eat the flesh, *per se*. Rather, they secrete toxins that break it down.

Necrotizing infections are rare—fewer than 1,000 cases occur each year in the US—but the fatality rate is quite high at 25% to 30%. These infections spread very rapidly—if you marked the edge of an infection with a pen, you might see the redness creep past the mark in as little as one hour.

What to look for: Skin redness and/or swelling that's warm to the touch. The initial infection, which can follow even a minor cut or puncture wound, resembles cellulitis. But a necrotizing infection is far more painful. As the infection progresses, you may develop very large, fluid-filled purple blisters (bullae), a high fever (104°F or higher), disorientation and a rapid heartbeat. If you develop any of these symptoms, seek immediate medical attention at a hospital emergency department.

Treatment: Intravenous antibiotics and surgery, sometimes requiring amputation, to remove infected tissue.

To reduce your risk of developing a necrotizing infection: Thoroughly clean even minor cuts and scrapes. Apply an over-the-counter antibiotic ointment, such as Neosporin or bacitracin, and keep the area covered with a clean dressing until the area is completely healed.

FOLLICULITIS

This skin infection occurs at the root of a hair (follicle) and may produce a small pimple —or, less often, a larger, more painful pimple called a boil. Folliculitis tends to be more common in people with diabetes (which reduces resistance to infection) and those who live in hot, humid climates (excessive perspiration promotes growth of the bacterium that causes folliculitis).

What to look for: A small, white pimple at the base of a hair. Boils, also called abscesses, are larger than pimples (sometimes an inch or more in diameter), with a greater volume of pus. They tend to be warmer than the surrounding skin and can be intensely painful.

Treatment: The small pimples caused by folliculitis often disappear on their own within several days. Applying a topical antibiotic several times a day can prevent the infection from spreading. Apply a warm, moist compress (for 15 minutes four times daily for one to two days) to tender pimples or boils to help them drain.

Painful or unusually large boils should be lanced, drained and cleaned by a doctor. *Do not* "pop" them yourself. The risk for infection is high—and boils can be caused by MRSA. Antibiotics usually aren't necessary when boils are professionally drained and cleaned.

To reduce your risk of developing folliculitis: Wash your hands several times daily with soap...and take a daily shower or bath. If you have chronic, recurrent boils, use antibacterial soap.

Abdominal Pain

Mark A. Stengler, NMD, licensed naturopathic medical doctor in private practice, Encinitas, California... adjunct associate clinical professor at the National College of Natural Medicine, Portland, Oregon...author of *The Natural Physician's Healing Therapies* and co-author of *Prescription for Natural Cures* (both from Bottom Line Books).

By the time she consulted me, 57-year-old Sue was fed up. For four decades, she had suffered from unpredictable bouts of burning abdominal pain that occurred about once a month and lasted for days. Each attack was accompanied by excessive burping and a bitter taste.

Over the years, Sue had consulted half a dozen gastroenterologists and had numerous tests—including ultrasound and endoscopy —but no abnormalities had been found. Six years ago, she had taken antibiotics for several months after being diagnosed with an infection of *Helicobacter pylori* (the bacterium that causes stomach ulcers), but relief was temporary. Sue also took *pantoprazole* (Protonix), a prescription heartburn drug that reduces stomach acid. It did ease her heartburn but did not alleviate her sporadic abdominal pain.

A stool test showed undigested meat fibers, indicating poor protein digestion. This made sense, since Sue was still taking the acid-suppressing medication. It also showed an overgrowth of the fungus *Candida albicans* —a common side effect of antibiotics, which destroy beneficial bacteria in the digestive tract that keep fungi in check.

Blood tests showed no signs of a food allergy but did show a deficiency of vitamin B-12, which is common in people with low levels of the stomach acids that promote absorption of certain nutrients. A B-12 deficiency also can result from excessive alcohol use—clearly the case for Sue, who had several alcoholic drinks per day. Sue also smoked daily and sometimes indulged in sweets and spicy foods—all of which contribute to inflammation, especially of the digestive system.

Since Sue's abdominal pain was not the result of any single cause, we took an integrated approach. She agreed to reduce her smoking by half, cut back to three alcoholic drinks weekly, avoid spicy fare and limit foods that contain simple sugars, such as soda and white bread. She began taking a daily B-12 supplement and, to reduce inflammation, an ingestible blend of aloe vera juice plus *deglycyrrhizinated* licorice root (DGL), available at health-food stores. (These shouldn't be used while pregnant or nursing.) I prescribed the homeopathic remedy *Chelidonium majus* (from the juice of a plant with the same name), to take at the first sign of abdominal pain (from Remedy Source, 301-610-6649, *www.remedysource.com*).

A month later, Sue reported that the Chelidonium majus brought quick relief during bouts of pain. Her attacks were less frequent and milder, and the burping and bitter taste had disappeared—all results of improved digestion and decreased stomach irritation. I prescribed a supplement of antifungal herbs, including oregano oil and *pau d'arco* (from the *taheebo tree*), to halt the Candida overgrowth. After several months, Sue was able to stop using her heartburn medication—and her abdominal pain became a thing of the past.

Drink Water to Prevent Back Pain

Depending on your age and spinal health, the shock-absorbing discs in your spine are 70% to 90% water. If a person is not adequately hydrated, increased back stiffness may result.

Self-defense: Drink about one-half ounce of water per pound of body weight.

Also: Use proper lifting techniques (bend with your knees and keep the object as close to you as possible)...and maintain a healthy weight. If back pain is severe or accompanied by leg weakness, numbness or fever, seek immediate attention. This could be a sign of something more serious like a disc herniation, circulatory problems, infection or cancer.

Daniel A. Shaye, DC, certified chiropractic rehabilitation doctor, Williamsburg, Virginia.

No Surgery! Technique to Fight Back Pain

Conrado Estol, MD, director, Neurological Center for Treatment and Rehabilitation, Buenos Aires.

Arya Nick Shamie, MD, chief, spine surgery, Wadsworth Veterans Administration, and medical director, University of California at Los Angeles Comprehensive Spine Center.

American Academy of Neurology annual meeting, Miami Beach.

A technique to alleviate debilitating lower back and neck pain, developed over a quarter-century ago by French doctor Philippe Souchard is receiving new attention after preliminary research discovered that it quickly improved the quality of life for a majority of patients.

The Souchard global postural re-education (GPR) method addresses posture correction in problem areas by targeting entire muscle groups, rather than individual muscles. These muscle chains are slowly stretched and elongated over multiple therapy sessions to relieve pressure on pinched spinal nerves. The technique is non-surgical and does not involve prescription medications.

THE STUDY

Study author Conrado Estol, MD, of the Neurological Center for Treatment and Rehabilitation in Buenos Aires treated 102 Argentinian men and women, ages 25 to 91, for four years. All had been afflicted with severe back or neck pain for an average of seven months prior to the start of the study.

Prior to receiving GPR, all the men and women had already been prescribed at least one traditional remedy for a minimum of six months, including nonsurgical treatments, such as regular physical therapy, anti-inflammatory drugs, acupuncture, epidural injections or simply rest.

None of the traditional remedies had helped diminish symptoms among the patients treated. All of the patients said they had experienced at least some disruption to their daily routine as a result of their pain.

"Most cases of lower back pain and neck pain go away spontaneously while the patient is being worked up or just starting physical therapy," says Dr. Estol. "Intractable back pain is very rare nowadays, but these people were not going to improve on their own in four or five days. Some of these patients couldn't walk."

Following an initial week in which they received two therapies, all of the patients were placed on a five-month regimen of once-weekly GPR, administered in a combination of standing, sitting and lying positions. During the therapy sessions, patients were taught breathing techniques, and were instructed in a special home-exercise program.

According to Dr. Estol, 85% of the patients noticeably improved after the first three weeks of GPR. By the end of the study period, 90% were able to resume their normal daily routines. Only 6% said they continued to experience some pain when engaging in demanding sports activity, while 4% gained no apparent benefit from GPR.

After almost two years of follow-up, none of the patients who appeared to benefit from GPR reported any back pain relapse.

"I am extremely enthusiastic. It's a very safe method, and I think we're proving it works," says Dr. Estol, who has been exploring the promise of GPR for more than 14 years.

EFFECTIVE FOR ALL?

"Not only is GPR an effective non-surgical solution to back pain, but a softer, less brisk alternative to traditional physical therapy," Dr. Estol says. But he notes that his study focused only on people experiencing the most severe and enduring kind of back pain.

"GPR appears to be effective, but, of course, people should always get evaluated first by a physician with expertise before they choose a treatment," he adds.

Arya Nick Shamie, MD, chief of spine surgery at Wadsworth Veterans Administration in Brentwood, California, agrees that informed medical advice is in order whenever back pain persists beyond two weeks or is the result of an accident. Once the doctor determines the need for treatment, Dr. Shamie is not so sure GPR is the best option.

"Back pain is such a mixed soup of various problems, and this study lumps all sorts of diagnoses into one group," cautions Dr. Shamie, who is also medical director at UCLA Comprehensive Spine Center. "A patient with sciatic pain, and another with degenerative disc disease and another with a cyst in his spine—if you group all of these patients together and suggest this one form of physical therapy is going to treat them all, it's not so compelling."

Dr. Shamie notes that in Dr. Estol's study, no other form of therapy was studied alongside GPR as a "control" group to provide comparison.

To learn more about back pain, visit the American Academy of Orthopaedic Surgeons at *www.aaos.org*.

Natural Prescriptions For Laryngitis

Jamison Starbuck, ND, naturopathic physician in family practice in Missoula, Montana. She is past president of the American Association of Naturopathic Physicians and a contributing editor to The Alternative Advisor: The Complete Guide to Natural Therapies and Alternative Treatments *(Time-Life).*

There's no mistaking the husky, whispered voice that accompanies laryngitis. Often due to a viral infection, laryngitis also can cause your voice to sound hoarse or crackle into a variety of unexpected pitches. Typically occurring with a sore or dry throat, a cough and, in some cases, fever and fatigue, laryngitis frequently is related to a cold, bronchitis or sinusitis. It also can be due to overuse of the voice or irritation from smoke or air pollution. Because there are so many potential causes of laryngitis, it's a good idea to see your doctor for an exam to rule out a bacterial infection, such as from *Strep*. Fortunately, there are a number of natural strategies that are safe and effective at limiting the length and severity of laryngitis.

Since laryngitis indicates inflammation of the vocal cords, it's crucial to rest your voice as much as possible for several days.

To accelerate healing of laryngitis—or a sore throat (without laryngitis)...

• **Use slippery elm.** This demulcent (soothing) herb relieves inflamed mucous membranes including those of the throat. Lozenges, which are available at health-food stores, are probably the most convenient form of slippery elm. Use the lozenges according to the instructions on the label. Another option is slippery elm powder.

How to prepare: Add one teaspoon of slippery elm powder to one-quarter cup of applesauce. Eat this four times a day.

• **Soothe your throat with a botanical spray.** Typically made from demulcent and antiseptic herbs (such as those mentioned below), a throat spray can effectively relieve the symptoms of laryngitis. Look for a botanical throat spray at a health-food store or make your own by combining equal parts of the individual tinctures of echinacea, hyssop, osha and marshmallow.

How to prepare: To six ounces of warm water, add one-half ounce of each tincture. Add two teaspoons of honey and stir until the honey dissolves. Put this mixture in a small spray bottle and spray directly on the back of the throat every two waking hours. (You can store this mixture in a sealed jar.)

• **Try homeopathic remedies.** My patients have reported very good results when using either of these homeopathic remedies: *Causticum*, used when hoarseness is accompanied by a raw sore throat and/or cough or a sore throat due to overuse of the voice...or *Phosphorus*, used when laryngitis is painless or accompanied by extreme thirst and anxiety.

What to do: Take two pellets of a 30C potency of either remedy (under the tongue), 20 minutes before or after eating, twice daily for no more than three days. (Taking the remedy longer may lead to irritation.)

If your laryngitis lasts for more than two weeks or recurs every few weeks, there may be a more serious problem. Heavy smoking, gastroesophageal reflux disease (chronic heartburn) or benign or malignant growths on the vocal cords can lead to chronic laryngitis. See your doctor for an evaluation.

14

Prevent & Cope With Diabetes

Reverse Diabetes Just by What You Eat

ut calories and keep careful track of the fat, protein and carbohydrates (including sugar) you eat—those are the usual dietary recommendations for adults with type 2 diabetes (commonly referred to as adult-onset or non-insulin-dependent diabetes).

Trap: In my experience, many people who follow these recommendations still don't reap the promised benefits—weight loss, reduced need for medication and fewer complications.

My approach is dramatically different—and it works. My research team and I conducted a series of studies with hundreds of patients, and we discovered that it is possible to improve blood-sugar levels through diet alone.

Big payoff: People can now control—and even reverse—their type 2 diabetes. While the diet won't reverse type 1 (or juvenile) diabetes,

it will reduce risk for diabetic complications and help to minimize use of insulin.

WHERE IT STARTS

If you have type 2 diabetes, your body has become resistant to insulin, the hormone that carries glucose (sugar) into your cells, where it is used for energy.

Potential cause: Tiny droplets of fat have accumulated inside your muscle cells and are interfering with their ability to use insulin. Glucose can't get into your cells properly, which means that it builds up in your blood instead.

What if you could remove that accumulated fat from inside your cells? You would improve your body's ability to use insulin, get your blood sugar under control—and possibly even reverse your type 2 diabetes.

Neal D. Barnard, MD, adjunct associate professor of medicine at the George Washington University School of Medicine and Health Sciences and president of the nonprofit Physicians Committee for Responsible Medicine. He is author of numerous books, including *Dr. Neal Barnard's Program for Reversing Diabetes* (Rodale). *www.pcrm.org*

417

The best way to do this is by changing the way you eat. *With my three-step program, you can eat as much as you want of certain foods, because this approach focuses solely on what you eat, not how much...*

THE THREE-STEP PROGRAM

1. Avoid all animal products, including red meat, poultry, fish, dairy and eggs, as well as dishes and baked goods containing these ingredients. Animal protein is harmful to the kidneys. And the principal ingredient of dairy products, even low-fat or nonfat, is sugar in the form of lactose.

2. Minimize fats, and food made with fats, including cooking oils, salad dressings, mayonnaise, margarine and peanut butter, plus fried foods and naturally fatty foods, such as avocados and olives.

3. Consume lots of fruits, vegetables and whole grains. These foods are low on the glycemic index—meaning that they act slowly on your blood sugar.

Best choices: Whole-grain breads (wheat, pumpernickel, rye), other whole grains (barley, oats, bulgar, brown rice and corn), plus beans, lentils, sweet potatoes (which contain natural sugar but do not raise blood sugar rapidly), green vegetables, most fruits (except watermelon and pineapple, which are naturally sugary) and tofu. Nuts and seeds are also good in small amounts—unless you need to lose weight. In that case, it's best to avoid them.

Also: Herbal or regular tea and coffee are fine. Skip the soda and fruit juice, though, as these drinks are high on the glycemic index. I recommend avoiding diet soda as well. Although the reasons are not clear, people who stop drinking diet soda often lower their blood glucose. I also advise that you take a daily multivitamin/mineral supplement and a daily vitamin D supplement of 1,000 international units.

Bonus: If you follow these guidelines, you'll get plenty of fiber, which has many health benefits including helping to control blood sugar. And don't worry—you'll get enough protein from eating beans, leafy green vegetables, seeds and nuts.

MAKING THE CHANGE

If this all sounds like a very low-fat "vegan" diet, that's because it is. *To help yourself ease into this new program...*

• **Throw out all animal products and oils and foods that contain them.**

• **Make a list of foods you like that fit into the plan.** Then go to the store and buy a week's worth so you can test-drive the diet.

Helpful: There are plenty of healthy convenience foods on the market, like frozen cheese-free veggie pizza with a whole-wheat or rice crust, low-fat vegetarian chili and frozen vegan enchiladas.

• **Follow my plan to the letter for three weeks.** Your blood sugar should start to drop within the first week and will continue to improve. Your blood pressure may drop as well. You'll have more energy, and you may lose some weight (up to a pound a week). By the end of the third week, you won't be able to imagine going back to your old way of eating.

Our cravings go away because of a simple biological fact—we crave today what we had yesterday. Once you've gotten your diabetes under control, you can treat yourself to small amounts once in a while of, say, chocolate and other favorite foods. You may even find that you're satisfied with more healthful substitutes, such as strawberries drizzled with chocolate syrup instead of a candy bar.

Best of all, after a few months, you may be able to cut back or eliminate some of your medications.

Note: Always discuss medication changes with your doctor first.

GET MOVING

I recommend exercise as something you add to a healthy diet, not as a substitute for eating better.

Best: If you can manage a brisk walk for half an hour a day (or longer!), definitely do it.

If you are overweight or have joint or heart problems, you may not be able to do much exercise when you start the diet. Before long, however, you'll feel so much better, you'll want to start moving. And once you find a form of exercise that's appropriate for you—and that you enjoy—exercise becomes a lot more fun...and your diabetes becomes even less of a health concern.

More from Dr. Neal Barnard...

Delicious Recipe

To make the dietary changes to reverse diabetes, use the free resources on the Physicians Committee for Responsible Medicine Web site (*www.pcrm.org*). You can ask questions, join our online support group and find recipes to help you stick with your diabetes-busting diet. *Tasty example...*

ALMOST INSTANT BLACK BEAN CHILI

½ cup water
1 medium-sized onion, chopped
2 medium-sized cloves garlic, minced
1 small bell pepper, diced fine
½ cup crushed tomatoes or tomato sauce
2 15-oz cans black beans, including liquid
1 4-oz can diced chilies
1 tsp ground cumin

In a large skillet or pot, heat the water. Add onion, garlic, and pepper. Cook over high heat —stirring often—for about 5 minutes or until onion is translucent. Add remaining ingredients and simmer—stirring occasionally—for about 15 minutes or until flavors are blended. Makes 6 cups.

Stay-Well Secrets for People with Diabetes or Prediabetes

Theresa Garnero, advanced practice registered nurse (APRN), certified diabetes educator (CDE) and clinical nurse manager of the Center for Diabetes Services at the California Pacific Medical Center in San Francisco. She is author of *Your First Year with Diabetes: What to Do, Month by Month* (American Diabetes Association).

We've all heard that diabetes is on the rise in the US, but few people realize the degree to which older adults are disproportionately affected.

Frightening statistic: Nearly one out of every three Americans over age 65 has diabetes,

the highest rate among all age groups. Another one out of three older adults has a precursor to diabetes known as "prediabetes"—defined as a fasting blood sugar (glucose) level of 100 mg/dL to 125 mg/dL.

Many people downplay the seriousness of diabetes. That's a mistake. Because elevated glucose can damage blood vessels, nerves, the kidneys and eyes, people with diabetes are much more likely to die from heart disease and/or kidney disease than people without diabetes—and they are at increased risk for infections, including gum disease, as well as blindness and amputation. (Nerve damage and poor circulation can allow dangerous infections to go undetected.)

And diabetes can be sneaky—increased thirst, urination and/or hunger are the most common symptoms, but many people have no symptoms and are unaware that they are sick.

Despite these sobering facts, doctors rarely have time to give their patients all the information they need to cope with the complexities of diabetes. Fortunately, diabetes educators—health-care professionals, such as registered nurses, registered dietitians and medical social workers—can give patients practical advice on the best ways to control their condition.*

Good news: Most health insurers, including Medicare, cover the cost of diabetes patients' visits with a diabetes educator.

What you've probably never been told about diabetes...

SAVVY EATING HABITS

• **Most doctors advise people with diabetes or prediabetes to cut back on refined carbohydrates,** such as cakes and cookies, and eat more fruits, vegetables and whole grains. This maximizes nutrition and promotes a healthy body weight (being overweight greatly increases diabetes risk). *Other steps to take...*

• **Drink one extra glass of water each day.** The extra fluid will help prevent dehydration, which can raise glucose levels.

• **Never skip meals—especially breakfast.** Don't assume that bypassing a meal and fasting

*To find a diabetes educator near you, consult the American Association of Diabetes Educators, 800-338-3633, *www.diabeteseducator.org*.

for more than five to six hours will help lower glucose levels. It actually triggers the liver to release glucose into the bloodstream.

Better strategy: Eat three small meals daily and have snacks in between. Start with breakfast, such as a cup of low-fat yogurt and whole-wheat toast with peanut butter or a small bowl of whole-grain cereal and a handful of nuts.

Good snack options: A small apple or three graham crackers. Each of these snacks contains about 15 grams (g) of carbohydrates.

•**Practice the "plate method."** Divide a nine-inch plate in half. Fill half with vegetables, then split the other half into quarters—one for protein, such as salmon, lean meat, beans or tofu…and the other for starches, such as one-third cup of pasta or one-half cup of peas or corn. Then have a small piece of fruit. This is an easy way to practice portion control—and get the nutrients you need.

Ask yourself if you are satisfied after you take each bite. If the answer is "yes," stop eating. This simple strategy helped one of my clients lose 50 pounds.

•**Be wary of "sugar-free" foods.** These products, including sugar-free cookies and diabetic candy, often are high in carbohydrates, which are the body's primary source of glucose. You may be better off eating the regular product, which is more satisfying. Compare the carbohydrate contents on product labels.

GET CREATIVE WITH EXERCISE

If you have diabetes or prediabetes, you've probably been told to get more exercise. Walking is especially helpful. For those with diabetes, walking for at least two hours a week has been shown to reduce the risk for death by 30% over an eight-year period. For those with prediabetes, walking for 30 minutes five days a week reduces by about 60% the risk that your condition will progress to diabetes. *But if you'd like some other options, consider…***

•**"Armchair workouts."** These exercises, which are performed while seated and are intended for people with physical limitations to standing, increase stamina, muscle tone, flexi-

**Consult your doctor before starting a new exercise program.

420

bility and coordination. For DVDs, go to *www.armchairfitness.com* or call 800-453-6280.

Cost: $29.95 per DVD.

•**Strength training.** This type of exercise builds muscle, which burns more calories than fat even when you are not exercising.*** Use hand weights, exercise machines or the weight of your own body—for example, leg squats or bicep curls with no weights. Aim for two to three sessions of strength training weekly, on alternate days.

•**Stretching**—even while watching TV or talking on the phone. By building a stretching routine into your daily activities, you won't need to set aside a separate time to do it. If your body is flexible, it's easier to perform other kinds of physical activity. Stretching also promotes better circulation. Before stretching, do a brief warm-up, such as walking for five minutes and doing several "arm windmills." Aim to do stretching exercises at least three times weekly, including before your other workouts.

CONTROL YOUR BLOOD GLUCOSE

If you are diagnosed with diabetes, blood glucose control is the immediate goal. Self-monitoring can be performed using newer devices that test blood glucose levels.

Good choices: LifeScan's OneTouch Ultra …Bayer's Contour…or Abbott Laboratories' FreeStyle.

The hemoglobin A1C test, which is ordered by your doctor and typically is done two to four times a year, determines how well glucose levels have been controlled over the previous two to three months.

If you have prediabetes: Don't settle for a fasting glucose test, which measures blood glucose after you have fasted overnight. It misses two-thirds of all cases of diabetes. The oral glucose tolerance test (OGTT), which involves testing glucose immediately before drinking a premixed glass of glucose and repeating the test two hours later, is more reliable. If you can't get an OGTT, ask for an A1C test and fasting glucose test.

***If you have high blood pressure, be sure to check with your doctor before starting a strength-training program—this type of exercise can raise blood pressure.

If you have diabetes or prediabetes, you should have your blood pressure and cholesterol checked at every doctor visit and schedule regular eye exams and dental appointments. *In addition, don't overlook...*

• **Proper kidney testing.** Doctors most commonly recommend annual microalbumin and creatinine urine tests to check for kidney disease. You also may want to ask for a *glomerular filtration rate* test, which measures kidney function.

• **Meticulous foot care.** High glucose levels can reduce sensation in your feet, making it hard to know when you have a cut, blister or injury. In addition to seeing a podiatrist at least once a year and inspecting your own feet daily, be wary of everyday activities that can be dangerous for people with diabetes.

Stepping into hot bath water, for example, can cause a blister or skin damage that can become infected. To protect yourself, check the water temperature on your wrist or elbow before you step in. The temperature should be warm to the touch—not hot.

STAY UP TO DATE ON MEDICATIONS

Once diabetes medication has been prescribed, people with diabetes should review their drug regimen with their doctors at every visit. *Insulin is the most commonly used diabetes drug, but you may want to also ask your doctor about these relatively new medications...*

• **DPP-4 inhibitors.** These drugs include *sitagliptin* (Januvia), which lowers glucose levels by increasing the amount of insulin secreted by the pancreas. DPP-4 inhibitors are used alone or with another type of diabetes medication.

• **Symlin.** Administered with an injectable pen, *pramlintide* (Symlin) helps control blood glucose and reduces appetite, which may help with weight loss. It is used in addition to insulin, not on its own.

If you have prediabetes or diabetes: Always consult a pharmacist or doctor before taking any over-the-counter products. Cold medicines with a high sugar content may raise your blood glucose, for example, and wart removal products may cause skin ulcers. Pay close attention to drug label warnings.

Free Web Site Helps Control Diabetes

Log on to *www.sugarstats.com* to keep track of your blood glucose levels...medication usage...food intake...and exercise. People with diabetes can use the free site to help manage their disease and share information with their health-care providers.

Do You Have Prediabetes?

Annals of Family Medicine.

If you are age 65 or older, you are at increased risk for prediabetes regardless of the characteristics described below. For this reason, you should ask your doctor about receiving a fasting glucose test.

If you are under age 65, answer the following questions. Speak to your doctor about receiving a fasting glucose test if you score 5 or higher.

Age	Points
20–27	0
28–35	1
36–44	2
45–64	4
Sex	
Male	3
Female	0
Family History of Diabetes	
No	0
Yes	1
Heart Rate (beats per minute)	
Less than 60	0
60–69	0
70–79	1
80–89	2
90–99	2
Greater than 100	4

To determine your heart rate, place the tips of the first two fingers lightly over one of the blood vessels in your neck or the pulse spot inside your wrist just below the base of your thumb. Count your pulse for 10 seconds and multiply that number by 6.

High Blood Pressure

No	0
Yes	1

Body Mass Index (BMI)

Less than 25	0
25–29.9	2
30 or greater	3

To determine your BMI, consult the National Heart, Lung and Blood Institute Web site, *www.nhlbi.nih.gov* (search BMI calculator).

compared with 21% of those with diabetes alone, 17% of those with arthritis alone and 11% of those with neither condition.

Theory: People with both arthritis and diabetes remain inactive because they are concerned about worsening pain and joint damage, both of which can be exacerbated by excess body weight.

If you have arthritis and diabetes: Try arthritis-friendly workouts, such as walking, cycling and swimming, to help control your arthritis and diabetes.

Charles Helmick, MD, lead scientist, arthritis program, Centers for Disease Control and Prevention, Atlanta.

Self-Defense for Women with Diabetes

The death rate for women with diabetes has not declined, even though the rate for men with diabetes has declined by 43% over the last three decades.

Likely reason: The primary cause of death in people with diabetes is cardiovascular disease—which appears to be diagnosed and managed less efficiently in women.

Self-defense: Women with diabetes should be in the regular care of a physician and alert to symptoms such as chest and abdominal discomfort, shortness of breath and unexplained ankle swelling.

Ronald B. Goldberg, MD, professor of medicine, biochemistry and molecular biology, University of Miami Miller School of Medicine, and principal investigator for the university's Diabetes Prevention Program. He also is associate director of the Diabetes Research Institute, also in Miami.

Important for Diabetes: Secret to Protecting Your Liver

Excess fat in the liver can lead to cirrhosis and liver failure, especially in diabetes patients, necessitating dialysis or a transplant. Liver fat was reduced by an average of 34% among type 2 diabetes patients who did 45 minutes of moderate aerobic exercise (walking, cycling) plus 20 minutes of weight lifting three times weekly for six months. Waistlines shrank an average of two inches.

Kerry Stewart, EdD, professor of medicine, Johns Hopkins University School of Medicine, Baltimore, and leader of a study of 77 diabetes patients, reported at the annual meeting of the American Association of Cardiovascular and Pulmonary Rehabilitation.

Hip Fracture Common in Diabetics

In an analysis of 16 studies involving 836,941 people, researchers found that people with diabetes were 70% more likely to fracture a hip than nondiabetics. The reason has not yet been determined.

Inactivity Danger

When researchers analyzed physical activity among adults with both arthritis and diabetes, nearly 30% of them were sedentary,

If you have diabetes: Ask your doctor if you should have an annual bone density test.

Mohsen Janghorbani, PhD, professor of epidemiology, School of Public Health, Isfahan University of Medical Sciences, Isfahan, Iran.

Indian Herb Fights Diabetes

Mark A. Stengler, NMD, licensed naturopathic medical doctor in private practice, Encinitas, California... adjunct associate clinical professor at the National College of Natural Medicine, Portland, Oregon...author of *The Natural Physician's Healing Therapies* and co-author of *Prescription for Natural Cures* (both from Bottom Line Books).

Salacia oblonga is an herb commonly used in traditional Ayurvedic medicine to treat diabetes and obesity. Researchers fed 66 people with type 2 diabetes test meals on three separate occasions. Study participants were given a high-carbohydrate liquid meal or the liquid meal plus Salacia oblonga (S. oblonga) at a dosage of either 240 milligrams (mg) or 480 mg.

Result: Compared with the control meal alone, the 240-mg dose of S. oblonga lowered blood sugar by 14%...and the 480-mg dose lowered it by 22%. The amount of insulin, a hormone that regulates blood sugar, produced in response to the meal was reduced by 14% and 19%, respectively (high insulin contributes to inflammation in the body). These reductions were especially impressive given the high-carb meal (carbs raise blood sugar and insulin).

This herb prevents carbohydrates from being broken down in the digestive tract, allowing less glucose into the bloodstream—and resulting in lower blood glucose and insulin levels. Studies have shown it to be safe, and side effects are uncommon. People with mild-to-moderate elevation in glucose levels, as well as those with diabetes, should talk to their doctors about S. oblonga.

Note: Three study authors are employed by Abbott Laboratories, which funded the research. However, other studies with humans also have shown the benefits of S. oblonga.

More from Dr. Stengler...

Diabetes Medication Danger

Researchers at Wake Forest University have found that Avandia and Actos, two drugs that control type 2 diabetes, can almost double the risk for hip fractures in women.

Both medications—*rosiglitazone* (Avandia) and *pioglitazone* (Actos)—belong to a class of drugs known as *thiazolidinediones*. This is not the first time that these drugs have made headlines. In 2007, it was found that those who took rosiglitazone were at increased risk for heart attack. The FDA required warnings about heart attack and congestive heart failure to be added to rosiglitazone's label.

In the pharmaceutical industry, drugs are monitored through a practice known as post-marketing surveillance. Health-care professionals and the public voluntarily let the FDA know about any adverse effects experienced while using a drug. Manufacturers also are required to report any adverse events involving their drugs. Neither system is reliable. The disturbing new findings about Avandia and Actos emphasize the need for more rigorous monitoring and reporting of side effects.

Many patients with diabetes can reduce or eliminate the need for medication with proper diet and exercise, along with certain natural supplements—including chromium... ginseng...and PolyGlycoplex (also known as PGX), a blend of fiber including glucomannan and Pycnogenol (extract from pine bark). If you must take medication to control your diabetes, talk to your physician about drugs other than Avandia and Actos. *Metformin* (Glucophage) has a long history as a reliable diabetes medication.

Drug Helps Block Diabetes in People with Early Symptoms

Drug helps prevent diabetes in people with early symptoms, reports Ralph A.

DeFronzo, MD. About 21 million people in the US have impaired glucose tolerance, a pre-diabetic condition that is diagnosed through blood tests. According to recent research, impaired glucose tolerance is 81% less likely to turn into full-blown diabetes if patients take the prescription drug *pioglitazone* (Actos).

Possible side effects: Weight gain...edema (swelling)...increased fracture risk in post-menopausal women.

Ralph A. DeFronzo, MD, professor of medicine and diabetes chief, University of Texas Health Science Center, San Antonio, and leader of a study of 602 people with impaired glucose tolerance, presented at the 68th Scientific Sessions of the *American Diabetes Association*.

Are You Taking Byetta?

A few people with diabetes taking the drug Byetta have died after developing pancreatitis. There have been about six deaths involving pancreatitis among the one million people who have used Byetta since the Food and Drug Administration approved the drug in 2005.

But: The pancreatitis may not have caused the deaths—one patient weighed more than 400 pounds and had extensive gallstones... another had a relapse of leukemia.

Bottom line: No drug is completely safe. In Byetta's case, the benefits may far outweigh the risks.

The late Stanley Mirsky, MD, clinical professor of metabolic diseases, Mount Sinai School of Medicine in New York City and coauthor of *Diabetes Survival Guide* (Ballantine).

Improved Diabetes Monitor

One group of type 1 diabetes patients did conventional blood tests several times daily. Another group used tiny sensors (which patients place under the skin every few days using an insertion device) to continuously monitor blood sugar. With constant feedback on when to eat or take insulin, sensor users had better blood sugar control—reducing risk for diabetes complications. Prescription sensor systems cost about $10 per day. Some insurance plans cover them.

Roy W. Beck, MD, PhD, executive director, Jaeb Center for Health Research, Tampa, and head of a study of 322 diabetes patients, published in *The New England Journal of Medicine*.

Measure Sugar Before Eating

Diabetics should measure blood sugar before meals to best establish their long-term blood sugar levels. Premeal sugar level is more closely aligned with long-term levels than standard blood sugar measurements taken two hours after a meal. Postmeal levels are still important to measure the effects of the meal on blood sugar.

Important: Those with diabetes should work to maintain a low-sugar and low-carbohydrate diet.

The late Stanley Mirsky, MD, clinical professor of metabolic diseases, Mount Sinai School of Medicine, New York City, and coauthor of *Diabetes Survival Guide* (Ballantine).

Better Insulin Therapy

In a five-year study, researchers followed 1,300 diabetes patients who received insulin therapy using either syringes to inject insulin extracted from a vial...or insulin pens, which contain a needle and a premeasured dose of the drug. The insulin pen group had average annual health-care costs nearly $17,000 lower than those who used syringes (due to lower total hospital costs, for example, and fewer trips to emergency rooms).

Theory: When using an insulin pen, there is less risk of getting an incorrect dose.

If you use a syringe for insulin therapy: Ask your doctor if switching to an insulin pen would be appropriate for you.

Rajesh Balkrishnan, PhD, professor of pharmacy, Ohio State University, Columbus.

A Spoonful of Vinegar Helps the Blood Sugar Go Down

Adding vinegar to a meal slows the glycemic response—the rate at which carbohydrates are absorbed into the bloodstream—by 20%.

Reason: The acetic acid in vinegar seems to slow the emptying of the stomach, which reduces risk for *hyperglycemia* (high blood sugar), a risk factor for heart disease, and helps people with type 2 diabetes to manage their condition.

Ways to add vinegar to meals: Use malt vinegar on thick-cut oven fries...marinate sliced tomatoes and onions in red-wine vinegar before adding the vegetables to a sandwich...mix two parts red wine vinegar with one part olive oil, and use two tablespoons on a green salad.

Carol S. Johnston, PhD, RD, director, nutrition program, Arizona State University, Mesa, and coauthor of a study published in *Diabetes Care.*

Eye Scan for Diabetes

An experimental test uses specialized photographs of the eye to detect tissue damage caused by diabetes. The test—called *flavoprotein autofluorescence* (FA) imaging—is noninvasive and faster than blood-glucose testing—and could allow an earlier diagnosis.

University of Michigan Kellogg Eye Center

Older Treatment Beats New One for Saving Eyesight

Several years ago, early reports of success suggested that injection of steroids into the eye was a promising new treatment for diabetic macular edema (retinal swelling).

Surprising study: After two years of treatment, vision had worsened substantially in 28% of diabetes patients treated with steroids ...but in only 19% of patients given the traditional laser therapy. Steroid users also had more side effects, including cataracts and increased eye pressure.

David Brown, MD, ophthalmologist and retina specialist, Methodist Hospital, Houston, and local principal investigator of a study of 693 people, published in *Ophthalmology.*

Hearing Loss Tied to Diabetes

When researchers recently analyzed hearing test results and related questionnaires for about 5,000 Americans, they found that hearing loss was about twice as common in people who had diabetes than in those without diabetes.

Theory: Diabetes may cause hearing loss by damaging nerves and blood vessels in the inner ear.

If you have been diagnosed with diabetes: Ask your doctor to refer you to a hearing specialist (audiologist), so you can receive a hearing test.

Catherine Cowie, PhD, director, diabetes epidemiology program, National Institute of Diabetes and Digestive and Kidney Diseases, Bethesda, Maryland.

Diabetes Linked to Colon Cancer

In a recent analysis of data for 45,000 women, those with diabetes were 1.5 times more likely to develop colorectal cancer during an eight-and-a-half-year period than women without diabetes.

Theory: Elevated levels of insulin (a hormone that helps regulate blood sugar) may stimulate cancer-cell growth. These findings are believed to apply to men as well.

If you have diabetes: Control your blood sugar levels, and ask your doctor how often you should have a colonoscopy.

Andrew Flood, PhD, assistant professor, division of epidemiology and community health, University of Minnesota, Minneapolis.

Wow! Fat Hips May Prevent Diabetes

Abdominal fat increases a person's risk for type 2 diabetes, but fat on the hips may protect against diabetes.

How: Fat just beneath the skin on hips and thighs actually may improve insulin sensitivity (the ability of the body's cells to recognize and properly respond to insulin).

Theory: Subcutaneous fat produces adipokines, hormones that have beneficial effects on glucose metabolism.

C. Ronald Kahn, MD, vice-chairman, Joslin Diabetes Center, Mary K. Iacocca Professor of Medicine, Harvard Medical School, Boston, and leader of an animal study published in *Cell Metabolism.*

Secret Recipe for Fighting Diabetes

In a recent study, 24 herbs and spices were analyzed and found to contain high levels of polyphenols, which are antioxidant compounds that block the formation of inflammation-promoting substances that raise diabetes risk. Levels were highest in ground cloves...followed by cinnamon (shown in earlier research to help fight diabetes)...sage...marjoram...tarragon...and rosemary.

Instead of seasoning with salt: Consider trying these herbs and spices.

James L. Hargrove, PhD, associate professor, department of foods and nutrition, University of Georgia, Athens.

Is It Easy to Identify Diabetes?

Steven V. Edelman, MD, clinical professor of medicine at University of California, San Diego, Veterans Affairs Medical Center, and founder and director of the not-for-profit education organization Taking Control of Your Diabetes, both in San Diego. *www.tcoyd.org*

With type 1 diabetes, the pancreas produces little or no insulin, a hormone needed to convert sugar into fuel for cells. This soon leads to excessive thirst and hunger, frequent urination, weight loss, lethargy and blurry vision.

However, the more common type 2 diabetes—in which the body's cells do not use insulin properly—often causes no symptoms in the early stages.

You could have the disease for five years or more before developing telltale signs, including those above plus slow-healing sores, frequent vaginal and/or bladder infections, and patches of dark, thickened skin.

Best: Talk to your doctor about diabetes risk factors—high cholesterol, high blood pressure, excess weight, history of gestational diabetes, family history of diabetes or being of African American, Native American, Latino, Pacific Islander or Asian descent.

OJ Raises Risk

It only takes one cup of orange juice per day to raise diabetes risk, according to new research.

Reason: The juice's high sugar content causes a spike in blood glucose levels.

Diabetes Care.

Leafy Greens May Cut Diabetes Risk

In an 18-year study of 71,346 women, those who increased their intake of leafy, green vegetables (such as spinach or kale) by one additional half-cup serving daily had a 9% lower risk, on average, for diabetes than those who ate less of these vegetables.

Theory: Leafy, green vegetables are rich in magnesium, which is associated with lower diabetes risk.

Self-defense: Aim to eat at least one cup daily of leafy greens.

Lydia A. Bazzano, MD, PhD, assistant professor of epidemiology, Tulane University Health Sciences Center, New Orleans.

The Diabetes Risk-Reduction Plan

JoAnn E. Manson, MD, DrPH, professor of medicine and women's health at Harvard Medical School and chief of the division of preventive medicine at Brigham and Women's Hospital, both in Boston. A lead investigator for two important studies on women's health, Dr. Manson is coauthor of *Hot Flashes, Hormones & Your Health* (McGraw-Hill).

The statistics are shocking—23% of Americans age 60 and up now have diabetes, a deadly disease that can lead to heart disease, stroke, blindness, amputation, kidney failure and coma. Yet the Nurses' Health Study (NHS), which tracked 84,941 women for 16 years, suggests that about 90% of cases could be prevented.

With type 2 diabetes (the most common form), either the pancreas does not produce enough insulin (a hormone needed to convert glucose into energy) or the body's cells ignore insulin. Certain risk factors cannot be helped—a family history of diabetes…a personal history of polycystic ovary syndrome or diabetes during pregnancy…delivering a baby with a birth weight of nine pounds or more… or being non-Caucasian. However, the majority of risk factors are within your control.

• **Avoid "diabesity."** Researchers coined this term to emphasize the interconnection between obesity and diabetes. In the NHS, obese women were 10 times more likely to get diabetes than women of normal weight.

Theory: Fat cells—particularly those deep inside the belly—produce hormones and chemical messengers that trigger inflammation so that cells become resistant to insulin. Even modest weight loss can cut diabetes risk in half.

• **Stand, don't sit.** Just getting off the couch can help. NHS participants had a 14% increased risk for diabetes for every two hours per day spent watching TV—and a 12% decreased risk for every two hours per day spent standing or walking around at home.

Even better: A brisk one-hour walk daily can reduce diabetes risk by 34%.

• **Skip soda and fruit punch.** Sugar-sweetened soft drinks are the largest single source of calories in the US diet. Daily soda drinkers tend to consume more calories, gain more weight and develop diabetes more often than people who seldom drink soda.

Wise: Drink water or unsweetened beverages instead.

• **Choose the right fats.** Polyunsaturated fats—found in corn oil, soybean oil, nuts and fish—may affect cell membranes in a way that improves insulin use. Avoid trans fats—found in some deep-fried fast foods, stick margarines and packaged snack foods—which may have the opposite effect.

• **Limit red meat.** In the NHS, a one-serving-daily increase in red meat (beef, pork, lamb) or processed meat (cold cuts, hot dogs) increased diabetes risk by 26% and 38%, respectively.

Theory: Excessive heme iron (the type of iron in meat) and/or sodium nitrate (a preservative) may damage the pancreas.

• **Go for whole grains.** Compared with refined grains (white flour, white rice), whole grains minimize blood sugar fluctuations, easing demands on the pancreas...and provide more magnesium, which makes insulin more effective.

• **Consider coffee.** In studies involving about 200,000 people, drinking four to six cups of coffee daily was associated with a 28% reduction in diabetes risk compared with drinking two or fewer cups daily. Chlorogenic acid, an antioxidant in regular and decaf coffee, may make cells more responsive to insulin.

Trouble Sleeping? You May Be at Risk

Women who take longer than 30 minutes to fall asleep have a higher risk for diabetes, heart disease and stroke.

Reason: These women tend to have higher levels of insulin...inflammatory proteins that are linked to heart disease...and fibrinogen, a protein that is associated with stroke and heart attack.

Best: If you often have difficulty sleeping, talk to your doctor about the risks and ways to fall asleep.

Edward Suarez, PhD, associate professor, department of psychiatry, Duke University Medical Center, Durham, North Carolina, and leader of a study of 210 people, published in *Brain, Behavior and Immunity.*

Depression Linked To Diabetes

Researchers followed 4,681 people (average age 73) for 10 years, screening them annually for signs of depression. People with a high number of depression symptoms were 50% to 60% more likely to develop type 2 diabetes than those who were not depressed.

Theory: Depressed people may be more vulnerable to diabetes because they typically have high levels of the stress hormone cortisol, which can reduce insulin sensitivity (the body's ability to respond to insulin).

If you have been diagnosed with depression: Ask your doctor to give you a screening for diabetes.

Mercedes R. Carnethon, PhD, associate professor of preventive medicine, Feinberg School of Medicine, Northwestern University, Chicago.

Is Diabetes Sneaking Up On You?

Cynthia R. Green, PhD, founder and director of the Memory-Enhancement Program at Mount Sinai School of Medicine, New York City, and president of Memory Arts, LLC, which provides memory fitness training, Montclair, New Jersey. She is author of *Total Memory Workout: 8 Easy Steps to Maximum Memory Fitness* (Bantam). *www.totalbrainhealth.com*

For many women, a diagnosis of diabetes seems to come like a bolt out of the blue, with little or no warning. This is worrisome, because once the disease has developed, it can bring on a multitude of health problems. Yet if women at risk are identified when still in the prediabetic stages, the condition is much easier to control and its consequences are far less severe.

Most people know that being overweight increases the likelihood of developing diabetes —but few people recognize the various hidden risk factors that can contribute to the disease.

UNRECOGNIZED RISK FACTORS

Insulin resistance is a prediabetic condition in which the body's cells do not efficiently use the hormone insulin to regulate blood sugar levels. Often this progresses to type 2 diabetes, in which the body no longer produces enough insulin or the cells ignore the insulin.

Here are seven risk factors for insulin resistance and/or diabetes. *If any apply to you, talk to your doctor now—before diabetes creeps up on you...*

• **You are of African-American, Hispanic, Asian or Native American descent.** For unknown reasons, people within these ethnic groups are at increased risk for diabetes.

• **Your mother or father has or had diabetes.** If a parent developed the disease by age 50, your risk is about one in seven—or one in 13 if the parent was diagnosed after age 50. Having a sibling with diabetes also increases your risk.

• **You had high blood sugar when pregnant.** During pregnancy, a woman's insulin resistance rises, so the pancreas needs to produce more insulin. If the pancreas can't meet this demand, you develop high blood sugar. If the insulin shortage is severe, you may develop gestational diabetes (diabetes caused by pregnancy). This usually goes away after the baby is born, but it's a clue that your pancreas doesn't produce plentiful levels of insulin. The amount it does make will be enough to do the job if you maintain a normal weight, but if you gain weight, you may not be able to produce enough insulin to supply your larger body.

• **Your mother had gestational diabetes when she was pregnant with you.**

Theory: Animal studies suggest that excess blood glucose in the fetus's system may be harmful, "programming" the baby to be prone to diabetes in the future.

• **You weighed nine pounds or more at birth—which suggests that your mother may have had undiagnosed gestational diabetes.** Babies born to mothers with gestational diabetes often are large. As the mother's extra blood glucose goes through the placenta, the baby receives more energy than he/she needs to grow—excess energy that is stored as fat.

• **You're 45 or older.** A woman's risk for diabetes rises in midlife, especially after menopause. The reasons are unclear but may be related to the weight gain that often accompanies menopause.

• **You have *polycystic ovary syndrome* (PCOS),** a disorder characterized by irregular menstrual periods, excessive hair growth, acne, obesity and/or insulin resistance. PCOS affects up to 10% of women of reproductive age. We don't know the exact cause, but researchers believe PCOS is linked to excess insulin, which may stimulate ovaries to produce excess androgens (male hormones, such as testosterone). Women with PCOS usually have high blood sugar and are at greater risk for developing diabetes.

LESSER-KNOWN DANGERS

Why is it so important to protect yourself from diabetes? In part because the disease itself can have grave consequences—including seizures, blindness, kidney failure, coma and nerve and/or circulatory problems that can lead to loss of limbs and even death.

Diabetes also increases your risk for other serious diseases.

Reason: Because diabetics cannot use their blood sugar efficiently, excess amounts stay in the bloodstream. *Left untreated, this can lead to...*

• **Heart disease.** Before menopause, women usually have less risk for heart disease than men of the same age—but diabetes erases this female advantage. Diabetic women of any age are more prone to cardiovascular problems than are women without diabetes. Over time, high blood glucose levels lead to increased buildup of fatty plaque on the insides of the blood vessel walls. These plaque deposits impede the flow of blood and cause the arteries to harden, raising your risk for heart attack and stroke.

• **Breast cancer.** Being obese increases a woman's risk for breast cancer after menopause. Many researchers believe that type 2 diabetes, independent of obesity, also increases risk—perhaps due to insulin's effects on estrogen, a hormone that is linked to breast cancer.

• **Other cancers.** Every cancer studied shows a small but consistent increase in incidence among overweight diabetics.

SELF-PROTECTION

You can decrease your risk for developing diabetes—or for suffering severe consequences if you do have the disease. *To optimize your health...*

• **Maintain a normal weight.** If you are overweight, losing even a small amount can improve insulin resistance and lower blood sugar levels.

• **Exercise more,** even if all you do is add some walking to your daily routine. Try to work up to a brisk 30-minute walk most days. Exercise reduces insulin resistance.

• **Eat sensibly.** Focus on fruits, vegetables and whole grains. Ask your doctor for a referral to a diabetes educator for help working out the best diet for you.

• **Take appropriate medications,** if necessary, to help keep your blood sugar at normal levels. Also be conscientious about taking any other medications—for high blood pressure, for example—as prescribed by your doctor.

Snoring in Pregnancy Could Signal Blood Sugar Trouble

Northwestern University, news release.

P regnant women who snore regularly are more likely to develop gestational diabetes, recent research has found.

WHAT IS GESTATIONAL DIABETES?

In gestational diabetes, pregnant women who had not previously been diagnosed with diabetes develop high blood sugar levels. It is estimated to occur in about 4% of pregnant women, and those who develop it are at higher risk for type 2 diabetes later in life.

Gestational diabetes can cause problems for the baby, too.

Some of the risks to the baby include: being large for gestational age, which may lead to delivery complications; low blood sugar levels; obesity later in life; and impaired sugar tolerance or metabolic syndrome later in life.

THE STUDY

In the study, 189 healthy women completed a sleep survey when they were between six and 20 weeks pregnant, and again in their third trimester.

The researchers found that pregnant women who were frequent snorers—defined as snoring at least three nights per week—had a 14.3% chance of developing gestational diabetes, and among women who did not snore the risk was only 3.3%.

Taking into account other factors that could increase the risk of gestational diabetes—body mass index, age, race and ethnicity—the researchers found that there was still an association between frequent snoring and the disease, according to researchers at Northwestern University.

"Sleep disturbances during pregnancy may negatively affect your cardiovascular system or metabolism," said study author Francesca Facco, MD, an assistant professor of obstetrics and gynecology at Northwestern University's Feinberg School of Medicine. She is also maternal and fetal medicine physician at Northwestern Memorial Hospital. Both are in Chicago.

The study, which the authors said is the first to link snoring and gestational diabetes, was presented at the Associated Professional Sleep Societies annual meeting, in Seattle.

POSSIBLE EXPLANATIONS

"Snoring may be a sign of poor air flow and diminished oxygenation during sleep that can cause a cascade of events in your body," Dr. Facco explained. "This may activate your sympathetic nervous system, so your blood pressure rises at night. This can also provoke inflammatory and metabolic changes, increasing the risk of diabetes or poor sugar tolerance."

Although the cause for the link between snoring and gestational diabetes in not well understood, Dr. Facco suggested that it could be due to weight gain and fluid retention, which could cause increased airway resistance.

ADVICE

"If snoring is bothering a woman who is pregnant, she should seek a consultation with a sleep specialist," Dr. Facco said.

More study is needed to shed light on the association between snoring and gestational diabetes, which could lead to new interventions to treat pregnant women with sleep disorders.

Both Types of Diabetes Increase Stroke Risk

Type 1 (insulin-dependent) diabetes and type 2 (non-insulin-dependent) diabetes increase risk of ischemic stroke, triggered by a blood clot that blocks a blood vessel in the brain. Type 1 also is linked to hemorrhagic stroke, triggered by a vessel bleeding into the brain.

Self-defense: If you have either type, ask your doctor about controlling your stroke risk factors.

Mohsen Janghorbani, PhD, professor of epidemiology, department of epidemiology and biostatistcs, School of Public Health, Isfahan University of Medical Sciences, Iran, and lead author of a study of 116,316 women, published in *Diabetes Care*.

Do Environmental Toxins Cause Diabetes?

Mark A. Stengler, NMD, licensed naturopathic medical doctor in private practice, Encinitas, California...adjunct associate clinical professor at the National College of Natural Medicine, Portland, Oregon...author of *The Natural Physician's Healing Therapies* and co-author of *Prescription for Natural Cures* (both from Bottom Line Books).

Few people would dispute that the root cause of diabetes often is a high-calorie diet that's loaded with simple sugars but deficient in fiber, combined with a lack of exercise. Yet it is increasingly clear that in a world full of man-made chemicals, environmental toxins are contributing to the growing epidemic of diabetes.

How so? Certain toxic chemicals can...

• **Destroy the special beta cells** of the pancreas that are responsible for producing insulin, the hormone that regulates blood glucose (sugar) levels.

• **Interfere with the activity of cell receptors** that transport glucose into muscle and fat cells.

• **Exert an estrogenlike effect** that can further impair the cell receptors' ability to use insulin.

NEED-TO-KNOW FACTS ABOUT DIABETES

Insulin is required to transport glucose into our cells for energy production. A deficiency of insulin is the main cause of type 1 diabetes. Of the 20.8 million Americans with diabetes, 5% to 10% have type 1.

Far more common in the US is type 2 diabetes, in which the body's cells ignore insulin, allowing excess amounts of this hormone to build up in the blood. As cells become less effective at accepting and using insulin, blood glucose levels rise. Often, this causes the pancreas to pump out even more insulin.

The dangers: Excess glucose can damage kidneys, nerves and eyes...and excess insulin promotes harmful widespread inflammation and boosts cholesterol production, raising cardiovascular disease risk.

An additional 54 million Americans have the prediabetic condition insulin resistance (in which cells do not properly use the hormone insulin to regulate blood sugar). Insulin resistance is the root of a common health problem called syndrome X or metabolic syndrome, which is characterized by elevated insulin and glucose levels...elevated blood fats (particularly cholesterol and triglycerides)...high blood pressure...overall weight gain...and body fat accumulation around the waist. Insulin resistance frequently leads to type 2 diabetes.

THE CASE AGAINST TOXINS

How many types of toxins are found in the modern-day human body? No one knows. There may be as many as 75,000 man-made chemicals in the environment, so it's reasonable to estimate that several hundred and possibly many more are lodged within us. Since toxins are stored primarily in fatty tissue, being overweight may increase one's toxicity risk.

The federal Centers for Disease Control and Prevention (CDC) researches chemical accumulation in Americans (as measured in blood and urine samples) and publishes its findings biannually in its National Report on Human Exposure to Environmental Chemicals. The report includes data on 219 chemicals—from toxic metals (such as mercury, lead, barium and uranium) to pesticides to cigarette smoke—found in air, water, food, soil, dust and consumer products.

The CDC reported that cadmium (a by-product of cigarette smoke) was detected at alarming levels in 5% of adult Americans—probably due in part to secondhand smoke. Cadmium can cause kidney damage (to which diabetics are vulnerable) and weaken bones.

Most of the subjects also had many pesticides in their bodies. An earlier CDC report revealed that, among pesticides for which a so-called "acceptable" exposure level has been established, two—*chlorpyrifos* (Dursban) and *methyl parathion*—were found in amounts that exceeded the supposedly safe levels by as much as 4.6 times. Pesticides disrupt the cells' ability to accept glucose.

Other studies show that military veterans who were exposed to dioxin—a toxic chemical produced during manufacturing processes—have an increased incidence of diabetes. The US Department of Veterans Affairs has added type 2 diabetes to its list of diseases associated with exposure to the dioxin-containing herbicide Agent Orange, used in the Vietnam War.

A study in the journal *Epidemiology* showed that women with high blood levels of *polychlorinated biphenyls* (PCBs) had a greater risk of diabetes. PCBs are man-made chemicals used as coolants and lubricants. Production in the US halted in 1977, but PCBs break down slowly and are still found in water, soil, plants, animals and fish.

Another recent study involving more than 2,000 Americans published in *Diabetes Care* found a striking association between diabetes and blood levels of six persistent *organic pollutants* (POPs), including PCBs and various pesticides. These pollutants were found in about 80% of the people tested.

If you are concerned about known or unknown exposure to pesticides, dioxin or other toxic chemicals, talk to your doctor about getting blood and/or urine tests to measure the levels of toxins in your body.

POLLUTANT SELF-PROTECTION

Take steps to minimize buildup of the harmful toxins that can lead to diabetes and other health problems. (Supplements below are sold at health-food stores, generally are safe and can be taken indefinitely.) *General recommendations for adults...*

• **Eat organic plant foods,** which are grown without harmful pesticides.

• **Select poultry and eggs labeled "free range" and organic** (meaning that the animals were not constantly caged and were not fed antibiotics or hormones).

• **Get more fiber from fruits, vegetables, grains, nuts and seeds.** Fiber promotes proper digestive function, so toxins can be eliminated via urine and stool. Fiber also binds with toxins, preventing them from circulating through the body.

• **Drink fresh vegetable juice daily.** Beets, celery, parsley, carrots and burdock root all can be juiced and supply nutrients that aid in detoxification.

• **Supplement daily with a green-food** formula that includes *chlorella, spirulina* and wheatgrass. This supports liver and kidney detoxification by binding to toxic metals, which then can be excreted.

Try: Greens+ from Orange Peel Enterprises (800-643-1210, *www.greensplus.com*).

• **Take a daily multivitamin and mineral supplement** to support liver function.

• **Take milk thistle extract** daily to aid liver and kidney detoxification.

A good brand: Nature's Way Super Thisilyn (800-962-8873, *www.naturesway.com*).

• **Also, take a daily probiotic supplement** containing beneficial bacteria, such as *Lactobacillus acidophilus* and *bifidobacterium*, to detoxify the digestive tract.

• **Exercise.** Sweating releases toxins stored in fat.

• **Consider a series of four weekly colonics each year** (a holistic doctor can provide a referral). This infusion of water into the rectum flushes out waste from the lower end of the colon for more complete elimination than bowel movements provide.

432

• **Take a sauna weekly to clear toxins from cells.**

• **Purify water at home** by installing a reverse osmosis filtering system on each tap…a chlorine-removal filter on your showerhead…and a charcoal filter on your main waterline.

Toxin in Plastics Is Linked to Diabetes

Bisphenol A (BPA), a chemical commonly found in hard plastics, such as water bottles and some baby bottles, already has been linked to cancer.

Recent finding: People who have high amounts of BPA in their bloodstreams are more than twice as likely to have diabetes than people who have little or no BPA.

Theory: BPA acts like the hormone estrogen, which can increase levels of insulin and cause chronically elevated blood sugar, both of which are associated with insulin resistance and diabetes.

Frederick vom Saal, PhD, curators' professor, division of biological sciences, University of Missouri, Columbia, and leader of a study of 1,455 adults, published in *The Journal of the American Medical Association.*

Chamomile Tea May Fight Diabetic Damage

An animal study suggests that chamomile tea can help prevent diabetic complications, such as blindness, nerve damage and kidney failure, by lowering blood glucose levels and reducing levels of enzymes linked to nerve, eye and kidney damage.

Atsushi Kato, MD, department of hospital pharmacy, University of Toyama, Japan, and coauthor of a study published in *Journal of Agricultural and Food Chemistry.*

When Wounds Won't Go Away…

Steven J. Kavros, DPM, podiatrist, assistant professor of orthopedic surgery and certified wound specialist at Mayo Clinic in Rochester, Minnesota. He has published several papers on diabetic and vascular wound care in peer-reviewed medical journals.

If you get a scrape or other superficial wound, it usually heals in a week or two. But some wounds don't go away so quickly—especially if you're an older adult, are confined to a bed or wheelchair, or have diabetes or some other condition that interferes with your blood flow.

Latest development: New, highly effective therapies and the proliferation of wound-care centers staffed by doctors and other health-care professionals (often located at large medical centers or university hospitals) are helping to prevent amputations, life-threatening infections and other serious complications.*

WHY WOUNDS BECOME CHRONIC

If a wound doesn't heal within six weeks, it is considered chronic and requires special care. Poor blood flow, which cuts off the supply of oxygen and nutrients that are needed for healing, is a common cause of chronic wounds.

Basic care for all chronic wounds usually involves cleansing (to remove foreign matter and bacteria-laden debris)…debridement (to remove dead and damaged tissue)…and dressing (often treated with a medicinal preparation, such as an antimicrobial solution, to prevent the growth of bacteria).

COMMON CHRONIC WOUNDS

• **Diabetic foot ulcers.** Among Americans with diabetes, 15% will develop a foot ulcer, and many of them will ultimately require amputation of the foot—usually because the patient has developed a life-threatening condition, such as gangrene (decay and death of tissue due to insufficient blood supply).

Why are people with diabetes at such high risk for foot ulcers?

*To find a wound-care specialist in your area, consult the American Board of Wound Management (202-457-8408, *www.abwmcertified.org*).

The disease not only impairs healthy blood flow, but also inhibits the body's ability to fight infection. In addition, neuropathy (a type of nerve damage that often occurs in people with diabetes) can cause nerve pain and decrease sensation, so pressure and injury may go unnoticed.

Diabetic ulcers typically occur at points of prolonged or repeated pressure on the skin and underlying tissue—for example, the big toe or front part of the foot.

Self-defense: People with diabetic foot ulcers should wear properly fitting shoes. They also may need a podiatrist to check for abnormalities in their gaits, perhaps with the aid of a computerized scan of pressure points on their feet. Special shoe inserts (orthotics) can help adjust the position of the foot to relieve pressure points.

• **Venous ulcers.** When veins, which carry blood back to the heart, don't function properly, blood can pool in the legs, causing swelling and discoloration and disrupting the supply of fresh blood with its oxygen and bacteria-fighting immune cells. This sets the stage for venous ulcers to develop.

Self-defense: The main treatment for a venous ulcer is compression (wrapping the leg, under a doctor's supervision, with an elastic bandage or special stocking to reduce swelling and improve blood flow). Venous ulcerations that don't respond to standard therapy may require surgery to close off the failing veins, which improves blood flow back to the heart and reduces venous pressure in the leg.

• **Arterial ulcers.** Atherosclerosis, the build-up of fatty deposits (plaque) that narrows the coronary arteries, also may impair circulation to the limbs. If circulation is further inhibited by a tiny blood clot, tissue may die, causing an arterial ulcer, typically on the toes or an ankle.

Self-defense: The most effective treatments for arterial ulcers are much like those used for coronary artery disease—the doctor may thread a catheter into the affected artery and inflate a balloon to open it up, possibly inserting a stent (tiny wire mesh tube) to keep it open.

A severe blockage may require bypass surgery—as with a coronary bypass, a blood vessel (taken from elsewhere in the body) is implanted to "bypass" the blockage.

• **Pressure ulcers.** Also known as bedsores, these afflict people who are confined to a bed or wheelchair. Immobility causes constant pressure, which cuts off circulation (for example, in the tailbone). About 9% of hospitalized patients develop pressure ulcers, usually during the first two weeks of their stay.

Self-defense: Pressure ulcers require the same basic care as other chronic wounds. Bedsores often can be prevented by regularly changing an immobile person's position (every two hours), which distributes pressure more evenly.

BREAKTHROUGH THERAPIES

A chronic wound is a magnet for bacteria—the dead tissue and moisture provide a hospitable environment for germs to thrive.

Recent development: A treatment available at many wound-care centers uses low-frequency ultrasound to break up biofilm (a microscopically thin layer of film containing bacteria) on the wound. This stimulates the production of cells that fill in the wound with new tissue and help keep the area clean.

Caution: Notify your physician promptly if your wound shows signs of infection, such as pain, odor, redness, pus or streaks along the affected limb, or if you have a fever (above 99°F). Infections require antibiotic treatment.

Wounds that refuse to heal despite treatment may require one of the other latest therapies typically available at wound-care centers…

• **Cell therapy involves placing a bioengineered skin substitute over the wound.** This film-like material secretes substances that stimulate your own cells to grow tissue that will close the wound. Cell therapy is often used for resistant diabetic or venous ulcers.

• **Hyperbaric oxygen therapy,** which is mainly used for diabetic ulcers, involves sitting or lying for about 90 minutes in a room or chamber that contains 100% oxygen at two to three times normal air pressure. Breathing this supercharged air promotes wound healing by raising oxygen levels in the blood.

• **Negative pressure wound therapy,** which is used for diabetic and arterial ulcers, involves placing a sponge or foam dressing over the wound and attaching a device that suctions off waste fluids and infectious material, thus stimulating the growth of new tissue.

Neuropathy—Ways To Get Relief

John D. England, MD, Grace Benson Professor and chairman of the department of neurology at Louisiana State University Health Sciences Center School of Medicine in New Orleans. Dr. England has published more than 100 professional articles about neuropathy and other disorders and was lead author of the recent *AAN* guidelines on peripheral neuropathy.

Peripheral neuropathy—damage, disease or dysfunction of nerves outside the brain and spinal cord—is a condition that affects an estimated 20 million Americans. It has more than 100 known causes, including diabetes, autoimmune disorders, infections and more.

If identified early, neuropathy may disappear with proper treatment. But until recently, there were no specific criteria for doctors to use when diagnosing the nerve disorder. As a result, a patient might go for months or even years without getting a proper diagnosis for symptoms (such as numbness, tingling, burning or stabbing pain, a feeling of pins and needles or weakness) that typically occur in the hands and/or feet.

Latest development: Updated guidelines by the American Academy of Neurology can help patients get a prompt diagnosis and effective treatment that reduces their risk for permanent nerve damage.

THE DIAGNOSIS

Peripheral neuropathy can have various symptoms because there are many possible causes. If you suffer any of the symptoms mentioned above, see your primary care physician and describe them in as much detail as possible. You may be referred to a neurologist.

Your doctor will want to know…

• **Do you have weakness or feel clumsy at times?** Because nerves stimulate muscles, some neuropathies result in a loss of strength, causing patients to lose balance, trip and/or feel clumsy.

• **Where did you first notice the symptoms?** Peripheral neuropathy typically starts in the areas of the body farthest from the spinal cord, usually the feet and/or hands.

• **Did the symptoms occur simultaneously on both sides of the body**—for example, in both feet—or on only one side? Peripheral neuropathy symptoms usually occur simultaneously on both sides of the body. If you experience symptoms on only one side, other possible causes, such as multiple sclerosis or a stroke, must be considered.

Be sure to tell your doctor about: All medications you have taken in the last year or are currently taking. *Among the drugs that can cause peripheral neuropathy…*

• **Chemotherapy drugs,** such as *vincristine* or *cisplatin.*

• **Antibiotics,** including *metronidazole* (Flagyl) or *nitrofurantoin* (Macrodantin).

• **Anticonvulsants,** such as *phenytoin* (Dilantin).

In addition, excessive doses of vitamin B-6 (*pyridoxine*) can cause peripheral neuropathy.

IDENTIFYING THE CAUSE

To find the cause of peripheral neuropathy, you should receive blood tests for…

• **High blood sugar (glucose).** This could indicate diabetes or glucose intolerance (impaired ability to convert glucose to energy). When prolonged, glucose elevation damages small blood vessels, leading to slow nerve death.

To prevent further nerve damage: Control blood glucose through diet and/or the use of insulin and, if necessary, other diabetes medication.

• **Vitamin deficiency.** As many as one in three adults over age 50 does not efficiently absorb vitamin B-12, a nutrient required for proper nerve function. Vitamin B-12 deficiency also can result from heavy drinking or a poor diet. Because vitamin B-12 is found only in animal foods, such as meat, poultry and dairy products, some vegetarians are at increased risk for a deficiency unless they take a supplement.

To prevent further nerve damage: Ask your doctor about monthly vitamin B-12 injections and/or daily B-12 oral supplements.

•**Infection and/or inflammation.** A complete blood count (CBC) and a test for the inflammation marker C-reactive protein (CRP) can help identify infections that can cause neuropathy, such as Lyme disease…HIV… hepatitis…and syphilis.

To prevent further nerve damage: Begin treatment immediately with an antibiotic or other medication.

WHAT OTHER TESTS CAN TELL

The blood tests described above can usually identify the general cause of neuropathy, but other tests that may be needed include…

•**Nerve conduction study (NCS).** With this noninvasive test, electrodes are placed on the surface of the skin—on the hands and feet, for example—and mild electric shocks are delivered to help measure the speed of nerve signals. Some types of neuropathy, such as Charcot-Marie-Tooth disease (a hereditary disorder), strip the nerves of their protective coating (myelin), causing nerve impulses to travel more slowly.

•**Electromyography (EMG).** Often performed with NCS, this test helps evaluate the health of nerves that control muscles. A needle-thin electrode is inserted through the skin and into a muscle to track electrical activity that gives clues to the causes of muscle weakness.

•**Skin and nerve biopsies.** By taking a skin sample, doctors can examine the small nerve fibers that cause pain or numbness. A nerve biopsy can find less common causes of inflammation, including deposits of abnormal proteins, or unusual infections, such as leprosy.

THE BEST TREATMENT

If you identify neuropathy early, symptoms may disappear with proper treatment, such as improved blood sugar control or medication to treat infection or inflammation. By stopping the disease process, you often can avoid additional nerve damage.

Too often, however, nerve damage is permanent—and pain and numbness continue indefinitely.

In these cases, you should…

•**Get some exercise.** Physical activity helps maintain your physical abilities and prevent disabilities, such as muscle contractures (shortening of muscles). Exercise also triggers the release of natural painkilling compounds called *endorphins.*

For minor neuropathy, the best exercises include low-impact activities, such as walking and bicycling. Water exercises, which can build strength without risk for injury from falling, are especially good for people who have balance problems. Aim to exercise for 30 minutes three to four times weekly—as tolerated.

•**Avoid neuropathy-related injury.** If pain signals are blunted, cuts and blisters are easily ignored and may become infected.

To prevent injury: Don't go barefoot… wash and examine your feet daily…and moisturize with a lotion or cream, when necessary, to avoid cracking skin.

•**Relieve the pain.** Pain can reduce your quality of life, limit your activities and may even "rewire" your brain so that your discomfort becomes more difficult to treat. *Best to try…*

•Topical pain relievers. When applied to the hands or feet, topical analgesics can relieve pain intensity in some people by reducing nerve sensation. *Example:* Prescription lidocaine creams and patches. *Common side effects:* Temporary tenderness at the application site.

•Antidepressant medications. Relatively new antidepressants called *selective serotonin and norepinephrine reuptake inhibitors* (SSN-RIs) can increase levels of the brain chemicals serotonin and norepinephrine, both of which help regulate mood. The drugs inhibit pain impulses so that they don't "register" in awareness. *Examples: Venlafaxine* (Effexor) and *duloxetine* (Cymbalta). *Common side effects:* Nausea, dry mouth and insomnia.

•Anti-epileptic medications. Developed to control seizures, these drugs can intercept the transmission of pain signals. *Examples: Pregabalin*

(Lyrica)…and *gabapentin* (Neurontin). *Common side effects:* Sleepiness and dizziness.

•Centrally acting analgesics. These drugs bind to specific receptors in the brain to block pain and alter the patient's emotional response to the sensations. There is a risk for dependency with these drugs, so they are used only as a last resort. *Examples: Oxycodone* (OxyContin)…and *hydrocodone* and *acetaminophen. Common side effects:* Sleepiness, dizziness and gastrointestinal upset.

The Virus Cure for Diabetes

M. William Lensch, PhD, Affiliate Faculty, Harvard Stem Cell Institute, HHMI/Children's Hospital Boston, Harvard Medical School.

We're accustomed to thinking of viruses as "bad guys" that the world would be better without—but now that scientists have used a virus to transform a non-insulin-producing pancreatic cell into one that produced insulin, we may need to reconsider that position. Adding to the achievement is that the "programming" of the cell was done without use of sometimes controversial stem cells. This is a major breakthrough in the field of regenerative medicine, which aims to regrow or repair missing or damaged tissue.

In the study, which was published in the journal *Nature*, Douglas A. Melton, PhD, co-director of the Harvard Stem Cell Institute, and his fellow researchers used a modified virus to activate three key genes in non-insulin-producing pancreatic cells in mice. Within three days, the "infected" cells started producing insulin—far faster than the several weeks it's known to take to transform stem cells into specific organ tissues.

The findings are incredibly exciting for other researchers in the field of regenerative medicine as well. "This paper really got a lot of people's attention," says M. William Lensch, PhD, affiliate faculty at the Harvard Stem Cell Institute, who wasn't himself involved with Dr. Melton's research. "It expands the possible universe of where regenerated cells can come from and how to get there—that's exciting."

Though remarkable, it's important to note that this type of cell reprogramming is still a long way from becoming a viable mainstream treatment—it has yet to be tried in humans, and long-term safety is still to be determined. Nonetheless it deserves attention because of the thinking behind it—the idea that you can quickly, relatively easily and with no political debate, change a cell that's close to what's needed into exactly what's needed, perhaps to treat cancer, liver disease, cardiovascular disease and more.

15

Cancer Updates

What Most People Still Don't Know About Breast Cancer

 **M**ost women know to tell their doctors about any new breast lumps. But a lump is not the only potential warning sign of breast cancer. As a breast cancer surgeon who also has survived this disease, I know many subtle signs of breast cancer that initially may go unnoticed.

In my own case, the first clue was not a lump—but rather a tiny area of retracted skin on my breast. The mammogram I received the next day appeared normal, but I knew to follow up with an ultrasound (an imaging test using high-frequency sound waves). This test revealed a tumor, which a biopsy later confirmed was malignant.

Important facts that could save your life—or that of a loved one…

• **A swollen, red, warm and/or tender breast can indicate breast cancer.** Such symptoms can mean an infection, but they also can be caused by inflammatory breast cancer, a rare condition in which cancer cells clog the lymphatic channels in the breast skin, preventing the lymph fluid from draining.

Self-defense: If you're diagnosed with a breast infection that doesn't clear within one week of antibiotic treatment, your doctor should order a mammogram and arrange for a skin biopsy to check for inflammatory breast cancer.

A newly developed lump in the breast is the most common sign of breast cancer, but other red flags include…

• Thickened, red skin in one breast.

Carolyn M. Kaelin, MD, MPH, founding director of the Comprehensive Breast Health Center at Brigham and Women's Hospital, surgical oncologist at Dana Farber Cancer Institute and an assistant professor of surgery at Harvard Medical School, all in Boston. Dr. Kaelin is author of *Living Through Breast Cancer* and coauthor of *The Breast Cancer Survivor's Fitness Plan* (both from McGraw-Hill).

•Any dimpling, puckering or retraction (small depression) of breast skin.

•Nipple scaling, flaking or ulceration.

•A newly inverted nipple.

•Spontaneous discharge from one nipple. (*Note:* This can also occur at least six months after breastfeeding or miscarriage.)

•A lump in the underarm.

•Persistent pain in one breast (this usually indicates a benign cyst, but it should be assessed).

•**Mammograms miss about 10% to 20% of breast cancers.** Even so, studies suggest that among women who undergo annual screenings, mammograms may reduce the breast cancer death rate by as much as 65%. And the technology continues to improve. According to a study published recently in *The New England Journal of Medicine*, newer digital mammography (which provides computer-generated images that can be enlarged and/or enhanced) is up to 28% more accurate than film mammography in detecting cancers in women who are under age 50, premenopausal or who have dense breast tissue (breasts that have a much greater proportion of dense tissue than fat). Digital mammography is becoming widely available in the US.

Self-defense: If you have a lump or another suspicious symptom and have already had a normal mammogram, request an ultrasound. This test can distinguish between fluid-filled and solid masses. It's a rare breast cancer that eludes both a mammogram and ultrasound.

•**Some breast cancer risk factors are not well-known.** More than 75% of breast cancers occur in women over age 50. You're at higher risk if you've been taking combination estrogen/progesterone hormone replacement therapy for at least five years…if you began menstruating before age 12 or stopped after age 55…if you've never had children or had your first child after age 30…and/or if you consume more than one to two alcoholic drinks daily. Dense breast tissue on a mammogram has recently been identified as an independent risk factor.

You also are at higher risk for breast cancer if one or more of the following is true: A first-degree relative (mother, sister or daughter) has had breast cancer…a family member was diagnosed with breast cancer when younger than age 40 or before menopause…a family member had cancer in both breasts…or you have a family history of ovarian cancer. This constellation of factors could suggest the presence of a mutated gene, such as the BRCA1 or BRCA2, which may be inherited.

STAY-WELL STRATEGIES

There's no way to predict or prevent every breast cancer, but you can lower your chances of developing or dying from the disease.

Here's how…

•**Maintain a healthy weight.** Gaining weight and being overweight raise the likelihood of developing a breast malignancy—and worsen your prognosis if you already have this type of cancer.

Reason: Body fat produces estrogen, which is one of the factors that increase breast cancer risk.

•**Stay active.** Exercise helps prevent breast cancer—probably by decreasing circulating estrogen. Newer research suggests that it also may improve long-term survival odds for those previously treated for the disease. In a recently published *Journal of the American Medical Association* study, breast cancer patients who walked or engaged in another moderate exercise three to five hours weekly were 50% less likely to have a recurrence or to die prematurely than women who exercised less than one hour weekly.

Best choice: Aerobic exercises, such as walking, jogging or cycling.

•**Weight-bearing exercises,** such as walking or weight-lifting, also help to minimize bone loss—a significant advantage, since chemotherapy can lead to osteoporosis. (Chemotherapy can damage the ovaries, reducing estrogen levels and inducing early menopause in premenopausal women, which greatly accelerates bone loss.)

Self-defense: In addition to performing regular weight-bearing exercise, women with breast cancer should take a daily calcium supplement (1,000 mg for those ages 31 to 50…and 1,200 mg for those ages 51 or older) plus at least 800 international units (IU) of vitamin D. If you've had chemotherapy, experienced premature menopause or take an aromatase inhibitor (a drug used to treat postmenopausal breast cancer patients), ask your doctor what levels of calcium and vitamin D intake are right for you.

The breast cancer preventive drug *tamoxifen* has also been shown to conserve bone while reducing malignancies in high-risk women by as much as 50%.

Downside: Tamoxifen increases risk for blood clots, stroke and uterine cancer.

Some studies have shown the osteoporosis drug *raloxifene* (Evista) to be as effective as tamoxifen for preventing breast cancer and preserving bone in postmenopausal women —with lower risk for uterine cancer. Raloxifene was recently approved by the FDA as a breast cancer preventive drug for postmenopausal women. Tamoxifen is still the preferred drug for premenopausal women.

Best: Ask your doctor if either drug may be appropriate for you.

LATEST ADVANCES

• **Aromatase inhibitors (AIs)** may offer even more powerful protection against breast cancer recurrence and death for postmenopausal women than tamoxifen. Whereas tamoxifen works by blocking estrogen from binding with cancer cells, AIs work by inhibiting estrogen production in fat tissues—our primary source of the hormone after menopause.

In a recent British study, breast cancer patients who switched from tamoxifen to an AI called *exemestane* (Aromasin) were 17% less likely to see their breast cancer spread to other organs, had a 15% lower chance of dying within about five years than women who stayed on tamoxifen, and had a 44% lower risk of developing cancer in the opposite breast. AIs do not appear to raise risk for endometrial cancer as tamoxifen does, but AIs do speed bone loss and are not effective for premenopausal women.

• **Newly developed tests** are enabling doctors to look at the genetic makeup of tumors and predict with increasing accuracy which are likely to recur or metastasize.

In the past, breast cancer patients had been routinely prescribed chemotherapy, usually following surgery, since doctors had no way of knowing which cancers would return and become fatal. New tests, which include "tumor profiling" (a more detailed analysis of the tumor than biopsy alone), take some of the guesswork out of deciding who will benefit most from chemotherapy and who is most likely to do just fine without it.

Good News on Breast Cancer

Breast cancer is claiming fewer lives. There has been a 24% decrease in breast cancer–related deaths since 1990.

Reasons: Mammography screening that detects tumors early…and innovative drug therapy, particularly the drug *tamoxifen*, given to prevent recurrence.

Ismail Jatoi, MD, PhD, director, Breast Care Center, department of surgery, National Naval Medical Center, Bethesda, Maryland, and author of a study of 235,000 women, published in *Journal of Clinical Oncology*.

How to Make Sure Your Mammogram Is Right

Obese women have a 20% greater risk of receiving false-positives on mammograms than women of normal weight. This can lead to unnecessary and invasive follow-up tests.

Helpful: Have mammograms performed at the same facility each year so that you establish a baseline against which the radiologist can compare each test.

Joann G. Elmore, MD, MPH, associate professor of medicine and epidemiology, University of Washington, Seattle, and leader of a study of 100,622 mammography screenings, published in *Archives of Internal Medicine*.

Size Matters When It Comes to Cancer Risk

Women with different-sized breasts have a greater risk for breast cancer than women whose breasts are almost the same size.

Recent finding: Risk increases by 50% for every 100-milliliter difference in breast volume (about half a cup size).

Theory: Mutations that cause asymmetry may be linked to breast cancer.

Diane Scutt, PhD, director of research in health sciences, faculty of medicine, University of Liverpool, UK, and leader of a study of more than 500 women, published in *Breast Cancer Research*.

Digital Test That's More Accurate Than Mammogram for Most Women

Etta D. Pisano, MD, professor of radiology, Medical University of South Carolina, Charleston.
Rowan T. Chlebowski, MD, chief of medical oncology, Harbor-UCLA Medical Center, Torrance, California.
Robert A. Smith, PhD, director, cancer screening, American Cancer Society.
The New England Journal of Medicine.
American College of Radiology Imaging Network.

Compared with standard mammograms, which are recorded on film, computer-based digital mammograms are more accurate for more than half of the women who get breast cancer screenings, a large study has discovered.

Women who have dense breast tissue, those who are younger than age 50 and those who are premenopausal would benefit from digital mammograms, the researchers say.

THE STUDY

In the study, lead author Etta D. Pisano, MD, formerly a professor of radiology and biomedical engineering at the University of North Carolina School of Medicine, and her colleagues evaluated data on 42,760 asymptomatic women who were screened for breast cancer using both digital and film mammography.

"Overall, film and digital mammography were equally accurate," Dr. Pisano says. "But for women with dense breasts, women under age 50 and women who were pre- and perimenopausal, digital was significantly better. The kinds of cancer that the digital [mammography] found and film missed were important cancers—the kind that kill women," she notes.

"For the 65% of women who had improved accuracy, they should get that kind of mammography," Dr. Pisano says. "But for other women, there is no benefit of digital over film, and it's more expensive."

THE TREND TOWARD DIGITAL

Dr. Pisano adds that digital mammography will eventually replace film mammography. "There is a trend toward digital, mainly for the other advantages that it offers," she says. These advantages include the ease of storing and retrieving digital images, and the ability to make these images part of a patient's electronic medical record.

Rowan T. Chlebowski, MD, chief of medical oncology at Harbor-UCLA Medical Center, says, "Even without a clinical benefit, digital would replace film. With the current mandate for electronic medical records, you are going to have a hard time getting a film mammogram into an electronic medical record.

"This study makes it more reasonable to go for the investment now, because you get an immediate clinical payoff," he adds.

DON'T WAIT

All the experts agree that women need to get screened for breast cancer, and not wait for digital screening if it is not available in their area.

"The finding that digital mammography is more accurate than film mammography in women under age 50 and women with medium and high breast density is an important finding that should lead to improvements in screening programs," says Robert A. Smith, PhD, director of cancer screening for the American Cancer Society.

However, although the availability of digital mammography screening is increasing, it is unclear how soon—or even whether—it will entirely replace film mammography, he adds.

"The important thing is that women receive mammograms on a regular basis, regardless of which technology they use," Dr. Smith says.

"Younger women and women with denser breasts should not forego their regular mammograms if digital mammography is not available. While this study showed an advantage with digital imaging in these groups, it should be remembered that traditional film mammography also is effective," Dr. Smith adds.

Dr. Pisano agrees. "It is important that women get screened when they are supposed to be screened and not wait to get a digital [mammography]. If there is film available, it's better than nothing."

Better Breast Cancer Detection

Mammography plus ultrasound helps detect small cancers in dense breast tissue, which occurs in almost half of women. In the densest breast tissue, mammograms alone detect less than half of all invasive tumors. Adding ultrasound raises the detection rate to 97%.

Thomas M. Kolb, MD, radiologist in private practice, New York City, and leader of a study of breast cancer detection in 11,220 women, published in *Radiology*.

Should You Have a Digital Mammography?

In a study of 42,760 women, digital mammographies (which take electronic images of the breast and store them in a computer) yielded more accurate results than standard film mammography for women younger than age 50 who were premenopausal or perimenopausal (when the ovaries begin producing less estrogen) and had dense breast tissue (characterized by more glands and less fat). For other women, there was no significant difference in accuracy between the two screening methods.

Theory: Digital mammography images can be magnified or otherwise manipulated for more accurate readings.

Self-defense: If you are a premenopausal or perimenopausal woman under age 50 with dense breasts, ask your doctor about receiving digital mammography.

Etta D. Pisano, MD, professor of radiology, Medical University of South Carolina, Charlston.

Is Breast Thermography A Good Alternative to A Mammogram?

Thermography should not be used as a substitute for mammography. In thermography, special infrared cameras are used to detect and map heat that is produced in different parts of the body. Some cancers show up as "hot spots" because new blood vessels are forming rapidly there.

However: The technique is unreliable. The rate of false-negatives (cancers that go undetected) and false-positives (nonmalignant areas that show up as hot spots and require further testing) is unacceptably high.

Mammography remains the most useful breast-cancer screening test. The American Cancer Society recommends annual mammograms for women age 40 and over—and earlier or more frequently for women at increased risk.

Phil Evans, MD, FACR, professor of radiology and director of the Center for Breast Care, University of Texas Southwestern Medical Center at Dallas.

Osteoporosis Drug Reduces Breast Cancer Risk

An osteoporosis drug, recently approved by the FDA for postmenopausal women, has been proven to significantly decrease the risk of breast cancer.

Recent finding: *Raloxifene* (Evista), a prescription drug used to treat osteoporosis in postmenopausal women, decreases the risk of invasive breast cancer by 58% in women who don't have a family history of the disease...and by 89% in women with a family history. Raloxifene is believed to reduce estrogen's tumor-promoting effects.

Marc E. Lippman, MD, former John G. Searle Professor and chair of the department of internal medicine, University of Michigan, Ann Arbor, and leader of a study of raloxifene and breast cancer, published in *Clinical Cancer Research*.

Lower Risk of Dying From Breast Cancer By 50%

Michelle D. Holmes, MD, DrPH, associate professor of medicine, Harvard Medical School, Boston.

A substantial number of studies have established that regular exercise such as walking is associated with a reduced risk of developing breast cancer, but a new study suggests that regular exercise may be associated with a significantly lower risk of dying from the disease in those battling breast cancer.

The study, led by Michelle D. Holmes, MD, DrPh, associate professor of medicine at Harvard Medical School, analyzed data from 2,987 women with breast cancer who took part in the long-range Nurses' Health Study. This study revealed that walking one to three hours a week at a moderate pace was associated with a 20% reduced risk for breast cancer death...walking three to five hours weekly was associated with a 50% reduced risk. Interestingly, walking five to eight hours a week was associated with a reduced risk of 44%...and walking more than eight hours a week was associated with a reduced risk of 40%. However, it is unclear why this is so. Most important is that, with exercise, there was significant improvement in risk for cancer death.

FACTORS AFFECTING THE STUDY

The immediate question, of course, was whether the women who were healthy enough to walk were more likely to survive anyway. Accordingly, they also conducted an analysis based on the stage of cancer, from one to three (precluding stage-four cancer, in which the disease has spread).

Surprisingly, they discovered that walking appeared to benefit the stage-three group the most. The exercise was associated with a reduced risk of 68%, apparently disproving the idea that those with more advanced disease and poorer health wouldn't do as well. However, there were fewer women in this group (about 260 total), and further studies are important. Dr. Holmes added that a contributing factor might be that women diagnosed with more advanced cancer may be more motivated to adopt a healthy lifestyle.

A LITTLE GOES A LONG WAY

Although the study focused on walking, the women participated in a number of aerobic activities, including bicycling, hiking, tennis, swimming and jogging, as well as aerobics classes. The study designers evaluated these in terms of activity units and translated that to the equivalent number of hours of walking. It's encouraging for women in treatment to learn that they don't need to walk a great deal to gain benefit. A mere three to five hours of walking a week was the optimum amount of time associated with decreased risk for death. Right now, theories abound for why walking is so beneficial for breast cancer patients. The good news is that it does seem to be beneficial.

Breast Cancer Patients Benefit from Yoga

In a recent study of breast cancer survivors, it was found that engaging in the Iyengar method—one of the more active forms of yoga—during treatment for breast cancer promotes psychological well-being...benefits the immune system...and generally improves patients' quality of life.

Sally E. Blank, PhD, associate professor, program in health sciences, Washington State University, Spokane, and researcher of a study of breast cancer survivors, presented at a meeting of the American Physiological Society.

Breakthrough Treatment Zaps Breast Cancer

Virgilio Sacchini, MD, associate attending physician of breast disease, Memorial Sloan-Kettering Cancer Center, and associate professor of surgery, Weill Medical College of Cornell University, both in New York City.

Louis B. Harrison, MD, clinical director, Continuum Cancer Centers of New York, chairman, radiation oncology, Beth Israel Medical Center and St. Luke's-Roosevelt Hospital Center and professor of radiation oncology, Albert Einstein College of Medicine, all in New York City.

Doctors are investigating an exciting new treatment alternative for women with breast cancer—intraoperative radiation therapy (IORT). Instead of six weeks of conventional external radiation, this technique entails one highly intensified, 20-minute dose of radiation during cancer surgery.

This is a tremendous breakthrough, reports Virgilio Sacchini, MD, associate attending physician of breast disease at Memorial Sloan-Kettering Cancer Center and associate professor of surgery, Weill Medical College of Cornell University, both in New York City. He has been using IORT on breast cancer patients in this country and in Milan, Italy, since 1997. Following surgery, a woman who has been treated with IORT does not have to suffer through six weeks of radiation treatments.

NEW FOR BREAST CANCER... OLD HAT FOR OTHER CANCERS

IORT's highly specialized technique is an established treatment method for head and neck cancers, colorectal cancers, abdominal and pelvic tumors and thoracic malignancies. Its application for breast cancer is more recent. In IORT, a large dose of radiation is applied directly to the area from which the tumor was just removed during surgery. Specially equipped operating rooms allow the transmission of the radiation with greater intensity and localization.

To learn more about this innovative technique, we spoke with Louis B. Harrison, MD, a pioneer in the development and practice of intraoperative radiation therapy and clinical director of the Continuum Cancer Centers, which offer state-of-the-art cancer care at New York City hospitals, including Beth Israel and St. Luke's-Roosevelt.

According to Dr. Harrison, IORT affords two primary benefits...

• **It optimizes radiation to the cancer.**

• **It minimizes danger to the surrounding healthy organs.**

A primary difference between IORT and conventional external radiation is that you could never apply such a large dose of radiation under normal conditions because, postoperatively, other organs would be in the way of the radiation beam and would be harmed by it. In IORT, the radiation is applied during surgery, when other organs are more easily moved out of the way.

AN INTEGRAL NEW TOOL IN BREAST-CONSERVING TREATMENT

The choice facing women with breast cancer is either to have breast-conserving treatment (such as a lumpectomy) or a modified radical mastectomy, in which the surgeon removes the whole breast, most or all of the lymph nodes under the arm and possibly the lining of the chest muscles. The smaller of the two chest muscles may also be taken out to make it easier to remove the lymph nodes. In women with early-stage breast cancer—tumors that are no more than two centimeters without palpable lymph nodes are considered clinical stage one—research shows that there is no difference in outcome between these two treatment options.

Radiation, which is an integral part of breast conserving treatment, is used after a lumpectomy to prevent recurrence. Two to three weeks after surgery, most women begin six weeks of radiation therapy, with such possible side effects as fatigue, localized reddening of the skin and swelling of the breast.

How did this variation—IORT—come about? The rationale behind IORT is that 85% of breast cancer recurrences take place in the same area, or quadrant, as the primary tumor. So doctors asked themselves, *Instead of treating the whole breast over time, why not apply a one-time dose of intense radiation to this single area?* This is possible only when radiation is administered during surgery.

IORT HAS SIGNIFICANT ADVANTAGES

In addition to fewer treatments and less damage to surrounding tissue, Dr. Sacchini says the advantages of a single dose of radiation during surgery are huge…

- **Shorter treatment means less psychological distress and faster return to a normal life.**
- **IORT is less expensive than conventional radiation.**
- **IORT eliminates the side effects associated with six weeks of radiation therapy.**

Note: Although a single large dose of radiation may cause fibrosis, or breast hardening, this normally disappears in five to six months.

IMPROVED QUALITY OF LIFE

There are distinct psychological advantages to IORT as well. While it is distressing to be in the hospital for surgery and IORT, it's far more distressing to undergo surgery and then spend hours in a waiting room week after week before undergoing radiation therapy.

Dr. Sacchini is also concerned about the logistical issues that face women following surgery, such as the inconvenience of making trips regularly to receive radiation treatment. In an earlier study, he notes that women who lived farther from radiation facilities were more likely to choose mastectomy over lumpectomy.

And when all is said and done, it's a relief for women to address their cancer, take care of it and resume their normal lives as quickly as possible. IORT makes this more possible than conventional radiation.

IORT IS NOT FOR EVERYONE

Although the advantages of IORT treatment are becoming increasingly clear, this procedure is not for everyone. IORT is appropriate only for women with small, confined tumors, usually in clinical stage one of the disease. Tumors must be less than two centimeters in size, and there must be only one tumor (with no satellite cancers).

Age is also an issue. Younger women have higher rates of recurrence, even in other quadrants, explains Dr. Sacchini. Most treatment centers limit the procedure to women in their late forties and over.

IORT is still considered an experimental procedure, but it is gradually being adopted by more treatment centers across the country. So far, the results look promising for one more weapon in the war against breast cancer.

For more information, visit the Cancer Treatment Centers of America Web site *www.cancercenter.com* (search "IORT for Breast Cancer").

Foods That Lower Risk For Breast Cancer

Eating dark green or deep orange vegetables and fruits that are rich in carotenoids reduces the risk for estrogen-receptor-negative cancers by 13%. Eat spinach, broccoli, cantaloupe, carrots, apricots and other dark green or orange fruits and vegetables.

Review of data from 18 studies involving more than 1 million women by researchers at Harvard School of Public Health, Boston, published in *Nutrition Action Healthletter.*

Promising Breast Cancer Vaccine

Ruth Lerman, MD, specialist in breast disease, William Beaumont Breast Care Center, Royal Oak, Michigan.

As vaccine research advances, scientists are taking on a variety of new conditions, including various forms of cancer.

Like many of the cutting-edge treatments, breast cancer vaccines are currently experimental and limited to women with advanced disease. However, scientists see vaccination as a way to prevent future breast cancer in women at high risk due to personal or family histories.

HARNESSING THE POWER OF THE IMMUNE SYSTEM

To learn more about this growing branch of cancer research, we spoke with Ruth Lerman, MD, a three-time breast cancer survivor who specializes in breast disease at the William Beaumont Breast Care Center, located in Royal Oak, Michigan. She explained that, in patients with cancer, the immune system may not recognize cancer cells as a threat, so they are left free to grow. But, according to Dr. Lerman, vaccination stimulates the immune system to actively recognize and destroy breast cancer cells throughout the body.

NEW VACCINE SHOWS PROMISE

A small government study performed at Walter Reed Army Medical Center in Washington, DC, involved women whose cancer had spread to the lymph nodes. All had previous treatment that included surgery, radiation and/or chemotherapy, and afterward experienced no evidence of breast cancer. However, because the cancer had already spread, they remained at high risk.

A breast cancer vaccine was administered in six monthly injections to 14 of these women. It targeted a growth-stimulating protein known as HER2/neu, which is present in large quantities in one-third of women with breast cancer. The vaccine caused no serious side effects, and cancer recurred in only two women (those who had

the weakest immune response to the vaccine). In contrast, in a control group of 20 unvaccinated women with similar medical histories, the disease recurred much more quickly.

LOOKING TOWARD THE FUTURE

Although many scientists are excited about the possibilities of breast cancer vaccines, more research is needed. For example, in the Walter Reed study, will the vaccinated women continue to resist a breast cancer recurrence for longer than the women who didn't receive the vaccine? Only time will tell. Larger clinical trials are also planned for women whose cancer is confined to the breast.

The bottom line? While immunotherapy may never totally vanquish cancer or replace other strategies, such as chemotherapy, it has a good chance to become one more powerful weapon in our cancer-fighting arsenal.

For more information, contact the American Cancer Society at *www.cancer.org*.

New Technique Detects Breast Cancer Earlier

Mayo Clinic news release.

A technique that uses a specially designed gamma camera was found to improve the detection of small breast tumors, according to a study.

TECHNIQUE ALLOWS EARLIER DETECTION

A team from the Mayo Clinic in Rochester, Minnesota, used the technique, called *molecular breast* imaging, on 40 women who had suspicious mammogram findings.

The imaging detected 33 of the 36 malignant lesions confirmed in 26 of the women during surgery.

Overall, molecular breast imaging had an 86% detection rate of small breast tumors.

"By optimizing the camera to detect smaller breast lesions, this technique should aid in the detection of early-stage breast cancer, something that was not possible with conventional gamma cameras," says Michael O'Connor, PhD, a Mayo Clinic radiologist.

BETTER THAN MAMMOGRAPHY

Mammography uses differences in the anatomic appearance of tumors and normal tissue to detect breast cancer. These differences can be subtle and can often be obscured by dense breast tissue.

In contrast, molecular breast imaging detects cancer by identifying differences in the metabolic behavior of tumors and normal tissue.

"Approximately 25% to 40% of women have dense breast tissue, which decreases the chance that a cancer will be visible on their mammograms," says Douglas Collins, MD, another Mayo radiologist.

"With molecular breast imaging, the visibility of the tumor is not influenced by the density of the surrounding tissue, so this technique is well-suited to find cancers in women whose mammograms may not be very accurate," Dr. Collins explains.

Common Ingredient Doesn't Cause Breast Cancer

Breast cancer is not linked to *acrylamide*, commonly found in potato chips, bread, coffee, cereal and other fried, baked or roasted high-carbohydrate foods. Acrylamide is currently classified as a probable human carcinogen because, in high doses, it has been found to cause cancer in laboratory animals.

Recent finding: Women who consumed large amounts of foods that contain acrylamide did not increase their risk of developing breast cancer.

Important: Additional studies are needed to determine if acrylamide causes other cancers.

Lorelei Mucci, PhD, assistant professor of epidemiology, Harvard School of Public Health, Boston.

HRT and Breast Cancer Risk

The late John R. Lee, MD, Sebastopol, California–based family practitioner who pioneered the study and use of natural progesterone. Dr. Lee was coauthor of *What Your Doctor May Not Tell You About Breast Cancer: How Hormone Balance Can Help Save Your Life* (Grand Central Publishing).

Medical experts have done an about-face on the supposed health advantages of *hormone-replacement therapy* (HRT). This shift in thinking is long overdue. Some doctors have been warning women about the potential dangers of hormones for years. Now there's strong evidence that even the standard HRT regimen can cause breast cancer.

THE ESTROGEN FACTOR

The problem is, doctors are prescribing the wrong hormone. Conventional wisdom has held that menopause is caused by estrogen deficiency. This belief was supported by the fact that supplemental estrogen alleviated hot flashes in menopausal women. However, the majority of women going through menopause are deficient in progesterone—*not* estrogen.

Why is progesterone so important? To begin with, it is just as critical as estrogen in preventing osteoporosis. Estrogen slows down bone loss, but progesterone is responsible for the formation of new bone tissue. In addition, progesterone works to counteract the breast cancer–promoting effect of estrogen.

That's why maintaining a proper balance of these two hormones is so important. Ideally, a woman's ratio of progesterone to estrogen should be between 200:1 and 300:1. If this ratio drops below 200:1—meaning there's too little progesterone—*estrogen dominance results*. Symptoms of this dangerous condition include difficulty sleeping, anxiety, headaches, increased body fat, swollen or tender breasts, bloating, fatigue, irritability and diminished sex drive.

Even more ominous, estrogen dominance activates the normally dormant cancer-causing gene Bcl-2.

A statistical link between estrogen dominance and breast cancer has emerged. In one study of 3,000 breast cancer patients, more than 99% had estrogen dominance. Among healthy women, the majority did not have estrogen dominance.

DANGERS OF HRT

Many women on HRT have a progesterone/estrogen ratio far lower than it should be. *This occurs for two reasons...*

•**HRT increases estrogen levels**—often unnecessarily. As a *Lancet* article pointed out, even in the minority of instances where women do require estrogen supplements, the necessary dose is usually just 0.25 milligram (mg)—less than half the .625 mg that is typically prescribed.

•**HRT supplements contain no natural progesterone.** Instead, they use a synthetic progesterone called *progestin*. Progestin does not provide as much protection against uterine cancer as does natural progesterone. Furthermore, progestin does *not* have progesterone's protective effect against breast cancer.

While progesterone benefits a woman's body by building up bone, contributing to the normal function of blood clotting and blood sugar levels, progestin has a long list of toxic side effects, including increased risk for stroke, fluid retention, epilepsy and asthma.

Many women *not* on HRT may also be at increased risk for breast cancer due to estrogen dominance caused by...

•Birth control pills, which can block the body's production of progesterone.

•Working a night shift under artificial light and sleeping during the day. Doing so inhibits progesterone production.

•A diet high in sugar and starches or low in green, leafy vegetables.

•Prolonged stress, which increases the sensitivity of the body's estrogen receptors.

•Eating meat from cattle that have been given estrogen supplements to boost their weight.

STABILIZING HORMONE LEVELS

Every woman should get her estrogen and progesterone levels tested—and discuss the results with her doctor.

Blood tests do *not* accurately reflect the level of active hormones. A saliva test,* which measures the amount of "free," or biologically active, hormones in the body, is essential for an accurate reading.

If testing reveals a progesterone/estrogen ratio below 200:1, some doctors recommend using a topical progesterone cream, which enters the bloodstream more efficiently than pills.

The cream, which can be applied to your palms, chest and neck, is sold over-the-counter. It costs about $12 to $30. Look for key words, such as "progesterone" or "natural progesterone." The cream is sold under many brand names, including Awakening Woman, Femgest, and Renewed Balance.

Most postmenopausal women must use 15 to 20 mg of cream every day (which is equivalent to about one-quarter teaspoon) for several months before regaining their progesterone/estrogen balance.

After three months, have your progesterone and estrogen levels tested again to make sure you're taking an adequate dose.

If saliva tests reveal low levels of progesterone and estrogen, ask your doctor about supplementing the progesterone cream with oral estrogen. Start with a dose of 0.3 mg daily (currently the lowest dose you can get). Have another saliva test done after three months to recheck your hormone levels.

*To obtain a mail-order saliva test, contact Genova Diagnostics (800-522-4762 or *www.gdx.net*)...or ZRT Laboratory (866-600-1636 or *www.zrtlab.com*). *Typical costs:* $50 and up.

Potent Anticancer Agent: Vitamin D

Vitamin D can drive down mortality rates from 16 types of cancer, including breast and ovarian, by up to 70%. As a possible cancer preventive, be sure to get at least 1,000 IU of vitamin D-3 (cholecalciferol—not D-2, ergocalciferol, which is less effective) in summer and 2,000 IU in winter. For most people, it is best to take 1,500 IU daily in supplement form.

William B. Grant, PhD, founding director, Sunlight, Nutrition and Health Research Center, *www.sunarc.org*.

Making Sense of Your Pap Test Results

Alan G. Waxman, MD, professor of obstetrics and gynecology at University of New Mexico School of Medicine and medical director of UNM Women's Health Clinic at University of New Mexico Health Sciences Center, both in Albuquerque. Dr. Waxman is a leading authority on cervical cancer screening and prevention.

Y ou probably have a Pap test every one to three years—as you should! The test reveals cancer of the *cervix*, the internal gateway between the vagina and the uterus. More importantly, the Pap detects problematic changes *before* cells become cancerous, when the condition is most easily treated.

Before the Pap test was developed, cervical cancer was the number-one cause of cancer deaths in women...now it ranks 15th. But the fight is not yet won. In the US, 70% of new cervical cancers are diagnosed in women who have not had regular Pap tests or whose abnormal results were not followed up with appropriate additional testing for and treatment of precancerous lesions.

If you are among the three million to four million US women per year whose Pap results are "abnormal," you probably are confused about what this means and what to do next. *The answers you need...*

CANCER CULPRIT: HPV

Cervical cancer is almost always caused by infection with *human papillomavirus* (HPV). Of the more than 100 strains of this sexually transmitted virus, 15 are linked to cervical cancer. Nearly 80% of sexually active women become infected at some point, but usually HPV disappears on its own, so HPV testing is not done routinely.

However: Occasionally, HPV persists and, over many years, can cause cellular changes that lead to cervical cancer.

What happens: Like any virus, HPV can take over a cell and alter its DNA. The purpose of the Pap test is to detect and grade precancerous HPV-infected cells so doctors can provide the appropriate subsequent tests and treatments to prevent the cells from progressing to cancer.

During a Pap test, the doctor uses a small brush or spatula to scrape two types of cells from the cervix—*squamous cells* from the epithelium (skin) on the surface of the cervix... and mucus-producing *glandular cells* from the endocervical canal, the narrow channel that runs from the cervix into the uterus.

The cells are transferred to a glass slide...or to a vial of liquid preservative (such as the ThinPrep or SurePath brand). Slides made from the liquid are easier to analyze. If the Pap results are abnormal, the remaining liquid can be tested for HPV.

TEST INTERPRETATION

Within a few weeks of your Pap smear, your health-care provider should notify you of the test results. If you are told simply that your results are abnormal, ask for the *specific term* for your type of abnormality. Then check the list below for an explanation of the term. The follow-up recommendations given are appropriate for most adult women. (Guidelines for adolescents and pregnant women differ— consult your doctor.)

A Pap test result of...

•**NEGATIVE**—or *negative for intraepithelial lesion for malignancy*—means results are normal and cervical cells look fine.

About 90% of Paps are negative.

What's next: No action is needed until your next regularly scheduled Pap test. If you are under age 30, have a Pap every one to two years. If you are 30 or older and have had three consecutive negative Paps, your doctor may suggest waiting two to three years between tests because your risk is low and cervical cancer grows slowly.

•**ASC-US**—or *atypical squamous cells of undetermined significance*—are slightly abnormal but not obviously precancerous. Caution is warranted—about 13% of ASC-US abnormalities are associated with a more serious or "high-grade" lesion called *HSIL* (described later).

What's next: Your doctor will recommend one of three courses...

1. Repeat the Pap test after six months and again after another six months. Most women return to normal by the first repeat test—but two tests are needed for confirmation. If both repeat tests are normal, you don't need to do anything until your next annual Pap.

•If your second test result also is ASC-US, your doctor will do a *colposcopy* (examination of the cervix using a magnifying instrument) and perhaps a *biopsy* (removal and analysis of a small tissue sample) of any abnormal area.

•If your second or third Pap test indicates a "low-grade" lesion called *LSIL* or if it indicates HSIL, see these categories below.

2. Do an HPV test. If it is negative, your risk of developing HSIL is just 1.4%. If the HPV test is positive, your HSIL risk is 27%—so you need a colposcopy.

3. Skip additional tests and get a colposcopy. This is best if your most recent previous Pap result also showed ASC-US, LSIL or HSIL.

•**ASC-H** is a subcategory of atypical squamous cells with specific characteristics that *might* indicate HSIL.

What's next: Colposcopy and biopsy of any abnormal areas.

•**LSIL**—or *low-grade squamous intra-epithelial lesion*—may indicate a viral skin infection, but in about 27% of cases, it hides high-grade changes.

What's next: Colposcopy and biopsy. If the biopsy is negative or if it confirms LSIL, your doctor should follow you carefully over the next year—repeating the Pap test twice at six-month intervals or doing an HPV test after 12 months. Low-grade changes usually regress without treatment. Even if the LSIL persists for two years, often the best course is to do additional Pap and/or HPV testing rather than to treat the lesion.

•**HSIL**—or *high-grade squamous intra-epithelial lesion*—indicates more advanced precancerous changes. Fewer than one-third of these lesions disappear on their own. If not removed, they are likely to become cancerous.

What's next: Colposcopy and biopsy. *Depending on the findings, your doctor may recommend one of the following surgical treatments...*

•*Loop electrosurgical excision procedure* (LEEP). With this office procedure, abnormal tissue of the cervical lining is cut out using a loop of very thin, heated wire.

•*Cone excision.* In the operating room, the doctor typically uses a scalpel or laser to remove a cone-shaped area from the cervical lining and underlying tissue.

•*Ablation.* This office procedure uses either extreme cold (cryotherapy) or extreme heat (laser) to destroy abnormal cervical tissue.

Once the surgery is over, have a Pap test after six months or an HPV test after 12 months to make sure the HSIL hasn't come back.

•**AGC**—or *atypical glandular cells*—are slightly abnormal glandular cells, usually from the endocervical canal or squamous tissue of the cervix.

What's next: Colposcopy and biopsy, including sampling of the endocervical canal... plus an HPV test. A biopsy of the *endometrium* (uterine lining) also is needed if you are age 35 or older...have abnormal menstrual bleeding ...or had Pap results showing abnormal endometrial cells.

•If your biopsy and HPV test are negative, have a repeat Pap and HPV test in one year.

•If the biopsy is negative but HPV is positive, repeat the Pap test and HPV test after six months. If either test is abnormal, have another colposcopy and biopsy.

•If the biopsy is positive, the abnormal area is treated surgically.

•**AIS**—or *endocervical adenocarcinoma in situ*—indicates a high risk for cancer in the endocervical canal, where it often cannot be seen with colposcopy.

What's next: Biopsy and, if necessary, cone excision.

Make Sure Your Pap Test Is Accurate

It is best to abstain from intercourse for 48 hours beforehand—or have your partner use a condom. With a routine exam that includes testing for cervical cancer, semen could contaminate the cell sample and lead to false negative Pap test results...if you have a *human papillomavirus* (HPV) test, your partner's DNA rather than yours could inadvertently be tested. If you're having a pelvic exam to evaluate vaginal discharge, semen may alter the appearance and pH of the discharge, hindering identification of an infection. For similar reasons, also avoid douching or using vaginal medication for 48 hours prior to your exam.

Julie L. Laifer, MD, attending physician, department of obstetrics/gynecology, Bridgeport Hospital–Yale New Haven Health, Bridgeport, Connecticut. Also in private practice in Trumbull, Connecticut, she specializes in natural approaches to women's health.

Detecting Ovarian Cancer Long Before It Turns Deadly

Robert P. Edwards, MD, professor of obstetrics, gynecology and reproductive sciences at University of Pittsburgh School of Medicine, director of gynecologic oncology research and vice chairman of clinical affairs at Magee-Womens Hospital, and senior investigator at Magee-Womens Research Institute, all in Pittsburgh.

Some cancers of the female reproductive tract have obvious early warning signs. For uterine cancer, it's bleeding after menopause. For cervical cancer, it's a Pap smear that shows abnormal cells. But ovarian cancer—cancer of the glands that produce eggs and manufacture the hormones estrogen and progesterone—often has no obvious symptoms.

Reasons: In the spacious abdominal cavity, a tumor can grow undetected for years…and cancer cells can silently spread via the peritoneal fluid in the abdominal cavity.

Result: Among women whose ovarian cancer is caught and treated early—while it is still confined to the ovary—the five-year survival rate is 93%. Unfortunately, of the estimated 22,000 women in the US who are newly diagnosed with ovarian cancer each year, 80% already have cancer that has spread to other parts of the body. For them, the five-year survival rate could be just 20% to 30%.

Self-defense: Determine your level of risk, then follow the protective guidelines below.

Important: Watch for the subtle, easy-to-miss warning signs of ovarian cancer (see page 452).

AT HIGH RISK

The average woman's risk for ovarian cancer is relatively small—for every 100 women, fewer than two get the disease. However, certain factors significantly worsen these odds. For instance, for every 100 women who inherit a mutated form of the genes linked to breast cancer (BRCA1, BRCA2), 16 to 60 of them—depending on the specific mutation—are likely to develop ovarian cancer.

You are at high risk if any of these apply…

•**Two or more first-degree relatives** (mother, sister, daughter) have had ovarian or breast cancer.

•**Three or more second-degree relatives** (grandmother, aunt) have had ovarian or breast cancer.

•**You have a personal history of breast cancer diagnosed before menopause.**

You are at intermediate-high risk if…

•**You have one first-degree relative who has had ovarian cancer.**

Self-defense: If your risk is high or intermediate-high, maximize your chances for early detection…

•**Get genetic counseling.** The counselor precisely maps your family history to determine if genetic testing (for instance, for the BRCA1 and BRCA2 genes) is appropriate. Genetic counseling is available at many university-based cancer centers.

Referrals: National Cancer Institute, 800-422-6237, *www.cancer.gov.*

•**Have frequent screening tests.** *At least once per year, see your gynecologist for a…*

•Pelvic exam, during which the doctor manually examines the ovaries and uterus.

•Transvaginal ultrasound, in which a probe is placed in the vagina to check for ovarian tumors.

•Blood test for CA-125, a protein produced by ovarian cancer cells. *Recent study:* This test detected about half of early-stage ovarian cancers

...and about 80% when used with a symptom questionnaire among high-risk women.

If any of these test results are suspicious, your doctor may order a magnetic resonance imaging (MRI) or computed tomography (CT) scan.

• **Consider a laparoscopic exam.** A thin, lighted tube inserted via a small incision in the navel region allows the doctor to visually examine the ovaries.

• **Ask your doctor about preventive surgery.** Surgical removal of the ovaries (oophorectomy) reduces the odds of ovarian cancer by about 95%. (It does not provide 100% protection because microscopic cancer cells already may have existed prior to the surgery.) Insurance generally covers the cost.

Downside: If you are premenopausal, oophorectomy leads to abrupt menopause, which may cause severe hot flashes, mood swings and vaginal dryness. Hormone therapy can ease these symptoms—but may increase risk for breast cancer and heart disease.

AT SLIGHTLY INCREASED RISK

Even if you are not at high or intermediate-high risk, your chances of getting ovarian cancer may be above average. *Studies have linked increased risk with the following factors...*

• **Age.** Two-thirds of ovarian cancer patients are 55 or older.

• **Ethnicity.** The disease is most common among Caucasians.

• **Menstrual history.** Ovulation increases ovarian cancer risk. If you began to menstruate before age 12 and/or reached menopause after age 55, your risk is greater.

• **No history of oral contraceptive use.** The Pill prevents ovulation, so women who have taken it for at least two years are at lower risk.

• **History of infertility.** This link may be due to increased ovulation and/or decreased progesterone.

• **History of endometriosis (overgrowth of the tissue lining the uterus).** The link is unclear but may be due to increased inflammation.

The more of these risk factors you have, the more vital it is to get annual pelvic exams.

Also, ask your doctor if a CA-125 blood test and ultrasound are warranted for you.

AT AVERAGE RISK

Unfortunately, there is no reliable screening test for ovarian cancer that is appropriate for women who have no risk factors. Studies show that on average, periodic ultrasounds and/or CA-125 testing provide no benefit for women at average risk—no increased level of detection, no lower death rate from the disease—but do lead to unnecessary tests and even surgeries when small cysts are mistaken for cancer.

Several new blood and urine screening tests have received much publicity lately. Called *proteomics*, this emerging field of research seeks to identify biomarkers for ovarian cancer. But although the early news about these tests was promising, subsequent larger studies showed that none were effective in increasing cancer detection or survival.

Bottom line: If you're at average risk, the only recommended screening tool for ovarian cancer is the all-important annual pelvic exam.

More from Dr. Edwards...

Suspicious Symptoms

Though ovarian cancer often produces no obvious symptoms, in about 60% of cases it does have some subtle warning signs. *See your gynecologist without delay if you experience any of the following...*

• **Abdominal swelling or bloating**
• **Pelvic pressure or abdominal pain**
• **Feeling full quickly when eating**
• **Urgent and/or frequent urination.**

These same symptoms can be caused by irritable bowel syndrome or urinary incontinence. *However, they are more likely to indicate ovarian cancer when symptoms...*

• **Appeared within the last year**
• **Are severe**
• **Occur almost every day**
• **Last for more than a few weeks.**

Better Ovarian Cancer Treatment

Researchers compared the care that gynecologic oncologists, gynecologists and general surgeons provided to 3,000 women ages 65 or older who had surgery for early-stage ovarian cancer.

Result: Patients treated by the gynecologic oncologists and gynecologists had half the mortality rate (2.1% versus 4%) of those treated by general surgeons.

Self-defense: Women diagnosed with ovarian cancer should seek treatment by a gynecologic oncologist. To find one, contact the Society of Gynecologic Oncology, 312-235-4060, *www. sgo.org.*

Craig C. Earle, MD, former associate professor of medicine, Harvard Medical School, Boston.

Cancer Risk

Women with a history of precancerous cervical lesions have twice the average risk for eventually developing cervical or vaginal cancer.

Best: These women should continue to get annual Pap smear tests for at least 25 years after cervical lesions occur.

Björn Strander, MD, gynecologist, Sahlgren's University Hospital, Sweden, and leader of a study of 132,493 women, published in *British Medical Journal.*

Tea Lowers Ovarian Cancer Risk

In a study of 61,057 women ages 40 to 76, those who drank two or more cups of tea (primarily black tea) per day were 46% less likely to develop ovarian cancer over a 17-year period, compared with those who didn't drink tea.

Theory: Tea contains polyphenols, potent antioxidants that may inhibit tumor growth.

Self-defense: Women should drink at least two cups of tea daily to receive this cancer-fighting benefit.

Susanna C. Larsson, PhD, researcher, National Institute of Environmental Medicine, Karolinska Institutet, Stockholm, Sweden.

Better Cervical Cancer Screening

In a study including 1,305 women ages 40 to 50, researchers analyzed the results of Pap smears and testing for human papillomavirus (HPV), a common cause of cervical cancer.

Result: Twenty-one percent of the women who tested positive for HPV at the beginning of the study developed cervical cancer or precancerous cervical lesions within a 10-year period, even though the results of their Pap smears, which also had been performed at the beginning of the study, were negative.

If you are over age 40: Ask your gynecologist about receiving an HPV test with your PAP smear.

Susanne Krüger Kjær, MD, DMSc, professor, Danish Cancer Society, Copenhagen.

Smoking and Cervical Cancer

Smoking increases risk for cervical cancer in women who are infected with the *human papilloma virus* (HPV). Smokers who have HPV are 14 times more likely to develop cervical cancer than smokers who don't have HPV—but nonsmokers with HPV are only six times more likely to get cervical cancer than nonsmokers without HPV.

Researchers from the department of medical epidemiology and biostatistics, Karolinska Institute, Stockholm, Sweden, and leaders of a study of 738 people, published in *Cancer Epidemiology, Biomarkers and Prevention.*

Seemingly Harmless Symptoms That May Be Red Flags for Cancer

Amy P. Abernethy, MD, program director of the Duke Cancer Care Research Program and associate director of the Cancer Control Program at the Duke Comprehensive Cancer Center, both in Durham, North Carolina. Dr. Abernethy is also an associate professor of medicine in the division of medical oncology at the Duke University Medical Center.

If you are one of the estimated 1.5 million people in the US who will be told you have cancer this year, much of your medical fate will depend on how advanced the malignancy is when it is diagnosed.

When cancer is caught early—before the abnormal cells multiply and spread—the odds of defeating the disease improve dramatically.

Problem: Because cancer is tricky—early symptoms most often (but not always) are painless, and they often mimic common noncancerous conditions—many people ignore red flags that could help them get an early diagnosis.

For the best possible chance of beating cancer: Be alert for subtle symptoms of the disease. Here are nine such cancer symptoms that you should never ignore—and how to distinguish them from more benign causes.*

1. Difficulty swallowing. When you swallow, you've probably had the uncomfortable or painful experience of food getting stuck—for example, high in the esophagus or in the middle of the upper chest.

It may be cancer if: You have this sensation all or most times that you eat, and it's usually not painful. Difficulty swallowing is common in people with esophageal or stomach cancer and may be a sign that a tumor is obstructing the esophagus or that inflammation and scarring have narrowed the opening. Inflammation can be a precursor to cancer and also can indicate that a malignant tumor has irritated surrounding healthy tissue.

Because difficulty swallowing evolves slowly, many people adjust the way they eat, taking smaller bites, chewing longer and perhaps

*Important: If you have a troubling symptom that is not listed in this article, see your doctor.

even switching to a diet that is mostly liquid. If eating becomes difficult—for any reason—see a doctor.

2. Excessive bleeding and/or unexplained bruising. Leukemia causes a shortage of blood platelets (cellular elements responsible for clotting), which results in easy and excessive bleeding and unexplained bruising. (Normal bleeding, such as that caused by a cut, should stop after application of direct pressure.)

It may be cancer if: You have an unusual number of unexplained nosebleeds (for example, not due to dry air, a common trigger) and/or develop unexplained bruises (a change in frequency or severity from the norm) that tend to be painful when touched, dark purple and large (the size of a fist or bigger).

Important: Bleeding gums may be a sign of poor dental care or a serious medical problem, such as leukemia. If brushing causes bleeding, see your dentist for an evaluation to determine the cause.

3. Exhaustion. Everyone gets tired, but extreme fatigue due to cancer is quite different. Although all cancers can cause fatigue, this symptom is most common with colon cancer, leukemia and other cancers that may cause anemia.

It may be cancer if: For no apparent reason, you experience overwhelming and debilitating fatigue similar to that caused by the flu.

Important: Fatigue due to cancer is sometimes mistaken for depression.

Key difference: A person with depression often lacks the will and desire to perform daily activities, while a person with fatigue related to cancer wants to stay active but lacks the physical ability to do so.

4. Fever and night sweats. The presence of cancer causes a storm of chemical processes as the body ramps up its immune defenses to fight cancer cells. Fever is one indication that your immune system is fending off an illness, such as a cold or the flu, or even cancer.

It may be cancer if: You have fevers (typically 100°F or higher) that come and go over a period of days or weeks. Cancer-related fevers occur most often at night—often along with drenching night sweats.

Important: Menopausal women often have hot flashes that may lead to night sweats—but sweats due to menopause also occur during the day. Anyone who experiences night sweats—including menopausal women who have night sweats but no daytime hot flashes—should see a doctor.

5. Lumps. Any new, firm, painless lump that is growing in size or that is bigger than a nickel should be immediately examined by a doctor. Worrisome lumps typically feel firmer than the tip of your nose, while spongy or painful lumps are less of a concern. Lumps can be caused by several types of cancer, including breast, testicular and throat malignancies, and melanoma (skin cancer).

The immune response launched by your body when it is fighting a serious disease—including cancer—may lead to enlarged lymph nodes (the small filtering structures that help prevent foreign particles from entering the bloodstream). Painful and/or swollen lymph nodes are common signs of infection and usually return to normal size within a few days of the infection resolving.

It may be cancer if: Enlarged lymph nodes do not return to normal size and/or have the characteristics described above.

Helpful: Lymph nodes can be found throughout the body, but enlarged ones are easiest to feel behind the neck (at the base of the skull or behind the ears)…in the armpit… in the groin (at the junction of the torso and leg)…in the hollowed space above the collarbone (clavicle)…in back of the knee…and at the crook of the elbow.

6. Persistent cough. Longtime smokers get used to coughing, so they tend not to notice this important symptom of lung cancer. Nonsmokers can experience persistent cough as well, which also can be a symptom of other cancers, including malignancies of the throat and esophagus.

It may be cancer if: You have a cough—with or without breathlessness—that persists for longer than one month. Coughing up blood also can be a cancer symptom.

7. Skin changes. Most people know that changes in a mole can be a sign of skin cancer. But the moles that are most prone to cancerous changes are the type that are flat (as opposed to raised or bumpy in shape).

It may be cancer if: You have a mole that becomes darker…changes color…changes shape (especially in an asymmetrical pattern) …or grows larger. Guidelines recommend seeing a doctor if you have a mole that grows larger than a pencil eraser, but don't wait to see your doctor if you have a mole that undergoes any of the changes described above.

Important: A sore that doesn't heal also can be skin cancer. (In healthy people, most superficial wounds heal within days.)

8. Stumbles or falls. If you suddenly become clumsy, it may signal a neurological problem, such as nerve damage from diabetes or multiple sclerosis, or it could be a sign of a brain tumor.

It may be cancer if: Your clumsiness is accompanied by confusion, difficulty concentrating and an inability to move your arms and/or legs. Although paralysis is an obvious sign that something is wrong, it is rarely the first sign of a brain tumor. Check with your doctor immediately if your body's basic functions change in any way.

9. Unexplained weight loss. If you experience significant weight loss (about 10 pounds or more of your body weight) that is not a result of an intentional weight-loss regimen, it often is a symptom of a potentially serious medical condition, such as cancer or depression.

It may be cancer if: Weight loss is due to a reduced appetite. Always see your doctor promptly if you experience unexplained weight loss.

More from Amy P. Abernethy, MD…

Cancer Alerts for Women

Cancer symptoms that women should watch for include…

•**Breast lumps or changes.** Any new lump in the breast should be seen by a physician—especially if the lump is painless. Don't wait to see if it goes away in a month or two. Breast cancer may also cause thickening of the skin…swelling…and/or changes in breast size or shape.

•**Nipple changes.** Report to your doctor any changes in the shape of your nipple…liquid discharge (especially if tinged pink from blood)…inversion of the nipple (in which the nipple projects into the breast mound)…and/or a scaly rash around the nipple.

•**Abdominal changes.** Bloating and abdominal pain can result from a number of gynecologic, urologic or gastrointestinal issues. Oncologists become concerned when a woman has more than one symptom at a time—for example, ovarian cancer can lead to bloating, abdominal pain, increased urinary frequency and/or urgency, constipation and loss of appetite.

•**Postmenopausal bleeding.** Any vaginal bleeding after menopause may signal cancer of the ovaries, uterus or cervix.

The Cancer Recovery Diet

The late Mitchell Gaynor, MD, former clinical assistant professor of medicine at Weill Cornell Medical College of Cornell University in New York City. He is author of *Nurture Nature/Nurture Health* (Nurture Nature), and *Sounds of Healing: A Physician Reveals the Therapeutic Power of Sound, Voice and Music* (Broadway).

When you are facing cancer, it is more important than ever to follow a nutritious diet that strengthens your immune system and helps your body detoxify. This often is challenging, however, because some cancer treatments interfere with the body's ability to take in or use nutrients. *Cancer patients undergoing chemotherapy and/or radiation often experience…*

•**Damage to salivary glands resulting in a dry mouth,** difficulty swallowing and unpleasant changes in taste.

•**Nausea and vomiting.**

•**Impaired absorption of nutrients and calories** due to changes in the normal intestinal bacteria.

These factors and the resulting loss of appetite deplete the body's stores of nutrients and can lead to excessive weight loss that impedes

your recovery, strains your immune system and adds to fatigue.

The following nutrition plan is designed for cancer patients undergoing treatment—as well as for those who finished treatment within the past year—to help rebuild nutrient reserves. All supplements below are sold at health-food stores and/or online.

Important: Discuss your diet and supplement use with your oncologist—this helps the doctor determine the best treatment and follow-up regimen for you. *What to do…*

•**Eat plenty of protein.** Protein helps repair body tissues and prevent unwanted weight loss. It also helps minimize the memory and concentration problems ("chemo brain") common among patients on chemotherapy. The recommended dietary allowance (RDA) for women is 38 grams (g) of protein per day and for men it is 46 g—but for cancer patients, I recommend at least 70 g per day.

Example: With breakfast, include one egg (7 g) and eight ounces of unsweetened soy milk (8 g)…with lunch, a cup of lentil soup (10 g) and eight ounces of low-fat yogurt (12 g)…as a snack, two ounces of almonds (12 g)…with dinner, three ounces of chicken or fish (21 g) or one cup of soybeans (29 g).

Helpful: Consider a protein supplement— such as Biochem Sports Greens & Whey, which provides 20 g of protein per one-ounce serving.

•**Have eight ounces of low-fat yogurt or kefir daily.** Check labels and choose unsweetened brands with live active cultures of *lactobacillus acidophilus* and *bifidobacterium.* Chemotherapy and radiation destroy beneficial bacteria in the gut. Restoring them with probiotics helps alleviate nausea, optimizes immune system function and reduces production of cancer-promoting chemicals.

Alternative: Try a probiotic supplement that contains at least one billion colony forming units (CFUs) per gram. Choose coated capsules to protect the probiotics from stomach acids. Take on an empty stomach upon awakening and also one hour before lunch and dinner.

Good brand: Natren Healthy Trinity (866-462-8736, *www.natren.com*).

• **Boost fiber.** This combats constipation, a common side effect of chemotherapy. Aim for six to 10 servings of whole grains daily.

Examples: One slice of whole-grain bread …one-half cup of cooked brown rice, rolled barley, millet or buckwheat…one-half cup of old-fashioned oatmeal.

Also eat seven to 10 servings of fruits and vegetables daily, which provide fiber and cancer-fighting *phytonutrients* (plant chemicals). If you have lost your taste for vegetables, have juice instead—it is easier to swallow. Carrots, celery, watercress and beets make delicious juices. Juicers are sold at kitchenware stores ($50 and up).

• **Focus on anti-inflammatory foods.** The same enzyme (called COX-2) that causes inflammation also may increase levels of compounds that allow cancer cells to grow. Lowering the body's inflammatory response may be protective.

Best: Eat cold-water fish (salmon, sardines, herring, mackerel, cod) at least three times per week—these are rich in anti-inflammatory omega-3 fatty acids. I recommend avoiding tuna, swordfish and shark, which may contain mercury and other metals.

Alternative: Take 2.5 g of a fish oil daily with food.

Also helpful: Use curry powder liberally to spice up vegetables, meats and poultry—it is a natural anti-inflammatory.

• **Eat foods rich in calcium, magnesium and vitamin D.** These bone-building nutrients are especially important for cancer patients who take steroid medication to control nausea, because steroids can weaken bones. Increase your intake of foods that provide calcium (low-fat dairy, fortified cereals, leafy green vegetables)…magnesium (nuts, beans, quinoa)…and vitamin D (fish, fortified dairy). Also supplement daily with 1,500 mg of calcium citrate…400 mg of magnesium…and 1,000 international units (IU) of vitamin D-3.

• **Minimize intake of sugar and white flour.** Eating these foods temporarily increases your levels of *insulin-like growth factor* (IGF), which has hormonelike effects. Although the long-term consequences are unclear, some research suggests a link between high IGF levels and cancer, especially of the breast and colon.

• **Drink plenty of fluids.** Dehydration contributes to decreased salivation…promotes inflammation…and stresses the kidneys and liver, making it harder for these organs to detoxify the body. Drink at least six eight-ounce glasses of water, broth or tea per day.

Beneficial: Green tea contains compounds that may inhibit *angiogenesis* (creation of blood vessels that feed cancer cells).

• **Opt for organic.** Conventionally grown produce often has pesticide and herbicide residues that stress the liver. Choose free-range chicken and beef from grass-fed cows to minimize exposure to antibiotics and hormones in the feed of nonorganic animals. Remove the skin from poultry and fish before cooking, even if organic—skin tends to store a high concentration of toxins.

Helpful: A dietitian who specializes in oncology nutrition can help monitor your nutrient intake and recommend alternatives if certain foods are difficult to eat.

Referrals: Academy of Nutrition and Dietetics, 800-877-1600, *www.eatright.org.*

Herbs Affect Chemo

Black cohosh*, often recommended to breast cancer patients to relieve menopausal symptoms, changes the potency of some chemotherapy drugs.

Self-defense: Be sure your doctor knows all of the supplements and over-the-counter remedies you take. To check interactions, go to the Medline Plus Web site (*www.nlm.nih. gov/medlineplus*) and click on "Drugs and Supplements."

Sara Rockwell, PhD, professor of therapeutic radiology and pharmacology, Yale University School of Medicine, New Haven, and leader of a study of black cohosh to control menopausal symptoms after breast cancer, published in *Breast Cancer Research and Treatment.*

*The US Food and Drug Administration does not regulate herbal supplements. Check with your physician before taking any of these products. Some may interact with prescription medications.

What Even Nonsmokers Need to Know About Lung Cancer

Joan H. Schiller, MD, professor of internal medicine, hematology and oncology, and deputy director of the Simmons Comprehensive Cancer Center at University of Texas Southwestern Medical Center at Dallas. She is president of the not-for-profit National Lung Cancer Partnership. *www.nationallungcancerpartnership.org.*

Each year, lung cancer claims the lives of more women than breast, ovarian and uterine cancers *combined*. Equally startling is that 20% of women who develop lung cancer *never smoked* (compared with 10% of men). *Why women must take care...*

• **One in 16 women in the US will develop lung cancer in her lifetime.**

• **Some studies show that current and former women smokers are at greater risk** for lung cancer than men who have smoked equal amounts.

• **Lung cancer typically appears at a younger age in women,** with 9% of female patients diagnosed before age 50.

• **Lung cancer deaths are declining in men but not in women.**

There are two main types of this disease. *Non–small cell* lung cancer accounts for about 80% of cases...*small cell* lung cancer is rarer but more aggressive.

Good news: There are a number of strategies that help prevent lung cancer...steps that increase the odds of detecting the disease early, when treatment is most successful...and cutting-edge therapies that bring new hope for lung cancer patients.

PREVENTION PLAN

The most important thing you can do to prevent lung cancer is to not smoke.

Reality: Cigarettes are linked to 87% of all lung cancer deaths. *Yet whether or not you ever smoked, you can do more to stay safe...*

• **Avoid smokers.** Secondhand smoke is almost as dangerous as smoking yourself. Do not allow anyone to smoke in your home or car. When in another person's house or vehicle, go to a different room or open a window if someone lights up. Avoid public places where smoking is permitted.

• **Reduce radon exposure.** This invisible, odorless radioactive gas, produced by the breakdown of uranium in soil and water, increases lung cancer risk. Test your home's air yourself (kits start at about $12). If levels are high, install an air venting system (about $1,200 to $1,500). If your home has a private well, test your water, too. If radon levels in your water are high, consider a water-filtration system ($1,500 to $5,000, depending on levels). Retest your home every two years.

• **Ask your doctor about diet.** In one study, women whose diets included the most *boron* (a trace element) were less likely to get lung cancer than those whose diets had the least.

Sources: Almonds, hazelnuts, peanuts... apples, pears, raisins...beans, broccoli, salad greens...coffee.

In another study that involved only men, those who regularly drank red wine had a reduced risk for lung cancer. No such studies have yet been done on women. If you choose to drink, have no more than one glass per day —drinking more may increase risk for various health problems.

If you are a smoker...

• **Quit.** Your lung cancer risk will never drop to zero, but it will decrease as your lungs begin to recover. Cutting down is not good enough —the number of cigarettes smoked daily is less influential than the number of years you smoked.

Helpful: Visit *www.smokefree.gov* for information and support...ask your doctor about prescription and over-the-counter drugs that reduce cigarette cravings.

• **Avoid beta-carotene supplements.** Studies showed that beta-carotene supplements, in dosages averaging 20 milligrams (mg) to 30 mg per day, increased lung cancer risk in smokers. Multivitamins typically contain less than 1 mg of beta-carotene, so the risk with these probably is minimal. However, multivitamins designed to promote good vision often have extra beta-carotene—so they are not your best choice.

If you are a former smoker...

• **Acknowledge your risk.** Up to half of all lung cancers in the US occur in former smokers. So while your lung health did start to improve the day you quit smoking, a significant cancer risk remains for 20 years or more.

DETECTION AND DIAGNOSIS

The five-year survival rate is 56% for patients whose non–small cell lung cancer was diagnosed before it spread to other parts of the body—but 2% for those diagnosed at the most advanced stage. *For early detection…*

• **Review your family history.** New research suggests that people who have a strong family history of lung cancer (three or more blood relatives) plus certain genetic variations have a fivefold increased risk for lung cancer—even if they do not smoke.

Best: If several close relatives have or had lung cancer, your doctor should monitor you closely.

• **Watch for warning signs.** If you smoke, you probably have a long-standing cough due to chronic airway irritation—but see your doctor if coughing worsens, brings up more phlegm or produces blood. If you do not smoke, tell your doctor about any persistent cough.

Other signs: A change in your voice… recurrent sore throats, bronchitis or pneumonia …shortness of breath, wheezing…swelling in the neck or face…difficulty swallowing.

Testing: When a patient has such symptoms, diagnostic testing is warranted. This typically includes microscopic analysis of cells in sputum, *bronchoscopy* (fiber-optic airway exam) and/or chest X-ray. If findings are suspicious, a patient usually is given a *low-dose spiral computed tomography* (CT) scan, which creates a detailed three-dimensional image from a series of X-rays. A tissue biopsy also may be done.

NEW HOPE FOR PATIENTS

Emerging therapies are improving the odds for lung cancer patients. *Advances have occurred in the areas of…*

• **Targeted drug therapies.** Unlike chemotherapy, which affects the whole body, targeted therapies help stop cancer cell growth while sparing healthy tissues.

Example: The medication *bevacizumab* (Avastin) blocks formation of the blood vessels that feed non–small cell cancer tumors. Though not a cure, such treatment helps prolong lives.

• **Chemotherapy.** Improved drugs help patients live longer and more comfortably, with less nausea, hair loss and other side effects.

• **Radiation.** Newest techniques deliver higher radiation doses to tumors while minimizing damage to surrounding tissues.

• **Surgery.** Non–small cell cancer patients generally have better survival rates when tumors and surrounding lung tissue are removed.

New: Video-assisted thoracic surgery techniques make this extensive operation less invasive, reducing pain and speeding recovery.

More information: Free to Breathe, 608-833-7905, *www.freetobreathe.org*. Under "Lung Cancer Info," click on "Treatment," then "Clinical Trials" to learn about ongoing research on the latest therapies.

Does Teflon Cause Cancer?

Ronald Melnick, PhD, senior toxicologist with National Institute of Environmental Health Sciences, a division of the National Institutes of Health, Research Triangle Park, North Carolina.

Teflon has not been found to cause cancer. Perfluorooctanoic acid (PFOA), a chemical used in the synthesis of Teflon, has been labeled a "likely carcinogen" by a panel advising the Environmental Protection Agency. But Teflon pans do not emit PFOA when used properly.

Teflon cookware might emit a small amount of PFOA when heated to extreme temperatures —for example, when a frying pan has been left empty on a heated burner for an extended period. Even then, it has not been established that overheated Teflon produces a dangerous amount of PFOA. Still, it wouldn't be unreasonable to dispose of a Teflon pan that has been left empty on a heated burner.

Approximately 95% of the population has some amount of PFOA in their bloodstream—but most of this PFOA likely comes from stain- and water-repelling treatments used on carpets and fabrics. Grease-resistant food packaging, such as microwave popcorn bags and cardboard fast-food boxes, also might contain small amounts of PFOA.

The fact that PFOA is in our bodies does not mean that we're all going to die from PFOA-related cancers. Individuals who have worked in factories where PFOA is produced, and perhaps some people who live in neighboring areas, seem to have the highest levels of PFOA.

Support Helps Survival

In a recent study, mid-stage breast cancer patients attended a "psychological intervention program" consisting of 26 counseling sessions in one year. They learned ways to reduce stress, increase social support, improve diet and exercise, and comply with cancer treatment.

Encouraging results: Compared with a control group that did not attend the program, study participants were 45% less likely to have a cancer recurrence and 56% less likely to die from breast cancer during the seven- to 13-year follow-up.

If you have cancer: Your doctor or a mental health professional can refer you to a psychological intervention program in your area. Or to find a support group in your area, contact the Cancer Care Counseling Line at 800-813-4673.

Barbara Andersen, PhD, professor of psychology at the Comprehensive Cancer Center at The Ohio State University in Columbus and leader of a study of 227 patients.

Biopsy Alert

Susan L. Blum, former editor, *Bottom Line/Health*, 3 Landmark Square, Stamford, Connecticut 06901.

When pathologists at Johns Hopkins University School of Medicine took a second look at more than 6,000 biopsy samples previously analyzed at other institutions, the results were shocking. Almost two out of every 100 analyses were erroneous. Nearly 25% of the misdiagnoses mistook a benign growth for a cancer.

Scary: Six percent gave patients an "all clear" when in fact they had cancer.

As a result of these errors, some healthy patients underwent grueling cancer treatment—unnecessarily. And some cancer patients failed to receive needed treatment.

Why so many potentially life-threatening errors? Jonathan I. Epstein, MD, professor of pathology at Johns Hopkins and lead author of the study, says that the trend is the ironic result of medical progress.

New, less invasive techniques such as needle biopsies are easier on patients, since they remove less tissue. But that gives pathologists smaller samples to examine—which means signs of disease may be missed.

Also, earlier biopsies are now the norm, thanks to cancer screening procedures like blood tests and mammograms. But early biopsies are more likely to be ambiguous…and the potential for "false-positives" greater.

To protect yourself, Dr. Epstein advises patients to have biopsy samples double-checked by a pathologist specializing in the tissue type under scrutiny.

The Anticancer Diet: Cut Your Risk in Half

Diana Dyer, RD, nutritionist based in Ann Arbor, Michigan. She is a cancer survivor and author of *A Dietitian's Cancer Story* (Swan). Her Internet site at *www.cancerrd.com* provides links to cancer-research organizations and anticancer menus.

For the first time, researchers have announced that a large, randomized and placebo-controlled study—thought to be one of the highest standards of scientific research—strongly suggests that diet reduces cancer rates.

In this study, 2,437 women who had early-stage breast cancer were randomly chosen to follow a low-fat diet (33.3 grams [g] of fat daily) or a higher-fat diet (51.3 g daily). After five years, there was a reduction of more than 20% in breast cancer recurrence in the low-fat group.

The study didn't prove that a low-fat diet can reduce cancer in women without a history of the disease. Nor did it look at other nutritional factors, such as the consumption of fiber, fruits and vegetables, etc.

But more and more oncologists are convinced that future research will continue to demonstrate that good nutrition can help guard against most types of malignancies.

A CANCER-PROTECTION PLAN

Diana Dyer, a registered dietitian and three-time cancer survivor, has reviewed all the latest studies and interviewed top researchers to create an anticancer nutrition plan.

Even if you consume ample amounts of fiber (25 to 30 g daily) and try to eat broccoli and other cruciferous vegetables as often as possible, you may be surprised to learn that there is much more you can do to curb your cancer risk.

PRODUCE: NINE A DAY

For years, US dietary guidelines recommended five daily servings of fruits and vegetables. Now five to nine daily servings (one-half cup equals one serving) are recommended.

In addition to providing fiber, fruits and vegetables are the best sources of antioxidants and other plant chemicals that inhibit damage of a cell's DNA and fight the inflammation that causes normal cells to become cancerous.

What most people don't know: Only about 22% of all Americans eat five servings of fruits and vegetables daily. If you're getting only two daily servings but increase your intake to five daily servings, you could potentially reduce the risk for some cancers, such as esophageal and colorectal, by 20% to 50%. More daily servings provide even greater protection. *To maximize the cancer-fighting effect, eat produce with the highest levels of antioxidants…*

•**Vegetables.** Kale, beets, red peppers, broccoli, spinach, sweet potatoes and corn. Try a stir-fry with olive oil and many of these veggies…or top a pizza with them.

•**Fruits.** All berries, including blueberries and strawberries, plums, oranges, red grapes and pink grapefruit.

FAT: IT MUST BE THE RIGHT KIND

The average American diet includes 33% fat. Excessive fat—especially the saturated fat found in lunch meats, prime rib and other red meats and full-fat dairy products, such as butter, milk, cheese and sour cream—produces carcinogens that increase cancer risk.

What most people don't know: To maximize the absorption of fat-soluble—and cancer-fighting—phytochemicals and nutrients found in vegetables and fruits, 16% to 18% of your diet *should* be from healthful fat, such as monounsaturated fat.

Helpful: To add healthful monounsaturated fat to your diet, use olive oil for salads, sautéing, etc.

Avoid saturated fat altogether, or follow these suggestions…

•**Buy only very lean meats.** Limit portion sizes to two to three ounces (about the size of a deck of cards) per meal.

•**Always use reduced-fat or fat-free dairy products.**

•**Minimize the use of margarine, shortening and liquid vegetable oils.**

FISH: IT FIGHTS CANCER, TOO

The omega-3 fatty acids found in wild salmon, light tuna and other cold-water fish are known to protect the heart.

What most people do not know: Omega-3s interact with other molecules in the body to help reduce inflammatory changes that can promote cancer. Aim for two to three servings of fish weekly. Or use one to two tablespoons of ground flaxseed meal daily. It's high in *alpha-linolenic acid* (ALA), a beneficial omega-3.

Caution: Avoid all blackened fish. High-heat cooking and grilling produce carcinogens that increase cancer risk. If you do grill, marinate fish or meats in vinegar, lime juice, teriyaki sauce or other marinades, and turn once a minute. This reduces the production of carcinogens by approximately 90%.

461

USE HERBS AND SPICES OFTEN

Garlic, anise and other herbs as well as ginger and other spices used in cooking contain high levels of anticancer phytochemicals. To increase flavor, add herbs and spices to your foods instead of salt, sugar or fat.

What most people don't know: Cutting or smashing fresh garlic 10 minutes before cooking will preserve higher levels of its anticancer compounds.

SOY: A LITTLE GOES A LONG WAY

Soybeans contain numerous anticarcinogenic compounds, including the phytoestrogen genistein. Phytoestrogens are plant chemicals that mimic the effects of natural estrogen—and help prevent it from causing cancerous changes in cells in women and men.

Just one daily serving of soy (one cup of soy milk, one-half cup of tofu, one-half cup of soybeans) may reduce the risk for some breast and prostate cancers.

What most people don't know: Soy foods, such as soybeans, tofu and tempeh, also are good sources of cancer-fighting omega-3s.

Caution: Soy foods may *increase* the risk for hormone-sensitive cancers, such as some breast or prostate malignancies—or reduce the effects of the anticancer drug *tamoxifen*. Patients diagnosed or at risk for these types of cancers should ask their doctors or a registered dietitian whether soy foods are appropriate.

The Breast Cancer Risk That's as Bad as the Gene

Chaya Moskowitz, PhD, associate attending biostatistician at Memorial Sloan Kettering Cancer Center in New York City and lead author of a study on breast cancer risk among childhood cancer survivors presented at a recent meeting of the American Society of Clinical Oncology.

I t's tough to think of kids battling cancer…but it's great to know that most children now beat the disease. Nevertheless, as they reach adulthood, some childhood cancer survivors need to be extra-wary about yet another cancer threat, a recent study reveals.

Researchers looked at long-term data (the median follow-up period was 26 years) on 1,268 female childhood cancer survivors who had been treated with radiation to the chest. It's not news that radiation raises a person's risk for future cancers—but what was surprising was the degree to which risk increased.

How the numbers stacked up: Among childhood cancer survivors who had received chest radiation, 24% developed breast cancer by age 50…the median age at diagnosis was just 38. Risk was especially elevated among women who as children got high doses of chest radiation to treat Hodgkin lymphoma (cancer of the immune system)—their rate of 30% was comparable to the 31% rate that the researchers estimated for women who carry the BRCA1 gene mutation.

It is worrisome to note that only about half of women treated with chest radiation as youngsters follow the current breast cancer screening guidelines from the Children's Oncology Group, a consortium supported by the National Cancer Institute. Those guidelines recommend that childhood cancer survivors who received 20 Gy (the unit of measure for radiation) or more to the chest area undergo twice-yearly clinical breast exams, annual mammograms and annual breast MRIs starting at age 25 or eight years after radiation, whichever comes later. And the new study findings suggest that these same guidelines also may be appropriate for women who were treated with lower chest radiation dosages, researchers said.

Childhood cancer survivors: Talk to your doctor about breast cancer screening—and make sure that he or she is aware of your chest radiation treatment history.

16

Heart Health and Stroke Alerts

Heart Disease: What Women—and Their Doctors—Often Overlook

Most women now know that heart disease is their single greatest health risk—greater than stroke and all cancers, including breast malignancies, combined.

However, many doctors still associate heart disease with men—and overlook it in women. That's partially because a woman's symptoms of heart disease or a heart attack are different from symptoms in men—but no less dangerous.

Consider these facts…

• **A woman has a one in two lifetime risk of dying from heart disease.** (Her lifetime risk of dying from breast cancer is one in 25.)

• **Women are twice as likely as men to die in the first few weeks following a heart attack.**

Fortunately, recent research has revealed ways to help protect women.

DELAYED ONSET

Heart disease in women tends to become apparent about 10 years later than it does for men. The same risk factors that cause men to have heart attacks in middle age are initially masked in women by the protective effects of estrogen, which is associated with healthy cholesterol levels. After menopause, sharp declines in estrogen dramatically increase a woman's risk for heart attack.

DIFFERENT SYMPTOMS

The "classic" heart attack symptoms, such as crushing chest pain or pain that radiates down an arm, can affect women, but is more common

Nieca Goldberg, MD, cardiologist and nationally recognized pioneer in women's heart health. Her New York City practice, Total Heart Care, focuses primarily on caring for women. Dr. Goldberg is clinical associate professor of medicine and medical director of the New York University Women's Heart Program. She is author of The Women's Healthy Heart Program *(Ballantine).*

in men. Women have their own classic symptoms, which doctors often fail to recognize.

They include...

- **Unusual fatigue.**
- **Heart palpitations.**
- **Pressure or pain in the upper abdomen.**
- **Back pain or symptoms resembling indigestion.**

Angina, mild to severe chest pain caused by insufficient blood to the heart and often the initial symptom of a heart attack, occurs less often in women than in men. Women are more likely than men to suffer *angina-equivalent* symptoms—shortness of breath, tightness or tingling in the arm and/or lower chest.

Doctors who don't recognize heart attack symptoms in women may delay lifesaving treatments—and women may not go to a hospital because they don't understand the significance of the symptoms.

MISSED RISK FACTORS

About 80% of women who die suddenly of a heart attack have modifiable risk factors, such as obesity or a history of smoking, but women are less likely to receive adequate counseling regarding preventive strategies.

Important: Because heart disease is strongly associated with lifestyle issues, women must begin addressing key risk factors, such as weight, exercise levels, diabetes and smoking, years before menopause.

DIFFERENT LIPID PROFILES

Elevated cholesterol levels can be associated with heart disease in men as well as in women—but elevated levels of blood fats known as triglycerides present a greater risk for women, even when their cholesterol levels are low. Women with high triglycerides also tend to have high total and LDL cholesterol, and low levels of HDL cholesterol.

Recommendation 1: A woman's triglycerides should be less than 150 mg/dL. Her HDL should be 50 mg/dL or higher, and her LDL should be less than 100 mg/dL. In men, triglycerides and LDL levels should be the same, and HDL should be 40 mg/dL or higher.

A recent study published in the journal *Circulation* found that nearly two-thirds of women

at very high risk for heart disease had unacceptably high levels of cholesterol, but only about one-third were receiving statins or other appropriate medication, as recommended by the American Heart Association.

Recommendation 2: Every woman age 20 or older should ask her doctor for a fasting lipoprotein profile, which measures total, LDL and HDL cholesterol, along with triglycerides (a 12-hour fast ensures that triglycerides are not falsely elevated). If the first test is normal, repeat it in five years. Abnormal tests are usually repeated in six months to a year, following medical or lifestyle interventions to control cholesterol and triglyceride levels.

INSUFFICIENT TESTING

When women undergo angiography, an imaging test that examines the blood vessels of the heart, doctors usually find that they have fewer diseased arteries than the typical male patient—yet women have a higher death rate from heart disease. This is primarily because women often have other conditions, such as hypertension, diabetes or even heart failure, that increase risk for heart attack and stroke but aren't treated as aggressively as they are in men.

Important: Every woman should know her blood pressure...her cholesterol levels...and other heart disease risk factors. If her doctor doesn't routinely order these tests—and recommend treatment when required—she should insist on it.

A standard test for heart disease is the exercise stress test, in which a person walks on a treadmill while being monitored by an electrocardiogram (ECG), a test that measures the electrical activity of the heartbeat.

The stress test increases the work of the heart and reveals angina or other symptoms that are present only during exertion. The test can help detect coronary artery disease in men about 90% of the time—but for reasons that are not yet known, it is not as accurate in women.

In about half of cases, women with coronary artery disease who receive an ECG during a stress test will appear to have normal coronary arteries. This false-negative reading may occur if a woman doesn't achieve a high enough heart rate during the test, or if beta blocker or other medications she's taking keep her heart rate artificially low.

Important: Women with heart disease symptoms should get a stress test that includes imaging studies, such as a nuclear exercise stress test (which involves the injection of a radioactive substance to produce images of the heart muscle) or an exercise echocardiogram (which uses ultrasound waves to view the heart). These tests provide more accurate results and are typically covered by insurance.

ASK ABOUT ASPIRIN

Doctors routinely recommend aspirin therapy for patients with an elevated risk for heart disease.

Recent finding: Aspirin does not reduce the risk for heart attack in healthy women under age 65...and is more likely to cause gastrointestinal upset or bleeding problems in women than in men. In women over age 65, the heart benefits of aspirin may outweigh the risks for stomach problems.

In my opinion, women with heart disease or risk factors benefit from taking aspirin. Get your doctor's advice before starting aspirin therapy.

OVERLOOKED STRESS

Women often must balance more life roles and responsibilities than men but may feel that they have less control at home or in the workplace. This situation can foster anxiety, anger or depression, all of which are major risk factors for heart disease, according to reliable scientific studies.

Elevated stress hormones, particularly cortisol and adrenaline, raise blood pressure and/or heart rate. Elevated cortisol levels also increase the coronary arteries' susceptibility to plaque buildup. Central adiposity, a condition associated with elevated cortisol and characterized by accumulations of abdominal fat, greatly increases heart disease risk.

Women with untreated depression and/or high levels of anxiety or stress should talk to a counselor or therapist. Social support also helps.

In a recent pilot study, women with heart disease participated in either coed exercise sessions using weight machines...or joined a women-only aerobics class. Levels of depression and anxiety were significantly decreased in the aerobics group, probably because of the social support the women got from working out with each other.

Best Time for a Stress Test

Get a treadmill stress test if you have two or more risk factors for heart disease—high blood pressure, high cholesterol, diabetes, family history, sedentary lifestyle, obesity, smoking or are over age 65. Also get tested if you notice any change in ability to do normal activities or any heart disease symptoms. Chest pain is the most common symptom—but in women, signs include shortness of breath, fatigue, nausea, and pain in the jaw, shoulder or back.

Suzanne Steinbaum, DO, attending cardiologist and director of the Women and Heart Disease Program at Lenox Hill Hospital in New York City and a leading expert on women and heart disease. www.srsheart.com

The Heart Disease Tests That Work Best for Women

Nieca Goldberg, MD, cardiologist and nationally recognized pioneer in women's heart health. Her New York City practice, Total Heart Care, focuses primarily on caring for women. Dr. Goldberg is clinical associate professor of medicine and medical director of the New York University Women's Heart Program. She is author of The Women's Healthy Heart Program (Ballantine).

Heart disease can sound so ominous that many women assume they have nothing to worry about if they are not suffering obvious symptoms, such as chest pain or shortness of breath. That's not so.

Although men who have heart disease typically develop symptoms in their 40s or 50s, women usually don't experience symptoms until their 60s—about 10 years after menopause.

But that does not mean that women's hearts are necessarily safe when they are younger.

What most women don't realize: Arteries can clog little by little, perhaps even starting in adolescence. That's why it's so important to start early to prevent heart disease.

DIAGNOSIS DILEMMAS

Part of the problem in diagnosing heart disease in women is that its symptoms can be so vague—fatigue, shortness of breath during exertion, anxiety, light-headedness. It's common for a woman to go from doctor to doctor but hear repeatedly that the problem is "just nerves," ordinary fatigue or stress.

If you experience any of the symptoms above, make an appointment with your doctor and insist on being evaluated for heart disease.

There is no single test for heart disease. Among the many possible diagnostic tools are tests for blood pressure, cholesterol levels, heart rhythm, heart muscle function and blood vessel problems. Some work well for women—and some do not. *What you must know...*

• **Electrocardiogram (ECG).** This test gives a graphic record of the heart's electrical impulses and is commonly used to see if the heart is damaged. It is quick, painless and noninvasive. However, even when a woman does have heart disease, her ECG may appear normal.

• **Exercise ECG (stress test).** Sometimes the earliest signs of heart disease are evident only when a person is active. This type of ECG can detect clogged arteries by measuring heart function and blood pressure while you walk on a treadmill.

Sometimes this test is unreliable in women, so you may be sent for a *nuclear exercise electrocardiogram* (in which a radioactive substance is injected during exercise) to confirm the result. This test is more accurate than a regular stress test but may give false-positive results in large-breasted women.

Another concern: Even after a positive stress test, doctors are less likely to send women for more testing.

• **Angiogram.** This test is typically used in people who have abnormal stress test results. A dye is injected into the arteries and an X-ray is taken, allowing the doctor to see the degree of arterial blockage caused by the buildup of cholesterol.

However, women with heart disease can have "normal" angiogram results. That is because a woman's cholesterol plaque tends to be more evenly distributed throughout the arteries than a man's is. When this occurs, arteries can be stiffened and diseased by excess cholesterol, but the test might not show it. In addition, women are more likely to have disease in the tiny arteries of the heart—a condition that is difficult to detect.

If you have symptoms of heart disease but previous tests are inconclusive, consider requesting a newer test called computed tomography (CT) coronary angiography. It creates 3-D images of blockages in the arteries. Unfortunately, the test is not typically covered by health insurance and costs approximately $2,000.

BEST TREATMENTS

If you have heart disease, your prognosis largely depends on how quickly and effectively you are treated. *Options include...*

• **Medication.** A variety of drugs—such as beta-blockers, calcium channel blockers, nitroglycerin preparations, aspirin and cholesterol-lowering statins—may be prescribed either by themselves or in some combination to help control heart disease.

Problem: Most big studies on heart disease medication have been conducted on men, not women—so there is little accurate information about the drugs' effects on women. For instance, despite generally being smaller in size, women often are given the same dosages as men—increasing women's risk for side effects, such as insomnia and depression.

Solution: To minimize risk for side effects, ask your doctor to start with the lowest effective dose and then increase the dose only as needed.

• **Surgery.** *Common surgical procedures for heart disease include...*

• Angioplasty, in which a deflated balloon is inserted into a blocked artery and expanded, pushing the blockage aside.

• Stenting, in which a small mesh tube is inserted to hold the artery open.

• Coronary bypass surgery, in which disease-free blood vessels from your leg or elsewhere in the body are used to "bypass" blocked heart arteries.

Problems: Women who undergo bypass surgery have a higher risk for stroke during and after surgery than men—in part because they may be more likely to have untreated high blood pressure or diabetes. After heart surgery, women also are more likely to experience postsurgical internal bleeding and/or continue having heart disease symptoms.

Strategy: These problems should not prevent you from getting one of these procedures if it is needed. Afterward, however, your doctor should monitor you with extra care.

Self-defense: If you have heart disease, it is best to be treated by a cardiologist. To find one near you, contact the American Medical Association (800-621-8335, *www.ama-assn.org*).

HEART ATTACK WARNING SIGNS

Even when heart disease leads to a heart attack, symptoms may not be recognized. A study published in the journal *Circulation* showed that among the 515 women studied who had a heart attack, 78% had at least one of the symptoms listed below a month or more before the attack.

The following heart attack symptoms are common in women—but too many doctors fail to identify them...

• **Unusual fatigue.**

• **Any unusual breathlessness during normal activities or at rest.**

• **Nausea.**

• **Dizziness.**

• **Lower chest discomfort.**

• **Back pain.**

• **Upper abdominal pressure or discomfort.**

The "classic" heart attack symptoms below apply to both men and women...

• **Pressure or pain in the center of the chest,** spreading to the neck, shoulder or jaw.

• **Chest discomfort with nausea, sweating or fainting.**

If you think you may be experiencing symptoms of a heart attack, call 911. Too many women worry unnecessarily about feeling embarrassed if they go to the hospital and their "heart attack" turns out to be nothing.

Don't Overlook This Test

Women 65 and older with a history of heart disease or who have ever smoked should be screened for abdominal aortic aneurysm (AAA), advises K. Craig Kent, MD. An AAA is a bubblelike swelling in the aorta (the main artery).

Burst AAAs kill 30,000 Americans every year. Because the majority of victims are older men, Medicare pays for AAA screening only for men ages 65 to 75 who have ever smoked. But women who are at risk should consider paying for the test themselves—the five- to 10-minute test costs only $40 to $50.

K. Craig Kent, MD, chief of vascular surgery, New York–Presbyterian Hospital/Weill Cornell Medical Center, New York City, and leader of a study of 17,540 people, published in Journal of Vascular Surgery.

Low Testosterone May Raise Heart Disease Risk

In a recent study, postmenopausal women who had low levels of free testosterone (the amount not bound to blood proteins) were twice as likely to have coronary heart disease or to suffer a stroke or heart attack as women with higher levels.

Gail Laughlin, PhD, assistant professor of family and preventive medicine, University of California, San Diego, and leader of a study of 678 women, reported in The Medical Post.

Heart Disease, the #1 Killer of Women

Harvey S. Hecht, MD, FACC, director, cardiovascular computed tomography, Lenox Hill Heart and Vascular Institute of New York, and past president of the Society for Atherosclerosis Imaging.

With all the fund-raising and public relations efforts surrounding breast cancer, women often overlook their number-one killer—heart disease. The reality is that one-third of all women develop cardiovascular problems by age 45. And each year, more women die from heart disease than from the next seven causes of death combined. We naively think of cardiac issues as a male problem. Not even close…women face special challenges with heart disease.

VAGUE SYMPTOMS CAN BE MISLEADING

A major concern is that women experience much more subtle heart attack symptoms than do men. In place of or in addition to chest discomfort, women may have shortness of breath, fatigue, back discomfort, nausea and dizziness. These complaints are often underestimated by both women and their doctors or are mistaken for signs of other disorders.

Harvey S. Hecht, MD, FACC, warns that this can be a life-threatening error, as timing is everything when it comes to heart attack intervention. The sooner the treatment, the better your chances of survival. The hope is that women will team up with their doctors to prevent heart disease, and with increased awareness, they will also be better equipped to recognize dangerous warning signs.

HEART-HEALTHY GUIDELINES

Finally dispensing with the one-size-fits-all perspective, the American Heart Association (AHA) issued guidelines to aggressively reduce the risk for heart disease and stroke in women. The guidelines urge women to get regular heart checkups, during which blood pressure and cholesterol levels are evaluated, just as they get regular breast exams…and to treat risk factors, such as high blood cholesterol and high blood pressure, at lower thresholds than in the past.

The guidelines base the aggressiveness of treatment on whether a woman is at a low, intermediate or high degree of risk for heart attack within the next 10 years, according to a standardized scoring method developed by the Framingham Heart Study in Massachusetts.

Risk is based on such factors as age, blood pressure, cholesterol levels and smoking status. Low risk means that a woman has a less than 10% chance of suffering a heart attack within the next 10 years…intermediate risk is a 10% to 20% chance…and high risk means that a woman is at a greater than 20% risk of suffering a heart attack within the next 10 years.

The American Heart Association's recommendations include…

•**All women should be assessed** for their heart disease risk beginning as early as age 20. They should get regular heart checkups along with their annual physical exam from a physician.

•**If blood pressure measures 140/90 or higher,** women should take antihypertensive (blood-pressure-lowering) medication.

•**Because of the risk of bleeding,** strokes and stomach problems, only women at high risk should take aspirin daily.

•**Women should not take hormone-replacement therapy (HRT)** to prevent heart disease. Recent studies have indicated that HRT may actually have harmful consequences to women's cardiovascular health.

•**Since they have shown no individual heart-healthy benefits** in several large clinical trials, the guidelines are not in favor of beta-carotene or vitamin E supplements.

•**All women should follow a healthy diet,** get regular exercise and refrain from smoking.

EARLY SCREENING IS OPTIMAL

Dr. Hecht is also a strong believer in early screening and treatment. He is a leader in the development of electron beam tomography (EBT), a new screening tool that does not use needles or dyes, and is 98% accurate in detecting coronary artery disease in its earliest stages. Available in most major cities, the scan works by detecting the presence of coronary calcium, an indicator of plaque. When plaque composed of fatty cholesterol and calcium deposits accumulates on the walls of arteries, blood vessels narrow. The plaque can then rupture, causing a heart attack.

Dr. Hecht recommends EBT for all women over the age of 55...women age 45 and over with any risk factors...and women under age 45 with a striking family history of premature heart disease (such as a parent, brother or sister who had a heart attack).

Early screening also makes early intervention possible, and Dr. Hecht is a strong advocate of "interventional lipidology," a practice that combines early detection of coronary atherosclerosis by EBT with aggressive drug treatment of cholesterol disorders.

PREVENTION AND INTERVENTION: THE EARLIER, THE BETTER

To prevent heart disease, Dr. Hecht recommends adhering to a heart-healthy diet, exercise, weight control and no smoking. If screening indicates that a woman is at high risk for a heart attack, he strongly advises taking more aggressive measures, such as using medication to control cholesterol. If symptoms of a heart attack occur, remember that every second counts—call 911 and get immediate assistance.

For more about women and heart disease, visit the Web site *www.heart.org*.

Heart Warning—Don't Drink to Excess

Women who drank alcohol to the point of intoxication at least once a month were six times as likely to suffer a heart attack (not necessarily while drinking) as women who drank at least monthly but not enough to be intoxicated.

Best: Never drink to the point of intoxication.

Joan M. Dorn, PhD, associate professor, department of social and preventive medicine, University of Buffalo, and leader of a study of 1,885 women, published in *Addiction*.

The Hidden Condition Doctors Miss— Microvascular Disease

C. Noel Bairey Merz, MD, director of the Women's Heart Center and the Preventive and Rehabilitative Cardiac Center at Cedars-Sinai Heart Institute in Los Angeles and professor of medicine at the David Geffen School of Medicine at University of California, Los Angeles.

You're awake (again!) in the middle of the night, worrying about your finances, when suddenly you feel a stab of pain in your chest. It's not the first time such chest discomfort has accompanied stress. What's happening?

Answer: You may have small vessel heart disease, or coronary *microvascular disease* (MVD). By impairing blood flow in the heart's tiniest arteries—the twigs of the arterial tree—MVD can lead to a heart attack or heart failure.

When the Women's Ischemic Syndrome Evaluation (WISE) study began several years ago, MVD was found to play a major role in heart disease in women. You may never have heard of MVD—and your primary care physician may know next to nothing about it—even though it affects up to three million American women, most of them over age 45. *What women must know about this potentially deadly disease...*

WOMEN'S ARTERIES ARE DIFFERENT

Scientists don't yet know the exact cause of MVD, but they are focusing on several likely factors. Because men are far less prone to MVD, a key to understanding the disease seems to lie in the ways in which arteries differ between the sexes. *Women's arteries are...*

• **More likely to spasm.** Women have much larger variations in hormone levels, day to day and over a lifetime, than men do. Such variations may affect arteries, which have hormone receptors, and lead to *vascular reactivity*— arteries that are likely to spasm, limiting or halting blood flow.

• **Smaller.** It is not only that women, on average, are smaller than men. Even after adjusting for average body area, women have relatively smaller arteries—perhaps because they have less *testosterone*, a hormone that powers tissue growth. The tinier the blood vessel, the more vulnerable it is to spasm.

•**Prone to smoother plaque.** Plaque is a fatty material that builds up on inner walls of arteries, impairing blood flow. In men, plaque typically forms big lumps. Although women may have as much plaque as men, in women it often spreads out smoothly and evenly—which makes it harder to detect.

DIFFICULT TO DIAGNOSE

Many women with MVD have the classic signs of heart disease—*angina* (chest pain) and/or shortness of breath upon minor exertion, such as when walking up stairs. To check for heart disease, doctors typically begin with a *stress test*, which measures heart function and blood pressure while the patient walks on a treadmill. If results suggest a problem, the patient is given an *angiogram*—an injection of dye into the arteries followed by an X-ray to detect blockages.

Problems: With MVD, the angiogram may not find threatening obstructions in large blood vessels because smooth plaque is not easily detected…and the test may not be sensitive enough to find abnormalities in small blood vessels.

Result: The woman is assured that she does not have heart disease—though in fact she does. Because she goes untreated, she continues to be at high risk for heart attack or heart failure.

What many doctors don't know: Persistent chest pain and an abnormal stress test *are* indications of MVD—and sufficient reason for treatment—even when the angiogram is normal.

Many doctors also are not aware that about 50% of women with MVD do *not* have the typical "exertional" symptoms. Instead, these women have angina when they're upset or stressed—even if they are sitting or lying down.

Reason: Anxiety or stress can trigger the release of stress hormones, such as *adrenaline*, that can affect the small blood vessels and bring on angina. Yet doctors may not recognize the link between this type of "nonexertional" chest pain and heart disease.

Self-defense: If you have persistent chest pain but your doctor says that you don't have heart disease, get a second opinion. This is especially important if your doctor attributes your symptoms to heartburn, hiatal hernia or gallbladder disease even though tests do not confirm any of those diagnoses and treating those conditions does not stop the pain. To find a cardiologist who is knowledgeable about MVD, I suggest contacting a top medical center for a referral.*

Best: A *coronary reactivity test* is the gold standard for determining the extent and severity of—and the most appropriate treatment for—MVD. First, a wire is inserted into a coronary artery and blood flow is measured…then a substance that dilates small blood vessels is injected, and blood flow is measured again. Currently, the test is available at only a limited number of medical centers. As knowledge of MVD increases, the test should become more widely available. Ask your cardiologist if this test is appropriate for you. Insurance may cover the test.

MVD TREATMENTS

Treatment of MVD aims to ease symptoms and reduce risk factors for heart attack and heart failure. *Treatment may include…*

•**Lifestyle changes.** As with any form of heart disease, follow your doctor's guidelines for eating a heart-healthy diet with no more than 30% of calories from fat…doing aerobic exercise, such as brisk walking, for 30 minutes a day…maintaining a healthy weight… managing stress…and not smoking.

•**Medication.** *Your doctor may prescribe one or more drugs…*

•A beta-blocker to block the action of adrenaline, thereby slowing heartbeat, lowering blood pressure and easing angina.

•An ACE inhibitor to reduce heart attack risk by blocking production of angiotensin, a compound that narrows arteries.

*Among the top medical centers that treat MVD are Cedars-Sinai Medical Center in Los Angeles…Emory University Hospital in Atlanta…Harvard Medical School's Brigham and Women's Hospital in Boston…Mayo Clinic in Rochester, Minnesota…Stanford University School of Medicine in Stanford, California…and University of Florida at Gainesville.

• Baby aspirin, taken at 81 milligrams (mg) daily, to reduce the risk for artery-clogging blood clots.

• Statin medication to lower LDL "bad" cholesterol.

• Ranolazine, nitroglycerine and/or a calcium channel blocker to improve blood flow.

• **Enhanced external counterpulsation therapy (EECP).** Inflatable pressure cuffs are wrapped around the legs from the calves up to the hips. The cuffs inflate and deflate in time with the heartbeat, improving circulation and blood vessel health.

Drawback: EECP treatment requires a one-hour session, five days a week, for seven weeks. While EECP has not been clinically tested specifically for MVD, it has been proven to be effective for easing angina in cases of heart failure—and many experts say that EECP has helped their MVD patients whose angina was not sufficiently relieved by lifestyle changes and medication.

Half a Million Heart Attacks Per Year...and Most Have No Prior Symptoms

Prediman K. Shah, MD, director of the division of cardiology and the Atherosclerosis Research Center at Cedars-Sinai Heart Center in Los Angeles. He is a professor of medicine at the David Geffen School of Medicine at the University of California, Los Angeles, and was the leader of the Screening for Heart Attack Prevention and Education (SHAPE) Task Force editorial committee.

Up to 50% of people who have a first heart attack—which often results in sudden death—don't experience prior chest pain, shortness of breath or other red flags for cardiovascular disease. A heart attack is their first and only symptom.

In the past, cardiologists relied solely on the presence of risk factors—a family history of heart disease, smoking, diabetes, etc.—to identify "silent" heart disease.

Recent approach: An international task force of leading cardiologists has issued new guidelines that could prevent more than 90,000 deaths from cardiovascular disease each year in the US. Most of these patients have no prior symptoms.

RISK FACTORS AREN'T ENOUGH

Most heart attacks and many strokes are caused by atherosclerosis, buildup of cholesterol and other substances (plaque) within artery walls.

Over time, increasing accumulations of plaque can compromise circulation—or result in blood clots that block circulation to the heart (heart attack) or brain (stroke).

Plaque can accumulate for decades within artery walls without causing the arterial narrowing that results in angina (chest pain) or other symptoms. Even patients with massive amounts of plaque may be unaware that they have heart disease until they suffer a heart attack or sudden death.

RECOMMENDED TESTS

Guidelines created by the Society for Heart Attack Prevention and Eradication (SHAPE) Task Force call for noninvasive screening of virtually *all* asymptomatic men ages 45 to 75 and women ages 55 to 75.* The tests can detect arterial changes that are present in the vast majority of heart attack patients. The SHAPE Task Force identified two tests—a computed tomography (CT) scan of the coronary arteries and an ultrasound of the carotid arteries in the neck—that are more accurate than traditional risk-factor assessments in identifying high-risk patients.

Most patients require only one of these tests. Which test is recommended will depend on insurance coverage and/or other underlying health conditions and risk factors. Although these tests are widely available, health insurers do not always cover the cost, which ranges from about $200 to $400 each.

• **Coronary artery screening.** Calcium within the coronary arteries always indicates that a patient has atherosclerosis (whether or

*Screening for adults age 75 or older is not recommended because they are considered at high risk for cardiovascular disease based on their age alone.

471

not blockages are present). Calcium is a marker of actual disease, not just the *risk* of disease.

What's involved: The patient is given a CT scan of the heart and three coronary arteries. Undressing isn't required—the test is noninvasive and takes about five to 10 minutes.

Dozens of images are taken during the test and then analyzed with computer software. If calcium is present, it's given a score based on severity. A score of 0 is ideal…less than 100 indicates moderate atherosclerosis…100 to 400 represents a significant problem…and more than 400 is severe.

In patients with a score of 0 (no calcium is present), the risk of having a heart attack or stroke over the next 10 years is 0.1%. Patients with a score of 400 or higher are 20 to 30 times more likely to have a heart attack or stroke than those with a score of 0.**

•**Carotid ultrasound.** This test measures the *intima media thickness* (the gap between the inside of the blood vessel wall and a layer called the media) of the carotid arteries. It also measures the amount of plaque that may be present.

A thickening of the intima media (the values are adjusted for age and sex) is a predictor of stroke as well as heart attack. The presence of any plaque is a red flag—patients who have plaque in the carotid arteries generally will also show evidence of plaque in the coronary arteries.

What's involved: The patient lies on an examination table while a technician moves a *transducer* (a device that emits and receives ultrasound signals) over the carotid arteries on both sides of the neck. Like the CT scan, the test is noninvasive. It takes about 45 to 90 minutes to complete.

TREATING SILENT HEART DISEASE

With screening tests, doctors can target high-risk patients more precisely—and recommend appropriate treatment. The aggressiveness of treatment should be proportionate to the risk level.

**Coronary artery calcium scoring is not recommended as a screening tool for coronary heart disease in low-risk patients because of high false-positive rates. It may be recommended for intermediate/high-risk individuals. See your doctor.

It's possible that drugs to reduce levels of existing plaque will be on the market within the next few years. *Until then, patients diagnosed with asymptomatic cardiovascular disease (based on one of the above tests) should…*

•**Get a stress test.** Patients who test positive for calcium or plaque in the coronary or carotid arteries should undergo a cardiac stress test. The test, which uses an electrocardiogram, involves walking on a treadmill or riding a bicycle. The test detects impediments in circulation through the coronary arteries and identifies abnormal heart rhythms (arrhythmias) that can occur during exercise in patients with heart disease. Nuclear stress tests (which involve the use of radioactive dye) or echocardiogram (a type of ultrasound) stress tests generally are more reliable than simple electrocardiogram tests.

Patients with significant blockages in the coronary arteries may require invasive procedures, such as angioplasty or bypass surgery, to restore normal circulation to the heart.

•**Control cholesterol and blood pressure.** They're two important risk factors for heart attack and stroke—and both are modifiable with medication and/or lifestyle changes. A patient who tests positive for asymptomatic cardiovascular disease needs to treat these conditions much more aggressively than someone without it. For cardiovascular health, aim for a blood pressure of no more than 110 mmHg to 120 mmHg systolic (top number) and 70 mmHg to 80 mmHg diastolic (bottom number). An ideal LDL "bad" cholesterol level is no more than 70.

Most patients can significantly lower blood pressure and cholesterol with lifestyle changes—exercising for 30 minutes at least three to four times a week…losing weight, if necessary …eating less saturated fat and/or trans fat… and increasing consumption of fruits, vegetables, whole grains and fish.

Other risk factors to control: Smoking, obesity, diabetes, as well as emotional stress/ anger, which may lead to a heart attack or angina. It's important to control all of these risk factors because they can amplify each other— for example, a sedentary lifestyle promotes obesity, which can lead to diabetes—or have a cumulative effect that's much more dangerous than an individual risk factor.

For more on silent heart disease, consult the Society for Heart Attack Prevention and Eradication, a nonprofit group that promotes heart disease education and research, 877-742-7311, *www.shapesociety.org.*

"Runner's High" May Help Your Heart

In a recent study on rats, *opioids*—the body chemicals created when you do strenuous aerobic exercise that cause the euphoria called "runner's high"—appear to protect the heart from damage if a heart attack occurs.

Eric Dickson, MD, head, department of emergency medicine, University of Iowa, Iowa City, and leader of a study published in *American Journal of Physiology: Heart and Circulatory Physiology.*

Never Have a Stroke— Specific Steps For Women

Lori Mosca, MD, PhD, MPH, director of the New York–Presbyterian Hospital Preventive Cardiology Program in New York City, *www.hearthealthtimes.com.* She is professor of medicine at Columbia University Medical Center, past-chair of the American Heart Association Council on Epidemiology, and author of *Heart to Heart: A Personal Plan for Creating a Heart-Healthy Family* (HCI).

For women, stroke prevention is even more important than it is for men. There are steps you can take now to reduce your risk.

Reasons: Between the ages of 45 and 54, women are more than twice as likely as men to have a stroke, according to a recent study from the University of California, Los Angeles. Even when treated with state-of-the-art medication, women of all ages are at greater risk than men for suffering serious disability after a stroke. And regardless of age, female stroke patients are more likely to die than male stroke patients are. *What you need to know...*

STROKE PREVENTION STRATEGIES

A stroke is a "brain attack" that occurs when a blood vessel that carries oxygen and nutrients to the brain gets blocked by a clot (an ischemic stroke) or leaks or bursts (a hemorrhagic stroke). Either way, cells in the affected area of the brain are starved of oxygen. This can impair a person's ability to function, often irreparably.

Risk factors for stroke build up over years, even decades. *To slash your stroke risk...*

1. Know your numbers. Get a checkup that includes tests for the risk factors below. *Discuss with your doctor how your results compare with these ideal measurements...*

- **Blood pressure**—less than 130/80.
- **Total cholesterol**—less than 200.
- **LDL (bad) cholesterol**—no more than 100 for most women.
- **HDL (good) cholesterol**—greater than 50.
- **Triglycerides (blood fats)**—less than 150.
- **Fasting blood glucose (sugar)**—less than 100.
- **Body mass index (a ratio of height to weight)**—18.5 to 24.9, with higher numbers indicating excessive weight. Calculate your body mass index at *www.nhlbi.nih.gov* (search "BMI Calculator").
- **Waist circumference**—35 inches or less.

2. Determine your risk level based on new American Heart Association (AHA) guidelines. This will help you and your doctor develop a personalized prevention program.

- You're at high risk if you've already had a stroke...or have diabetes or coronary heart disease.
- You're at risk if you smoke...have high blood pressure...or have a condition called metabolic syndrome, characterized by symptoms such as a thick waist, higher-than-normal blood glucose, high triglycerides and low HDL cholesterol.
- Your risk factor level is optimal if you eat a heart-healthy diet...exercise regularly...and have none of the risk factors listed above.

For more risk-assessment tools, visit *www.hearthealthtimes.com*, the Web site for the New York–Presbyterian Hospital Preventive Cardiology Program.

3. Exercise every day at moderate intensity. Being active helps lower blood pressure and keeps your weight in check.

Concern: Being overweight by as little as 10 pounds boosts stroke risk. To lose weight, you should log 60 to 90 minutes of exercise daily. Consistency is important because it keeps blood vessels healthy and metabolism functioning optimally.

4. Eat to beat stroke. Build your diet mostly on fruits, vegetables and whole grains. Eat fish twice a week, preferably fatty kinds, such as herring. Limit sodium to less than 2,300 mg a day by reducing salt added to foods and avoiding high-sodium prepared foods (check nutrition labels). Avoid trans fats, such as partially hydrogenated vegetable oils and shortening. Keep saturated fat low—less than 7% of total calories if possible—by limiting meats and nonskim dairy foods. Consume no more than 300 mg daily of dietary cholesterol. Limit alcohol to one drink daily. Avoid fried foods. Opt for baked, boiled, broiled, steamed or sautéed foods.

5. Make informed decisions about medications that affect hormones. Taking estrogen for menopausal symptoms or a selective estrogen receptor modulator (SERM), such as *tamoxifen*, for breast cancer treatment may raise stroke risk. The longer you take such medications, the greater your risk.

6. Consider aspirin. For women age 65 and over, taking aspirin daily (typically 75 mg to 162 mg) may prevent the blood clots that cause the most common type of stroke and may protect against heart disease. Aspirin therapy also may make sense for women under age 65 who are at high risk for stroke.

Do not take aspirin without first discussing it with your doctor. Aspirin therapy can *increase* your risk for stroke if you have uncontrolled high blood pressure. It also can cause gastrointestinal bleeding. That's why women under age 65 who are not at high risk for stroke generally are advised against taking daily aspirin—the risks may outweigh the benefits.

7. Stop smoking. Smoking increases blood pressure and blood clotting, both of which can set the stage for stroke. Women who smoke and take oral contraceptives are at even greater risk for stroke. Studies show that the more individual, group or telephone smoking-cessation counseling you get, the better your chances of quitting.

Helpful: Use medication, such as nicotine replacement, to reduce cravings.

8. Don't ignore troubling symptoms, such as heart palpitations. A common risk factor for stroke is atrial fibrillation (AF)—an irregular, rapid heart rhythm that causes abnormal blood flow and increases the likelihood of a clot. AF increases a woman's stroke risk fivefold. Other AF symptoms include light-headedness, weakness, confusion and/or difficulty breathing. If you have symptoms of AF, see your doctor—blood-thinning drugs, such as aspirin or *warfarin* (Coumadin), can lower your risk for clots and stroke.

9. Talk to your doctor about other medications that reduce risk factors. If efforts to improve your lifestyle habits aren't enough to reduce your risk, talk to your doctor about adding drug therapy. For instance, thiazide diuretics and other prescription drugs can help control blood pressure…niacin or fibrate medication can increase HDL (good) cholesterol.

More from Dr. Lori Mosca…

One Word That Can Save a Life —FAST

Stroke is a medical emergency that requires immediate care. Brain cells starved of oxygen die and do not regenerate. *To remember the sudden symptoms of stroke, think of the word "FAST"…*

• **Face.** Sudden numbness or weakness of the face, especially on one side…severe headache…dizziness…vision trouble.

• **Arm and leg.** Sudden numbness or weakness of the arm and/or leg, especially on one side…trouble walking…loss of coordination.

•**Speech.** Sudden confusion and trouble speaking or understanding speech.

•**Time.** Time is critical—if you think you or someone else is having a stroke, call 911.

Latest Developments in Stroke Rehab

Michael Reding, MD, associate professor of neurology at Weill Medical College of Cornell University, New York City. He is medical director of the Stroke Rehabilitation Program at the Burke Rehabilitation Hospital, one of the premier rehabilitation centers in the country, White Plains, New York.

Most stroke patients require rehabilitation to recover their physical skills and to regain the ability to live independently. Recent developments in stroke rehabilitation are helping patients recover better and faster, perhaps even several years after the stroke.

The following therapies are the latest approaches to stroke recovery. Check with the stroke centers in your area about what is available.

ARMS AND LEGS

Stroke patients often require physical therapy for arm or leg weakness or immobility. Repetitive physical movements prevent muscle atrophy and enhance brain cells in the area surrounding the stroke damage. *Breakthrough therapies....*

•**Robotic therapy.** MIT researchers have developed the tabletop robot MIT-Manus, which significantly improves arm mobility—and may be more effective than conventional physical therapy.

How it works: The patient puts his/her lower arm and wrist into a brace attached to the robot. A video screen prompts the patient to perform arm exercises, such as connecting dots on the screen. The robot monitors movement and increases or decreases resistance as required—and even moves the arm if the patient is unable to do so. The robot can move the arm thousands of times in a single session and detects (and responds to) movements and muscle tension that are too subtle for the patient to notice.

Patients who use robotic therapy have muscle strength scores that are about twice as high as those undergoing traditional physical therapy.

Most patients enjoy the interactive nature of this "video game" therapy. It gives immediate feedback and boosts their motivation to keep trying. Between 18 and 36 sessions are needed.

•**Bilateral arm training with rhythmic auditory cueing (BATRAC).** When patients move both the damaged arm and the healthy arm together (bilateral movement), the healthy side of the brain promotes better functioning in the side damaged by stroke.

How it works: The patient works with an occupational therapist for about an hour several days a week. He performs movements to the beat of a metronome or other auditory device. He moves both arms simultaneously—for example, moving arms away from the body, then moving them back in. Early studies indicate that patients treated with BATRAC have greater improvements in upper-extremity motor function than those treated with conventional therapy.

•**Constraint-induced movement therapy.** When a stroke victim has trouble moving a limb, damage to the brain's sensory cortex may cause him to lose awareness of that hand, arm or leg—and he stops moving it entirely.

How it works: In constraint-induced therapy, placing the healthy limb in a sling forces the patient to use the disabled limb and thereby regain movement control. This approach requires the patient to practice for up to six hours a day for several weeks. He might be asked to pick up a block of wood, sweep floors, throw balls or draw pictures repeatedly.

The therapy is performed in a clinic setting, often in groups to encourage participation and enhance motivation. Studies show that this approach results in improvements in motor function and muscle strength.

WALKING

Patients in conventional rehabilitation programs typically use canes or leg braces for support. For safety reasons, they walk slowly, and they may not reach their optimal level of recovery.

• **Body weight support.** With body weight support, patients can more than double their speed. Faster walking hastens recovery and prepares patients for the types of movements they will need in daily life, such as quickly crossing a street.

How it works: The patient is suspended in a harness attached to a weight-support system. The harness prevents the patient from falling, so he can increase the speed of the treadmill and push himself harder. The harness adjusts to support more or less of the patient's body weight, depending on his progress.

SWALLOWING

Many patients experience difficulty swallowing (dysphagia). Traditionally, speech therapists teach patients how to initiate normal swallowing movements.

• **VitalStim therapy.** Electricity applied to the neck stimulates the muscles involved in swallowing to activate at the appropriate times. This approach is effective in as little as one week.

How it works: Electrodes are placed on the neck. Electrical currents stimulate muscles in the throat to contract. The treatment, lasting 20 to 30 minutes, may be repeated 10 or more times over a week. It retrains the brain to stimulate involuntary swallowing movements.

Drawbacks: This does not work for all patients. Many require speech therapy sessions. Also, the treatment may be uncomfortable—it causes a feeling of tightness in the neck, as though one is being grabbed by the throat.

VISION

• **Visual retraining.** Stroke victims who suffer vision damage can gain significant improvement from a technique called visual retraining, or vision restoration therapy.

How it works: The patient fixes his eyes on a spot on a monitor, then clicks a button when he becomes aware that another dot has appeared in the periphery. This stimulates neurons in the visual center of the brain. Sessions usually are 30 minutes, twice daily, for six months.

A study presented at the American Stroke Association International Conference in February reported that patients were able to detect 62% of the peripheral dots after six months, compared with 54% when they began. Follow-up studies show that 70% of patients maintain the improvement more than a year later.

BEWARE OF DEPRESSION

Depression is common in stroke patients in the first year. One study found that patients who suffer poststroke depression are 3.5 times more likely to die within 10 years than those who aren't depressed.

Stroke patients should be evaluated for depression and, if diagnosed, given appropriate treatment—therapy and/or antidepressants. Treatment can greatly improve patients' motivation and increase their rate of recovery.

The Latest Blood Pressure Control Diet

C. Tissa Kappagoda, MD, PhD, professor of medicine, preventive cardiology program, University of California, Davis. Dr. Kappagoda has published more than 150 medical journal articles on heart health.

For the first time, high blood pressure that is uncontrolled is more common in women than in men—yet women are less likely to be prescribed treatment, such as blood pressure–lowering medication. High blood pressure, or hypertension, doesn't hurt or cause other obvious warning signs, but it damages arteries in ways that can lead to stroke, heart attack, kidney problems and cognitive impairment. *More concerns for women...*

• **Hypertension now affects nearly one in four American women.** Rates in women are rising even as rates in men are falling.

• **About 35% of women with hypertension go untreated.**

Blood pressure is the force that blood exerts against the arterial walls. It is reported as two numbers. The top number, or *systolic pressure*, is the pressure as the heart pumps. The bottom number, or *diastolic pressure*, is the pressure as the heart rests between beats. Normal, healthy blood pressure is below 120/80 millimeters of mercury (mmHg)…hypertension is diagnosed at 140/90 mmHg or higher.

Problem: Up to 70% of people who are told that they are fine because their blood pressure is in the "high normal" range actually are *at serious risk*. Systolic pressure of 120 to 139 and/or diastolic pressure of 80 to 89 indicates *prehypertension*—which often progresses to hypertension.

Good news: You can significantly reduce blood pressure by changing what you eat. You must do more than just cut back on salt —although following this common advice helps—but the simple strategies below are worth the effort.

If you already have hypertension or have "high normal" blood pressure…are at risk due to being overweight or having a family history of blood pressure problems…or simply want to be as healthy as possible, this diet is for you.

Bonus: These habits often lead to weight loss—which also lowers blood pressure.

HAVE MORE…

• **Berries.** Berries are high in *polyphenols*, micronutrients that relax blood vessels.

Study: Hypertension patients who ate berries daily for two months lowered their systolic blood pressure by up to seven points—which could reduce risk for heart-related death by up to 15%.

Action: Eat one cup of fresh or frozen berries daily.

• **Fat-free milk.** A study found that people who ingested the greatest amounts of low-fat dairy were 56% less likely to develop hypertension than those who ate the least.

Theory: The active components may be the milk proteins *whey* and/or *casein*, which help blood vessels dilate.

Action: Have eight to 16 ounces of fat-free milk per day. Evidence suggests that fat-free milk is best—higher fat milk and other dairy products may not work as well.

• **Potassium-rich produce.** Potassium counteracts the blood pressure–raising effects of sodium.

Recent study: Prehypertension patients with the highest sodium-to-potassium intake were up to 50% more likely to develop cardiovascular disease within 10 to 15 years, compared with those who had the lowest ratio.

Action: Among the generally recommended five or so daily servings of fruits and vegetables, include some potassium-rich choices, such as bananas, citrus fruits, lima beans, potatoes and sweet potatoes (with skin), tomatoes and yams. Talk to your doctor before increasing potassium if you take blood pressure or heart medication (diuretic, ACE inhibitor or ARB blocker) or if you have kidney problems.

• **Fiber.** Studies suggest that fiber lowers blood pressure, though the mechanism is unknown. The fiber must come from food—fiber supplements do not offer the same benefit.

Action: Check food labels, and aim for at least 25 grams of fiber daily.

Good sources: Whole fruits (juice has less fiber)…raw or lightly cooked vegetables (overcooking reduces fiber)…beans and lentils… high-fiber breakfast cereals…and whole grains, such as barley, brown rice, oats, quinoa and whole wheat.

EAT LESS…

• **Meat.** Often high in cholesterol and saturated fat, meat contributes to the buildup of plaque inside arteries—a condition called *atherosclerosis*. Hypertension significantly increases the risk that atherosclerosis will lead to a heart attack or stroke.

Action: If you have been diagnosed with both atherosclerosis and hypertension, a good way to reduce your cardiovascular risk is to adopt a vegetarian or near-vegetarian diet.

Also: Avoid other sources of saturated fats, such as high-fat dairy, and palm oil.

If you are concerned about getting enough protein, increase your intake of plant proteins.

Good sources: Soy foods (edamame, soy milk, tofu)…beans, lentils, peas…nuts and seeds.

If you have hypertension or prehypertension but no atherosclerosis, limit yourself to no more than three weekly four-ounce servings of animal protein, and stick with low-fat meat, fish or poultry.

• **Salt.** Sodium raises blood pressure by increasing blood volume and constricting blood vessels. Some people are more sensitive to salt than others—but limiting dietary salt is a good idea for everyone.

Recommended: Healthy people up to age 50 should limit sodium to 2,300 mg per day (about one teaspoon of salt)…older people and anyone with prehypertension or hypertension should stay under 1,500 mg daily (about two-thirds of a teaspoon of salt).

Action: Instead of salt, add flavor with pepper, garlic and other seasonings. Do not use seasoning blends that contain salt. Avoid processed and canned foods unless labeled "low sodium."

PROS AND CONS OF…

• **Red wine.** Like berries, red wine contains heart-healthy polyphenols.

But: Polyphenols relax blood vessels only when exposure time is short, as with light-to-moderate alcohol consumption. Heavy drinking actually *reduces* the blood vessels' ability to relax, negating polyphenols' benefits.

Advised: If you choose to drink alcohol, opt for red wine and have no more than one glass per day.

Alcohol-free option: Polyphenol-rich unsweetened dark grape juice.

• **Coffee, tea and soda.** Some evidence links caffeine to increased blood pressure.

Advised: Opt for caffeine-free beverages.

Good choice: Herbal tea. A recent study suggests that drinking three cups daily of a blend that includes the herb hibiscus can lower systolic blood pressure by about seven mmHg.

• **Chocolate.** Small studies suggest that dark chocolate helps lower blood pressure.

Theory: Cocoa contains antioxidant *procyanidins*, which boost the body's production of *nitric oxide*, a chemical that relaxes blood vessels.

But: Chocolate is high in sugar and fat, both of which contribute to weight gain.

Advised: If you want an occasional dessert, one-half ounce of dark chocolate is a good choice.

Melatonin Reduces Blood Pressure

Mark A. Stengler, NMD, licensed naturopathic medical doctor in private practice, Encinitas, California…adjunct associate clinical professor at the National College of Natural Medicine, Portland, Oregon…author of *The Natural Physician's Healing Therapies* and co-author of *Prescription for Natural Cures* (both from Bottom Line Books).

A randomized, double-blind study involved 18 women, ages 47 to 63, half with hypertension being successfully controlled with ACE inhibitor medication and half who had normal blood pressure. For three weeks, participants took either 3 mg of time-released melatonin (a supplement typically used to promote sleep) or a placebo one hour before bed. They were then switched to the other treatment for another three weeks. After taking melatonin for three weeks, 84% of the women had at least a 10 mmHg decrease in nocturnal (nighttime) systolic and diastolic blood pressure, while only 39% experienced a decrease in nocturnal blood pressure after taking the placebo. The reduction was the greatest in those with controlled hypertension. In both groups, no change was found in daytime blood pressure readings. Previous studies have found similar results when men with untreated hypertension took melatonin.

My view: Melatonin, a hormone produced by the pineal gland in the brain, is secreted in response to darkness and promotes a normal sleep cycle. A deficiency of melatonin may prevent relaxation of the cardiovascular and nervous systems, increasing blood pressure. (Normally, heart rate and blood vessel constriction decrease at night.) While people with hypertension often monitor their daytime blood pressure, they usually are unaware of their readings at night. This can be a mistake. High nighttime blood pressure is just as important as high daytime pressure. For people with high blood pressure whose levels also tend to be elevated at night, I recommend taking 3 mg of time-released melatonin one hour before bed. To determine if you have elevated blood pressure at night, use a home blood pressure monitor to test levels several times during the day and twice a night (at midnight and 4:00 am) for three days.

Caution: Consult your doctor before trying melatonin. It may require an adjustment to your blood pressure medication. Women who are pregnant or breastfeeding, as well as those taking birth control pills, should not use melatonin.

Blood-Pressure Medication Warning

Women on certain blood-pressure medications are at increased risk of dying from heart disease. When used together with diuretics in women with hypertension but no history of heart disease, calcium channel blockers—a class of drugs that includes *diltiazem* (Cardizem) and *amlodipine* (Norvasc)—increased risk more than a beta-blocker or ACE inhibitor taken with a diuretic. Calcium channel blockers used alone also increased risk, compared with diuretics used alone.

Self-defense: Consult your physician. Don't stop taking any blood pressure medication on your own.

Sylvia Wassertheil-Smoller, PhD, professor and head of epidemiology, Albert Einstein College of Medicine, Bronx, New York, and leader of a study of 30,219 women, published in *Journal of the American Medical Association.*

Natural Ways to Lower Your Blood Pressure

The late Robert Kowalski, former medical journalist in Los Angeles, author of several books, including *The Blood Pressure Cure—8 Weeks to Lower Blood Pressure Without Prescription Drugs* (Wiley).

Evidence clearly shows that risk for stroke and heart attack increases with blood pressure that is above 120/80.

When elevated blood pressure doesn't respond to lifestyle modifications, such as sodium restriction and increased activity, doctors frequently prescribe medications. But these drugs often have serious side effects, including fatigue, loss of energy, dizziness on standing, chronic cough and loss of libido. As a result, many patients don't take their medication as prescribed.

Good news: Based on decades of dialogue with top medical researchers, I've found that the natural treatments described below have each been shown to lower systolic blood pressure (the top number) from a few points to 20 points, with a proportional drop in diastolic pressure (the bottom number). Used in combination, these treatments can produce a drop of 20 points or more depending on how regularly you follow the recommendations—that is enough to reduce the blood pressure of many hypertensive patients to safe levels *without* medication.

Step 1: **Get your blood pressure tested by your doctor.** Hypertension often produces no symptoms. The only way to know if your blood pressure is elevated is to have it checked by a professional. Devices in pharmacies and other places are frequently abused and not calibrated often enough and therefore may be inaccurate.

Step 2: **Buy a home monitor if you have even slightly elevated blood pressure.** Get one that uses an upper-arm cuff (it's more accurate than a wrist cuff). All models using an upper-arm cuff made by Omron have been reviewed and approved by the British Hypertension Society, considered the gold standard of approval.

Cost: $60 to $100.

Check your blood pressure at different times of day—in the morning, after meals, on the weekend, when you're under stress—to learn how your blood pressure fluctuates. Also, have your doctor check your machine against his periodically for accuracy.

Step 3: **Adopt a Mediterranean-style diet.**

Lowering effect: Up to 20 points systolic, when followed strictly...moderate adherence will produce lesser, but still beneficial, results. *Eat from the following general categories of foods, including...*

• **Fruits and vegetables.** Eat nine to 10 daily servings. This isn't as much as it sounds. A big bowl of vegetable soup, for example, provides three servings of vegetables. The more variety and colors, the better.

Reason: Different colors indicate different types of polyphenols (substances in plants found to lower blood pressure).

• **Whole grains,** such as barley, oats, rye and wheat.

Reason: Polyphenols in whole grains increase the elasticity of the arteries.

• **Nuts.** Research shows that people who eat a daily serving of nuts are less likely to develop cardiovascular disease or have heart attacks than those who don't.

Strategy: Since nuts are fattening, eat only a handful or so 20 to 30 minutes before dinner. This has the added advantage of taking the edge off your appetite—you'll consume fewer calories at dinner and lose weight if you need to.

• **Seafood.** Eat at least two servings a week of cold-water fatty fish, such as mackerel, salmon and albacore tuna. For added benefits, take a daily fish oil tablet containing at least 250 mg each of the omega-3 fatty acids DHA and EPA, which have been shown to enhance cardiovascular health.

• **Lean meat.** Choose lean cuts, such as loin and tenderloin. For poultry, go with white meat chicken and turkey over dark meat. Avoid duck.

• **Nonfat and low-fat dairy products,** including cheeses, yogurt and milk—if you choose to eat dairy.

• **Heart-healthy cooking oils.** Use canola and olive oil, which are rich in monounsaturated fats. Research has shown that replacing saturated fats and partially hydrogenated oils with monounsaturated oils lowers LDL (bad) cholesterol and raises HDL (good) cholesterol.

Strategy: When eating bread, dip it in olive oil instead of using butter or margarine. Switching to healthy oils alone can produce a six- to 10-point drop in systolic blood pressure.

Step 4: **Balance your intake of sodium, potassium, magnesium and calcium.**

Lowering effect: Six to eight points systolic per mineral.

These four minerals are electrolytes that your body's cells need to function. For years, doctors have recommended eating less sodium to lower blood pressure. But studies have shown that reducing sodium alone has only a minimal effect on blood pressure. It's more important to balance mineral intake by selectively reducing sodium while increasing your intake of potassium, magnesium and calcium.

To reduce sodium intake: Since most dietary sodium comes from packaged foods, avoid snack foods, fast foods and canned foods, including soups, unless labeled low sodium. Eat frozen rather than canned vegetables. If you do eat canned vegetables, halve their sodium content by pouring out the water in the can and rinsing the food in tap water.

To increase potassium intake: Cook food using a salt substitute containing potassium chloride, available at supermarkets next to the regular salt (any brand is good). Also eat high-potassium foods, including potatoes, sweet potatoes, honeydew melon, cantaloupe, acorn and winter squash, avocado, dried figs and apricots, prunes, dates, raisins, bananas, orange juice, tomato puree (low-salt variety) and lima beans.

To increase magnesium and calcium intake: Take a daily supplement containing 150 mg magnesium and 300 mg calcium.

Step 5: **Walk for 30 minutes or get a similar amount of exercise, at least four days a week.**

Lowering effect: Six to 8 points systolic. Regular physical activity increases the flexibility and health of arteries by lowering levels of the stress hormones *cortisol* and *norepinephrine.*

Step 6: **Lose weight.**

Lowering effect: One point systolic for every two pounds lost. Weight is a risk factor for increased blood pressure when waist circumference exceeds 35 inches for women and 40 inches for men.

Step 7: **Take three or four "mini vacations" per day.**

Lowering effect: More than 10 points systolic.

How it works: Find a quiet place, sit down, close your eyes and breathe deeply for two to three minutes. Imagine that your chest is a big balloon, and inflate it as far as possible, then suck in a couple of extra puffs if you can. Hold a moment, then slowly deflate the balloon.

Research shows that, repeated three or four times daily, this will produce a permanent, significant drop in blood pressure.

***Step 8:* Drink a cup of hot cocoa 30 minutes before bedtime.**

Lowering effect: Six to 10 points systolic. Dark cocoa added to skim milk is rich in polyphenols...holding the mug in your hands is relaxing...and the milk contains calcium and *tryptophan* (an essential amino acid present in proteins), which improves sleep—further lowering blood pressure. Be sure to use dark chocolate—the darker the better. Milk chocolate and white chocolate have scarce benefit.

Step 9:* Take the following supplements daily.

Lowering effect: 8 to 10 points systolic each.

• **Lyc-O-Mato (150 mg),** a tomato extract supplement that promotes heart health. It contains lycopene, phytoene, phytofluene, tocopherols and beta-carotene. Sold in pharmacies and health-food stores (*www.lycored.com*).

• **MegaNatural BP grape seed extract** (300 mg), made by Polyphenolics (*www.polyphenolics.com*). This patented supplement has been clinically proven to lower blood pressure.

• **Sustained-release arginine** (six 350-mg capsules, three each in the morning and evening), an artery-relaxing amino acid.

Two brands: EP L-Arginine SR, made by Endurance Products (*www.endur.com*) and SR Perfusia, made by Thorne Research (*www.thorne.com*). These are the only sustained-release arginine products currently available. Immediate-release arginine will not lower blood pressure.

• **Pycnogenol** (100 to 200 mg), a pine bark extract. While many products claim to contain pine bark, use only products that contain Pycnogenol, a patented version clinically demonstrated to lower blood pressure.

*Always check with your doctor before taking supplements.

Vision Loss Link

With *retinal vein occlusion* (RVO), blood vessels in the eye become blocked and may rupture, damaging eyesight.

Recent finding: Having high blood pressure more than tripled a person's risk for RVO...high cholesterol more than doubled RVO risk.

Best: Get regular eye exams, and control blood pressure and cholesterol.

Joel G. Ray, assistant professor, division of endocrinology and metabolism, St. Michael's Hospital, University of Toronto, Canada, and lead author of an analysis of 21 studies, published in *Archives of Ophthalmology*.

Statins Lower Blood Pressure

Statin drugs reduce both systolic (top number) and diastolic blood pressure to a modest but significant degree.

Helpful: If your doctor is considering starting you on both a statin and a medication for high blood pressure, ask whether it might be prudent to wait and see whether the statin alone reduces blood pressure enough.

Beatrice A. Golomb, MD, PhD, associate professor of medicine, University of California, San Diego, School of Medicine, and leader of the ongoing UCSD Statin Effects Study.

Cholesterol—the Surprising Facts You Really Must Know

Mary P. McGowan, MD, director of the Cholesterol Treatment Center at Concord Hospital in Concord, New Hampshire, and an assistant professor of medicine at the University of Massachusetts Medical Center in Worcester. She is board certified in internal medicine and cholesterol metabolism and coauthored *50 Ways to Lower Your Cholesterol* (McGraw-Hill).

The dangers of cholesterol have received a lot of attention, but very few people realize that they still don't have all the information they need to truly understand this crucial health issue.

For example, most people believe that cholesterol is always bad for you. The fact is, your body needs some cholesterol to produce certain hormones and make healthy cells. It's just that more than half of all Americans have far more cholesterol in their bodies than they need for good health.

Some people with elevated cholesterol, such as those with genetic cholesterol disorders or a history of heart disease, need to take a cholesterol-lowering statin drug and/or other prescription medications to keep their cholesterol in check. But many others can get good results without the potential side effects and expense of such drugs.

Mary P. McGowan, MD, is a leading expert on cholesterol metabolism. Here she provides insight on how to correct elevated cholesterol—or avoid it in the first place.

IMPORTANT ISSUES TO DISCUSS

When reviewing your cholesterol profile, you and your doctor should discuss…

• **What medications you are taking.** Some medications that are widely used to treat other conditions can raise LDL "bad" cholesterol and/or lower HDL "good" cholesterol. This includes some diuretics and beta-blockers (both commonly used for high blood pressure) and progestin hormones (commonly used in hormone replacement therapy).

In some cases, you may be able to switch to a different drug in the same class that does not negatively affect cholesterol levels as much as the one you are taking.

Examples: Indapamide is a diuretic that tends not to hurt cholesterol levels…*carvedilol* (Coreg) is a beta-blocker that usually does not adversely affect cholesterol…and micronized progestin, such as Prometrium, has been found to be the progestin with the least negative impact on cholesterol.

• **Your family history.** Only about 25% to 30% of the cholesterol in your body comes from your diet. This means that roughly 70% to 75% of your body's cholesterol doesn't come from food—it is made by your liver and often influenced by your genes.

Some people simply have good genes when it comes to cholesterol, but others need to work hard to control their cholesterol levels.

SMART FOOD CHOICES

• **Think beyond oat bran.** High-fiber foods, such as oat bran, have been highly publicized for their ability to help reduce cholesterol. But not all fiber sources have this effect—for example, wheat bran, one of the most common fiber sources in the American diet, does nothing to get total cholesterol to the desirable level of less than 200 milligrams per deciliter (mg/dL). Thats because fiber must be *soluble* (dissolvable in water) to improve cholesterol levels.

Sources of soluble fiber you may not know about: Kidney beans, navy beans, apples, oranges, prunes, grapefruit and Brussels sprouts. Psyllium, which is derived from the husks of seeds from the herblike shrub *Plantango ovata*, is another excellent source of soluble fiber. Its found in some cereals, such as All-Bran Bran Buds and Smart Bran… and in over-the-counter (OTC) fiber products such as Metamucil.

• **Check out butter substitutes.** Butter has a lot of saturated fat—and most people who like it tend to use a lot of it. Saturated fat impairs the livers ability to remove LDL cholesterol from the blood.

Instead of butter: Try olive oil or canola oil on your toast in the morning. But remember, while olive oil is healthful, it is high in calories (100 calories per tablespoon), so don't pour it on. Consider using a mister.

If you prefer the taste of butter, replace it with products that contain plant stanols or sterols, which are derived from vegetable oils and wood pulp. Both of these plant-derived compounds lower LDL cholesterol by inhibiting its absorption by the intestine. Plant stanol esters are found in Benecol spread…plant sterols are in Smart Balance spread. Both products are widely available at supermarkets.

Important: When patients' cholesterol levels don't improve on one of these products, they're usually not getting enough—you need to eat an average of two tablespoons daily. Try "light" versions (which have 50 calories per tablespoon versus 70 or 80).

•**Snack on pistachios.** Walnuts and almonds are well-known sources of omega-3 fatty acids, a kind of healthful fat that can help reduce LDL cholesterol. But if you would like more variety, recent research has found that pistachios also have the same benefits. Just be sure to limit yourself to no more than a handful (about 1.5 ounces) of pistachios (or walnuts or almonds) per day—nuts are high in calories.

EXERCISE COUNTS

Exercise is essential to maintaining healthy levels of triglycerides (blood fats). Exercise also improves HDL cholesterol levels but has less impact on LDL.

Aim for a minimum of 30 minutes three days a week—but you are likely to get a greater cholesterol benefit if you exercise daily. Be sure to consult your doctor before you begin an exercise routine.

SUPPLEMENTS TO CONSIDER

If a low-fat diet and exercise have not helped you achieve optimal cholesterol levels, and you prefer to not take a statin, you may want to ask your doctor about trying…

•**Red yeast rice—but don't buy the wrong kind.** This supplement, which is made by culturing a red yeast on rice, has been shown in some studies to reduce LDL by roughly 20% when 1,200 mg is taken twice daily with meals.

Important new research: When 12 red yeast rice extracts were tested, tremendous variability was found in the products' levels of *monacolins,* the active ingredient. The levels of total monacolins ranged from 0.31 mg to 11.15 mg per capsule. Scientists also found that one-third of the supplements contained high levels of *citrinin,* a toxic contaminant derived from fungus that may harm the kidneys.

Choose a product made by a large, well-known manufacturer—such companies generally have more quality control. Rare side effects of red yeast rice include headache, stomachache or bloating, gas and dizziness. Avoid drinking grapefruit juice with red yeast rice—the combination can increase the risk for liver damage.

•**Niacin.** This powerful B vitamin can reduce LDL cholesterol by up to 20% and raise HDL by as much as 35%. Niacin also reduces triglycerides by up to 25%.

Typical dose: About 1,000 mg daily.

Niaspan, (niacin extended-release tablet or NERT—niacin is its active ingredient), is taken once a day and is generally safer for the liver than OTC niacin, which must be taken three times daily. Both forms can cause flushing and should be taken at bedtime (so flushing occurs during sleep) and with a snack (to avoid stomachache). If you use OTC niacin, avoid niacinamide, a "cousin" of niacin. Niacinamide does not cause flushing but also has no effect on cholesterol.

To lessen flushing: Take 325 mg of aspirin a half hour before you take either type of niacin. Aspirin has a blood-thinning effect, so be sure to consult your doctor if you have a history of stomach ulcers, anemia, kidney or liver disease or take blood thinners. Also avoid hot beverages, alcohol, hot showers and spicy foods around the time you take the niacin. Anyone taking niacin or Niaspan should have his/her liver function periodically tested by a physician.

Say Yes to Soy

Women who substituted soy nuts (dry-roasted soybeans) for red meat for eight weeks had a 9.5% decrease in LDL (bad) cholesterol, reducing risk for cardiovascular disease, and a 5.1% decrease in blood sugar levels, lowering risk for diabetes, according to a recent study. These risk factors also improved when women substituted textured soy protein (imitation meat made from soy) for red meat.

Leila Azadbakht, PhD, department of nutrition, School of Health, Isfahan University of Medical Sciences, Isfahan, Iran, and leader of a study of postmenopausal women on the Dietary Approaches to Stop Hypertension (DASH) diet, published in *The American Journal of Clinical Nutrition.*

Should Women Take Statin Drugs?

Judith Walsh, MD, MPH, associate clinical professor of medicine, University of California, San Francisco.

Beatrice A. Golomb, MD, PhD, associate professor of medicine, University of California at San Diego.

There is mounting evidence that statin drugs such as Lipitor or Zocor are not the cure-all for women that they are touted to be for men.

In fact, of all the major studies done on the effects of statins, fewer than 10% of the participants have been women. And when their results were looked at separately, there was no evidence to show that the benefits seen for men were also present for women.

WHAT'S A WOMAN TO DO?

Judith Walsh, MD, MPH, associate clinical professor of medicine at the University of California, San Francisco, says that based on research results, the odds of statins preventing just one cardiovascular event in women are very low.

A better strategy: Talk to your doctor about all your risk factors, and ask about alternatives to statins, such as all-natural *policosanol*.

"Your [total] cholesterol number must be interpreted in terms of the rest of your general health," she explains. "You must look at all the overall risk factors, one of which is age. A healthy woman at the age of 70 is already at risk for heart problems, simply because she is 70. That is an age when the likelihood of cardiovascular problems increases. Other risk factors are high blood pressure, diabetes, smoking or family history of premature heart disease."

More and more doctors are beginning to look into this issue, including Beatrice A. Golomb, MD, PhD, associate professor of medicine at the University of California at San Diego.

According to Dr. Golomb, "The people who benefit from statins are middle-aged men. Benefits to the heart do extend to women as well, but benefits to survival have not been shown to do so."

Statin Not Proven to Cut Women's Risk

Clinical trials of cholesterol-lowering *atorvastatin* (Lipitor) found evidence that the drug reduced heart attack risk for men—but not women. Ads for Lipitor fail to disclose this. Statins can have serious side effects—review pros and cons with your doctor.

Theodore Eisenberg, JD, professor of law, adjunct professor of statistical sciences, Cornell Law School, Ithaca, New York, and coauthor of a meta-analysis of drugs' effects on cardiovascular risk, published in *Journal of Empirical Legal Studies*.

Five More Ways to Lower Heart Attack Risk

Michael Mogadam, MD, clinical associate professor of medicine at George Washington University School of Medicine in Washington, DC. He is also author of *Every Heart Attack Is Preventable: How to Take Control of the 20 Risk Factors and Save Your Life* (LifeLine).

Most Americans know all of the traditional heart disease risk factors—lack of physical activity, high cholesterol, high blood pressure, diabetes, obesity and smoking. Although these are important, there also are lesser-known risk factors. *Ways to avoid them…*

• **Boost your HDL level.** Though high LDL ("bad") cholesterol has long been considered the major culprit in heart attack risk, low HDL ("good") cholesterol actually is the bigger risk factor, especially in women. About 70% of women and half of all men with coronary artery disease (CAD) have low HDL cholesterol.

What to do: If you're a woman with HDL below 55 or a man with HDL below 45, take steps to boost your good cholesterol. Engaging in regular, vigorous exercise can raise HDL levels by 10% to 15%. Limiting carbohydrates to less than 45% of your daily diet and increasing monounsaturated fats (found in olive, canola and hazelnut oils) can raise HDL levels by 10%. Cholesterol-lowering statin drugs also may raise HDL levels by as much as 10%. Taking

1,500 milligrams (mg) of the B vitamin niacin under the supervision of a health-care provider can raise HDL by 25% to 30%.

Note: At high doses, niacin can cause side effects, such as flushing, liver problems and irregular heart rhythm.

Warning: Low-fat diets invariably lower HDL levels, which may actually *increase* heart attack risk. To ensure a healthy cholesterol ratio, don't simply eliminate fats from your diet. Monounsaturated and nonhydrogenated polyunsaturated fats should provide up to 30% of your daily calories.

Good sources: Olive oil, canola oil, nuts and avocados.

• **Determine your LDL size.** LDL cholesterol particles come in two sizes—large (type A) and small (type B). A predominance of type B particles increases risk of CAD by 300% to 500%, *even when LDL levels are normal* (less than 100).

Reason: Small LDL particles pass through the inner lining of coronary arteries more easily, possibly triggering a heart attack.

What to do: If you have low HDL cholesterol levels (below 45 for men and below 55 for women), particularly if any family members developed CAD before age 55, have your LDL particle size measured. This simple blood test is widely available, and many insurers now cover the cost.

The best way to decrease your type-B LDL count is to eat a healthful diet comprised of 30% fat, mostly in the form of monounsaturated fats, and limit carbohydrate intake to no more than 45% of total calories.

To boost your intake of beneficial omega-3 polyunsaturated fats, eat two to three seafood meals weekly. Choose the fattier fish, such as salmon and tuna.

Self-defense: Pregnant and lactating women should ask their doctors about limiting intake of fish due to its mercury content.

Avoid the trans-fatty acids and the omega-6 polyunsaturated fats found in margarine, fried foods, baked goods, corn and safflower oils.

• **Know your birth weight.** A low birth weight is a significant and independent risk factor for heart attack, hypertension and diabetes in adulthood. Research has shown that people who weighed less than 5.5 pounds at birth are three times more likely to develop CAD than people who weighed more than 7.5 pounds at birth.

What to do: Tell your doctor if you had a low birth weight (less than 5.5 pounds)—and show him/her this article.

If you were a very small baby, ask your doctor to test regularly for other coronary risk factors, such as hypertension, elevated cholesterol, diabetes and LDL particle size.

• **Choose heart-healthy beverages.** The heart-protective benefits of alcohol have been well-established. When consumed in moderation (one glass daily for women and no more than two glasses daily for men), wine, beer and mixed drinks reduce CAD by 30%.

Researchers now know that water also may play a role in preventing heart attack. Physicians at Loma Linda University recently reported that drinking five or more glasses of water daily (versus two or fewer) reduces fatal heart attack risk in men by 51% and in women by 35%.

Water seems to protect against heart attacks by making blood less likely to clot. Minerals in hard tap water, such as calcium and magnesium, also may help guard against heart disease.

What to do: Drink from six to eight 8-ounce glasses of water daily. Ask your local water utility if your water is hard (mineral rich) or soft. Even soft water from the tap may be a healthier choice than filtered bottled waters, which can be stripped of minerals.

Helpful: Consider installing a faucet-mounted home water filter that removes waterborne parasites from your water but doesn't filter out the beneficial minerals.

Good brands: Moen and Culligan.

• **Take folic acid.** This B vitamin has been shown to lower levels of homocysteine, a protein in the blood that significantly increases risk for cardiovascular disease when it is elevated. Folic acid also lowers the risk for heart attack and stroke.

What to do: Eat more folic acid–rich foods, such as spinach, asparagus, lima beans, wheat germ and fortified cereals. If your homocysteine level is greater than 15, you may need to take a folic acid supplement daily.

17

Tired All the Time?

Anemic? You May Need More Than Iron

When there is a shortage of hemoglobin in the red blood cells, the amount of oxygen being carried through the circulatory system is insufficient to meet all of the body's needs. This is called anemia.

The condition affects at least twice as many women as men. Among its symptoms are fatigue, shortness of breath, dizziness, depression and cloudy thinking. Because these symptoms have many other possible causes (and because the mild form of the disease often causes no symptoms), anemia often goes undiagnosed and untreated.

Although some people think of anemia as a "young woman's disease," it affects postmenopausal women, too. In fact, anemia hits seniors hard, increasing their risk for cognitive dysfunction (such as problems remembering to take

medication or pay bills)…physical impairment (for instance, difficulty getting up from a chair, walking or maintaining balance) …hospitalization…and death. *How to protect yourself…*

ALL-IMPORTANT IRON

Among anemia's various causes, the most common is iron deficiency. Iron is crucial for production of hemoglobin, a protein needed to form healthy red blood cells. Premenopausal women are particularly prone to iron-deficiency anemia because menstruation and pregnancy drain the body of iron.

But: Many women who enter menopause with an undiagnosed iron deficiency continue to be anemic—because their iron stores are never adequately replenished. Others become

---

John Neustadt, ND, medical director of Montana Integrative Medicine in Bozeman. He is a regular contributor to the medical journal *Integrative Medicine,* an editor of the textbook *Laboratory Evaluations for Integrative and Functional Medicine* and author of *A Revolution in Health through Nutritional Biochemistry* (iUniverse). *www.drjohnneustadt.com*

anemic after menopause due to blood loss—for instance, from a gastrointestinal problem.

Self-defense: If you have persistent fatigue or other signs of anemia (see page 488), ask your doctor for a blood test called a complete blood count (CBC) to measure hemoglobin levels. At the same time, specifically request that your blood also be tested for ferritin, the primary form of iron storage in the body. Even if your CBC is normal, the more sensitive ferritin test may reveal an iron deficiency.

Trap: The so-called "normal" level of ferritin for women is from 12 nanograms per milliliter (ng/mL) to 150 ng/mL—a range so broad that it is nearly useless.

Recommended: If your ferritin level is below 50 ng/mL, take action.

You may think that the solution is to eat iron-rich red meats, dark green leafy vegetables, legumes, dried fruits and seeds. Providing about 3 milligrams (mg) to 10 mg of iron per serving, these foods do help healthy women meet the recommended daily allowance of 18 mg of iron per day before menopause (or 27 mg during pregnancy) and 8 mg after menopause.

However, for an anemia patient, it is nearly impossible to get enough iron from diet alone—because it takes a lot of iron to replenish depleted stores.

Protocol: For my female anemia patients, I recommend daily iron supplements at a dosage of 2 mg to 3 mg per kilogram (2.2 pounds) of body weight. For a 135-pound woman, for instance, that is 123 mg to 184 mg of iron daily. After three months, I retest to see if ferritin levels have normalized.

Problem: Ferrous gluconate and other commonly prescribed iron supplements often cause nausea, indigestion and/or constipation. Worse, less than half of the iron in such supplements actually is absorbed by the body.

Better: Some studies show that a chelated form—in which the iron is combined with an amino acid—decreases digestive upset and increases absorption.

Options: Nature's Plus Chewable Iron with Vitamin C & Herbs (800-645-9500, *www.naturesplus.com*)...Solgar Chelated Iron (877-765-4274, *www.solgar.com*)...and FerroSolve, a brand that I formulated (800-624-1416, *www.nbihealth.com*). A nutrition-oriented doctor can advise you on how much iron to take and for how long.

For best absorption, take iron with orange juice or another source of vitamin C. Do not take iron within 30 minutes of drinking tea, coffee or red wine—these contain tannins, compounds that block iron absorption. Iron can interact with and/or reduce absorption of certain drugs, so your doctor should advise you about when to take each dose.

Important: If you are postmenopausal, in addition to treating your iron deficiency, your doctor needs to check for underlying causes.

Examples: Hemorrhoids, colon polyps and ulcers may cause hidden bleeding that leads to anemia.

Caution: Where there is no diagnosis of iron deficiency, the normal upper daily limit for iron is 45 mg. Iron supplements should be taken only with a doctor's okay—among people with the genetic disorder hemochromatosis, excess iron can lead to joint and organ damage.

A VITAMIN PROBLEM

The second most common type of anemia is caused by a deficiency of vitamin B-12. Seniors are especially at risk because aging diminishes intrinsic factor, a substance in the digestive tract lining that aids vitamin B-12 absorption. Up to 15% of people over age 60 have vitamin B-12–deficiency anemia. Blood tests can confirm the diagnosis.

Dietary sources of vitamin B-12 include shellfish, salmon, red meat, eggs and dairy products. However, diet alone generally will not correct this type of anemia...and many oral vitamin B-12 supplements are not well absorbed by the body. Some doctors instead recommend weekly intramuscular B-12 injections, continuing indefinitely in some cases.

Pain-free option: Daily sublingual supplements—lozenges placed under the tongue to dissolve—of B-12 may be quickly absorbed into the bloodstream.

Dosage: 2,500 micrograms (mcg) daily until B-12 levels normalize, or indefinitely if needed.

More from Dr. Neustadt...

Test Yourself for Anemia

Anemia, a shortage of hemoglobin (the protein that carries oxygen), may cause...

- **Cold or numb hands and feet**
- **Concentration and memory problems**
- **Cracks at the corners of the mouth**
- **Depression**
- **Dizziness**
- **Fatigue**
- **Leg or muscle cramps**
- **Nails that look scooped out**
- **Pale skin**
- **Pica (abnormal hunger for nonfoods, such as paper or dirt)**
- **Rapid or irregular heartbeat**
- **Shortness of breath**
- **Walking and balancing problems.**

Self-test: Looking in a mirror, gently pull down your bottom eyelid and check the color on the inside of the lid...next, check the inner lining of your cheek. If either is white rather than pink, you may have anemia. If you are not "in the pink" or if you have any of the symptoms above, see your doctor.

Anemia Impairs Brain Function

Researchers gave 354 women ages 70 to 80 cognitive tests as well as blood tests to check for anemia.

Result: Women with mild anemia scored up to five times worse on the cognitive tests than those who did not have anemia.

Theory: When red blood cell levels are too low, blood carries less oxygen to the brain, leading to cognitive decline.

Self-defense: If you have symptoms of anemia (see above), see your doctor.

Paulo H.M. Chaves, MD, PhD, assistant professor of medicine and epidemiology, Johns Hopkins University, Baltimore.

Iron Out Fatigue

Cathy Carlson-Rink, ND, registered midwife in British Columbia. She is an instructor of obstetrics and pediatrics, Boucher Institute of Naturopathic Medicine, New Westminster, British Columbia.

National Institutes of Health Office of Dietary Supplements, *http://ods.od.nih.gov/factsheets/iron.*

US Food and Drug Administration, *www.fda.gov.*

It used to be that if you ate right, exercised and took Geritol for "iron-poor blood," everything would be "okay." Somehow, the health concern about iron deficiency seems to have gotten lost amid the mass of other medication marketing. Yet, iron deficiency is the number-one deficiency in women and the leading cause of fatigue in women between the ages of 15 and 50. Women in their childbearing years are especially susceptible to this problem because of the monthly loss of iron in menstrual fluid.

According to Cathy Carlson-Rink, an ND and registered midwife in British Columbia, as many as one in four American women are iron deficient, and the tragedy is that this deficiency is easily preventable.

EVEN A MILD DEFICIENCY CAN BE HARMFUL

A shortage of iron in the blood deprives cells of the oxygen they require to burn the body's fuel. Even a mild deficiency can rob you of energy and leave you feeling constantly tired or even exhausted. Your concentration may become so impaired that you find it difficult to complete simple tasks. Still worse, Dr. Carlson-Rink warns that a mild iron deficiency can be linked to PMS, depression, impaired fertility and pregnancy complications.

Symptoms of iron deficiency include...

- **Pale skin**
- **Brittle hair and nails**
- **Pale, dark circles under the eyes**
- **Rapid pulse**
- **Fatigue and weakness**
- **Impaired work and school performance**
- **Slow cognitive and social development during childhood**

•**Increased susceptibility to infections, such as colds and flu**

•**Shortness of breath**

•**Heart palpitations**

•**Poor concentration**

•**Poor sleep**

•**Cold hands and feet**

THREE STAGES OF IRON DEFICIENCY

Although iron deficiency is harmful and may be a prelude to anemia, the condition often escapes doctors' attention. Iron deficiency can be detected with a simple blood test to measure serum ferritin (the storage form of iron). Yet this test is seldom performed.

Dr. Carlson-Rink says that there are three stages of iron deficiency…

•**The body's iron stores (serum ferritin) begin to drop.**

•**Red blood cells decrease in size and color.**

•**Hemoglobin levels decline.**

Common tests for iron check only hemoglobin, she notes, which isn't affected until the third and more serious stage of iron deficiency has been reached. It is better to measure serum ferritin to catch a problem earlier.

WHO NEEDS IRON?

While women of childbearing years are at greatest risk for iron deficiency, Dr. Carlson-Rink adds that it's not just women who may require additional iron. Teenagers—both male and female—with poor eating habits or who are having growth spurts require a boost in iron, as do people with gastrointestinal disorders who do not absorb iron effectively. Conversely, iron deficiency is uncommon among most postmenopausal women and adult men. Some research confirms that people who engage in regular, intense exercise (jogging, cycling and even swimming) require more iron.

GET SUFFICIENT IRON IN YOUR DIET

Iron deficiency often can be prevented simply by eating plenty of iron-rich foods. According to the US Food and Drug Administration (FDA), the Daily Value (DV) for iron—that is, the average daily requirement for women of childbearing age—is 18 mg.

Note: Men, children and older people of both sexes need less iron…pregnant and nursing women require more. Men age 19 and older require 8 mg daily. The iron requirement for pregnant women increases to 27 mg per day.

Good dietary sources of iron include…

•**Lean meats, fish and poultry.** There are two forms of dietary iron—heme and nonheme. Heme iron, which is found in red meats, fish and poultry, is more easily absorbed by the body. Nonheme iron is found in plant foods and is the form added to enriched products such as cereals.

•**Plant foods,** including beans, tofu, apricots, raisins and leafy, dark green vegetables such as spinach, kale, bok choy, collards and seaweed. One cup of boiled lentils provides 35% of your daily iron requirement…one-half cup of firm raw tofu or boiled spinach provides 20%.

Note: While breakfast cereal manufacturers tout their iron fortification, Andrew L. Rubman, ND, warns that the form of iron used is not easily absorbed by the body, so it has a limited benefit.

Vegetarians may need to take in twice as much iron as meat eaters because of the lower intestinal absorption of iron from plant foods. Also, proper iron absorption is dependent upon adequate protein levels. Vegetarians who do not get adequate protein may not be able to store or transport absorbed iron very well. To improve absorption, eat iron-rich plant foods in combination with a good source of vitamin C, such as citrus fruits. Dr. Carlson-Rink notes that it is better to eat spinach steamed rather than raw—raw spinach contains compounds called oxalates that decrease iron absorption.

WHEN SUPPLEMENTS ARE NECESSARY

If you fail to take in enough iron through diet alone, it's time to consider supplementation. According to Dr. Carlson-Rink, iron is best taken apart from the nutrients calcium, vitamin E, magnesium, manganese and zinc, which interfere with its absorption. She advises taking iron as a single liquid supplement and recommends the brand Floradix (an organic plant-based liquid iron supplement distributed by Flora Inc. of British Columbia, *www.florahealth.com*). The suggested dosage for women of childbearing age is 18 mg daily. If you are anemic, check with your doctor regarding the appropriate level.

That said, it is equally important not to take in too much iron. Iron overload can be a problem, with some researchers suggesting that excess iron is implicated in heart disease and rheumatoid arthritis. High doses can cause gastrointestinal side effects such as nausea, constipation and abdominal distress. Excess supplementation typically leads to darkened stools. Be sure to consult with a trained health practitioner before starting iron supplementation.

Bottom line: If you feel tired for no reason, check it out. Ask your doctor about a serum ferritin test. Relief may be as near as the pantry or refrigerator.

Note: Dr. Carlson-Rink is a spokesperson for Flora Inc., the company that markets Floradix.

Gluten Intolerance Can Cause Anemia

Mark A. Stengler, NMD, licensed naturopathic medical doctor in private practice, Encinitas, California... adjunct associate clinical professor at the National College of Natural Medicine, Portland, Oregon...author of *The Natural Physician's Healing Therapies* and co-author of *Prescription for Natural Cures* (both from Bottom Line Books).

Mary, a 41-year-old homemaker, was suffering from a constellation of troubling symptoms—fatigue, dizziness, hair loss and a menstrual cycle that was irregular and quite heavy. It had been a year since she had seen a doctor, so besides giving her a complete physical exam, I ran a standard blood panel.

Results: She had anemia, severe iron deficiency that was preventing her body from making enough healthy red blood cells.

I asked Mary about health issues that could be causing this deficiency. Was she a vegetarian (and possibly not getting enough iron in her diet)? Did she notice any dark color in her stool (which can indicate bleeding in her digestive tract)? Did she have bleeding hemorrhoids? The answer to all of my questions was no. I suspected that she was anemic as a result of her heavy menstrual cycles. Such heavy bleeding can be caused by a variety of factors, including fibroids (benign tumors in the uterus) or a hormonal imbalance.

First it was important to regulate Mary's cycle and reduce the blood loss. I put her on supplements of natural progesterone, a hormone, as well as intravenous infusions of iron. Her red blood cell count built up quickly, and after four treatments, I switched her to oral iron capsules. Mary felt much better, and her periods and blood tests had normalized. It seemed that we had solved her problem. To be safe, I kept her on maintenance iron.

But several months later, she was back in my office, describing how she was once again feeling tired and dizzy. Blood work revealed that she was severely anemic and deficient in ferritin, a protein found inside cells that stores iron so that your body can use it later. A normal ferritin level is 12 nanograms per milliliter (ng/ml) to 150 ng/ml. Mary's level was just 2 ng/ml. Her menstrual cycle was still regular, so I became concerned that she was bleeding internally.

Additional blood work revealed that Mary had celiac disease, an autoimmune disorder triggered by an intolerance to gluten, a type of protein found in wheat, rye, barley and most oat products. A colonoscopy revealed a specific type of damage to her intestinal wall, confirming the diagnosis.

In people with celiac disease, the body's immune system reacts to what it perceives as an invader, causing damage to the intestines and destruction of red blood cells—as well as hormonal imbalances in women that can create irregular menstrual cycles. Nearly three million Americans (1 in 133) suffer from celiac disease, according to new research from the University of Maryland Center for Celiac Research. The condition never goes away, but it can be managed by eating a gluten-free diet. I cautioned Mary to read labels carefully, because gluten is a common "hidden" ingredient in foods such as soy sauce, potato chips, soups and candy.

Good news: Mary adapted well to a gluten-free diet. Now she is no longer anemic and is feeling much more energetic and healthier overall.

Help for Fibromyalgia

Mark A. Stengler, NMD, licensed naturopathic medical doctor in private practice, Encinitas, California... adjunct associate clinical professor at the National College of Natural Medicine, Portland, Oregon...author of *The Natural Physician's Healing Therapies* and co-author of *Prescription for Natural Cures* (both from Bottom Line Books).

Fibromyalgia is a chronic condition characterized by muscle pain and sore spots called tender points. It may be linked to an inability to produce or use *adenosine triphosphate* (ATP), an energy-carrying molecule essential for muscle function.

Several natural substances improve cellular energy production, reduce pain signals from cells and boost a person's overall energy. They are sold in health-food stores and generally are safe. Try the natural sugar ribose (5 g in powder form, twice daily, mixed with water)...magnesium (250 mg two or three times daily)...malic acid (1,200 mg twice daily)...and vitamin-like coenzyme Q10 (200 mg to 300 mg daily). To improve sleep, you can take sublingual (under the tongue) tablets of the hormone melatonin (1 mg to 3 mg) an hour before bedtime. On this regimen, most people improve within two weeks. If not, the cause may be a deficiency of the thyroid hormones needed to stimulate energy production in cells. If blood tests confirm the diagnosis, bioidentical hormone replacement therapy may be warranted.

Fibromyalgia Is Real

Many patients are told that fibromyalgia symptoms—chronic muscle pain, tender spots, fatigue—are imagined.

But: Imaging tests of fibromyalgia sufferers showed above-normal blood flow in areas of the brain involved in pain perception and below-normal blood flow in regions affecting emotional responses to pain.

Eric Guedj, MD, Centre Hospitalo-Universitaire de la Timone, Marseille, France, and lead author of a study of 30 fibromyalgia patients, published in *Journal of Nuclear Medicine.*

Exercise Fights Fibromyalgia

A four-month program of walking, stretching and strength training relieved symptoms and improved physical function in women with fibromyalgia for the next six months. Mental health, fatigue and depression also improved, especially in women who also participated in an educational program about managing fibromyalgia symptoms. For more information, contact the National Fibromyalgia & Chronic Pain Association, *www.fmcpaware.org.*

Daniel S. Rooks, ScD, assistant professor of medicine, Harvard Medical School, Boston, and leader of a study of 207 women, published in *Archives of Internal Medicine.*

More Supplements for Fibromyalgia Relief

The amino acid *5-hydroxytryptophan* (5-HTP) can relieve musculoskeletal and other symptoms, such as insomnia—take 100 milligrams (mg) three times daily. Do not take 5-HTP if you use an antidepressant or an antianxiety drug.

Also helpful: 500 mg of calcium twice daily and 250 mg of magnesium twice daily. Consult your physician before starting any supplement.

Mark A. Stengler, NMD, licensed naturopathic medical doctor in private practice, Encinitas, California... adjunct associate clinical professor at the National College of Natural Medicine, Portland, Oregon...author of *The Natural Physician's Healing Therapies* and co-author of *Prescription for Natural Cures* (both from Bottom Line Books).

Fibromyalgia Relieved By Water Exercise

I n an eight-month study of 33 women with fibromyalgia (characterized by painful muscles, ligaments and tendons), those who participated in a supervised exercise program in a heated swimming pool for 60 minutes three times weekly had fewer symptoms than non-exercisers.

Theory: Warm water induces relaxation, which helps fight pain. Ask your doctor if water workouts are an option for you.

Narcís Gusi, PhD, professor, University of Extremadura, Cáceres, Spain.

Supercharge Your Energy —and Your Metabolism

Mark A. Stengler, NMD, licensed naturopathic medical doctor in private practice, Encinitas, California... adjunct associate clinical professor at the National College of Natural Medicine, Portland, Oregon...author of *The Natural Physician's Healing Therapies* and co-author of *Prescription for Natural Cures* (both from Bottom Line Books).

I magine a simple nutritional protocol that not only boosts your metabolism but also your energy levels! It is one I prescribe in my clinic daily—and I want to share it with you.

Even if you are in good shape and in relatively good health, you probably don't have the vitality that came so naturally when you were younger. Many of my patients also complain about putting on weight even when they still eat and exercise much as they did when they were younger. You already know that carrying excess weight contributes to or complicates a multitude of serious conditions—among them diabetes, arthritis, heart disease, and several types of cancer. Carrying even a few extra pounds makes us feel slower...less ready to live with energy and zest...older.

Many people are resigned to these changes, assuming that slowing down and fattening up

are inevitable parts of aging. Not so! You can't turn back the clock, but you can rev up your metabolism so it is closer to where it was when you were younger. In recent years, I have had great success prescribing "metabolism super-chargers"—critical nutrients that revitalize the bodys energy production. My patients tell me that these substances give them more energy, and I have seen many patients of all ages lose excess pounds.

THE ENERGY THIEVES

Your *basal metabolic rate* (BMR) is the speed at which your body burns calories while at rest. When it slows, as it usually does with age, you burn fewer calories.

Result: Your energy level begins to flag... you gain weight.

But what is "energy" to our bodies? Heres a brief (I promise!) biology refresher to help you understand.

Our physical strength, stamina and vigor originate within cell structures called *mitochondria*. Mitochondria generate *adenosine triphosphate* (ATP), a chemical that affects our metabolism and produces energy—both the fuel that cells need to do their work and the vitality we feel in our bodies.

As we age, mitochondrial function gradually declines...as does the actual number of mitochondria.

One reason: The numerous toxins to which the body is exposed over the years, including environmental metals and other pollutants, radiation, alcohol, infections...hormone imbalances, such as hypothyroidism...inherited mitochondria mutations...some medications ...and, in elite athletes, the stress caused by chronically overexercising—ultimately damage some mitochondria and interfere with replication of new mitochondria cells.

Decreased mitochondrial function also contributes to diseases. The mitochondrias slowed ability to make ATP is often a common denominator of two conditions that involve extreme fatigue—chronic fatigue syndrome and some cases of fibromyalgia. (There are many possible causes of fibromyalgia—and a study in *Journal of the American College of Nutrition* showed that ATP production may be one of them.)

Chronic heart disease often follows decreased ATP production, and it appears that heart failure is caused by a lack of ATP production in the heart muscle cells. Other age-related conditions seem to cause decreased ATP production as well. These include ischemic heart disease (due to blocked arteries)...angina...arrhythmia...Alzheimer's disease...Parkinson's disease...and Huntington's disease.

Be on the lookout for more mitochondria research in the future—the National Institutes of Health Division of Strategic Coordination recently designated "Functional Variations in Mitochondria" as one of six priority areas for funding in the next few years.

THE NATURAL WAY
TO BOOST YOUR ENERGY

Considerable research demonstrates that certain natural nutrients, taken as supplements, can increase energy by directly increasing mitochondrial functioning and ATP production. In other words, they can supercharge your metabolism. Healthful foods do boost metabolism, but not enough to make a real difference in energy or weight to people who need help in those areas.

My suggestion: For three months, take all of the following nutrients daily (there is no one energy supplement that combines these nutrients in the amounts I recommend). All are available at many drug stores and most health-food stores. Then assess whether your energy has increased and whether it feels as if your weight has become easier to control with appropriate food choices and exercise. I find that most people experience an energy boost (if you don't experience this, stop taking the supplements), and about 75% of patients find that this regimen helps with weight control. If you are pleased with your increased energy, you can continue to take these supplements indefinitely—as I do.

●**Coenzyme Q10 (CoQ10).** This nutrient is found in every cell in the body and is required for ATP production. It is a potent antioxidant, helping to protect mitochondria from damage. Researchers at the Southeastern Institute

of Biomedical Research in Bradenton, Florida, examined 20 women with chronic fatigue syndrome who became so exhausted after even mild exercise that they required bed rest. Testing revealed that 80% of them were deficient in CoQ10. After three months of taking 100 milligrams (mg) of CoQ10 daily, they were able to exercise for twice as long, and 90% of them showed fewer symptoms of fatigue—or none at all. The generally recommended dosage is 100 mg once daily with a meal. For people with severe fatigue—those who have trouble carrying out daily activities—I advise taking 100 mg two or three times each day with meals. Continue the higher dosage for a few months. When your energy level improves, try to cut back to 100 mg daily. CoQ10 is a mild blood thinner so if you are on blood-thinning medication it is particularly important to consult your doctor before taking this supplement.

●**L-Carnitine.** This chemical derived from the amino acids *lysine* and *methionine* exists in most cells and serves a dual purpose—it transports long-chain fatty acids into the mitochondria to be used as fuel...and removes waste products such as lactic acid and ammonia. I was particularly impressed by the results of a study at the University of Catania, Italy, on the beneficial effects of L-carnitine. For the study, 66 centenarians were divided into two groups. For six months, one group took two grams (g) of L-carnitine once a day and the other took a placebo. The study authors concluded that the L-carnitine helped to reduce body fat...increase muscle mass...increase the capacity for physical activity...minimize fatigue...and improve cognitive functions, such as arithmetic, memory and orientation (an awareness of one's environment with reference to time, place, and people). My recommended dosage is 1,500 mg (that's 1.5 grams) twice daily. Side effects are uncommon, but can include digestive upset—in which case, take it with food or reduce your dosage slightly.

●**Resveratrol.** Recently publicized as the "healthful" component of red wine in animal studies, this potent antioxidant has been shown to help increase the number of mitochondria in muscles and other tissues and to reduce fat deposits in the body. Resveratrol activates the *SIRT1 gene*, which promotes longevity, and also contributes to better glucose and insulin control in men with type 2 diabetes (which leads to better energy and weight control). In my practice, I am also finding that resveratrol helps with metabolism in general.

My colleague, Carrie Louise Daenell, ND, in Denver, works extensively with fatigue and weight issues. She has her patients take all the nutrients discussed here and says that 75% of her patients improve in energy and weight—but, she adds, it is resveratrol that seems to give the greatest benefits for weight control.

My recommended resveratrol dosage for adults to improve metabolism and weight control: 125 mg daily. It is generally well tolerated, though occasionally people experience nausea or loose stool—in which case take with food or start with a lower dose and build up over time.

• **D-ribose.** This is a type of sugar found in all the body's cells. It helps to restore energy by prompting the mitochondria to recycle ATP that has broken down...and it acts as another fuel source besides glucose, especially in the muscles and in particular the heart. In a study at The Fibromyalgia and Fatigue Centers in Dallas, patients with either fibromyalgia or chronic fatigue syndrome were given 5 g of d-ribose three times daily for between 15 and 35 days. Patients had few side effects, and 66% showed significant improvement in energy, sleep, mental clarity, pain intensity and overall well-being. My recommended dosage of d-ribose for the average person is 5 g twice daily. If you feel light-headed after taking d-ribose, take it with meals. Although d-ribose is a type of sugar, it is safe for people with type 2 diabetes.

You aren't likely to hear much talk about mitochondrial dysfunction from practicing physicians in the conventional Western medical community. That's because researchers are just beginning to demonstrate that it is very common and plays an important role in our metabolism, energy levels and weight. Furthermore, as I mentioned earlier, new research

is on the horizon. The recommendations you read here are well ahead of the curve, but you can adapt them into your life now. These plus a healthful diet and regular exercise should enable you to enjoy vibrant energy, a greater zest for life—more happiness!

More from Mark Stengler, NMD...

Clues to the Causes Of Fatigue

To identify and treat the root cause of an individuals fatigue, doctors must take into account all accompanying symptoms.

Here are some of the clues I look for...

IF YOU EXPERIENCE FATIGUE AND...	THE CAUSE MAY BE...
Mood swings, memory problems, low back pain...	Adrenal fatigue
A history of root canal problems...	Bacterial infection
Chest pain, heart palpitations...	Congestive heart failure
Yellow skin, unexplained weight loss...	Hepatitis
Hot flashes, weight gain, reduced muscle mass...	Hormone deficiency
Dizziness, nausea, clammy skin...	Hypotension
Low body temperature, weight gain, dry skin...	Hypothyroidism
History of flulike symptoms or mononucleosis...	Viral infection

---

Also from Mark Stengler, NMD...

Would You Pass the Energy Test?

If you are among the many people with energy or weight issues, a simple urine test can help measure whether your mitochondria are firing on all cylinders. This test, which you can take at home and send to a lab, measures organic acids that are involved in cellular energy production—*lactic acid, pyruvic acid, fumaric acid* and several others. The test measures dozens of markers that can indicate specific problems within the mitochondria and help pinpoint the cause.

Possible causes: Nutritional deficiencies, toxic metals (mercury, lead, etc), and *dysbiosis* (overgrowth of harmful bacteria or yeast). The test must be ordered by a licensed healthcare practitioner.

Ask your doctor to contact Genova Diagnostics (800-522-4762, *www.gdx.net*) for its *Metabolic Analysis Profile* test or Integrative Psychiatry (800-385-7863, *www.integrativepsy chiatry.net*) for its *Organix* test. Your doctor can interpret the results for you.

And finally from Mark Stengler, NMD…

Trouble with Fatigue? Restore Your Energy

D octor, I'm so tired—and I've felt this way for years." I often hear this complaint from patients. Persistent exhaustion is often caused by nutritional deficiencies and lifestyle choices. Below I outline steps for restoring energy. Unless noted, supplements below are sold at health-food stores and generally are safe.

NUTRITION & FATIGUE

Within all of the body's trillions of cells are energy-producing units known as mitochondria. When a person is inadequately nourished, mitochondria cannot produce enough energy to dispel fatigue. *Causes…*

- **Low-nutrient diet.** If you eat junk foods scarce in vitamins and minerals, your body cannot function well.

Obvious fix: Eat more fruits, vegetables, legumes, nuts, seeds and whole grains…limit high-fat and high-sugar foods. Yet even with a healthful diet, a nutrition boost usually is needed. Depending on the severity of your problem, take one or more—or even all—of the supplements below (listed in order of importance). Continue until energy returns.

- D-ribose, a sugar, at 5 grams (g) two times daily.

- Coenzyme Q10 (CoQ10), a vitamin-like substance, at 300 mg daily.

- The supplement *nicotinamide adenine dinucleotide* (NADH), which comes from niacin, at 15 mg daily.

- Magnesium at 400 mg daily.

- L-carnitine, an amino acid, at 2,000 mg daily.

Get a blood test to check levels of iron, a mineral essential for carrying oxygen to cells. Underlying causes of low iron (digestive tract bleeding, heavy menstruation) should be treated, but during recovery, iron supplementation alleviates fatigue. Do not take iron unless tests reveal a deficiency—excess iron damages the liver.

- **Digestive problems.** Sluggish digestion—signaled by gassiness, bloating and fatigue after eating—stems from lactose intolerance, gluten intolerance or another digestive disorder. As blood stagnates in the digestive organs, less blood is available to carry energizing oxygen and nutrients to the rest of the body. Atrophic gastritis (chronic inflammation of the stomach lining) affects up to 30% of adults age 50 and older. Caused by persistent infection, it impairs absorption of energizing vitamin B-12. *For better digestion, take one or more of the following…*

- **Betaine hydrochloride** (Betaine HCl), a beet extract that mimics stomach acid, at one to two capsules with each meal or as directed on the label. Do not use if you have an ulcer or gastritis.

- **Full-spectrum digestive enzymes,** which break down food, at one to two capsules with each meal or as labeled. Check with your doctor first if you have an ulcer or gastritis.

- **Probiotics** (beneficial intestinal bacteria) at 5 billion colony-forming units (CFU) daily.

- **Vitamin B-12,** taken sublingually (dissolved under the tongue), at 100 micrograms (mcg) to 200 mcg daily.

Fast-acting alternative for severe fatigue: Weekly injections of a B-vitamin complex (consult a nutrition-oriented doctor).

495

• **Nutrient-depleting medications.** Beta-blockers (for high blood pressure and heart disease) and cholesterol-lowering statins can cause deficiencies of the CoQ10 that helps create energy in cells. Heartburn drugs, such as *omeprazole* (Prilosec) and *esomeprazole* (Nexium), impair nutrient absorption by suppressing stomach acid. The fatigue often eases when patients switch to natural alternatives. For instance, blood pressure may be lowered with CoQ10, calcium, magnesium and hawthorn extract...heartburn may be eased with oral aloe vera, herbal *deglycyrrhizinated licorice root* (DGL) and homeopathic nux vomica. Consult a holistic doctor for dosages.

• **Blood sugar imbalance.** If blood sugar is too low, cells lack fuel for normal activity. If blood sugar is too high, the hormone insulin is not properly carrying sugar into cells. In either case, eat balanced proportions of protein, carbohydrates, beneficial fats (from fish, nuts and seeds) and fiber. *Also, take one or more of the following (check with your doctor first if you take diabetes medication)...*

• Magnesium at 400 to 600 mg daily.

• Chromium, a mineral, at 500 mcg daily.

• B-vitamin complex at 100 mg daily.

• Cinnamon extract at 500 mg daily.

LIFESTYLE LINKS

Are you "so busy" that you spend no more than five or six hours in bed each night? Cut back on activities to get eight hours of sleep nightly. If that does not alleviate fatigue, consider other possible causes.

• **Insomnia.** Up to 15% of adults have chronic insomnia.

Recommended: Take an early evening walk...listen to relaxing music before bed...retire by 10:30 pm. Also take 200 mg daily of the relaxing amino acid L-theanine...or take sublingual melatonin, a hormone that regulates the body clock, at 3 mg one hour before bed (ask your doctor first if you take blood pressure medication).

Caution: Melatonin can interfere with oral contraceptives.

• **Alcohol or drug use.** Alcohol is a depressant that impairs sleep and nutrient absorption. *Methamphetamine* (Desoxyn), a stimulant sold by prescription to treat obesity and attention-deficit hyperactivity disorder, interferes with sleep and appetite. This drug, commonly called meth, is often abused and is widely available in "street drug" form. People with severe fatigue should not drink alcohol or take stimulants.

Supplements can reduce cravings for alcohol and stimulants by correcting nutritional deficiencies, stabilizing blood sugar and balancing brain chemicals that affect mood.

Daily dosages: The amino acids L-tyrosine (900 mg), L-tryptophan (400 mg), L-glutamine (2,000 mg in divided doses)...a B-vitamin complex (100 mg)...and chromium (500 mg).

• **Exposure to toxins.** Toxic metals interfere with enzymes involved in cellular energy production. Exposure to mercury can come from metal dental fillings and contaminated fish...lead, from old plumbing...aluminum, from unfiltered tap water, antacids and antiperspirants...and arsenic, from unfiltered tap water and contaminated shellfish. Urine tests or hair analysis confirms toxicity.

Treatment: A chelating drug that pulls metals out of the body's tissues so that they can be excreted...and detoxifying supplements of chlorella (an algae), vitamin C and the amino acid glutathione. See a holistic doctor for an appropriate regimen. Once toxins are removed from the body and their sources eliminated, toxin-related fatigue should abate.

Many people with persistent exhaustion are depressed. If fatigue began first, depression may stem from the frustrating limitations that exhaustion imposes on a person's lifestyle—so treating the underlying cause leads to improvement in mood.

If the problem developed after a major upset (loss of a job, death of a loved one), the depression may have led to the fatigue. Urine tests can help identify imbalances in neurotransmitters (brain chemicals) that affect mood.

If a traumatic experience has left you feeling exhausted all the time, you may want to seek out psychiatric help.

496

Depression should be treated. Medical doctors often prescribe pharmaceutical antidepressants, such as *escitalopram* (Lexapro) or *sertraline* (Zoloft), but I rarely recommend them—these drugs worsen fatigue. *Instead I prescribe supplements of amino acids that boost neurotransmitter levels naturally…*

- 5-hydroxytryptophan (5-HTP) at 100 mg twice daily.

- S-adenosyl-L-methionine (SAMe) at 800 mg daily.

- L-tryptophan at 500 mg twice daily.

Generally, patients see improvement in both mood and energy within two to six weeks.

Feeling Tired All the Time?

Jamison Starbuck, ND, naturopathic physician in family practice in Missoula, Montana. She is past president of the American Association of Naturopathic Physicians and a contributing editor to The Alternative Advisor: The Complete Guide to Natural Therapies and Alternative Treatments *(Time-Life).*

All too often, conventional medical practitioners mistakenly assume that fatigue is a red flag for depression—especially if the patient complains only of a vague yet constant tiredness. But fatigue typically results from a complex constellation of physical and emotional issues. That's why treatment should be based on an assessment of the patient's physical health and lifestyle. *Before you see your doctor with a complaint of fatigue, spend two weeks completing this checklist…*

- **Monitor your breathing.** Shallow breathing, which is commonly caused by anxiety, fear and poor posture, reduces your oxygen supply and, as a result, often leads to fatigue. To monitor your breathing, pay attention to your breathing patterns throughout the day. In addition, practice deep breathing for five minutes several times a day.

What to do: As you inhale deeply, allow your lungs to fully expand (your belly should rise if you're doing this correctly), then exhale to a count of five. If you have trouble taking a deep breath, or if you cough or wheeze during deep breathing, discuss this with your physician. These reactions could be signs of disease or injury.

- **Note your caffeine intake.** If you need more than 20 ounces of a caffeinated beverage to get through the day, ask your doctor to order blood tests to check your levels of blood sugar (glucose) and the adrenal hormones *dehydroepiandrosterone* (DHEA) and cortisol as well as your thyroid function (TSH, T3 and T4). Each may be linked to fatigue.

- **Do a media and computer "fast" for the weekend.** Keeping up with media reports is enough of a job. When you add in the deluge of information most of us receive via the computer, it can be a tremendous energy drain. A time-out will tell you if you need to cut back on these activities.

- **Keep a diet diary for one week.** Each day, write down what you eat and drink and a description of your energy levels in the morning, afternoon and evening. Look for patterns. Skipping meals and consuming foods that can trigger allergic reactions, such as wheat, dairy, eggs or soy, are common causes of fatigue. Not drinking enough plain water, which is important to overall physiological function, also may be a culprit.

My advice: Drink one-half ounce of plain water for every pound of body weight—for example, if you weigh 150 pounds, drink 75 ounces of water daily.

- **Assess your emotional state.** Fatigue can result from painful emotions, such as grief or anger, but some doctors are too quick to prescribe an antidepressant. It's often better to first try keeping a journal, talking to a close friend and/or meeting with a counselor.

Of course, fatigue can be caused by medical conditions, such as diabetes, anemia and even cancer. That's why you should see a doctor if your fatigue does not improve after trying these steps. If you experience extreme fatigue accompanied by pain, fever or disorientation, see your doctor immediately.

Tired? Moody? Adrenal Fatigue May Be to Blame

Mark A. Stengler, NMD, licensed naturopathic medical doctor in private practice, Encinitas, California... adjunct associate clinical professor at the National College of Natural Medicine, Portland, Oregon...author of *The Natural Physician's Healing Therapies* and co-author of *Prescription for Natural Cures* (both from Bottom Line Books).

The epidemic of exhaustion affecting so many Americans today may have at its root a condition that is common and easy to correct—yet that condition often goes unrecognized by medical doctors. The culprit is adrenal fatigue (AF).

Adrenal glands produce stress hormones in response to stressful situations. With AF, the hormone response mechanism is so overwhelmed that it becomes ineffective. AF is usually triggered by long periods of mental, emotional or physical stress, and it is worsened by poor nutrition and unhealthful lifestyle choices.

In my estimation, 20% of Americans suffer from some degree of AF. And I find that this disorder often causes—or contributes to—the development of numerous other illnesses, particularly chronic fatigue syndrome and diabetes. When AF is correctly diagnosed and treated, the other conditions often are relieved as well.

STRESS HORMONE FACTORY

Located on top of each kidney is a crescent-shaped adrenal gland. The hormones these glands secrete affect blood pressure, heart rate, metabolism, liver function, immunity and the body's response to stress. Although the adrenal glands produce many hormones, two in particular become depleted in cases of AF—*dehydroepiandrosterone* (DHEA) and cortisol.

• **DHEA.** The body converts DHEA into estrogen and testosterone. Abnormally low DHEA levels may contribute to cardiovascular disease, autoimmune disorders, poor resistance to infection, diabetes, weight gain, osteoporosis, sexual dysfunction, menopausal symptoms and mood disorders. DHEA also plays a role in aging. On average, the citizens of the Japanese Island of Okinawa (one of the world's longest-living people) have much higher DHEA levels at age 70 than Americans do—30% higher for men and 172% higher for women.

• **Cortisol** plays an important role in fighting infection...stabilizing blood sugar...controlling the body's use of proteins, carbohydrates and fats...and regulating the sleep cycle. Cortisol is secreted at higher levels during the fight-or-flight response to stress, providing a burst of energy, heightened alertness and decreased pain sensitivity. But when cortisol levels are elevated for long periods, production by the adrenal glands drops. Insufficient cortisol can make you prone to fatigue, infection, allergies, diabetes and thyroid dysfunction.

Depletion of DHEA and cortisol adversely affects the way your body handles stress, inflammation, blood sugar regulation, energy production, immune response and cognitive function. That's why AF can be a contributing factor in a surprising number of ailments (see "Conditions Associated with Adrenal Fatigue" on page 500). A weakened immune response plays a part in cancer as well as in recurring infections, particularly of the respiratory tract. And poor regulation of blood sugar can contribute to both diabetes and alcoholism (alcoholics often crave simple sugars, which are found in alcohol, so improving blood sugar balance can help reduce alcohol cravings).

MAKING THE DIAGNOSIS

Conventional medical doctors often don't recognize AF—even though the condition was described in medical literature in the early 20th century. It was known then as hypoadrenia, which means low- or under-functioning adrenal glands.

If you show signs of AF (see "Adrenal Fatigue Symptoms," page 500), your best bet for diagnosis and treatment is to see a holistic doctor. For a referral, consult the American College for Advancement in Medicine (800-532-3688, *www.acam.org*). *In addition to assessing your symptoms, the doctor may perform...*

• **Saliva testing to measure cortisol levels.** This test is more accurate than a blood test. A pattern of low cortisol levels throughout the day indicates AF. I ask patients to collect saliva samples in test tubes upon waking...before lunch...in the late afternoon...and before bed. Cortisol levels are normally highest in the morning and decrease throughout the day. People with severe AF usually have below-normal cortisol readings during at least two of the four time periods. I also use a saliva test that measures the DHEA level in the morning, when it is normally highest.

Saliva testing of cortisol levels is used by many research institutions, particularly to assess the effects of stress. Several commercial labs offer saliva hormone testing—including Quest Diagnostics, the nation's largest conventional medical lab, which is used by medical and naturopathic doctors. To use Quest, you must have a prescription for the test from a doctor. A lab I have used for years that usually doesn't require a doctor's order is ZRT in Beaverton, Oregon (866-600-1636, *www.zrt lab.com*). The adrenal function test, including four cortisol samples and a morning DHEA reading, costs about $150, which is not covered by insurance. If your state does not allow residents to order lab testing directly (check the list on the ZRT Web site), you can order the kits at the same price through my clinic (call 760-274-2377).

Blood pressure measurements, taken three times—first while you lie on your back, then when you sit upright and again when you stand up. Normally, systolic (top number) and diastolic (bottom number) blood pressure will increase between 5 mm Hg and 10 mm Hg from the first reading to the third. If blood pressure drops, it may indicate AF—the adrenal glands may not be producing the stress hormones needed to maintain blood pressure.

Pupil testing, performed in a darkened room. A practitioner shines a flashlight from the side across one eye, and the pupil should continue to get smaller. With AF, the pupil first contracts and then dilates again.

HEALING STRATEGIES

Lifestyle changes and treatment reduce symptoms in most people with AF in four to six weeks. In severe cases, full recovery may take several months. *My advice…*

•**Curb stress.** A hectic lifestyle sets the stage for AF. Are you working too hard? Is your job emotionally draining? Are your relationships unsatisfying? Try to alleviate stress and seek out emotional support.

•**Get enough rest.** Go to bed by 10 pm, and aim for eight to nine hours of sleep nightly. Whenever possible, take a 15- to 30-minute nap after lunch, even if you're getting the required amount of sleep. On weekends, nap for an hour or two.

If you have insomnia, it's vital that your sleep problems be resolved. Take a walk in the early evening or listen to relaxing music. One hour before bedtime, take 100 mg to 200 mg of 5-*hydroxytryptophan* (5-HTP), an amino acid that increases brain serotonin levels and promotes relaxation…or take 0.5 mg to 3 mg of melatonin, a hormone that induces sleep. Both are available at health-food stores.

•**Eat right.** People with AF are prone to blood sugar swings that sap energy, so it is imperative to eat breakfast. I also recommend between-meal snacks, such as whole-grain toast or whey protein drinks. My favorite is Jay Robb's Whey Protein, which is naturally sweetened. It is available at major health-food stores and at *www.jayrobb.com* (877-529-7622). Almonds, walnuts and macadamia nuts are good snack foods, since they provide protein for blood sugar stabilization. Avoid simple sugars, such as those found in fruit juice and soda, as well as processed grains, such as white breads and pastas. These trigger a quick spike and subsequent drop in blood sugar levels.

Don't severely restrict salt intake unless you have high blood pressure. People with AF often benefit from salt because it helps maintain blood volume and proper circulation. Aim for 2,400 mg of sodium daily. Limit caffeinated beverages, such as coffee, tea and cola, to one cup daily because caffeine stimulates the already overtaxed adrenal glands. Avoid alcohol, which contains simple sugars.

•**Exercise in moderation.** Too little exercise is harmful, since exercise helps balance stress hormones. But overexercising worsens fatigue.

General guideline: If you're exhausted after your workout or feel more worn-out than usual the next day, you're doing too much. Start by walking 15 minutes daily. As your adrenal glands recover, you can gradually increase to 45 minutes of moderately intense exercise daily.

• **Avoid lung irritants.** Cigarette smoke, air pollution and allergens can worsen AF by stimulating cortisol release. If you smoke, please quit. Avoid secondhand smoke, and reduce exposure to allergy triggers with a high-efficiency particulate air (HEPA) filter.

• **Clear up infections.** Acute and chronic respiratory infections as well as other types of infections can exacerbate AF symptoms. To speed recovery, work with a holistic doctor, who can recommend natural immune boosters, such as the herb astragalus.

HELPFUL SUPPLEMENTS

The following nutritional supplements are invaluable in promoting adrenal function. Take them until you recover. All are available at health-food stores. (Do not use if you are pregnant or breastfeeding.)

• **Adrenal glandular extract** (AGE) is made from cow or sheep adrenal tissue. It contains growth factors (substances that promote cell healing and regeneration) and nutrients that support gland function and adrenal repair. Take one to two tablets, two to three times daily, on an empty stomach. If you get a headache, have insomnia or feel jittery, lower the dosage.

• **Ashwagandha** is an herb used traditionally in Ayurvedic medicine for normalizing adrenal gland function. I like Jarrow's Sensoril Ashwagandha, which uses a form of the herb that has been well studied and standardized. Take one to two capsules of this product daily on an empty stomach. Side effects are rare.

Caution: Individuals with diabetes and high blood pressure should check with their doctor before using Ashwagandha.

• **Rhodiola rosea,** an herb that has been extensively researched, supports normal adrenal function. Paradise Herbs' Dual Action Rhodiola is standardized to 3% to 5% rosavins (the active ingredient). Take 500 mg twice daily, on an empty stomach. If you feel jittery, try a lower dose.

• **Vitamin C** is needed for the adrenal glands to synthesize hormones. I recommend 1,000

mg to 2,000 mg twice daily. Reduce the dosage if you develop loose stools.

For severe cases of AF, hormone support with DHEA and cortisol may be required. This therapy should be administered by a knowledgeable doctor. The goal is to reduce the workload of the adrenal glands so they can heal. Over time, the hormone replacement can be reduced, then discontinued once the adrenals are functioning optimally.

For more information on AF, I recommend the book *Adrenal Fatigue: The 21st Century Stress Syndrome* by James Wilson, ND (Smart Publications).

ADRENAL FATIGUE SYMPTOMS

Patients with AF typically experience exhaustion plus one or more of the following...

• **Light-headedness upon standing up**
• **Mood swings, especially irritability**
• **Decreased ability to cope with stress**
• **Low libido**
• **Poor concentration**
• **Impaired memory**
• **Slow recovery from illness**
• **Low back pain**
• **Salt and/or sugar cravings**
• **Inability to lose or gain weight, despite calorie reduction or increase**

CONDITIONS ASSOCIATED WITH ADRENAL FATIGUE

Although AF is not the direct cause of all the conditions below, it can be a factor in...

• **Alcoholism**
• **Arthritis**
• **Asthma**
• **Exercise burnout** (becoming ill after intense workouts)
• **Autoimmune disorders,** such as lupus and multiple sclerosis
• **Cardiovascular disease**
• **Chronic fatigue syndrome**
• **Depression and/or anxiety**
• **Diabetes or hypoglycemia** (low blood sugar)
• **Insomnia**
• **Menopausal symptoms**
• **Osteoporosis**
• **Recurring infections**

When Fatigue Just Won't Go Away

Leo Galland, MD, director, Foundation for Integrated Medicine, New York City. He is author of *The Fat Resistance Diet* (Three Rivers Press). Dr. Galland is a recipient of the Linus Pauling award.

I feel totally drained and exhausted," said Susannah, age 36, who had been a runner for most of her life. "There are times when I can barely stand up." In addition to training for marathons, Susannah also had a successful consulting business and was raising a young child. But about a year before she came to see me as a patient, she found herself unable to complete her marathon training schedule.

Susannah's doctor thought that she had been overtraining and advised her to take a break. Within six months, she found that even moderate exertion (such as climbing stairs) made her feel weak, dizzy and nauseated. On top of that, she also was losing weight that she couldn't afford to lose. Susannah's doctor ran a series of blood tests, looking for signs of anemia, infection or thyroid problems. All of the results were normal. Susannah consulted three specialists —a psychiatrist, a neurologist and a rheumatologist. No medical diagnosis was made.

When I first saw Susannah, I carefully reviewed her medical records, took a detailed medical history and conducted a thorough physical examination. Two subtle findings struck me as very important. The first was her skin—it had a bronze tone, even though she had sandy-colored hair, spent little time outdoors and avoided the sun. The other finding was buried in the mass of laboratory test results—her blood potassium level was slightly elevated. A high potassium reading is usually caused by a laboratory error. But when it is combined with weight loss, fatigue and bronze skin tone, high potassium suggests malfunctioning adrenal glands.

The adrenals are a pair of walnut-sized glands, one located above each kidney. By secreting a variety of hormones, including corticosteroids (cortisone-like hormones, such as cortisol), these glands regulate responses to stress and inflammation and control the levels of salt and water in the body. Adrenal defects are actually quite common but are often overlooked because the levels of hormones produced by the glands normally fluctuate so much that abnormal adrenal function can be hard to measure. Clinical researchers have identified adrenal defects in the majority of patients with chronic fatigue and in patients with autoimmune disorders, such as rheumatoid arthritis and polymyalgia rheumatica (marked by aching and stiff muscles, primarily in the shoulders and hips).

I frequently test for abnormal levels of adrenal hormones in my practice and often find them. Intolerance to stress (becoming very fatigued due to any stress) and exertion is an early symptom of malfunctioning adrenal glands. The function of the adrenal glands is regulated by a complex network of hormones called the hypothalamic pituitary-adrenal (HPA) axis. The hypothalamus, a small area at the base of the brain, decides whether your body needs more or less corticosteroid and signals your pituitary gland, which lies just beneath it. The pituitary secretes a hormone called adrenal corticotropic hormone (ACTH), which stimulates the adrenals to produce more corticosteroid. Adrenal malfunction can be caused by a defect at any level of the HPA axis.

In Susannah's case, I suspected that her problem was Addison's disease (underactive adrenal glands that can lead to a deficiency of adrenal hormones). In response to the malfunctioning adrenal glands, the pituitary gland releases large quantities of ACTH in a desperate attempt to increase the secretion of corticosteroid from the adrenals. Skin bronzing is a side effect of ACTH. President John F. Kennedy suffered from adrenal deficiency for most of his life. In fact, some medical experts have attributed his perpetual "tan" to Addison's disease.

I was able to confirm Susannah's diagnosis with additional laboratory tests. While her corticosteroid levels were low but still within the "normal" range, her ACTH levels were very high, and she was experiencing an immune reaction against her own adrenal glands. Her own immune system was attacking her

501

adrenals, causing them to fail. Administering low doses of oral cortisone to correct the corticosteroid deficiency returned her to her normal state of health. She will continue cortisone therapy indefinitely. Because she is taking cortisone in low doses to replace a deficiency, the side effects associated with this drug, such as cataracts and easy bruising, are not likely to occur.

CORRECT DIAGNOSIS: ADDISON'S DISEASE

Lesson for all: If you suffer from disabling fatigue, make sure that your doctor tests the adrenal hormone levels in your blood and saliva.

Natural Help for Multiple Sclerosis

Mark A. Stengler, NMD, licensed naturopathic medical doctor in private practice, Encinitas, California... adjunct associate clinical professor at the National College of Natural Medicine, Portland, Oregon...author of *The Natural Physician's Healing Therapies* and co-author of *Prescription for Natural Cures* (both from Bottom Line Books).

D onna, 70, dragged herself into my office three years ago. Her complaints —muscle weakness and stiffness, fatigue, irritability and sensitivity to noise—were all due to multiple sclerosis (MS), a disease she had battled since age 21.

MS is a degenerative autoimmune disease in which immune cells attack the body's nerves. It damages the myelin sheath (fatty tissue that surrounds and protects nerve fibers), disrupting the flow of electrical impulses between the brain and the nerves. Symptoms may flare up when a patient is stressed or has a viral infection, such as a cold or the flu. Conventional treatment includes the immune-regulating drug *interferon* (Betaseron) or *glatiramer* (Copaxone), which suppresses immune activity against the myelin sheath...and steroids or chemotherapy to reduce inflammation. These therapies can have serious side effects, including depression and flulike symptoms.

Research suggests that a deficiency of vitamin B-12 may be associated with the development of MS. B-12 aids in repairing the myelin sheath, so B-12 injections help to prevent and treat MS flare-ups. To relieve Donna's symptoms, I prescribed B-12 injections twice weekly, plus a daily sublingual (under the tongue) B-12 supplement. After a month, she had more energy, strength and flexibility...was less irritable...and was less bothered by noise.

I urged Donna to increase her intake of essential fatty acids (EFAs), found in fish, walnuts, almonds and pistachios. I also recommended a high-potency fish oil supplement and a gamma linoleic acid (GLA) supplement in the form of evening primrose oil. To encourage her, I showed Donna studies by the late Roy Swank, MD, a professor of neurology at the University of Oregon, which found that a diet limited in saturated fat (from meat and dairy foods) and hydrogenated oils (from margarines and baked goods made with vegetable oils) and rich in polyunsaturated fatty acids (from fish oil and vegetables) helps to halt the progression of MS.

I also tested Donna's blood level of vitamin D and found that it was low. Vitamin D is a critical nutrient for proper immune function, including prevention of auto-immune disorders. MS is more common in higher latitudes where sunlight—a key source of vitamin D— is limited. A study published in *The Journal of the American Medical Association* reported that higher levels of vitamin D in the body may reduce the risk of developing MS by up to 62%. For Donna, I prescribed 1,000 international units (IU) of vitamin D daily, taken in addition to the multivitamin/mineral formula she was already using.

Since she began this treatment three years ago, Donna has had only occasional minor flare-ups, for which she receives twice-weekly B-12 injections. In general, her condition is well controlled with just one monthly B-12 injection, plus the sublingual B-12 and the vitamin D supplements. She no longer requires steroid medication—and she says that despite having had MS for almost 50 years, she's now in better health overall than her septuagenarian friends.

Is Your Thyroid Making You Sick?

Richard Shames, MD, and Karilee Shames, RN, PhD, coauthors of *Thyroid Power* (William Morrow) and *Feeling Fat, Fuzzy, or Frazzled?* (Plume). They are in private practice at the Preventive Medical Center of Marin in San Rafael, California. Their Web site is *www.feelingfff.com*.

Weight gain, joint pain, dry skin and exhaustion are just a few of the many possible symptoms of hypothyroidism (low levels of thyroid hormone). Consequences of hypothyroidism range from the annoying to the potentially life-threatening—yet it is one of the most overlooked and undertreated health problems in the US. *Facts...*

•**Women are five to eight times more likely than men** to suffer from the condition.

•**Only about half of people with hypothyroidism** (also called "low thyroid") may ever be diagnosed.

•**Even when diagnosed, patients often are not given vital information about lifestyle factors** that worsen the condition and natural therapies that can help.

WHEN THYROID HORMONE IS LOW

Thyroid hormone regulates metabolism, the intricate interplay of chemical processes that release energy and replenish cells. The hormone is produced by the thyroid gland, a butterfly-shaped gland in the neck. Thyroid hormone is needed for proper function of every part of the body—which is why hypothyroidism can cause a wide variety of symptoms (see page 504).

Low thyroid can develop at any time. The main causes are autoimmune disorders, in which the immune system attacks the body's own tissues. Family history, diet and stress can increase risk for hypothyroidism. *Symptoms vary depending on your stage of life...*

•**Perimenopause.** As production of the hormone estrogen declines, menstrual periods become irregular...and premenstrual symptoms, such as bloating, breast tenderness and mood swings, may worsen. For women with low thyroid, merely bothersome changes transform into "super-PMS."

•**Menopause.** Low thyroid can prompt early onset of menopause. It also can exacerbate menopause symptoms, such as hot flashes, insomnia, vaginal dryness and memory problems. The usual treatment for severe menopause symptoms is estrogen therapy—but for women with low thyroid, this may make things worse.

Reason: Estrogen may increase proteins that circulate in the blood and prevent thyroid hormone from reaching tissues that need it.

•**Postmenopause.** Hypothyroidism symptoms tend to worsen after menopause. More than 20% of postmenopausal women suffer from fatigue, weight gain, sluggishness and mental fogginess brought on by low thyroid. Hypothyroidism raises LDL (bad) cholesterol, total cholesterol and triglycerides (blood fats), increasing heart disease risk.

Diagnosis: There are two main types of thyroid hormone—T4 and the more potent T3. Also important is thyroid stimulating hormone (TSH), produced by the pituitary gland, which promotes production of T4 and T3. In blood tests, high levels of TSH indicate that the thyroid gland is not functioning optimally.

Testing concerns: The TSH range that many doctors consider normal doesn't call attention to cases of borderline low thyroid that should be corrected...and many doctors do not order an accurate test for T3 levels.

Best: If you have symptoms of low thyroid, see a holistic doctor, who may order alternative saliva, urine and/or blood tests to detect low thyroid as well as suggest lifestyle changes and/or medications that can correct the problem.

THYROID-BOOSTING LIFESTYLE

For optimal thyroid function...

•**Limit exposure to fluoride and chlorine.** These chemicals may be toxic to the thyroid. Don't use fluoridated toothpaste...avoid household products containing chlorine bleach...use a carbon block filtration system for your drinking water.

• **Know which "healthful" foods to limit.** Some otherwise beneficial foods—such as broccoli, brussels sprouts, cabbage, cauliflower, mustard greens, soy, spinach and turnips—have compounds that slow thyroid hormone production. Limit these foods to one serving daily, and cook them to deactivate the compounds.

• **Choose all-natural or organic food** to limit exposure to chemical additives and pesticide residues that may impair thyroid function.

THYROID-BOOSTING SUPPLEMENTS

The more symptoms you have, the more important it is to give your thyroid gland the nutrients it needs. *I generally recommend taking a daily multivitamin/mineral supplement, plus...*

• **Antioxidants.** These fight inflammation that may impair thyroid function.

Daily dosages: Vitamin A up to 10,000 IU ...vitamin C up to 2,000 mg...and vitamin E up to 400 IU.

Alternative: A combination formula that also provides iodine, zinc and ashwaganda, such as Thyroid Action by Puritan Pride (800-645-1030, *www.puritan.com*).

• **Selenium.** This mineral is involved in hormone production.

Dosage: 200 micrograms (mcg) daily.

• **Amino acids.** These are the raw materials from which thyroid hormone is constructed. Supplement daily with an amino acid mix labeled "free-form aminos." Choose a brand that contains the especially effective L-taurine and L-glutamine.

THYROID HORMONE REPLACEMENT

For severe hypothyroidism, your doctor may recommend thyroid hormone replacement. *Options...*

• **Synthetic thyroid hormone medication,** such as *levothyroxine* (Synthroid) or *liothyronine* (Cytomel). It may require trial-and-error to figure out which drug and dosage work best for you.

• **Prescription natural thyroid medication made from animal thyroid glands.** For some people, these perform better than synthetics. Good brands include Armour Thyroid and Nature-Throid.

To find a physician knowledgeable about natural approaches as well as medications that treat thyroid problems, contact the Academy of Integrative Health & Medicine (858-240-9033, *www.aihm.org*).

Symptoms of Low Thyroid

See your doctor if you have more than three of the following...

• **Constipation**
• **Depression**
• **Dry, pale skin**
• **Excess weight and trouble losing weight**
• **Fatigue, low energy**
• **Hair loss**
• **Infertility**
• **Insomnia**
• **Irritability and/or anxiety**
• **High cholesterol**
• **Heavy menstrual periods**
• **Joint pain or stiffness**
• **Low libido**
• **Memory problems**
• **Muscle weakness**
• **Nodules (lumps) on the thyroid gland**
• **Puffy face**
• **Severe menopausal symptoms**
• **Severe premenstrual syndrome**
• **Sensitivity to cold**

Natural Remedies for a Sluggish Thyroid

Ellen Kamhi, PhD, RN, board-certified holistic nurse and clinical instructor at Stony Brook University's School of Medicine and New York Chiropractic College, Seneca Falls. She is author of *Definitive Guide to Weight Loss* and coauthor of *The Natural Medicine Chest* (both from Natural Nurse, 800-829-0918, *www.naturalnurse.com*).

D o you feel tired most of the time? Are you gaining weight for no apparent reason? A sluggish thyroid may be to blame. Though just 3% of all Americans suffer from an underactive thyroid, or hypothyroidism (sometimes referred to as a sluggish thyroid), as many as 10% to 15% of Americans have a subclinical (mild) hypothyroid condition. Because hypothyroidism often underlies other health conditions, the number of people who have the disorder may be even higher, perhaps as high as one in three.

Untreated hypothyroidism can lead to serious medical problems, including reduced immunity, high cholesterol and high blood pressure.

Recent finding: A study published in *Archives of Internal Medicine* reported that even mild changes in thyroid function are associated with an increased risk for mortality in patients with cardiac disease.

The good news is that a sluggish thyroid often can be corrected naturally.

If your doctor doesn't discover a thyroid problem but you have many of the symptoms (see previous article), visit a holistic practitioner who may have a better understanding of hidden thyroid issues.

NATURAL REMEDIES

Lifestyle changes can go a long way toward correcting a sluggish thyroid...

• **Consume natural sources of iodine.** If you're low in iodine, it can lead to a thyroid deficiency. The best sources of iodine are iodized salt, sea vegetables, such as seaweed, as well as eggs and shellfish, including lobster, shrimp and crab. You will need 100 micrograms (mcg) to 120 mcg of iodine a day. A three-ounce serving of shrimp—or one egg—contains about 30 mcg.

Also, to ensure a healthy metabolism, eat a balanced diet that includes adequate amounts of protein (beef, poultry, fish, eggs and milk products, such as yogurt and cottage cheese), whole grains and plenty of vegetables. Whenever possible, opt for organic foods—pesticides and herbicides have been linked to thyroid disorders.

• **Eat foods rich in vitamin E and selenium.** Studies reported in *Biofactors* and *European Journal of Endocrinology* indicate that vitamin E and selenium can revitalize an underactive thyroid. Vitamin E is in various foods, including wheat germ, whole-grain cereals, nuts, avocados, green leafy vegetables and fish. Try to consume a total of 400 international units (IU) per day. One tablespoon of wheat germ oil has 30 IU...one ounce of almonds has 10 IU.

Selenium is in seafood, liver, poultry, red meat and grains—aim for 200 mcg a day. A four-ounce serving of most fish has 50 mcg to 75 mcg of selenium...four ounces of turkey breast has 33 mcg.

• **Exercise.** The latest research on hypothyroidism suggests that thyroid dysfunction may be linked to stress. A study published in *Annals of the New York Academy of Science* found that exercise helps reestablish healthy thyroid function by decreasing the overall impact of stress. Aim for 30 minutes a day of any form of exercise.

Thyroid Disorders May Increase Glaucoma Risk

W hen researchers reviewed health data for 12,376 adults, they found that those diagnosed with glaucoma were 38% more likely to have had a thyroid disorder, such as hypothyroidism (underactive thyroid) or hyperthyroidism (overactive thyroid).

Theory: Thyroid disease causes chemical deposits to develop in the blood vessels that circulate blood to the eye, causing increased pressure within the eyeball (a hallmark of glaucoma).

If you are diagnosed with a thyroid condition: See an ophthalmologist to be screened for glaucoma, which can be treated if detected at an early stage.

Gerald McGwin, Jr., PhD, professor, department of epidemiology, surgery and ophthalmology, University of Alabama at Birmingham.

Thyroid Disease Could Be Causing Your Energy Crisis

Richard L. Shames, MD, thyroid specialist in private practice at the Preventive Medical Center of Marin in San Rafael, California. He is coauthor of *Thyroid Power: 10 Steps to Total Health* (William Morrow).

A merica is in the grip of an energy crisis. Millions of men and women drag themselves around from day to day, feeling fatigued, unable to work productively or enjoy life. Many suffer additional ills, such as depression, anxiety, digestive misery, headaches and muscle pains.

What is their problem? It could be that they have low levels of thyroid hormone.

Trouble with the butterfly-shaped gland located at the base of the throat is surprisingly common—and since the symptoms of hypothyroidism are vague and nonspecific, thyroid disorders often go undetected.

THE MASTER GLAND

The thyroid functions much like a gas pedal for the entire body. Its hormones penetrate every cell to regulate the body's energy-producing "machinery." Too little thyroid hormone, and your organs can slow down—with consequences that range from irritating to devastating.

According to estimates, 5% of adult Americans have hypothyroidism. But recent surveys show that actually double that number—one in 10 Americans—have the problem. Moreover, among women who are in menopause, *one in five* has hypothyroidism.

Why the epidemic? No one knows for sure. But some endocrinologists theorize that the thyroid is affected by air pollution, pesticides and other chemical pollutants...increased radiation exposure from power plants, microwaves and cell phones...and chronic psychological stress.

Regardless of the reason, hypothyroidism can cause symptoms as diverse as the body systems the gland regulates.

In addition to the fatigue, low energy and mild depression that occur so frequently, many people with the condition have difficulty controlling their weight because their metabolism is sluggish. They may also feel cold when others are comfortable.

Additional problems that may point to thyroid disorder include allergies...dry skin, eczema or adult acne...poor concentration or forgetfulness...difficulty swallowing...or recurrent infections.

GETTING DIAGNOSED

Because the symptoms can have a number of causes, doctors* often mistake thyroid problems for another condition, such as menopause, irritable bowel syndrome or rheumatoid arthritis.

To avoid misdiagnosis, blood tests to assess thyroid function should be a routine part of any physical checkup—especially for people over age 35.

Make even more sure to have your thyroid checked if anyone in your family (even an aunt or a cousin) has had thyroid problems or a condition, such as diabetes or prematurely gray hair, which often suggests thyroid malfunction.

Caution: The most common test, which measures the levels of thyroid-stimulating hormone (TSH), sometimes gives a "false negative" (a normal reading even when there is thyroid trouble).

It's wise to follow up an all-too-frequent negative result with tests that can detect levels of the thyroid hormone thyroxine (T4), which the body converts into thyronine (T3).

Ask for: Free T3 and free T4 tests.

*To locate a thyroid specialist in your area, check the Top Thyroid Doctors Directory at *www.thyroid-info.com*.

TREATMENT—THE HORMONE GAME

Standard treatment for low thyroid levels is a daily dose of T4. But getting good results sometimes requires a little fine-tuning.

There are several brands of synthetic T4, or *levothyroxine*, including Synthroid, the largest seller and one of the most prescribed drugs in America. Others include Levoxyl... and Unithroid. These formulations are not always equal. Some people fare much better on one than another. Unfortunately, it's impossible to tell in advance which will be best for you.

If symptoms persist for six months despite T4 treatment, ask your doctor about switching brands.

It may be that no brand of T4 hormone will do the job because your body can't convert it into T3 properly. If this is the case, doctors often recommend adding a synthetic form of T3, called *liothyronine* (Cytomel). This more active hormone works on its own and boosts the effectiveness of T4 to help your body restore normal function. But in many instances, a better approach is a natural thyroid extract that contains both T3 and T4.

Bonus: Brands of natural thyroid hormone, such as Armour Thyroid and Westhroid, cost less than synthetic preparations.

WATCH YOUR DIET

Even the best medical regimen needs nutritional help. To keep your thyroid healthy, minimize exposure to chemicals found in processed foods. *Eat natural foods—without preservatives, additives or artificial sweeteners. Also take daily supplements that contain...*

- **Vitamin A**—10,000 international units (IU).
- **Vitamin C**—500 milligrams (mg).
- **Vitamin E**—400 IU. Check amount with your doctor.
- **Vitamin B complex**—At least 50 mg each of B-1, B-3, B-5 and B-6.
- **Folic acid**—800 micrograms (mcg).
- **Zinc**—25 mg.
- **Selenium**—200 mcg.
- **Manganese**—20 mg.

The thyroid needs iodine to function, but deficiencies of this mineral are largely a thing of the past due to Americans' high consumption of iodized salt. Especially if you live near a coast, you may be getting too much iodine, which is harmful to the thyroid.

To reduce iodine intake: Buy noniodized salt and minimize sodium intake by avoiding salty snacks and other high-sodium foods.

Fluoride is highly toxic to the thyroid. Don't use fluoridated toothpaste. If your water supply is fluoridated, drink bottled water.

What Is Graves' Disease?

Graves' disease is a condition in which an overactive thyroid produces excessive levels of thyroid hormones in the bloodstream and puts organs, including the heart and brain, into overdrive. Symptoms include rapid heartbeat, tremors, anxiety, weight loss, intolerance to heat, swelling of the neck and sometimes protruding eyes. The primary cause is an inherited autoimmunity—an overactive immune system that wrongly targets the thyroid gland. Graves' disease usually can be treated by blocking thyroid hormone production through the use of medication, such as *methimazole* (Tapazole), or alternative therapy, such as acupuncture. If such treatment is not successful, your doctor may recommend removing the thyroid gland with surgery or a radioactive medicine.

Richard L. Shames, MD, thyroid specialist, Preventive Medical Center of Marin, San Rafael, California, and author of *Thyroid Power* (William Morrow).

Thyroid Medication— Natural vs. Synthetic

Mark A. Stengler, NMD, licensed naturopathic medical doctor in private practice, Encinitas, California... adjunct associate clinical professor at the National College of Natural Medicine, Portland, Oregon...author of *The Natural Physician's Healing Therapies* and co-author of *Prescription for Natural Cures* (both from Bottom Line Books).

For low thyroid function, should you take a synthetic thyroid hormone, or a natural product?

The body produces two main thyroid hormones—T4 and the more potent T3. Normally, the liver converts T4 into T3. Sometimes this conversion does not occur effectively, due to genetics…diabetes or liver disease…nutritional deficiencies, especially of selenium and/or beta-carotene…or a hormone imbalance, such as low progesterone (in men as well as women) or high cortisol or insulin levels.

Natural prescription thyroid medications, including Armour Thyroid and Nature-Throid, contain both T4 and T3. Synthetic versions, such as Synthroid, contain only T4. People who are able to convert T4 into T3 may do fine on a synthetic brand, so if you feel well and your blood test results are good, you need not switch. However, for many people, changing to natural thyroid medication brings relief from low-grade fatigue and slow metabolism. Do not take natural thyroid medication if you are allergic to pork, because the product is made from the thyroid glands of pigs.

How MS Patients Can Beat Fatigue

Aaron Miller, MD, professor of neurology, medical director of the Corinne Goldsmith Dickinson Center for Multiple Sclerosis, Mount Sinai School of Medicine, New York City.

Fatigue is a common problem for people with multiple sclerosis (MS). Researchers have recently concluded that regular exercise is one of the few things that may help patients feel better.

It's important for all MS patients, at every stage of the disease, to participate in some kind of exercise program because it has been consistently shown to reduce fatigue, according to Aaron Miller, MD, medical director of the Corinne Goldsmith Dickinson Center for Multiple Sclerosis at the Mount Sinai School of Medicine in New York City. Physical activity in general helps to stabilize blood sugar, reducing inflammation. It also gives patients a psychological boost, and increases endorphins and other brain chemicals that may affect fatigue. He feels that aerobic exercise should be primary (and says even running is fine for many people), but that resistance exercise and other types are also worthwhile. For patients in more advanced stages, with limited mobility, exercise works to strengthen the muscles that still function, thereby easing the body's overall work load. Although there is no evidence that exercise makes any difference in the course of the illness, it may help the patient to tolerate some symptoms better.

Dr. Miller offers one cautionary note: Exercise elevates body temperature, which is problematic for some people with MS. He says the increase in body temperature does nothing to worsen the disease, but it can exacerbate uncomfortable symptoms. However, this can be considered an annoyance, and not dangerous, and is not a reason to stop. You could set up fans in front of your treadmill, or limit workouts to air-conditioned environments. (For information from the Multiple Sclerosis Association of America, go to *www.mymsaa.org.*)

Index

516

Ovaries, 32, 56, 357, 429, 439
  freezing of, 53–54
  hysterectomy and, 90–91
  removal of, 90–91, 93, 452
Overflow incontinence, 175, 180
Overweight, 8, 92, 207, 213, 242,
  274, 396, 407, 505
  cancer and, 429, 439
  diabetes and, 104–105, 419, 428,
    429, 430
  exercise and, 307, 327–28
  fertility and, 56, 57
  MSG and, 273
  stroke and, 474
  See also Obesity
Ovulation, 34, 53, 83, 100, 452
  irregular, 16, 56
  test for, 164
Oxalate, 489
Oxidative stress, 62, 367
Oxybenzone, 342
Oxybutynin (Ditropan), 388
Oxybutynin gel (Gelnique), 177
Oxycodone (OxyContin), 356, 437
Oxygen, 159, 191, 212, 215, 291–92,
  297, 338, 357, 410, 495
  hyperbaric therapy and, 434–35
Oxytocin, 145, 148, 241, 253, 262

P
Pain, 23, 161, 390–416
  See also specific kinds of pain
Paint, 168
Pancreas, 301, 421, 426, 427, 428, 431
  cancer of, 216
Pancreatitis, 424
Panties, 197
Pap tests, 93–94, 109, 449–51, 453
Paralysis, 159
Paraphenylenediamine (PPD),
  169, 341
Parkinson's disease, 169, 180, 248,
  288, 330, 359, 387
Paroxetine (Paxil), 40, 377
Parsley, 220, 295
Past, reminiscing about, 125
Pasta, 273, 337, 338, 364
Patience, 11, 114,
Patient advocacy groups, 42
Pau d'arco, 414
Paxil (*paroxetine*), 40, 377
Peaches, 186, 337
Peanut butter, 267, 294, 299,
  338, 418
Peanuts, 188, 338, 458
  allergy to, 61, 152
Pedicures, 350
Pelvic exams, 16, 93, 451
Pelvic floor disorder, 98
Pelvic floor exercises, *see* Kegel
  (pelvic floor) exercises
Pelvic inflammatory disease (PID),
  96–97
Pelvic organ prolapse, 98
Pelvic pain, 2, 60, 84, 98, 196, 410
Pelvis, 178
Pepcid (*famotidine*), 205, 206, 360

Peppermint, 258
Peppermint leaf, 28
Peppermint oil, 182, 271
Peppermint tea, 182, 186
"Pepper remedy," 24
Peppers, 184, 291, 338, 361,
  367, 461
Perfluorooctanoic acid (PFOA),
  459–60
Perimenopause, 16, 92, 100–101,
  357, 503
Periodic limb movement disorder
  (PLMD), 236, 237
Periodontal disease, 215–17,
  353–55, 419
Periodontitis, 353, 354
Periostat, 203
Peripheral artery disease, 161
Peripheral neuropathy, 355,
  435–37
Perlane, 332
Persistent genital arousal disorder
  (PGAD), 113
Persistent organic pollutants
  (POPs), 432
Persistent sexual arousal syndrome
  (PSAS), 113
Personal-care products, 24–25
Personal trainers, 317, 327
Pertussis (whooping cough), 154,
  156, 165
Pesticides, 169, 365, 432, 507
  birth defects and, 71
  in produce, 170, 457
Pets, 26, 155, 174, 348
PGE2, 30
Pharmaceutical companies, 107
  free coupons for, 46
  patient-assistance programs of, 39,
    40–41, 45–46
  post-marketing surveillance
    and, 423
Pharmacists, 42
Pharmacy benefit managers, 41
Pharynx, cancer of, 19
Phenytoin (Dilantin), 216, 435
Phlebectomy, 214
Phlegm, dark-colored, 154
Phosphatidylserine, 277, 278
Photodynamic therapy, 374
Phthalates, 169–70
Physical abuse, 241
Physical therapy (PT), 196, 401,
  405, 415
  fascia and, 410–12
Physicians' desk reference (PDR), 46
Phytochemicals, 291, 293, 461, 462
Phytoestrogens, 33, 304, 378
Phytonutrients, 273, 456
Piezoelectric effect, 381
Pilates exercises, 311, 350, 405
Pillar, the, 192
Pillows, 235, 399
Pimples, 25
Pineapple, 103, 219, 292, 338,
  408, 418
Pine nuts, 267–68

Pinkeye, 173
Pinolenic acid, 279–80
Pioglitazone (Actos), 423
Pituitary gland, 2, 56, 83, 501
Placental corticotropin-releasing
  hormone (pCRH), 77–78
Plans, marital problems and, 137
Plantar fasciitis, 397
Plaque, 2, 162, 232, 429, 465, 466,
  468–69, 470
  amyloid, 30, 31, 366, 367, 370, 371
  gum, 217, 354
Plastics, 433, 460
Plastic surgery, *see* Cosmetic surgery
Platinol (*cisplatin*), 435
Platitude-offers, 264
Plavix (*clopidogrel*), 289
Plumpers, 346
Pneumonia, 154, 159, 207, 356, 459
  prevention of, 156–57
  vaccination against, 6, 166
Podiatrists, 193, 397, 421, 434
Poison ivy, 347–48
Pollen, 219
Polybrominated diphenyl ethers
  (PBDEs), 169
Polychlorinated biphenyls
  (PCBS), 432
Polycystic ovary syndrome (PCOS),
  91–92, 93, 357, 364, 427, 429
Polyglycoplex (PGX), 423
Polymyalgia rheumatica, 501
Polyphenols, 273, 300, 337, 353,
  426, 453, 477, 478, 480, 481
Polyphenon E/Kunecatechins
  (Veregen), 208–10
Pomegranates, pomegranate juice,
  228, 276, 304–5
Porcelana, 333
Pork, 229, 292, 299, 338, 407,
  427–28
Positive, accentuating of, 128
Positive mental imagery, 277–78
Postherpetic neuralgia (PHN), 409
Post-nasal drip (upper-airway
  cough syndrome), 155
Post-traumatic stress disorder
  (PTSD), 238
Posture, 313, 315, 380–81
Potassium, 34, 293–94, 299, 305,
  311, 349, 378, 477, 480, 502
Potatoes, 184, 220, 293–94, 352,
  361, 404
Poultry, 220, 229, 298, 299, 359,
  364, 369, 371, 432, 489, 505
  red wine and, 300
Power Plate workout, 330
Powwows, 261
Pramlintide (Symlin), 421
Prayer, 224, 277–78
Prebiotics, 190
Prediabetes, 419–24, 428–29, 431
Prednisone, 20
Preeclampsia, 64–65, 68
Preeclampsia Foundation, 65
Pregabalin (Lyrica), 436–37

Roche Labs Patient Assistant
Foundation, 41
Romance, 117–18, 127–30
Rosemary, 32, 170, 426
Rosemary oil, 199
Rosiglitazone (Avandia), 423
Ruler body, exercise for, 319, 320–21
Runner's high, 473
Runner's knee, 329
Running, 381, 405
Ruscogenins, 188
Rx Outreach, 41

S

Saccharomyces boulardii, 184
S-adenosylmethionine (SAMe), 226,
  227, 497
Sadness, 225, 227, 230, 237, 249
Safflower oil, 170, 184, 201, 272
Sage, 31–32, 33, 426
St. John's wort, 158, 226, 227
Salacia oblonga, 423
Salads, 220, 267, 338, 391, 458
Salicylates, 402–3
Salicylic acid, 202
Saline solution for nasal irrigation,
  153
Saliva, 354
Saliva tests, 448, 499, 503
Salmon, 75, 230, 242, 276, 282,
  287, 288, 295, 298, 299, 337, 338,
  369, 404, 408, 480
    cancer and, 456
    mood-boosting and, 226,
    228, 230
Salt, 15, 36, 105, 218, 426, 478,
  499–500, 502, 506, 508
Sanctura (*trospium*), 177, 388
Sanding, 332–33
Sardines, 242, 276, 282, 287, 288,
  298, 304, 337, 369, 404, 408
    cancer and, 457
    mood-boosting and, 226, 228
Sauerkraut, 179, 210, 289
Saunas, 220, 348–49, 432
Saw palmetto, 198–99, 339
Scalp, itchy, 200
Scalpel sculpting, 332
Scars, 66–67, 332–33, 343
Sciatica, 399–400
Scientific studies, Web sites on, 51
Sclerotherapy, 187, 213, 214, 333
Scopolamine (Transderm Scop), 182
Seasonal affective disorder
  (SAD), 227
Sebum, 198, 202
Secondary gains, 143
Secrets, keeping, 253, 262
Sedentary lifestyle, 422, 427, 465, 472
  varicose veins and, 213, 214
Seeds, 201, 228, 272, 273, 364, 371,
  418, 487
Seizures, 167
Seldane (*terfenadine*), 20
Selective estrogen receptor
  modulator (SERM), 474

Selective serotonin and
  norepinephrine reuptake
  inhibitors (SSN-RIs), 436
Selective serotonin reuptake
  inhibitors (SSRIs), 246, 377
Selenium, 211, 226, 293, 296, 337, 493
  thyroid and, 504, 505, 507
Selenomethionine, 296
Self-esteem, 238, 246, 256
Self-intimacy, 135–36
Self-worth, 126
Semen, 450–51
Senses, paying attention to, 349
Sensoril, 363
Sensoril ashwagandha, 198
Separations, marital, 75, 137
Sepia, 341
Serenity, 242, 350
Serotonin, 23, 113, 225, 227, 228,
  246, 365, 370, 436, 499
    love personality and, 119, 120
Serotonin/norepinephrine
  reuptake inhibitors (SNRIs), 377
Sertraline (Zoloft), 42, 107, 108, 497
7-Minute workout, 324–25
Sex, 102–16, 160, 377
  aging and, 106–8, 113–15
  asexuality and, 108
  chemical attraction and, 112, 119
  chocolate vs., 115
  D4 receptor gene and, 116
  erectile dysfunction and, 102–3,
    106, 109, 110, 114
  falling asleep after, 103–4, 148
  fear and, 109
  female testosterone and, 109, 116
  foreplay and, 102, 105
  great at any age, 111–12
  G-spot and, 111–12
  headaches and, 104
  kissing and, 104, 126
  loss of interest in, 227, 251
  love personality and, 120, 121
  male sweat and, 108
  marriage and, 102–4, 126, 127–128,
    131, 133–36
  oral, 103
  orgasms and, 103, 108–12, 113, 149
  premarital, 94, 113
  reasons for having, 109
  sleep disturbances and, 115, 358
  talking about, 113, 115, 133–35
  "too old" for, 102
  vaginal infections and, 116
  See also Libido
Sexsomnia, 115
Sex therapists, sex therapy, 97, 107,
  109, 113, 114, 135, 142
Sex toys, 103, 105
Sexual assault, 237
Sexual intercourse, 94, 178
  beyond, 114
  painful, 84, 96–97, 102, 114, 116
Sexually transmitted diseases,
  95–96, 97
Sexual medicine clinics, 109
Shampoos, 169, 200

Shangri-la Diet, 268–69
Shellfish, allergy to, 151–53, 184, 404
Shingles, 164–65, 408–9
Shoes, 193, 194, 196, 356, 362, 434
  inserts for, 50
  magnetic insoles for, 410
  orthotic for, 397
  removing, 174
Shopping, 254–55, 316
Shoulder press, 308
Shoulders, 308, 313
  pain in, 401–2, 465
Showers, 346, 347
Shrimp, 152, 299, 338
Shrinkage, 380–81
Shrug muscle stretch, 411
Side kick, 312
Sildenafil (Viagra), 42, 103, 109,
  110–11
Simethicone (Gas-X), 186
Simvastatin (Zocor), 42
Singulair (*montelukast*), 155
Sinusitis, 31, 155
Sitagliptin (Januvia), 39, 421
Skin, 161, 201–204, 303, 331–38,
  342–47, 436, 488, 502, 504
    acne, 92, 116, 202–4, 332, 338
    birthmarks, 343
    calendula spray for, 28
    cancer, 5, 30, 94, 287, 337, 345,
    455
    chemical peel for, 332
    cold-weather care for, 345–46
    dark, 287, 383
    eczema, 72, 334
    exfoliants for, 26
    from the inside out care of,
    336–38
    itchy, flaky or dry, 25, 112, 334
    keratosis pilaris, 202
    liver spots, 217, 333
    non-surgical rejuvenation of,
    335–36
    poison ivy and, 347–48
    psoriasis, 200, 201, 212, 230
    scars, 66–67, 332–33, 343
    shingles, 164–65, 408–9
    sores, 214
    sunscreen, 286, 336, 342, 344–45
    warm-weather care for, 343–45
    wrinkles, 331, 332–33, 335–37
Skin-prick test, 152
Sleep, 153, 160, 167, 227, 233–37,
  251, 489
  aging and, 356, 357–58, 370
  chronic fatigue and, 494, 496, 499
  depression and, 230, 234, 357
  deprivation of, 8, 107, 211, 251,
    447; *See also* Insomnia
  diabetes and, 234, 358, 428, 430
  falls and, 356, 357
  marriage and, 129
  memory and, 372
  men vs. women and, 234
  solutions for problems of,
    235–37, 357–58, 491
Sleep aids, 42, 43, 356